The
International Critical Commentary
on the Holy Scriptures of the Old and
New Testaments.

PLANNED AND FOR YEARS EDITED BY

THE LATE REV. PROFESSOR SAMUEL ROLLES DRIVER, D.D., D.LITT.

THE REV. ALFRED PLUMMER, M.A., D.D.

THE LATE REV. PROFESSOR CHARLES AUGUSTUS BRIGGS, D.D., D.LITT.

THE EPISTLES OF ST. PAUL
TO THE THESSALONIANS

A

CRITICAL AND EXEGETICAL COMMENTARY

ON THE

EPISTLES OF ST. PAUL TO THE THESSALONIANS

BY

JAMES EVERETT FRAME

PROFESSOR OF BIBLICAL THEOLOGY, UNION THEOLOGICAL
SEMINARY, NEW YORK

EDINBURGH
T. & T. CLARK, 38 GEORGE STREET

PRINTED IN GREAT BRITAIN BY
MORRISON AND GIBB LIMITED
FOR
T. & T. CLARK, EDINBURGH
NEW YORK: CHARLES SCRIBNER'S SONS

FIRST IMPRESSION 1912
SECOND IMPRESSION . . . 1946

CONTENTS

	PAGE
ABBREVIATIONS	vii
INTRODUCTION	1
§ I. FOUNDING OF THE CHURCH OF THE THESSALONIANS	1
(1) FROM ANTIOCH TO PHILIPPI	1
(2) FROM PHILIPPI TO THESSALONICA . . .	1
(3) FOUNDING OF THE CHURCH	2
(4) CHARACTER OF THE CHURCH	5
§ II. THE FIRST LETTER	8
(1) FROM THESSALONICA TO CORINTH . . .	8
(2) PLACE, DATE, AND OCCASION	9
(3) CONTENTS	12
(4) DISPOSITION	17
§ III. THE SECOND LETTER	18
(1) OCCASION	18
(2) PLACE, DATE, AND PURPOSE	19
(3) CONTENTS	20
(4) RELIGIOUS CONVICTIONS	24
(5) DISPOSITION	27
§ IV. LANGUAGE AND PERSONAL EQUATION	28
(1) WORDS	28
(2) PHRASES	32
(3) PERSONAL EQUATION	34
§ V. AUTHENTICITY OF I	37
(1) EXTERNAL EVIDENCE	37
(2) BAUR'S CRITICISM	37
(3) PRIORITY OF II	38
(4) THEORIES OF INTERPOLATION	39
§ VI. AUTHENTICITY OF II	39
(1) ANTECEDENT PROBABILITY	39
(2) HISTORY OF THE CRITICISM	39
(3) OBJECTION FROM ESCHATOLOGY	43
(4) OBJECTION FROM LITERARY RESEMBLANCES	45
(A) STATEMENT OF THE CASE	45
(B) HYPOTHESIS OF FORGERY	51
(5) HYPOTHESIS OF GENUINENESS	53

CONTENTS

	PAGE
§ VII. THE TEXT	55
§ VIII. COMMENTARIES	59
COMMENTARY	67
INDEXES:	
I. SUBJECTS AND AUTHORS	315
II. GREEK WORDS AND PHRASES	319

ABBREVIATIONS

AJT. = *The American Journal of Theology* (Chicago).

Ambst. = Ambrosiaster.

BDB. = Brown, Driver, Briggs, *Heb.-Eng. Lexicon.*

Bl. = F. Blass, *Grammatik des neutestamentlichen Griechisch* (1896, 1902²).

BMT. = E. D. Burton, *Syntax of the Moods and Tenses in N. T. Greek* (1898³).

Born. = Bornemann.

Bousset, *Relig.* = W. Bousset, *Die Religion des Judentums im neutestamentlichen Zeitalter* (1906²).

Calv. = Calvin.

Charles, *Eschat.* = R. H. Charles, *Eschatology, Hebrew, Jewish, and Christian* (1899).

Chrys. = Chrysostom.

Deiss. *BS.* = A. Deissmann, *Bibelstudien* (1895).
NBS. = *Neue Bibelstudien* (1897).
Light = *Light from the Ancient East* (1910) = *Licht vom Osten* (1909³).

De W. = De Wette.

Dob. = Ernst von Dobschütz,

EB. = *The Encyclopædia Biblica* (London, 1899– 1903; ed. J. S. Black and T. K. Cheyne).

EGT. = *The Expositor's Greek Testament* (ed. W. R. Nicoll, 1897–1910).

Einl. = *Einleitung in das N. T.*

Ell. = Ellicott.

Ephr. = Ephraem Syrus.

ERE. = *Encyclopædia of Religion and Ethics* (ed. J. Hastings, 1909 *ff.*).

Exp. = *The Expositor* (London; ed. W. R. Nicoll).

Exp. Times = *The Expository Times* (Edinburgh; ed. J. Hastings).

Find. = G. G. Findlay.

GGA. = *Götting. Gelehrte Anzeigen.*

GMT. = W. W. Goodwin, *Syntax of the Moods and Tenses of the Greek Verb* (1890).

Grot. = Hugo de Groot (Grotius).

Hatch, *Essays* = E. Hatch, *Essays in Biblical Greek* (1889).

HC. = Holtzmann's *Handcommentar zum Neuen Testament.*

HDB. = Hastings' *Dictionary of the Bible* (1898–1904).

ICC. = *International Critical Commentary.*

Introd. = *Introduction to the N. T.*

vii

JBL. = *The Journal of Biblical Literature* (New York).

JTS. = *The Journal of Theological Studies.*

Kennedy, *Last Things* = H. A. A. Kennedy, *St. Paul's Conceptions of the Last Things* (1904). *Sources* = *Sources of N. T. Greek* (1895).

Lft. = Lightfoot.

Lillie = John Lillie, *Epistles of Paul to the Thessalonians, Translated from the Greek, with Notes* (1856).

Lün. = Lünemann.

Lxx. = *The Old Testament in Greek* (ed. H. B. Swete, 1887–94).

Meyer = *Kritisch-exegetischer Komm. über das N. T.*

Migne, *PG.* = *Patrologiæ series græca.*

PL. = *Patrologiæ series latina.*

Mill. = George Milligan.

Moff. = James Moffatt.

Moult. = James Hope Moulton, *A Grammar of N. T. Greek,* I (1906).

NKZ. = *Neue kirchliche Zeitschrift.*

PRE. = *Real-Encyclopädie für protest. Theologie u. Kirche* (3d ed. Hauck, 1896–1909).

RTP. = *Review of Theology and Philosophy.*

Ruther. = W. G. Rutherford, *St. Paul's Epistles to the Thess. and Corinthians. A New Translation* (1908).

SBBA. = *Sitzungsberichte der königlich. Preuss. Akad. der Wissenschaften zu Berlin.*

Schürer = E. Schürer, *Geschichte des Jüdischen Volkes im Zeitalter Jesu Christi* (4th ed., 1901–9).

SH. = Comm. on Romans in *ICC.* by W. Sanday and A. C. Headlam.

SHS. = C. A. Briggs, *General Introduction to the Study of Holy Scripture* (1899).

SK. = *Studien und Kritiken.*

SNT. = *Die Schriften des N. T.* (1907–8; ed. J. Weiss).

Sod. = Hermann Freiherr von Soden.

Soph. *Lex.* = E. A. Sophocles, *Greek Lexicon of the Roman and Byzantine Periods* (revised by J. H. Thayer, 1887, 1900).

Thay. = Joseph Henry Thayer, *Greek-English Lexicon of the N. T.* (1889).

Th. Mops. = Theodore of Mopsuestia, *in epistolas Pauli commentarii* (ed. H. B. Swete, 1880–82).

Tisch. = Tischendorf.

TLZ. = *Theologische Literaturzeitung.*

TS. = *Texts and Studies* (Cambridge).

TU. = *Texte und Untersuchungen zur Geschichte der altchristlichen Literatur.*

Vincent = M. R. Vincent, *Word Studies in the N. T.*, vol. IV, 1900.

Viteau = J. Viteau, *Étude sur le Grec du N. T.* (I, 1893, II, 1896).

Volz, *Eschat.* = Paul Volz, *Jüdische Eschatologie von Daniel bis Akiba* (1903).

Weiss = B. Weiss in *TU.* XIV, 3 (1896).

WH. = *The New Testament in the Original Greek* (1881; I, Text, II, Introduction and Appendix).

Witk. = St. Witkowski, *Epistulæ Privatæ Græcæ* (1906).

Wohl. = Wohlenberg.

WS. = P. W. Schmiedel, 8th ed. of Winer's *Grammatik* (1894 *ff.*).

Zim. = F. Zimmer, *Der Text der Thessalonicherbriefe* (1893).

ZNW. = Preuschen's *Zeitschrift für die neutestamentliche Wissenschaft.*

ZTK. = *Zeitschrift für Theologie und Kirche.*

ZWT. = *Zeitschrift für Wissenschaftliche Theologie.*

N. B. The Old Testament is cited from the Greek text (ed. Swete), the New Testament from the text of WH., and the Apostolic Fathers from the *editio quarta minor* of Gebhardt, Harnack, and Zahn (1902). For Ethiopic Enoch (Eth. En.), Slavonic Enoch (Slav. En.), Ascension of Isaiah (Ascen. Isa.), Assumption of Moses (Ass. Mos.), Apocalypse of Baruch (Apoc. Bar.), Book of Jubilees (Jub.), and Testaments of the Twelve Patriarchs (Test. xii), the editions of R. H. Charles have been used; for the Psalms of Solomon (Ps. Sol.), the edition of Ryle and James; and for the Fourth Book of Ezra (4 Ezra), that of Bensly and James.

By I is meant 1 Thessalonians and by II, 2 Thessalonians.

INTRODUCTION.

§ I. FOUNDING OF THE CHURCH OF THE THESSALONIANS.

(1) *From Antioch to Philippi.*—It was seventeen years after God had been pleased to reveal his Son in him, and shortly after the momentous scene in Antioch (Gal. $2^{11\,ff.}$) that Paul in company with Silas, a Roman citizen who had known the early Christian movement both in Antioch and in Jerusalem, and with Timothy, a younger man, son of a Gentile father and a Jewish mother, set forth to revisit the Christian communities previously established in the province of Galatia by Paul, Barnabas, and their helper John Mark. Intending to preach the gospel in Western Asia, they made but a brief stay in Galatia and headed westward presumably for Ephesus, only to be forbidden by the Holy Spirit to speak the word in Asia; and again endeavouring to go into Bithynia were prevented by the Spirit of Jesus. Having come down to Troas, Paul was inspired by a vision to undertake missionary work in Europe; and accordingly set sail, along with the author of the "we"-sections, from Troas and made a straight course to Samothrace, and the day following to Neapolis; and from thence to Philippi (Acts 15^{40}–16^{11}). The experiences in that city narrated by Acts (16^{12-40}), Paul nowhere recounts in detail; but the persecutions and particularly the insult offered to the Roman citizenship of himself and Silas (Acts 16^{37}) affected him so deeply that he could not refrain from telling the Thessalonians about the matter and from mentioning it again when he wrote his first letter to them (I 2^2).

(2) *From Philippi to Thessalonica.*—Forced by reason of persecution to leave Philippi prematurely (I 2^2 Acts 16^{39-40}), Paul and Silas with Timothy (I 2^2; he is assumed also by Acts to be

I

present, though he is not expressly named between 16³ and 17¹⁴), but without the author of the "we"-sections, took the *Via Egnatia* which connected Rome with the East, travelled through Amphipolis and Apollonia, and arrived, early in the year 50 A.D., at Thessalonica, a city placed *in gremio imperii nostri*, as Cicero has it (*de prov. consul.* 2), and a business and trade centre as important then to the Roman Empire as it is now to the Turkish Empire, Saloniki to-day being next after Constantinople the leading metropolis in European Turkey.

Thessalonica had been in existence about three hundred and sixty-five years and a free city for about a century when Paul first saw it. According to Strabo (330²¹·²⁴, ed. Meineke), an older contemporary of the Apostle, it was founded by Cassander who merged into one the inhabitants of the adjacent towns on the Thermaic gulf and gave the new foundation the name Thessalonica after his wife, a sister of Alexander the Great. "During the first civil war, it was the headquarters of the Pompeian party and the Senate. During the second, it took the side of Octavius, whence apparently it reached the honour and advantage of being made a 'free city' (Pliny, *H. N.* IV¹⁰), a privilege which is commemorated on some of its coins" (Howson). That it was a free city (*liberae conditionis*) meant that it had its own βουλή and δῆμος (Acts 17⁵?), and also its own magistrates, who, as Luke accurately states, were called politarchs (Acts 17⁶).

Howson had already noted the inscription on the *Vardár* gate (destroyed in 1867) from which it appeared that "the number of politarchs was seven." Burton, in an exhaustive essay (*AJT*. 1898, 598–632), demonstrated, on the basis of seventeen inscriptions, that in Thessalonica there were five politarchs in the time of Augustus and six in the time of Antoninus and Marcus Aurelius.

On Thessalonica in general, see Howson in Smith's *DB*. and Dickson in *HDB*. where the literature, including the dissertation of Tafel, is amply listed. On *Roads and Travel*, see Ramsay in *HDB*. V, 375 ff.

(3) *Founding of the Church.*—In the time of Paul, Thessalonica was important, populous, and wicked (Strabo 323, 330²¹; Lucian, *Lucius* 46, ed. Jacobitz). Various nationalities were

represented, including Jews (I 2$^{15-16}$ II 3^2 Acts 17^2 ff.). Quite naturally, Paul made the synagogue the point of approach for the proclamation of the gospel of God, for the Christ, whose indwelling power unto righteousness he heralded, is of the Jews according to the flesh; and furthermore in the synagogue were to be found a number of Gentiles, men and women, who had attached themselves more or less intimately to Judaism either as proselytes or as φοβούμενοι (σεβόμενοι) τὸν θεόν (see Bousset, *Relig.*^{2}, 105), and who would be eager to compare Paul's gospel both with the cults they had forsaken for the austere monotheism and rigorous ethics of Judaism and with the religion of Israel itself. In such Gentiles, already acquainted with the hopes and aspirations of the Jews, he was almost certain to win a nucleus for a Gentile Christian community (*cf.* Bousset, *op. cit.*, 93), even if he had confined his ministry to the synagogue, as the account of Acts at first reading seems to intimate.

According to that narrative (Acts 17^2 ff.), Paul addressed the synagogue on three, apparently successive, Sabbath days, making the burden of his message the proof from Scripture that the Messiah was to suffer and rise again from the dead, and pressing home the conclusion that the Jesus whom he preached was the promised Christ. The result of these efforts is stated briefly in one verse (17^4) to the effect that there joined fortunes with Paul and Silas some Jews, a great number of the σεβόμενοι ῞Ελλη-νες, and not a few women of the best society. It is not put in so many words but it is tempting to assume that the women referred to were, like "the devout Greeks," Gentile proselytes or adherents, although Hort (*Judaistic Christianity*, 89) prefers to assume that they were "Jewish wives of heathen men of distinction." However that may be, it is interesting to observe that even from the usual text of Acts 17^4 (on Ramsay's conjecture, see his *St. Paul the Traveller*, 226 ff.) it is evident that the noteworthy successes were not with people of Jewish stock but with Gentile adherents of the synagogue.

Of the formation of a Christian community consisting almost wholly of Gentiles, the community presupposed by the two letters, the Book of Acts has nothing direct to say. In lieu thereof, the author tells a story illustrating the opposition of the Jews and accounting for the enforced departure of Paul from Thessalonica. Jealous of Paul's successful propaganda not only with a handful of Jews but also with those Gentiles who had been won over wholly or in part to the Jewish faith, the Jews took occasion to gather a mob which, after parading the streets and setting the city in an uproar, attacked the house of Jason in the hope of discovering the missionaries. Finding only Jason at home, they dragged him and some Christians before the politarchs and preferred the complaint not simply that the missionaries were disturbing the peace there as they had been doing elsewhere in the empire, but above all that they were guilty of treason, in that they asserted that there was another king or emperor, namely, Jesus,—an accusation natural to a Jew who thought of his Messiah as a king. The politarchs, though perturbed, did not take the charge seriously, but, contenting themselves with taking security from Jason and the others who were arrested, let them go.

> Just how much is involved in this decision is uncertain. Evidently Jason and the rest were held responsible for any conduct or teaching that could be interpreted as illegal; but that Paul was actually expelled is doubtful; and that Jason and the others gave security for the continued absence of Paul is unlikely, seeing that the converts were surprised at his failure to return. See on I 2^{18} and cf. Knowling on Acts 17^9 in EGT.

Of the preaching on the Sabbath Paul has nothing to say, or of the specific case of opposition, unless indeed the persecution of Jason was one of the instances of hardness of heart alluded to in I $2^{15\text{-}16}$. On the other hand, while Acts is silent about missionary work apart from the synagogue, Paul intimates in the course of his *apologia* (I $2^{7\text{-}12}$) that he was carrying on during the week a personal and individual work with the Gentiles that was even more important and successful than the preaching on the Sabbath of which alone Luke writes. It is quite to be expected that the Apostle would take every opportunity to speak informally about the gospel to every one he met; and to point out especially to those Gentiles, who had not expressed an interest in the God of his fathers by attaching themselves to the synagogue, the absurdity of serving idols, and to urge them to forsake their dead and false gods and turn to the living and true God and to his Son Jesus, who not only died for their sins but was raised again from the dead in order to become the indwelling power unto righteousness and the earnest of blessed felicity in the not distant future when Jesus, the rescuer from the coming Wrath, would appear and gather all believers into an eternal fellowship with himself (I 1^{9-10} 4^{9-10} II 2^{13-14}).

(4) *Character of the Church.*—His appeal to the Gentiles succeeded; in spite of much opposition, he spoke courageously as God inspired him (I 2^2), not in words only but in power, in the Holy Spirit and in much conviction (I 1^5); and the contagious power of the same Spirit infected the listeners, leading them to welcome the word which they heard as a message not human but divine, as a power of God operating in the hearts of believers (I $1^{6\ ff.}$ $2^{13\ ff.}$), creating within them a religious life spontaneous and intense, and prompting the expression of the same in those spiritual phenomena (I 5^{21-22}) that appear to be the characteristic effect of Paul's gospel of the newness of life in Christ Jesus.

But although the gospel came home to them with power, and a vital and enthusiastic religious life was created, and a community of fervent believers was formed, there is no reason for supposing that the circle of Christians was large, unless we are determined to press the πλῆθος πολύ of Acts 17^4. The necessities of the case are met if we imagine a few men and women meeting together in the house of Jason, the house in which Paul lodged at his own expense (II 3^7), and which was known to the Jews as the centre of the Christian movement; for it was there that they looked for the missionaries and there that they found the "certain brethren."

Nor must we expect to meet among the converts "many wise after the flesh, many mighty, and many noble." To be sure, we hear later on of such important Thessalonians as Aristarchus (who was a Jew by birth, Acts 20^4 27^2 Col. 4^{10} Phile. 24), Secundus (Acts 20^4) and Demas (Col. 4^{14} Phile. 24 2 Tim. 4^{10}); but it cannot be affirmed with confidence that they belonged to the

original group. Apart then from a few Gentile women of the
better class (Acts 17²), the bulk of the Christians were working
people. That they were skilled labourers like Paul is by no
means clear; evident only is it that, hospitable and generous
as they were (I 4¹⁰), they were poor, so poor indeed that Paul
supported himself by incessant toil in order not to make any
demands upon the hospitality either of Jason his host or of any
other of the converts, and that he welcomed the assistance sent
him by the Philippians (Phil. 4¹⁶) probably on their own initiative.

This little circle of humble Christians quickly became as dear
to Paul as the church of their fellow-Macedonians at Philippi.
He did not insist upon the position of preponderance which
was his by right as an apostle of Christ, but chose to become
just one of them, a babe in the midst of them. As a nurse
cherishes her own children, so in his affection for them he gave
them not only the gospel of God but his very self as well. Like
as a father deals with his own children, so he urged each one of
them, with a word of encouragement or a word of warning as the
need might be, to walk worthily of God who calls them into his
own kingdom and glory (I 2⁶⁻¹²). When he tried, in his first letter to them, to put into words his love for those generous, affectionate, and enthusiastic workingmen, his emotion got the better
of his utterance: "Who is our hope or joy or crown to boast in
—or is it not you too—in the presence of our Lord Jesus when he
comes? Indeed, it is really you who are our glory and our joy"
(I 2¹⁹⁻²⁰). It is not surprising that on his way to Corinth, and
in Corinth, he received constantly oral reports from believers
everywhere about their faith in God and their expectancy of the
Advent of his Son from heaven (I 1⁷⁻¹⁰). And what he singles
out for emphasis in his letters, their faith, hope, and love, their
brotherly love and hospitality, their endurance under trial, and
their exuberant joy in the Spirit, are probably just the qualities
which characterised them from the beginning of their life in
Christ.

It was indeed the very intensity of their religious fervour that
made some of them forget that consecration to God is not simply

religious but moral. He had warned them orally against the danger (I 4²), but was obliged to become more explicit when he wrote them later on (I 4³⁻⁸). Others again, it may be assumed though it is not explicitly stated, aware that the day of the Lord was near and conscious that without righteousness they could not enter into the kingdom, were inclined to worry about their salvation, forgetting that the indwelling Christ was the adequate power unto righteousness. Still others, influenced by the pressure of persecution and above all by the hope of the immediate coming of the Lord, became excited, and in spite of Paul's example of industry gave up work and caused uneasiness in the brotherhood, so that Paul had to charge them to work with their own hands (I 4¹¹) and had to say abruptly: "If any one refuses to work, he shall not eat" (II 3¹⁰). These imperfections however were not serious; they did not counterbalance the splendid start in faith and hope and love; had he been able to stay with them a little longer, he could have helped them to remove the cause of their difficulties. Unfortunately however, as a result of the case of Jason, he was compelled to leave them sooner than he had planned.

It has been assumed in the foregoing that Paul was in Thessalonica not longer than three weeks. There is nothing incredible in the statement of Acts (17²), if the intensity of the religious life and the relative smallness of the group are once admitted. To be sure, it is not impossible that Luke intends to put the arrest of Jason not immediately after the three Sabbaths but at a somewhat later date, and that consequently a sojourn of six weeks may be conjectured (cf. Dob.). The conjecture however is not urgent nor is it demanded by the probably correct interpretation of Phil. 4¹⁶. That passage indicates not that the Philippians repeatedly sent aid to Paul when he was in Thessalonica but only that they sent him aid (see note on I 2¹⁸). There is no evidence that either Paul or the Thessalonians requested assistance; it came unsolicited. Hence the time required for the journey on foot from Philippi to Thessalonica, about five or six days, does not militate against the assumption of a stay in Thessalonica lasting not longer than three weeks. See on this, Clemen, *NKZ.*, 1896, VII, 146; and *Paulus*, II, 158; also, more recently, Lake, *The Earlier Epistles of St. Paul*, 1911, 64 *ff*.

§ II. THE FIRST LETTER.

(1) *From Thessalonica to Corinth.*—No sooner had Paul left Thessalonica than he was anxious to return. "Now we, brothers, when we had been bereaved of you for a short time only, out of sight but not out of mind, were excessively anxious to see you with great desire, for we did wish to come to you, certainly I Paul did and that too repeatedly, and Satan stopped us" (I 2[17-18]). To the happenings in the interval between his departure and the sending of Timothy from Athens, Paul does not allude; from Acts however (17[10-15]) it appears that directly after the arrest of Jason, the brethren sent away Paul and Silas by night westward to Beroea, a land journey of about two days. In that city, the missionaries started their work, as in Thessalonica, with the synagogue and had success not only with the Gentile adherents of Judaism, men and women, but also with the Jews themselves. When however the Jews of Thessalonica heard of this success, they came to Beroea, stirred up trouble, and forced Paul to leave (*cf.* also I 2[15-16]), after a stay of a week or two. Accompanied by an escort of the brethren, Paul travelled to the coast and, unless he took the overland route to Athens, a journey of nine or ten days, set sail from Pydna or Dion for Athens (a voyage under ordinary circumstances of two full days) leaving behind directions that Silas and Timothy follow him as soon as possible.

From Paul, but not from Acts, we learn that they did arrive in Athens and that, after the situation in Thessalonica had been discussed, decided to send Timothy back immediately to strengthen the faith of the converts and prevent any one of them from being beguiled in the midst of the persecutions which they were still undergoing (I 3[1 ff.]; on the differences at this point between Acts and Paul, see McGiffert, *Apostolic Age*, 257). Whether also Silas and Timothy had heard rumours that the Jews, taking advantage of Paul's absence, were maligning his character and trying to arouse the suspicion of the converts against him by misconstruing his failure to return, we do not know. At all events, shortly after the two friends had arrived, and Timothy had started back for Macedonia, Paul, after a sojourn of a fortnight or more, departed from Athens and in a day or two came to Corinth, whether with Silas or alone (Acts 18¹) is unimportant.

(2) *Place, Date, and Occasion.*—Arriving in Corinth early in the year 50 A.D., Paul made his home with Prisca and Aquila, supported himself by working at his trade, and discoursed every Sabbath in the synagogue. Later on, Silas and Timothy came down from Macedonia and joined hands with Paul in a more determined effort to win the Jews to Christ, only to meet again the same provoking opposition that they had previously met in Macedonia. Paul became discouraged; but Timothy's report that the Thessalonians, notwithstanding some imperfections, were constant in their faith and love and ever affectionately thinking of Paul, as eager to see him as he was to see them, cheered him enormously (I 3⁶⁻¹⁰).

Bacon (*Introd.*, 58) dates the arrival in Corinth early in the spring of 50 A.D.; *cf.* also C. H. Turner (*HDB.*, I, 424). According to Acts 18¹¹, Paul had been in Corinth a year and six months before Gallio appeared on the scene and left Corinth shortly after the coming of the proconsul (18¹⁸). From an inscription in Delphi preserving the substance of a letter from the Emperor Claudius to that city, Deissmann (*Paulus*, 1911, 159–177) has shown that Gallio took office in midsummer, 51, and that, since Paul had already been in Corinth eighteen months when the proconsul of Achaia arrived, the Apostle "came to Corinth in the first months of the year 50 and left Corinth in the late summer of the year 51." Inasmuch as Paul had probably not been long in Corinth before Timothy arrived, and inasmuch as the first letter was written shortly after Timothy came (I 3⁶), the date of I is approximately placed in the spring of 50 and the date of II not more than five to seven weeks later.

From the oral report of Timothy and probably also from a letter (see on I 2¹³ 4⁹· ¹³ 5¹) brought by him from the church, Paul was able to learn accurately the situation and the needs of the brotherhood. In the first place he discovered that since his departure, not more than two or three months previously, the Jews had been casting wholesale aspersions on his behaviour during the visit and misinterpreting his failure to come back;

and had succeeded in awakening suspicion in the hearts of some
of the converts. Among other things, the Jews had asserted
(I 2^{1-12}) that in general Paul's religious appeal arose in error,
meaning that his gospel was not a divine reality but a human
delusion; that it arose in impurity, hinting that the enthusiastic
gospel of the Spirit led him into immorality; and that it was
influenced by sinister motives, implying that Paul, like the pagan
itinerant impostors of religious or philosophical cults (*cf.* Clemen,
NKZ., 1896, 152), was working solely for his own selfish advantage. Furthermore and specifically the Jews had alleged
that Paul, when he was in Thessalonica, had fallen into cajoling
address, had indulged in false pretences to cover his greed, and
had demanded honour from the converts, as was his wont, using
his position as an apostle of Christ to tax his credulous hearers.
Finally, in proof of their assertions, they pointed to the unques-
tioned fact that Paul had not returned, the inference being that
he did not care for his converts and that he had no intention
of returning. The fact that Paul found it expedient to devote
three chapters of his first letter to a defence against these at-
tacks is evidence that the suspicion of some of the converts was
aroused and that the danger of their being beguiled away from
the faith was imminent. In his defence, he cannot withhold an
outburst against the obstinate Jews (I 2^{15-16}) who are the instigators of these and other difficulties which he has to face; but
he betrays no feeling of bitterness toward his converts. On the
contrary, knowing how subtle the accusations have been, and
confident that a word from him will assure them of his fervent
and constant love and will remove any scruples they may have
had, he addresses them in language of unstudied affection. His
words went home; there is not the faintest echo of the *apologia*
in the second epistle.

In the second place, he discovered that the original spiritual
difficulties, incident to religious enthusiasm and an eager expectation of the coming of the Lord, difficulties which his abrupt departure had left unsettled, still persisted, and that a new
question had arisen, due to the death of one or more of the converts. In reference to the dead in Christ, they needed not only

encouragement but instruction; as for the rest, they required not new teaching but either encouragement or warning. "The shortcomings of their faith" (I 3¹⁰) arose chiefly from the religious difficulties of the weak, the faint-hearted, and the idle. (1) The difficulty of "the weak" (οἱ ἀσθενεῖς I 5¹⁴) was that as pagans they had looked upon sexual immorality as a matter of indifference and had perhaps in their pagan worship associated impurity with consecration to the gods. What they as Christians needed to remember was that consecration to the true and living God was not only religious but ethical. Whether they had actually tumbled into the abyss or were standing on the precipice is not certain. At all events, Paul's warning with its religious sanction and practical directions (I 4³⁻⁸) sufficed; we hear nothing of "the weak" in the second letter. (2) The second class chiefly in mind are "the faint-hearted" (οἱ ὀλιγόψυχοι I 5¹⁴), those, namely, who were anxious not only about the death of their friends but also about their own salvation. (a) Since Paul's departure, one or more of the converts had passed away. The brethren were in grief not because they did not believe in the resurrection of the saints but because they imagined, some of them at least, that their beloved dead would not enjoy the same advantages as the survivors at the coming of the Lord. Their perplexity was due not to inherent difficulties with Paul's teaching, but to the fact that Paul had never discussed explicitly the question involved in the case. Worried about their friends, they urged that Paul be asked by letter for instruction concerning the dead in Christ (I 4¹³⁻¹⁸). (b) But the faint-hearted were also worrying about themselves. They knew that the day of the Lord was to come suddenly and that it would catch the wicked unprepared; they remembered that Paul had insisted that without blameless living they could not enter into eternal fellowship with the Lord; but they forgot that the indwelling Christ is the power unto righteousness and the pledge of future felicity, and in their forgetfulness were losing the assurance of salvation. They needed encouragement and received it (I 5¹⁻¹¹). Of these faint-hearted souls, we shall hear even more in the second letter (II 1³⁻2¹⁷). (3) The third class of which Paul learned com-

prised the idle brethren (οἱ ἄτακτοι I 5¹⁴). With the enthusiastic conviction that the Lord was coming soon, with the
constant pressure of persecution, and with the stimulus of Paul's
presence removed, some of the brethren had resumed their idle
habits with their train of poverty and meddlesomeness in the
affairs of the brotherhood. It would appear (see note on I 4¹¹)
that they had sought assistance from the church and had been
refused on the ground that Paul had clearly said that if a man
refused to work, he could receive no support. Perhaps the idlers
had asked for money "in the Spirit," a misuse of spiritual gifts
that tempted "those that laboured among them," that is, those
who took the lead in helping and warning, to despise the charismata (I 5¹⁹⁻²²). At all events, the leading men seem not to have
been overtactful; and when they intimated that they would
report the matter to Paul and ask for instructions, the idlers
retorted that they would not listen to the reading of Paul's letter (I 5²⁷). There was undoubtedly blame on both sides; clearly
the peace of the brotherhood was disturbed. Still the trouble
did not appear serious to Paul, judging from the answer which
he sent (I 4¹¹⁻¹²; cf. 5¹²⁻¹⁴· ²¹⁻²²· ²⁶⁻²⁷·). But in spite of Paul's letter, as we shall see, the idle brethren continued to be troublesome (II 3¹⁻¹⁷).

(3) *Contents.*—With this situation in mind,—the excellence
of their faith and love in spite of the temptations of the weak, the
discouragement of the faint-hearted, and the unbrotherly conduct
of the idlers; and their personal affection for Paul, notwithstanding the insinuations of the Jews, Paul began, not long after
the arrival of Timothy (I 3⁶) to dictate our first epistle. The
first three chapters are given to a review of his attitude to the
church from its foundation, and to a defence both of his behaviour when he was there (1⁵⁻²¹⁶) and of his failure to return
(2¹⁷⁻3¹⁰). Even the prayer (3¹¹⁻¹³) that closes the double thanksgiving (1²⁻2¹²; 2¹³⁻3¹⁰) begins with the petition that God and
Christ may direct his way to them. Tactfully disregarding the
shortcomings, Paul thanks God, as he remembers their work of
faith, labour of love, and endurance of hope, for the election of
the readers, the certainty of which is known from the presence

of the Spirit controlling not only the converts who welcomed the
gospel with joy in spite of persecution and became a model assembly to believers everywhere, but also the attitude of the missionaries whose preaching was in the Spirit and whose behaviour
was totally unselfish ($1^{2\text{-}10}$). Coming directly to the charges of
the Jews, Paul, conscious both of the integrity of his motives and
of his unselfish love (the theme is heard already in δι' ὑμᾶς 1^5)
and aware of the openness of his religious appeal, reminds his
friends that he came not empty-handed but with a gospel and
a courageous power inspired by God ($2^{1\text{-}2}$). Wherever he goes,
he preaches as one who has no delusions about the truth, for
his gospel is of God; who has no consciousness of moral aberration, for God has tested him and given him his commission; and
who has no intention to deceive, for he is responsible solely to
God who knows his motives ($2^{3\text{-}4}$). In Thessalonica, as his readers know, he never used cajoling speech, never exploited the gospel to further his own ambition, and never required honour to be
paid him, even if he had the right to receive it as an ambassador
of Christ ($2^{5\text{-}6}$). On the contrary, he waived that right, choosing
to become just one of them, a babe in the midst of them; waived
it in unselfish love for his dear children. Far from demanding
honour, he worked with his hands to support himself while he
preached, in order not to trespass upon the hospitality of his
friends ($2^{7\text{-}9}$). The pious, righteous, and blameless conduct of
which they were ever aware proves his sincerity as a preacher
(2^{10}). Not as a flatterer but as a father, he urged them one and
all, by encouragement or by solemn appeal, to behave as those
who are called of God unto salvation in his kingdom and glory
($2^{11\text{-}12}$). Having thus defended his visit, he turns again to the
welcome which they gave him and his gospel ($2^{13\text{-}16}$ resuming
$1^{6\text{-}10}$). Rightly they thank God, as he does, that they welcomed
the word which they heard as God's word, as a power operating
in their hearts, attesting the genuineness of their faith by their
steadfast endurance in the persecutions at the hands of their
fellow-countrymen. It is however the Jews who are egging on
the Gentiles,—the Jews who killed the prophets and the Lord
Jesus and persecuted us, and who are not pleasing to God
and are against humanity, hindering us from preaching to Gen-

tiles unto their salvation. They have hardened their hearts; their sins are filling up; and the judgment is destined to come upon them at last (2 13-17).

Turning next to the insinuation of the Jews that he did not want to return, he reminds his orphaned children that from the moment he left them, he had been excessively anxious to see them and had repeatedly wished to return. Indeed nothing less than Satan could have deterred him. Far from not caring for them, he insists in words broken by emotion that it is above all they who are his glory and joy (2 17-20). Determined no longer to endure the separation, the missionaries, he says, agreed to send Timothy to encourage them in their faith and prevent their being beguiled in the midst of their persecution. As the Jews had singled out Paul for attack, he is at pains to add that he too as well as his companions had sent to know their faith, for he is apprehensive lest the tempter had tempted them and his work should turn out to be in vain (3 1-5). The return of Timothy with the good news of their spiritual life and their personal affection for Paul gave him new courage to face his own trials. "We live if you stand fast in the Lord." Words fail to express the abundance of joy he has in their faith, as he prays constantly to see them and help them solve their spiritual difficulties (3 6-10). But whether or not his prayer will be answered, God and Christ, to whom he prays, will increase their love and will inwardly strengthen them, so that they will be unblemished in holiness when the Lord Jesus comes (3 11-13).

Even as he prays for brotherly love and a blameless life, he seems to have in mind the needs of the idlers and the weak. At all events, the *apologia* finished, he takes up the imperfections of the group, dealing chiefly with the difficulties of the weak, the idlers, and the faint-hearted. He begins the exhortations (4 1-5 22) tactfully, urging not his own authority but that of the indwelling Christ, and insisting graciously that he has nothing new to say and that, since they are already doing well, he can only bid them to do so the more (4 1-2). At the same time, he does not withhold his exhortations. Speaking first of all of the weak, he urges that true consecration is moral as well as religious and demands imperatively sexual purity. He suggests the practical remedy that fornication may be prevented by respect for one's wife and that adultery may be prevented by marrying not in the spirit of lust but in the spirit of holiness and honour. Then, as a sanction for obedience, he reminds them that Christ punishes impurity; that God calls them not for impurity but for holiness; that to sin is to direct a blow not against the human but against the divine, even the Spirit, the consecrating Spirit that God gives them (4^{3-8}).

As to brotherly love, concerning which they had written, Paul remarks first of all and tactfully that, as they are practising it, instruction is unnecessary; but then proceeds to urge them in general to abound the more in that love and specifically, reiterating what he had said orally in reference to idleness, to strive to be tranquil in mind, undisturbed by the nearness of the advent, to mind their own business, not meddling in the affairs of the brotherhood, and to work with their hands, in order to win the respect of unbelievers and to avoid dependence upon the church for support (4^{9-12}).

Taking up the new point, the question of the faint-hearted in reference to the dead in Christ, he replies that his purpose in giving this new instruction is that they, unlike the unbelievers, who do not have the hope in Christ, should not sorrow at all. For it is certain, both on the ground of the believer's experience in Christ and of a word of Jesus, whose point is summarised, that the surviving saints will not anticipate the dead at the *Parousia.* In fact, when the Lord comes, the dead in Christ will arise first; then the survivors will be snatched up at the same time with the risen dead and all together, with no advantage the one over the other, will meet the Lord in the air. "And so we shall always be with the Lord" (4^{13-18}). With this encouraging teaching, he turns to the personal anxieties of the faint-hearted. They know, he says, as well as he that the day of the Lord will come suddenly and will take unbelievers by surprise; but they are not unbelievers that the day of the Lord should surprise them. To be sure they must be morally prepared, armed with faith, hope, and love; but they need not be discouraged about the outcome, for God has appointed them to salvation, the indwelling Christ has enabled them to be blameless, and Christ died for their sins in order that all believers, surviving or dead, may at the same time have life together with Christ. "Wherefore encourage one another and build up each other, as in fact you are doing" (5^1-11).

With a renewed exhortation, the need of a deeper brotherly love being in mind, he urges all to appreciate those who labour among them, leading and admonishing, and to regard them highly because of their work. Recognising that the idlers are not alone to blame for disturbing the peace of the brotherhood, he adds: "Be at peace among yourselves" (5^12-13). With a further exhortation, he sets forth the proper attitude of all to each of the three classes prominently in mind since 4^1: "Warn the idlers, encourage the faint-hearted, cling to the weak" (5^14). Then follows a word to all in view of the persecutions and the temptation to revenge, and in view also of the friction in the brotherhood: "Be slow to anger; see to it that no one retaliates an injury, but seek earnestly the good within and without" (5^14d-15). In spite of these difficulties, "always rejoice, continually pray, in everything give thanks, for this is God's will operating in Christ for you" (5^16-18). Finally, in view both of the disparagement and of the misuse of spiritual gifts, he exhorts: "Quench not the gifts of the Spirit, do not make light of cases of prophesyings; on the other hand, test all gifts of the Spirit, holding fast to the good and holding aloof from every evil kind" (5^19-22). Recognising however that his exhortations (4^1-5^22), especially to ethical consecration (4^3-8) and to brotherly love and peace (4^9-12 5^12-13) are of no avail without the help of God; and recognising further the necessity of the consecration not only of the soul but of the body (4^3-8), a consecration impossible unless the Spirit of God as immanent in the individual be inseparably bound to the human personality, body and soul, he prays first in general that God would consecrate them through and through, and then specifically that he would keep their spirit, the divine element, and their soul and body, the human element, intact, as an undivided whole, so that they might be morally blameless when the Lord comes. That this petition will be granted is certain, for God the faithful not only calls but consecrates and keeps them blameless to the end ($5^{23\text{-}24}$).

When you pray without ceasing (5^{17}), brothers, he says in closing, remember not only yourselves but us as well (5^{25}). Greet for us the brothers, all of them, with a holy kiss (5^{26}). Then having in mind the assertion of some of the idlers that they would give no heed to his letter, Paul adjures the brethren that his letter be read to all without exception (5^{27}). "The grace of our Lord Jesus Christ be with you" (5^{28}).

(4) *Disposition.*—The first epistle may be thus divided:

I. Superscription 1^1
    A. The Apologia 1^2–3^{13}
II. Thanksgiving 1^2–3^{10}
    (1) Visit and Welcome $1^{2\text{-}10}$
    (2) Visit $2^{1\text{-}12}$
    (3) Welcome; the Jews $2^{13\text{-}16}$
    (4) Intended Visit $2^{17\text{-}20}$
    (5) Sending of Timothy $3^{1\text{-}5}$
    (6) Timothy's Return and Report $3^{6\text{-}10}$
III. Prayer $3^{11\text{-}13}$
    B. The Weak, The Idlers, The Faint-hearted, etc. 4^1–5^{27}
IV. Exhortations 4^1–5^{22}
    (1) Introduction $4^{1\text{-}2}$
    (2) True Consecration $4^{3\text{-}8}$
    (3) Brotherly Love $4^{9\text{-}10\,a}$
    (4) Idleness $4^{10\,b\text{-}12}$
    (5) The Dead in Christ $4^{13\text{-}18}$
    (6) Times and Seasons $5^{1\text{-}11}$
    (7) Spiritual Labourers $5^{12\text{-}13}$
    (8) Idlers, Faint-hearted, Weak $5^{14\,a\text{-}c}$
    (9) Love $5^{14\,d\text{-}15}$
    (10) Joy, Prayer, Thanksgiving $5^{16\text{-}18}$
    (11) Spiritual Gifts $5^{19\text{-}22}$
V. Prayer $5^{23\text{-}24}$
VI. Final Requests $5^{25\text{-}27}$
VII. Benediction 5^{28}

2

§ III. THE SECOND LETTER.

(1) *Occasion.*—It is impossible to determine with exactness the reasons that led to the writing of the second epistle. The internal evidence of II, upon which we must rely, permits only a tentative reconstruction of the course of events in the interval between the sending of I and the composition of II. We may assume however that the first letter did not have quite the effect that a visit from Paul would have had. To be sure, whatever suspicion the readers may have entertained as to Paul's motives during and since his visit was dispelled by his affectionate words in defence of himself. It is evident also that his warning to the weak was effectual, being fortified by the help of the brethren, who, as he had requested, held to the weak, tenderly but firmly supporting them. On the other hand, the idle brethren continued to be meddlesome, Paul's command, reiterating what he had said orally (I 4^{11}), not having had the desired effect. This failure may have been due in part to the fact, for which Paul is not responsible, that the majority, who had been urged to admonish the idlers (I 5^{14}) had not been tactful in performing their function (II 3^{13. 15}); and in part to the fact, for which again Paul is not to blame, that some of the brethren had imagined that Paul had said, either in an utterance of the Spirit, or in an uninspired word, or in the first epistle, something that was interpreted to mean that the day of the Lord was actually present (II 2^2). This disquieting statement, innocently attributed to Paul, perhaps by some of the excited idlers, affected not only the idle brethren as a whole but the faint-hearted as well. Already anxious about their salvation (I 5^{1-11}), they became unsettled and nervously wrought up (II 2^2); and naturally enough, for if they deemed themselves unworthy of salvation, and if it was true that the day of the Lord had actually dawned, then there was no time left for them to attain that blamelessness in holiness, that equipment of faith, hope, and love upon which the first letter had insisted (I 3^{13} 5^8) as essential to the acquisition of salvation; and the judgment, reserved for unbelievers, would certainly come upon them.

Unable either to relieve the anxiety of the faint-hearted or to bring the idlers to a sense of duty, the leaders sent a letter (see notes on $1^{3. 11}$ 3^{1-5}) to Paul by the first brother (3^{11}) who was journeying to Corinth. Reflecting the discouragement of the faint-hearted, they write remonstrating with Paul for his praise of their faith, love, and endurance, intimating that they were not worthy of it. Though they are praying that God may consider them worthy of the kingdom, they fear that he may not deem them worthy (1^{3-12}). They tell Paul of the assertion, attributed to him, that the day of the Lord is present, and the effect which it had both on the faint-hearted and on the idlers; and they ask advice specifically concerning the advent of the Lord and the assembling unto him (II 2^1). It may be conjectured that "those who labour among you" (I 5^{12}) had informed the idle brethren that they would report their conduct to Paul; and that some of these idlers had retorted that they would give no heed to the commands of Paul by letter (II 3^{14}), and would not even listen to the reading of the expected reply, intimating that they could not be sure that the letter would be genuine (II 3^{17}).

(2) *Place, Date, and Purpose.*—Such a letter as we have postulated will have been sent shortly after the receipt of I. The new situation which it recounts is not new in kind but a natural development of tendencies present during the visit and evident in the first letter. Hence if we allow two or three weeks for I to reach Thessalonica, a week for the preparation of the reply, and two or three weeks for the reply to get to Corinth, then an interval between I and II of five to seven weeks is ample enough to account for the situation in Thessalonica suggested by II. Indeed, apart from the increased discouragement of the faint-hearted and the continued recalcitrance of some of the idle brethren, there is nothing to indicate a notable change in the church since the visit of Timothy. Persecutions are still going on (II 1^4; cf. 2^{17} $3^{3 ff.}$), and the Jews are evidently the instigators of the same (II 3^2); the endurance of the converts is worthy of all praise (II 1^4); and the increase of faith and love (II 1^3) indicates not a large growth numerically but an appreciative recognition of progress in things essential, the fulfilment in part of the prayer

in I 3¹². In Corinth, likewise, the situation since the writing of I has not changed materially; Silas and Timothy are still with Paul (II 1¹); and the opposition of the Jews (Acts 17⁵ ᶠ·), those unrighteous and evil men whose hearts are hardened (II 3²; cf. I 2¹⁴⁻¹⁶), persists, so much so that Paul would gladly share with the converts the relief which the *Parousia* is to afford (II 1⁷). On the whole, then, the available evidence points to the assumption that the second epistle was written from Corinth in the spring of 50 A.D. not more than five to seven weeks after the first epistle.

The second epistle is not a doctrinal treatise on the Antichrist, as if 2¹⁻¹² were the sole point of the letter, but a practical exhortation, written by request and designed to encourage the faint-hearted and to admonish the idlers. The description of the judgment in 1⁶ ᶠ·, the allusions to the premonitory signs in 2³⁻⁸, and the characterisation of the advent of the *Anomos* (2⁹⁻¹²), placed significantly after his destruction (2⁸), are manifestly intended not to convey new information but to encourage the faint-hearted by reminding them of his oral instructions,—an employment of teaching for practical needs which is characteristic of Paul, as the passage in another Macedonian letter suggests (Phil. 2⁵ ᶠ·). In reference to the second purpose of II, it is to be observed that since the idleness and meddlesomeness have increased, it is necessary to supplement the injunctions of I (4¹¹⁻¹² 5¹⁴) by the severer command that the majority hold aloof from the idle brethren, avoid association with them; at the same time it is significant that the last word is only a repetition of what was said in the first letter (5¹⁴), with an added covert admonition of the somewhat tactless majority: "Do not regard him as an enemy but admonish him as a brother" (II 3¹⁵). To encourage the faint-hearted (II 1³–2¹⁷) and to warn the idlers (II 3¹⁻¹⁷) is the two-fold purpose of this simple, tactful, pastoral letter.

(3) *Contents.*—After the superscription (1¹⁻²) which differs from that in I only in having ἡμῶν after πατρί, expressing the sense of common fellowship in the Father, and in having after εἰρήνη the usual "from God our Father and the Lord Jesus

Christ," making explicit the source of divine favour and spiritual prosperity, Paul enters upon the thanksgiving (1^{3-10}) and closely related prayer (1^{11-12}) which together form an unbroken sentence of over two hundred words, liturgical in tone and designed to encourage the faint-hearted. In spite of what they have written, he ought, he insists, to thank God, as is proper under the circumstances, because their faith and brotherly love abound, so much so that he himself, contrary to their expectations, is boasting everywhere of their endurance and faith in the midst of persecutions. They need not worry (though the brethren as a whole are addressed, the faint-hearted are chiefly in mind) about their future salvation, for their splendid endurance springing from faith is positive proof that God the righteous judge will, in keeping with his purpose, deem them worthy of entrance into the kingdom, on behalf of which they as well as he are suffering. It will not always be well with their persecutors, for God, as righteous in judgment, will recompense them with affliction, as he will recompense the afflicted converts with relief from the same, a relief which Paul also will share. God will do so at the great assize (described in 1^{7b-10} not for the sake of the description but for the encouragement of the believers) when the wicked, those, namely, who do not reverence God and do not obey the gospel of our Lord Jesus, will receive as their punishment separation forever from Christ, on the very day when the righteous in general and (with an eye to the faint-hearted) all who became believers (for the converts believed the gospel addressed to them) will be the ground of honour and admiration accorded to Christ by the attendant angels. To reach this happy consummation, to be acquitted in that day, Paul prays, as the converts likewise prayed, that God will fill them with goodness and love, in order that finally the name of the Lord Jesus may be honoured in virtue of what they are and they may be honoured in virtue of what his name has accomplished. This glorification and blessed consummation, he assures them, is in accordance with the divine favour of our God and of the Lord Jesus Christ (1^{3-12}).

A little impatient that they have forgotten the instructions which he had given them orally and at a loss to understand how anything he had said in the Spirit, orally, or in his previous letter could be misconstrued to imply that he was responsible for the assertion that the day of the Lord is present, and yet recognising the agitation of the faint-hearted by reason of the assertion, and their need of encouragement, Paul turns to the specific question put to him "as to the coming of our Lord Jesus Christ and our assembling unto him" and exhorts them not to let their minds become easily unsettled and not to be nervously wrought up by the assertion, however conveyed and by whatever means attributed to him, that the day of the Lord is actually present. Allow no one to delude you, he says, into such a belief whatever means may be employed. Then choosing to treat the question put, solely with reference to the assertion and ever bearing in mind the need of the faint-hearted, he selects from the whole of his previous oral teaching on times and seasons only such elements as serve to prove that the assertion is mistaken, and reminds them that the day will not be present until first of all the apostasy comes and there is revealed a definite and well-known figure variously characterised as the man of lawlessness, the son of destruction, etc., allusions merely with which the readers are quite familiar, so familiar indeed that he can cut short the characterisation, and appeal, with a trace of impatience at their forgetfulness, to the memory of the readers to complete the picture (2^{1-5}).

Turning from the future to the present, he explains why the apostasy and the revelation of the *Anomos* are delayed. Though the day of the Lord is not far distant,—for there has already been set in operation the secret of lawlessness which is preparing the way for the apostasy and revelation of the *Anomos*, still that day will not be actually present until that which restrains him in order that the *Anomos* may be revealed only at the time set him by God, or the person who now restrains him, is put out of the way. Then and not till then will the *Anomos* be revealed. But of him the believers need have no fear, for the Lord will destroy him; indeed his *Parousia*, inspired by Satan and attended by outward signs and inward deceit prompted by falsehood and unrighteousness, is intended not for believers but for unbelievers. These are destined to destruction, like the son of destruction himself, because they have destroyed themselves by refusing to welcome the heavenly guest, the influence of the Spirit designed to awaken within them the love for the truth which is essential to their salvation. As a consequence of their refusal, God as righteous judge is bound himself (for it is he and not Satan or the *Anomos* who is in control) to send them an inward working to delude them into believing the falsehood, in order that at the day of judgment they might be condemned, all of them, on the ground that they believed not the truth but consented to unrighteousness (2$^{6-12}$).

With a purposed repetition of 1^3, Paul emphasises his obligation to thank God for them, notwithstanding their discouraged utterances, because, as he had said before (I 1$^{4\,f\cdot}$), they are beloved and elect, chosen of God from everlasting, called and destined to obtain the glory of Christ. As beloved and elect, they should have no fear about their ultimate salvation and no disquietude by reason of the assertion that the day is present, but remembering the instructions, received orally and in his letter, should stand firm and hold those teachings. Aware however that divine power alone can make effective his appeal, and aware that righteousness, guaranteed by the Spirit, is indispensable to salvation, Paul prays that Christ and God, who in virtue of their grace had already commended their love to Christians in the death of Christ and had granted them through the Spirit inward assurance of salvation and hope for the ultimate acquisition of the glory of Christ, may grant also to the faint-hearted that same assurance and strengthen them in words and works of righteousness (2$^{13-17}$).

With these words of encouragement to the faint-hearted, he turns to the case of the idle brethren. Wishing to get their willing obedience, he appeals to the sympathy of all in requesting prayer for himself and his cause, and commends their faith. Referring to some remarks in their letter, he observes that if the idlers are disposed to excuse themselves on the ground that the tempter is too strong for them, they must remember that Christ is really to be depended on to give them power to resist temptation. Inasmuch as they have in Christ this power, Paul in the same Christ avows his faith in them that they will gladly do what he commands; indeed they are even now doing so. But to make his appeal effective, the aid of Christ is indispensable, —the power that will awaken in them a sense of God's love and of the possession of that adequate endurance which is inspired by Christ (3^{1-5}). Having thus tactfully prepared the way, he takes up directly the question of the idlers. He commands the brethren as a whole to keep aloof from every brother who lives as an idler, a command issued not on his own authority but on that of the name of Christ. He is at pains to say that he is urging nothing new, and gently prepares for the repetition of the original instruction by referring to the way in which he worked to support himself when he was with them, so as to free them from any financial burden, strengthening the reference by reminding them that although he was entitled to a stipend as an apostle of Christ, he waived the right in order that his self-sacrificing labour might be an example to them. Then after explaining the occasion of the present command, he enjoins the idlers, impersonally and indirectly and with a tactfully added "we exhort," to work and earn their own living with no agitation about the day of the Lord. With a broad hint to the majority as to their attitude to the idle brethren, he faces the contingency of disobedience on the part of some of the idlers. These recalcitrants are to be designated; there is to be no association with them. But the purpose of the discipline is repentance and reform. Once more the majority are warned: "Do not treat him as an enemy but warn him as a brother" (3^{6-15}). Since the command alone may not succeed in restoring peace to the brotherhood, Paul finally prays that Christ, the Lord of peace, may give them a sense of inward religious peace, and that too continually in every circumstance of life (3^{16}). Anticipating that some of the idlers may excuse their refusal to listen to Paul's letters on the ground that they are not his own, Paul underscores the fact that he is wont to write at the end a few words in his own hand (3^{17}). The benediction closes the pastoral letter (3^{18}).

(4) *Religious Convictions.*—The religious convictions expressed

or implied in II are Pauline. As in I so in II, the apocalyptic and the mystic are both attested. Though the former element is more obvious because of the circumstances, the latter is present as an equally essential part of the gospel, "our gospel" (2^{14}), to use the characteristic designation of the convictions that he had held for over seventeen years. Central is the conviction, inherited by Paul from the early church (*cf.* Acts 2^{36}) and constant with him to the end (Phil. 2^{11}), that Jesus is Christ and Lord. Of the names that recur, Our (The) Lord Jesus Christ ($2^{1.\ 14.\ 16}\ 3^{8}$; $1^{1.\ 2}\ 2^{12}\ 3^{6.\ 12}$), Our (The) Lord Jesus ($1^{8.\ 12}$; 1^{7}) Christ (3^{5}) and The Lord ($1^{9}\ 2^{2.\ 13}\ 3^{1.\ 3.\ 4.\ 5.\ 16.\ 16}$), the last, ὁ κύριος, is characteristic of II as compared with I (*cf.* II 3^{1-5} with Phil. 4^{1-5}). Though there is no explicit mention either of his death (*cf.* 2^{16}) or of his resurrection, the fact that he is Lord and Christ presupposes both that he is raised from the dead and that he is soon to usher into the kingdom of God all those who have been deemed worthy (1^{5}). This day of the Lord (2^{2}) is not actually present, as some had asserted, but it is not far distant (2^{7}). In that day (1^{10}), when the Lord comes (2^{1}) or is revealed from heaven (1^{7}), he will destroy the *Anomos* (2^{8}), execute judgment on unbelievers ($1^{6.\ 8-9}$), the doomed (2^{9-12}), by removing them eternally from his presence; and will bring salvation ($2^{10.\ 13}$) and glory (2^{14}) to all believers (1^{10}), those, namely, who have welcomed the love for the truth (2^{10}) and have believed the gospel preached to them ($1^{10}\ 2^{14}$) when they were called ($1^{11}\ 2^{14}$).

The exalted Lord does not however confine his Messianic activities to the day of his coming; he is already at work in the present. To him either alone ($3^{5.\ 16}$) or with the Father (2^{16}), prayer is addressed; and from him with the Father come grace ($1^{2}\ 2^{12.\ 16}$) and peace (1^{2}; *cf.* 3^{16}); he is with the believers (3^{16}), the faithful Lord who strengthens them and guards them from the Evil One (3^{3}) and gives them an eternal encouragement, good hope, and endurance ($2^{16}\ 3^{5}$). In these passages it is not always easy to tell whether Paul is thinking of the Lord who is at the right hand of God (Rom. 8^{34}) or of the Lord who is in the believers (Rom. 8^{10}). However that may be, it is important to observe that the Lord to Paul is not only the being enthroned with God and ready to appear at the last day for judgment and salvation but also, and this is distinctive, the permanent indwelling power unto righteousness, the ground of assurance that the elect and called will enter into the glory to be revealed, the first fruits of which they now enjoy. And this distinctive element underlies the utterances of this epistle, especially of $1^{11\text{-}12}$ and $2^{13\text{-}17}$. It is the indwelling Lord in whom the church of the Thessalonians exist (1^1), in whom also Paul has his confidence in reference to the readers (3^4) and gives his command and exhortation (3^{12}). The same Lord within inspires the gospel (3^1) and equips the persecuted with an endurance that is adequate (3^5). It is the Spirit, to whom equally with the Lord Paul ascribes the divine operations, that accounts for the charismata (2^2) and prompts consecration to God and faith in the truth (2^{13}). And it is either the Spirit or the Lord who is the means by which God fills the readers with goodness and love (ἐν δυνάμει 1^{11}; cf. ἐν θεῷ 1^1).

Faith in Jesus the Christ and Lord ($1^{3\cdot\,4\cdot\,11}$) or faith in the gospel (1^{10} 2^{13}) which he inspires (3^1) and which Paul proclaims (1^{10} 2^{14}) is the initial conviction that distinguishes the believers (1^{10}) from the Jews (3^2) and all others who have believed the lie of the *Anomos* with its unrighteousness ($2^{9\text{-}12}$). This faith is apparently prompted by the Spirit, the heavenly guest that seeks to stir within the soul the love for the truth unto salvation (2^{10}) and that inspires the consecration of the individual body and soul to God, and faith in the truth of the gospel (2^{13}). To be sure, the love for the truth may not be welcomed; in that case, God who controls the forces of evil, Satan and his instrument the *Anomos*, himself sends an inward working to delude the unbelievers into believing the lie, so that their condemnation follows of moral necessity; for they themselves are responsible for being in the category of the lost. On the other hand, if the promptings of the Spirit are heeded, then the activities of the Spirit continue in believers; a new power (1^{11}) enters into their life to abide permanently, a power whose presence is manifested not only in extraordinary phenomena (2^2) but in ethical fruits such as (*cf.* Gal. $5^{22\,f\cdot}$, 1 Cor. $13^{1\,ff\cdot}$, and Rom. $12^{6\,ff\cdot}$) love (the work of faith 1^{11}), brotherly love (1^3 3^{15}), peace (3^{16}), goodness (1^{11}), encouragement (2^{16}), hope (2^{16}), endurance (3^5 1^4), and, in fact, every good work and word (2^{17}); and a power unto righteousness that insures the verdict of acquittal at the last day ($1^{5.\ 11}$), and the entrance into the glory of the kingdom, foretastes of which the believer even now enjoys.

Since there are no errorists in Thessalonica, such as are to be found later in Colossæ dethroning Christ from his supremacy, there is no occasion for an express insistence upon his pre-eminence. It is thus noteworthy in II not only that the Lordship of Jesus is conspicuous but also that in 2^{16} as in Gal. 1^1 he is named before the Father. There are no Judaists in Thessalonica; hence it is not significant that the categories prominent in Galatians (a letter which Zahn, McGiffert, Bacon, Lake, and others put before I and II), namely, law, justification, works, etc., are absent from II as from I. Furthermore, since the situation does not demand a reference to the historical or psychological origin of Sin, it is not surprising that we hear nothing either in II or in I of Sin, Adam, Flesh. In fact, it happens that in II there is no explicit mention either of the death or of the resurrection of Christ. What is emphasised in II along with the apocalyptic is the indwelling power of the Lord or the Spirit, the source of the moral life and the ground of assurance not only of election from eternity but also of future salvation ($1^{5.\ 11-12}$ 2^{13-17}), an emphasis to be expected in a letter one of the two purposes of which is to encourage those whose assurance of salvation was wavering.

(5) *Disposition.*—The second letter may thus be divided:

I. Superscription 1^{1-2}
  A. Encouraging the Faint-hearted 1^3–2^{17}
II. Thanksgiving and Prayer 1^{3-12}
    (1) Assurance of Salvation 1^{3-10}
    (2) Prayer for Righteousness 1^{11-12}
III. Exhortation 2^{1-12}
    (1) Why the Day is not present 2^{1-8}
    (2) Destruction of the *Anomos* 2^8
    (3) *Parousia* of the *Anomos* only for the doomed 2^{9-12}

IV. Thanksgiving, Command, and Prayer 2¹³⁻¹⁷
    (1) Assurance of Salvation 2¹³⁻¹⁴
    (2) Hold fast to Instructions 2¹⁵
    (3) Prayer for Encouragement and Righteous-
    ness 2¹⁶⁻¹⁷
B. Warning the Idlers 3¹⁻¹⁷
V. Finally 3¹⁻⁵
    Transition to the Idlers
VI. Command and Exhortation 3⁶⁻¹⁵
    The Case of the Idlers
VII. Prayer for Peace 3¹⁶
VIII. Salutation 3¹⁷
IX. Benediction 3¹⁸

§ IV. LANGUAGE AND PERSONAL EQUATION

(1) *Words.*—The vocabulary of the letters is Pauline. The presence of words either in I or in II which are not found elsewhere in the N. T., or which are found either in I or in II and elsewhere in the N. T. but not elsewhere in Paul (the Pastoral Epistles not being counted as Pauline), indicates not that the language is not Pauline, but that Paul's vocabulary is not exhausted in any or all of the ten letters here assumed as genuine. Taking the text of WH. as a basis, we find in I about 362 words (including 30 particles and 15 prepositions) and in II about 250 words (including 26 particles and 14 prepositions). Of this total vocabulary of about 612 words, 146 (including 20 particles and 13 prepositions) are found both in I and in II.

Two hundred and ninety-nine of the 362 words in I (about 82 per cent) and 215 of the 250 words in II (about 86 per cent) are found also in one or more of the Major Epistles of Paul (*i. e.* Rom. 1, 2 Cor. Gal.). If we added to the 299 words of I some 19 words not found in one or more of the Major Epistles but found in one or more of the Epistles of the Captivity (*i. e.* Eph. Phil. Col. Phile.), then 318 of the 362 words in I (about 88 per cent) would appear to be Pauline; and similarly if we added to the 215 words of II some 7 words not found in one or more of the Major Epistles but found in one or more of the Epistles of the Captivity, then 222 of the 250 words in I (about 89 per cent) would appear to be Pauline.

Of the 146 words common to I and II all but 4 are also found in one or more of the Major Epistles. These 4 are Θεσσαλονικεύς I 1¹ II 1¹ (Acts 20⁴ 27²); κατευθύνειν I 3¹¹ II 3⁵ (Lk. 1⁷⁹); ἐρωτᾶν I 4¹ 5¹² II 2¹ (Phil. 4³; Gospels, Acts, 1, 2 Jn.); and περιποίησις I 5⁹ II 2¹⁴ (Eph. 1¹⁴; Heb. 10³⁹ 1 Pet. 2⁹).—The 19 words in I and in the Epistles of the Captivity but not in the Major Epistles are ἀγών 2² (Phil. Col. Past.); ἀκριβῶς 5² (Eph.); ἀπέχεσθαι 4³ 5²² (Phil. Phile. ἀπέχειν; Past. ἀπέχεσθαι); ἄμεμπτος 3¹³ (Phil.); δίς 2¹⁸ (Phil.); ἐρωτᾶν 4¹ (II, Phil.); θάλπειν 2⁷ (Eph. 5²⁹); θώραξ 5⁸ (Eph.); καθεύδειν 5⁶· ⁷· ¹⁰ (Eph.); καταλείπειν 3¹ (Eph.); μεθύσκεσθαι 5⁷ (Eph.); παρρησιάζεσθαι 2² (Eph.); περικεφαλαία 5⁸ (Eph.); περιποίησις 5⁹ (II, Eph.); πληροφορία 1⁵ (Col.); πρόφασις 2⁵ (Phil.); σβεννύναι 5¹⁹ (Eph.); φίλιπποι 2² (Phil.); and ὑπερεκπερισσοῦ 3¹⁰ 5¹³ (Eph. 3²⁰).—The 7 words in II and in the Epistles of the Captivity but not in the Major Epistles are αἱρεῖσθαι 2¹³ (Phil.); ἀπάτη 2¹⁰ (Col. Eph.); ἐνέργεια 2⁹· ¹¹ (Phil. Col. Eph.); ἐρωτᾶν 2¹ (I, Phil.); ἰσχύς 1⁹ (Eph.); κρατεῖν 2¹⁵ (Col.); and περιποίησις 2¹⁴ (I, Eph.).—Of these 19 + 7 = 26 words, two are common to I and II (ἐρωτᾶν and περιποίησις); and four others are distinctively Pauline, in that they do not occur in the N. T. apart from Paul (ἐνέργεια; θάλπειν; περικεφαλαία; and ὑπερεκπερισσοῦ).

Of the 44 (362 − 318 = 44) words of I which are not found in the Major Epistles or in the Epistles of the Captivity, 20 are also not found elsewhere in the N. T., 22 are found elsewhere in the N. T. but not elsewhere in Paul, and 2 are common to I and II. Again, of the 28 (250 − 222 = 28) words of II which are not found in the Major Epistles or in the Epistles of the Captivity, 10 are also not found elsewhere in the N. T., 16 are found elsewhere in the N. T. but not elsewhere in Paul, and 2 are common to II and I.

In the subjoined lists, an asterisk indicates that the word is not found in the Lxx.

(a) Words in I but not elsewhere in the N. T.: ἀμέμπτως 2¹⁰ 5²³; ἀναμένειν 1¹⁰; *ἀπορφανίζεσθαι 2¹⁷; ἄτακτος 5¹⁴; ἐκδιώκειν 2¹⁵; ἐνορκίζειν 5²⁷; ἐξηχεῖσθαι 1⁸; *θεοδίδακτος 4⁹; κέλευσμα 4¹⁶; *κολακία 2⁵; ὀλιγό-ψυχος 5¹⁴; ὀλοτελής 5²³; ὁμείρεσθαι 2⁸; ὁσίως 2¹⁰; περιλείπεσθαι 4¹⁵· ¹⁷;

*προπάσχειν 2²; *σαίνεσθαι 3³; *συμφυλέτης 2¹⁴; τροφός 2⁷; and ὑπερβαίνειν 4⁶.

(b) Words in II but not elsewhere in the N. T.: *ἀτακτεῖν 3⁷; ἀτάκτως 3⁶·¹¹; *ἔνδειγμα 1⁶; ἐνδοξάζεσθαι 1¹⁰·¹²; ἐνκαυχᾶσθαι 1⁴; *καλοποιεῖν 3¹³; περιεργάζεσθαι 3¹¹; σημειοῦσθαι 3¹⁴; τίνειν 1⁹; and ὑπεραυξάνεσθαι 1³.

(c) Words in I and elsewhere in N. T. but not elsewhere in Paul: Ἀθῆναι 3¹; αἰφνίδιος 5³; ἀληθινός 1⁹; ἀληθῶς 2¹³; ἀπάντησις 4¹⁷; *ἀρχάγγελος 4¹⁶; ἀσφάλεια 5³; εἴσοδος 1⁹ 2¹; ἡσυχάζειν 4¹¹; κτᾶσθαι 4⁴; ὁλόκληρος 5²³; παραμυθεῖσθαι 2¹¹ 5¹⁴; τοιγαροῦν 4⁸; ὑβρίζειν 2²; ὠδίν 5³; ἀντέχεσθαι 5¹⁴; γαστήρ 5³; διαμαρτύρεσθαι 4⁶; ἐναντίος 2¹⁵; ἐφιστάναι 5³; νήφειν 5⁶·⁸; and παραγγελία 4². The last seven words are in I, in one or more of the Pastorals, and elsewhere in the N. T., but not elsewhere in Paul.

(d) Words in II and elsewhere in N. T. but not elsewhere in Paul: ἀναιρεῖν 2⁸; ἀποστασία 2³; ἄτοπος 3²; δίκη 1⁹; ἐπισυναγωγή 2¹; θροεῖσθαι 2²; καταξιοῦν 1⁵; μιμεῖσθαι 3⁷; σαλεύειν 2²; σέβασμα 2⁴; φλόξ 1⁸; ἀξιοῦν 1¹¹; ἐπιφάνεια 2⁸; ἡσυχία 3¹²; κρίσις 1⁵ and μήτε 2². The last five words are in II, in one or more of the Pastorals, and ἐπιφάνεια excepted, elsewhere in N. T. but not elsewhere in Paul. While ἐπιφάνεια appears elsewhere in N. T. only in the Pastorals, the phrase in II 2⁸ ἡ ἐπιφάνεια τῆς παρουσίας αὐτοῦ is unique in the Gk. Bib.

(e) Words common to I and II and found elsewhere in N. T. but not elsewhere in Paul: Θεσσαλονικεύς I 1¹ II 1¹ (Acts 20⁴ 27²) and κατευθύνειν I 3¹¹ II 3⁵ (Lk. 1⁷⁹).

None of the words in the five lists above can be strictly called un-Pauline.

Attention has often been called to the consideration that II contains very few words which are found in Paul but not elsewhere in the N. T., except such as it has in common with I. As a matter of fact, the same criterion applied to I demonstrates that II is relatively better off than I in this respect. Apart from the two words common to I and II which are found elsewhere in Paul but not elsewhere in the N. T. (ἐπιβαρεῖν I 2⁹ II 3⁸ 2 Cor. 2⁵ and μόχθος I 2⁹ II 3⁸ 2 Cor. 11²⁷), there are only 12 of the 216 words in I (362−146 common = 216) and 8 of the 104 words in II (250−146 common = 104) which are found elsewhere in Paul but not elsewhere in the N. T.

(a) Words found in I and Paul (except II) but not elsewhere in the N. T.: ἀγιωσύνη 3¹³ (Rom. 1⁴ 2 Cor. 7¹); ἀδιαλείπτως 1³ 2¹³ 5¹⁷ (Rom. 1⁹); ἔκδικος 4⁶ (Rom. 13⁴); εὐσχημόνως 4¹² (Rom. 13¹³ 1 Cor. 14⁴⁰); θάλπειν

2⁷ (Eph. 5²⁹) πάθος 4⁵ (Rom. 1²⁶ Col. 3⁵); περικεφαλαία (5⁸ Eph. 6¹⁷); πλεονεκτεῖν 4⁶ (2 Cor. 2¹¹ 7² 12¹⁷· ¹⁸); προλέγειν 3⁴ (2 Cor. 13² Gal. 5²¹); στέγειν 3¹· ⁵ (1 Cor. 9¹² 13⁷); ὑπερεκπερισσοῦ 3¹⁰ 5¹³ (Eph. 3²⁰); and φιλοτιμεῖσθαι 4¹¹ (Rom. 15²⁰ 2 Cor. 5⁹).

(b) Words found in II and Paul (except I) but not elsewhere in the N. T.: ἀγαθωσύνη 1¹¹ (Rom. 15¹⁴ Gal. 5²² Eph. 5⁹); εἴπερ 1⁶ (Rom.ᵗᵉʳ 1 Cor.ᵇⁱˢ 2 Cor. 5³); ἐνέργεια 2⁹· ¹¹ (Eph. Phil. Col.); στέλλεσθαι 3⁶ (2 Cor. 8²⁰); συναναμίγνυσθαι 3¹⁴ (1 Cor. 5⁹· ¹¹); and ὑπεραίρεσθαι 2⁴ (2 Cor. 12⁷).

On the other hand, the vocabulary of I is relatively somewhat richer than II in specifically Pauline words, if we reckon as specific such words as are found in I and II (apart from words common to both) and elsewhere in the N. T., but elsewhere chiefly in Paul including one or more of the Major Epistles.

(a) Words found in I and elsewhere in N. T. but elsewhere chiefly in Paul including one or more of the Major Epistles, II being excepted: ἀγνοεῖν 4¹³; ἀκαθαρσία 2³ 4⁷; ἀναπληροῦν 2¹⁶; ἀξίως 2¹²; ἀρέσκειν 2⁴· ¹⁵ 4¹; ἀσθενής 5¹⁴; δοκιμάζειν 2⁴; δουλεύειν 1⁹; εἴδωλον 1⁹; εἰρηνεύειν 5¹³; ἐκλογή 1⁴; ἐξουθενεῖν 5²⁰; ἔπειτα 4¹⁷; ἐπιποθεῖν 3⁶; εὐχαριστία 3⁹; καθάπερ 2¹¹ 3⁶· ¹² 4⁵; καύχησις 2¹⁹; μεταδιδόναι 2⁸; μιμητής 1⁶ 2¹⁴; μνεία 1² 3⁶; νήπιος 2⁷; περισσοτέρως 2¹⁷; ποτέ 2⁵; συνεργός 3²; ὑστέρημα 3¹⁰; and φθάνειν 2¹⁶ 4¹⁵.

(b) Words found in II and elsewhere in N. T. but elsewhere chiefly in Paul including one or more of the Major Epistles, I being excepted: ἄνεσις 1⁷; ἀνέχεσθαι 1⁴; ἀποκάλυψις 1⁷; ἐνιστάναι 2²; ἐνκακεῖν 3¹³; ἐξαπατᾶν 2³; εὐδοκία 1¹¹; καταργεῖν 2⁸; κλῆσις 1¹¹; and νοῦς 2².

(c) Words common to I and II, found elsewhere in N. T. but elsewhere chiefly in Paul including one or more of the Major Epistles, may here be added: ἁγιασμός I 4³· ⁴· ⁷ II 2¹³; ἀνταποδιδόναι I 3⁹ II 1⁶; εἴτε I 5¹⁰ II 2¹⁵; ἐνεργεῖσθαι I 2¹³ II 2⁷; ἐπιστολή I 5²⁷ II 2²· ¹⁵ 3¹⁴· ¹⁷; θλίβειν I 3⁴ II 1⁶· ⁷; εὐδοκεῖν I 2⁸ 3¹ II 2¹²; κόπος I 1³ 2⁹ 3⁵ II 3⁸; νουθετεῖν I 5¹²· ¹⁴ II 3¹⁵; ὄλεθρος I 5³ II 1⁹; παράκλησις I 2³ II 2¹⁶; πλεονάζειν I 3¹² II 1³; and στήκειν I 3⁸ II 2¹⁵.

It is generally conceded that the vocabulary of I is Pauline; and the same may be said with justice of II. Even when the literary resemblances between I and II are taken into account, it is to be remembered that of the 146 words common to I and II all but four are to be found in one or more of the Major Epistles of Paul; and that two of these four recur in one or more of the Epistles of the Captivity, the remaining two being θεσσαλονικεύς, and the good Lxx. word κατευθύνειν. Nägeli's estimate of the vocabulary of II is at least not an overstatement: "Taking it on the whole, the lexical situation of this letter yields nothing essential either for the affirmation or for the negation of the question of authenticity" (*Wortschatz des Paulus*, 1905, 80).

(2) *Phrases.*—More significant than the vocabulary of I and II are the phrases and turns of thought. Two groups have been compiled, one in which the phrases are apparently unique, the other in which they are more or less specifically Pauline. The lists are not exhaustive, but the impression conveyed by them is that as with the vocabulary so with the phrases the resourceful mind of Paul is at work.

In the following lists, an asterisk indicates that the phrase is apparently not in the Lxx.; Lxx. = reminiscence from the Lxx.; and Lxx. cit. = a citation from the Lxx.

(1) *Unique Phrases.*—(a) Phrases in I but not elsewhere in N. T.: * ἅμα σύν 4¹⁷ 5¹⁰; διδόναι πνεῦμα εἰς 4⁸ (Lxx.); * εἰς τὸν ἕνα 5¹¹; ἔμπροσθεν with divine names 1³ 2¹⁹ 3⁹· ¹³; * ἐν βάρει εἶναι 2⁶; * ἐρωτᾶν καὶ παρακαλεῖν 4¹ (Papyri); * ἔχειν εἴσοδον πρός τινα 1⁹; καθάπερ οἴδατε 2¹¹ (cf. καθὼς οἴδατε 2²· ⁵ 3⁴); * πρὸς καιρὸν ὥρας 2¹⁷ (Latinism in κοινή?); * θεὸς ζῶν καὶ ἀληθινός 1⁹; κατευθύνειν τὴν ὁδὸν πρός 3¹¹ (Lxx.); * ἡ ὀργὴ ἡ ἐρχομένη 1¹⁰; ἡ πίστις ἡ πρὸς τὸν θεόν 1⁸; οἱ περιλειπόμενοι 4¹⁵· ¹⁷; * πράσσειν τὰ ἴδια 4¹¹ (classic); * σαλπίγξ θεοῦ (apocalyptic? cf. 1 Cor. 15⁵²); στέφανος καυχήσεως 2¹⁹ (Lxx.); * υἱοὶ ἡμέρας 5⁵, The next two may have been coined by Paul: * ὁ κόπος τῆς ἀγάπης 1³ and * ἡ ὑπομονὴ τῆς ἐλπίδος 1³. The following have a distinctively Pauline flavour: διὰ τοῦ Ἰησοῦ 4¹⁴; διὰ τοῦ κυρίου Ἰησοῦ 4²; ἐν τῷ θεῷ ἡμῶν 2²; ἐν θεῷ πατρί 1²; οἱ νεκροὶ ἐν χριστῷ 4¹⁶ (cf. 1 Cor. 15¹⁸ Rev. 14¹³); and οἱ κοιμηθέντες διὰ τοῦ Ἰησοῦ 4¹⁴.

(b) Phrases in II, but not elsewhere in N. T.: * διδόναι ἐκδίκησίν τινι 1⁸; * ἐκ μέσου γίνεσθαι 2⁷; ἐν παντὶ τρόπῳ 3¹⁶ (cf. Phil. 1¹⁸); εὐδοκεῖν τινι 2¹² (Lxx.); * εὐχαριστεῖν ὀφείλομεν 1³ 2¹³; ἡγεῖσθαι ὡς 3¹⁵ (Lxx.); * στηρίζειν καὶ φυλάσσειν 3³; * τίνειν δίκην 1⁹ (classic); * ἀπάτη ἀδικίας 2¹⁰; * ἄτοπος καὶ πονηρός 3²; * ἐνέργεια πλάνης 2¹¹; κατευθύνειν τὰς καρδίας 3⁵ (Lxx.); * περιπατεῖν ἀτάκτως 3⁶· ¹¹; * πιστεύειν τῇ ἀληθείᾳ 2¹²; * πιστεύειν τῷ ψεύδει 2¹¹; * πίστις ἀληθείας 2¹³ (cf. Phil. 1²⁷); * σαλευθῆναι ἀπὸ τοῦ νοός 2². The influence of apocalyptic may be felt in * ἄγγελοι δυνάμεως 1⁷; ἀνελεῖ τῷ πνεύματι τοῦ στόματος 2⁸ (Lxx.); * ὁ ἄνθρωπος τῆς ἀνομίας 2³; ὁ ἀντικείμενος κτλ. 2⁴ (Lxx. in part); ἀπὸ τῆς δόξης τῆς ἰσχύος 1⁹ (Lxx. cit.); * ἡ ἐπιφάνεια τῆς παρουσίας 2⁸; * ὁ κατέχων ἄρτι 2⁷; * τὸ κατέχον 2⁶; * τὸ μυστήριον τῆς ἀνομίας 2⁷; ὄλεθρος αἰώνιος 1⁹; ὅταν

ἔλθῃ κτλ. 1¹⁰ (Lxx. in part). The following may have been coined by
Paul: *ἡ ἀγάπη τῆς ἀληθείας 2¹⁰; *ἐλπὶς ἀγαθή 2¹⁶; εὐδοκία ἀγαθωσύνης 1¹¹; τὸ μαρτύριον ἡμῶν 1¹⁰ (cf. εὐαγγέλιον 2¹⁴); *παράκλησις
αἰωνία 2¹⁶; *τρέχειν καὶ δοξάζεσθαι 3¹; *ἡ ὑπομονὴ τοῦ χριστοῦ 3⁵. The
following have a distinctively Pauline flavour: *ἐν θεῷ πατρὶ ἡμῶν 1¹;
*τὸ εὐαγγέλιον τοῦ κυρίου ἡμῶν Ἰησοῦ 1⁸; ὁ θεὸς ὁ πατὴρ ἡμῶν 2¹⁶; *ὁ
κύριος τῆς εἰρήνης 3¹⁶ (cf. I 5²²); and πιστὸς δέ ἐστιν ὁ κύριος 3³.

(c) Phrases in I and elsewhere in N. T., but not elsewhere in Paul:
δέχεσθαι τὸν λόγον 1⁶ 2¹³; ἐν μέσῳ cum gen. 2⁷; καθὼς οἴδατε 2²· ⁵ 3⁴;
λόγος ἀκοῆς 2¹³; ὁ πειράζων 3⁵; υἱοὶ φωτός 5⁵.

(d) Phrases in II and elsewhere in N. T., but not elsewhere in Paul:
ἀνθ'ὧν 2¹⁰; ἀπ' ἀρχῆς 2¹³; ἀπὸ προσώπου 1⁹ (Lxx. cit.); διδόναι εἰρήνην
3¹⁶; δικαία κρίσις 1⁵ (cf. Rom. 2⁵); ἐν ἁγιασμῷ πνεύματος 2¹³ (1 Pet.
1²); ἐν πυρὶ φλογός 1⁸ (Lxx.); ἐν τῇ ἡμέρᾳ ἐκείνῃ 1¹⁰ (Lxx. cit.); ἔργῳ καὶ
λόγῳ 2¹⁷; ἐσθίειν ἄρτον 3⁸· ¹²; κρατεῖν τὰς παραδόσεις 2¹⁵ (cf. 1 Cor. 11²);
πάντες οἱ πιστεύσαντες 1¹⁰; ὁ υἱὸς τῆς ἀπωλείας 2³.

(e) Phrases common to I and II, but not elsewhere in N. T.: ἀδελφοὶ
ἠγαπημένοι ὑπὸ τοῦ θεοῦ (κυρίου) I 1⁴ II 2¹³ (Lxx. with Paul's ἀδελφοί);
αὐτοὶ γὰρ οἴδατε I 2¹ 3² 5² II 3⁷; ἐν θεῷ πατρὶ (ἡμῶν) I 1¹ II 1¹ and ἐν
κυρίῳ Ἰ. Χ. I 1¹ II 1¹ 3¹² (ἐν is distinctively Pauline); ἐρωτῶμεν δὲ ὑμᾶς
ἀδελφοί I 5¹² II 2¹ (for παρακαλοῦμεν, due to infrequent use of ἐρωτᾶν in
Paul); καὶ γὰρ ὅτε I 3⁴ II 3¹⁰; (τὸ) ἔργον (τῆς) πίστεως I 1³ II 1¹²;
αὐτὸς ὁ κύριος I 3¹¹ 4¹⁶ II 2¹⁶ 3¹⁶ (cf. Rom. 8¹⁶· ²⁶ 1 Cor. 15²⁸ 2 Cor. 8¹⁹ ℵ).

(f) Phrases common to I and II, found elsewhere in N. T., but not
elsewhere in Paul: αὐτὸς ὁ θεός I 3¹¹ 5²³ II 2¹⁶ (Rev. 21³); καὶ διὰ τοῦτο
(I 2¹³ II 2¹¹); ὁ λόγος τοῦ κυρίου I 1⁸ (4¹⁵) II 3¹ (cf. Col. 3¹⁶); νυκτὸς καὶ
ἡμέρας I 2⁹ II 3⁸; προσεύχεσθε περὶ ἡμῶν I 5²⁵ II 3¹ (Heb. 13¹⁸; cf.
Col. 4²).

(2) Pauline Phrases.—(a) Phrases in I and Paul except II but not
elsewhere in N. T. Unless otherwise indicated, they are found in one or
more of the Major Epistles: ἅπαξ καὶ δίς 2¹⁸ (Phil. 4¹⁶; Lxx.); εἰς κενόν
3⁵; ἐν παντί 5¹⁸; ἐν πολλῷ (πολλῇ) 1⁵· ⁶ 2²· ¹⁷ ἐπὶ τῶν προσευχῶν 1²; ἀρέσκειν θεῷ 2⁴·¹⁵ 4¹; διὰ τοῦ κυρίου ἡμῶν Ἰ. Χ. 5⁹; ἐν φιλήματι ἁγίῳ 5²⁶;
εἶναι σὺν κυρίῳ 4¹⁷ (Phil. 1²³); ἐν κυρίῳ Ἰησοῦ 4¹; ἐργάζεσθαι ταῖς χερσίν
4¹¹; τὸ εὐαγγέλιον τοῦ χριστοῦ 3²; εὐχαριστεῖν πῷ θεῷ 1² 2¹³; ζῆν σὺν
αὐτῷ 5¹⁰; ἡμεῖς οἱ ζῶντες 4¹⁵· ¹⁷ (2 Cor. 4¹¹); οὐ θέλομεν ὑμᾶς ἀγνοεῖν
4¹³; ὁ θεὸς καὶ πατὴρ ἡμῶν 1³ 3¹¹· ¹³; θεὸς μαρτύς 2⁵·¹⁰ ὁ καλῶν ὑμᾶς 2¹²
5²⁴; περιπατεῖν ἀξίως τοῦ θεοῦ 2¹² (Col. 1¹⁰); στήκετε ἐν κυρίῳ 3⁸ (Phil.
4¹); and συνεργοὶ τοῦ θεοῦ 3².

(b) Phrases in II and Paul except I but not elsewhere in N. T. Unless
otherwise indicated, they are found in one or more of the Major
Epistles: μή with aor. subj. of prohibition in third person 2³ (1 Cor.
16¹¹ 2 Cor. 11¹⁶); position of μόνον 2⁷ (Gal. 2¹⁰); ἐπιστεύθη with impersonal subject 1¹⁰ (Rom. 10¹⁰); ὡς ὅτι 2² (2 Cor. 5¹⁹ 11²¹); οἱ ἀπολλύμενοι 2¹⁰; ὁ ἀσπασμὸς τῇ ἐμῇ χειρὶ Παύλου 3¹⁷; μὴ ἐνκακήσητε καλοποιοῦντες

3

3¹³ (Gal. 6⁹); θεὸς πατὴρ ἡμῶν 1¹; ὁ λόγος ἡμῶν 3¹⁴ (2 Cor. 1¹⁸); παρακαλεῖν τὰς καρδίας 2⁷ (cf. Col. 2² 4⁸ Eph. 6²²); πεποιθέναι ἐν κυρίῳ 3⁴
(Phil. 2²⁴; cf. Rom. 14¹⁴); and ὑπακούειν τῷ εὐαγγελίῳ 1⁸ (Rom. 10¹⁶).

(c) Phrases in I and elsewhere in N. T. but elsewhere chiefly in Paul
including one or more of the Major Epistles, II being excepted: ἐν παντὶ
τόπῳ 1⁸; οἱ ἔξω 4¹²; ἐπιποθεῖν ἰδεῖν 3⁶; τὸ εὐαγγέλιον τοῦ θεοῦ 2². ⁸. ⁹;
θέλημα τοῦ θεοῦ 4³ 5¹⁸; ὁ θεὸς τῆς εἰρήνης 5²³; οἱ λοιποί 4¹³ 5⁶; and πάντες οἱ πιστεύοντες 1⁷. To this list should be added ἐν χριστῷ Ἰησοῦ 2¹⁴
5¹⁸ and ἐν χριστῷ 4¹⁶; and perhaps the following: ἐν πνεύματι ἁγίῳ 1⁵;
θεὸς ζῶν 1⁹; ἰδεῖν τὸ πρόσωπον 2¹⁷ 3¹⁰; ὁ λόγος τοῦ θεοῦ 2¹³; οἱ πιστεύοντες 2¹⁰. ¹³; and χρείαν ἔχειν 1⁸ 4⁹. ¹² 5¹.

(d) Phrases in II and elsewhere in N. T. but elsewhere chiefly in Paul
including one or more of the Major Epistles, II being excepted: ἐν ὀνόματι 3⁶; παρὰ θεῷ 1⁶; and perhaps the following: ἡ ἀγάπη τοῦ θεοῦ 3⁵;
ἡ ἀποκάλυψις τοῦ κυρίου Ἰησοῦ 1⁷ (1 Cor. 1⁷); διωγμοὶ καὶ θλίψεις 1⁴
(Rom. 8³⁵); πάσχειν ὑπέρ 1⁵ (Phil. 1²⁹); and σημεῖα καὶ τέρατα 2⁹ (Rom.
15¹⁹ 2 Cor. 12²).

(e) Phrases common to I, II and Paul but not found elsewhere in N.
T.: ἄρα οὖν I 5⁶ II 2¹⁵; τὸ εὐαγγέλιον ἡμῶν I 1⁵ II 2¹⁴; ·ὁπος καὶ μόχθος
I 2⁹ II 3⁸; (τὸ) λοιπὸν ἀδελφοί I 4¹ II 3¹; πρὸς τὸ μή cum inf. I 2⁹ II 3⁸.

(f) Phrases common to I, II Paul and found elsewhere in N. T. The
following are characteristic of Paul: ἐν κυρίῳ I 3⁸ 5¹² II 3⁴; χάρις ὑμῖν
καὶ εἰρήνη I 1¹ II 1²; θεὸς πατήρ I 1¹ II 1². The following are not
characteristic: ὁ θεὸς ἡμῶν I 2² 3⁹ II 1¹¹. ¹² (1 Cor. 6¹¹); ἡμέρα κυρίου I
5² II 2²; ἡ πίστις ὑμῶν I 1⁸ 3². ⁵. ⁶. ⁷. ¹⁰ II 1³. ⁴; ἡ παρουσία τοῦ κυρίου
(ἡμῶν Ἰ. Χ.) I 3¹³ 4¹⁵ 5²³ II 2¹ (1 Cor. 15²³); πῶς δεῖ I 4¹ II 3⁷ (Col. 4⁶);
and στηρίζειν καὶ παρακαλεῖν I 3² II 2¹⁷ (inverted order); cf. Rom. 1¹¹.

(3) *Personal Equation.*—It is generally felt that the personality back of the words and phrases of the first letter is none
other than that of Paul. Characteristic of him and characteristic of that letter are warm affection for his converts, confidence
in them in spite of their shortcomings, tact in handling delicate
pastoral problems, the consciousness of his right as an apostle
and the waiving of the same in love, the sense of comradeship
with his readers in all things, and the appeal for their sympathy
and prayers. So conspicuously Pauline is the personal equation
of I that it is unnecessary to illustrate the point. But it is also
frequently felt that the personal qualities revealed in I are lacking in II, that indeed the tone of II is rather formal, official,
and severe. This impression arises in the first instance from
the fact that there is nothing in II corresponding to the *apologia*

to which three of the five chapters of I are devoted and in which the personal element is outspoken. Omit the self-defence from I and the differences in tone between I and II would not be perceptible. This estimate is likewise due to the failure to read aright Paul's purpose, with the result that the clew to his attitude is lost. The impression of formality and severity is however quite mistaken; as a matter of fact the treatment of both the faint-hearted and the idlers is permeated by a spirit of warm personal affection. Paul knows his Macedonians too well, trusts their love for him too deeply to be greatly disturbed either by the forgetfulness of the one class or the disobedience of the other. It is his love for them all that prompts him at the start to praise not only their growth in faith but also, despite the friction in the brotherhood, their increase in brotherly love; and to surprise them by saying that contrary to their expectations he is boasting everywhere of their endurance and faith.

From his love springs his confidence in them notwithstanding their continued shortcomings. He is quite sure that the faint-hearted are more in need of encouragement than of warning and so he directs every word in the first two chapters, including the description of judgment, the allusion to premonitory signs, and the characterisation of the advent of the *Anomos*, to the single end of assuring these brethren beloved by the Lord that they are as certain of future salvation as they are of being elected and called. His slight impatience at their forgetfulness (2^5) is free from brusqueness and his sole imperative, based on their assurance of salvation and supported by prayer, to hold fast the instructions (2^{15}) is dictated by a fatherly concern. He is likewise confident that the idlers, in spite of their neglect of his injunction given once orally and again by letter, will do, as they indeed are doing, what he commands (3^4), and so includes them in his praise of the faith and brotherly love of the church (1^4). Furthermore, from his love arises also the tact with which the two parish problems before him are managed. One or two illustrations will suffice to make this clear. In $1^{8\ ff.}$ Paul is describing the judgment in reference to unbelievers and saints in general; suddenly with ἐν πᾶσιν τοῖς πιστεύσασιν (v. [10]), he changes from the general to the specific, intimating by the "all" that the faint-hearted belong to the number of the saints, and by the unexpected aorist participle that, as the explanatory parenthesis ("for our testimony to you was believed") declares, they had believed the gospel which he had preached to them. The description then closes with the assurance that that day is a day not of judgment but of salvation for believers, specifically the faint-hearted among them. The same tact is evident in 2^{9-12} where after announcing the destruction of the *Anomos*, he comes back to his *Parousia*, an infringement of orderly description prompted by the purpose of showing that the advent of the Lawless One is intended not for the faint-hearted believers but solely for the doomed. Even more conspicuously tactful is the treatment of the idlers. He approaches the theme in 3^{1-5} by expressing his confidence that the brethren will do what he commands as indeed they are doing; then, addressing the group as a whole but having in mind the majority, he gives his command, not on his own authority but on that of Christ, to hold aloof from the idlers, qualifying the directness of the injunction by observing that his order is not new but the original teaching, and persuading obedience by referring to his own example of industry. When he addresses the idlers (3^{12}), he does so indirectly and impersonally, and softens the command with an exhortation. Indeed, throughout the discussion, he insists that the idlers are brothers (3^6), even the recalcitrants among them (3^{15}); that the purpose of discipline is reform; and, most notably, that the majority are not without blame in their treatment of the erring brothers (3^{13}), his final injunction being so worded as to leave the impression that the majority needed admonition as well as the idlers: "And do not regard him as an enemy but warn him as a brother" (3^{15}).

But affection, confidence, and tact are not the only characteristics of Paul that appear in II as well as in I. There is also the sense of fellowship with the readers which appears unobtrusively in 1^5 "for which you too as well as we suffer"; and in 1^7 "relief with us";—touches so genuinely Pauline as to be fairly inimitable. There is further the characteristic appeal for the sympathy and prayers of his friends in 3¹⁻², a passage too in which he delicately compliments their faith (καθὼς καὶ πρὸς ὑμᾶς). And there is finally the assertion of his right as an apostle to a stipend, and the voluntary waiving of the same in love in order that he may not burden his poor friends with the maintenance and support to which he was entitled (3⁷ ˢ·).

If this estimate of the personal equation of II is just, then in this respect as in respect of the words and phrases, II as well as I is entitled to be considered, what it claims to be, a genuine letter of Paul.

§ V. AUTHENTICITY OF I.

The positive considerations already advanced in the preceding sections are sufficient to establish the Pauline authorship of I, unless one is prepared to assert that Paul never lived or that no letter from him has survived. Curiously enough it is the certainty that I is Pauline that seems to account (cf. Jülicher, *Einl.*⁶ 56) for the revival in recent years of an earlier tendency either to doubt seriously or to deny altogether the authenticity of the second epistle.

(1) *External Evidence.*—The external evidence for the existence and Pauline authorship of I is no better and no worse than that for Galatians. Following the judicious estimate of *The New Testament in the Apostolic Fathers*, 1905, it may be said that "the evidence that Ignatius knew I is almost *nil*" (cf. I 5¹⁷ ἀδιαλείπτως προσεύχεσθε with Ign. Eph. 10¹ and I 2⁴ οὐχ ὡς ἀνθρώποις ἀρέσκοντες ἀλλὰ θεῷ with Ign. Rom. 2¹). The παιδεύετε οὖν ἀλλήλους καὶ εἰρηνεύετε ἐν αὐτοῖς of Hermas Vis. III 9¹⁰ does not certainly come from I 5¹³ ᶠ·; nor does the θεοδί-δακτοί of Barn. 21⁶ depend on I 4⁹. On the other hand, I like Galatians was in Marcion's N. T. (cf. Moff. *Introd.* 69 f.), and of course from Irenæus on was accepted as Pauline and canonical by all branches of the church.

(2) *Baur's Criticism.*—While Schrader (*Der Apostel Paulus*, V, 1836, 23 ff.) was the first to question the authenticity of I, it was Baur (*Paulus* 1845, 480 ff.) who made the most serious inroads against the tradition and succeeded in convincing some (*e. g.* Noack, Volkmar, Holsten) but not all (*e. g.* Lipsius, Hilgenfeld, Holtzmann, Pfleiderer, Schmiedel) of his followers that the letter is spurious. Four only of his reasons need be mentioned (cf. Lün. 11-15): (*a*) The un-Pauline origin is betrayed

by the "insignificance of the contents, the want of any special aim and of any definite occasion" (Lün.). The last two objections are untenable and the first overlooks the fact that Paul's letters are not dogmatic treatises but occasional writings designed to meet practical as well as theoretical difficulties, and that I everywhere presupposes on the part of its readers a knowledge of the distinctive Pauline idea of the indwelling Christ or Spirit as the power unto righteousness and the pledge of future salvation. (b) It is contended that I depends both on Acts and on the Pauline letters, especially 1, 2 Cor. To this it is replied that to pronounce I as a "mere copy and echo of 1, 2 Cor. is a decided error of literary criticism" (Moff. Introd. 70), and that the very differences between Acts and I point not toward but away from literary dependence (McGiffert, EB. 5041). (c) More elusive is the objection that I reveals a progress in the Christian life which is improbable, if a period of only a few months had elapsed between the founding of the church and the writing of I. But the evidence adduced for this judgment is unconvincing. The fact that the fame of the little group has spread far and wide ($1^{7\text{-}8}$), that they have been hospitable to their fellow-Macedonians (4^{10}), or that Paul has repeatedly desired to see them (2^{18} 3^{10}) is proof not of the long existence of the community but of the intensity and enthusiasm of their faith. Indeed the letter itself, written not later than two or three months after Paul's departure, reveals the initial freshness and buoyancy of their faith and love. Even the shortcomings betray a recent religious experience (cf. Dob. 16–17). (d) Finally it is argued that $4^{14\text{-}18}$ while not disagreeing with 1 Cor. 15^{22} is in its concreteness unlike Paul. But on the other hand, waiving the antecedent probability in favour of Paul's use of apocalyptic, and the distinctively Pauline οἱ νεκροὶ ἐν χριστῷ, it is to be observed that 4^{17} indicates that he expects to survive until the Parousia. It is not likely that a forger writing after Paul's death would have put into his mouth an unrealised expectation (Lün.).

(3) Priority of II.—The supposed difficulties in I have been removed by some scholars not by denying the Pauline authorship but by assuming that II was written before I. Grotius (see on II 2^{13}) for example supposed that II was addressed to Jewish Christians who along with Jason had come to Thessalonica from Palestine before Paul had preached there; and that II 3^{17} is proof that II is the first letter of Paul to the Thessalonians. The priority of II was defended also by Laurent, Ewald, and others (cf. J. Weiss on 1 Cor. 16^{21} and see, for details, Lün. 169–173, Dob. 20–21, or Moff. Introd. 75). Some colour is lent to this hypothesis by the consideration that the case of the idlers in II $3^{6\ \text{ff.}}$ yields a clearer insight into the meaning of I $4^{11\text{-}12}$ and 5^{14} (νουθετεῖτε τοὺς ἀτάκτους) than these passages themselves at first blush afford, and that it is not impossible that the severer discipline of II may have been followed by the less severe of I. On the other hand, II 2^{15} 3^{17} naturally refer not to a lost letter but to I; and ἐπισυναγωγή (II 2^1), which is not treated

in 2¹⁻¹² is an allusion to I 4¹³⁻¹⁸. Furthermore, the evidence of II 1³ ᶠ· 1¹¹ 2¹ 3¹⁻⁵ (see notes on these verses) suggests that II is a reply to a letter from Thessalonica written after the receipt of I. Finally the reference to growth in faith and love (II 1³) is an advance on I 1² ᶠ· and a fulfilment in part of the prayer of I 3¹². There is therefore no compelling reason for departing from the tradition, as early as Marcion, that I is prior to II.

(4) *Theories of Interpolation.*—More ingenious than convincing is the theory of Robert Scott (*The Pauline Epistles*, 1909, 215 ff.) to the effect that I and II are made up of two documents, one by Timothy (chs. 1–3 of I and ch. 3 of II) and the other by Silas (chs. 4–5 of I and chs. 1–2 of II), documents completed and edited by Timothy somewhere between 70 and 80 A.D. An interesting element in the conjecture is that chs. 1–3 of I depend largely on Phil. and slightly on 2 Cor.

Minor glosses have been suspected in 2¹⁴⁻¹⁶ (*cf.* Schmiedel, *ad loc.*) or at least in 2¹⁶ ᶠ· (Schmiedel, Drummond, Moff. *et al.*), in 5²³ ᶠ· (*cf. EB.* 5041), in 5²⁷ (*cf.* Moff. *Introd.* 69) and elsewhere; but in no one of these instances is the suspicion warranted, as the exegesis will show.

§ VI. AUTHENTICITY OF II.

(1) *Antecedent Probability.*—Since the internal evidence of II reveals a situation which is thoroughly intelligible on the assumption of genuineness, and since the language, personal equation, and religious convictions of the letter are Pauline, it is antecedently probable that the ancient tradition assigning the epistle to Paul is to be accepted.

The external evidence of II is slightly better than that for I. To be sure, little stress is to be laid on Ign. Rom. 10³ ἐν ὑπομονῇ 'I. X.=3⁵ or on the similarity in respect of apocalyptic utterances between II and Barn. 15⁵ 18², Did. 16¹ ᶠ·, or Justin Martyr *dial.* 32¹² 110⁶ 116⁵. On the other hand, Polycarp addresses the Philippians in 11³ with the words of 1⁴, and in 11⁴ (*et non sicut inimicos tales existimetis*) with the words of 3¹⁵. "In spite of the fact that both these passages occur in the part of Polycarp for which the Latin version alone is extant, his use of 2 Thess. appears to be very probable" (*N. T. in Ap. Fathers*, 95). Furthermore II like I has a place in Marcion's N. T. and has from Irenæus on been accepted as canonical and Pauline by all sections of the church.

(2) *History of the Criticism.*—Though the antecedent probability tells in favour of the genuineness of II, yet there are ad-

mitted difficulties which to some scholars appear so serious as to compel them either to speak doubtfully of the authorship or to assume that II proceeds from the hand not of Paul but of a *falsarius*. As the sketch of the history of criticism, given below, hopes to make clear, the difficulties are mainly two in number, the alleged contradiction between the eschatological utterances of II $2^{1\text{-}12}$ and I $5^{1\text{-}11}$ and the confessedly close literary resemblances between II and I. Both of these difficulties, it is to be remarked, proceed on the assumption (Kern, Holtzmann, Schmiedel, Wrede, and others) that I is a genuine letter of Paul.

(a) *Against Genuineness.*—The first to question seriously the genuineness of II (see especially Born. 498 *ff.*) was J. E. C. Schmidt (1801) who, on the ground of the eschatology of $2^{1\text{-}12}$ in general, of the alleged discrepancies between $2^{1\text{-}12}$ and I $4^{13}\text{-}5^{11}$, and of the supposed references to forged letters in 2^2 3^{17}, thought that at least $2^{1\text{-}12}$ was a Montanistic interpolation; but who later (1804) denied the letter as a whole to Paul. De Wette at first (*Einl.* 1826) agreed with Schmidt, but afterward when he published his commentary (1841) withdrew his support. Apparently the exegesis of II became easier on the assumption of genuineness.

One of the most important contributions, both on account of its insight and on account of its influence on Baur (*Paulus*, 1845, 480 *ff.*), Holtzmann (*Einl.* 1885, 1892³; *ZNW.* 1901, 97–108; and finally *N. T. Theol.* 1911², II, 213–215), Weizsäcker (*Das Apostolische Zeitalter*, 1886, 258–261 = 1892², 249–251), Pfleiderer (*Urchristentum*, 1887, 1902²), Schmiedel (1889, 1893²), Wrede (*Die Echtheit des zweiten Thessalonicherbriefes*, 1903), von Soden (*Urchristliche Literaturgeschichte*, 1905, 164–168), Weinel (*Biblische Theol. des N. T.* 1911, 500), and others, is unquestionably that of Kern, *Ueber 2 Thess.* $2^{1\text{-}12}$. *Nebst Andeutungen über den Ursprung des zweiten Briefes an die Thessalonicher* (Tübinger Zeitschrift für Theologie, 1839, Zweites Heft, 145–214). After a careful exposition of $2^{1\text{-}12}$ (145–174) and a sketch of the history of interpretation (175–192), Kern looks for the origin of the prophecy in the historical situation of the writer (193 *ff.*) and finds that the apocalyptic picture is an application by a Paulinist of the legend of the Antichrist to the belief in *Nero Redivivus*. "The Antichrist, whose appearance is expected as imminent, is Nero; the things that restrain him are the circumstances of the world of that time; the person that restrains him is Vespasian, with his son Titus who had just besieged Jerusalem. What is said of the apostasy reflects the abominable wickedness that broke out among the Jewish people in their war against the Romans" (200). This unfulfilled prophecy belongs to the years between 68–70 A.D. and could not therefore be written by Paul (207). After referring briefly to the difficulty in 3^{17}, Kern sketches (211–213) the manner in which II depends on I, indicating in passing both the Pauline and un-Pauline elements in II. The first letter, he thinks, with its historical situation was excellently adapted to the creation of a second in which the apocalyptic picture, conceived by the spirit of the Paulinist, could be imparted to his Christian brethren. The passage 2^{1-12}, which is the pith of the whole matter, is preceded by an introduction and followed by an exhortation, both drawn from the genuine letter of Paul (214).

The same conclusion was reached by Weizsäcker who held that the purpose of II is the desire to impart 2^{1-12}, while the rest of the letter is solely a framework designed to encircle it with the authority of Paul, an intention revealed by the imitation, with corresponding changes, of the first letter. Unlike Kern, however, Weizsäcker, in presenting his case, says nothing of the theory of *Nero Redivivus*, but points first of all, in evidence of spuriousness, to the striking relation of II to I both in the similarity of the historical situation and in the correspondence in their contents of separate parts of II to certain sections of I; although, he observes, the whole of II does not correspond in extent and arrangement to the whole of I. Schmiedel held with Kern to the theory of *Nero Redivivus*, but indicated in greater detail than he the literary dependence of II on I, while Holtzmann (1892) put into the forefront of the debate the differences between II and I in respect of eschatology.

Between 1892 and 1901, the investigations into apocalyptic of Gunkel, Bousset, and Charles suggested not only the naturalness in Paul of such a passage as 2^{1-12} but also that the legend of *Nero Redivivus* is not the clew to the interpretation of that difficult section. Charles indeed (*Ascension of Isaiah*, 1900, LXII) gave convincing reasons for concluding that Schmiedel's theory which regards 2^{1-12} as a Beliar-Neronic myth (68–70 A.D.) "is at conflict with the law of development as well as with all the evidence accessible on the subject."

A new impetus was given to the discussion by Holtzmann in 1901, who while still insisting that 2^{1-12} and I $4^{13}-5^{11}$ present mutually exclusive views of the future, called attention anew to the literary dependence of II upon I; and by Wrede independently in 1903, who subjected the literary relations to an exhaustive examination and strengthened the theory of Kern as to the intentional dependence of II upon I. To Wrede, however, the argument from eschatology was convincing not of itself but only in connection with the main argument from literary dependence. Since, however, a date as early as 70 for a forgery is difficult to maintain, he was compelled to place II at the close of the first or at the beginning of the second century, a date which Hilgenfeld (1862) had already suggested on the strength of the assumption that "the mystery of iniquity" presupposes the rise of the gnostic heresies. Finally Hollmann (*ZNW*. 1904, 28–38), while recognising that the literary relation of II and I, the lack of the personal equation in II, and the statement of II 2^2 when compared with 3^{17} are difficulties, is inclined with Holtzmann to lay the stress on the alleged discrepancies between 2^{1-12} and I 5^{1-11}. Unlike his predecessors, Hollmann acknowledges the important part that the idlers play in II and accordingly suggests that the eschatological situation at the end of the century, which evoked from II the correction that the *Parousia* is postponed, had been causing among other things the flight from labour. The forger selects for his purpose elements of the legend of Antichrist because of the theory of *Nero Redivivus* current in his day, forgetting entirely or else treating figuratively the allusion to the temple.

(b) *For Genuineness.*—The arguments of Kern failed to convince Lünemann (1850), Lightfoot (Smith's *DB.* 1870, 3222 ff.; *Biblical Essays*, 1893, 253 ff.*, printed from lecture notes of 1867), Auberlen and Riggenbach (in Lange, 1864 = Lillie's edition 1868), Jülicher (*Einl.* 1894), Bornemann (1894), Briggs (*Messiah of the Apostles*, 1895), Zahn (*Einl.* 1897), B. Weiss (*Einl.*³ 1897), McGiffert (*Apostolic Age*, 1897, 252 ff.), Charles (*Ascen. Isa.* 1900, LXII), Vincent (*Word Studies*, IV, 1900), Bacon (*Introd.* 1900), Askwith (*Introd. to the Thess. Epistles*, 1902), Wohlenberg (1903), Lock (*HDB.* 1903, IV, 743 ff.) and many others. The rebuttal, however, is addressed mainly not to the argument from literary dependence but to that from the differences in eschatology. On the other hand, McGiffert, who in his *Apostolic Age* (*loc. cit.*) had accepted the style of II as genuinely Pauline and had considered the arguments in favour stronger than those against the authenticity, published in 1903 (*EB.* 5041 ff.), after a fresh examination of the problem made independently of Holtzmann (1901) and Wrede (1903), a modification of his previous position. In this important discussion which reveals a keen sense of the relevant, he waives as secondary the arguments from differences in eschatology and in style, and puts significantly into the foreground the argument from literary dependence. While admitting that the evidence as a whole points rather toward than against the Pauline authorship, he concludes that "it must be recognised that its genuineness is beset with serious difficulties and that it is at best very doubtful."

But in spite of the serious obstacles which the suggestion of Kern in its modern form puts into the way of accepting confidently the Pauline authorship of II, it may be said fairly that the tendency at present is favourable to the hypothesis of genuineness; so for example Wernle (*GGA.* 1905, 347–352), Findlay (1904), Clemen (*Paulus*, 1904, I, 114 ff.), Vischer (*Paulusbriefe*, 1904, 70 f.), Heinrici (*Der litterarische Charracter der neutestamentlichen Schriften*, 1908, 60), Milligan (1908), Bousset (*ERE.* 1908, I, 579), Mackintosh (1909), von Dobschütz (1909), Moffatt (*EGT.* 1910; *Introd.* 1911), Knowling (*Testimony of St. Paul to Christ* 1911³, 24–28), Harnack (*SBBA.* 1910, 560–578), Dibelius (1911), Lake

(*The Earlier Epistles of St. Paul*, 1911), Deissmann (*Paulus*, 1911, 14), and many others.

(c) *Other Hypotheses.*—(1) J. E. C. Schmidt (1801) found in 2¹⁻¹² a Montanistic interpolation and Michelsen (1876) in 2¹⁻⁹ a Jewish Christian apocalypse; Paul Schmidt (1885) discovered in 1⁵⁻¹² and 2² ᵇ⁻¹² evidences that a genuine letter of Paul had been worked over by a Paulinist in A.D. 69. The difficulty with these and similar theories of interpolation, apart from the question of the validity of the literary criteria, is the fact that in removing 2¹⁻¹² one of the two salient purposes of the letter is destroyed. "As a matter of fact, the suggestion of Hausrath (*Neutestamentliche Zeitgeschichte*[2] 3, 198) that this passage is the only genuine part of the epistle is much more plausible" (McGiffert, *EB.* 5043). For other theories of interpolation, see Moff. 81 *f.* (2) Spitta (*Zur Geschichte und Litteratur des Urchristentums*, 1893, I, 111–154) assigns II, except 3¹⁷⁻¹⁸, to Timothy (*cf.* also Lueken, *SNT.* II, 21), a theory which is incompatible with the obvious exegesis of 2⁵ (see Mill. lxxxix *ff.*). On Scott's proposal, *v. supra*, p. 39. (3) Bacon (*Introd.* 74) suggests that the linguistic peculiarities of II may be explained by the assumption that the amanuensis of II is different from that of I. (4) On the theory of Grotius, *v. supra*, p. 38; on that of Harnack, *v. infra*, p. 53.

The history of the criticism outlined above tends to show that the two main objections to the authenticity of II are, as Kern pointed out in 1839, the literary resemblances between II and I, and the alleged discrepancy in respect of eschatology between II 2¹⁻¹² and I 5¹⁻¹¹, both objections depending on the assumption that I is genuine.

(3) *Objection from Eschatology.*—The first of the two main objections to the genuineness of II is based on the alleged inconsistency between II 2¹⁻¹² and I 5¹⁻¹¹. According to II 2⁵, the converts had been taught that certain signs would precede the *Parousia*; but according to I 5¹⁻¹¹ they know accurately that the day comes as a thief at night, that is, suddenly and unexpectedly. These two elements of the original teaching are, it is argued, mutually exclusive; and since Paul cannot be inconsistent, and cannot have changed his opinions within the short interval between the composition of I and II, the reference in II to premonitory signs betrays a later hand. To this objection it has been urged with force (1) generally that in apocalyptic literature both the idea of the suddenness of the coming of the day of the Lord and the idea of premonitory signs constantly appear together; and (2) specifically that the natural inference

from I 5^{1-4} is that the readers are acquainted with the teaching of Paul that certain signs will herald the approach of the Lord. Signs and suddenness are not mutually exclusively elements in apocalyptic; and the mention of the suddenness but not the signs in I 5^{1-11} and of the signs but not the suddenness in II 2^{1-12} is evidence not of a contradiction in terms but of a difference of emphasis due to a difference of situation in Thessalonica.

In I 5^{1-11}, Paul is not concerned with giving new instruction either on times and seasons in general or in particular on the suddenness of the coming of the day; he is interested solely in encouraging the faint-hearted to remember that though the day is to come suddenly upon all, believer and unbeliever alike, it will not catch the believer unprepared, the tacit assumption being that the readers already know accurately about the times and seasons including, as II 2^5 expressly declares, a knowledge of the premonitory signs. In II 2^{1-12}, Paul is writing with the same faint-hearted persons in mind and with the same purpose of encouragement, but he is facing a different situation and a different need. The faint-hearted have become more discouraged because of the assertion, supported, it was alleged, by the authority of Paul, that the day of the Lord had actually dawned. In order to show the absurdity of that opinion, it became necessary for Paul to remind them of his oral teaching on premonitory signs. Though the reminder was of itself an encouragement, Paul took the pains to add for the further encouragement of the faint-hearted that the advent of the *Anomos* (2^{9-12}) is intended not for them, but for unbelievers, the doomed who destroyed themselves by refusing to welcome the love for the truth unto their salvation. Since the converts are aware of this teaching about the signs, it is necessary only to allude to it; and the allusions are so indistinct that no one hearing the words for the first time could fully understand them. A different situation occasions a different emphasis; signs and suddenness are not incompatibles in apocalyptic.

On the question of signs and suddenness as a whole, see Briggs *Messianic Prophecy*, 1886, 52 *ff.*; *Messiah of the Gospels*, 1894, 156 *ff.*, 160 *ff.*; and *Messiah of the Apostles*, 1895, 550 *ff.* Against the contention of

Schmiedel, Holtzmann, Hollmann, and others that I 5¹⁻¹¹ and II 2¹⁻¹² are mutually exclusive, see Briggs, *Messiah of the Apostles*, 91 *ff.*; Spitta (*op. cit.* 129 *ff.*); McGiffert (*EB.* 5042); Clemen (*Paulus*, I, 118); Zahn (*Introd.* I, 253); Moff. (*Introd.* 80*f.*); and the commentaries of Find. (lii), Mill. (lxxxv *f.*), and Dob. (38 *f.*). Wrede candidly admits that were it not for the literary dependence of II on I, there would be little force in the argument from eschatology.

(4) *Objection from Literary Resemblances.*—The second and more important of the two main objections to the authenticity of II is based on the literary resemblances between II and I. These similarities, it is contended, are so close and continuous as to make certain the literary dependence of II upon I and to exclude as a psychological impossibility the authorship of II by Paul, if, as is generally assumed, II is addressed to the same readers as I and written about three months after I.

(*A*) *Statement of the Case.*—(*a*) In presenting the case for the literary dependence of II on I, care must be taken not to overstate the agreements or to understate the differences (see especially Wernle, *op. cit.*). It is said for example: "New in the letter is the passage 2¹⁻¹² (more accurately 2²⁻⁹· ¹¹⁻¹²), the evident prelude thereto 1⁵· ⁶· ⁹· ¹², and finally the epistolary material 2¹⁵ 3². ¹³· ¹⁴· ¹⁷. The entire remainder is simply excerpt, paraphrase, and variation of the larger letter, often in fact elaborated repetition of parallel passages of the same" (Holtzmann, *ZNW.* 1901, 104; so also in *Einl.*³ 1892, 214). Much truer to the facts is the estimate of McGiffert (*EB.* 5044; *cf.* Dob. 45): "the only new matter in the second (letter) is found in 1⁵⁻¹² 2²⁻¹²· ¹⁵ 3¹⁻⁵· ¹⁰· ¹³ ᶠ· ¹⁷ (though) even within these passages there is more or less dependence upon I. The remainder of the epistle, about a third of the whole, is simply a more or less close reproduction of the first epistle." That is to say, the new matter comprises about two-thirds of the epistle, a rather large proportion when it is recalled that the *apologia* of the first three chapters of I does not recur in II, and that only two of the three classes chiefly exhorted in the last two chapters of I are treated in II.

In the paragraphs that follow, only the salient points of resemblance and difference are mentioned; for an exhaustive discussion, see Wrede (*op. cit.*).

(*b*) The most striking and at the same time most important feature in the resemblances between II and I is the epistolary outline, formally considered. No other two extant letters of Paul agree so closely in this respect. At the same time there are differences, and II has new material of its own. The following table may serve to visualise the outline:

I	II
παῦλος ... χάρις καὶ εἰρήνη ... 1^{1}	idem ... 1^{1-2a}
	ἀπὸ θεοῦ πατρός κτλ ... 1^{2b}
εὐχαριστοῦμεν ... $1^{2}-2^{12}$	εὐχαριστεῖν ὀφείλομεν ... 1^{3-10}
	προσευχόμεθα ... 1^{11-12}
$(4^{1}\ 5^{12})$ ...	ἐρωτῶμεν ... 2^{1-12}
εὐχαριστοῦμεν ... $2^{13}-3^{10}$	ὀφείλομεν εὐχαριστεῖν ... 2^{13-14}
	στήκετε ... 2^{15}
αὐτὸς δὲ ὁ θεός ... καὶ κύριος. 3^{11-13}	αὐτὸς δὲ ὁ κύριος ... καὶ θεός ... 2^{16-17}
λοιπόν ... 4^{1-2}	τὸ λοιπόν ... 3^{1-2}
ἐρωτῶμεν $4^{1}\ 5^{12}\ (4^{1}-5^{22})$ ...	$(2^{1})\ (παρακαλοῦμεν\ 3^{12})$ ...
(5^{25}) ...	προσεύχεσθε περὶ ἡμῶν ... 3^{1-2}
$(πιστὸς\ ὁ\ καλῶν\ 5^{24})$ ...	πιστὸς δέ ἐστιν ὁ κύριος ... 3^{3}
	πεποίθαμεν ἐν κυρίῳ ... 3^{4}
$(3^{12.\ 11})$ ...	ὁ δὲ κύριος κατευθύναι ... 3^{5}
οὐ θέλομεν δὲ ὑμας ἀγνοεῖν ... 4^{13-18}	
περὶ δὲ τῶν χρόνων καὶ τῶν καιρῶν ... 5^{1-11}	
	παραγγέλλομεν ... 3^{6-15}
	παρακαλοῦμεν 3^{12} ...
αὐτὸς δὲ ὁ θεὸς τῆς εἰρήνης ... 5^{23}	αὐτὸς δὲ ὁ κύριος τῆς εἰρήνης ... 3^{16a}
	ὁ κύριος μετὰ πάντων ὑμῶν ... 3^{16b}
πιστὸς ὁ καλῶν ... 5^{24}	(3^{3}) ...
προσεύχεσθε καὶ περὶ ἡμῶν ... 5^{25}	(3^{1}) ...
ἀσπάσασθε ... 5^{26}	ὁ ἀσπασμός ... 3^{17a}
	σημεῖον ... 3^{17b}
ἐνορκίζειν ... 5^{27}	
ἡ χάρις ... μεθ' ὑμῶν ... 5^{28}	idem ... 3^{18}

The striking similarity between the two outlines, apart from the superscription and the salutation and benediction, consists in the double thanksgiving, the first prayer with αὐτός, the λοιπόν, and the second prayer with αὐτός. But even within the agreement there are differences, for example, ὀφείλομεν II $1^{3}\ 2^{13}$; the position of κύριος in 2^{16}; the contents of the section introduced by λοιπόν, and κύριος for θεός in II 3^{16a}. Moreover, II adds new material, for example, προσευχόμεθα

(1¹¹; *cf.* Phil. 1⁹) after the first thanksgiving; ἐρωτῶμεν (2¹⁻¹²; to be sure 2¹ = I 5¹²; the exhortation is natural, for the purpose is not to censure but to encourage); the imperative στήκετε after the second thanksgiving; and the ὁ κύριος μετὰ πάντων ὑμῶν (3¹⁶) after the second prayer with αὐτός.

(*c*) The author of II, though he follows in the main the epistolary outline of I and centres his reminiscences about the corresponding sections in II, does not draw these reminiscences entirely from the corresponding epistolary sections in I; that is to say, II 1³⁻⁴ does not come wholly from I 1²⁻⁴, nor II 2¹⁶⁻¹⁷ from I 3¹¹⁻¹³, nor II 3¹⁻⁵ from I 4¹⁻² nor II 3¹⁶ from I 5²³. Evidently the author of II is not a slavish copyist, as is for example the author of the epistle to the Laodiceans (*cf.* Lightfoot, *Colossians and Philemon*, 285 *f.*) who starts with Gal. 1¹ and then follows the order of Philippians for sixteen out of twenty verses, and ends with Col. 4¹⁶ (Dob. 45–46). In fact, apart from the formal agreements in the main epistolary outline, the striking thing is not the slavish dependence of the author of II on I, but the freedom with which he employs the reminiscences from I and incorporates them in original ways into new settings.

In II 1³⁻⁴, little stress should be laid on the common epistolary formula εὐχαριστεῖν τῷ θεῷ πάντοτε περὶ ἡμῶν; more important is the new ὀφείλομεν which along with καθὼς ἄξιόν ἐστιν reveals the encouraging purpose of the first two chapters, as the exegesis will show. The ὑπεραυξάνει and πλεονάζει, indicating the inward growth of the church, come not from I 1²⁻⁴ but from the equally redundant πλεονάσαι καὶ περισσεύσαι of I 3¹²; the prayer for brotherly love is fulfilled. The ἑνὸς ἑκάστου is drawn not from I 1²⁻⁴ but if necessary from I 2¹². Instead, however, of repeating "the work of faith," "the labour of love," and "the endurance of hope" (I 1²), or the faith, hope, and love of I 5⁸, he confines himself to faith and love, the points which Timothy, in reporting the situation in I 3⁶, had emphasised. Then instead of saying that it is unnecessary to speak of their faith (I 1⁸⁻⁹), he is at pains to say that, contrary to their expectations, he is boasting everywhere not of their faith and love, but of their endurance and faith in persecutions, which reminds one more of I 3² than of 1² ᶠ. It is evident that the writer of II 1³⁻⁴ draws not simply from I 1²⁻³ but from I 3¹² 2¹² 3⁶ 3² and if ἄξιον, which controls καταξιωθῆναι (II 1⁵) and ἀξιώσῃ (II 1¹¹), must have a basis, from ἀξίως 2¹².

In the prayer II 2¹⁶⁻¹⁷ (αὐτὸς δέ κτλ.), which corresponds to I

3¹¹⁻¹³, the only resemblance to I 3¹¹⁻¹³, apart from the initial phrase (and II puts Christ before God as in Gal. 1¹), is ὑμῶν τὰς καρδίας and στηρίξαι. But the collocation στηρίζειν καὶ παρακαλεῖν (cf. Rom. 1¹²) occurs in I 3². Surely the unique phrase παράκλησιν αἰωνίαν does not owe its origin simply to ἡ παράκλησις ἡμῶν I 2³.

Most interesting is the section beginning with τὸ λοιπόν in II 3¹⁻⁵, which introduces the command to the idlers in 3⁶⁻¹⁵, when compared with the corresponding section in I 4¹⁻² (λοιπόν κτλ.) which introduces the exhortations of 4³–5²². It is interesting because II 3¹⁻⁵ draws nothing from I 4¹⁻² except the λοιπόν, unless παραγγελίας ἐδώκαμεν suggests παραγγέλλομεν and καθὼς καὶ περιπατεῖτε accounts for καὶ ποιεῖτε καὶ ποιήσετε. Rather καθὼς παρελάβετε (cf. 1 Cor. 15¹ Gal. 1⁹ Phil. 4⁹ Col. 2⁶) παρ' ἡμῶν (I 4¹) appears first in II 3⁶ κατὰ τὴν παράδοσιν ἣν παρελάβετε παρ' ἡμῶν; and τὸ πῶς δεῖ ὑμᾶς περιπατεῖν (I 4¹) appears first in II 3⁷ πῶς δεῖ μιμεῖσθαι ὑμᾶς, the resulting combination εἰδέναι πῶς δεῖ being found also in Col. 4⁶ and 1 Tim. 3¹⁵. But the αὐτοὶ γὰρ οἴδατε of II 3⁷ comes not from οἴδατε γάρ I 4², but rather from the αὐτοὶ γὰρ οἴδατε of I 2¹ or 3³. But to return to II 3¹⁻⁵; vv. ¹⁻² are new and fit nicely into the situation at Corinth; οὐ γὰρ πάντων ἡ πίστις betrays a mood similar to that in I 2¹⁵⁻¹⁶; προσεύχεσθε ἀδελφοὶ περὶ ἡμῶν (Heb. 13¹⁸; cf. Col. 4²) is not a slavish reproduction of I 5²⁵ as the omission of καί and the changed position of ἀδελφοί indicate. To be sure, ὁ λόγος τοῦ κυρίου occurs elsewhere in Paul only I 1⁸ (4¹⁶), though Col. 3¹⁶ has ὁ λόγος τοῦ χριστοῦ; but κύριος is characteristic of II compared with I, and in 3¹⁻⁵, as in Phil. 4¹⁻⁵, occurs four times. In II 3³, πιστὸς δέ ἐστιν ὁ κύριος ὅς agrees with I 5²⁴ only in πιστός and ὅς; στηρίξει (2¹⁷) need come neither from I 3² nor from 3¹³ (cf. Rom. 1¹¹ 16²⁵), and φυλάξει is used elsewhere in Paul only with νόμος. In II 3⁴, πεποίθαμεν ἐν κυρίῳ (Phil. 2²⁴), which is characteristic of Paul, does not occur in I; παραγγέλλομεν is not quite παραγγελίας ἐδώκαμεν (4²); and καὶ ποιεῖτε καὶ ποιήσετε resembles I 4¹⁰ or 5¹¹ more than 4¹. In II 3⁵, ὁ δὲ κύριος κατευθύναι ὑμῶν τὰς καρδίας reminds one of ὑμᾶς δὲ ὁ κύριος (I 3¹²), of κατευθύναι (3¹¹), and of ὑμῶν τὰς καρδίας (3¹³; II 2¹⁷). It will be remembered that of the 146 words common to I and II, κατευθύνειν, Θεσσαλονικεύς, ἐρωτᾶν (Phil.), and περιποίησις (Eph.) are the only ones not found in one or more of the Major Epistles of Paul; and that κατευθύνειν τὰς καρδίας is a good Lxx. phrase. If now we follow the order of allusions in II 3¹⁻⁵ to I, we shall have I 4¹ (λοιπόν), 5²⁵ (προσεύχεσθε), 1⁸ (ὁ λόγος τοῦ κυρίου), 2¹⁵⁻¹⁶ (οὐ γὰρ πάντων ἡ πίστις), 5²⁴ (πιστός), 3² or 3¹³ (στηρίξει), [Phil. 2²⁴ πεποίθαμεν ἐν κυρίῳ], 4¹⁰ or 5¹¹ (ποιεῖτε), 3¹² (ὁ δὲ κύριος), 3¹¹ (κατευθύναι), 3¹³ (ὑμῶν τὰς καρδίας). It is evident that the writer of II 3¹⁻⁵ does not take much from the corresponding I 4¹⁻², but rather mingles scattered reminiscences from I with his new material (vv. ¹⁻². ⁴ᵃ ⁵ᵇ).

Finally, II 3¹⁶ agrees with the corresponding I 5²³ only in the initial αὐτὸς δὲ ὁ θεὸς τῆς εἰρήνης, and even so θεός becomes κύριος. The prayer itself is different. Then, instead of the πιστός clause (I 5²⁴), II inserts the new ὁ κύριος μετὰ πάντων ὑμῶν.

(d) Apart from the epistolary outline, there are few lengthy agreements in the phrases common to I and II.

The superscription of II 1¹⁻² differs from that in I 1¹ in adding ἡμῶν to πατρί and ἀπὸ θεοῦ πατρός κτλ. to εἰρήνη. While ἐν θεῷ πατρὶ (ἡμῶν) and ἐν κυρίῳ 'I. X. (also II 3¹²) are not found elsewhere in N. T., the ἐν is distinctively Pauline; moreover, both χάρις καὶ εἰρήνη and θεὸς πατήρ are characteristic of Paul. In the first thanksgiving, the πάντοτε περὶ πάντων ὑμῶν of I 1² recurs in II 1³ without πάντων; furthermore πάντοτε περὶ ὑμῶν II 1¹¹ 2¹³ agrees not with I 1² or 2¹³ but with II 1³. The first prayer with αὐτός (II 2¹⁶) agrees with I 3¹¹ in the mention but not in the order of the divine names; and the second prayer with αὐτός (II 3¹⁶) has Lord not God of peace (I 5²³). The προσεύχεσθε κτλ. of II 3¹ is not identical with I 5²⁵. Striking is ἐρωτῶμεν δὲ ὑμᾶς ἀδελφοί (II 2¹ I 5¹²), for in this phrase we expect παρακαλοῦμεν; but ἐρωτᾶν is found in Phil. and of course frequently in the papyri. The briefest agreement in the epistolary outline is τὸ λοιπόν II 3¹ = λοιπόν I 4¹. In this connection may also be noted ἀδελφοὶ ἠγαπημένοι ὑπὸ κυρίου which, though it occurs in the second thanksgiving of II (2¹³) is a purposed reminiscence of ἀδελφοὶ ἠγαπημένοι ὑπὸ τοῦ θεοῦ in the first thanksgiving of I (1⁴). The idea of election though not the word is present in both contexts (ἐκλογή I 1⁴; εἵλατο, ἐκάλεσεν, περιποίησιν II 2¹³⁻¹⁴).

Apart from the epistolary outline, the agreements are seldom lengthy. Furthermore, the setting of the phrases in II is usually different from their setting in I. The two lengthiest agreements occur in II 3⁸⁻¹⁰; the first (3⁸) ἐν κόπῳ καὶ μόχθῳ (I 2⁹ τὸν κόπον ἡμῶν καὶ τὸν μόχθον) νυκτὸς καὶ ἡμέρας ἐργαζόμενοι πρὸς τὸ μὴ ἐπιβαρῆσαί τινα ὑμῶν appears in a different context in I 2⁹ and is a purposed reminiscence (see note on II 3⁸); the following elements in it are found elsewhere in Paul but not elsewhere in the N. T.: κόπος καὶ μόχθος (2 Cor. 11²⁷ κόπῳ καὶ μόχθῳ), πρὸς τὸ μή with infin., and ἐπιβαρεῖν (2 Cor. 2⁵; nowhere else in Gk. Bib.); on the other hand νυκτὸς καὶ ἡμέρας is found elsewhere in N. T. but not elsewhere in Paul. The second (3¹⁰), καὶ γὰρ ὅτε (not elsewhere in N. T.) ἦμεν πρὸς ὑμᾶς (cf. 2⁵ ὢν πρὸς ὑμᾶς) appears in a different connection in I 3⁴. Briefer reminiscences are αὐτοὶ γὰρ οἴδατε II 3⁷ (I 2¹ 3² 5²) and ἔργον πίστεως II 1¹² (I 1³) which are not found elsewhere in the N. T.; καὶ διὰ τοῦτο II 2¹¹ (I 2¹³) and ὁ λόγος τοῦ κυρίου II 3¹ (I 1⁸ 4¹⁶) which are found elsewhere in N. T. but not elsewhere in Paul; ὁ θεὸς ἡμῶν II 1¹¹· ¹² (I 2² 3⁹ I Cor. 6¹¹), ἡμέρα κυρίου II 2² (I 5²), ἡ πίστις ὑμῶν II 1³· ⁴ (I 1⁸ 3²· ⁵· ⁶· ⁷· ¹⁰), ἡ παρουσία τοῦ κυρίου (ἡμῶν 'I. X.) II 2¹ (I 3¹³ 4¹⁵ 5²³ I Cor. 15²³), πῶς δεῖ II 3⁷ (I 4¹ Col. 4⁶), and στηρίζειν καὶ

4

παρακαλεῖν II 2¹⁷ (I 3²; cf. Rom. 1¹²), which are found elsewhere in N. T. and elsewhere in Paul; and ἄρα οὖν ἀδελφοί II 2¹⁵ (I 5⁶ Rom. 8¹²), τὸ εὐαγγέλιον ἡμῶν II 2¹⁴ (I 1⁵) which are found elsewhere in Paul but not elsewhere in N. T.

(e) In the passage 1⁵–2¹², which consists of new material, there is but slight evidence of literary dependence on I, although knowledge of I is presupposed. In this material, distinctively Pauline elements occur.

In I 1⁴⁻¹⁰ the stress is laid on election evidenced by the reception of the word in great θλίψις, and not on judgment (1¹⁰); but in II 1⁵⁻¹⁰, the emphasis is put not so much on election as on the certainty of acquittal in judgment. This certainty is due to the fact of their endurance and faith, and the judgment is sketched in vv. ⁷⁻¹⁰. It is not strange that θλίψις occurs in both passages; but ὀργή (I 1¹⁰) is not in II nor διωγμός (II 1⁴) in I. The ἐν τῇ ἀποκαλύψει τοῦ κυρίου Ἰησοῦ ἀπ᾽ οὐρανοῦ of II 1⁷ is not a literary dependence on I 4¹⁶, καταβήσεται ἀπ᾽ οὐρανοῦ; "his angels of power" is unique in Gk. Bib. and does not come from I 3¹³; the saints, ἐκδίκησις and ὄλεθρος come respectively not from I 3¹³ 4⁶ 5³ but from the Lxx. In II 1¹¹⁻¹², ἔργον πίστεως is the only certain reminiscence of I (1³), for ὁ θεὸς ἡμῶν is found not only in I 2² 3⁹ but elsewhere in Paul, as well as elsewhere in the N. T. and Lxx.; πάντοτε περὶ ὑμῶν comes not from I 1² but from II 1³. In II 2¹, ἐπισυναγωγή refers to I 4¹³⁻¹⁸ but is not discussed in 2¹⁻¹²; ἐπιστολῆς in 2² refers to I.

The Pauline elements have already been mentioned: εἴπερ (1⁶), the touch μεθ᾽ ἡμῶν (1⁷), ὑπακούειν τῷ εὐαγγελίῳ (1⁸), πᾶσιν leading to the ὅτι clause with ἐπιστεύθη (1¹⁰), ὡς ὅτι (2²), and οἱ ἀπολλύμενοι (2¹⁰); see further the notes ad 1⁵–2¹².

(f) The freedom with which the author of II gives expression to Pauline convictions is illustrated in 2¹³⁻¹⁴.

In II 2¹³ the epistolary outline of I 2¹³ is followed, but the new ὀφείλομεν purposely repeats II 1³. The "brethren beloved by the Lord" (not God as in I 1⁴) is an intentional reference to I 1⁴; but what follows is not a slavish combination of ἐκλογή (I 1⁴), ὁ καλῶν (I 2¹² or 5²⁴), τὸ εὐαγγέλιον ἡμῶν (I 1⁵), περιποίησιν (I 5⁹) and δόξαν (I 2¹²), but is a fresh and vigorous statement of Pauline convictions, sweeping from everlasting to everlasting, akin to I 5⁹ but not betraying literary dependence on the same. In the midst thereof come the effective but in Paul unusual ἀπ᾽ ἀρχῆς, ἁγιασμὸς πνεύματος (1 Pet. 1²), and πίστις ἀληθείας (due to v. ¹²). A similar freedom is witnessed also in II 1¹¹⁻¹² (see notes ad loc.).

(g) Finally it is interesting to observe that from II 3⁶⁻¹⁵ it is possible to get a clearer picture of the situation presupposed by

I 4¹¹⁻¹² and 5¹⁴ (νουθετεῖτε τοὺς ἀτάκτους) than from those passages themselves. II at this point explains I.

The statement that II 3⁶⁻⁹. ¹¹⁻¹² is a reproduction of I 2⁶⁻⁹ 4¹¹⁻¹² 1⁶⁻⁷ 5¹⁴ is misleading. Were it not for the context in which περιπατεῖν ἀτάκτως (II 3⁶. ¹¹) and ἀτακτεῖν (3⁷) appear, we should not be certain that νουθε- τεῖτε (cf. II 3¹⁵) τοὺς ἀτάκτους (I 5¹⁴) referred not to the disorderly in general, as I 4¹¹⁻¹² allows, but specifically to the idlers. The author of II thus betrays at this point first-hand acquaintance with the situa- tion faced in I.

The μιμεῖσθαι of 3⁷ refers to work not to suffering (I 1⁶ 2¹⁴ μιμηταί); τύπον in view of Phil. 3¹⁷ is a natural word for "example" without re- course to the τύπον of I 1⁷; the idea of waiving apostolic right in love (3⁹) appears in a different setting in I 2⁶⁻⁷, and the language in which it is expressed agrees not with I 2⁶⁻⁷ but with 1 Cor. 9⁴ ᶠ·; and although 3⁹ and I 2⁷⁻⁸ alike hint at self-sacrifice, μεταδοῦναι τὰς ψυχάς does not suggest διδόναι τύπον. Furthermore, the lengthy agreement of 3⁸ with I 2⁹ is intentional, that of 3¹⁰ with I 3³ accidental, as II 2⁵ suggests. These facts, coupled with the tactful treatment of the case of the idlers, es- pecially the significant emphasis in 3¹⁵, which is far from *Kirchenzucht*, with the ethical turn in οὐ θέλει (3¹⁰) and with the quite Pauline ἐν κυρίῳ (3¹²), point distinctly to the hand of Paul.

(B) *Hypothesis of Forgery.*—Notwithstanding the fact that the greater part of the material in II is new, that, aside from the agreements in the epistolary outline of I and II, the reminis- cences from I but rarely occur in the corresponding sections of II, that these reminiscences are worked over freely and mingled with new material, and that II 3⁶⁻¹⁵ reflects an intimate and first- hand acquaintance with the situation presupposed by I 4¹¹⁻¹² 5¹⁴, it is nevertheless held that it is quite as easy to imagine that a later writer familiar with I and with the style of Paul imitated I for his own purpose, as that Paul himself wrote II. Since then it is a psychological impossibility for Paul to have written II to the same persons a few months after I, the alternative is a forger.

But apart from the consideration that those who support the hypothesis of forgery fail to indicate what are the criteria for a psychological impossibility in such a case, it is to be observed that it is difficult, if not impossible, to determine what the pur- pose of the forger is and why he hits on I as the point of departure for his pseudepigraphon.

It is sometimes urged that II is written to take the place of I. Were this true, the reason for the forgery would be patent. But as both Mc-Giffert (*EB*. 5042) and Wrede (60) insist, there is no indication of an intention to "save Paul's reputation and set him right with the Thess. after his death, by showing that he had not expected the consummation as soon as I seemed to imply" (McGiffert). In fact, 2^{15} intimates that the authority of I is formally recognised (Wrede). Hence "the sole purpose of the eschatological passage is clearly to put a stop to the fanaticism to which the belief in the speedy consummation was giving rise" (McGiffert; so essentially Kern, 214, Weizsäcker, 250, and Wrede, 67–69).

To this it may be rejoined: (1) The internal evidence of the second letter reveals not one but two purposes, to encourage the faint-hearted who had become more despondent by reason of the assertion that the day is present and to warn more sharply the idlers who since the writing of I had become more troublesome. Hollmann recognises this twofold purpose in that he affirms that the forger united closely the strained eschatological situation and the flight from labour. (2) If 2^{1-12} is designed as a corrective of prevailing wrong impressions as to the imminence of the *Parousia*, it chooses an extremely obscure method of illuminating the minds of the readers. On the assumption of genuineness, the reason for the obscurity is clear; the Thessalonians, since they knew the teaching already, needed only to be reminded of it. (3) Neither Kern nor Wrede has succeeded in explaining just why I is seized upon as the point of departure for the pseudepigraphon. (4) It is admittedly (Wrede, 37 *f*. and McGiffert, *EB*. 5042) difficult to believe that a letter could be sent to the Thessalonians and be accepted by them as Pauline before Paul's death; or to believe that a letter addressed to them but not really intended for them could have gained currency as Pauline in Paul's lifetime. It is necessary therefore to go beyond the sixties, down even to the end of the first or even to the beginning of the second century in order to make a forgery intelligible. But the further one goes beyond 50 A.D. the harder it is to account for that intimate acquaintance with the situation implied by I, which is revealed especially in II 3^{6-15}. (5) There is no essential incompatibility between I 5^{1} ff. and II 2^{1-12}, between signs and suddenness, as both McGiffert and Wrede concede. (6) At every point the exegesis of II is easiest on the assumption of genuineness. (7) The hypothesis of forgery proceeds on the supposition that it is a psychological impossibility for Paul to have written II a few months after I to the same people. But criteria for distinguishing what is psychologically possible or impossible to Paul are not adduced. The only evidence that throws any light on the matter is the statement of Paul to another Macedonian church: "To go on writing the same things is not tedious to me, while to you it is safe" (Phil. 3^{1}). To be sure, there are no objective criteria to go by; no two other extant letters of Paul in which two out of the three situations in one letter are treated in a second letter written less than three months later. On the assumption of genuineness, it is evident that it was important for Paul to remember I, for its utterances at certain points had been misconstrued by some. And since, according to Phil. 3^1, Paul could write the same things if necessary, the presence in II of reminiscences, apart from the epistolary outline, is natural, especially if II is a reply to a letter which the Thessalonians sent to Paul asking advice concerning the faint-hearted and the idlers, a letter written after their reading of I and after their failure to cope successfully with the difficulty created by the assertion that the day of the Lord was actually present. Indeed, it is not improbable that, as Zahn (*Introd.* I, 250; *cf.* Moff. *Introd.* 76) suggests, Paul read over the original draft of I before he dictated II, for in the light of Cicero's usual habit (*cf.* Zahn, *loc. cit.*) and of similar evidence from the papyri (*cf.* Deiss. *Light*, 227 *f.*), it may be assumed that the letters of Paul were usually revised after dictation and copied, the copy being sent, and the original draft retained by Paul or his secretary. At the same time, it is strange that the epistolary outline of II should agree so closely with that of I. But strangeness is not identical with psychological impossibility.

(5) *Hypothesis of Genuineness.*—Since the antecedent probability, namely, the intelligibility of the historical situation implied by II, the language, the personal equation, and the religious convictions, is distinctly in favour of Pauline authorship, and since the objection to the genuineness on the score of alleged discrepancies between I $5^{1\ ff.}$ and II 2^{1-12} is not insuperable, the hypothesis of genuineness may be assumed as the best working hypothesis in spite of the difficulties suggested by the literary resemblances, especially the striking agreement in the epistolary outline.

Harnack, however (*op. cit.*), like Wrede, is convinced that it is psychologically impossible for II to have been written by Paul a few months after I to the same address, although the criteria for determining psychological impossibility are not stated. But he is equally confident that II is thoroughly Pauline. The only way then out of the conclusion that II is a forgery is the postulate that there were two churches in Thessalonica, one the main church composed of Gentiles, the other a kind of annex made up of Jews; and that I was addressed to the Gentile and II to the Jewish church. Although Paul ordered the former to see to it that the latter should hear the first epistle read (I 5^{27}), yet he was aware that the exhortations in reference to impurity, a sin to which Gentiles were susceptible, and in reference to eschatology (new teaching in I 4^{13-18}, and simple in I 5^{1-11}), had in mind mainly if not wholly the problems of the Gentile Christians. Accordingly, in order to meet the specific needs of the Jewish Christians who were steeped in eschatology and had begun to believe that the day of the Lord was present, and who were also idle (for although the Gentiles were idle, the Jews were the conspicuous idlers, as the severe reproof of II 3⁶⁻¹⁵ shows), he writes the second letter at the same time as I, or a few days after I. Though both types of Christians were dear to Paul, yet the letter to the Jewish annex, while not unfriendly, lacks the warm tone and the intimate friendliness of I, is in fact somewhat severe (3¹² ᶠ·), official and ceremonious (ὀφείλομεν 1³ 2¹³). This postulate, once made, is worked out with the brilliance familiar to readers of his discussion of the Priscan authorship of Hebrews.

Waiving the suggestion that the hypothesis would be relieved of one difficulty if the traditional assertion that II is severe, official, and ceremonious were dispensed with altogether, two important difficulties may be suggested, one that the evidence adduced for the existence of a separate Jewish Christian group is not quite conclusive, and the other that the psychological difficulty that prompts the postulate is not entirely removed. As to the first point, Harnack assumes that the O. T. colouring in II suggests Jewish Christian readers, an assumption which is disputable; also that the Gentiles had had no instruction in eschatology beyond the simplest teaching as to the suddenness of the day and the necessity for watchfulness, an assumption difficult not only in the light of I 5² ᶠ·, but also of I 4¹⁶⁻¹⁷ where Paul includes in his new teaching apocalyptic details which, on the theory of simplicity, are irrelevant. Furthermore, while Acts 17⁴ states that the preaching in the synagogue succeeded with a few Jews and with a great many Gentiles, men and women, who as adherents of the synagogue may be presumed to have been acquainted with the Messianic hopes of the Jews in their apocalyptic expression, still it has nothing to say of the formation of two separate Christian groups. Still further, the first letter betrays no knowledge of the existence of more than one Christian assembly in Thessalonica, for the "all" in 5²⁷ obviously suggests not an annex of Jewish Christians but recalcitrants, most probably some of the idle brethren, within the one church of the Thessalonians. Moreover, the reading ἀπαρχήν (see note on 2¹³), which did not suggest the hypothesis but which to Harnack is objective evidence in favour of it, is less suitable than ἀπ' ἀρχῆς in a context designed to assure the readers of their certainty of salvation. The second important difficulty with this plausible hypothesis is that the psychological impossibility which prompts it is not entirely eliminated, for although the presence of reminiscences is adequately accounted for, the surprising similarity of the epistolary outline is not.

Lake (*Exp. Times*, Dec. 1910, 131–3, and *The Earlier Epistles of St. Paul*, 1911, 83 ff.) inclines to think that Harnack's theory complies with all the conditions of the problem; Dibelius and Knopf (*TLZ*. 1911, 455–457) speak hesitatingly.

§ VII. THE TEXT.

The text of Westcott and Hort is followed almost without exception in the commentary. The nomenclature is that of Gregory, *Die Griechischen Handschriften des N. T.* 1908 and *Text Kritik des N. T.* III, 1909 (*cf.* Souter, *Nov. Test. Graece*, 1910). The various readings are taken from the apparatus of Tischendorf (*Nov. Test. Graece*, vol. II, ed. 8, 1872) and of Souter.

> The various readings from Greek manuscripts, versions, and patristic writers have been cited in the interest of exegesis. The following authorities have been most serviceable: Zimmer (*Der Text der Thessalonicherbriefe*, 1893), B. Weiss (*Textkritik der Paulinischen Briefe*, in *TU.*[2] 1896), and the textual notes in the commentaries of Findlay and Dobschütz.

(1) *Greek Manuscripts.*—From the lists in Gregory (*op. cit.*) and von Soden (*Die Schriften des N. T.*, begun in 1902 and now (1912) nearing completion), it would appear that about six hundred Greek manuscripts contain 1, 2 Thess. wholly or in part. The twenty-one uncials among them may be briefly enumerated as follows:

א (e a p r). *Cod. Sinaiticus*, saec. iv, now at St. Petersburg. Edited by Tischendorf, its discoverer, in 1862. Photographic reproduction by H. and K. Lake, Oxford, 1911. Contains I and II complete.

A (e a p r). *Cod. Alexandrinus*, saec. v, now in the British Museum. Edited by Woide in 1786. Facsimile by E. M. Thompson, 1879. Contains I and II complete.

B (e a p r). *Cod. Vaticanus*, saec. iv, now in the Vatican Library. Photographic reproduction by Cozza-Luzi, Rome, 1889, and by the Milan firm of Hoepli, 1904. Contains I and II complete.

C (e a p r). *Cod. Ephraemi Rescriptus*, saec. v, now in the National Library at Paris. The N. T. fragments were edited by Tischendorf in 1843. Contains I 1^2 $\epsilon\upsilon\chi\alpha\rho\iota\sigma\tau\sigma\upsilon\mu\epsilon\nu$—2^8 $\epsilon\gamma\epsilon\nu\eta\theta\eta\tau\epsilon$.

D (p). *Cod. Claromontanus*, saec. vi, Graeco-Latin, now in the National Library at Paris. Edited by Tischendorf in 1852. Contains I and II complete.

[E] *Cod. Sangermanensis*, saec. ix, now at St. Petersburg. A copy of D.

F (p). *Cod. Augiensis*, saec. ix, Graeco-Latin, now in the Library of Trinity College, Cambridge. An exact transcript by Scrivener, 1859. Contains I and II complete.

G (p). *Cod. Boernerianus*, saec. ix, now in the Royal Library at Dresden. "It is closely related to F, according to some the archetype of F" (Souter). Edited by Matthaei, 1791. *Im Lichtdruck nachgebildet*, Leipzig (Hiersemann), 1909. Contains I and II complete.

H (p). *Cod. Saec. vi*. Most of the forty-one leaves now known are in the National Library at Paris; the remainder are at Athos, Moscow, St. Petersburg, Kiev, and Turin. The fragments at Kiev contain 2 Cor. 4^{2-7}, 1 Thess. 2^{9-13} ($\mu\nu\eta\mu\rho\nu\epsilon\nu\epsilon\tau\epsilon \ldots \epsilon\sigma\tau\iota\nu \ \alpha\lambda\eta\theta\omega\varsigma$) and 4^{4-11} ($\epsilon\alpha\nu\tau\sigma\nu \ \sigma\kappa\epsilon\nu\sigma\varsigma \ldots \phi\iota\lambda\sigma\tau\iota\mu\iota\sigma\theta\alpha\iota$); *cf.* H. Omont, *Notice sur un très ancien manuscrit*, etc. 1889.

I (p). *Cod. Saec. v*. Ms. 4 in the Freer Collection at Detroit, Michigan. This manuscript is a "badly decayed fragment, now containing many short portions of the epistles of Paul. It is written on parchment in small uncials and probably belongs to the fifth century. . . . Originally contained Acts and practically all of the epistles but not Revelation. . . . While no continuous portion of the text remains, many brief passages from Eph. Phil. Col. Thess. and Heb. can be recovered" (H. A. Sanders, *Biblical World*, vol. XXI, 1908, 142; *cf.* also Gregory, *Das Freer-Logion*, 1908, 24). The fragments of Thess., a collation of which Prof. Sanders kindly sent me, contain I $1^{1-2.9-10}$ $2^{7-8.14-16}$ $3^{2-4.11-13}$ $4^{8-9.16-18}$ $5^{9-11.23-26}$ II $1^{1-3.10-11}$ $2^{5-8.15-17}$ 3^{8-10}.

K (a p). *Cod. Mosquensis*, saec. ix, now at Moscow. Collated by Matthaei, 1782. Contains I and II complete.

L (a p). *Cod. Angelicus*, saec. ix, now in the Angelican Library at Rome. Collated among others by Tischendorf (1843) and Tregelles (1845). Contains I and II complete.

P (a p r). *Cod. Porphyrianus*, saec. ix, now at St. Petersburg. Edited by Tischendorf (1865). Contains I and II except I 3^5 μηκετι—ημεις οι 4^{17}.

Ψ (e a p). *Cod. Saec. viii–ix*, now at Mount Athos. Contains I and II complete.

048 (a p). *Cod. Saec. v*, now in the Vatican Library, a fragmentary palimpsest. Contains I 1^{1-2} with the short codex title.

049 (a p). *Cod. Saec. viii–ix*, now at Mount Athos. Contains I 1^1–2^{13} ανθρωπων.

056 (a p). *Cod. Saec. x*, now in the National Library at Paris. I and II were collated by Van Sittart (Gregory, *Text Kritik*, 296).

075 (p). *Cod. Saec. x*, now in the National Library at Athens (Gregory, *ibid.* 309).

0111 (p). *Cod. Saec. vii* (?), now in the Royal Museum at Berlin, a fragment containing only II 1^1–2^2, mutilated in 1^{1-4} and 1^{11}–2^2. Printed in Gregory (*ibid.* 1075 ff.).

0142 (a p). *Cod. Saec. x*, now in the Royal Library at Munich. Contains I and II complete.

0150 (p). *Cod. Saec. ix* (Gregory, *ibid.* 1081), now at Patmos.

0151 (p). *Cod. Saec. ix or x* (Gregory, *ibid.* 1081), now at Patmos.

These uncials may be summarised as to date thus: Saec. iv (אB), v (ACI. 048), vi (DH.), vii (0111), viii–ix (Ψ 049), ix (EFGKLP. 0150), ix–x (0151), and x (056. 075. 0142).

There are about 585 minuscules which contain I and II complete or in part. Of these the following 38 appear to be the oldest: Saec. ix (1430. 1862. 1900); ix–x (33. 1841); x (1. 82. 93. 221. 454. 456. 457. 605. 619. 627. 920. 1175 (I 1^{10}–2^{21} is lacking). 1244. 1739. 1760. 1770. 1836. 1845. 1870. 1880. 1891. 1898. 1905. 1920. 1954 (I 1^1–2^5 is lacking). 1997. 1998. 2110. 2125); x–xi (1851 (II 3^{7-18} is lacking). 1910. 1912. 1927).

The leading minuscules, according to SH. (lxv) are: 33 (saec. ix-x), 1912 (saec. x-xi), 104. 424. 436. 1908 (saec. xi), 88. 321 (saec. xii), 263 (saec. xiii-xiv), 5. 489 (saec. xiv), and 69 (saec. xv), one of the Ferrar Group.

(2) *Versions*.—The following versions are occasionally quoted: Latin including Old Latin and Vulgate (Vulg.), Syriac Vulgate (Pesh.), Coptic in the Bohairic dialect (Boh.), and Armenian (Arm.).

(*a*) *Latin*. Witnesses for the Old Latin are the Latin of the bilinguals D (E) F G, namely, d (e) f (?) g (?); r (saec. vii, a fragment now in Munich containing Phil. 4^{11-23} and 1 Thess. 1^{1-10}, discovered and edited by Ziegler, *Italafragmente der Paulinischen Briefe*, 1876); X^2 (saec. vii-viii, now in the Bodleian; according to Wescott (Smith's *DB*. 3458 *f*.) it agrees in many cases with d almost or quite alone); also the citations of the Speculum (=m; edited by Weihrich in the Vienna Corpus, xii, 1887; contains I 2^{1-14} 4^{1-16} 5^{6-22} II 1^{3-12} 3^{6-15}); and of Ambrosiaster (= Ambst., quoted from a collation which Prof. Souter was good enough to send me), and others. The Vulgate is cited from Nestle's edition (*Nov. Test. Graece*, 1906); there are occasional references to the Vulgate codices Amiatinus (=am.; saec. viii) and Fuldensis (=fuld.; saec. vi). On the Latin versions, see Kennedy in *HDB*. III, 47-62 and Burkitt in *EB*. 4992 *ff*.

(*b*) *Syriac*. According to Burkitt (*EB*. 4998 *ff*.), "no manuscript of the Old Syriac version of the Pauline Epistles is known to have survived." The Syriac Vulgate or Peshitta, of which some sixty-seven manuscripts are available for Paul (Gregory, *Text Kritik*, 520 *f*.), owes its origin (so Burkitt) to Rabbula, Bishop of Edessa (411–435 A.D.), and represents a revision of an older Syriac translation. On the Syriac versions including the later revisions of Philoxenus (A.D. 508) and Thomas of Harkel (A.D. 616), see Burkitt (*op. cit.*).

(*c*) *Coptic.* The Bohairic is cited from Horner: *Coptic Version of the N. T. in the Northern Dialect*, III, 1905.

N. B. In the library of Mr. J. Pierpont Morgan, of New York, there are about fifty manuscripts in the Sahidic dialect of the Coptic, formerly in the Coptic Monastery of St. Michael, in the Fayyûm. Prof. Hyvernat, the future editor, announces that the N. T. is represented by three complete gospels (Mt. Mk. and Jn.; Lk. is incomplete), fourteen letters of Paul, the two of Peter, and the three of John (*JBL*. XXXI, 1912, 55).

(*d*) *Armenian*. On this version, see Conybeare in *HDB*. I, 153 *f*.

§ VIII. COMMENTARIES.

Commentaries and annotations on Thessalonians are unexpectedly numerous. The list given in the following paragraphs does not pretend to be exhaustive.

On the history of interpretation, the following commentators are important: Crocius, Pelt, Lillie, Dobschütz, and especially Bornemann (1–7 and 538–708).

(1) In the early church, the most important commentators are the Antiochans Chrysostom, Theodore of Mopsuestia, and Theodoret in Greek; also Ephraem in Syriac, and Ambrosiaster and Pelagius in Latin.

For patristic commentators, see the notes in Swete's edition of Th. Mops. on the Minor Epistles of Paul, and Turner's article, *Greek Patristic Commentaries on the Pauline Epistles* in *HDB*. V, 484–531. Origen is apparently the first commentator on our letters; but only one definite comment is extant, I 4$^{15-17}$ (quoted by Jerome, *Ep.* 119). The commentaries of the Antiochans Theodore of Heraclea, the pupil of Lucian, Apollinaris of Laodicea, and Diodore of Tarsus, the teacher of Chrys. and Th. Mops., are known, if at all, only in fragments (*cf.* Cramer, *Catenae*, 1841–44). The homilies of Chrysostom, eleven on I and five on II (ed. F. Field, Oxford, 1885) have influenced not only the gatherers of catenae in the Middle Ages but every comm. down to the present. Equally an Antiochan, but less homiletical and more exegetical than Chrys. is his friend Theodore of Mopsuestia († c. 429) whose work on the Minor Epistles of Paul is fully extant in a Latin translation and partly in the original (ed. H. B. Swete, *Th. Mops. in epistolas Pauli*, Cambridge, 1880–1882, and enriched by invaluable notes). This work is "the first and almost the last exegetical book produced in the ancient church which will bear any comparison with modern commentaries" (G. H. Gilbert, *Interpretation of the Bible*, 1908, 135). Theodoret of Cyrrhus († 457), a pupil of Theodore, gathers from him and Chrys. and aims at conciseness of expression. Less penetrating than they, he is still an Antiochan in method (ed. Marriott, Oxford, 1852, 1870).

Of Ephraem Syrus († 373), a few notes on Paul have been preserved in Armenian; these were translated into Latin and published by the Mechitarist Fathers, Venice, 1893.

Two important Latin commentators of the fourth century are Ambrosiaster and Pelagius. By the former is meant the work on Paul published along with the works of Ambrose in Migne (*PL.* 17); see

Souter, *TS*. VII, 4, 1905. The text of Pelagius, bound up with the works of Jerome in Migne (*PL*. 30, 670 *ff*.), is corrupt; but of Ms. cxix in the Grand Ducal Library at Karlsruhe, Souter (in a paper read before the British Academy, Dec. 12, 1906, and published 1907: *Comm. of Pelagius on the Epistles of Paul*) says, "it is pure Pelagius, perhaps the only copy in existence."

(2) "In the Middle Ages, exegesis consisted chiefly in the reproduction of the expositions of the fathers, in collections and compilations, called epitomes, glosses, postilles, chains." "The traditional principle of exegesis became more and more dominant, and alongside of this the allegorical method was found to be the most convenient for reconciling Scripture with tradition. The literal and the historical sense was almost entirely ignored" (Briggs, *SHS*. 453 *f*.).

Among the later Greeks, the most important is John of Damascus († c. 760; Migne, *PG*. 95). On Œcumenius and the other Greek catenists, *e. g.* Theophylact and Euthymius Zigabenus, both of whom died in the early twelfth century, see Turner (*op. cit.*).

The most important commentators in Latin are the scholastic master Thomas Aquinas († 1274) and Nicolaus de Lyra, the free but faithful converted Jew († 1340). Mainly compilers are Florus Diaconus († c. 860; Migne, *PL*. 119) who for Paul gathered together the stray comments of Augustine (*cf.* Born. 559); Haymo (? † 853; Migne, *PL*. 117, 765 *ff*.); Rabanus Maurus († 856; Migne, *PL*. 112, 539 *ff*.) and his pupil Walafrid Strabo († 849; Migne, *PL*. 114, 615 *ff*.) who was *auctoritas* to Peter Lombard († 1164); Atto († 961; ed. Burontius, Vercelli, 1768); Hervaeus Burgidolensis († 1150; Migne, *PL*. 181, 1355 *ff*.; follows Augustine freely); and Dionysius the Carthusian († 1471) the new edition of whose works begun in 1896 contemplates forty-five quarto volumes; a fruitful but unoriginal compiler.

(3) In the sixteenth century, the Protestant Reformers agreed with the humanists, of whom Erasmus is the conspicuous example, in going back to the Hebrew and Greek text of Scripture and in giving the grammatical and literal sense over against the allegorical, but "insisted that Scripture should be its own interpreter and that it was not to be interpreted by tradition or external ecclesiastical authority" (Briggs, *SHS*. 456). Of the three great exegetes, Luther, Zwingli, and Calvin, the greatest is Calvin.

Erasmus († 1536) edited the annotations of the Italian humanist Laurentius Valla († 1457) in 1505, and a paraphrase of his own on all of Paul in 1521. Luther did not comment on our letters. Calvin's comm. on Thess. appeared in 1539 (best edition in *Corpus Ref.* 52, 1895, 133–218) and Zwingli's in 1526 (ed. *opera exeget.* 1581, vol. IV). "Worthy to stand by their side" (Briggs) are Bugenhagen (1524), Bullinger († 1575) and Musculus († 1563). Beza's *Annotationes in N. T.* (1565) should be mentioned. Melanchthon did not, but his friend Camerarius (*Notatio*, 1554) and his pupil Strigel (*Hypomneumata*, 1565) did comment on our epistles.

The immediate successors of the Reformers "had somewhat of their spirit, although the sectarian element already influenced them in the maintenance of the peculiarities of the different national churches" (Briggs, *SHS.* 457). Calvinists are Hyperius († 1564), Marloratus (1561), Hemmingsen († 1600), Aretius († 1574), Zanchius († 1590) and Piscator (1589). Lutherans are Flacius (1570), Hunnius († 1603), Georgius Major († 1574) and Selnecker († 1592). In Britain we have John Jewel whose sermons, edited by John Garbrand (1583), are the first exposition of our epistles in English; and Robert Rollock, principal or first master of the Univ. of Edinburgh, whose Latin commentary (1598) was followed by his lectures, in English (1606).

Among Roman Catholic commentators or scholiasts are Faber Stapulensis († 1512), Gagnaeus († 1549), Catharinus (1551), Clarius († 1555), Sasbout (1561), Zegers († 1559), Arias († 1598), Serarius († 1609), and Estius († 1613).

(4) The seventeenth century is marked by the exegetical activity of the British Puritans such as Edward Leigh and Matthew Poole, and by the revival in Holland of the spirit of Erasmus in the person of Hugo de Groot who combined sound classical learning with a keen historical sense. Like Grotius is Hammond who insisted on the plain, literal, and historical meaning.

On seventeenth-century exegesis in Britain, see especially Briggs, *SHS.* 459–469. Leigh's *Annotations upon all the N. T.* was published in 1650. Several of the scholars whom he used in addition to Grotius have commented upon our epistles, as for example Drusius (1612, 1616) and de Dieu (1646), the Dutch divines; John Cameron († 1625), the Scot who worked chiefly in France; John Mayer (1631); and William Sclater (*Exposition with notes on 1 Thess.* 1619; *Briefe Exposition with notes on 2 Thess.* 1627; this brief exposition runs to 598 quarto pages). The annotations of the Westminster divines covering the whole Bible went into a second edition, 2 vols., in 1651. The great compilation *Critici*

Sacri was published in 1660, 9 vols. "Among the last of the Puritan works on the more learned side was the masterpiece of Matthew Poole" (Briggs, *op. cit.* 467) entitled: *Synopsis Criticorum*, 1669 *ff.* in five folio volumes (1, 2 Thess. in vol. IV, 1676, col. 943–1004). Poole's *English Annotations on the Holy Bible* was completed by his friends and published in 1685.

The *annotationes ad V. et N. T.* of Grotius was published in Amsterdam in 1641 *ff.* Hammond's *Paraphrase and Annotations* on the N. T. appeared in 1653 and was done into Latin by Clericus in 1698.

Other British expositors may be named: William Bradshaw (*A plaine and pithie Exposition* of 2 Thess. 1620, edited by Thos. Gataker); Timothie Jackson (1621, on 2 Thess.); David Dickson (*expositio analytica omnium apost. epp.* 1645; English in 1659 by W. Retchford); Thomas Case (1670; this is not a comm. on 1 Thess. but an exposition of I 4^{13-18} entitled *Mount Pisgah: or a prospect of heaven*); James Fergusson (1674; brief exposition of 1, 2 Thess.); J. Fell (1675; on Paul's letters); Richard Baxter (1684; paraphrase on N. T. with notes doctrinal and practical); William Burkitt (1700; on the N. T.); and Daniel Whitby (*Paraphrase and Commentary on the N. T.* 1703). Other Continental commentators are Vorstius († 1622); Cappelus († 1624); Gomarus († 1641); Diodati († 1649); Calixtus († 1656); Haak (1637; in English, 1657, under title of *Dutch Annotations*, etc.); Slichting (the Socinian, † 1661; Thess. was finished in 1660); Crocius (*comm. in omnes epp. Pauli minores*, ed. 1663, 3 vols.); Calovius (1672-76; a Lutheran who corrects Grot.); and Cocceius († 1669). Among Roman Catholic scholars are Stevart (1609; on 1, 2 Thess.); Justinianus (1612-13); Cornelius a Lapide (1614); Bence (1628; depends on Estius); Menochius (1630; praised by Grot.); Tirinus (1632); Fromond († 1653; depends on Estius); Leander of Dijon (1663); Mauduit (1691); Quesnel (1687; moral reflections in French); and Bernardinus a Piconio (1703 in Latin; 1706 in French. Often reprinted; *cf.* A. H. Prichard, 1888-90). The Roman Church had its Poole in John de la Haye: *Biblia Magna* (1643, 5 vols.) and *Biblia Maxima* (1660, 19 vols.).

(5) In the eighteenth century, the most important commentator is Bengel (*Gnomon*, 1742). But Ernesti's principles of interpretation (1761) found fruit in Schott (1834). Flatt (1829) is influenced by Storr, and Pelt (1830) by Schleiermacher.

The attention of the eighteenth century is given to the text (Bentley, Mill, Bengel, Semler, Griesbach), and to the gathering of parallels from profane literature (Wolf, Kypke, Koppe, Rosenmüller, and especially Wetstein in his N. T. (1751)), from Philo (Loesner), and from rabbinical sources (Schöttgen and Meuschen). The revival of Biblical studies especially in Germany toward the end of the century (see Briggs, *SHS.* 469 *ff.*), due to Lessing, Herder, Semler, Eichhorn, and others, prepared the way for modern methods of interpretation in the nineteenth century.

British expositors of the eighteenth and the first half of the nineteenth century are mainly practical: Matthew Henry (vol. VI, 1721); Philip Doddridge (1739–56); Edward Wells († 1727); George Benson (1 Thess. 1731; 2 Thess. 1732); John Guyse († 1761); John Gill (1746–48); John Wesley (1754; depends in part on Bengel, Doddridge, and Guyse); Thomas Scott (1788–92); also John Lindsay († 1768); Thomas Pyle († 1756); John Philips (1751; on 1 Thess.); Samuel Chandler († 1766; ed. N. White, 1777); James Macknight (1787 and 1795); Thomas Coke (1803; depends on Doddridge); Adam Clarke (1810–25); James Slade (1816); T. Belsham († 1829); P. N. Shuttleworth (1829); W. Trollope (1828–34); Edward Burton (Greek Test. 1831); S. T. Bloomfield (Greek Test. 1832); Charles Eyre (1832); Granville Penn (1837; annotations on N. T.); E. Barlee (1837); W. Bruce (1836); and W. Heberden (1839).

Continental scholars: Laurentius (1714; the first comm. in German, according to Dob.); J. Lange (1729); Turretin († 1737; ed. 1, 2 Thess. 1739); Heumann († 1764); Zachariä (1770); Matthaeus (1785); and Olshausen (vols. 1–4, 1830; English by A. C. Kenrick, 1858).

Roman Catholic interpreters: Natalis Alexander (1710); Rémy (1739); Calmet († 1739); Gregorius Mayer (1788); and Massl (1841–48).

(6) From De Wette (1841) to the present, commentaries on our epistles are many and excellent. (1) *German.* Koch (on 1 Thess. 1849); Lünemann (in *Meyer*, 1850; 1878⁴ in English by Gloag, 1880); Auberlen and Riggenbach (in Lange's *Bibelwerk*, 1864); J. C. K. Hofmann (1862²); P. W. Schmidt (on 1 Thess. 1885); Zöckler (in *Kurzgefasster Komm.* 1887); P. W. Schmiedel (in Holtzmann's *Handcomm.* 1892²); W. Bornemann (in *Meyer*, 1894); B. Weiss (1896, 1902²); Wohlenberg (in Zahn's *Komm.* 1903); Lueken (in *SNT.* 1907²); E. von Dobschütz (in *Meyer*, 1909); and M. Dibelius (in Lietzmann's *Handbuch*, 1911). (2) *Dutch.* Baljon (1907). (3) *British.* Alford (Greek N. T. 1849–61); Jowett (1855); Ellicott (1858); Lightfoot († 1889; *Notes on Epistles of St. Paul*, 1895); James Drummond (in *International Handbooks*, 1899); Findlay (in *Cambridge Greek Test.*, 1904); George Milligan (1908); and

Moffatt (in *EGT*. 1910).   (4) *American*. John Lillie (*The Epistles of Paul to the Thess.*, *Translated from the Greek with Notes*, 1856; and his English edition of Auberlen and Riggenbach, 1868. Lillie's is the most important American work done on our epistles); Henry Cowles (*Shorter Epistles of Paul*, etc. 1879; popular); W. A. Stevens (in *American Comm.* 1890); and E. T. Horn (in *Lutheran Comm.* 1896).

Excellent examples of scholarly exposition with a practical purpose are Lillie (*Lectures*, 1860); John Hutchinson (1884); and especially James Denney (in *Expositor's Bible*, 1892) and H. J. Holtzmann (on 1 Thess.; ed. E. Simons, 1911).

Roman Catholic scholarship is represented in German by Bisping (1854, 1865²), Röhm (on 1 Thess. 1885), Schäfer (1890), and Gutjahr (1900); in English by MacEvilly (1856); in French by Maunory (1881); and in Latin by Pánek (1886).

In addition to Ewald's *Die Bücher des neuen Bundes* (1870) and Reuss's *La Bible* (1874-80), the following commentators may be named: (1) *German*. Baumgarten-Crusius (ed. Schauer, 1848); and the practical works of Havemann (1875) and Goebel (1887, 1897²). (2) *British*. T. W. Peile (1851-2); J. Turnbull (1854); Webster and Wilkinson (Greek Test. 1855-61); A. S. Patterson (1857); Wordsworth (Greek N. T. 1856-60); A. R. Fausset (in *Pocket Bible*, 1862-3); E. Headland and H. B. Swete (1863-66); C. J. Vaughan (on 1 Thess. 1864); John Eadie (ed. W. Young, 1877); A. J. Mason (in Ellicott's *N. T. Comm.* 1879?); William Alexander (in *Speaker's Comm.* 1881); F. A. Malleson (*The Acts and Epistles of St. Paul*, 1881); Marcus Dods (in Schaff's *Popular Comm.* 1882); P. J. Gloag (in *Pulpit Comm.* 1887); M. F. Sadler (1890); Findlay (in *Cambridge Bible for Schools and Colleges*, 1891); G. W. Garrod (1899-1900; analysis with notes); V. Bartlet (in *Temple Bible*, 1902); W. F. Adeney (in *New Century Bible*, 1907?); R. Mackintosh (in *Westminster N. T.* 1909); and H. W. Fulford (Thess. and Pastorals, 1911). Practical are A. R. Dallas (*Cottager's Guide*, vol. I, 1849); J. B. Sumner ("Expository lectures," 1851); H. Linton ("Paraphrase and notes on Paul," 1857); J. Edmunds ("plain and practical" comm. on 1, 2 Thess. 1858); C. D. Marston ("Expositions on the Epp. of N. T." 1865); W. Niven ("Family readings on 1, 2 Thess." 1875); R. V. Dunlop ("Lectures on 1 Thess." 1882); G. W. Clark (1903); and A. R. Buckland (1906). (3) *American*. The explanatory and practical notes of Albert Barnes (1846) and the Family Bible of Justin Edwards (1851) may be mentioned.

N. B. Of the commentators named in the preceding paragraphs, a score or more have been particularly helpful to the present editor: Chrysostom, Theodore of Mopsuestia, Ambrosiaster, Calvin, Grotius, Hammond, Poole, Bengel, De Wette, Lünemann, Lillie, Ellicott, Auberlen and Riggenbach, Denney, Schmiedel, Bornemann, Lightfoot, Wohlenberg, Findlay, and especially Milligan and von Dobschütz.

COMMENTARY ON THE FIRST EPISTLE TO THE THESSALONIANS.

I. SUPERSCRIPTION (1^1).

Paul and Silvanus and Timothy to the assembly of Thes-
salonians in God the Father and the Lord Jesus Christ.
Grace to you and peace.

1. The superscription, which is to be distinguished from the address written "on the outside or on the cover of the folded letter" (Dèissmann, *Light*, 148), comprises, as in contemporary letters, the name of the writer in the nominative, the people addressed in the dative, and the greeting. Although it is the shortest of extant Pauline superscriptions, it contains the essential points of the more developed forms, not simply the names of writers and recipients but also the divine names God the Father and the Lord Jesus Christ, and the characteristically Pauline "grace and peace." The Holy Spirit is mentioned in no superscription and in but one benediction (2 Cor. 13^{13}).

The inscription ΠΡΟΣ ΘΕΣΣΑΛΟΝΙΚΕΙΣ Α (אBAK, *et al.*), like the inscriptions and subscriptions in most Mss. and like the introductions (ὑποθέσεις) in some Mss., is editorial and seems to presuppose a *corpus Paulinum* with some such title as ΕΠΙΣΤΟΛΑΙ ΠΑΥΛΟΥ. For elaborations of this briefest form of inscription (*e. g.* in DGF with a prefixed ἄρχεται; in P with a prefixed παύλου ἐπιστολή, or in G with a prefixed ἄρχεται and an added πρώτη ἐπιστολή), see von Soden, *Schriften des N. T.* I, 294 *ff.* For the influence of contemporary literature upon the general form and many phrases of the Pauline and other N. T. letters, see Deissmann, *BS.* 187 *ff.*, *EB.* II, 1323 *ff.*, and *Light;* Rendel Harris, *Exp.*[5] VIII, 161 *ff.*, 401 *ff.*; Robinson, *Ephesians*, 275 *ff.*; Mill. 121 *ff.*; and Moff. *Introd.* 44 *ff.* Useful selections from contemporary letters may be found in Lietzmann, *Griechische Papyri*, 1905; Witkowski, *Epistulae graecae privatae*, 1906; and Mill. *Selections from the Greek Papyri*, 1910.

Since Silvanus and Timothy were with Paul in Thessalonica when the church was established and with him in Corinth when both our letters were written (Acts 18[5]; *cf.* 2 Cor. 1[19]), it is natural to find the three names associated in the superscription. Paul takes precedence as he is the leading spirit and the letter is his in a peculiar sense; Silvanus, the Silas of Acts, comes next; and Timothy, who was not only a helper but a preacher (2 Cor. 1[19]), as youngest comes last. While the letter is Paul's, the exceptionally frequent appearance of "we" where it is natural to think primarily not of an epistolary plural but of Paul and his companions suggests an intimacy of association in writing which is not true of 1 Cor. where Sosthenes is joined with Paul in the superscription, nor of 2 Cor. Col. Phile. Phil. where Timothy is joined with Paul.

It is generally admitted that "we" may be used in various senses including that of the epistolary plural (*cf.* not only Paul (1 Cor. 9[11] and 9[15]), but also Polybius, Josephus, and the papyri); but it is observed with force by Mill. (131–132) that owing to the "special circumstances under which the two epistles were written, we shall do well to give its full weight to this normal use of the plural in them, and to think of it as including St. Paul's two companions along with himself wherever on other grounds this is possible"; *cf.* Zahn, *Introd.* I 209 *ff.* On the other hand, Dob. thinks that though the associated authors may be in mind they have no prerogatives whatever (67–68); see Dick, *Der schrift-stellerische Plural bei Paulus*, 1900.

The form Σιλβανός (DG; *cf.* B in 1 Pet. 5[12]) is regular in the papyri (Mill.); *cf.* P. Oxy. 335 (*c.* 85 A.D.) where Παῦλος sells Σιλβανός the sixth part of a house in the Jewish quarter. Our Silvanus is a Jew and a Roman citizen (Acts 16[37]); *cf.* Schmiedel, *EB.* 4514 *ff.* Timothy was of mixed Gentile and Jewish blood; whether a Roman citizen or not is unknown; *cf.* Moff. *EB.* 5074 *ff.*

The designation ἀπόστολος does not appear in the superscription of the Macedonian letters and Philemon; it appears in that of Gal. 1, 2 Cor. addressed to communities in which Judaists attacked Paul's apostleship (Phil. 3[2 ff.] refers to unbelieving Jews as Lipsius, McGiffert, and most recently Dob. (117) insist); in that of Rom., a community not founded by him and not sharing his distinctive views, to which he is presenting his gospel; and in that of Col. Eph., churches founded by his converts whose Christianity he vouches for.

τῇ ἐκκλησίᾳ Θεσσαλονικέων. There is but one Christian group in Thessalonica; it is small numerically, unless πλῆθος

πολύ (Acts 17⁴) is to be pressed, but intense in faith (v. ⁸; *cf.*
Rom. 1⁸ Col. 1⁶· ²³); and it assembles perhaps in the house of
Jason.

The numerical strength of the church in the house of Prisca and Aquila
(1 Cor. 16¹⁹ Rom. 16⁵) is computed by Gregory (*Canon and Text of the
N. T.* 524) to be at least fifty. Whether the church in Thess. that Paul
addressed was as large as that is quite unknown.

No good reasons have been adduced to show why we have here and in II
1¹ (*cf.* Col. 4¹⁶) the *nomen gentilicium* Θεσσαλονικεύς instead of the name
of the place (Gal. 1² 1 Cor. 1² 2 Cor. 1¹). The view of von Soden (*SK.*
1885, 274) that Paul "under the influence of the fresh impression of his
success thinks of the inhabitants as already as a whole in touch with the
church," is unlikely in the light of the similar τῇ Λαοδικέων ἐκκλησίᾳ
in Col. 4¹⁶. Equally obscure is the fact that I, II, Gal. 1, 2 Cor. Phile.
are addressed to the "church" or "churches" (*cf.* Phil. 1¹ σὺν ἐπισκόποις
καὶ διακόνοις) while Rom. Col. Eph. are addressed to the saints and
brethren.

ἐν θεῷ πατρὶ καὶ κυρίῳ 'I. X. This phrase, found only here
and (with ἡμῶν after πατρί) in II 1¹ and to be attached closely
to the preceding as in 2¹⁴, specifies the Christian character of
the ἐκκλησία in contrast with the civic assembly of the Gentiles and the theocratic assembly of the Jews (Chrys.). The
omission of τῇ after θεσσ., which on the analogy of Gal. 1²²
might have been retained, serves to accentuate the closeness of
the attachment. Both the phrase as a whole and its component parts ἐν θεῷ πατρί (II 1¹) and ἐν κυρίῳ 'I. X. (II 1¹ 3¹²)
are peculiar to our letters.

The ἐν, however, is the ἐν of the characteristic Pauline phrases
ἐν Χριστῷ 'Ιησοῦ (2¹⁴ 5¹⁸ and often in Paul), ἐν Χριστῷ (4¹⁶
and often in Paul), ἐν κυρίῳ (3⁸ 5¹² II 3⁴ and often in Paul),
ἐν κυρίῳ 'Ιησοῦ (4¹ Rom. 14¹⁴ Eph. 1¹⁵ Phil. 2¹⁹), ἐν Χριστῷ
'Ιησοῦ τῷ κυρίῳ ἡμῶν (1 Cor. 15³¹ Rom. 6²³ 8³⁹ Eph. 3¹¹, but
not in I, II), ἐν πνεύματι (v. ⁵; Rom. 8⁹ 9¹, etc.), and ἐν τῷ θεῷ
(2²; Col. 3³ Eph. 3⁹, but not Rom. 2¹⁷ 5¹¹). The relation of the
human and divine indicated by ἐν is local and realistic; the
human is in the atmosphere of the divine. There is presupposed
the indwelling of God (1 Cor. 14²⁵ 2 Cor. 6¹⁶), Christ (Rom. 8¹⁰),
or the Spirit (Rom. 8⁹· ¹¹) as an energising (*cf.* 1 Cor. 12¹⁶
Phil. 2¹³) power both ethical and permanent. Hence when a

man is in Christ or the Spirit, terms interchangeable as regards the operations, or in God, or when a man is possessed by them (ἔχειν Rom. 8¹⁹ 1 Cor. 7⁴⁰), he is as such under the control of a divine power that makes for newness of life (*cf.* ἐν δυνάμει πνεύματος Rom. 15¹³· ¹⁹). The divine air which the human breathes is charged, so to speak, with ethical energy.

> The new in these phrases with ἐν is neither the realism of the relation nor the grammatical form (*cf.* ἐν κυρίῳ Hab. 3¹⁸; ἐν πνεύματι Ezek. 11²⁴ 37¹) but the combination of ἐν with Χριστῷ, a combination due to Paul's experience of Christ as Spirit and Lord. For influences on Paul's conception, see Gunkel (*Die Wirkungen des Geistes*, 1888, 100 *ff.*); Deissmann (*Die neutestamentliche Formel in Christo Jesu*, 1892); Volz (*Der Geist Gottes*, 1910, 198 *ff.*); Reitzenstein (*Die hellenistischen Mysterienreligionen*, 1910) and a critique of the same in Schweitzer's *Geschichte der Paulinischen Forschung*, 1911, 141–184, especially 170 *ff.*; Deissmann's *Paulus*, 1911, 87 *ff.*; and Percy Gardner's *Religious Experience of St. Paul*, 1911. An analogy to Paul's phrase is found in ἐν πνεύματι ἀκαθάρτῳ (Mk. 1²³) and ἔχειν πνεῦμα ἀκάθαρτον (Mk. 3³⁰); the man is in the demon because the demon is in the man as an energising (*cf.* II 2⁷ Eph. 2²; also II 2⁹· ¹¹) force; δαίμονος γὰρ οὐσία ἐνέργεια (Reitzenstein, *Poimandres*, 352²⁴).

θεῷ πατρί. The omission of the articles indicates that the phrase had long been fixed for Paul (*cf.* also II 1² (BD) Gal. 1¹ 1³ (BD) Eph. 6²³ Phil. 2¹¹). The name Father, inherited by the Master (*cf.* Bousset, *Relig.* 432 *ff.*) and put into the central place in his teaching, is confirmed as primary in Paul's redemptive experience. It is striking that this name occurs in passages giving fervent expression to his religious life, and that it is joined usually with the name Christ, *e. g.* in the superscriptions, thanksgivings (1³ 2 Cor. 1³ Col. 1³ 3¹⁷ Eph. 1³ 5²⁰), prayers (3¹¹· ¹³ II 2¹⁶ Rom. 15⁶ Eph. 6²³), and the like (1 Cor. 8⁶ 15²⁴· ²⁸ 2 Cor. 11³¹ Rom. 6⁴ Eph. 2¹⁸ 4⁶). It is probable that as Paul insists that no man can say κύριος Ἰησοῦς but in the Holy Spirit (1 Cor. 12³), so he would insist that no man can say Ἀββά ὁ πατήρ (Gal. 4⁶ Rom. 8¹⁵) but in the same Spirit. At all events, Paul's specifically Christian name of the God of both Jews and Gentiles (Rom. 3²⁹) is "God the Father of our Lord Jesus Christ," "Our Father."

κυρίῳ 'I. X. In these words both the primitive (Acts 2³⁶) and
the Pauline convictions about Jesus are summed up: he is Messiah and Lord. The Lordship of Jesus (1 Cor. 12³ Rom. 10⁹),
Jesus Christ (1 Cor. 8⁶ Rom. 13¹⁴ Phil. 2¹¹), Christ Jesus (2 Cor.
4⁵ Col. 2⁶) is the essence of the Pauline experience; it receives
conspicuous emphasis in the second epistle (see on II 2¹³).
While both 'Ιησοῦς Χριστός and Χριστὸς 'Ιησοῦς have already
become proper names, the Messianic connotation of Χριστός is
not lost (cf. Rom. 9⁵ 2.Cor. 5¹⁰ Phil. 1¹⁵ Eph. 1¹⁰, etc.). It is
Jesus the Messiah who is Lord.

On the divine names in I, II, see Mill. 135–140. Dob. (60–61) explains the placing of Χριστός before 'Ιησοῦς (e. g. 2¹⁴ 5¹⁸), to which SH.
(3 ff.) call attention, as due to the ambiguity of the *casus obliqui* of 'Ιησοῦς;
for apart from Rom. 8³⁴ 2 Cor. 4⁵ Col. 2⁶, the order X. 'I. appears only in
the formulæ Χριστοῦ 'Ιησοῦ and ἐν Χριστῷ 'Ιησοῦ, while Paul writes continually κυρίου 'I. X. and ἐν κυρίῳ 'I. X.

χάρις ὑμῖν καὶ εἰρήνη. This phrase, common to all the
ten Pauline superscriptions, bears, like the phrase ἐν Χριστῷ,
the stamp of Paul's experience. It is likewise the shortest Pauline præscript. χάρις, used here in its widest sense, is the favour
of God by which he acquits all sinners, Jews and Gentiles, solely
on the principle of faith and grants them freedom from the power
of sin and newness of life in Christ or the Spirit. εἰρήνη is the
spiritual prosperity enjoyed by the recipients of the divine favour.
What is expressed in all the other letters of Paul (except Col. 1²
which adds only "from God our Father"), namely, that grace
and peace come from God the (our) Father and the Lord Jesus
Christ, is already implied in ἐν θεῷ κτλ. There is, however, no
reason either here or in Col. for attaching χάρις to the clause
with ἐν.

In coining, as he apparently does coin, this form of greeting,
Paul is less influenced by current epistolary phrases than by
his conviction that the blessings of the promised Messianic kingdom (Is. 9⁵ Ps. 72³) are realised only through the grace of God
in Christ.

It is generally assumed (cf. Fritzsche on Rom. 1⁷ or Zahn on Gal. 1²)
that the Pauline greeting is suggested both by the Semitic and the Greek.

The influence of the Aramaic in εἰρήνη (Ezra 4¹⁷ 5⁷ Dan. 3³¹⁽⁹⁸⁾ 6²⁶; see BDB. *sub* שׁלם) may have been felt (*cf.* also Apoc. Bar. 78² where Syriac suggests ἔλεος καὶ εἰρήνη); but it is doubtful (Robinson, *Ephesians*, 141) whether χάρις has anything to do with χαίρειν (Jas. 1¹ Acts 15²³ 23²⁶), for in some papyri at least (Witk. 22 *ff.* Ἀλκαῖος Σωσιφάνει χαίρειν. χάρις τοῖς θεοῖς πολλή or θεῷ πλείστη χάρις), χαίρειν is the greeting and χάρις the thanksgiving. On the other hand, *cf.* 2 Mac. 1¹ χαίρειν . . . καὶ εἰρήνην ἀγαθήν (Nestle, *Exp. Times*, 1911, vol. XXIII, 94).

The word χάρις is rare in the Prophets and Psalms but frequent in the Wisdom literature. Paul's usage has affected Luke and First Peter. The Johannist prefers ἀλήθεια to χάρις. εἴη or (since in later Gk. the optative tends to disappear) ἔστω is to be supplied, in accordance with Semitic (Dan. 3⁹⁸ Lxx. 1 Pet. 1², etc.), not Greek (which demands χάριν *sc.* λέγουσιν) usage. The position of ὑμῖν serves to distinguish both χάρις and εἰρήνη (Bl. 80²). It is doubtless "pedantry to reflect on the fact that the readers as Christians possess already that grace, that hence only an increase of the same could be desired for them" (Dob.). Most editors omit with BGF Orig. Pesh. Arm. f g r Vulg. the usual clause with ἀπό. The insertion of the same by אADKLP, *et al.*, is more explicable than its omission.

II. THANKSGIVING (1²–3¹⁰).

In the thanksgiving (1²–3¹⁰; *cf.* 1² 2¹³ 3⁹) and closely related prayer (3¹¹⁻¹³) covering the major portion of the letter, Paul reviews his attitude to the church during his visit (1²–2¹⁶) and during the interval between his enforced departure and the writing of I (2¹⁷–3¹⁰). Though he praises without stint the faith and love of his converts, hardly mentioning the imperfections that exist (3⁸·¹⁰), and though his words pulsate with warmest affection, yet a tone of self-defence is heard throughout. The constant appeal to the knowledge or memory of the readers as regards his behaviour (1⁵ 2¹⁻¹²), the reference to oral reports which concern not only them but him (1⁹), the insistence on the fact that the writers desired—Paul himself repeatedly—to return (2¹⁷⁻²⁰), the statement that the writers, Paul especially, had determined to send Timothy (3¹⁻⁵), and finally the prayer that the writers may return (3¹¹)—all serve to intimate that Paul is defending both his conduct during the visit and his failure to return against the allegations, not of the converts, not of Judaizers (for there are none in Thessalonica), not of the Gentile persecutors (2^{14}), for they are not attacked, but, as the ominous outburst (2^{15-16}) suggests, of the Jews.

It may be conjectured that the Jews, after Paul's departure, were maligning his conduct and misconstruing his failure to return. Indeed they may well have been the real instigators of Gentile persecutions. Though it is unlikely that the converts actually distrusted Paul (3^{6}), it is not improbable that they were wrought up and worried by the representations of the Jews, especially since Paul did not return. Whether he had heard of the matter before he despatched Timothy is uncertain but altogether probable. That the self-defence arises purely from a suspicion of Paul without any basis of fact (Dob. 106–107) is unlikely. In the light of 2^{15-16}, the Jews not the Gentiles (*cf.* Zahn, *Introd.* I, 217–218) are the accusers.

(1) *Visit and Welcome* (1^{2-10}).

Paul thanks God, as he bears in mind the spiritual excellence of the readers, for their election, the certainty of which is inferred from the presence of the Spirit controlling not only the converts who welcomed the gospel in spite of persecutions (vv. $^{6-10}$; *cf.* 2^{13-16}), but also the preachers themselves (vv. $^{5.~9a}$; *cf.* 2^{1-12}).

^{2}*We thank God always for you all, making mention of you when we pray, ^{3}bearing in mind continually your work resulting from faith, and your activity prompted by love, and your endurance sanctioned by hope in our Lord Jesus Christ in the presence of our God and Father, ^{4}because we know, brothers beloved by God, that you have been chosen, ^{5}from the fact that the gospel we preach did not come to you with words only but also with power, and in the Holy Spirit and much conviction,—as you know the kind of men we became to you for your sake; ^{6}and (from the fact that) you became imitators of us and of the Lord, welcoming the Word in the midst of great persecution with the joy that the Holy Spirit gives, ^{7}so that you became a model community to all the believers in Macedonia and in Achaia: ^{8}for starting from you the Word of the Lord has sounded out not only in Macedonia and Achaia but in every place your faith in God has gone out, so that we need not utter a word about you, ^{9}for they themselves are reporting about us what kind of*

*visit we paid you, and (about you) how you turned to God leaving
behind those idols of yours, for the purpose of serving the living and
genuine God* [10]*and of awaiting his Son who comes down out of the
heavens, whom he raised from the dead,—Jesus who delivers us
from the judgment that is coming.*

The epistolary arrangement of I (χάρις 1[1]; εὐχαριστοῦμεν 1[2]–3[10];
αὐτὸς δέ 3[11-13]; ἐρωτῶμεν 4[1]–5[22]; προσεύχεσθε 5[25]; ἀσπάσασθε 5[26]; χάρις
5[28]) may be compared with BGU, 423 (saec. ii, A.D., quoted by
Robinson, *op. cit.* 276): πλεῖστα χαίρειν, εὔχομαι, εὐχαριστῶ . . . ὅτι,
ἐρωτῶ, ἄσπασαι, ἐρρῶσθαί σε εὔχομαι. Some of the phrases in v. [2 ff.]
may be compared with P. Lond. 42 (saec. ii, B.C., quoted by Deiss.
BS. 209 *ff.*): οἱ ἐν οἴκῳ πάντες σου διαπαντὸς μνείαν ποιούμενοι . . .
ἐπὶ μὲν τῷ ἐρρῶσθαί σε εὐθέως τοῖς θεοῖς εὐχαριστοῦν; with BGU, 632
(saec. ii, A.D., quoted by Robinson, *op. cit.* 276): μνίαν σου ποιούμενος;
and with 1 Mac. 12[11].

As in the papyri, so also in Paul's letters, there is freedom in the use
both of the general epistolary outline and of the separate phrases. In
Paul, the simplest thanksgiving is II 1[3] Rom. 1[3]. This is expanded in I 1[4]
Col. 1[4] Phile. 5 by a causal participle without ὅτι; in 1 Cor. 1[4] by clauses
with ἐπί and ὅτι; in Phil. 1[3 ff.] with two clauses with ἐπί and a causal
participle. In Phil. and our letter, the thanksgiving is full, while Gal.
has no thanksgiving. In 2 Cor. and Eph., the O. T. εὐλογητὸς ὁ θεός
takes the place of εὐχαριστοῦμεν.

From Paul's usage we may assume that περὶ πάντων ὑμῶν is to be
taken not with μνείαν ποιούμενοι but with εὐχαριστοῦμεν (hence a
comma after ὑμῶν), as the simpler form (1 Cor. 1[4] Rom. 1[8]) suggests;
that μνημονεύοντες is parallel to and an expansion of μνείαν ποιούμενοι,
as δεόμενος (Rom. 1[10]; contrast Phile. 4 Eph. 1[16]) indicates; and that
εἰδότες is a causal participle depending on εὐχαριστοῦμεν, while ὅτι
depends not on the latter but on the former. Doubtful is the reference
of ἀδιαλείπτως and ἔμπροσθεν; *v. infra.*

2. εὐχαριστοῦμεν κτλ. Thankfulness is not only felt but
is expressed to God, and that too always and for all; in saying
πάντων, Paul is thinking not of their imperfections (3[10]) but
of their faith and love and personal affection (3[6]).

Inasmuch as Paul always uses the article in the phrase εὐχαριστεῖν
τῷ θεῷ, τῷ is not significant in this case. Born. (69) presses the article
to mean "the one God" in contrast to the pagan gods. But quite apart
from the lack of definiteness in the use of the article (Bl. 46[6]), it is to be
noted that ὁ θεός is more frequent than θεός in Paul; in I the proportion

is about three to one, in Romans slightly greater; and in Col. all but two of the twenty-three cases have the article; cf. I 4⁶ with Gal. 4⁹.—Both πάντοτε (except Rom. 1¹⁰) and περὶ ὑμῶν (except Phile. 4) follow εὐχαριστεῖν in the initial thanksgivings of Paul. πάντοτε, a late word, is rare in the Lxx. (Sap. 11²¹ 19¹⁸) but common in Paul (3⁶ 5¹⁶ II 1¹¹, etc.). ἀεί occurs a score or more times in the Gk. Bib. (cf. 2 Cor. 4¹¹ 6¹⁰); ἑκάστοτε but once (2 Pet. 1¹⁵).—For περί, we have ὑπέρ in Phil. 1³ Col. 1³ (v. l.); the distinction between them is fading away (Moult. I, 105).

μνείαν ποιούμενοι κτλ. This participial clause defines πάντοτε (cf. Phile. 4). ἐπὶ τῶν προσευχῶν ἡμῶν = προσευ-χόμενοι (Col. 1³); ἐπί = "in the time of." Each time that they are engaged in prayer, the writers mention the names of the converts (contrast μνημονεύειν v.³ and μνείαν ἔχειν 3⁶) and give thanks for them.

While both ποεῖσθαι μνείαν περί τινος and ποιεῖσθαι μνείαν τινός (cf. Job. 14¹³ Ps. 110⁴ Is. 32¹⁰) are classic, epistolary usage favours the latter construction. ὑμῶν is to be supplied. Its omission is due both here and Eph. 1¹⁶ to the περὶ (ὑπὲρ) ὑμῶν; its retention by CDG, et al., is influenced by Rom. 1¹⁰ Phile. 4 (cf. I 3⁶ Phil. 1³ and papyri). ἡμῶν instead of μου (Rom. 1¹⁰ Eph. 1¹⁶ Phile. 4) is natural, since Silvanus and Timothy are associated with Paul in the thanksgiving.—The distinction between ἐν ταῖς προσευχαῖς (Dan. Lxx. 9¹⁸· ²⁰; Ign. Mag. 14¹ Trall. 13¹ with μνημονεύειν; cf. Paul in Rom. 15³⁰ Col. 4¹²) and ἐπὶ τῶν προσευχῶν is probably slight; cf. 1 Mac. 12¹¹.

3. ἀδιαλείπτως μνημονεύοντες. "Bearing in mind continually." This participial clause, parallel to the defining temporal clause μνείαν ποιούμενοι, suggests the immediate ground of the thanksgiving, while the third parallel εἰδότες gives the ultimate ground (Find.). The never-failing memory of the spiritual excellence of the converts prompts the expression of thanks at every season of prayer.

Whether ἀδιαλείπτως is to be taken with μνημονεύοντες (Chrys. Dob. Dibelius, et al.) or with ποιούμενοι (Ephraem, Pesh. Vulg. and G (which capitalises Μνημονεύοντες) Wohl. Mill. Moff. et al.) cannot be determined. In view of the freedom of epistolary usage, the analogy of 1 Mac. 12¹¹ Rom. 1¹⁰ P. Lond. 42 (διαπαντὸς μνείαν ποιούμενοι) is not decisive. ἀδιαλείπτως is used with μνείαν ποιεῖσθαι (Rom. 1⁹; cf. 1 Mac. 12¹²), εὐχαριστεῖν (2¹³), and προσεύχεσθαι (5¹⁷; cf. Ign. Eph. 10¹; Hermas Sim. IX 11⁷; and Polyc. 4³ ἐντυγχάνειν).—Since μνημονεύειν with gen.

(Gal. 2¹⁰ Col. 4¹⁸) refers to the thought not to its expression in prayer before God, it is better to take ἔμπροσθεν κτλ. not with the distant μνημονεύοντες but with the adjacent Ἰησοῦ Χριστοῦ (Lft. Mill. Dob.), as indeed the position of the clause and the analogy of 3¹³ make probable (but see Lillie, *ad loc.*).

ὑμῶν . . . Χριστοῦ. The genitives are somewhat bewildering and the interpretations are various. The most favoured solution is that which joins ὑμῶν with ἔργου, κόπου, ὑπομονῆς, and which explains τῆς πίστεως, τῆς ἀγάπης, and τῆς ἐλπίδος as subjective genitives, and τοῦ κυρίου as an objective genitive qualifying ἐλπίδος. The stress is laid not on faith alone but on the work that results from faith; not on love alone but on the toilsome activity prompted by love; not on endurance alone but on the endurance that is inspired by the hope in Christ. The three phrases τὸ ἔργον τῆς πίστεως, ὁ κόπος τῆς ἀγάπης, and ἡ ὑπομονὴ τῆς ἐλπίδος may be the coinage of Paul; at least they are not found elsewhere in the Gk. Bib. (except II 1¹¹ ἔργον πίστεως; Heb. 6¹⁰ reads not τοῦ κόπου τῆς ἀγάπης but simply τῆς ἀγάπης), or in the Apostolic Fathers.

Lillie notes that Olshausen and Steiger (1832 on 1 Pet. 1²) connect τοῦ κυρίου with all three gen. πίστεως, ἀγάπης and ἐλπίδος, a view to which Dob. inclines. But love to God (Rom. 8²⁸ 1 Cor. 2⁹ 8³) or Christ (1 Cor. 16²² Eph. 6²⁴) is rare in Paul compared with the love of God or Christ for men. On the name ὁ κύριος ἡμῶν Ἰ. Χ. (5⁹· ²³· ²⁸ II 2¹· ¹⁴· ¹⁶ 3¹⁸), see below on 2¹⁹.

τοῦ ἔργου τῆς πίστεως. The work of faith is the activity that faith inspires, that is, love in all its manifestations (as in II 1¹¹).—τοῦ κόπου τῆς ἀγάπης. "The toilsome activity prompted by love." In this unique phrase, minted from the situation, it is uncertain whether Paul has in mind manual labour necessary to support missionary propaganda, or the laborious missionary effort as such (3⁵), or both. Love is not to be restricted to φιλαδελφία.—τῆς ὑπομονῆς τῆς ἐλπίδος. "The endurance inspired by hope." This unique phrase differs from ἡ ἐλπὶς τῆς ὑπομονῆς (4 Mac. 17⁴) in that the emphasis is upon endurance. Hope, whose object is Christ (Col. 1²⁷), is the confident expectation of spiritual prosperity after death, the hope of salvation (5⁸), the good hope (II 2¹⁶) originating in Christ, a hope that those who are not in Christ do not share (4¹³).

ὑπομονή (II 1⁴ 3⁵) is frequent in 4 Mac. (e. g. 15³⁰) in the sense of καρτερία. In 1 Clem. 5⁷ Paul himself is ὑπομονῆς μέγιστος ὑπογραμμός. In II 3⁵ the only adequate endurance is that inspired by Christ.

ἔμπροσθεν κτλ. Hope in Christ suggests the day of the Lord when all men must appear before God. For the unbeliever, it is a day of destruction (1¹⁰ 5³ II 1⁹), but for the believer, a day of salvation (1¹⁰ 3¹³ 5⁹), the fruition of hope. The Judge here is not Christ (2 Cor. 5¹⁰) but God (Rom. 14¹⁰), and that too the God and Father of us Christians. As in 2¹⁹ 3¹³, ἔμπροσθεν is attached loosely to the immediately preceding words.

ὁ πατήρ (Rom. 6⁴ Eph. 2¹⁸ 3¹⁴ Col. 1² v. l.), ἀββά ὁ πατήρ (Gal. 4⁶ Rom. 8¹⁵), ὁ θεὸς πατήρ (Col. 1¹² (א) 3¹⁷), θεὸς ὁ πατήρ (1 Cor. 8⁶ Col. 1¹² FG), ὁ θεὸς καὶ πατήρ (1 Cor. 15²⁴ Eph. 5²⁰), ὁ θεὸς καὶ πατὴρ τοῦ κυρίου ἡμῶν Ἰ. Χ. (Rom. 15⁶ 2 Cor. 1³ Eph. 1³ Col. 1³ (אA; BCDG omit καί) 2 Cor. 11³¹ D) do not occur in I, II. We have, however, θεὸς πατήρ (1¹ II 1² (BD) Gal. 1¹ 1³ (BD) Eph. 6²³ Phil. 2¹¹), θεὸς πατὴρ ἡμῶν (II 1¹ Gal. 1³ (אA) Rom. 1⁷ 1 Cor. 1³ 2 Cor. 1² Col. 1² Eph. 1² Phil. 1² Phile. 3), and ὁ θεὸς καὶ πατὴρ ἡμῶν (1³ 3¹¹· ¹³ Gal. 1⁴ Phil. 4²⁰). Unique is II 2¹⁶ whether we read θεὸς ὁ πατὴρ ἡμῶν (BD) or ὁ θεὸς ὁ πατὴρ ἡμῶν (אG). Paul does not use ὁ θεὸς ἡμῶν καὶ πατήρ or πατὴρ θεός (Sir. 23⁴).

4. εἰδότες = ὅτι οἴδαμεν. The causal participle (cf. Phil. 1⁶ Col. 1³ Phile. 4) introduces the ultimate ground of the thanksgiving, namely, the election of the readers. Of this election Paul is assured both from the fact that (ὅτι v.⁵) the gospel which he preached, the gospel through which God calls men unto salvation (II 2¹⁴), came home to them with the power of the Spirit, and from the fact that (sc. ὅτι before ὑμεῖς v.⁶) the same Spirit operated in the believers, as could be plainly inferred from the welcome they gave to the Word and its messengers in spite of great persecution. It is significant both that here, as Calvin observes, Paul infers the pretemporal election of the readers from the fruits of the Spirit, and that it is taken for granted that the readers understand what ἐκλογή means, an evidence that this idea formed an integral part of the gospel of God proclaimed in Thessalonica.

ἀδελφοὶ ἠγαπημένοι ὑπὸ τοῦ θεοῦ. The frequency of ἀδελφοί in I is indicative of Paul's love for his converts. This affectionate address is strengthened by "beloved by God," a phrase which like "beloved by the Lord" (II 2¹³) is unique in the N.T., though equivalent in sense to ἀγαπητοὶ θεοῦ (Rom. 1⁷). The connection of this phrase with ἐκλογή makes plain that election proceeds from the love of God (cf. Is. 41⁸⁻⁹ where ἐκλέγεσθαι is parallel to ἀγαπᾶν).

Moses in Sir. 45¹ is ἠγαπημένος ὑπὸ θεοῦ καὶ ἀνθρώπων; Israel in Baruch 3³⁷ is ἠγαπ. ὑπ' αὐτοῦ (i. e. "our God"); and Solomon in Neh. 13²⁶ is ἀγαπώμενος τῷ θεῷ; cf. Ep. to Diogn. 4⁴ where ἐκλογή and ἠγαπημένους ὑπὸ θεοῦ appear together and Ign. Trall. init. of the holy church ἠγαπ. θεῷ πατρὶ 'Ι. Χ. More frequently we have in this phrase, as in II 2¹³, κυρίου; for example, Benjamin in Deut. 33¹² and Issachar in Test. xii Iss. 1¹ are ἠγαπ. ὑπὸ κυρίου; and Samuel in Sir. 46¹³ is ἠγαπ. ὑπὸ κυρίου αὐτοῦ. See further Col. 3¹² 1 Cor. 15⁵⁸, etc.—ἀδελφοί μου (Rom. 7⁴ 15¹⁴ 1 Cor. 1¹¹ 11³³ 14³⁹ Phil. 3¹), ἀδελφοί μου ἀγαπητοί (1 Cor. 15⁵⁸ Phil. 4¹), ἀγαπητοί (Rom. 12¹⁹ 2 Cor. 7¹ 12¹⁹ Phil. 4¹), ἀγαπητοί μου (1 Cor. 10¹⁴ Phil. 2¹²), do not occur in I, II as forms of address. The simple ἀδελφοί of address occurs about 20 times in 1 Cor., 14 in 1 Thess., 10 in Rom., 9 in Gal., 7 in 2 Thess., 6 in Phil., 3 in 2 Cor., and twice in Phile. (ἀδελφέ). But no one of these addresses appears in Col. or Eph. On the Christian use of ἀδελφοί, cf. Harnack, Mission,² I, 340 ff.; on the pagan use, Deiss. BS. 82 f. and Witk. 38, note 1. It is doubtful whether τοῦ before θεοῦ is to be retained (ℵACKP) or omitted (BDGL; cf. Weiss, 72).

τὴν ἐκλογὴν ὑμῶν. "The election of you," that is, "that you have been chosen," namely, by God, as always in Paul. The eternal choice of God, "the divine purpose which has worked on the principle of selection" (SH. ad Rom. 9¹¹), includes, according to II 2¹⁴, not only the salvation of the readers but also the means by which or the state in which salvation is realised.

The words ἐκλέγεσθαι (1 Cor. 1²⁷ ff. Eph. 1⁴), ἐκλεκτός (Rom. 16³³), ἐκλεκτοὶ θεοῦ (Rom. 8³³ Col. 3¹²), and ἐκλογή (Rom. 9¹¹ 11⁵· ⁷· ²⁸) are rare in Paul. ἐκλογή does not occur in the Lxx. For its use in Ps. Sol., see the edition of Ryle and James, 1891, 95 f. κλῆσις (II 1¹¹), καλεῖν (2¹² 4⁷ 5²⁴) is the historical calling mediated by the preaching of the gospel (II 2¹⁴).

5. ὅτι . . . ἐγενήθη. We infer your election from the fact that (ὅτι = "because" as in II 3⁷ Rom. 8²⁷ 1 Cor. 2¹⁴) the Spirit

was in us who preached (v. [5]) and in you who welcomed the Word
(vv. [6-10]). By saying "our gospel came" instead of "we came
with the gospel" (2 Cor. 10[14]), Paul puts the emphasis more
upon the message as the means of realising God's call than upon
the bearers of the message. The presence of the Spirit is the
central fact in Paul's experience and the test of its validity.
Hence such passages as Gal. 3[2] 1 Cor. 12[2] Rom. 8[15] and the inevitable 2 Cor. 13[13].

That ὅτι = *quia* (Vulg.) is the usual view. εἰδότες . . . ἐκλογὴν . . .
ὅτι = οἴδαμεν ὅτι (that) ἐκλήθητε ὅτι (because), as in Rom. 5[4-5] 8[28-29]
Phil. 4[15-16]. An alternative interpretation takes ὅτι as an object clause
further explaining ἐκλογήν. Since, however, ἐκλογήν of the original purpose of God is not exactly the equivalent of the ὅτι clause, ἐκλογήν is
held to mean "the manner of your election" and ὅτι "how that" (Lft.
Mill.). In support of this view, 2[1] 1 Cor. 16[15] 2 Cor. 12[3-4] should not be
adduced, or Rom. 11[3] where τὸν καιρόν is resumed by ὥρα. On the
other hand, 1 Cor. 1[26], especially if ἐκλήθησαν be not supplied, might be
considered a parallel, although βλέπετε is not εἰδότες. But this alternative view is not "exegetically satisfactory" (Ell.).—The passive
ἐγενήθη = ἐγένετο is frequent in Lxx.; in the N. T. it is found chiefly
in Paul, Heb. Mt. Of the score or more instances in Paul, eight appear
in 1[5]-2[14]; *cf.* Bl. 20[1].

In Lxx., γίνεσθαι πρός or ἐπί with accus. or ἐν with dat. are frequent
as also γίνεσθαι εἰς for nominative (I 3[5]; *cf.* 2[1]), but otherwise γίνεσθαι
εἰς is rare. It is used with persons (Ezek. 23[10] 2 Mac. 12[5]) or things
(3 Reg. 13[32]; Judg. 17[8] A ἐγενήθη εἰς ὄρος where B has ἦλθεν ἕως ὄρους).
On γίνεσθαι = ἔρχεσθαι, *cf.* 1 Cor. 2[1. 3] and the prophetic phrase λόγος
κυρίου ἐγενήθη (ἐγένετο) πρός. In Paul, we expect with persons either
πρός (1 Cor. 2[3] 16[10] and here ADG) or ἐν (so below ℵAC with ὑμῖν);
εἰς here and Gal. 3[14] may be equivalent to the dative (I 4[8]; *cf.* Bl. 39[5];
κηρύσσειν εἰς 2[9] where ℵ has dative as in 1 Cor. 9[27]), or to πρός. For
the interchange of εἰς and πρός with γίνεσθαι, *cf.* Lk. 1[44] Acts 10[13] 26[6] 13[32].
ἐν = "with" (2 Cor. 2[1]) or "clothed with" (1 Cor. 4[21]); *cf.* Moult. I, 61.

τὸ εὐαγγέλιον ἡμῶν. "Our gospel" (II 2[14] 2 Cor. 4[3]; *cf.*
Rom. 2[16] 16[25]) is the gospel with which Paul and his associates
have been intrusted (2[4]) and which they preach (Gal. 2[2]). The
author of the gospel is God (τὸ εὐαγγέλιον τοῦ θεοῦ 2[2. 8. 9]
Rom. 1[1] 15[16] 2 Cor. 11[7]) or Christ (τὸ εὐαγγέλιον τοῦ Χριστοῦ
3[2] Gal. 1[7] 1 Cor. 9[12] 2 Cor. 2[12] 9[13] 10[14] Rom. 15[19] Phil. 1[27]; τοῦ
υἱοῦ αὐτοῦ Rom. 1[9]). "The gospel" (τὸ εὐαγγέλιον 2[4] and

frequently in Paul) represents Paul's convictions about Christianity, the good news of the grace of God unto salvation proclaimed in the prophets and realised in Christ (Rom. 1²) by whose death and resurrection the Messianic promise is mediated to all believers. Only such elements of this comprehensive gospel are explicitly treated in a given letter as the specific need requires (cf. Dob. 81 f.). Hence, for the purpose of determining the content of the gospel, what is said implicitly may be more important than what is accentuated. For example, the gospel preached in Thessalonica had to do not simply with faith in the living and true God and ethical consecration to him, not simply with the *Parousia* and Judgment, but also with God's election and calling, the significance of the death of Christ (5⁹), the new life in Christ or the Spirit, and the attendant spiritual gifts (5¹⁹ ⁸·).

On the origin and meaning of εὐαγγέλιον, see Zahn (*Introd.* II, 377–379), Mill. (141–144), Dob. (86), and Harnack, *Verfassung und Recht*, 1910, 199 *ff.* (also in English). The use of εὐαγγέλιον to designate the good news unto salvation may have originated in Palestinian Christianity. In the Lxx. (and Test. xii, Ps. Sol.), the singular does not occur. A papyrus of the third century (A.D.) seems to read ἐπεὶ γνώστης ἐγενόμην τοῦ εὐαγγελίου (Deiss. *Light*, 371). בשרה = "good tidings" is rendered in Lxx. by εὐαγγελία (2 Reg. 18²⁰· ²⁷ 4 Reg. 7⁹ and (according to Harnack but not Swete) 2 Reg. 18²⁵); while בשרה = "reward for good tidings" (see BDB.) is translated by the plural εὐαγγέλια (2 Reg. 4¹⁰ 18²²). For the plural εὐαγγέλια = "good news" in the Priene inscription, see Deiss. (*op. cit.* 371).

In Paul's usage, the genitive in εὐαγγέλιον θεοῦ is subjective, pointing to the fact that God, ὁ ἐνεργῶν (Phil. 2¹³) in Paul, inspires the message preached (*cf.* I 2¹³); it is ἐν τῷ θεῷ that the missionaries speak the ˙ gospel of God (2²). Similarly the genitive in εὐαγγέλιον Χριστοῦ is subjective (Zahn; Harnack, 217–218, against Dob.). The indwelling Christ speaks in Paul (2 Cor. 13³) and reveals the gospel (Gal. 1¹²). Such a view of the genitive does not preclude references to the content of the gospel (2 Cor. 4⁴ Eph. 1¹³ 6¹⁵) or the employment of κηρύσσειν Χριστόν (1 Cor. 1²³, etc.) or εὐαγγελίζεσθαι αὐτόν (Gal. 1¹⁶), for when Paul preaches Christ he preaches not only Christ but the plan of salvation conceived by God, promised by the prophets, and realised in the death and resurrection of Christ (Harnack, *op. cit.* 235).

Like εὐαγγέλιον but with a distinctively O. T. flavour is the rarer ὁ λόγος (1⁶ Gal. 6⁶ Col. 4³), ὁ λόγος τοῦ θεοῦ (2¹³ 1 Cor. 14³⁶ 2 Cor. 2¹⁷ 4² Phil. 1¹⁴ Col. 1²⁵) and ὁ λόγος τοῦ κυρίου (1⁸ II 3¹ = Χριστοῦ Col. 3¹⁶); *cf.*

Harnack (*op. cit.* 245 *f.*). This word is the word which God or Christ in Paul speaks, a divine not a human oracle (2¹³) which comes to Paul as it came to the prophets (*cf.* Rom. 9⁶). The content of the word is occasionally specified as truth (2 Cor. 6⁷ Col. 1⁵ Eph. 1¹³), life (Phil. 2¹⁶), the cross (1 Cor. 1¹⁸), or reconciliation (2 Cor. 5¹⁹).—The gospel is also the proclamation (τὸ κήρυγμα 1 Cor. 1²¹; μου 1 Cor. 2⁴; ἡμῶν 1 Cor. 15¹⁴) which Jesus Christ inspires (Rom. 16²⁵); or the testimony (τὸ μαρτύριον) which God (1 Cor. 2¹) or Christ (1 Cor. 1⁶) inspires and which Paul and his associates proclaim (II 1¹⁰; *cf.* εὐαγγέλιον 1⁸).—On the Pauline gospel, see further J. Weiss, *Das älteste Evangelium,* 1903, 33 *ff.,* and J. L. Schultze, *Das Evangelium im ersten Thess.* 1907.

λόγῳ . . . δυνάμει. The stress is laid on the manner of the coming of the gospel: "clothed not only with a form of words but also," and significantly, "with power," that is, with a reality back of the form, and that too a divine reality as the added ἐν πνεύματι ἁγίῳ explains.

Unlike the Corinthians, the Thessalonians did not object to Paul's style, for we have not οὐκ... ἀλλά (1 Cor. 2³ ᶠ· 4¹⁹⁻²⁰ where λόγος and δύναμις are mutually exclusive) but οὐκ... μόνον... ἀλλά. δύναμις refers not to the results of power, the charismata in general, or those specifically associated with σημεῖα καὶ τέρατα (2 Cor. 12¹²)—in which case we should expect δυνάμεις (but *cf.* II 2⁹) or an added phrase (Rom. 15¹⁹ ἐν δυνάμει σημείων καὶ τεράτων)—but to the power itself, as the contrast with λόγῳ and the explanatory πνεύματι indicate.—ἐν with πνεύματι as with λόγῳ and δυνάμει is ultimately local; to be clothed with the Spirit is to be in the Spirit. There is no reference to glossolalia in πνεῦμα. Furthermore ἐν δυνάμει καὶ ἐν πνεύματι is not a hendiadys, though the operation of the Spirit is in its essence δύναμις (1 Cor. 2⁵ of God; 1 Cor. 5⁴ 2 Cor. 12⁹ of Christ; 1 Cor. 2⁴ Rom. 15¹³· ¹⁹ of the Spirit; *cf.* ἐν δυνάμει II 1¹¹).

καὶ πληροφορίᾳ πολλῇ. Closely connected with ἐν πνεύματι ἁγίῳ (omit ἐν before πληροφορίᾳ with ℵB) and resulting from the indwelling of the Spirit, is the inward assurance, *certa multa persuasio* (Beza), of the missionaries (*cf.* 2² ἐπαρρησιασάμεθα ἐν τῷ θεῷ ἡμῶν).

πληροφορία is rare in Gk. Bib. (Col. 2² Heb. 6¹¹ 10²²; *cf.* 1 Clem. 42²); the verb is less rare (*e. g.* Eccl. 8¹¹ Rom. 4²¹ 1 Clem. 42³; and in papyri; *cf.* Deiss. *Light,* 82 *f.*). Of the meanings "fulness" or "conviction," the latter is more appropriate here; see Hammond on Lk. 1¹ and Lft. on Col. 2². The phrase ἐν πολλῇ (πολλῷ) happens to occur in the N. T. only in Paul, the adjective preceding (2². ¹⁷ Rom. 9²²) or following (1⁵· ⁶ 1 Cor. 2³ 2 Cor. 6⁴) the noun.

6

καθὼς οἴδατε κτλ. "As you know what sort of men (οἷοι = quales; cf. 2 Cor. 12²⁰) we became in your eyes for your sakes." The connection appears to be: "We preached the gospel in the power of the Spirit and in full persuasion of its divine reality. That means that we preached not for our own selfish interests, as the Jews insinuate, but solely for your advantage, as you know." The theme of self-defence here struck is elaborated in 2¹⁻¹² where the appeal to the knowledge of the readers in confirmation of Paul's statements becomes frequent.

καθὼς οἴδατε (2². ⁵ 3⁴), αὐτοὶ γὰρ οἴδατε (2¹ 3³; 5² II 3⁷), καθάπερ οἴδατε (2¹¹), οἴδατε (4² II 2⁶), μνημονεύετε (2⁹; II 2⁵), μάρτυς (2⁵. ¹⁰) occur chiefly in the thanksgiving (1²–3¹⁰), especially 2¹⁻¹². καθώς (13 times in I) is later Gk. for καθά which Paul does not use; cf. καθάπερ (2¹¹ 3⁶. ¹² 4⁵). —The reading ὑμῖν (ℵAC) has been assumed with WH.; ἐν ὑμῖν (BDG) is preferred by Tisch. Zim. Weiss, Dob. In Rom. 10²⁰, ℵAC read εὑρέθην τοῖς, ἐγενόμην τοῖς with Is. 65¹, while BD insert ἐν in each instance. The ἐν interprets the simple dative; 2¹⁰ is a good parallel, but γίνεσθαι ἐν λόγῳ 2⁵ is quite different, and 2⁷ has ἐν μέσῳ as we should expect after νήπιοι. The simple ὑμῖν is a dative of reference (2¹⁰), expressing neither advantage nor disadvantage, and importing scarcely more than "before."—On δι' ὑμᾶς, cf. 1 Cor. 4⁶ 2 Cor. 4¹⁵ 8⁹ Phil. 1²⁴.

6. The sentence is getting to be independent, but ὅτι (v. ⁵) is still in control: "and from the fact that you became," etc. The proof of election is the presence of the Spirit not only in the preachers (εὐαγγέλιον ἡμῶν) but also in the hearers who welcomed the word (ὑμεῖς δεξάμενοι) with joy in the midst of great persecution. To be sure, Paul mentions first not the welcome but the imitation. But the two things are inseparable, if we take δεξάμενοι as a participle not of antecedent action, "when you had welcomed," but of identical action, "in that you welcomed." μιμηταὶ ἡμῶν κτλ. "Imitators of us and above all of the Lord" (ipsius Domini, Ambst.). Paul's consciousness of his own integrity (1 Cor. 4⁴), due to the power of Christ in him (Gal. 2²⁰), permitted him to teach by example (1 Cor. 11¹) as well as by precept. As an example not simply of endurance but of joy in persecutions, he could point to himself and especially to Christ. Some knowledge of the life of Jesus on the part of the readers is here presupposed (cf. Gal. 3¹). μετὰ χαρᾶς πνεύματος ἁγίου.

The inward joy which is the accompaniment (μετά) of external
persecution, and which is cogent proof of election, is an enthusiastic happiness (Phil. 1²⁵) due to the new δύναμις operating in
the believers, the power of the Spirit (Gal. 5²² Rom. 14¹⁷) or
Christ (Phil. 3¹ 4⁴·¹⁰).

Although θλίψις alone is the point of comparison in 2¹⁴, and although
Paul, who frequently refers to the sufferings of Christ (2 Cor. 5¹ Phil. 3¹⁰
Rom. 8¹⁷), does not elsewhere refer to Christ's joy in suffering, yet Chrys.
is right in finding the point of comparison here in θλίψις μετὰ χαρᾶς.
The context alone here as elsewhere (II 3⁷·⁹ 1 Cor. 4¹⁶ 11¹ Phil. 3¹⁷ 4⁹
Gal. 4¹²) determines the scope of imitation. ἐν θλίψει = ἐν μέσῳ θλίψεως;
external persecution (Acts 17⁵ ᶠᶠ· and the like) is meant (3²·⁷ II 1⁴·⁶;
cf. 2 Cor. 1⁸), not distress of mind (2 Cor. 2⁴).—δέχεσθαι, as the contrast
with παραλαμβάνειν (2¹³) shows, means not simply "receive," but "receive willingly," "welcome." The phrase δέχεσθαι τὸν λόγον (only here
and 2¹³ in Paul) is used by Luke (Lk. 8¹³ Acts 8¹⁴ 11¹ and especially 17¹¹)
but not by Lxx.; it is equivalent to δέχεσθαι τὸ εὐαγγέλιον (2 Cor. 11⁴).
—κύριος is not θεός (A) but Christ, as always in I, II (Mill. 135-140).—
B inserts καί before πνεύματος conforming to δυνάμει καὶ πνεύματι v. ⁵.
—On μετά of accompaniment, cf. 3¹³ 5²⁸ II 1⁷ 3¹²·¹⁶·¹⁸.—On joy in
suffering, cf. 2 Cor. 6¹⁰ 13⁹ and especially 7⁴ 8².

7. ὥστε γενέσθαι κτλ. The actual result of their imitation of
Christ and Paul is that the Thessalonians became themselves an
example to all the Christians "in Macedonia and in Achaia," the
two provinces constituting Greece since 142 B.C. In the matter
of how one ought to welcome the gospel, the taught have become
the teachers. Knowledge of their progress came to Paul not
only from Timothy's report (3⁶) but also from other news that
kept coming to him in Corinth (ἀπαγγέλλουσιν v. ¹⁰).

In the mainly Pauline phrases πάντες οἱ πιστεύοντες (Rom. 3²² 4¹¹;
cf. Rom. 1¹⁶ 10⁴ Acts 13³⁹), ὑμεῖς οἱ πιστεύοντες (2¹⁰·¹³; Eph. 1¹⁹ 1 Pet.
2⁷), and οἱ πιστεύοντες (Gal. 3²² 1 Cor. 1²¹ 14²²; Jn. 6⁴⁷), the present
tense is timeless. Paul does not use the aorist (cf. Mk. 16¹⁷ Acts 2⁴⁴
4³² Heb. 4³) in these expressions except in II 1¹⁰.—The reading τύπος is
necessary in Rom. 5¹⁴ 6¹⁷ and certain in II 3⁹ Phil. 3¹⁷. τύποι is secure
in 1 Cor. 10⁶. On the analogy of II 3⁹ Phil. 3¹⁷ 4 Mac. 6¹⁹ τύπον is here
to be read with BD. τύπους (אAC) may be due to ὑμᾶς.

8-10. The general drift of these verses is clear, but some of
the details are obscure. The statement (v. ⁷) that the readers

have become a pattern to all the Christians in Greece may well have surprised the Thessalonians. But the explanation (vv. ⁸ ᶠ·) must have been a greater surprise, for it is added that news of the gospel as proclaimed in Thessalonica and of the Christianity of the readers has spread not only in Greece (v. ⁷) but everywhere, as if v. ⁷ had ended with πιστεύουσιν. The point of vv. ⁸ ᶠ· is not that Paul himself is everywhere extolling the readers, as he probably did (II 1⁴), for ἡμᾶς (v. ⁸) and αὐτοί (v. ⁹) are designedly contrasted; not that the readers are boasting at home and abroad of their spiritual life, even if they might have boasted of the gospel, for ἀφ᾽ ὑμῶν is not ὑφ᾽ ὑμῶν; but that other people, believers everywhere, whose names are not given, keep telling Paul in Corinth both about the visit he paid and about the conversion of the Thessalonians. These reports make unnecessary any words from Paul.

Difficulty arises only when we try to make Paul more definite than he is. He does not say who carried the news everywhere, but says only that the gospel which he preached has sounded out and the faith of the converts has gone out. He does not specify the indirect objects of λαλεῖν and ἀπαγγέλλουσιν, nor does he define αὐτοί. It may perhaps be conjectured that αὐτοί means the believers everywhere, that is, some of them. In this case, the αὐτοί are probably not those who bring the news to Greece and other parts from Thessalonica, but those who make reports to Paul. The indirect object of λαλεῖν may be the αὐτοί, that of ἀπαγγέλλουσιν, Paul and his associates. λαλεῖν rather than γράφειν here suggests oral reports. To be sure, περὶ ὑμῶν (v. ⁹ B, et al.) is the easier reading, but περὶ ἡμῶν prepares better for ὁποίαν ἔσχομεν. Paul writes from the standpoint of Corinth where the reports keep coming in; hence not ἀπήγγειλαν or ἀπήγγελλον, as if Berœa or Athens were in mind, but the progressive present ἀπαγγέλλουσιν.

8. This verse, formally considered, is without asyndeton, unless recourse is had to the unnecessary expedient of placing a colon after κυρίου or τόπῳ. The obscurity lies in the fact (1) that v. ⁸ (γάρ) explains not solely, as we should expect, why the readers became "a model to all Christians in Greece," but also why they became a pattern to all believers everywhere; and in the fact (2) that after τόπῳ, where the sentence might naturally end, a second and, in the argument, a more important subject

is introduced, ἡ πίστις ὑμῶν, which is not synonymous with ὁ λόγος τοῦ κυρίου, and a second predicate ἐξελήλυθεν which is prose
for ἐξήχηται. Materially considered, this verse is concerned
not with the method by which the news of the gospel and of the
faith of the readers is brought everywhere, whether by Paul, by
travelling Thessalonians, or by other Macedonians (cf. 4¹⁰), but
with the fact that the word of the Lord and their faith have actually spread, a fact that makes it unnecessary for Paul himself
to say anything about this model community.

It is hardly worth while tampering with an innocent anacoluthon (see
Lillie for a conspectus of attempts) whether by conjecturing ᾧ = ἐν ᾧ
after τόπῳ and translating "in every place into which your faith has
gone forth"; or by putting a colon after κυρίου (Lün. Born. Wohl.
et. al.), a procedure which introduces a formal asyndeton and hints that
the parallel subjects are synonymous. Simpler is it to let the balanced
sentence remain untouched (Lft. Schmiedel, et al.), in which case ἐξήχηται κτλ. explains only ἐν τῇ Μακεδονίᾳ . . . Ἀχαίᾳ (v. ⁷) and ἡ πίστις
κτλ. explains πᾶσιν τοῖς πιστεύουσιν (v. ⁷).—In ὁ λόγος τοῦ κυρίου there
is a covert allusion to Paul as a preacher in the Spirit and in much conviction (v. ⁵), and in ἡ πίστις a clear reference to the welcome which the
converts gave (v. ⁶). Each of these points recurs in vv. ⁹⁻¹⁰ and 2¹⁻¹².
¹³⁻¹⁶. In passing, be it observed that vv. ²⁻¹⁰ form a single sentence;
hence after Ἀχαίᾳ (v. ⁷) a colon is to be placed and also after λαλεῖν τι
(v. ⁸).

ἀφ' ὑμῶν κτλ. "Starting from you, the word of the Lord (the
word that Christ inspires) has sounded forth." The parallel
ἐξελήλυθεν and the similar ἡ ἀφ' ὑμῶν ὁ λόγος τοῦ θεοῦ ἐξῆλθεν
(1 Cor. 14³⁶) suggests that ἀπό (which might = ὑπό; cf. Bl. 40³)
is here local, marking the Thess. "as the simple terminus a quo
of the ἐξηχεῖσθαι" (Ell.).

Whether ἐξήχηται implies the sound either of a trumpet (Chrys.) or
of thunder (Lft.) is uncertain; it may mean simply "has spread." The
word itself is rare in the Gk. Bib. (active in Joel 3¹⁴ Sir. 40¹³, middle in
3 Mac. 3² (Ven.) and here); cf. Lk. 4³⁷ ἦχος with 4¹⁴ φήμη. Before Ἀχαίᾳ,
ἐν τῇ is retained by אCD, et al., a reading perhaps conformed to v. ⁷
(Weiss); cf. Acts 19²¹ where אB omit and AD retain τήν before Ἀχαίαν.
If with B, et al., ἐν τῇ is omitted, then Greece as a whole is contrasted with
the rest of the world.—The ἐν with ἐξήχηται and ἐξελήλυθεν (cf. Lk. 7¹⁷)
may be interpreted with the older grammarians to mean "not only the

arrival of the report, but its permanence after its arrival" (Lün.), as, indeed, the perfects of resultant action likewise suggest. Recent grammarians (Bl. 41¹ and Mill.) are inclined not to press the point, in view of the frequency in later Gk. of ἐν for εἰς.—After οὐ (μή) μόνον ... ἀλλά, Paul adds καί except here and Phil. 2¹²; but to insert καί here with KL is to fail to observe that the omission is purposed, for ἐν παντὶ τόπῳ includes Macedonia and Achaia (Bl. 77¹³).—ἐν παντὶ τόπῳ is a pardonable hyperbole (1 Cor. 1² 2 Cor. 2¹⁴; cf. Rom. 1⁸ Col. 1⁶). As Paul is not speaking with geographical accuracy, it is unnecessary to assume that since he left Thessalonica he went beyond Greece or that he has Galatia or Rome in mind.

ἡ πίστις ὑμῶν ἡ πρὸς τὸν θεόν. The repetition of the article serves to make clear the object toward which their faith is turned and also to suggest a contrast (Ell.) between their present attitude to God and their past pagan attitude to idols. The phrase is rare in the Greek Bible (4 Mac. 15²⁴ (א) 16²²) but frequent in Philo (cf. Hatch, *Essays*, 86 f.).

With πίστις and πιστεύειν Paul uses εἰς (Col. 2⁵ Phile. 5 v. l.), ἐν (Col. 1⁴ Gal. 3²⁶ Eph. 1¹⁵), ἐπί (Rom. 4⁵) and πρός (Phile. 5 v. l.). ἡ πίστις ὑμῶν (3². ⁵· ⁶· ⁷· ¹⁰ II 1³· ⁴) is frequent in Paul (Rom. 1⁸· ¹², etc.) and elsewhere (Jas. 1³, etc.). ἐξέρχεσθαι, a rare word in Paul, is used with εἰς (Rom. 10¹⁸) and πρός (2 Cor. 8¹⁷).

λαλεῖν has to do strictly with the utterance as such, λέγειν with the content of the utterance (SH. on Rom. 3¹⁹), as when we say: "he speaks well but says nothing."

On λαλεῖν with accus., cf. 2² Phil. 1¹⁴ Rom. 15¹⁸ (τι). Observe the parallelism of ὥστε ... γάρ in vv. ⁷⁻⁸· ⁸⁻⁹. On ὥστε μή, cf. 1 Cor. 1⁷ 2 Cor. 3⁷. The common χρείαν ἔχειν with infin. only here and 4⁹ 5¹ in Paul. The reading ὑμᾶς (B, *et al.*) for ἡμᾶς is probably conformation to ὑμῶν after πίστις.

9. αὐτοὶ γάρ κτλ. There is no need for us missionaries (ἡμᾶς) to speak, for they themselves, that is, such believers from Greece and elsewhere as happen to be in Corinth (αὐτοί in contrast with ἡμᾶς) keep reporting (ἀπαγγέλλουσιν is a progressive present) to us, first of all and somewhat unexpectedly, about us (περὶ ἡμῶν), namely, what kind of a visit we paid you, and then about you, "how you turned," etc. It is unnecessary to remark that Paul's version of the report need not be literal. As he

writes, he has in mind the insinuations of the Jews (v. ⁵ 2¹⁻¹²);
hence περὶ ἡμῶν is put first.

αὐτοί is *constructio ad sensum* as αὐτοῖς Gal. 2². ἀπαγγέλλειν (1
Cor. 14²⁵) is frequent in Lxx. and Luke; ἡμῖν is to be understood.
The reading περὶ ὑμῶν (B) misses the point of contrast between visit
and welcome. *adnuntiatis* (r), which Rendel Harris prefers, is due to
the supposed difficulty in περὶ ἡμῶν (Dob.).—The indirect interrogative
ὁποῖος (Gal. 2⁶ 1 Cor. 3¹³), which is rare in Gk. Bib., expresses like
οἷοι (v. ⁵) the quality of the visit.—εἴσοδος in Lxx. is used both of the
action (Mal. 3²) and of the place (Ezek. 42⁹). ἔχειν εἴσοδον πρός appears to be unique in Gk. Bib. (cf. 2¹); the reference is not to a door
opening into their hearts (cf. Marc. Aur. 5¹⁹ ἔχει εἴσοδον πρὸς ψυχήν
and Hermas Sim. IX, 12⁶), for that is excluded by 2¹; nor to the favourable reception (which even P. Oxy. 32 *peto a te ut habeat introitum ad te*
does not of necessity suggest), for the welcome is not mentioned until
πῶς ἐπεστρέψατε (cf. 2¹⁻¹² the visit; 2¹³ ff. the welcome); but simply to
the act of entering (Acts 13²⁴ Heb. 10¹⁹ 2 Pet. 1¹¹). εἴσοδος = παρουσία
"visit" (Phil. 1²⁶ 3 Mac. 3¹⁷); cf. also εἰσέρχεσθαι, εἰσπορεύεσθαι πρός
(Acts 16⁴⁰ 28³⁰).

καὶ πῶς ἐπεστρέψατε κτλ. "And" about you they report
"how you turned to God," etc. πῶς introduces a second object
clause parallel to ὁποίαν. In keeping with v. ⁸, faith in God is
singled out as the primary characteristic of the readers, but the
idea is expressed not, as we might expect, with ἐπιστεύσατε ἐν
τῷ θεῷ but, since Gentile rather than Jewish converts are in
mind, with a phrase perhaps suggested by the contrast with idols,
ἐπεστρέψατε πρὸς τὸν θεόν. In facing God, they turned their
backs on idols. These εἴδωλα are looked upon as dead (1 Cor.
12²) and false, not being what they purport to be. While the
idol in itself is nothing (1 Cor. 10¹⁹), communion with it brings
the worshipper under the power of the gods and demons who
are conceived as present at the ritual act, or as resident in the
idol, or, to the popular mind, as identified with the idol (1 Cor.
10²⁰). Unlike these dead and false idols, God is living and genuine, what he purports to be (contrast 1 Cor. 8⁵ Gal. 4⁸).

πῶς describes the fact (Ruth 2¹¹ Acts 11¹³) rather than the manner
(Sap. 6²² τί δέ ἐστιν σοφία καὶ πῶς ἐγένετο ἀπαγγελῶ), that is, πῶς
tends to become ὅτι (Bl. 70²). The ἐπί in ἐπιστρέφειν is directive as
in Gal. 4⁹ πῶς ἐπιστρέφετε πάλιν. ἐπιστρέφειν, rare in Paul, is frequent

in Lxx. In the phrase ἐπιστρέφειν . . . κύριον (θεόν), the Lxx. uses both ἐπί, which Luke prefers, and πρός (Lk. 17⁴ Acts 9⁴⁰ 2 Cor. 3¹⁶). The article in τὸν θεόν need not be pressed as Gal. 4⁸ indicates.—εἴδωλον (Rom. 2²² 1 Cor. 8⁴, etc.) in the Lxx. renders a variety of Hebrew words both proper and opprobrious. For the meaning of these words and for the forms of idolatry mentioned in the Bible, see G. F. Moore, *EB*. 2146 *ff*. The polemic against images begins with the prophets of the eighth century. "With the prophets of the seventh century begins the contemptuous identification of the gods of the heathen with their idols, and in the sixth the trenchant satire upon the folly of making gods of gold and silver, of wood and stone, which runs on through the later Psalms, Wisdom, Baruch, the Jewish Sibyllines, etc., to be taken up again by Christian apologists" (*op. cit.* 2158). See further Bousset, *Relig.* 350 *ff.* and Wendland, *Die hellenistische-römische Kultur*, 142.—θεὸς ζῶν (Rom. 9²⁶ = Hos. 1¹⁰ 2 Cor. 3³, etc.) is common in Gk. Bib. (Is. 37⁴· ¹⁷, etc.); ἀληθινός = "genuine" (Trench, *Synonyms*,¹² 27) appears only here in Paul as a description of God (*cf.* Jn. 17³ 1 Jn. 5²⁰ 2 Ch. 15³ 3 Mac. 2¹¹ 6¹⁸). The total phrase θεὸς ζῶν καὶ ἀληθινός seems to be unique in Gk. Bib. (καὶ ἀληθινῷ Heb. 9¹⁴ (AP) is a scribal reminiscence of our passage).

10. δουλεύειν καὶ ἀναμένειν. The positive turning to God, faith toward him, has a twofold purpose, religious consecration to him, a δουλεύειν θεῷ (Rom. 6²²) demanding righteousness of life (*cf.* 4³ ᶠ·); and a hope, hitherto unknown (4¹³), which awaits God's Son who comes (τὸν ἐρχόμενον) or comes down (τὸν καταβαίνοντα 4¹⁶) out of the heavens, to finish his work as rescuer, by freeing believers from the impending judgment.

On the infin. of purpose with ἐπιστρέφειν, *cf.* Rev. 1¹² Sap. 19² Eccl. 2²⁰. Like the Galatians (Gal. 4⁸ ᶠ·), the readers have exchanged a slavery to idols for a slavery to God. Usually Paul speaks of a slavery to Christ (δουλεύειν Rom. 12¹¹ 14¹⁸ 16¹⁸, etc.; δοῦλος Gal. 1¹⁰ Rom. 1¹, etc.). δουλεύειν κυρίῳ (Ps. 2¹¹ 99² Sir. 2¹, etc.) like ἐπιστρέφειν ἐπὶ (πρὸς) κύριον is a common phrase in the Lxx. On the meaning of δοῦλος in Paul, see Zahn on Rom. 1¹ (in Zahn's *Kommentar*).

ἀναμένειν (classical, Lxx.) appears only here in N. T. Paul does not use περιμένειν at all (Gen. 49¹⁸ Acts 1⁴) or μένειν transitively (Is. 8¹⁷ 2 Mac. 7³⁰ Acts 20⁵· ²³), choosing the stronger ἐκδέχεσθαι (1 Cor. 11³³ 16¹¹) and ἀπεκδέχεσθαι (Gal. 5⁵ Rom. 8¹⁹ ᶠ· 1 Cor. 1⁷ Phil. 3²⁰). The nearness of the thing expected is suggested by the very idea of waiting (*cf.* Is. 59¹¹).

τὸν υἱὸν αὐτοῦ . . . ᾿Ιησοῦν. The faith of the readers had to do not only with God but with his Son who is to come down out of the heavens, the Messiah of the apocalyptic hope. Specifically Christian is the phrase, explanatory of τὸν υἱόν, ὃν ἤγειρεν ἐκ τῶν νεκρῶν which intimates not only that the Messiah had lived and died but also that he is now, as ἐγερθείς, κύριος (cf. Rom. 4²⁴ 10⁹ Eph. 1²⁰). Likewise specifically Christian is the name Jesus; to Paul as to the Christians before him Ἰησοῦς is Χριστός and κύριος (see on 1¹). In the explanatory words τὸν ῥυόμενον ἡμᾶς κτλ. (a timeless participle), the function of Jesus as Messiah is stated negatively as that of deliverance or rescue from the judgment which though future is not far distant.

This is the only mention of Jesus as Son in our letter; the designation does not occur at all in II, Phil. Phile. For ὁ υἱὸς αὐτοῦ, cf. Gal. 1¹⁶ 4⁴· ⁶ Rom. 1³· ⁹ 5¹⁰ 8²⁹; 8³ (ἑαυτοῦ) 8³² (ἰδίου) 1 Cor. 1⁹ (+ Ἰ. Χ. τοῦ κυρίου ἡμῶν); for υἱὸς θεοῦ, cf. Gal. 2²⁰ 2 Cor. 1¹⁹ Rom. 1⁴ Eph. 4¹³; ὁ υἱός 1 Cor. 15²⁸; ὁ υἱὸς τῆς ἀγάπης αὐτοῦ (Col. 1¹³).—οὐρανός is rare in Paul compared with the gospels; the singular (11 times) and the plural (10 times) appear to be used interchangeably (cf. 2 Cor. 5¹⁻²). Paul may have shared the conception of seven heavens (Slav. En. 8¹ ff· 20¹ ff·; cf. 2 Cor. 12² ff·). ἐκ τῶν οὐρανῶν (Mk. 1¹¹ = Mt. 3¹⁷ Ps. 148¹ Sap. 9¹⁰) occurs only here in Paul, who prefers ἐξ οὐρανοῦ (Gal. 1⁸ 1 Cor. 15⁴⁷ 2 Cor. 5²) or ἀπ’ οὐρανοῦ (4¹⁶ II 1¹⁰).—Paul prefers ἐγείρειν to ἀνιστάναι (4¹⁴· ¹⁶ Eph. 5¹⁴) but ἀνάστασις (ἐξανάστασις) to ἔγερσις (Mt. 27⁵³). The phrase ἐγείρειν ἐκ νεκρῶν is not found in Lxx. (but cf. Sir. 48⁵). The reading ἐκ νεκρῶν (AC) is more usual in Paul than ἐκ τῶν νεκρῶν (אBD; cf. Col. 1¹⁸ Eph. 5¹⁴); see Weiss, 76.—ῥύεσθαι is frequent in Psalms and Isaiah. Paul uses ἐκ of things (Rom. 7²⁴ 2 Cor. 1¹⁰ Col. 1¹³) and ἀπό of persons (II 3²· Rom. 15³¹) with ῥύεσθαι, a point overlooked by CDG which read ἀπό here. For the historical name (ὁ) Ἰησοῦς, cf. 4¹⁴ Gal. 6¹⁷ Rom. 3²⁶ 8¹¹ 1 Cor. 12³ 2 Cor. 4⁵ ff· 11⁴ Phil. 2¹⁰ Eph. 4²¹ and Mill. 135.

ἐκ τῆς ὀργῆς τῆς ἐρχομένης. "From the wrath which is coming." This phrase seems to occur only here in the Gk. Bib. ἔρχεται, however, is used in a similar way in 5² Col. 3⁶ = Eph. 5⁶ (cf. ἔφθασεν 2¹⁶ and ἀποκαλύπτεται Rom. 1¹⁷ᶠ·). The choice of ἐρχομένη rather than μέλλουσα (Mt. 3⁷ = Lk. 3⁷; cf. Ign. Eph. 11¹) may have been determined by the fact that Paul purposes to express not so much the certainty (which the attributive participle present might indicate, *GMT.* 826) as the nearness of the judgment. Nearness involves certainty but certainty does not necessarily involve nearness. (ἡ) ὀργή (2¹⁶ 5⁹ Rom. 3⁵ 5⁹ 9²² 13⁴) is (ἡ) ὀργὴ (τοῦ) θεοῦ (Rom. 1[18] Col. 3[6] Eph. 5[6]), ἡ θεία ὀργή (4 Mac. 9[32]) as expressed in punishment and is equivalent to κρίσις (in Paul only II 1[5]), the eschatological judgment, as ἡμέρα ὀργῆς (Rom. 2[5]) indicates.

> The term ὀργή is Jewish; cf. especially Sir. 5[7]. On the phrase ἡμέρα ὀργῆς, cf. Zeph. 1[15]; on ἡ ἡμέρα ὀργῆς κυρίου, cf. Zeph. 1[18] 2[3] Ezek. 7[19] (A). On the idea of the day of judgment in the O. T. see Briggs, *Messianic Prophecy*, 1886, 487 ff. In Paul σωτηρία (σώζειν) and ζωή are often contrasted with ὀργή (e. g. 2[16] 5[9] Rom. 2[5 ff.] 5[9]).

(2) *The Visit of the Missionaries* (2[1-12]).

The account of the visit (2[1-12]; cf. 1[5. 8a. 9a]) takes the form of a self-defence against insinuations made by Jews. With the same subtlety that led them to accuse the missionaries of preaching another king, namely, Jesus (Acts 17[7]), the Jews were insinuating that the renegade Paul, like many a pagan itinerant preacher, was self-deluded, sensual, and deceiving, delivering his message in flattering words as a foil to cover selfish greed and requiring honour to be paid him. Paul's failure to return lent some colour to these assertions, and the converts became anxious. In his defence, Paul, speaking mainly for himself but including his associates, conscious both of the integrity of his motives and of the unselfishness of his love, and aware of the straightforwardness of his religious appeal, reminds his readers that he came not empty-handed but with a gospel and a courageous power inspired by God (vv. 1-2). Wherever he goes, he preaches as one with no delusion about the truth, for his gospel is of God; with no consciousness of moral aberration, for God had tested him and commissioned him to preach; with no intention to deceive, for he is responsible to God who knows his motives (vv. 3-4). Furthermore, when he was in Thessalonica, he never used cajoling speech, as the readers know, never used the gospel to exploit his ambitions, and never required honour to be given him, although he had the right to receive it as an apostle of Christ (vv. 5-6). On the contrary, he waived his right, becoming just one of them, not an apostle but a babe, and waived it in love for his dear children.

Instead of demanding honour, he worked incessantly to support himself while he preached, in order to save the readers from any expense on his account (vv. 7-9). His sincerity is evident from the pious, righteous, and blameless conduct which they saw in him (v. 10). Not as a flatterer but as a father, he urged them one and all, by encouragement and by solemn appeal, to behave as those who are called of God into his kingdom and glory (vv. 11-12).

The disposition of 21-12 is clearly marked by γάρ (vv. 1. 3. 5-6) and ἀλλά (vv. 2. 4. 7-12) and by the parallel comparisons attached to λαλοῦμεν (v. 4) and ὑμῶν (v. 8). The three points of v. 3 are met in the clause with ἀλλά (v. 4); and the three points of vv. 5-6 are met in vv. 7-12, the γάρ (v. 9) resuming and further elucidating ἀλλά (v. 7); thus ζητοῦντες δόξαν is considered in vv. 7-9, πλεονεξία in v. 10, and κολακία in vv. 11-12.— A careful exegesis of 23-8 is given by Zimmer in *Theol. Studien B. Weiss dargebracht*, 1897, 248-273.

[1]*Indeed you yourselves know, brothers, that the visit we paid you has not proved to be void of power.* [2]*On the contrary, although we had previously undergone suffering and insult in Philippi, as you know, still we in the power of our God took courage to tell you the gospel of God in the midst of much opposition.*

[3]*Indeed the appeal we are wont to make comes not from delusion nor from impurity nor with any purpose to deceive.* [4]*On the contrary, as we stand approved by God to be intrusted with the gospel, so we are wont to tell it, concerned not with pleasing men but God who tests our hearts.*

[5]*Indeed, we never once came before you with cajoling address, as you know, or with a pretext inspired by greed, God is witness,* [6]*or requiring honour of men—from you or from others, although we were ever able to be in a position of honour as Christ's apostles.* [7]*On the contrary, we became babes in the midst of you,—as a nurse cherishes her own children* [8]*so we yearned after you, glad to share with you not only the gospel of God but our very selves as well, for you had become dear to us.* [9]*You remember of course, brothers, our toil and hardship; night and day we worked for our living rather than put a burden on any of you while we preached to you the gospel of God.* [10]*You are witnesses and God as well how piously and right-*

eously and blamelessly we behaved in the sight of you believers.
¹¹As you know, we were urging you individually, as a father his own
children, both by encouragement ¹²and by solemn appeal, to walk
worthily of God who calls you into his own kingdom and glory.

1. αὐτοὶ γὰρ οἴδατε κτλ. With an explanatory γάρ, Paul resumes ὁποίαν εἴσοδον ἔσχομεν (1⁹) and takes up explicitly the
defence already touched upon in 1⁵ (which is strikingly parallel
to 2¹⁻²). Addressing the readers affectionately (ἀδελφοί as in 1⁴),
he recalls to their knowledge that the visit which he paid them
was not empty (κενή), meaning not that it was fruitless, for the
welcome by the converts (1⁶) is not resumed until v. ¹³; but that,
as the ἀλλά clause certifies, the visit was not empty-handed,
was not, as 1⁵ says, "in word only but also in power," for he came
with a gospel of which God is the author, and preached with a
courage (cf. 1⁵ πληροφορία) which was due to the power of God
operating in him (cf. 1⁵ ἐν δυνάμει καὶ ἐν πνεύματι ἁγίῳ). That
he thus preached, notwithstanding recent experiences of persecution and insult in Philippi and great opposition in Thessalonica,
is further proof of the divine inspiration both of his message and
of his power in proclaiming it.

> γάρ resumes and explains 1⁵ (Bengel) by way of 1⁹ where περὶ ἡμῶν
> is put significantly at the beginning. On αὐτοὶ γὰρ οἴδατε, see 1⁵;
> and on the construction οἴδατε τὴν . . . ὅτι, cf. 1 Cor. 3²⁰. The article
> (τήν) is repeated as in 1⁸ (ἡ πρός κτλ.). The perfect γέγονεν with which
> the aorists (1⁵ 2⁵· ⁷· ¹⁰) are to be contrasted denotes completed action;
> the facts of the visit are all in, and the readers may estimate it at its
> full value. ἡμῶν shows that Paul includes Silas and Timothy with him
> in the defence.

2. ἀλλὰ προπαθόντες κτλ. Using a strong adversative
(ἀλλά; cf. vv. ⁴· ⁷), he describes positively the character of his
visit and defines οὐ κενή (v. ¹). Equipped with a gospel inspired
by God (cf. vv. ⁴· ⁸· ⁹, and see note on τὸ εὐαγγέλιον ἡμῶν 1⁵)
and emboldened to preach by the indwelling power of their God
(ἐν τῷ θεῷ ἡμῶν), the visit of the missionaries was not devoid of
power. Paul had already told them of his persecution and especially (καί is perhaps ascensive as in 1⁶ καὶ τοῦ κυρίου) of the
illegal treatment previously experienced at Philippi, and had

mentioned the matter with feeling; for, as Lft. remarks, it was not the physical distress (προπαθόντες) that disturbed him but the insult (ὑβρισθέντες) offered to his Roman citizenship (Acts 16²² ᶠ·). He recalls the fact now (καθὼς οἴδατε; cf. 1⁵) for apologetic reasons (see above on v. ¹).

The aorist participles are of antecedent action and probably concessive. προπάσχειν (only here in Gk. Bib.) is one of the compounds with πρό which Paul is fond of using (3⁴ Gal. 3¹) even when there is no classic or Lxx. precedent (e. g. Gal. 3⁸· ¹⁷ Gal. 1² 2 Cor. 8⁶· ¹⁰ 9⁵). ὑβρίζειν, which Ruther. translates "to treat illegally," occurs only here in Paul and rarely in Lxx.—παρρησιάζεσθαι (here and Eph. 6²⁰ in Paul; frequent in Acts) denotes here, as λαλῆσαι shows, not "to speak boldly" (παρρησίᾳ λαλεῖν) but "to be bold," "to take courage" (cf. Sir. 6¹¹), fiduciam sumpsimus (Calv.). The aorist may be inceptive, "we became bold." According to Radermacher (Neutestamentliche Grammatik, 1911, 151), this ἐπαρρησιασάμεθα is only a more resonant and artificial expression for ἐτολμήσαμεν (cf. Phil. 1¹⁴) which an Attic author would have rather used, since ἐπαρρησιασάμεθα λαλῆσαι is ultimately a tautology. Paul does not elsewhere use πρός with λαλεῖν, but this directive preposition instead of a dative is natural after verbs of saying (cf. 2 Cor. 6¹¹ 13⁷ Phil. 4⁶).

ἐν τῷ θεῷ ἡμῶν. The missionaries are "in God" (see on ἐν θεῷ 1¹) because God is in them (ὑπ᾽ ἐκείνου ἐνδυναμούμενοι, Theophylact; cf. Phil. 4¹³). Characteristic of our epistles (3⁹ II 1¹¹· ¹²; 1 Cor. 6¹¹) and of Revelation (4¹¹ 5¹⁰ 7³ ᶠ· 12¹⁰ 19¹ ᶠ·) is ὁ θεὸς ἡμῶν. The ἡμῶν here (cf. τὰς καρδίας ἡμῶν v. ⁴) seems to refer primarily to the God whom Paul and his two associates preach (hence ἡμῶν, not μου Rom. 1⁸ 1 Cor. 1⁴ (ACD) 2 Cor. 12²¹ Phil. 1³ 4¹⁹ Phile. 4), but does not exclude the further reference to the converts and other believers who feel themselves in common touch with the Christian God, our God Father (1³ 3¹¹· ¹³ Gal. 1⁴ Phil. 4²⁰). There may be in ὁ θεὸς ἡμῶν a latent contrast with pagan idols and deities (1⁹).

Both κύριος ὁ θεὸς ἡμῶν (Mk. 12²⁹ Acts 2³⁹ Rev. 19⁶) and ὁ θεὸς ἡμῶν (Heb. 12²⁹ Lk. 1⁷⁸ Jude 4 2 Pet. 1¹) are frequent in Lxx. (e. g. Deut 11²² Ps. 43²⁰ 97³ Is. 40² Jer. 16¹⁰ 49⁴ Sap. 15¹ Baruch (passim); cf. πατὴρ ἡμῶν Tob. 13⁴) and express Israel's sense of devotion to her God, often in opposition tacit or expressed to the gods of other nations (cf. 1 Reg. 5⁷ Δαγὼν θεὸς ἡμῶν; also Acts 19³⁷ ἡ θεὸς ἡμῶν). For ἐν τῷ θεῷ μου, cf. 2 Reg. 32³⁰ = Ps. 17³⁰.

ἐν πολλῷ ἀγῶνι. "In the midst of much opposition" or "in great anxiety" (Vulg. *in multa sollicitudine*). Whether persecution is meant, as the reference to the experiences at Philippi at first suggests, or inward trouble, as the change from θλίψει (1⁶) to ἀγῶνι (*cf*. Heb. 12¹ Sap. 10¹²) may indicate, is uncertain.

Most comm. find here as in Phil. 1³⁰ a reference to outward troubles, whether persecutions (Ephr.), danger, or untoward circumstances of all sorts (*e. g.* De W. Lün. Ell. Lft. Mill. Born.). Since, however, ἀγών in Col. 2¹ refers to anxiety (*cf*. also ἀγωνίζεσθαι 1 Cor. 9²⁵ Col. 1²⁹ 4¹² and συναγωνίζεσθαι Rom. 15³⁰), it is not impossible that inward struggle is meant (so Fritzsche *apud* Lillie, and Dob.). In later Gk. ἀγών tends to mean "anxiety" (Soph. *Lex.* who notes Iren. I 2² ἐν πολλῷ πάνυ ἀγῶνι). Chrys., who speaks first of danger and then quotes 1 Cor. 2³, apparently understands ἀγών of both external and internal trouble; so Lillie: "at least this restriction (to the external) in the present case must be justified from the context, not from Paul's use of the word elsewhere."

3–4. The self-defence is continued with direct reference to the insinuation that the missionaries were of a kind with the wandering sophists, impostors, and propagandists of religious cults. First negatively (as v. ¹) it is said: "Indeed (γάρ as v. ¹) our appeal never comes from delusion, nor from impurity, nor is it ever calculated to deceive." Then positively (ἀλλά as v. ²): "On the contrary, we are wont to speak as men approved by God to be intrusted with the gospel, concerned not with pleasing men but God who tests our motives." The three specifications of v. ³ are not replied to formally but are nevertheless adequately met: Not ἐκ πλάνης, for the gospel is in origin divine not human; not ἐξ ἀκαθαρσίας, for the gospel has been committed to tested missionaries; and not ἐν δόλῳ, for our responsibility is not to men but to God who sounds the depths of our inner lives. ἡ παράκλησις ἡμῶν. "The appeal we make," taking up λαλῆσαι τὸ εὐαγγέλιον τοῦ θεοῦ. παράκλησις (often in Paul) may mean "summons," "address," "encouragement" (1, 2 Mac.; *cf*. II 2¹⁶) "comfort" (so usually in Lxx.). In this connection, however, as λαλῆσαι (v. ²) and λαλοῦμεν (v. ⁴) make evident, the address itself, not the content (διδαχή Chrys.), is meant; hence "appeal" (Lft.), and that too in virtue of ἐν τῷ θεῷ ἡμῶν and τὸ εὐαγγέλιον τοῦ θεοῦ, a religious appeal, not without reference to προφητεία (5²⁰ 1 Cor. 14¹·³⁹; Rom. 12⁸).

ἐστίν is to be supplied in view of λαλοῦμεν (v. ⁴). The habitual principle (Bengel) is intended. As the Thess. could have no direct knowledge of Paul's custom elsewhere, he does not in vv. ³⁻⁴ appeal to them in confirmation (contrast vv. ⁵ ᶠᶠ·).

ἐκ πλάνης. Our religious appeal does not come "from delusion," for our gospel is of God. πλάνη, as δόλῳ shows, is not "deceit" (active) but "error" (passive), the state of πλανᾶσθαι, "delusion" (Lillie). "Homo qui errat cannot but be undecided; nor is it possible for him to use boldness without consummate impudence and folly" (Cocceius, quoted by Lillie). οὐδὲ ἐξ ἀκαθαρσίας. "Nor does it come from an impure character." ἀκαθαρσία (elsewhere in N. T. only in Paul, except Mt. 23²⁷) regularly appears directly with πορνεία or in contexts intimating sexual aberration. Hence here, as 4⁷ Rom. 6¹⁹, the reference is not to impurity in general, not to covetousness, but to sensuality (Lft.). The traducers of Paul, aware both of the spiritual excitement (5¹⁹ᶠᶠ·) attending the meeting of Christian men and women and of the pagan emotional cults in which morality was often detached from religion, had subtly insinuated that the missionaries were no better morally than other itinerant impostors. That such propagandists would be repudiated by the official representatives of the cult would aid rather than injure a comparison intended to be as odious as possible.

"St. Paul was at this very time living in the midst of the worship of Aphrodite at Corinth and had but lately witnessed that of the Cabiri at Thessalonica" (Lft.). The exact nature of this latter cult, the syncretistic form which it assumed, and the ritual which it used are uncertain, but Lightfoot's phrase, "the foul orgies of the Cabiric worship," may not be too strong. The maligners of Paul may have had some features of this cult in mind when they charged him with ἀκαθαρσία. The cult of the κάβιροι or κάβειροι (perhaps from the root כבר; hence μέγαλοι, (δυνατοί, ἰσχυροί) θεοί) originated, it would appear, in Phœnicia and was carried thence to Lemnos, Samothrace (cf. Herod. 2⁵¹), Macedonia (cf. Lactant. div. instit. I, 15¹⁸ and Bloch, cols. 2533–34) and elsewhere, and became in the Hellenic-Roman period second in importance only to the Eleusinian mysteries. That it was well known in the seaport town of Thessalonica is evident from coins and from Jul. Firmicus Maternus (*de errore prof. relig.* 11). On the Cabiri, see Lft. *Bib. Essays*, 257 *ff.* where the older literature including Lobeck's *Aglaophanes*, 1202 *ff.* is given; also the articles by Hild (*Cabires* in *La Grande Encyc.* 606–610) and by Bloch (in Roscher, 1897), *Megaloi Theoi*, cols. 2522–2541.

οὐδὲ ἐν δόλῳ. "Nor is it with craft, with any purpose to deceive," for they are ever engaged in pleasing not men but God. Over against the ἐκ of origin, ἐν denotes the atmosphere of the appeal. It is not clothed with deception or deceit, that is, with any deliberate intention to deceive (Ell.). This charge may have suggested itself to the critics in view of the devices of sophists and the tricks of jugglers and sorcerers (*cf.* Chrys.) by which they sought to win the attention and the money of the crowd (*cf.* 2 Cor. 12^{16}).

> The reading οὐδέ before ἐν δόλῳ is well attested, but the οὔτε of KL after an οὐδέ has a parallel in Gal. 1^{12} (BEKL); *cf.* Bl. 77^{10}. Note in 1 Mac. ἐν δόλῳ (1^{30}), μετὰ δόλου (7^{10}), and δόλῳ (13^{17}).

4. With ἀλλά (as v. ^{2}), the origin and purpose of the λαλεῖν are positively affirmed. λαλοῦμεν "we are wont to speak" resumes ἡ παράκλησις ἡμῶν (v. ^{3}) and λαλῆσαι (v. ^{2}). As already noted, the points made in v. ^{3} are reckoned with: The gospel is of God, hence they are not deluded; they were commissioned to preach, hence their character is not unclean; they are pleasing not men but God, hence their appeal is not meant to deceive.

> On the correlation καθώς . . . οὕτως, *cf.* 2 Cor. 1^5 8^6 10^7, etc.; on οὐχ ὡς . . . ἀλλά, "not as such who . . . but as such who," *cf.* Col. 3^{22}.— Like Apelles (Rom. 16^{10}), they are δόκιμοι ἐν Χριστῷ; their λαλεῖν is ἐν τῷ θεῷ not ἐν δόλῳ.—ἀρέσκοντες (Gal. 1^{10}) indicates action going on; on the Pauline ἀρέσκειν θεῷ (2^{15} 4^1 Rom. 8^8; 1 Cor. 7^{32}), *cf.* Num. 23^{27} Ps. 68^{32}; on ἀρέσκειν ἀνθρώποις, *cf.* Gal. 1^{10}; on ἀνθρωπάρεσκος (Col. 3^{22} = Eph. 6^6), *cf.* Ps. 52^6.—On οὐ (Gal. 4^8 Phil. 3^3) with participle instead of μή (v. ^{15}), see *BMT.* 485.—δοκιμάζειν = "prove," "test" (of metals Sir. 2^5 34^{26}), as in Rom. 1^{28} Sir. 39^{34}; on the perfect "approve after test," *cf.* Sir. 42^8 2 Mac. 4^3.

τῷ δοκιμάζοντι τὰς καρδίας ἡμῶν. As the motive is in question, Paul refers to God as one who sounds the depths of the hearts, the inner life (Mk. 7²¹). ἡμῶν refers to Paul and his associates (contrast ὑμῶν 3¹³ II 2¹⁷ 3⁵).

In Psalms and Jeremiah, δοκιμάζειν of God's testing is frequent (*cf.* also Sap. 3⁶); *e. g.* Jer. 12³ καὶ σύ, κύριε, γινώσκεις με, δεδοκίμακας τὴν καρδίαν μου ἐναντίον σου; *cf.* also Ps. 16³, and with the possessive omitted, Jer. 11²⁰ 17¹⁰.

5. γάρ parallel to γάρ in vv. ¹· ³, resumes γάρ (v. ³) and further explains that what is true in general (vv. ³⁻⁴) of the principles of the missionaries, about which the readers could not know directly (hence no appeal to their knowledge in vv.³⁻⁴), is also true of their behaviour in Thessalonica of which the readers are directly aware (hence the καθὼς οἴδατε as in vv. ¹⁻²). As in vv. ¹· ³, the γάρ clause is negative; and again as in v. ³, there are three separate charges denied, each one being phrased differently: not ἐν λόγῳ κολακίας, not προφάσει πλεονεξίας, and not ζητοῦντες δόξαν. The points are similar to but not identical with those made in v. ³: ἐν λόγῳ κολακίας corresponds, indeed, rather closely to ἐν δόλῳ, but προφάσει πλεονεξίας is less specific than ἐξ ἀκαθαρσίας and is distinct from it in meaning, and ζητοῦντες δόξαν is quite different from ἐκ πλάνης. Following the γάρ clause (vv. ⁵⁻⁶) is the ἀλλά clause (vv. ⁷⁻¹²; *cf.* vv. ²· ⁴) in which the three points of vv. ⁵⁻⁶ are positively answered,—ζητοῦντες δόξαν in vv. ⁷⁻⁹, πλεονεξία in v. ¹⁰, and κολακία in vv. ¹¹⁻¹².

On οὔτε (vv. ⁵⁻⁶), *cf.* Rom. 8³⁸ ᶠᶠ· 1 Cor. 6⁹ ᶠᶠ·; on οὔτε γάρ . . . οὔτε . . . ἀλλά, *cf.* Gal. 6¹⁵.—ποτέ = "ever" is common in Paul and Lxx.— ἐγενήθημεν governs first a dative with ἐν (λόγῳ), then a dative without ἐν (προφάσει), and finally a participle (ζητοῦντες). Since γίνεσθαι = ἔρχεσθαι (1⁴), we may render: "Indeed we never came before you with cajoling address (ἐν as in 1⁴), nor using (dative of means) a pretext inspired by greed, nor demanding honour," etc. (participle of manner). —The ἐν before προφάσει, which Tisch. Zim. Weiss retain, is probably to be omitted as conformation to the first ἐν (BℵᶜWH. Dob.).

ἐν λόγῳ κολακίας. "With cajoling address." λόγος is here (as 1⁵) "speech," as λαλῆσαι, παράκλησις and λαλοῦμεν (vv. ²⁻⁴) demonstrate (Lün.). κολακία is either "flattery," the subordination of one's self to another for one's own advantage; or, as ἐν δόλῳ intimates, "cajolery," a word that carries with it the

7

additional notion of deception.   The genitive describes the character of the speech.   The hearers could tell whether Paul's address was straightforward or not; hence καθὼς οἴδατε.

ἐν λόγοις ἐκολάκευέ με καὶ μετὰ δόλου διὰ ῥημάτων ἐπαίνει (Test.
xii, Jos. 4¹). In classic usage (cf. Schmidt, Syn. 1879, III, 438 ff.), αἰκάλ-
λειν (not in Gk. Bib.) indicates flattery in the sense of complimentary
remarks designed to please; θωπεύειν (not in Gk. Bib.) means any kind
of subordination by which one gets one's own way with another;   while
κολακεύειν (1 Esd. 4³¹ Job 19¹⁷ Sap. 14¹⁷) hints at guile, a flattery calculated to deceive;   cf. Aristophanes, Eq. 46 ff. ἤκαλλ' ἐθώπευ' ἐκολάκευ'
ἐξηπάτα.   κολακία is only here in Gk. Bib.   Ell. notes Theophrastus
(Char. 2) and Aristotle (Nic. Eth. 4¹² ad fin.): "he who aims at getting
benefit for money and what comes through money is a κόλαξ."

προφάσει πλεονεξίας.   The "cloke of covetousness" is literally "pretext of greediness."   The point is that Paul did not use
his message as a foil to cover selfish purposes (cf. ἐπικάλυμμα
1 Pet. 2¹⁶).   As the appeal to God (θεὸς μάρτυς) indicates, the
motive is in question (cf. Chrys.).   The genitive is subjective,
"a pretext which greediness (Lft.) uses or inspires."   πρόφασις
here is not excuse but specious excuse (cf. Phil. 1¹⁸ Ps. 140⁴
Hos. 10⁴).   πλεονεξία is more general than φιλαργυρία and
denotes the self-seeking, greedy, covetous character of the
πλεονέκτης.

The context here does not allow a more specific meaning of πλεονεξία.
In the Lxx. (Judg. 5¹⁹ (A) Ps. 118³⁶ Hab. 2⁹, etc.), advantage in respect of
money is sometimes intended, cupidity. In 4⁶ below, it is joined with ἀκαθαρσία; but it "does not appear that πλεονεξία can be independently
used in the sense of fleshly concupiscence" (Robinson on Eph. 5⁵; but
see Hammond on Rom. 1²⁹ and Abbott in ICC. on Eph. 5⁵). Lft. (Col.
3⁵) translates: " 'greediness,' an entire disregard for the rights of
others."—On θεὸς μάρτυς (sc. ἐστίν as Rom. 1⁹), cf. not only Paul (Phil.
1⁸ 2 Cor. 1²³) but Jewish usage (e. g. Gen 31⁴⁴; 1 Reg. 20²³· ⁴² Sap. 1⁶ and
especially Test. xii, Levi 19³).

6. οὔτε ζητοῦντες κτλ.   "Nor did we ever come (v. ⁵) requiring honour," etc.   The participle of manner, in apposition to
the subject of ἐγενήθημεν (v. ⁵), introduces the third disclaimer,
which, like the other two (v. ⁵) may reflect the language of the
traducers (Zimmer).   Paul denies not that he received honour

from men, not that he had no right to receive it, but that he
sought, that is, required honour from men either in Thessalonica
or elsewhere.

δυνάμενοι ἐν βάρει κτλ. "Although we were ever (*sc. ποτέ*
from v. ⁵) able to be in a position of weight (*i. e.* honour) as
Christ's apostles." This concessive clause, subordinated to
ζητοῦντες δόξαν, qualifies the fact, "we never came requiring
honour," by asserting the principle (*cf.* II 3⁹) that the authority
to demand honour inheres in their place of preponderance as
Christ's apostles.

δόξα = "honour," as in classic usage. There is no evidence that it is
equivalent to *honor* in the later sense of *honorarium*. On the rare ζητεῖν
ἐκ, *cf.* Gen. 43⁸ Nah. 3¹¹ Ezek. 22³⁰; and for the rarer ζητεῖν ἀπό, *cf.*
Barn. 21⁶.—Since βάρος may mean not only "burden" (Gal. 6² 2 Cor. 4¹⁷
Sir. 13²) but also "importance" (as in later Gk.; *cf.* Soph. *Lex. sub voc.*
and βαρύς 2 Cor. 10¹⁰), it is possible to take ἐν βάρει εἶναι (a unique phrase
in Gk. Bib.) as equivalent to ἐν τιμῇ εἶναι (Chrys.), *in pondere esse*
(Calv.), the ἐν indicating the position in which they were able to stand
and from which, if necessary, they were able to exercise authority; "to
take a preponderant place" (Ruther.). On the other hand, ἐν βάρει
εἶναι may = βαρὺς εἶναι "to be burdensome." In a letter to the present
editor under date of March 15, 1910, Dr. Milligan writes that he "is
inclined to think the more literal idea of 'burden,' 'trouble' was certainly uppermost in the Apostle's thought and that the derived sense of
'*gravitas*,' '*honor*' was not prominent, if it existed at all." He calls
attention to P. Oxy. 1062¹⁴ (ii, A.D.) εἰ δὲ τοῦτό σοι βάρος φέρει; and
to BGU, 159⁵ (A.D. 210) οὐ δυνάμενος ὑποστῆναι τὸ βάρος τῆς λειτουργίας.
Assuming the translation "to be burdensome," expositors find a reference either (1) to the matter of a stipend (*cf.* v. ⁹ II 3⁸ 2 Cor. 12¹⁶ and
especially 2 Cor. 11⁹ ἀβαρῆ ἐμαυτὸν ἐτήρησα); so for example Theodoret, Beza (who takes πλεονεξία = φιλαργυρία), Grot. Flatt, Zim.
Drummond, and Field (*Otium Norv.* III, 122); or (2) to both the stipend
and the authority; so Chrys. Crocius (*non tantum de ambitione sed
et de avaritia*), Lft. Find. Wohl. Moff. and others. The immediate
context, however, does not distinctly suggest a reference to a stipend,
unless δόξα = *honorarium;* furthermore the omission of ὑμῖν (Dob.),
which Vulg. reads (*cum possemus vobis oneri esse*), makes the translation
"to be burdensome" less likely than "to be in honour," "*in pondere
esse*" (*cf.* Erasmus, Hammond, Pelt, De W. Lün. Ell. Schmidt, Schmiedel, Born. Dob.).—On Χριστοῦ ἀπόστολοι, *cf.* 2 Cor. 11³. Paul uses
ἀπόστολος not only of himself and the twelve, but also of Silvanus and
Timothy (here), Junias and Andronicus (Rom. 16⁷), Apollos (1 Cor. 4⁹),

Epaphroditus (Phil. 2²⁵). See further 2 Cor. 8²³ 11¹³ Acts 14¹⁴ and McGiffert, *Apostolic Age*, 648. The word ἀπόστολος occurs once in Lxx. (3 Reg. 14⁶ A). As after γέγονεν (v. ¹) and δόλῳ (v. ³), so after ἀπόστολοι, a comma is to be placed.

7. ἀλλὰ ἐγενήθημεν νήπιοι. "On the contrary, we became babes in the midst of you." ἀλλά is parallel to ἀλλά in v. ⁴ and controls vv. ⁷⁻¹², the γάρ (v. ⁹) resuming the ἀλλά here. A colon is to be put after ὑμῶν. Although they were entitled to demand honour as Christ's apostles, yet they waived that right, choosing to be not apostles but babes in the midst of them. To contrast with ἀπόστολοι and to fit ἐν μέσῳ ὑμῶν, we rather expect not an adjective but a noun. νήπιοι (Gal. 4¹· ³ 1 Cor. 13¹¹ Rom. 2²⁰, etc.), with its implication of the unripe and undeveloped, far from being meaningless (Schmidt) is a capital antithesis of ἀπόστολοι. Not only does νήπιοι fit the immediate context admirably, it is also in keeping with the spirit of brotherly equality that characterises Paul's attitude to his readers not only in I but also in II. He is just one of them, ὡς εἷς ἐξ ὑμῶν (Chrys.).

Not only is νήπιοι admirably adapted to the context, it is also the better attested reading (אBDCGF, Vulg. Boh. Ephr. Ambst. Orig. *ad* Mt. 19¹⁴) as Tisch. admits; and is accepted by WH. Zim. Baljon, Lft. Find. Wohl. Indeed WH. will not allow an alternative reading (*cf. App.*² 128). On the other hand, Weiss is equally insistent on ἤπιοι as alone worthy of attention (AEKLP, Pesh. Arm.; Tisch. Ell. Schmiedel, Born. Dob. Moff.). While on purely transcriptional grounds ἤπιοι may be accounted for by haplography or νήπιοι by dittography, internal evidence favours νήπιοι.—Six of the ten cases of νήπιοι in N. T. (including Eph. 4¹⁴ Heb. 5¹²) are found in Paul; ἤπιος is found in the Gk. Bib. only 2 Tim. 2²⁴. The objection (urged by Ell. Schmiedel, Born. and others) that νήπιοι "mars the metaphor" in the succeeding comparison (whose point, however, is not gentleness but unselfish love) is met by Lft. who observes that "rhetorical rules were as nothing compared with the object which he had in view." ἐν μέσῳ with gen. occurs only here in Paul; it is frequent elsewhere in Gk. Bib.

7-8. ὡς ἐὰν τροφός ... οὕτως κτλ. "As a nurse cherishes her own children so we yearning after you were glad to share not only the gospel of God but our very selves as well, because you had become dear to us." The change from νήπιοι to τροφός is due to a natural association of ideas. The point of the new meta-

phor is love, the love of a mother-nurse for her own children.
Not only did the missionaries waive their right to demand honour,
they waived it in motherly affection for their dear children (*cf.*
1⁵ δι' ὑμᾶς). No punctuation is necessary before οὕτως (*cf.* v. ⁴
and Mk. 4²⁶).

The construction is similar to Mk. 4²⁶ (AC) οὕτως . . . ὡς ἐὰν βάλῃ.
On the difference between ὡς ἐάν=ὡς ἄν (אA) with subjunctive indicating
the contingency of the act and ὡς with the indicative, note with Viteau
(I, 242) 2 Cor. 8¹² καθὸ ἐὰν ἔχῃ . . . καθὸ οὐκ ἔχει. τροφός here as elsewhere in Gk. Bib. (Gen. 35⁸ Is. 49²³ 4 Reg. 11² = 2 Ch. 22¹¹) is feminine.
θάλπειν = "to warm" is used of the mother-bird (Deut. 22⁶ Job 39¹⁴)
and of Abishag (3 Reg. 1². ⁴; *cf.* θερμαίνειν 1² ᵃ·); here and Eph. 5²⁹,
the secondary sense "to cherish" is appropriate (see Ell. on Eph. 5²⁹).
Neither τροφός nor θάλπειν suggests that the τέκνα are θηλάζοντα; hence
it is unnecessary to press the metaphor in the clause with οὕτως, as
some do (*e. g.* Lün.). Grot. compares Num. 11¹² λάβε αὐτὸν εἰς τὸν
κόλπον σου (Moses) ὡσεὶ ἄραι τιθηνὸς (nursing-father as Is. 49²³) τὸν
θηλάζοντα, a passage, which, according to Zimmer, may have been in
Paul's mind.—If ἑαυτῆς is emphatic, as in classic usage, the nurse is also
the mother; if it is = αὐτῆς (Bloomfield *apud* Lillie; *cf.* Moult. I, 87 *ff.*),
the nurse may or may not be the mother. Zimmer, accepting ἑαυτῆς as
emphatic (*cf.* v. ¹¹), but finding difficulty with the idea of a mother-nurse
in service, takes ἑαυτῆς metaphorically, understanding that the pro-
fessional nurse treats the children of her mistress as if they were "her
own"; *cf.* Chrys.: "Are they (the nurses) not more kindly disposed to
them (προσηνεῖς) than mothers ?"—ἑαυτοῦ in Paul, when used with the
article and substantive, has regularly, as in classic Gk., the attributive position (2⁸·¹² 4⁴ II 3¹²); the exceptions are Gal. 6⁴· ⁸ 1 Cor. 11⁵
(B) 2 Cor. 3¹³ (אD), where the position is predicate.

8. ὀμειρόμενοι ὑμῶν κτλ. "Yearning after you" (Lillie; *cf.*
ἐπιποθοῦντες 3⁶). With the affection of a mother-nurse, they
were eager to share not only what they had but what they were
(Schmidt), because, as is frankly said, the converts had become
dear to them, τέκνα ἀγαπητά (1 Cor. 4¹⁴ Eph. 5¹).

ὀμείρεσθαι (the breathing is uncertain) is found also in Job 3²¹ (Lxx.)
and Ps. 62² (Sym.). In meaning, it is similar to ἐπιποθεῖν and ἱμείρεσθαι
(see Wetstein, *ad loc.*); but the derivation is unknown (*cf.* WH. *App.*
151, 159; WS. 16⁶; Bl. 6⁴). Thackeray (*Gram. O. T. Greek*, I, 97, note 5),
following Moult., thinks the ὁ "comes from a derelict preposition ὤ.
There is therefore no connection between ὀμ. and ἱμείρεσθαι."—The

usual reading εὐδοκοῦμεν (B has ηὐδοκοῦμεν; so WH. Weiss) is not
here a present (2 Cor. 5⁸) but an imperfect, as ἐγενήθημεν (v. ⁷) and
ἐγενήθητε (v. ⁸) demand (*cf.* Zim.). εὐδοκεῖν is common in later Gk.
(*cf.* Kennedy, *Sources*, 131). In Lxx. θέλειν is sometimes a variant˷of
εὐδοκεῖν (Judg. 11¹⁷ 19¹⁰· ²⁵), sometimes a parallel (Ps. 50¹⁸) to it. In
papyri, εὐδοκεῖν is often used of consent to an agreement (P. Oxy. 261¹⁷
97²⁴; *cf.* Mill. *ad loc.*). In Paul, εὐδοκεῖν is frequent with infin. (3¹ Gal.
1¹⁵, etc.), but rare with ἐν (1 Cor. 10⁵ 2 Cor. 12¹⁰; Lxx. frequently) or
with dative alone (II 2¹²; *cf.* Sir. 18³¹ A); the construction with accus.,
with ἐπί and dat. or accus., or with εἰς does not appear in Paul.—The
construction μεταδιδόναι τί τινι is found also in Rom. 1¹¹ Tob. 7¹⁰ (B);
the accusative is of the part shared; hence μεταδοῦναι ψυχάς is not
a zeugma for δοῦναι ψυχὰς ὑπὲρ ὑμῶν. ψυχαί (2 Cor. 12¹⁵) is plural, for
Paul and his associates are in mind. ψυχή like καρδία (v. ⁴) is the inner
self. On ἑαυτῶν for ἡμῶν αὐτῶν, *cf.* WS. 22¹⁰; on οὐ μόνον ... ἀλλὰ καί,
see 1⁵.

διότι (2¹⁸ 4⁶) is regularly "because" in Gk. Bib.; in 2 Mac. 7³⁷, it
may mean "that" (Mill.); *cf.* WS. 5⁷ ᵈ. After ἀγαπητός in Paul we
expect a genitive (Rom. 1⁷) not a dative; but *cf.* Sir. 15¹³ καὶ οὐκ ἔστιν
ἀγαπητὸν τοῖς φοβουμένοις αὐτόν.

9. μνημονεύετε γάρ κτλ. "You remember of course brothers
(v. ¹)." The γάρ resumes ἀλλά (v. ⁷) and further illustrates οὔτε
ζητοῦντες δόξαν (v. ⁶). "Instead of requiring honour of you, we
worked hard and incessantly to support ourselves while we
preached to you the gospel of God" (*cf.* II 3⁸).

μνημονεύετε is indicative as οἴδατε (vv. ¹· ⁵· ¹¹) suggests. The accus.
with μνημονεύειν occurs only here in Paul; Lxx. has both gen. and accus. (*cf. v. l.* in Tob. 4¹⁹). The phrase κόπος καὶ μόχθος is Pauline (II 3⁸
2 Cor. 11²⁷); *cf.* also Jer. 20¹⁸ Test. xii, Jud. 18⁴. In fact in Paul μόχθος
always appears with κόπος (*cf.* Hermas, Sim. V, 6²). Beza, with Lillie's
approval, makes *labour, peine, travail* the equivalents respectively of
πόνος, κόπος, and μόχθος. Grot. (*cf.* Lft. and Trench, *Syn.* 102) considers κόπος passive, *in ferendo* and μόχθος active, *in gerendo*. Lft.
translates: "toil and moil."

νυκτὸς καὶ ἡμέρας κτλ. Without connecting particle (EKL
insert γάρ), the ceaselessness of the labour and the purpose of it
as a "labour of love" are indicated. They worked not through
the whole night and day (accus.) but during the night and day
(gen.). The purpose of this incessant labour (πρὸς τὸ μή II 3⁸
2 Cor. 3¹³) was to avoid putting upon the converts individually

or collectively a financial burden. ἐργαζόμενοι marks the circumstances attending the preaching. As in Corinth (1 Cor. 4¹² 9⁶)
where there were not many wise, mighty, or noble, so in Thessalonica (II 3⁸ᶠ·) where the converts were mainly working people,
Paul finds it necessary to work with his hands (4¹¹ 1 Cor. 4¹²
Eph. 4²⁸) for wages.

The phrase νυκτὸς καὶ ἡμέρας occurs in Paul elsewhere only 3¹⁰ and
II 3⁸; cf. 1 Tim. 5⁵ 2 Tim. 1³ Mk. 5⁵ Judith 11¹⁷. In the Lxx. the usual
order is ἡμέρας καὶ νυκτός (e. g. Josh. 1⁸ 3 Reg. 8⁵⁹, etc.; cf. Lk. 18⁷
Acts 9²⁴ Rev. 4⁸, etc.). ἐπιβαρεῖν, a late word, appears in Gk. Bib. elsewhere only in Paul (II 3⁸ 2 Cor. 2⁵) and is "nearly but not quite equivalent in meaning to καταβαρεῖν" (Ell.), which is found in Gk. Bib. only 2
Cor. 12¹⁶ and Mk. 14⁴⁰ (cf. καταβαρύνειν 2 Reg. 13²⁵, etc.). With κηρύσσειν,
Paul uses ἐν (Gal. 2² 2 Cor. 1¹⁹ Col. 1²³), εἰς (here, as Grot. notes, for
dative), or the dative (1 Cor. 9²⁷ and א here)—all permissible Attic constructions (Bl. 39⁴). The phrase κηρύσσειν τὸ εὐαγγέλιον τοῦ θεοῦ recurs
in Mk. 1¹⁴; cf. Gal. 2² Col. 1²³ Mk. 13¹⁰ 14⁹.

10. ὑμεῖς μάρτυρες κτλ. As vv. ⁷⁻⁹ referred to the charge of
ζητοῦντες δόξαν (v. ⁶), so this verse refers probably to the
charge of πλεονεξία (v. ⁵), and vv. ¹¹⁻¹² to that of κολακία. The
ἀλλά of v. ⁷ still controls, as the asyndeton (H inserts γάρ) suggests. The fact that Paul and his associates carried themselves
in a pious, righteous, and blameless manner (on the adverbs with
ἐγενήθημεν, cf. 1 Cor. 16¹⁰ Tob. 7¹¹) is evidence that they were
not using the gospel as a foil to cover greedy ambition (v. ⁵). As
witnesses of their behaviour, they invoke first, since the actual
conduct not the motive is mainly in mind, the believers, and then
to strengthen the appeal, God himself.

A man is ὅσιος who is in general devoted to God's service; a
man is δίκαιος who comes up to a specific standard of righteousness; and a man is ἄμεμπτος who in the light of a given
norm is without reproach. All three designations are common
in the Lxx. and denote the attitude both to God and to men, the
first two being positive, the third negative.

ὡς = "how" as in Phil. 1⁸. ὅσιος (not in Paul and rare in N. T.) is
common in Lxx. (especially Ps. Prov. Sap. Ps. Sol.); ὁσιοῦν (not in
N. T.) occurs in Sap. 6¹⁰ Ps. 17²⁶ 2 Reg. 22²⁶; ὁσιότης (Eph. 4²⁴ Lk. 1⁷⁵)
is found in Sap. and elsewhere in Lxx.; ὁσίως, in Gk. Bib. elsewhere only

Sap. 6¹⁰ 3 Reg. 8⁶¹, is frequent in 1 Clem.; *cf.* also P. Par. 63 (Deiss. *BS.* 211) πρὸς οὓς ὁσίως καὶ δικαίως πολιτευσάμενος.—ὅσιος and δίκαιος are frequently parallel (Pr. 17²⁶; *cf.* Sap. 9³ Lk. 1⁷⁵ 1 Clem. 48⁴). For ὅσιος and ἄμεμπτος, *cf.* Sap. 10¹⁵. δικαίως is more frequent than ὁσίως in Gk. Bib., but ἀμέμπτως is found elsewhere only 5²³ 3¹³ (BL) and Esther 3¹³ (13⁴); *cf.* 1 Clem. 44³⁻⁶ 63³. The adjective ἄμεμπτος (3¹³ Phil. 2¹⁵ 3⁶ Lk. 1⁶ Heb. 8⁷) is frequent in Job, sometimes (*e. g.* 1¹ 9²⁰, etc.) with δί-καιος.—The addition of τοῖς πιστεύουσιν to ὑμῖν is designed, if at all, not to contrast Paul's attitude to the non-Christians with his attitude to the Christians (so some older comm.), or his attitude to the converts as converts with that to the converts as pagans (Hofmann, Dob.), but simply to meet the charge that his attitude to the believers was influenced by selfish motives.

11–12. *καθάπερ οἴδατε κτλ.* Not as a *κόλαξ* (v. ⁵ *κολακία*) but as a *πατήρ* (1 Cor. 4¹⁵ Phil. 2²²), they urged the converts individually (*ἕνα ἕκαστον ὑμῶν*; *cf.* II 1³ Eph. 4⁷ Col. 4⁶), each according to his specific need, as the added *παραμυθούμενοι* and *μαρτυρόμενοι* intimate. The faint-hearted, they encouraged (5¹⁴ *παραμυθεῖσθε τοὺς ὀλιγοψύχους*); to the idlers (5¹⁴), they gave a solemn protest. *παρακαλεῖν* is general, *παραμυθεῖσθαι* and *μαρτύρεσθαι* specific. Hence *εἰς τό* is to be construed only with *παρακαλοῦντες* (*cf.* 2 Cor. 1⁴; also *δέομαι* below 3¹⁰ and *ἐρωτάω* II 2²). "We were urging both by encouragement and by solemn protest, that you walk," etc.

καθάπερ (3⁶· ¹² 4⁵), found frequently in Paul and in Exodus, is equivalent to the less Attic καθώς.—ὡς as in v. ¹⁰ = πῶς (GF).—παρακαλεῖν, a favourite word in Paul and susceptible of various translations, here means "urge," "exhort."—παραμυθεῖσθαι, a rare word in Gk. Bib. (5¹⁴ Jn. 11¹⁹· ³¹ 2 Mac. 15⁹), means here and 5¹⁴ not "comfort" but "encourage." On παρακαλεῖν and παραμυθεῖσθαι, *cf.* 1 Cor. 14³ Phil. 2¹ 2 Mac. 15⁸·⁹. μαρτύρεσθαι (Gal. 5³ Eph. 4¹⁷ Acts 20²⁶ 26²² Judith 7²⁸ 1 Mac. 2⁵⁶ ℵ) is stronger than παρακαλεῖν and means either "to call to witness" or "to protest solemnly"; in later Gk. (*cf.* Mill. *ad loc.* and 1 Mac. 2⁵⁶), it approximates μαρτυρεῖν (hence DG have here μαρτυρού-μενοι).—The participial construction (παρακαλοῦντες for παρεκαλοῦ-μεν) is quite admissible (*cf.* 2 Cor. 7⁵ and Bl. 79¹⁰). Some comm. repeat ἐγενήθημεν (v. ¹⁰), attaching the participle loosely; others supply a verb like ἐνουθετοῦμεν (Lft.).—The ὑμᾶς (which ℵ omits) after παρακαλοῦντες resumes ἕνα ἕκαστον ὑμῶν.

περιπατεῖν ἀξίως τοῦ θεοῦ κτλ. The object (*εἰς τό*) of the fatherly exhortation is that the readers conduct themselves in a

manner worthy of their relation to God who calls them, through
the preaching of the gospel (II 2¹⁴), into his own kingdom and
his own (*sc.* ἑαυτοῦ) glory. βασιλεία, an infrequent word in Paul
compared with the Synoptic Gospels, denotes the redeemed society of the future over which God rules, the inheritance of believers (Gal. 5²¹ 1 Cor. 6⁹· ¹⁰ 15⁵⁰; *cf.* Eph. 5⁵), and the consummation of salvation (II 1⁵ 1 Cor. 15²⁴). Foretastes of this sway
of God (Rom. 14¹⁷ ἐν πνεύματι ἁγίῳ; *cf.* 1 Cor. 4²⁰ Col. 4¹¹) or
of Christ (Col. 1¹³) are already enjoyed by believers in virtue of
the indwelling power of Christ or the Spirit. δόξα is parallel
with βασιλεία and suggests not only the radiant splendour of
God or of Christ (II 2¹⁴) but also the majesty of their perfection
(*cf.* Ps. 96⁶ Rom. 3²³).

περιπατεῖν ἀξίως τοῦ θεοῦ, found elsewhere in Gk. Bib. only Col. 1¹⁰
(κυρίου), is common in the Pergamon inscriptions (Deiss. *NBS.* 75 *f.*),
and appears also in the Magnesian inscriptions (Mill. *ad loc.*); *cf.*
πολιτεύεσθαι ἀξίως αὐτοῦ 1 Clem. 21¹ Polyc. 5².—περιπατεῖν like ἀνα-
στρέφεσθαι in the ethical sense is both a Hebrew and a Greek idiom.
KL read here, as in Col. 1¹⁰ Eph. 4¹, περιπατῆσαι.—τοῦ καλοῦντος (5²⁴
Gal. 5⁸ Rom. 9¹¹) is timeless like τὸν ῥυόμενον (1¹⁰). Paul prefers the
present to the aorist participle (Gal. 1⁶· ¹⁵ and אA here) of καλεῖν. On
εἰς after καλεῖν, *cf.* II 2¹⁴ 1 Cor. 1⁹ Col. 3¹⁵.—On βασιλεία θεοῦ, *cf.*
Sap. 10¹⁰ 2 Ch. 13⁸ Ps. Sol. 17⁴; on Christ's kingdom, *cf.* Col. 1¹³ Eph. 5⁵
2 Tim. 4¹· ¹⁸ Jn. 18³⁶. ἑαυτοῦ does not of necessity indicate a contrast
with Satan's kingdom (Col. 1¹³ Mk. 3²³ ff.). On the meaning of δόξα, see
Gray, *HDB.* II, 183 *ff.*; Kennedy, *Last Things,* 299 *ff.*; Gunkel, *Die
Wirkungen des heiligen Geistes,* 108 *ff.*; and SH. on Rom. 3²³.

(3) *Welcome in Persecutions; the Jews* (2¹³⁻¹⁶).

After the defence of his visit (2¹⁻¹²), Paul turns again (*cf.* 1⁶· ⁹)
to the welcome received. Repeating in v. ¹³ the thanksgiving of
1² ff., he points out that just as he is conscious of preaching God's
gospel (vv. ¹⁻⁴) so the readers welcomed his word as God's word.
That it is not a human word, as the Jews alleged, but a divine
word, operating in the hearts of believers, is demonstrated by
the fact that the readers welcomed it in spite of persecutions (v. ¹⁴
resuming 1⁶ ff.), persecutions at the hands of Gentiles similar to
those which the Jewish Christians in Judæa experienced at the

hands of Jews. Then remembering the constant opposition of
the Jews to himself in Thessalonica, Berœa, and Corinth, and
their defamation of his character since he left Thessalonica, and
the fact that though the Gentiles are the official persecutors yet
the Jews are the prompting spirits, Paul, in a prophetic outburst
(*cf.* Phil. 3¹ ᶠᶠ·), adds, neglecting negative instances, that the
Jews have always opposed the true messengers of God, killing
the prophets and the Lord Jesus, and persecuting Paul; and
prophesies that this their constant defiance is bound to result,
in accordance with the purpose of God, in the filling up of their
sins always, and in judgment at the day of wrath. Indeed, to
his prophetic vision, that day has come at last.

*¹³And for this reason, we too as well as you thank God continually,
namely, because when you had received from us the word which you
heard, God's word, you welcomed it, not as a word of men but as it
really is, as a word of God which also is operative in you who believe. ¹⁴For you, brothers, became imitators of the assemblies of God
in Judæa, those, namely, that are in Christ Jesus, in that you under-
went the same sufferings at the hands of your own countrymen, as
they themselves at the hands of the Jews—¹⁵the men who killed both
the Lord Jesus and the prophets, and persecuted us; who please
not God and are against all mankind ¹⁶in that they hinder us from
talking to the Gentiles with a view to their salvation,—in order that
they might fill up the purposed measure of their sins always; but
the wrath has come upon them at last.*

13. καὶ διὰ τοῦτο καὶ ἡμεῖς κτλ. "And for this reason we
too as well as you give thanks." διὰ τοῦτο refers, as the resumptive ὅτι shows, not to the entire contents of vv. ¹⁻¹² but to the
salient principle enounced in vv. ¹⁻⁴, namely, that the gospel is
not human, as the Jews alleged, but divine. The καί in καὶ
ἡμεῖς indicates a reciprocal relation between writers and readers.
As the Thessalonians, in their letter to Paul, thanked God that
they welcomed the gospel as a word from God, so now do the
missionaries reciprocate that thanksgiving.

διὰ τοῦτο like διό is frequent in Paul, but καὶ διὰ τοῦτο (Mk. 6¹⁴
= Mt. 14²; Lk. 14²⁰ Heb. 9¹⁵ Jn. 5¹⁶; Barn. 8⁷ Ign. Mag. 9² Hermas, Sim.
VII, 2, IX, 19¹ (καὶ διὰ τοῦτο καί as here)) occurs elsewhere in Paul only

II 2¹¹; hence D here and II 2¹¹ omits καί. It is probable that in Paul this consecutive and subordinating διὰ τοῦτο has always some reference to the preceding even when the primary reference, often general, is supplemented by a secondary, often specific, reference introduced by ὅτι as here and often in Jn. (cf. Gen. 11⁹ 21³¹, etc.; Diogn. 2⁶ Hermas Vis. III, 6¹), by ἵνα (2 Cor. 13¹⁰ Phile. 15), or by some other construction (II 2¹¹ 1 Cor. 11¹⁰ Heb. 9¹⁵). On διὰ τοῦτο καί, cf. 3⁵ Rom. 13⁶ Lk. 11⁴⁹ Mt. 24⁴⁴ Jn. 12¹⁸; on ὅτι = "because," Rom. 1⁸.—καί before ἡμεῖς, if it retains its classic force, is to be construed closely with ἡμεῖς. Its precise significance here is somewhat uncertain. In a similar passage (Col. 1⁹), Lft. observes that "καί denotes the response of the Apostle's personal feeling to the favourable character of the news" (so here Mill.). Wohl. thinks that Paul tacitly refutes the insinuation that he is not thankful to God. More plausible here (as in Col. 1⁹ Eph. 1¹⁶) is the conjecture of Rendel Harris (op. cit.; cf. Bacon, Introd. 73 and McGiffert, EB. 5038) that καί presupposes a letter from the Thess. to Paul (cf. 4⁹· ¹³ 5¹) in which they thanked God as Paul now thanks him. Dob. however, following the lead of Lietzmann (ad Rom. 3⁷), feels that καί is not to be joined closely with ἡμεῖς, but serves to emphasise the εὐχαριστοῦμεν with reference to εὐχαριστοῦμεν in 1². In support of this usage, Dob. refers to καὶ λαλοῦμεν in 1 Cor. 2¹³, which goes back to the λαλοῦμεν in 2⁶.

παραλαβόντες ... ἐδέξασθε. The distinction between the external reception (παραλαμβάνειν) and the welcome (δέχεσθαι) given to the word, a welcome involving a favourable estimate of its worth, was early recognised (cf. Ephr.). That the distinction is purposed, that Paul is tacitly answering the insinuation of the Jews that the word preached was not of divine but of human origin (vv. ¹⁻⁴) is suggested by the striking position of τοῦ θεοῦ (which leads P to put παρ' ἡμῶν before λόγον ἀκοῆς, and induces Schmiedel to consider τοῦ θεοῦ a gloss) and by the emphasis on the fact that this word, heard, received, and welcomed, also operates in the inner lives of believers.

λόγον ἀκοῆς = λόγον ὃν ἠκούσατε; cf. Sir. 42¹ λόγον ἀκοῆς = דבר שמע (Smend). Grot. notes Heb. 4² ὁ λόγος τῆς ἀκοῆς. The gen. is appositive. —Since παρά with gen. (rare in Paul) is used, apart from Rom. 11²⁷ (Lxx.), with verbs implying (II 3⁸) or stating the idea of receiving (e. g. παραλαμβάνειν 4¹ II 3⁶ Gal. 1¹²; δέχεσθαι Phil. 4¹⁸; κομίζεσθαι Eph. 6⁸), it is more natural to take παρ' ἡμῶν with παραλαμβάνειν than with ἀκοῆς, although, as Beza remarks, the sense is the same in either construction. On παραλαμβάνειν εὐαγγέλιον, cf. 1 Cor. 15¹ Gal. 1⁹.

οὐ λόγον ἀνθρώπων κτλ. "Not as a word of men but, as it really is, as a word of God." Since there is a distinction between παραλαμβάνειν and δέχεσθαι, the latter implying an estimate of worth, λόγον ἀνθρώπων and λόγον θεοῦ are to be taken predicatively. The precise point appears to be not that the word is true, for this is first stated in καθὼς ἀληθῶς ἐστίν, not that the hearers welcomed the word as if it were true, for there is no ὡς (contrast Gal. 4¹⁴), but that they welcomed the word as a word of God (cf. Ephr.). ὃς καὶ ἐνεργεῖται. Since λόγος receives the emphasis, ὅς refers not to θεοῦ but to λόγος. The καί indicates not only that the word is heard (ἀκοῆς), received (παραλαβόντες), and welcomed (ἐδέξασθε), but also that it is an active power (Rom. 1¹⁶) operating constantly (pres. tense) in (Col. 1²⁹) the hearts of believers. The word is living, for the power of God is in the believers (1¹ ἐν θεῷ) as it is in the missionaries (2² ἐν τῷ θεῷ ἡμῶν).

Eighteen of the twenty-one cases of ἐνεργεῖν in the N. T. occur in Paul. In the active, it is used of superhuman operations, usually divine but once (Eph. 2²) demonic. ἐνεργεῖσθαι (II 2⁷ 2 Cor. 4¹² Col. 1²⁹ Eph. 3²⁰; cf. Rom. 7⁵ 2 Cor. 1⁶ Gal. 5⁶) may be passive "to remind us that the operation is not self-originated" (Robinson, *Ephesians*, 247) or middle, without such a reminder (Mayor on Jas. 5¹⁶). It happens that ὑπό is never expressed. "In actual meaning ἐνεργεῖν and ἐνεργεῖσθαι come nearly to the same thing" (Robinson, *l. c.*). Grot. remarks: ἐνεργεῖσθαι *sono passivum sensu activum.* See further Robinson (*op. cit.* 241–247). —The Old Latins and some comm. (Ephr. Th. Mops. Piscator, Bengel, Auberlen) refer ὅς to θεός, an interpretation which is contextually improbable and which is precluded if ἐνεργεῖται is passive.

14. ὑμεῖς γὰρ μιμηταὶ...ὅτι ἐπάθετε. "For you became imitators, brothers, of the Christian congregations in Judæa in that you suffered." γάρ connects the points of welcome and steadfastness under persecution, and at the same time illustrates and confirms the reality of the indwelling word of God. The ὑπομονὴ ἐν θλίψει of 1⁶ is obviously resumed; but the persons imitated are not the missionaries and the Lord Jesus, but the Jewish Christians in Palestine, the analogy between them and the Thessalonians being that the former suffered (ἐπάθετε) at the hands of the Jews as the latter at the hands of the Gentiles.

The reason for referring to the persecutions in Judæa is unknown. It may be that the older churches are selected as pertinent examples of steadfastness to the younger communities; or that, and with greater probability (*cf.* Calv.), the Jews in Thessalonica had insinuated that Christianity was a false religion, inasmuch as the Jews, the holy people of God, were constrained to oppose it. If the latter surmise be correct, the force of Paul's allusion is that the Jews persecute the Christians because they always persecute the true followers of the divine will, and that it is the Jews who incite the Gentiles to harass the believers. ἐπάθετε may refer to a single event in the remoter (Gal. 1¹³ 1 Cor. 15⁹) or nearer (Dob.) past, or to a series of persecutions, considered collectively (*BMT*. 39ᶜ). In the latter case, the reference would include not only the case of Jason (Acts 17⁹), but the persecutions which continued since Paul's departure (3³), the Jews being the real cause of Gentile oppression in Thessalonica, as they were the actual persecutors in Judæa. The defence of his failure to return (2¹⁷–3¹³), which follows immediately after the prophetic outburst against the Jews, confirms the probability that the Jews are at the bottom of Gentile persecutions in Thessalonica after Paul's departure, as well as during his visit, and makes unnecessary the rejection of vv. ¹⁵⁻¹⁶ (Schmiedel) or of vv. ¹⁴⁻¹⁶ (Holtzmann, *Einl.* 214) as interpolation. τῶν ἐκκλησιῶν τοῦ θεοῦ. This phrase, mainly Pauline (II 1⁴ 1 Cor. 11¹⁶), might of itself denote Jewish assemblies or congregations, hence the distinctively Pauline ἐν Χριστῷ Ἰησοῦ (see on ἐν θεῷ 1¹) is added here, as in Gal. 1²², to specify the communities as Christian.

ἐκκλησία, the Greek term for the assembly of citizens (*cf.* Deiss. *Light*, 112 *ff.*), is used by Lxx. regularly for קהל and rarely for עדה; συναγωγή on the other hand usually renders the latter, and rarely the former. The terms are virtually synonymous in Jewish usage; *cf.* ἐκκλησία κυρίου (Deut. 23¹ ᶠᶠ· Mic. 2⁵ Neh. 13¹ (א; AB θεοῦ) 1 Ch. 28⁸); συναγωγὴ κυρίου (Num. 16³ 20⁴); also Pr. 5¹⁴: ἐν μέσῳ ἐκκλησίας καὶ συναγωγῆς (see Toy, *ad loc.* in *ICC*.) and 1 Mac. 3¹³ ἄθροισμα καὶ ἐκκλησίαν πιστῶν. How early the Christians began to restrict συναγωγή to the Jewish and ἐκκλησία to the Christian assembly is uncertain (*cf.* Jas. 2² and Zahn, *Introd.* I, 94 *f.*). The plural αἱ ἐκκλησίαι τοῦ Χριστοῦ occurs once in N. T. (Rom. 16¹⁶), but the singular ἡ ἐκκλησία τοῦ Χριστοῦ (αὐτοῦ) does not appear, except Mt. 16¹⁸ (μου), before Ignatius (Trall. *init.* and 1²). On τῶν οὐσων ἐν, *cf.* 1 Cor. 1² 2 Cor. 1¹.

τὰ αὐτά κτλ. "In that you suffered from your own fellow-citizens the same as they did from the Jews." The point of imitation, introduced by ὅτι, is obviously not the fact of παθεῖν but the steadfast endurance manifested under persecution. The comparison τὰ αὐτὰ καί... καθὼς καί is intended to express not identity but similarity. συμφυλέται are Gentiles as Ἰουδαίων shows.

After τὰ αὐτά (Rom. 2¹ 2 Cor. 1⁶ Phil. 3¹ Eph. 6⁹) we have not the expected ἅ (2 Cor. 1⁶) but the looser καθώς. Ell. cites Plato, *Phaed.* 86 A: τῷ αὐτῷ λόγῳ ὥσπερ σύ; *cf.* also Sap. 18¹¹ ὁμοίᾳ δὲ δίκη δοῦλος ἅμα δεσπότῃ κολασθείς, καὶ δημότης βασιλεῖ τὰ αὐτὰ πάσχων.—For the correlative καί in καὶ ὑμεῖς . . . καὶ αὐτοί, *cf.* Rom. 1¹³ and Bl. 78¹.—αὐτοί is *constructio ad sensum* for αὐταί; *cf.* Gal. 1²³ ἐκκλησίαι . . . ἀκούοντες.—πάσχειν is a kind of passive of ποιεῖν (Bl. 54²); hence ὑπό (D ἀπό); *cf.* Ep. Jer. 33 Mk. 5²⁶ Mt. 17¹².—D omits καὶ ὑμεῖς.

Like φυλέτης, a classic word not found in Gk. Bib., συμφυλέτης, only here in Gk. Bib., means either "tribesman" or "countryman" (*cf.* Hesychius: ὁμόεθνος); it is similar to συμπολίτης (Eph. 2¹⁹). The tendency in later Gk. to prefix prepositions without adding to the original force was condemned, as Ell. remarks, by the second-century grammarian Herodianus: πολίτης δημότης φυλέτης ἄνευ τῆς σύν. Paul, however, is fond of such compounds with σύν even when they do not appear in the Lxx. (*e. g.* Phil. 2² 3¹⁰· ¹⁷ 2 Cor. 6¹⁵ Gal. 1¹⁴, etc.).—ἴδιος, common in Gk. Bib., may in later Gk. mean either *proprius* (Vulg.) or *vester*.

The term Ἰουδαῖος (see Zahn, *Introd.* II, 306 *ff.*) is not of itself disparaging. It is frequently employed by Jews as a self-designation (Rom. 2¹⁷ Jer. 39¹² 45¹⁹, etc.). Paul, however, while he speaks of himself as of the seed of Abraham, of the tribe of Benjamin, a Hebrew and an Israelite (Rom. 11¹ 2 Cor. 11²² Phil. 3⁵), rarely if ever employs Ἰουδαῖος as a self-designation (Gal. 2¹⁵), but uses it of the Jew who finds in Christ the fulfilment of the law (Rom. 2²⁸), of the Jew contrasted with the Greek (so regularly as here), and of Judaism in contrast with Christianity (1 Cor. 10³² Gal. 1¹³ ᶠ·), no disparagement being intended by the word itself.

15-16. The past experiences in Thessalonica and Bercœa (Acts 17¹⁻¹⁵), the insinuations alluded to in vv.¹⁻¹²; and the present troubles in Corinth (3⁷; *cf.* Acts 18⁵ ᶠᶠ·) explain sufficiently this

prophetic denunciation of the Jews (*cf.* Phil. 3¹ ᶠᶠ·). The counts
are set forth in a series of five participles in close apposition with
τῶν Ἰουδαίων. Of these, the first two (ἀποκτεινάντων and ἐκδιωξάντων) are aorist and refer to the past: "who put to death
both the Lord Jesus and the prophets, and persecuted us," that
is, Paul, Silvanus, and Timothy (their experiences particularly
in Thessalonica and Berœa being looked at collectively). The
next two participles (μὴ ἀρεσκόντων, and ὄντων understood after
ἐναντίων) are present and describe the constant attitude of the
Jews, a description qualified by the fifth participle also present
(κωλυόντων, introduced without καί): "and who oppose the will
of God and the good of humanity in that they hinder us from
speaking to the Gentiles with a view to their salvation." For
such obstinacy, judgment is prepared. In accordance with the
purpose of God, the Jews are constantly filling up the measure
of their sins; and to the prophetic outlook of Paul, the wrath of
God has actually come upon them at last.

> The denunciation is unqualified; no hope for their future is expressed.
> The letters of Paul reveal not a machine but a man; his moods vary;
> now he is repressed (II 3² οὐ γὰρ πάντων ἡ πίστις), again he is outspokenly
> severe (Phil. 3¹ ᶠ·), and still again he is grieved, but affectionate and
> hopeful (Rom. 9¹ ᶠ· 11²⁵).

καὶ τὸν κύριον καὶ τοὺς προφήτας. "Both the Lord and
the prophets." καί ... καί correlates the substantives. The
"prophets" are not Christian but Hebrew (Rom. 1² 3²¹ 11³). By
separating τὸν κύριον from Ἰησοῦν, Paul succeeds in emphasising that the Lord of glory whom the Jews crucified (1 Cor. 2⁸)
is none other than the historical Jesus, their kinsman according
to the flesh (Rom. 9⁵).

> That the first two καί are correlative is the view of Ell. Lft. Dob.
> *et al.* and is confirmed by 1 Cor. 10³². Flatt, De W. Lillie, Auberlen,
> Lün. Schmiedel, *et al.*, interpret the first καί to mean "also." Erasmus
> and Schmidt translate "not only the Lord and the prophets but also us."
> —Some comm. take τοὺς προφήτας with ἐκδιωξάντων. Since, however,
> ἀποκτείνειν, a rare word in Paul, is used literally by him only here and
> Rom. 11³ = 3 Reg. 19¹⁰ (τοὺς προφήτας σου ἀπέκτειναν), the construc-
> tion with ἀποκτεινάντων suggested by the καί correlative is preferable,

apart from the consideration that the argument would be weakened were προφήτας attached to ἐκδιωξάντων (cf. Lk. 13³⁴ = Mt. 23³⁷).—For τῶν καί with participle, we might have had οἱ καί with finite verb (Rom. 8³⁴ 16⁷). On ἀποκτείνειν of the death of Jesus, cf. Acts 3¹⁵; also σταυροῦν (Acts 2³⁶ 4¹⁰ I Cor. 2⁸) and ἀναιρεῖν (Acts 2²³, etc.). On ὁ κύριος Ἰησοῦς, cf. 4² II 1⁷ 2⁸ I Cor. 16²³ 2 Cor. 4¹⁴ 11³¹ Eph. 1¹⁵ Phile. 5. According to Tert. (adv. Marc. 5¹⁵), Marcion prefixed ἰδίους to προφήτας (so KL, et al.), thus making the reference to the Hebrew prophets unmistakable.

καὶ ἡμᾶς ἐκδιωξάντων. "And persecuted us." It is uncertain whether ἐκδιώκειν here means "persecute" or "banish"; it is likewise uncertain whether the aorist indicates a single act of ἐκδιώκειν or a series of acts taken collectively. The word would recall to the readers the harassing experiences of Paul and his associates (ἡμᾶς) in Thessalonica and perhaps also in Berœa.

Ell. emphasises the semi-local meaning of ἐκ, and renders "drive out"; he sees a specific allusion to Acts 17¹⁰. But ἐκδιώκειν may be equivalent to διώκειν, as the use of these words and of καταδιώκειν in Lxx. suggests (cf. Kennedy, Sources, 37).

καὶ θεῷ μὴ ἀρεσκόντων κτλ. This present participle and the succeeding ἐναντίων (sc. ὄντων) state the constant obstinate attitude of the Jews to God and men, a statement to be understood in the light of the explanatory κωλυόντων κτλ. (v. ¹⁶), added without καί. The Jews please not God by resisting his purpose to save the Gentiles; they oppose all men not, as Tacitus (Hist. 5⁵) and others have it, in being *adversus omnes alios hostile odium*, but in being against the best interests of humanity, namely, their salvation. It is not talking to the Gentiles that the Jews are hindering but the talking to them with a view to their salvation (cf. Acts 17⁶ ᶠᶠ·), the λαλεῖν τὸ εὐαγγέλιον τοῦ θεοῦ (v. ²) εἰς περιποίησιν σωτηρίας (5⁹).

On Tacitus and the Jews, cf. Th. Reinach, *Textes Relatifs au Judaïsme*, 1895, 295 ff. ἐναντίος is rarely used of persons in the Gk. Bib. (cf. Num. 1⁵³ (AF) 2² and I Esd. 8⁵¹ πρὸς τοὺς ἐναντίους ἡμῖν). On ἀρέσκειν, see v. ⁴; on πάντες ἄνθρωποι, cf. Rom. 12¹⁷ ᶠ· I Cor. 15¹⁹ 2 Cor. 3² Phil. 4⁵, etc.; κωλύειν, I Cor. 14³⁹; λαλεῖν ἵνα, I Cor. 14¹⁹; ἵνα σωθῶσιν, I Cor. 10³³.—σώζειν and σωτηρία (5⁸⁻⁹ II 2¹³) are Jewish terms borrowed by the early Christians to designate the blessings of the age to come under the rule of God the Father. To Paul this salvation is future, though

near at hand (*cf.* Rom. 13¹¹); but there are foretastes of the future glory
in the present experience of those who possess the Spirit (Rom. 8²³), and
thus belong to the class "the saved" (1 Cor. 1¹⁸ 2 Cor. 2¹⁵; contrast
II 2¹⁰ οἱ ἀπολλύμενοι). σώζειν need not be negative except when ἀπὸ τῆς
ὀργῆς (Rom. 5⁹) or the like is mentioned (see on 1¹⁰).

εἰς τὸ ἀναπληρῶσαι κτλ. They killed both Jesus and the
prophets, they persecuted Paul and his fellow-missionaries, they
are hindering the Gentile mission, with the distinct purpose (εἰς
τό—not on their part but on God's part) of filling up the measure of their sins (B carelessly omits τὰς ἁμαρτίας) always.
Grammatically, εἰς τό with infin. (see v. ¹²) may denote either
purpose or conceived result; logically it may here denote purpose, for what is in result is to Paul also in purpose. The obstinacy of the Jews is viewed as an element in the divine plan.

> The metaphor underlying ἀναπληρῶσαι is to be found in the Lxx.
> (*cf.* Gen. 15¹⁶ Dan. 8²³ 2 Mac. 6¹⁴). A definite measure of sins is being
> filled up continually by each act of sin, in accordance with the divine
> decree. The aorist infin. is future in reference to the participles in the
> preceding context, but the tense of the infin. itself indicates neither action
> in progress nor action completed; it is indefinite like a substantive. The
> infinitive rather than the noun (*cf.* 2 Mac. 6¹⁴ πρὸς ἐκπλήρωσιν ἁμαρτιῶν)
> is chosen in reference to πάντοτε, the point of the adverb being the con-
> tinual filling up. This πάντοτε ἀναπληρῶσαι, while logically progressive,
> is regarded by the aorist collectively, a series of ἀναπληρῶσαι being
> taken as one (*cf. BMT.* 39).

ἔφθασεν δὲ ἐπ' αὐτούς κτλ. "But the wrath has come upon
them at last." ἡ ὀργή (that is, as DG, Vulg. explain, ἡ ὀργὴ τοῦ
θεοῦ; see 1¹⁰) is not so much the purposed or merited wrath (*cf.*
Sap. 19⁴) as the well-known principle of the wrath of God which
is revealed (Rom. 1¹⁸) in the ends of the ages (1 Cor. 10¹¹) in
which Paul lives, and which is shortly to be expressed in the
day of wrath (Rom. 2⁵). In view of the eschatological bearing
of ἡ ὀργή, the reference in ἔφθασεν (= ἦλθεν), notwithstanding ἡ ὀργὴ ἡ ἐρχομένη (1¹⁰), cannot be to a series of punish-
ments in the past (*cf.* the catena of Corderius on Jn. 3³⁶ in
Orig. (Berlin ed.) IV, 526: τὰς ἐπελθούσας ἐπ' αὐτοὺς θεη-
λάτους τιμωρίας); nor to a specific event in the past, whether
the loss of Jewish independence, or the famine (Acts 11²⁸), or

8

the banishment from Rome (Acts 18²; *cf.* Schmidt, 86–90); nor quite to the destruction of Jerusalem, even if Paul shared the view that the day of judgment was to be simultaneous with the destruction of Jerusalem; but must be simply to the day of judgment which is near at hand. ἔφθασεν is accordingly proleptic. Instead of speaking of that day as coming upon the sons of disobedience (Eph. 5⁶), he speaks of it as at last arrived. Such a proleptic use of the aorist is natural in a prophetic passage and has its analogy in the Lxx. (Dob. notes Hos. 9² ᶠ· 10⁵).

In the N. T. φθάνειν occurs, apart from Mt. 12²⁸ = Lk. 11²⁰, only in Paul, and is always equivalent to ἔρχεσθαι except in I 4¹⁵ where it is synonymous with προφθάνειν (Mt. 17²⁵). In the Lxx. it means regularly "to come"; occasionally "to anticipate" (Sap. 6¹³ 16²⁸; *cf.* 4⁷ Sir. 30²⁵). Elsewhere in Paul, φθάνειν is construed with εἰς (Rom. 9³¹ Phil. 3¹⁶; *cf.* Dan. (Th.) 4¹⁷· ¹⁹ 6²⁴ 12¹²) and ἄχρι (2 Cor. 10¹⁴). For ἐπί, *cf.* Mt. 12²⁸ = Lk. 11²⁰; Judg. 20³⁴· ⁴² Eccl. 8¹ᵃ (ἐπί and πρός) Dan. (Th.) 4²¹· ²⁵; for ἕως, *cf.* 2 Ch. 28⁹ Dan. (Th.) 4⁸ 7¹³ 8⁷.—For the use of the English perfect in translating the Greek aorist, *cf.* *BMT*. 46.

εἰς τέλος. "At last." That the temporal meaning of εἰς τέλος is here intended and that too not in the sense of "continually," "forever," but, as ἔφθασεν demands, "at last" is evident from the parallelism of the clauses:

ἀναπληρῶσαι   αὐτῶν   τὰς ἁμαρτίας   πάντοτε.
ἔφθασεν   ἐπ᾽ αὐτοὺς   ἡ ὀργὴ   εἰς τέλος.

For εἰς τέλος = *postremo*, *cf.* Stephanus, *Thes.* col. 9224. In the Lxx. εἰς τέλος (apart from εἰς τὸ τέλος of many Psalms and of Josh. 3¹⁶ F) is used both intensively "utterly," "completely," and temporally "forever" (Ps. 48¹⁰; *cf.* εἰς τὸν αἰῶνα as a variant reading (Ps. 9¹⁹) or as a parallel (Ps. 76⁷ 102⁹) of εἰς τέλος); but the translation "at last" is in no single case beyond question. In Gen. 46⁴ = Amos 9⁸, εἰς τέλος represents the so-called Hebrew infin. abs. (*cf.* Thackeray, *Gram. O. T. Greek*, I, 47, note 1). In Lk. 18⁵ "forever" = "continually" is equally possible with "finally." The difficulties in rendering εἰς τέλος may be observed in any attempted translation of 2 Clem. 19³ Ign. Eph. 14² Rom. 1¹ 10¹. In our passage, however, πάντοτε demands the temporal sense and that, too, because of ἔφθασεν, "at last."—When εἰς τέλος is taken intensively, ἔφθασεν is joined both with ἐπί and εἰς, and ὀργῆς is tacitly supplied after τέλος (*cf.* Job 23⁷ Ezek. 36¹⁰); or αὐτῶν is supplied after εἰς τέλος "to make an end of them" (De W.); or ἡ is supplied

before εἰς τέλος (the article could easily be omitted; *cf.* 2 Cor. 7⁷ 9¹³),
"the wrath which is extreme"; or πάντοτε is taken loosely for πάντως,
παντελῶς (Dob.). For a conspectus of opinions, see either Lillie or
Poole.—The reading of B Vulg. f is to be observed: ἐφθ. δὲ ἡ ὀργὴ
ἐπ᾽ αὐτοὺς εἰς τέλος. With this order, we may translate either "the
wrath has come upon them at last" or "the wrath which was against
them has come to its height" (*cf.* 2 Mac. 6¹⁵ πρὸς τέλος τῶν ἁμαρτιῶν
and 6¹⁴ πρὸς ἐκπλήρωσιν τῶν ἁμαρτιῶν; also Sap. 12²⁷ τὸ τέρμα τῆς κα-
ταδίκης ἐπ᾽ αὐτοὺς ἐπῆλθεν; and 2 Mac. 7³⁸). In the latter translation, φθάνειν is construed with εἰς as in Rom. 9³¹ Phil. 3¹⁶. The order
of B is, however, probably not original; it inverts for emphasis as in 5⁹
ἔθετο ὁ θεὸς ἡμᾶς (Zim.); furthermore the parallelism with v. ¹⁶ᶠ· is
broken. The reading ἔφθακεν (BD) makes explicit the prophetic sense
of ἔφθασεν; there is a similar variant in 1 Mac. 10²³ Cant. 2¹².—If the
literal sense of ἔφθασεν is insisted upon, and if of the many possible
references to the past the destruction of Jerusalem is singled out, then
either the entire letter is spurious (Baur, *Paulus*,² II, 97) or the clause
ἔφθασεν . . . τέλος is an interpolation inserted after 70 A.D. (*cf.* Schmiedel,
ad loc. and Moff. *Introd.* 73). In view of the naturalness of a proleptic aorist in a prophetic passage, the hypothesis of interpolation is
unnecessary (*cf.* Dob. and Clemen, *Paulus*, I, 114).

Relation of v. ¹⁶ᶜ *to Test. xii, Levi* 6¹¹. That notwithstanding the textual
variations there is a literary relation between our clause and Levi 6¹¹ is
generally admitted. But that Levi 6¹¹ is original to Levi is still debated.
Charles in his editions of the Test. xii (1908), following Grabe (*Spicileg.*
1700,² I, 138), holds that 6¹¹ is an integral part of the original text of Levi
and that Paul quotes it. The text which Charles prints (ἔφθασεν δὲ αὐτοὺς ἡ ὀργὴ τοῦ θεοῦ εἰς τέλος) is supported by c h (om. αὐτούς) i
and a e f (except that these three read not τοῦ θεοῦ but κυρίου), and
is apparently to be translated: "but the wrath of God has forestalled
them completely." In his English version Charles has: "but the wrath
of God came upon them to the uttermost," a translation that seems to
presuppose the text of b d g and the first Slavonic recension (d omits δέ
and prefixes διὰ τοῦτο; b S¹ invert the order to read: ἔφθασεν δὲ ἡ ὀργὴ
κυρίου ἐπ᾽ αὐτοὺς εἰς τέλος).—In favour of the view that Levi 6¹¹ in
some form is original to Levi, it is urged (1) that this passage, unlike 4⁴
ad fin. (where both Charles and Burkitt admit a Christian interpolation, although some form of ἀνασκολοπίζειν is attested), is not specifically Christian and hence is not likely to be an interpolation; and
(2) that 6¹¹ is prepared for by 6⁷ ᶠᶠ· where Levi sees that the ἀπόφασις
θεοῦ ἦν εἰς κακά against Shechem and the Shechemites. On this theory
Paul quotes Levi 6¹¹ from memory.—In favour of the view that Levi 6¹¹
is a Christian interpolation from Paul, it is urged (1) that the striking
parallelism of members already observed between our clause and v. ¹⁶ᵇ
points to the originality of v. ¹⁶ᶜ with Paul; (2) that the textual varia-

tions in Levi reflect those in Paul; for example, (a) ἡ ὀργή, which is used absolutely by Paul in a technical sense, does not appear in Test. xii, while ἡ ὀργὴ τοῦ θεοῦ is found both in Levi 6¹¹ and Reuben 4⁴; to be sure in Paul DEGF, Vulg. add τοῦ θεοῦ, but not ℵBAPKL (CH are wanting); (b) in b, S¹ of Levi 6¹¹, the order of words is that of B f Vulg. of Paul; (c) six of the nine Gk. Mss. of Levi (c h i a e f) omit the ἐπ', a reading similar to that of the catena of Corderius already noted: ἔφθασεν δὲ αὐτοὺς ἡ ὀργὴ εἰς τέλος; and (d) above all, the first Armenian recension omits Levi 6¹¹ altogether. (That εἰς τέλος is used absolutely in Test. xii elsewhere only in the poorly attested Levi 5⁶ is not significant, in the light of the frequent use of εἰς τέλος in the Lxx.). According to this theory, Levi 6¹¹, instead of being the original which Paul quotes, is an interpolation from Paul (the various Greek forms of the interpolation being influenced largely by the variants in Paul), and is thus an early witness to the presence in Paul of v. ¹⁶ ᶜ (Dob.).

The question may be considered as still unsettled. Conybeare (*RTP.* 1908, 375) seems to agree with Charles; Burkitt (*JTS.* 1908, 138) and Plummer (*Matthew*, 1909, xlvi) dissent; as does also Dob. (48), who, however, prefers (115) to leave it, in the present state of investigation, "*ganz unsicher*." Lock (*HDB.* IV, 746a) surmises that the "use of the phrase in the *Test. xii Patr.* perhaps shows that it was a half-stereotyped rabbinical formula for declaring God's judgment," but does not adduce any rabbinical parallels. Rönsch (*ZWT.* 1875, 278 *ff.*), according to Dob., finds the origin of both Levi 6¹¹ and our verse in a divergent conception of Gen. 35⁴ ᶠ· (*cf.* also Jub. 30²⁶). Burkitt (*op. cit.*) regards the text of Levi as "a Christian interpolation or at any rate as having been modified in language by the translator or by an editor who was familiar with 1 Thess."

(4) *The Intended Visit* (2¹⁷⁻²⁰).

These verses are to be joined closely to the succeeding sections of the epistolary thanksgiving, viz., the sending of Timothy (3¹⁻⁵), his return with a report on the whole favourable, though there were some deficiencies in their faith (3⁶⁻¹⁰), and the prayer that the apostles might be able to come back to Thessalonica (3¹¹⁻¹³). The emphasis upon the fact that they wanted to return, that Satan was the only power to hinder them, that Timothy, the trusted companion, is sent to take their place, and that they are praying God and Christ to direct their way to them, intimates rather strongly that 2¹⁷⁻3¹³, with its warm expressions of personal affection, is an apology for Paul's failure to return (*cf.* especially Calv.), prompted by the fact that the Jews (vv. [15-16]) had insinuated that he did not return because he did not want to return, did not care for his converts, an assertion which had made an impression on the warm-hearted and sensitive Thessalonians, in that it seemed to lend some colour to the criticism of Paul's conduct during his visit.

Although 2[17]–3[10] is a unit, we subdivide for convenience as follows: The Intended Visit (2[17-20]); The Sending of Timothy (3[1-5]); and Timothy's Return and Report (3[6-10]).

To allay their doubts, the readers are reminded (vv. [17-20]) that the apostles from the very moment that they had been bereaved of them were excessively anxious to see them, that Paul especially, the centre of the Jews' attack, had wished, and that too repeatedly, to see their faces again. Indeed, nothing less than Satan could have deterred them. Far from not caring for them, the missionaries insist, in language broken with emotion, on their eagerness to return, for is it not, they ask, above all, the Thessalonians who are the object of their glory and joy both now and in that day when the converts, having finished their race, will receive the victor's chaplet.

[17]*Now we, brothers, when we had been bereaved of you for a short time only, out of sight but not out of mind, were excessively anxious to see your faces with great desire,* [18]*for we did wish to come to you—certainly I Paul did, and that too repeatedly—and yet Satan stopped us.* [19]*For who is our hope or joy or chaplet to boast in—or is it not you too—in the presence of our Lord Jesus when he comes?* [20]*Indeed it is really you who are our glory and our joy.*

17. ἡμεῖς δέ. While δέ introduces a new point in the letter, the apology for his absence, it is also adversative, introducing a contrast not with ὑμεῖς (v. [14]) but with the Jews (vv. [15-16]; so Lün.). Over against the insinuation that Paul did not wish to return, that his absence meant out of mind as well as out of sight, he assures the distressed readers, with an affectionate address (ἀδελφοί), that he had been bereaved of them (ἀπορφανισθέντες is temporal, not both causal and temporal) only for a moment, a bodily absence that did not betoken forgetful-

ness, when he and his companions were excessively anxious to
return.

ἀπορφανισθέντες. Paul is not only τροφός (v. ⁷), νήπιος (v. ⁷),
and πατήρ (v. ¹¹), but also, if with Th. Mops. we press the metaphor here, ὀρφανός; for although ὀρφανός is used "with some
latitude of reference" (Ell. who notes *inter alia* Plato, *Phaed.*
239 E), yet the specific reference is here quite pertinent, as Chrys.
insists: "He says not χωρισθέντες ὑμῶν, not διασπασθέντες
ὑμῶν, not διαστάντες, not ἀπολειφέντες, but ἀπορφανισθέντες
ὑμῶν. He sought for a word that might fitly indicate his mental
anguish. Though standing in the relation of a father to them all,
he yet utters the language of orphan children that have prematurely lost their parent" (quoted by Lillie, *ad loc.*).

ἀπορφανίζεσθαι is found only here in Gk. Bib. Wetstein notes it
in Æschylus, *Choeph.* 247 (249). ὀρφανίζεσθαι (not in Gk. Bib.) takes
the gen. The ἀπό with ὑμῶν is in lieu of a gen. of separation; *cf.* 2 Clem.
2³: ἔρημος ἀπὸ τοῦ θεοῦ, and Bl. 40³.—ἀδελφοί frequently as here (*cf.* 2¹
4¹· ¹⁰· ¹³ 5¹· ¹²· ²⁵) but not always (1⁴ 2⁹· ¹⁴ 3⁷ 5⁴) marks the beginning of
a new section.

πρὸς καιρὸν ὥρας. This idiomatic expression for a very short
time is to be connected closely with ἀπορφανισθέντες. Calvin
observes: "It is not to be wondered at if a long interval should
give rise to weariness or sadness, but our feeling of attachment
must be strong when we find it difficult to wait even a very short
time." And the reason for the emphasis is that the Jews had
insinuated that Paul had no intention to return, no affection to
inspire such an intention.

The phrase πρὸς καιρὸν ὥρας, only here in Gk. Bib. appears to com-
bine the classic πρὸς καιρόν (1 Cor. 7⁵ Lk. 8¹³; Pr. 5³ Sap. 4⁴) and the
later πρὸς ὥραν (2 Cor. 7⁸ Gal. 2⁵ Phile. 15 Jn. 5³⁵); it is perhaps a Latinism in the κοινή; *cf. momento horae.*

προσώπῳ οὐ καρδίᾳ. "In face not in heart"; physically but
not in interest; "out of sight not out of mind" (Ruther.). The
phrase is interjected in view of the assertion of the Jews that
Paul's absence is intentional not enforced.

We have not τῷ σώματι οὐκ ἐν πνεύματι (cf. 1 Cor. 5³), not τῇ σαρκὶ οὐ τῷ πνεύματι (cf. Col. 2⁵), but, as in 2 Cor. 5¹², προσώπῳ οὐ καρδίᾳ. On the idea, cf. 1 Reg. 16⁷: ἄνθρωπος ὄψεται εἰς πρόσωπον ὁ δὲ θεὸς εἰς καρδίαν.

περισσοτέρως ἐσπουδάσαμεν κτλ. No sooner had we been separated than we became "anxious out of measure to see your face with passionate desire" (Ruther.). The verb receives two parallel modifiers, περισσοτέρως, in the elative sense of "excessively," and ἐν πολλῇ ἐπιθυμίᾳ. The repetition of a similar idea and the resumption of ἐσπουδάσαμεν in ἠθελήσαμεν (v. ¹⁸) serve to indicate not tautology, and not simply intensity of affection, but a tacit defence of Paul against the slanders of the Jews.

Since in later Gk. the comparative tends to usurp the function of the superlative, while the superlative tends to become an emphatic positive (Bl. 11³; Moult. I, 78, 236), it is probable that περισσοτέρως is here not comparative but elative as in 2 Cor. 7¹³ (περισσοτέρως μᾶλλον) and 7¹⁵ (where Bachmann (in Zahn's Komm.) notes a similar use in BGU, 380¹⁰). περισσῶς does not occur in Paul; περισσοτέρως is found chiefly in Paul (cf. 2 Cor.).—Interpreters who hold strictly to the comparative force of περισσοτέρως explain the meaning variously (see Lillie, ad loc.). (1) "The more fervently did we endeavour, as knowing the perils that beset you" (Fromond, Hofmann, Schmidt, Schmiedel); (2) the love of the apostles "instead of being lessened by absence was rather the more inflamed thereby" (Calvin, Lillie, Lft.); (3) "the repeated frustration of his attempts to get back to Thessalonica, far from deterring Paul from his intention, have rather still more stirred up his longing and increased his exertion to visit the believers in Thessalonica" (Born.; cf. Find. Wohl. Mill.).—Other expositors, taking περισσοτέρως as elative, find the reference in the confidence of Paul that the separation being external cannot in God's purpose be for long, a fact that prompts the eagerness to overcome the separation (cf. Dob. who refers to Phil. 1¹⁴· ²⁵).—σπουδάζειν (Gal. 2¹⁰ Eph. 4³) is always in the N. T. and occasionally in the Lxx. (Judith 13¹· ¹² Is. 21³) construed with the infinitive. τὸ πρόσωπον ὑμῶν ἰδεῖν (3¹⁰; cf. Col. 2¹ 1 Mac. 7³⁰) = ὑμᾶς ἰδεῖν (3⁶; Rom. 1¹¹ 1 Cor. 16⁷, etc.), as in P. Par. 47 (Witk. 64).—ἐπιθυμία is used here and Phil. 1²³ in a good sense. On πολλῇ, see on 1⁵. The phrase ἐν πολλῇ ἐπιθυμίᾳ is not the cognate dative (Lk. 22¹⁵ Gal. 5¹?), though this dative is common in Lxx. and occasional in classic Gk. (cf. Conybeare and Stock, Septuagint, 60–61). Note the various expressions of desire: σπουδάζειν, ἐπιθυμία, θέλειν, εὐδοκεῖν (3¹) and ἐπιποθεῖν (3⁶).

18. διότι ἠθελήσαμεν κτλ. "For we did wish to come to you." ἐσπουδάσαμεν becomes ἠθελήσαμεν and τὸ πρόσωπον ἰδεῖν becomes ἐλθεῖν πρὸς ὑμᾶς; the parallel expressions are virtually synonymous. The repetition is purposed, for he is defending himself and his associates; hence also he adds, "and Satan stopped us." Inasmuch, however, as the Jews had singled out Paul as the chief offender, he interjects ἐγὼ μὲν Παῦλος, καὶ ἅπαξ καὶ δίς. In the light of ἅπαξ καὶ δίς (Deut. 9¹³ 1 Reg. 17³⁹ Neh. 13²⁰ 1 Mac. 3³⁰), the first καί may be ascensive, and the interjected phrase as a whole be translated: "Certainly I Paul did (ἠθέλησα ἐλθεῖν) wish to come, and that too repeatedly."

διότι here as v. ⁸ is not "wherefore" (διό; so DᶜEKL) but "because"; a comma suffices after ἐπιθυμίᾳ. θέλειν (cf. 4¹³ II 3¹⁰ 1 Cor. 16⁷) occurs in Paul about twelve times as often as βούλεσθαι. In Paul it is difficult to distinguish between them, though θέλειν seems to pass into "wish," while βούλεσθαι remains in the realm of "deliberate plan." Had Paul here intended to emphasise distinct deliberation, he would probably have used βούλεσθαι as in 2 Cor. 1¹⁵. The actual resolve following σπουδάζειν and θέλειν comes first in ηὐδοκήσαμεν (3¹).—μέν occurs in every letter of Paul except II and Phile.; in about one-third of the instances it is *solitarium*.—Apart from the superscriptions and the ἀσπασμός (II 3¹⁷ 1 Cor. 16²¹ Col. 4¹⁸; cf. Phile. 19), Παῦλος appears in every letter of Paul except Rom. and Phil.—For ἐγὼ μέν, cf. 1 Cor. 5³; for ἐγὼ Παῦλος, 2 Cor. 10¹ Gal. 5² Eph. 3¹ Col. 1²³ Phile. 19.

The meaning of καὶ ἅπαξ καὶ δίς, a collocation found in Gk. Bib. only here, Phil. 4¹⁶ and Neh. 13²⁰ (א ᶜ· ᵃ; the correct reading is ἅπαξ καὶ δίς), is uncertain. Usually the four words are taken together to mean an indefinite succession of occurrences, "often," "repeatedly" (e. g. Grot. Pelt, Lft. Wohl. Dob.), or else, definitely (cf. Herod. II, 121, III, 148, cited by Wetstein on Phil. 4¹⁶ and Plato, *Phaed.* 63 E *init.*: καὶ δὶς καὶ τρίς= "both twice and thrice"), "both once and twice, that is, twice" (Mill.). Zahn, indeed (*Introd.* I, 204 f.; cf. Find.), conjectures that Paul attempted to return first when in Berœa and a second time when waiting in Athens for Silvanus and Timothy. In the Lxx., however, we have simply ἅπαξ καὶ δίς which in Deut. 9¹³ 1 Reg. 17³⁹ and Neh. 13²⁰ invites the translation "often," "repeatedly," and which in 1 Mac. 3³⁰ (ὡς ἅπαξ καὶ δίς) appears to mean καθὼς ἀεί, "as usual." Similar is the recurring phrase ὡς ἅπαξ καὶ ἅπαξ (1 Reg. 3¹⁰ 20²⁵ Judg. 16²⁰ 20³⁰· ³¹) which seems to mean καθὼς ἀεί (Judg. 16²⁰ A) or κατὰ τὸ εἰωθός (Num. 24¹). If the phrase in our passage is not καὶ ἅπαξ καὶ δίς but ἅπαξ καὶ δίς, then the first καί is ascensive: "and (καί) what is more, repeatedly (ἅπαξ καὶ δίς)"; and light is thrown on Phil. 4¹⁶: ὅτι καὶ ἐν Θεσσαλονίκῃ καὶ ἅπαξ καὶ δὶς εἰς τὴν χρείαν μοι ἐπέμψατε, which is to be rendered not, "for even in Thessalonica ye sent once and again unto my need," but, taking καὶ . . . καὶ correlatively (cf. Ewald, ad loc., in Zahn's Komm.), "for both (when I was) in Thessalonica and (καὶ) repeatedly (ἅπαξ καὶ δίς) (when I was in other places) you sent to my need." The point of Phil. 4¹⁶ is thus not that the Philippians sent help frequently to Paul in Thessalonica but simply sent help to him there (probably on their own initiative) and frequently elsewhere.

καὶ ἐνέκοψεν ἡμᾶς ὁ Σατανᾶς. "We were anxious to see you, we did wish to come to you, and yet Satan stopped us" (ἡμᾶς, that is, Paul and his two associates). The context gives an adversative turn to the copula (Vulg. sed). What particular obstacle Satan put in the way of their return, Paul does not tell us. Satan, however, did not thwart all of them permanently; they are able to send one of their number, Timothy, from Athens; and they are confident that God and Christ, to whom they pray (3¹¹) will direct their way to Thessalonica.

The reference to the work of Satan has been variously interpreted. (1) The illness of Paul is thought of as in 2 Cor. 12⁷ (so Simon, Die Psychologie des Apostels Paulus, 1897, 63). But as Everling remarks (Die paulinische Angelologie und Dämonologie, 1888, 74), the theory of illness does not fit Silvanus and Timothy. (2) Satan prevented them from returning in order to destroy the spiritual life of the converts and thus rob Paul of his joy in their chaplet of victory at the Parousia (so Kabisch, Die Eschatologie des Paulus, 1893, 27 f.). But as Dibelius (Die Geisterwelt im Glauben des Paulus, 1909, 56) observes, the chaplet of victory will be theirs if they continue steadfast under persecution; and furthermore, to make the victory sure, Paul himself need not return to Thessalonica (cf. 3¹¹⁻¹³). (3) Satan inspired the Politarchs to compel Jason and his friends to give bonds for the continued absence of Paul (so Ramsay, St. Paul the Traveller, 240; McGiffert, Apostolic Age, 249; Find. and others). This explanation, however, "renders it difficult to see why the Thessalonians did not understand at once how Paul could not return" (Moff.), and takes the force out of the insinuations of the Jews. (4) Hence it is safer to leave the reference indefinite as Paul does (Everling, Dibelius, Mill.), or at most to think of "the exigencies of his mission at the time being" (Moff.).

ἐνκόπτειν occurs in Gk. Bib. elsewhere only Gal. 5⁷ Acts 24⁴; ἐνκόπτεσθαι only Rom. 15²² 1 Pet. 3⁷. GF here and some minuscules in Gal. 5⁷ read ἀνέκοψεν (Sap. 18²³ 4 Mac. 13⁶; cf. 1³⁵ ℵ). The Satan of Job,

Zech. and 1 Ch. 21¹ is rendered in Lxx. by (ὁ) διάβολος except Job 2³ (A)
which like Sir. 21²⁷ has ὁ Σατανᾶς. For Σατάν, cf. 3 Reg. 11¹⁴· ²³. In Paul,
ὁ Σατανᾶς (II 2⁹; always with article except 2 Cor. 12⁷) is ὁ πειράζων
(3⁵), ὁ πονηρός (II 3²), ὁ θεὸς τοῦ αἰῶνος τούτου (2 Cor. 4⁴), ὁ ἄρχων τῆς
ἐξουσίας τοῦ ἀέρος, τοῦ πνεύματος τοῦ νῦν ἐνεργοῦντος ἐν τοῖς υἱοῖς τῆς
ἀπειθίας (Eph. 2²). On demonology in general, cf. Bousset, Relig.²
381 ff. and J. Weiss in PRE. IV, 408 ff.; in Paul, the works of Everling and Dibelius noted above.

19-20. τίς γὰρ ἡμῶν κτλ. In reply to the insinuation that
he does not return because he does not care for his converts, Paul
insists, with a compliment to their excellence, that he wanted
to come to them because they are really his glory and his joy.
As he thinks of them now and as he looks forward to the day when
Jesus is to come, when the Christian race in over, and the Thessalonians receive the triumphant wreath, he sees in them his
hope and joy, and in their victory his ground of boasting. His
words are broken with emotion: "For (γάρ introducing the motive of the ardent desire to return) who is our hope and joy and
chaplet of boasting?" The answer is given in v. ²⁰; but Paul
anticipates by an interjected affirmative question: "Or is it not
you as well as (καί) my other converts?" The καί before ὑμεῖς
is significant (cf. Chrys.): "Can you imagine that the Jews are
right in asserting that we do not care for you as well as for our
other converts?" This said, he finishes the original question
with the emphasis more on hope than on joy: "before our Lord
Jesus when he comes?" And finally he repeats the answer implied in ἢ οὐχὶ καὶ ὑμεῖς, but without καί, in v. ²⁰: "Indeed
(γάρ = certe, as Calvin notes) it is really (ἐστε) you who are our
glory and our joy."

τίς = "who" (Rom. 8³⁵); on τίς γάρ, cf. 1 Cor. 2¹¹ 4⁷ 2¹⁶ = Rom. 11³⁴.
As the hope is present, ἐστι is to be supplied; ἡμῶν goes with the three
nominatives. ἤ is usually disjunctive but sometimes the equivalent of
a copula (Bl. 77¹¹); it appears in all the Pauline letters; cf. ἢ οὐκ οἴδατε
(Rom. 11² 1 Cor. 6² ff.) or ἐπιγινώσκετε (2 Cor. 13⁵); ℵ here omits ἤ.
οὐχί is used frequently by Paul, chiefly in interrogative sentences (cf.
Rom. 3²⁹).—στέφανος (Phil. 4¹; 2 Tim. 4⁸ 1 Cor. 9²⁵) is here not the
royal crown (2 Reg. 12³⁰ 1 Ch. 20² Zech. 6¹¹· ¹⁴ Ps. 20³; see Mayor on
Jas. 1¹² and Swete on Mk. 15¹⁷ Rev. 2¹⁰) but the victor's wreath or
chaplet; Deiss. (Light, 312) notes a second-century A.D. inscription in the

theatre at Ephesus: ἠγωνίσατο ἀγῶνας τρεῖς, ἐστέφη δύο. καυχήσεως (obj. gen.) is the act of boasting. עֲטֶרֶת הַפְאָרֶת is rendered variously in Lxx.: στέφανος καυχήσεως (Ezek. 16¹² 23⁴² Pr. 16³¹), τρυφῆς (Pr. 4⁹), κάλλους (Is. 62³), δόξης (Jer. 13¹⁸) and ἀγαλλιάματος (Sir. 6³¹; so A in our passage).

ἔμπροσθεν κτλ. Paul's hope for his converts will be realised when they come "before our Lord Jesus," that is, ἔμπροσθεν τοῦ βήματος τοῦ Χριστοῦ (2 Cor. 5¹⁰; cf. 1 Thess. 1³ 3¹³ and contrast 3⁹), as ἐν τῇ παρουσίᾳ αὐτοῦ explains. When Jesus comes, arrives, is present, they will receive not ὀργή (as the Jews of v. ¹⁶) but σωτηρία (5⁹).

παρουσία is used untechnically in 1 Cor. 16¹⁷ 2 Cor. 7⁶⁻⁷ 10¹⁰ Phil. 1²⁶ 2¹² (cf. Neh. 2⁶ Judith 10¹⁸ 2 Mac. 8¹² 5²¹ 3 Mac. 3¹⁷). Whether the technical use (2¹⁹ 3¹³ 4¹⁵ 5²³ II 2¹. ⁸ 1 Cor. 15²³; cf. below II 2⁹ of ὁ ἄνομος) is a creation of the early church (Mill. 145 ff.; Dibelius) or is taken over from an earlier period (Dob.) is uncertain. (Test. xii, Jud. 22³ ἕως τῆς παρουσίας θεοῦ τῆς δικαιοσύνης is omitted by the Armenian; cf. Charles). Deiss. (Light, 372 ff.) notes that in the Eastern world παρουσία is almost technical for the arrival or visit of a king (cf. also Mt. 21⁵ Zech. 9⁹ Mal. 3¹) and that while the earthly king expected on his arrival to receive a στέφανος παρουσίας, Christ gives a στέφανος to believers ἐν τῇ παρουσίᾳ αὐτοῦ.—ὁ κύριος ἡμῶν Ἰησοῦς (3¹¹. ¹³ II 1⁸ Rom. 16²⁰ 1 Cor. 5⁴ 2 Cor. 1¹⁴) is less frequent in Paul than ὁ κύριος ἡμῶν Ἰ. Χ. (1³ 5⁹. ²³. ²⁸ II 2¹. ¹⁴. ¹⁶ 3¹⁸ Rom. 5¹. ¹¹ 15⁶. ³⁰ 1 Cor. 2². ⁷ ff. 15⁵⁷ 2 Cor. 1³ 8⁹ Gal. 6¹⁴. ¹⁸ Eph. 1³. ¹⁷ 5²⁰ 6²⁴ Col. 1³); hence GF add here Χριστοῦ.

ὑμεῖς γάρ ἐστέ κτλ. "Indeed it is really you who are the objects of our honour and our joy." ἐστε is significantly expressed, not to contrast the present with the future (Flatt; see Lillie, ad loc.) or with the past, but to contrast the reality of Paul's affection for his converts with the falsity of the insinuations of the Jews. χαρά is repeated from v. ¹⁹. δόξα is new, and may mean "glory" or "honour." In the latter case, the point may be that he does not demand honour from them (v. ⁶) but does them honour.

(5) *The Sending of Timothy* (3¹⁻⁵).

Although Satan had frustrated the immediate realisation of their desire to return, he was unable either to quench that desire (3^{11}) or to prevent the sending at least of Timothy. It is probable, as Calvin has observed, that vv. $^{1-5}$ are apologetic, but precisely what the situation is to which Paul speaks is uncertain. We may suppose that the Jews had alleged not only that the missionaries, and Paul in particular (2^{18} 3^5), had purposely left the converts in the lurch with no intention of returning, but also that the fact of Gentile persecution was evidence of the false character of the gospel preached (see on v. ^{14}). Reports of these slanders may have reached Paul and stimulated his eagerness to return. Unable himself to go back at once, he, with Silvanus, determines to send Timothy, a trusted friend, in his stead, and that too at no small cost, for he himself needed Timothy. The purpose of the sending is to strengthen and encourage the converts in the matter of their faith and thus prevent their being beguiled in the midst of their persecutions. As Paul had been singled out by the Jews as the object of attack, he is at pains to add that he too as well as Silvanus had sent to get a knowledge of their faith, for he is apprehensive that the Tempter had tempted them and that his work among them would turn out to be in vain. To the insinuation that their sufferings proved that the gospel which they had welcomed was a delusion, he tacitly replies, with an appeal to their knowledge in confirmation of his words (οἴδατε vv. $^{3-4}$, as in 2^{1-12}), by saying that Christianity involves suffering, a principle to which he had already alluded when he predicted affliction for himself and his converts, —a prediction which, as they know, was fulfilled.

¹*Wherefore, since we intended no longer to endure the separation, we resolved to be left behind in Athens alone, ²and sent Timothy, our brother and God's co-worker in the gospel of Christ, to strengthen you and encourage you about your faith, ³to prevent any one of you from being beguiled in the midst of these your afflictions. For you yourselves know that we Christians are destined to this; ⁴for when we were with you we were wont to tell you beforehand: "We Christians are certain to experience affliction," as indeed it has turned out and as you know.*

⁵*Wherefore, I too, since I intended no longer to endure the separation, sent him to get a knowledge of your faith, fearing that the*

Tempter had tempted you and that our labour might prove to be in vain.

1. διὸ μηκέτι κτλ. Since, after the shortest interval, we were anxious to see you because of our love for you, and since the immediate accomplishment of our desire was frustrated by Satan, "so then (διό summing up the main points of vv. [17-20]), since we intended no longer to endure τὸ ἀπορφανίζεσθαι ἀφ' ὑμῶν, we resolved (ηὐδοκήσαμεν being the climax of ἐσπουδάσαμεν (v. [17]) and ἠθελήσαμεν (v. [18])) to be left behind in Athens alone." The words καταλειφθῆναι ... μόνοι are emphatic, as Calvin observes. It was at some cost to Paul and Silvanus that they determined to be left behind, and that too alone, parting with so trusted and necessary a companion as Timothy. Such a sacrifice was an unmistakable testimony to their affection for the converts. "It is a sign of rare affection and anxious desire that he is not unwilling to deprive himself of all comfort for the relief of the Thessalonians" (Calvin).

διό (5[11]), like διὰ τοῦτο (v. [5] which resumes διό here) and ὥστε (4[18]), retains its consecutive force, even if it has lost its full subordinating force. B reads διότι, the only case in the N. T. epistles where διό is exchanged for διότι (Zim.); the reading of B may be due to μηκέτι (Weiss) or to διότι in 2[18] (Zim.).—On μηκέτι, cf. v. [5] Rom. 6[6] 2 Cor. 5[15], etc. If the classic force of μή with participles is here retained, then a subjective turn is to be given to μηκέτι: "as those who"; if not, μηκέτι = οὐκέτι. For the usage of μή and οὐ in later Gk., see *BMT.* 485, Bl. 75[1], and Moult. I, 231 *f.*—στέγειν, a Pauline word used with the accus. expressed (πάντα 1 Cor. 9[12] 13[7]) or unexpressed (here and v. [5]) occurs elsewhere in the Gk. Bib. only Sir. 8[17]: οὐ δυνήσεται λόγον στέξαι. The classic sense "cover" and derivatively "shelter," "protect," "conceal" is found also in Polybius (*e. g.* IV, 8[2], VIII, 14[5]); the meaning βαστάζειν, ὑπομένειν (Hesychius), likewise in Polyb. (*e. g.* III, 53[2], XVIII, 18[4]) fits all the N. T. instances better than "ward off" (which Wohl. here suggests); see especially Lft. *ad loc.* From Kypke (II, 213) down, Philo (*in Flac.* 526, ed. Mangey) is usually cited: μηκέτι στέγειν δυνάμενοι τὰς ἐνδείας. This passage has led many comm. to take στέγοντες here as = δυνάμενοι στέγειν; but the pres. part. probably represents an imperfect of intention (*cf. GMT.* 38), and is equivalent to μέλλοντες στέγειν. For ηὐδοκήσαμεν (אBP; εὐδοκ. ADGF) in the sense of "resolve," see above on 2[8]. While it is not certain, it is probable that the resolve was made when Paul and his two companions were in

Athens. In this case, the independent account of Acts must be supplemented by the inference that Silas and Timothy did come as quickly as possible to Athens (Acts 17¹⁴ ᶠ·).—Except in quotations, Paul does not elsewhere use καταλείπειν. The similar ὑπολείπειν occurs but once in Paul (Rom. 11³ cit.). The phrases καταλείπεσθαι or ὑπολείπεσθαι μόνος are quite common in Lxx., being employed either in contrast with others who have departed (Gen. 32²⁴ Judith 13² with ὑπολ.; cf. [Jn.] 8⁹ with καταλ.) or who have perished (Gen. 7²³ 42³⁸ Is. 3²⁶ 49²¹ 1 Mac. 13⁴ with καταλ.; Gen. 44²⁰ with ὑπολ.).

The "we" in vv. ¹⁻⁵ is difficult (see on 1¹). Were it true that θλίψεσιν (v. ³) refers solely to the persecutions that Paul experienced (Dob.), and that consequently the "we" of v. ⁴ refers to Paul alone, then it would be natural to take the "we" of v. ¹ as also referring simply to Paul, and to urge the consideration that a μόνοι which includes Silvanus weakens the argument. But it is by no means certain that θλίψεσιν (v. ³) has in mind only Paul; furthermore, κείμεθα (v. ³) and μέλλομεν (v. ⁴) may refer to Christians in general, while ἤμεν and προελέγομεν (v. ⁴) include not only Paul but Silvanus and Timothy. Above all, ἐγώ (v. ⁵) is naturally explained (cf. 2¹⁸) as purposely emphasising the fact that he as well as Silvanus had made the resolve to send Timothy, for the Jews obviously had directed their criticisms mainly against Paul. Hence the subject of ηὐδοκήσαμεν and ἐπέμψαμεν is Paul and Silvanus (cf. Mill.). —Failure to see the significance of the contrast between ἐγώ (v. ⁵) and the subject of ἐπέμψαμεν (v. ²) has led Hofmann and Spitta (Zur Geschichte und Litteratur des Urchristentums, 1893, I, 121 ff.), who rightly take the subject of ηὐδοκήσαμεν (v. ¹) to be Paul and Silvanus, to infer that Paul (v. ⁵) sent another person, unnamed, in addition to Timothy. But v. ⁶ speaks only of the return of Timothy, and the obvious object of ἔπεμψα here as of ἐπέμψαμεν (v. ²) is Τιμόθεον.

2. Τιμόθεον . . . συνεργὸν τοῦ θεοῦ κτλ. Timothy, who has already been called an apostle (2⁷), is here described not only as "our brother" (cf. 2 Cor. 1¹ Col. 1¹) but also, if the reading of D d e Ambst. be accepted, "God's fellow-labourer." The sphere in which (Rom. 1⁹ Phil. 4³) he works with God is the gospel which Christ inspires (see on 1⁴). The choice of such a representative honours the converts (Chrys.) and proves Paul's inclination to consult their welfare (Calv.).

The reading of B (καὶ συνεργόν), which Weiss and Find. prefer, yields excellent sense and attaches itself nicely to ἡμῶν (cf. Phil. 2²⁵ Rom. 16²¹). But if it is original, it is difficult to account for τοῦ θεοῦ in the other readings. If D is original, it is easy to understand (cf. Dob.

131) the suppression of the bold designation συνεργὸς τοῦ θεοῦ (else-where only 1 Cor. 3⁹) by the omission of τοῦ θεοῦ, the substitution of διάκονον for συνεργόν in אAP, Vulg. (διάκονον τοῦ θεοῦ; fuld. *domini*), and the conflated readings of GF (καὶ διάκονον καὶ συνεργὸν τοῦ θεοῦ) and DᶜKL, Pesh. (καὶ διάκονον τοῦ θεοῦ καὶ συνεργὸν ἡμῶν).—συνεργός, outside of Paul, appears in Gk. Bib. only 3 Jn. 8, 2 Mac. 8⁷ 14⁵; in Paul it is used with μου (Rom. 16³⋅ ²¹ Phile. 24 Phil. 4³) or ἡμῶν (Rom. 16⁹ Phile. 1; *cf.* 2 Cor. 8²³), with a thing (2 Cor. 1²⁴ Col. 4¹¹), and with θεοῦ (only here and 1 Cor. 3⁹). Timothy is thus not simply "our fellow-worker" (Rom. 16²¹) but "God's fellow-worker." Apart from אAPKL, *et al.*, here, Paul does not call Timothy a διάκονος τοῦ θεοῦ.

2–3ᵃ. εἰς τὸ στηρίξαι . . . τὸ μηδένα σαίνεσθαι κτλ. The primary purpose (εἰς τό) of Timothy's mission is to strengthen and encourage the converts in reference to (ὑπέρ = περί) their faith (1⁸). The secondary purpose, dependent on the fulfilment of the primary, is to prevent any person (τὸ μηδένα) from being beguiled in the midst of these their afflictions. Under the stress of persecutions, some of the converts might be coaxed away from the Christian faith by the insinuations of the Jews. In the phrase ἐν ταῖς θλίψεσιν ταύταις, ἐν is primarily local, though a temporal force may also be felt. Since Paul says not ἡμῶν but ταύταις, it is evident that he is thinking not of his own but of his converts' afflictions, as indeed ὑμᾶς and ὑμῶν (v. ²) intimate. Zahn (*Introd.* I, 218) observes: "The Tempter, who was threatening to destroy the Apostle's entire work in Thessalonica (3⁵), assumed not only the form of a roaring lion (1 Pet. 5⁸), but also that of a fawning dog (Phil. 3²) and a hissing serpent (1 Cor. 11³)."

Paul uses πέμπειν with εἰς τό and infin. elsewhere v. ⁵ II 2¹¹, with infin. of purpose (1 Cor. 16³; *cf.* 1 Mac. 13¹⁷ (אV) 2 Mac. 14¹⁹), and with ἵνα (2 Cor. 9³ Phil. 2¹⁹⋅ ²⁸; *cf.* Col. 4⁸ Eph. 6²²). It is a small matter who is the subject of στηρίξαι (*cf.* γνῶναι v. ⁵), whether Paul or Timothy, for in the last resort Timothy is the agent of Paul's purpose.—The collocation στηρίζειν and παρακαλεῖν occurs in the reverse order also in II 2¹⁷; *cf.* Rom. 1¹¹ Acts 14²² 15³².—ὑπέρ here and II 2¹ = περί (which DᶜL here read); on παρακαλεῖν ὑπέρ, *cf.* 2 Cor. 12⁸.—ὑμᾶς, to be supplied after παρακαλέσαι, is expressed by DᶜKL.—τὸ μή with infin., a good Pauline construction, is used appositively (Rom. 14¹³ 2 Cor. 2¹), predicatively (Rom. 14²¹ with adjective), and as the object of δεῖσθαι (2 Cor. 10²). Here τὸ μηδένα with infin. may be either in apposition with τὸ στηρίξαι (Lün. Born. Find.), or the object of παρακαλέσαι (Ell. Schmiedel, Wohl. Dob.), or the infin. of purpose (Bl. 71²), or better still, as in 4⁶, the infin. after an unexpressed verb of hindering (*GMT.* 811).

The meaning of σαίνεσθαι (only here in Gk. Bib.) is uncertain. (1) The usual view, that of the Fathers and Versions, interprets it to mean "to be moved" (κινεῖσθαι, σαλεύεσθαι) or "to be disturbed" (ταράττεσθαι, θορυβεῖσθαι); for the latter rendering, *cf.* Dob. who contrasts στηρίζειν (v. ²) and στήκειν (v. ⁸). (2) Lachmann (see Thay. *sub voc.*) conjectures from the reading of G (μηδεν ασι ενεσθαι) ἀσαίνειν = not λυπεῖν (Hesychius) but ἀσᾶειν = ἄχθεσθαι. (3) Nestle (*ZNW.* 1906, 361 *f.* and *Exp. Times*, July, 1907, 479) assumes σιένεσθαι = σιαίνεσθαι (*cf.* Mercati, *ZNW.* 1907, 242) and notes in Butler's *Lausiac Hist. of Palladius* (*TS.* VI,² 1904) the variant σκανδαλισθείς for σιανθείς. The meaning "to cause or feel loathing" fits all the passages noted by Nestle and Mercati (Dob.), but is not suitable to our passage. (4) Faber Stapulensis (*apud* Lillie: *adulationi cederet*) and others down to Zahn (*Introd.* I, 222 *f.*), starting from the Homeric literal sense of σαίνειν "to wag the tail," interpret σαίνειν in the derivative sense of "flatter," "cajole," "beguile," "fawn upon" (*cf.* Æschylus, *Choeph.* 194 (Dindorf): σαίνομαι δ' ὑπ' ἐλπίδος and Polyb. I, 80⁶: οἱ πλεῖστοι συνεσαίνοντο τῇ διαλέκτῳ). This meaning is on the whole preferable; it fits admirably the attitude of the Jews (*cf.* also Mill. *ad loc.*). Parallels to σαίνεσθαι were gathered by Elsner (II, 275 *f.*) and Wetstein (*ad loc.*).

3ᵇ–4. αὐτοὶ γὰρ οἴδατε κτλ. "I mention these persecutions of yours, for (γάρ) you yourselves are aware (*cf.* 2¹) that we Christians are destined to suffer persecution (κείμεθα; Calv. *ac si dixisset hac lege nos esse Christianos*). And I say you are aware that suffering is a principle of our religion, for (καὶ γάρ v. ⁴ resuming and further explaining γάρ v. ³) when we three missionaries were with you, we stated this principle in the form of a prediction repeatedly declared: "We Christians are certain to be afflicted." And the prophecy has proved true of us all as you know (2⁵)." It is to be observed that Paul not only states the prophecy and its fulfilment, but also appeals to the knowledge of the readers in confirmation of his statement. This appeal, in the light of the similar appeals in 2¹⁻¹², suggests that Paul is intending not only to encourage the converts but also at the same time to rebut the cajoling insinuations of the Jews who would coax the converts away from the new faith on the pre-tence that persecution is evidence that the gospel which they welcomed is a delusion.

εἰς τοῦτο = εἰς τὸ θλίβεσθαι. κεῖμαι εἰς (Phil. 1¹⁶ Lk. 2³⁴) does not occur in Lxx. (Josh. 4⁶ is not a parallel); it is equivalent to τέθειμαι εἰς (Bl. 23⁷; cf. Lk. 23⁵³ with Jn. 19⁴¹). Christians as such are "set," "appointed," "destined" to suffer persecution (cf. Acts 14²²). In εἶναι πρός (II 2⁵ 3¹⁰) as in παρεῖναι πρός (Gal. 4¹⁸· ²⁰ 2 Cor. 11⁹), πρός = "with," "bei," "chez" (cf. Bl. 43⁷). The phrase καὶ γὰρ ὅτε . . . ἦμεν recurs in II 3¹⁰. The imperfect προελέγομεν denotes repeated action; πρό is predictive as μέλλομεν shows; cf. Gal. 5²¹ 2 Cor. 13² Is. 41²⁶; and below 4⁶. The ὅτι before μέλλομεν may be recitative or may introduce indirect discourse unchanged. μέλλομεν is followed by the present infin. here and Rom. 4²⁴ 8¹³. It is uncertain whether μέλλομεν = κείμεθα "are certain to" or is a periphrasis for the future (Bl. 62⁴), "are going to." The construction καθὼς καὶ . . . καί is similar to that in 4⁶; "as also has happened," corresponding to the prediction, "and as you know," corresponding to their knowledge. The καί is implied in καθώς and is sometimes expressed (4¹· ⁶· ¹³ 5¹¹ II 3¹), sometimes not (1⁵ 2², etc.).

5. διὰ τοῦτο κἀγώ κτλ. Contrary to the slanders which you are hearing, "I too, as well as Silvanus, intending to stand the separation no longer, sent Timothy to get a knowledge of your faith." This verse obviously resumes v. ¹, though the purpose of the sending of Timothy is put in different language. As in 2¹⁸ (ἐγὼ μέν), so here the change from the plural to the singular (κἀγώ) is due to the fact that the Jews had singled out Paul as especially the one who, indifferent to the sufferings of the converts, had left them in the lurch with no intention of returning. The καί before ἐγώ is emphatic, "I too as well as Silvanus." That the object of ἔπεμψα is Τιμόθεον is plain not only from v. ¹ but from v. ⁶ which reports the return of Timothy only.

μή πως ἐπείρασεν κτλ. He sent to get a knowledge of their faith, "fearing that" (sc. φοβούμενος, and cf. Gal. 4¹¹) the Tempter had tempted them, that is, in the light of v. ³, that the Jews, taking advantage of the persecutions, had beguiled them from their faith; and fearing that, as the result of the temptation, the labour already expended might prove to be fruitless. The aorist indicative ἐπείρασεν suggests that the tempting has taken place, though the issue of it is at the time of writing

9

uncertain; the aorist subjunctive γένηται intimates that the work may turn out to be in vain, though that result has not yet been reached (*cf.* Gal. 2² μή πως εἰς κενὸν τρέχω ἢ ἔδραμον). The designation of Satan (2¹⁸) as ὁ πειράζων is found elsewhere in the Gk. Bib. only Mt. 4³; it is appropriate, for as Calvin remarks: *proprium Satanae officium est tentare* (*cf.* 1 Cor. 7⁵).

The construction of μή πως κτλ. assumed above (*cf. BMT.* 225 and Bl. 65²) is preferable to that which takes it as an indirect question (*cf.* Lk. 3¹⁵). The order of B τὴν ὑμῶν πίστιν puts an emphasis on ὑμῶν which is more suitable in v. ⁷. On the subject of γνῶναι, see on the subject of στηρίξαι v. ². εἰς κενόν, found in N. T. only in Paul, is a common phrase in the Lxx. *e. g.* with γίνεσθαι (as here; Mic. 1¹⁴), τρέχειν (Gal. 2² Phil. 2¹⁶), δέχεσθαι (2 Cor. 6¹), εἶναι (Lev. 26²⁰), and κοπιᾶν (Phil. 2¹⁶; Job 2⁹ 39¹⁶ Is. 65²² Jer. 28⁵⁸). For ὁ κόπος ἡμῶν, see 1³ and *cf.* 1 Cor. 15⁵⁸. The designation of Satan as ὁ πειράζων does not appear in Lxx. Test. xii, Ps. Sol. or in the Apostolic Fathers.

(6) *Timothy's Return and Report* (3⁶⁻¹⁰).

The apprehension that induced Paul to send Timothy is allayed by the favourable report of the religious and moral status of the converts and of their personal regard for him. From their faith which still kept hardy in trials, Paul derived courage to face his own privations and persecutions: "We live if you stand fast in the Lord." Transported by the good news, he cannot find adequate words to express to God the joy he has, as he prays continually that he might see them and amend the shortcomings of their faith. The exuberance of joy, the references to the visit (vv. ⁶· ¹⁰), the insistence that the joy is δι' ὑμᾶς (v. ⁹) and the thanksgiving περὶ ὑμῶν (v. ⁹) imply that the insinuations of the Jews are still in mind. The Tempter has tempted them but they have not succumbed. To be sure the exuberance of feeling, due not only to their personal affection for him, but also to their spiritual excellence, does not blind his mind to the fact that deficiencies exist, to which in 4¹ ᶠᶠ· he turns.

⁶*But now that Timothy has just come to us from you and has brought us good news of your faith and love, and has told us that you have been having a kindly remembrance of us always and have*

*been longing to see us as we too to see you,—⁷for this reason, brothers,
we became encouraged in you to face all our privations and persecutions through your faith, ⁸for now we live if you stand fast in the
Lord. ⁹Indeed, what adequate thanks can we return to God for you
for all the joy we express for your sake in the presence of our God,
¹⁰begging night and day most earnestly to see your face and make up
the deficiencies of your faith.*

6. ἄρτι δὲ ἐλθόντος κτλ. With δέ (*cf.* 2¹⁷), a new point in the
apologetic historical review of Paul's acts and intentions since
his departure from Thessalonica is introduced, the return and
report of Timothy. The selection of material is still influenced
by the criticisms directed by the Jews against Paul's character
and conduct. It is first stated that Timothy has but now (ἄρτι)
come from them to Paul and Silvanus, a fact that makes clear, as
Grotius has observed, that our letter was written not in Athens
but in Corinth, and that too under the fresh inspiration of the
report of Timothy. Although ἐλθόντος may be simply temporal,
it is probably also causal, as διὰ τοῦτο (v. ⁷) which resumes the
genitive absolute clause suggests.

> ἄρτι, which is to be joined with the gen. abs. (*cf.* 3 Mac. 6¹⁶) and not
> with παρεκλήθημεν, may refer either to the immediate present, "just
> now," "*modo*" (*cf.* Mt. 9¹⁸ Gal. 1¹⁰ 4²⁰ 2 Mac. 9¹⁸ (V) 3 Mac. 6¹⁶) or to
> the more distant past, "*nuper*" (*cf.* II 2⁷ 1 Cor. 13¹² 16⁷; also Poole,
> *ad loc.*) The former sense is preferable here as no contrast between
> the now and a more distant past is evident in the context. δέ is not
> in itself adversative, but introduces either a new section (2¹⁷ 3¹¹, etc.)
> or a new point within a section (2¹⁶ 3¹², etc.). ἀφ' ὑμῶν may be emphatic
> (Find.); it is from the Thessalonians that Paul desires news, and Tim-
> othy comes directly from them, bringing with him a letter. That Sil-
> vanus is already with Paul is the intimation of ἡμᾶς (but *cf.* Acts 18⁵).

εὐαγγελισαμένου κτλ. The word itself reveals the character
of the report; it is good news that the messenger brings. "Do
you see the exuberant joy of Paul? He does not say ἀπαγγεί-
λαντος (1⁹) but εὐαγγελισαμένου. So great a good did he think
their steadfastness (βεβαίωσιν) and love." The first element
in the good news is their excellence religiously (πίστις) and
morally (ἀγάπη); "in these two words, he indicates tersely *totam
pietatis summam*" (Calvin).

εὐαγγελίζεσθαι, "to bring good news," is a classic word (cf. Aristoph.
Eq. 642 f.) found in Lxx. (2 Reg.¯1²⁰ parallel with ἀναγγέλλειν, Ps. 39⁹
Is. 40⁹ 52⁷ 60⁶ 61¹, etc.) and N. T. (chiefly in Pauline and Lukan writings;
cf. Lk. 1¹⁹ 2²⁰ 3¹⁸, etc.). Paul uses it either absolutely in the technical
sense of preaching the gospel (1 Cor. 1¹⁷, etc.), or with εὐαγγέλιον
(Gal. 1¹¹ 1 Cor. 15¹ 2 Cor. 11⁷), πίστιν (Gal. 1²³), πλοῦτος Χριστοῦ, or
with Christ as the object (Gal. 1¹⁶; cf. Acts 5⁴² 8³⁵ 11²⁰ 17¹⁸). On the
word, see Mill. 141 ff. and Harnack, Verfassung und Recht, 199 ff.—
ἀγάπη for Paul as for Christ fulfils the law on the ethical side (Rom. 13¹⁰
Gal. 5¹⁴). The comprehensiveness of its meaning is made clear in 1 Cor.
13¹ ff. where the points emphasised are pretty much the same as those
in Gal. 5²²⁻²³ and Rom. 12⁶⁻²¹. Paul speaks regularly of divine love to
men (ἀγάπη τοῦ θεοῦ II 3⁵ Rom. 5⁵, etc.; τοῦ Χριστοῦ Rom. 8³⁵; τοῦ
πνεύματος Rom. 15³⁰), but he rarely speaks of man's love to God (1 Cor.
2⁹ 8³ Rom. 8²⁸) or Christ (1 Cor. 16²² Eph. 6²⁴).

καὶ ὅτι ἔχετε μνείαν κτλ. The second element in the good
news is personal; the Thessalonians have been having all along
(ἔχετε πάντοτε) a kindly remembrance of Paul, "notwithstanding the efforts of the hostile Jews" (Mill.). This constant remembrance is significantly revealed in the fact that they have
been all the time longing (ἐπιποθοῦντες; sc. πάντοτε) to see
the missionaries as the missionaries have been (sc. πάντοτε ἐπι-
ποθοῦμεν ἰδεῖν and cf. 2¹⁷ ff.) to see them.

ὅτι naturally goes with εὐαγγελισαμένου (cf. Acts 13³²); the change of
construction is more felt in English than in ̄Gk. But others supply
εἰπόντος or λέγοντος (Jer. 20¹⁵) before ὅτι.—Although πάντοτε sometimes precedes (4¹⁷ 5¹⁵. ¹⁶) and sometimes follows the verb (1² 2¹⁶ II 1³. ¹¹
2¹³), and hence could be here taken either with ἐπιποθοῦντες or with
ἔχειν μνείαν, yet the latter construction is to be preferred in the light
of 1² and Rom. 1¹⁰ (ποιεῖσθαι μνείαν ἀδιαλείπτως). In this case, the
present ἔχετε, because of the adverb of duration (πάντοτε), describes
an action begun in the past and still continuing at the time of speaking;
and is to be rendered: "And that you have had always," etc. (cf. BMT.
17).—ἀγαθός (5¹⁵ II 2¹⁶. ¹⁷) means here as in Rom. 5⁷ (Lft.) "kindly,"
"pleasant." It is doubtful whether ἐπιποθεῖν (a characteristic word
of Paul; cf. Rom. 1¹¹ Phil. 2²⁶) differs greatly from ποθεῖν (a word not
in Paul; cf Sap. 15⁵ ᶠ. with 15¹⁹). On καθάπερ (2¹¹) with comparative
καί, cf. 3¹² 4⁵ Rom. 4⁶ 2 Cor. 1¹⁴.

7. διὰ τοῦτο παρεκλήθημεν κτλ. The good news dispelled the
anxiety created by the situation in Thessalonica and gave him

courage to face his own difficulties. "Wherefore, because of the good news (διὰ τοῦτο resuming ἐλθόντος κτλ.) we became encouraged (cf. v. ² παρακαλέσαι) brothers (2¹⁷) in you (ἐφ' ὑμῖν) to face (ἐπί) all our privation and persecution through your faith." The first ἐπί denotes the basis of the encouragement; the second ἐπί the purpose for which it was welcome; and the διά the means by which it was conveyed, "through this faith of yours" (ὑμῶν being emphatic; contrast vv. ². ⁵).

> Grot. and Lillie take the first ἐπί = "on your account"; the second ἐπί is local with a touch of purpose in it (cf. Bl. 43³). On παρακαλεῖσθαι ἐπί, cf. 2 Cor. 1⁴ 7⁷; Deut. 32³⁶ Ps. 89¹³ 134¹⁴ 2 Mac. 7⁶. θλίψις is not distress of mind but as in 1⁶ "persecution" (cf. 2 Cor. 12¹⁰); ἀνάγκη is here not carking care (2 Cor. 9⁷) but "physical privation" (Lft.) as in 2 Cor. 6⁴: ἐν θλίψεσιν, ἐν ἀνάγκαις, ἐν στενοχωρίαις; see further Job 15²⁴ Zeph. 1¹⁵. ἐπὶ πάσῃ τῇ (v. ⁹ 2 Cor. 1⁴ 7⁴ Phil. 1²) is less frequent in Paul than ἐν πάσῃ τῇ (II 2⁹. ¹⁰; 3¹⁷ 1 Cor. 1⁵, etc.). Here and v. ⁹, πάσῃ may be comprehensive, the instances of privation and persecution being regarded as a unit, or may express heightened intensity (Dob.).

8. ὅτι νῦν ζῶμεν κτλ. "Through *your* faith," I say, "for now we live, if *you* stand fast in the Lord." Though at death's door constantly (Rom. 8³⁶ 1 Cor. 15³¹ 2 Cor. 6⁹ 11²³), he feels that he has a new lease of life (*recte valemus*, Calv.), if their faith stands unwavering in virtue of the indwelling power of Christ (Phil. 4¹), notwithstanding their persecutions (cf. II 1⁴) and the beguilement of the Jews.

> On the late Gk. στήκειν, built on ἕστηκα, see Bl. 17 and Kennedy, *Sources*, 158; and cf. Judg. 16²⁶ (B), 3 Reg. 8¹¹ (B; A has στῆναι), Ex. 14¹³ (A; B has στῆτε), Rom. 14⁴, etc. The phrase στήκετε ἐν κυρίῳ recurs in Phil. 4¹; on ἐν, see 1¹. The reading στήκετε (BAGF) is more original than στήκητε (אD); on ἐάν with indic., cf. 1 Jn. 5¹⁵ Mk. 11²⁵. It is not the form (*BMT.* 242, 247) but the fact of the condition that suggests that Paul here speaks "with some hesitation. Their faith was not complete" (Lft. who notes ὑστερήματα v. ¹⁰). If this is so, νῦν is not temporal but logical: "this being the case" (so Ell.).

9. τίνα γὰρ εὐχαριστίαν κτλ. The faith of the converts gave Paul and his associates not only life but joy (Chrys.), as γάρ, parallel to ὅτι and introducing a second and unqualified confirmation of διὰ τῆς ὑμῶν πίστεως, makes plain. This joy, which is not so much personal as religious, and which therefore finds its constant outlet ἔμπροσθεν τοῦ θεοῦ ἡμῶν (Dob.), is so excessive that Paul is unable to give God that adequate thanks which is his due. Although it is pointed out, over against the insinuations of the Jews, that it is none other than the converts for whom (περὶ ὑμῶν) he renders thanks to God, none other than they who are the basis of his joy (ἐπὶ πάσῃ τῇ χαρᾷ), and none other than they on whose account (δι᾽ ὑμᾶς; cf. 1⁵) he constantly expresses before the Christian God (ὁ θεὸς ἡμῶν; cf. 2²) his overwhelming feeling of joy, yet it is likewise indicated that it is God after all, not himself, not even the converts, that he must try to thank for their spiritual attainment.

On the co-ordinating γάρ in interrogative sentences, see Bl. 78⁶. εὐχαριστία, a favourite word of Paul, denotes for him not "gratitude" (Sir. 37¹¹ 2 Mac. 2²⁷) but the "giving of thanks" (Sap. 16²⁸ where it is parallel to ἐντυγχάνειν). ἀνταποδιδόναι, common in Lxx. and used by Paul either in a good sense as here and Ps. 115³ (Grot.) or in a bad sense (cf. II 1⁶ Rom. 12¹⁹ Deut. 32⁴¹), is probably stronger than ἀποδιδόναι (5¹⁵), and "expresses the idea of full, complete return" (Mill.). "What sufficient thanks can we repay?" (Lft.). Instead of τῷ θεῷ (ABEKL), אDFG read κυρίῳ, influenced doubtless by ἐν κυρίῳ (v. ⁸); similarly א reads at the end of v. ⁹ τοῦ κυρίου ἡμῶν.—For περὶ ὑμῶν, B alone has περὶ ἡμῶν, which is "sinnlos" (Weiss).—περί after δυνάμεθα ἀνταποδοῦναι is like that with εὐχαριστεῖν (1² II 1³ 2¹³, etc.). ἐπί indicates that joy, full and intense (πάσῃ; contrast ἐπὶ πάσῃ τῇ ἀνάγκῃ v. ⁸), is the basis of the thanksgiving; cf. 2 Cor. 9¹⁵. ᾗ before χαίρομεν stands not for ἐφ᾽ ᾗ (cf. 2 Cor. 7¹³), but either for the cognate dative χαρᾷ (Jn. 3²⁹ Is. 66¹⁰ B) or for the cognate accus. ἥν (Mt. 2¹⁰ Is. 39² אA, 66¹⁰ A, Jonah 4⁶). δι᾽ ὑμᾶς (Jn. 3²⁹) is stronger than the expected ἐφ᾽ ὑμῖν (cf. χαίρειν ἐπί Rom. 16¹⁹ 1 Cor. 13⁶ 16¹⁷ 2 Cor. 7¹³; Is. 39² Hab. 3¹⁸ and often in Lxx.). ἔμπροσθεν goes with χαίρομεν.

10. νυκτὸς ... δεόμενοι. It is in the atmosphere of intense joy that he prays unceasingly (νυκτὸς καὶ ἡμέρας as 2⁹) and exuberantly (ὑπερεκπερισσοῦ as 5¹³), not simply that he might see their face (as 2¹⁷) but also that he might make up the deficiencies of their faith (cf. v. ⁸). Both his desire to return which has been the point of his defence since 2¹⁷ and his desire to amend the shortcomings of their faith are suffused by the spirit of joy. The converts are thus tactfully assured both of the genuineness of his longing to see them and of his confidence that their imperfections are not serious. In passing, it is worth noting that the enthusiasm of his feeling does not prevent him from being aware of the existence of moral defects,—an interesting side-light on the ethical soundness of his religious feelings. δεόμενοι, loosely attached to χαίρομεν, prepares the way not only for the prayer (vv. ¹¹⁻¹³), namely, that God and Christ may direct his way to them (v. ¹¹), and that the Lord may increase their brotherly love and love in general (v. ¹²) and strengthen them to remove their defects, but also for the exhortations (4¹ ᶠᶠ·) in which there is a detailed and at the same time tactful treatment of the ὑστερήματα.

ὑπερεκπερισσοῦ is found in 5¹³ (אAP; BDGF read ὑπερεκπερισσῶς, a word occurring in 1 Clem. 20¹¹ but not in Lxx.), Eph. 3²⁰ and Test. xii, Jos. 17⁵, but not in Lxx. It is stronger than περισσοτέρως (2¹⁷) and ὑπερπερισσῶς (in Gk. Bib. only Mk. 7³⁷) and ἐκ περισσοῦ (Dan. (Th.) 3²²; Mk. 6⁵¹ v. l.). See Ell. on Eph. 3²⁰ and cf. Ambst. *abuntantissime*. εἰς τό introduces the object of δεόμενοι (*BMT.* 412). δεῖσθαι (Rom. 1¹⁰ Gal. 4¹², etc.), like ἐρωτᾶν (4¹ 5¹² II 2¹ Phil. 4³), is less frequent in Paul than παρακαλεῖν.—ὑστέρημα is found six times in Lxx., eight times in Paul, and once in Luke (Lk. 21⁴); it indicates a lack and is opposed to περίσσευμα (2 Cor. 8¹³ ᶠ·). It is joined with ἀναπληροῦν (1 Cor. 16¹⁷ Phil. 2³⁰; cf. Test. xii, Benj. 11⁵ 1 Clem. 38²), προσαναπληροῦν (2 Cor. 9¹¹ 11⁹) and ἀνταναπληροῦν (Col. 1²⁴) but not elsewhere in Gk. Bib. with καταρτίζειν. This word (Gal. 6¹ Rom. 9²², etc.; cf. προκαταρτίζειν 2 Cor. 9⁵), common in Lxx., means generally to render ἄρτιος, hence to "adjust" differences, "repair" things out of repair, "set" bows, "prepare" dishes, etc.; and here "make up," "make good" that which is lacking to complete faith. Since, however, the sense "*das Fehlende*" passes imperceptibly into that of "*Fehler*" (Dob.), as indeed 1 Clem. 2⁶ (where ὑστερήματα is parallel to παραπτώματα) and Hermas Vis. III, 2² (where it is parallel to ἁμαρτήματα) suggest, we may translate either "make up the deficiencies of your faith" (Lillie) or "amend the shortcomings of your faith" (Ruther.).

III. PRAYER (3¹¹⁻¹³).

With δέ, introducing a new section in the epistolary disposition of the letter, Paul passes from the superscription (1¹) and the thanksgiving (1²–3¹⁰) to the prayer (3¹¹⁻¹³). Both the desire

to see them (v. [10]) and the desire to amend the deficiencies of their
faith (v. [10]) are resumed as he turns in prayer to the supreme
court of appeal, God and Christ; but the emphasis in 3^{11-13} is
put less on the longing to see them (v. [11]), the apologetic interest underlying 2^{17}–3^{10}, than on the shortcomings of their faith
(vv. [12-13]), the ὑστερήματα of v. [10]. This change of emphasis
prepares the way for the exhortations (4[1 ff.]); in fact, when he
prays that Christ may make them abound in brotherly love as
well as in love (v. [12]) and may strengthen them inwardly so that
they may become blameless in saintliness when they appear before God at the last day when Jesus comes attended by his
glorious retinue of angels (v. [13]), it is not improbable that he
has more or less distinctly in mind the matter of φιλαδελφία
(4^{9-12}) and ἁγιασμός (4^{3-8}), to which, with λοιπόν (4^1), he forthwith addresses himself.

[11]*Now may our God and Father and our Lord Jesus himself
direct our way to you.* [12]*And as for you, may the Lord make you
to increase and abound in love toward one another and toward all
men, just as we too toward you,* [13]*in order that he may strengthen
your hearts (so that they may be) blameless in holiness in the presence
of our God and Father when our Lord Jesus comes with all his angels.*

11. αὐτὸς δὲ ὁ θεός κτλ. Since δέ introduces a new epistolary
division, and is not of itself adversative, it is unnecessary to
seek a contrast with the immediately preceding (v. [10]) or with
the remoter words: "and Satan hindered us" (2^{18}). Indeed the
prayer "to see your face" (v. [10]) is not contrasted with but is
resumed by the prayer that God and Christ "may open up and
direct our way to you *de medio eorum qui moram fecerunt verbo
nostro*" (Ephr.). While it is striking that in Paul's expressions
of religious feeling, in superscriptions, thanksgivings, prayers,
etc., the name of the Lord Jesus Christ stands next to the name
of the Father (see on θεῷ πατρί, 1^1), usually after but sometimes
before (II 2^{16} Gal. 1^1), it is even more striking that both names
should be unitedly governed by a verb in the singular (αὐτὸς ...
κατευθύναι; *cf.* II $2^{16 f.}$). The estimate of the lordship of Christ,
explicit in Colossians, is latent not only in 1 Cor. 8^6 but here, a
consideration that forbids (*cf.* Dob.) the taking of the ungram-

matical step of denying that αὐτός here includes both God and Christ as the objects of prayer.

Lillie, however, finds in δέ the idea both of transition and of slight opposition: "After all our own ineffectual attempts and ceaseless longings, may he himself, the hearer of our prayers (v. ¹⁰), direct our way unto you, and then will all Satan's hindrances be vain. (So Pelt, Schott, Lün.)." Characteristic of the prayers of I and II is the αὐτὸς δέ (θεός 5²³ II 2¹⁶; κύριος 4¹⁶ II 2¹⁶ 3¹⁶; *cf.* 2 Cor. 8¹⁹ ℵ) instead of the simple ὁ δέ (θεός Rom. 15¹³). These phrases (*cf.* also αὐτὸς ὁ υἱός 1 Cor. 15²⁸; αὐτὸ τὸ πνεῦμα Rom. 8¹⁶· ²⁶; αὐτὸς ὁ Σατανᾶς 2 Cor. 11¹⁴) are, except Rev. 21³ (αὐτὸς ὁ θεός), found in N. T. only in Paul. The αὐτός is either reflexive or an emphatic "he" (*cf.* Moult. I, 91). On ὁ κύριος ἡμῶν Ἰησοῦς (D omits Ἰησοῦς; GFKL add Χριστός), see on 2¹⁹. κατευθύνειν, rare in the N. T. (II 3⁵ Lk. 1⁷⁹) but common in Lxx., means "make straight," "make straight for" (*cf.* 1 Reg. 6¹²), and "guide," "direct," "prosper." κατευθύνειν ὁδόν (or διαβήματα) is likewise frequent in Lxx. (Ps. 5⁹ Judith 12⁸, etc.). On the πρός, *cf.* 1 Ch. 29¹⁸ 2 Ch. 20³³ Sir. 49³. In Paul, apart from μὴ γένοιτο (fourteen times), the optative of wishing with the third person is found only in our letters (vv. ¹¹⁻¹² 5²³ II 2¹⁷ 3⁵· ¹⁶), Rom. 15¹³ (followed by εἰς τό with infin.), and 15⁵ (followed by ἵνα); see further Phile. 20 and *BMT.* 176.

12. ὑμᾶς δὲ ὁ κύριος κτλ. The δέ introduces a new point and is here adversative, as the emphatic position of ὑμᾶς makes clear: "and as for you." "Such is our prayer for ourselves; but you, whether we come or not (Beng.: *sive nos veniemus, sive minus*), etc." (Lillie). This second petition, directed to the Lord alone (that is, not θεός (A) but Christ, as DGF, which add Ἰησοῦς, interpret,—Christ who is the indwelling power unto love), has in view the ὑστερήματα (v. ¹⁰). The love in which Christ will make them to increase and abound is defined both as φιλαδελφία, a love which though present (4⁹⁻¹⁰) needs to abound the more (4¹⁰⁻¹²), and as ἀγάπη, love to all men everywhere (5¹⁵ Gal. 6¹⁰). As an example of love, he points to himself (1⁶ II 3⁹; *cf.* Calv.): "As also (καθάπερ καί, v. ⁶) we increase and abound (*sc.* the intransitive πλεονάζομεν καὶ περισσεύομεν τῇ ἀγάπῃ and *cf.* 2 Cor. 9⁸) toward you." They are to love one another as he loves them.

πλεονάζειν, common in Lxx., is found in N. T. but once (2 Pet. 1⁸) outside of Paul (*cf.* II 1³); it means "increase," "multiply," "abound."

The transitive sense here is not infrequent in the Lxx. (*e. g.* Num. 26⁵⁴
2 Ch. 31⁵ Ps. 49¹⁹ 70²¹ Sir. 20⁸ (A) 32¹ Jer. 37¹⁹). περισσεύειν, frequent
in N. T. and seven times in Lxx., is virtually synonymous with πλεονάζειν.
The transitive occurs also in 2 Cor. 9⁸; *cf.* 2 Cor. 4¹⁵ Eph. 1⁸. "Do you
see the unchecked madness of love which is indicated by the words?
He says πλεονάσαι and περισσεύσαι instead of αὐξῆσαι" (Chrys.; *cf.*
II 1³). εἰς here, as in II 1³, may be taken closely with ἀγάπη, the article
being tacitly repeated and the verbs construed with the dative as in
2 Cor. 3⁹ Sir. 11¹²; or εἰς may be joined with the verbs (*cf.* πλεονάζειν
εἰς Phil. 4¹⁷; περισσεύειν εἰς Rom. 3⁷ 5¹⁵ 2 Cor. 1⁵, etc.), the dative
designating the sphere in which they are to increase and abound (*cf.*
περισσεύειν ἐν Rom. 15¹³ 1 Cor. 15⁵⁸, etc.).

13. εἰς τὸ στηρίξαι κτλ. The purpose of the prayer (εἰς τό;
cf. Rom. 15¹³) for love is that Christ (τὸν κύριον is the subject of στηρίξαι) may strengthen not their faith (v. ²) but their
hearts, their inward purposes and desires, with the result that
these hearts may be blameless (*cf.* 2¹⁰) in the realm of holiness.
The point appears to be that without the strong foundation of
love the will might exploit itself in conduct not becoming to
the ἅγιος, that is, specifically, as 4³⁻⁸ suggests, in impurity.
ἁγιωσύνη denotes not the quality (ἁγιότης), or the process
(ἁγιασμός), but the state of being ἅγιος, that is, separate from
the world and consecrated to God both in body and in soul (5²³).

Some comm. (*e. g.* Flatt, Pelt, Find. Dob.), influenced doubtless by
v. ², where, however, the στηρίξαι is specifically stated to be ὑπὲρ τῆς
πίστεως ὑμῶν, are inclined to think of the strengthening of faith to meet
trials, a strengthening resulting in holiness. στηρίζειν καρδίαν (II 2¹⁷
Ps. 111⁸ Sir. 6³⁷ 22¹⁶ Jas. 5⁸) differs from στηρίζειν ὑμᾶς (v. ²) only in
the expressed emphasis upon the inner life; *cf.* παρακαλεῖν with ὑμᾶς
(v. ²) and with καρδίας (II 2¹⁷). There is no indication here of fear as
the opposite of στηρίζειν καρδίαν (Sir. 22¹⁶ Ps. 111⁸) or of the thought
of perfect love casting out fear (1 Jn. 4¹⁷ ᶠᶠ·). ἀμέμπτους agrees with
καρδίας; to be supplied is either ὥστε αὐτὰς εἶναι or εἰς τὸ εἶναι αὐτάς;
cf. ὁλοτελεῖς (5²³), ἀνεγκλήτους (1 Cor. 1⁸) or σύμμορφον (Ph. 3²¹). The
reading ἀμέμπτως (BL. *et al.*; *cf.* 2¹⁰ 5²³) is due either to the verb or to a
difference of spelling (Zim.). ἁγιότης is rare in Gk. Bib. (2 Cor. 1¹²
Heb. 12¹⁰ 2 Mac. 15²); ἁγιωσύνη is more frequent (Rom. 1⁴ 2 Cor. 7¹
2 Mac. 3¹² Ps. 29⁵ 95⁶ 96¹² 144⁵); and ἁγιασμός (4³· ⁴· ⁷ II 2¹³) is still
more frequent (about ten times in Lxx. and ten times in N. T.; *cf.* Rom.
6¹⁹, etc.). BDEGF read ἁγιοσύνη; א and the corrected B ἁγιωσύνη,
"the usual change of o and ω" (Weiss); but A has δικαιοσύνη. On

the idea of holiness, see SH. on Rom. 1⁷ and Skinner and Stevens in *HDB*. II, respectively, 394 *ff.* and 399 *ff.*

ἔμπροσθεν κτλ. Only those whose love inspires purposes that are blameless in the sphere of holiness will find the day of the Lord a day not of wrath (1¹⁰ 2¹⁶) but of salvation (5⁹). In the light of v. ⁹, the reference might seem to be (*cf.* Chrys.) to a holiness not in the sight of men but "before our God and Father" (see on 1³); but in view of the next prepositional phrase, "in the coming of our Lord Jesus" (*cf.* 2¹⁹), it is evident that the day of the Lord is in mind when all must come before the βῆμα of Christ (2 Cor. 5¹⁰) or God (Rom. 14¹⁰) or both, when the same Father who demands holy love will test the hearts to see if they are free from blame in the realm of holiness.

μετὰ πάντων τῶν ἁγίων αὐτοῦ. "With all his holy ones." Whether ἅγιοι refers to angels or to saints is uncertain. (1) In favour of "angels" is the immediate connection with παρουσίᾳ, the time when Christ comes down from heaven at the voice of an archangel (4¹⁶), μετ᾽ ἀγγέλων δυνάμεως αὐτοῦ (II 1⁷). The picture of the accompanying retinue of angels is similar to that in Mk. 8³⁸ Mt. 25³¹ and Jude 14 = Enoch (Gk.) 1⁹. The αὐτοῦ, as Mt. 16²⁷ 24³¹ suggest, refers to Christ. Paul may have had in mind Zech. 14⁵: ἥξει ὁ κύριος μου καὶ πάντες οἱ ἅγιοι μετ᾽ αὐτοῦ. (2) In favour of "saints" is the usage of the N. T. where, apart from this passage, ἅγιοι = "saints"; the fact that πάντες οἱ ἅγιοι is a common turn in Paul (*cf.* οἱ ἅγιοι αὐτοῦ Col. 1²⁶); and possibly the fact that Did. 16⁷ interprets Zech. 14⁵ of the saints. In this case, because of the difficulty of conceiving the surviving saints coming *with* the Lord at his *Parousia*, and because of the difficulty, due to πάντες, of contrasting the departed and the living saints, it is necessary to place the scene implied by μετὰ πάντων κτλ. not immediately at the *Parousia*, as the present context seems to suggest, but later, namely, at the judgment, when Christ comes with all his consecrated ones, now glorified, ἔμπροσθεν τοῦ βήματος.

(1) In favour of "angels" are Grot. Hammond, De W. Lün. Edward Robinson (*Lex.* 1850), Schmiedel, Dob. Moff. Dibelius, and others; *cf.* Ascen. Isa. 4¹⁴ (with Charles's note) and Ps. Sol. 17⁴⁹ (with note of

Ryle and James). (2) In favour of "saints" are, in addition to those who unnaturally construe μετὰ τῶν κτλ. closely with στηρίξαι (Estius, Flatt, Hofmann, Wohl. *et al.*), Calv. Find. Briggs (*Messiah of the Apostles*, 85), Vincent, and others. (3) Still others (*e. g.* Bengel, Ell. Lillie, Lft. Mill.) include both angels and glorified men.—It is uncertain whether ἀμήν (אAD) is original (Zim.) or a liturgical addition (*cf.* Weiss, 104). WH. retain it in Paul only Rom. 15³³ 16²⁷ Gal. 6¹⁸; Rom. 1²⁵ 9⁵ 11³⁶ Gal. 1⁵ Eph. 3²¹ Phil. 4²⁰. In the N. T., apart from the unique usage in the words of Jesus (where a single *amen* in the Synoptic Gospels and a double *amen* in John begins the utterance), ἀμήν as in the O. T. is used at the end of a sentence. In the Lxx., however, ἀμήν is rare (*e. g.* 1 Ch. 16³⁶ 1 Esd. 9⁴⁷ Neh. 5¹³ 8⁶ Tob. 8⁸ 14¹⁵ 3 Mac. 7²² 4 Mac. 18²⁴); γένοιτο and ἀληθῶς also translate אמן (*cf.* the various renderings of Luke, ἀληθῶς, ἐπ᾽ ἀληθείας, πλήν, ναί, etc.). On the meaning of *amen*, see Massie in *HDB.* I, 80 *f.* and H. W. Hogg in *EB.* 136 *f.*

IV. EXHORTATIONS (4¹–5²²).

Formally speaking, Paul passes from the superscription (1¹), thanksgiving (1²–3¹⁰), and prayer (3¹¹⁻¹³) to the exhortations (4¹–5²²); materially speaking, he passes from the defence of his visit (1²–2¹⁶) and of his failure to return (2¹⁷–3¹³) to a tactful (*cf.* 4¹. ¹⁰ 5¹¹) treatment of the shortcomings of the faith of the readers (3¹⁰; *cf.* 3⁸. ¹²⁻¹³). These exhortations are not haphazard, but are designed to meet the specific needs of the community made known to Paul by Timothy and by a letter which Timothy brought. In fact, it would appear from 4⁹. ¹³ 5¹ (περὶ δέ; *cf.* 1 Cor. 7¹. ²⁵ 8¹ 12¹, etc.) that the Thessalonians had written specifically for advice concerning love of the brethren, the dead in Christ, and the times and seasons. Three classes of persons are chiefly in mind in 4¹–5²²: (1) The weak (4³⁻⁸; *cf.* οἱ ἀσθενεῖς 5¹⁴); (2) the idlers (οἱ ἄτακτοι 5¹⁴) who have been the main instruments in disturbing the peace of the brotherhood (4⁹⁻¹² 5¹²⁻¹³; *cf.* 5¹⁹⁻²²); and (3) the faint-hearted (οἱ ὀλιγόψυχοι 5¹⁴) who were anxious both about their dead (4¹³⁻¹⁸) and about their own salvation (5¹⁻¹¹). The only distinctly new point, not touched upon in the previous oral teaching of Paul, is the discussion of "the dead in Christ" (4¹³⁻¹⁸).

For convenience, we may subdivide the Exhortations as follows: (1) Introduction (4¹⁻²); (2) True Consecration (4³⁻⁸); (3) Brotherly

Love (4⁹⁻¹⁰ᵃ); (4) Idleness (4¹⁰ᵇ⁻¹²); (5) The Dead in Christ (4¹³⁻¹⁸); (6) Times and Seasons (5¹⁻¹¹); (7) Spiritual Labourers (5¹²⁻¹³); (8) The Idlers, The Faint-hearted, and The Weak (5¹⁴ᵃ⁻ᶜ); (9) Love (5¹⁴ᵈ⁻¹⁵); (10) Joy, Prayer, and Thanksgiving (5¹⁶⁻¹⁸); and (11) Spiritual Gifts (5¹⁹⁻²²).

(1) *Introduction to the Exhortations* (4¹⁻²).

In his introductory words, Paul appeals, in justification of his exhortations, not to his own authority but to the authority which both he and his readers recognise as valid, the indwelling Christ (ἐν κυρίῳ, διὰ κυρίου). He insists that he is asking of them nothing new, and that what he urges conforms to the instructions which they have already received and which they know. Finally, in emphasising that they are living in a manner pleasing to God, he can only ask and urge them to abound the more. These opening verses are general; the meaning of τὸ πῶς δεῖ and τίνας παραγγελίας becomes specific in 4³ ᶠᶠ·.

¹*Finally brothers we ask you and urge in the Lord Jesus that, as you have received from us instructions as to how you ought to walk and please God, as in fact you are walking, that you abound the more.* ²*For you know what instructions we gave you, prompted by the Lord Jesus.*

1. λοιπόν, ἀδελφοί. With λοιπόν, "finally," a particle of transition often found toward the end of a letter (Grot.: *locutio est properantis ad finem*), and with an affectionate ἀδελφοί (*cf.* 2 Cor. 13¹¹: λοιπόν, ἀδελφοί), Paul turns from the epistolary thanksgiving and prayer to the epistolary exhortation, from the more personal considerations to what remains to be said (Ambst. *quod superest*) about the deficiencies of the converts.

The reading is uncertain. The prefixed τό may be disregarded (Zim.); but as P in 2 Cor. 13¹¹ so most uncials here (אADEGFKL; WH.mg. Tisch. Zim. Weiss, Dob.) read λοιπὸν οὖν. Weiss (121) thinks that the omission of οὖν in B and in many minuscules and versions is due to a scribal error. Elsewhere, however, Paul uses both λοιπόν (1 Cor. 1¹⁶ 4² 2 Cor. 13¹¹) and τὸ λοιπόν (1 Cor. 7²⁹; plus ἀδελφοί, II 3¹, Phil. 4⁸; or plus ἀδελφοί μου, Phil. 3¹). Epictetus prefers λοιπόν to τὸ λοιπόν (*cf.* Bultman, *Der Stil der Paulinischen Predigt*, 1910, 101). If οὖν is read, the reference may still be in general to what has preceded (Lft.; *cf.* Dob.

who notes the οὖν in Rom. 12¹ Eph. 4¹, etc.) and not specifically to 3¹³, as many prefer (Ell.; *cf.* Lillie who remarks: "as working together with God to the same end"). For λοιπὸν οὖν in papyri, see Mill. *ad loc.* On the interpretation of vv. ¹⁻¹², see also Bahnsen, *ZWT.* 1904, 332–358.

ἐρωτῶμεν ὑμᾶς κτλ. "In the Lord Jesus we ask and urge you." On the analogy of παραγγέλλομεν καὶ παρακαλοῦμεν ἐν κυρίῳ Ἰ. Χ. (II 3¹²; *cf.* Rom. 14¹⁴ Eph. 4¹⁷), both verbs are to be construed with ἐν κυρίῳ Ἰησοῦ. In fact, ἐρωτᾶν and παρακαλεῖν are virtually synonymous (Œcumenius, *apud* Lillie: ταυτόν ἐστιν καὶ ἰσοδυναμεῖ), as the usage in papyri shows (*cf.* also Phil. 4²ᶠ· Lk. 7³ᶠ· Acts 16³⁹). The position of ὑμᾶς, after the first, not after the second verb, suggests not that the converts are in the Lord, which on other grounds is true, but that the apostles are in the Lord, the point being that the exhortation is based not on personal authority but on the authority of the indwelling Christ, which is recognised as valid by both readers and writers.

On the phrase, *cf.* P. Oxy. 744 (Witk. 97): ἐρωτῶ σε καὶ παρακαλῶ σε; and P. Oxy. 294 (Mill. *Greek Papyri*, 36): ἐρωτῶ δέ σε καὶ παρακαλῶ. Like δεῖσθαι, παρακαλεῖν is used of prayer to Christ (2 Cor. 12⁸); *cf.* P. Leid. K (Witk. 89): παρακαλῶ δὲ καὶ αὐτὸς τοὺς θεούς. ἐρωτᾶν like our "ask" and the Hebrew שאל is used in later Gk. for both "ask a question," "*interrogare*," and "ask a favour," "*rogare*" (*cf.* 2 Esd. 5¹⁰ Ps. 136³). The construction ἐρωτᾶν ἵνα, only here in Paul but quite common elsewhere (*cf.* Mk. 7²⁶ Lk. 7³⁶; P. Oxy. 744¹³ ᶠ·), is analogous to παρακαλεῖν ἵνα (II 3¹² 1 Cor. 1¹⁰ 16¹² 2 Cor. 9⁵ 12⁸). On the ἐν in ἐν (אA insert τῷ) κυρίῳ Ἰησοῦ, *cf.* Rom. 14¹⁴ Phil. 2¹⁹ Eph. 1¹⁵, and see on 1¹.

ἵνα . . . ἵνα. With ἵνα, Paul starts to introduce the object of the verbs of exhorting (*BMT.* 201); but before he gets to the goal he reminds the readers tactfully (1) that what he has to say is conformable to what they had received from him when he was with them; and (2) that they are in fact walking according to instructions received. When then he comes to the object of the verbs and repeats the ἵνα, he can only ask and urge them to abound the more.

Precisely what Paul intended to say when he began with the first ἵνα, whether περιπατῆτε καὶ ἀρέσκητε θεῷ, we do not know. Dob. observes that the Clementine Vulgate and Pelagius (but Souter thinks not) read *sic et ambuletis* = οὕτως καὶ περιπατῆτε, and take the second ἵνα in subordination to the first; a reading due to a corruption, within the Latin versions, of *ambulatis*. To avoid the pleonasm (Zim.), ℵAKL, *et al.*, omit the first ἵνα; KL, *et al.*, further soften by omitting καθὼς καὶ περιπατεῖτε.

καθὼς παρελάβετε κτλ. The first καθώς clause reminds them tactfully that what he has to say is not new but strictly conformable (καθώς) to the traditions and instructions which they had received (παρελάβετε; *cf.* Gal. 1⁹ 1 Cor. 15¹; II 3⁶ Phil. 4⁹ Col. 2⁶), those, namely, as v.² notes explicitly, that he had previously commanded διὰ τοῦ κυρίου. The teachings are here referred to generally and in the form of an indirect question: "As to how (τὸ πῶς) you ought to walk and so (καί) please God" (*cf.* Col. 1¹⁰). The καί is consecutive and "marks the ἀρέσκειν as the result of the περιπατεῖν" (Ell.; *cf.* Bl. 77⁶).

Paul as a Pharisee (Gal. 1¹⁴) and as a Christian has his παραδόσεις (II 2¹⁵ 3⁶ 1 Cor. 11²) or τύπος διδαχῆς (Rom. 6¹⁷; *cf.* 16¹⁷ 1 Cor. 4¹⁷ Col. 2⁷ Eph. 4²¹). Although he attributes his gospel to the immediate inspiration of the indwelling Christ or Spirit, yet the contents of the gospel are mediated by the Old Testament (*e. g.* Rom. 3²¹ 13⁹), late Judaism, words of Jesus (4¹⁵), and by the teaching of the primitive church (1 Cor. 11²³ 15²). On πῶς, see 1⁹; on τό introducing indirect questions, *cf.* Rom. 8²⁶ and Bl. 47⁵; on τὸ πῶς, Acts 4²¹; on πῶς δεῖ, II 3⁷ Col. 4⁶.

καθὼς καὶ περιπατεῖτε. This second tactful reminder, introduced by καθὼς καί (*cf.* 3⁴), is thoroughly in keeping with v. ¹⁰ 5¹¹ II 3⁴, and indicates of itself that the actual exhortation can only be for more such conduct. Hence the object of ἐρωτῶμεν καὶ παρακαλοῦμεν is, as expected: ἵνα περισσεύητε μᾶλλον, "that you abound even more in walking according to the instructions received."

On ἀρέσκειν, see 2⁴ and Deiss. *NBS.* 51; on περισσεύειν μᾶλλον, see v. ¹⁰ and *cf.* 2 Cor. 3⁹ Phil. 1⁹. Paul uses regularly the present subj. of περισσεύειν (1 Cor. 14¹² 2 Cor. 8⁷ 9⁸ Phil. 1²⁶); but B, *et al.*, here and BD, *et al.*, in Phil. 1⁹ read the aorist subj. as in 2 Cor. 4¹⁵.

2. οἴδατε γὰρ κτλ. "For you know what instructions we gave you." γάρ strengthens and confirms the point already made in the first clause with καθώς (v. ¹). This explicit appeal to

the knowledge of the readers shows how concerned Paul is in insisting that he is making no new requests.

"The emphasis, as Lünemann observes, rests on τίνας, and prepares the readers for the following τοῦτο, v. ³" (Ell.). Not until we come to ἀπέχεσθαι do we learn the content of τὸ πῶς δεῖ (v. ¹) and τίνας (v. ²). —For γάρ, cursive 33 reads δέ (cf. Gal. 4¹³). οἴδατε γάρ reminds us of the apologetic appeals in 1⁵ 2¹· ²· ⁵· ¹¹ 3³· ⁴; here also the reference is apologetic, but in a different sense; Paul would have his converts feel that he is not issuing new and arbitrary orders, but orders already given and prompted by the indwelling Christ (διὰ τοῦ κυρίου). παραγγελία is a military word occurring rarely in Gk. Bib. (literally in Acts 5²⁸ 16²⁴; of ethical orders, 1 Tim. 1⁵· ¹⁸ 1 Clem. 42³). διδόναι παραγ. is a late Gk. periphrasis for παραγγέλλειν (a common word in Gk. Bib.; cf. v. ¹¹ II 3⁴ ff.) similar to διδόναι ἐντολήν for ἐντέλλεσθαι (cf., in Jn. 14³¹, BL with ℵAD).

διὰ τοῦ κυρίου Ἰησοῦ. "Prompted by the Lord Jesus" (Lft.); loquente in nobis Spiritu Christi (Vatablus, apud Poole). The διά designates the Lord "as the causa medians through which the παραγγελίαι were declared; they were not the Apostle's own commands, but Christ's (οὐκ ἐμὰ γάρ, φησίν, ἃ παρήγγειλα, ἀλλ' ἐκείνου ταῦτα, Theophylact), by whose influence he was moved to deliver them" (Ell.). διὰ κυρίου is grammatically different from but essentially identical with ἐν κυρίῳ; the former is dynamic both in form and in meaning; the latter is static in form but dynamic in force (see on 1¹). Christians are "in" Christ or the Spirit because Christ or the Spirit is in them as a permanent energising activity. Since the divine is in them, it is "through" (διά) the divine as a mediating cause that they are empowered to do all things (Phil. 4¹³). The presence of both ἐν κυρίῳ (v. ¹) and διὰ κυρίου is here designed not to emphasise the apostolic authority of the writers but to point the readers to the divine source of authority which both readers and writers recognise as legitimate, the indwelling Christ. To be sure, Paul recognises his apostolic authority (2⁶ II 3⁹); no doubt it had of itself immense weight with the Thessalonians; but here he insists that just as when he was with them (2⁷) so now as he writes he is but one of them, relying as they do on Christ in them as the common source of divine authority.

Schettler, *Die paulinische Formel,* "*Durch Christus,*" 1907, gives an exhaustive study of διά with Χριστοῦ and its synonyms, θεοῦ and πνεύματος. While pressing his point somewhat rigorously, he succeeds in showing that διά indicates causal agency, and that the phrase "through Christ" denotes the activity of the spiritual Christ as agent in creation and salvation, and as an influence either in general or specifically in the life of prayer and the official legitimation of Paul (*cf. AJT.* 1907, 690 f.). For this διά, *cf.* 4¹⁴ 5⁹ II 2². A few minuscules (69. 441–2. 462) read here ἐν κυρίῳ 'I. (*cf.* II 3¹² where for ἐν κ. 'I. X., ℵᶜDᶜKL, *et al.*, read διά κ. 'I. X.); on this interchange of ἐν and διά, see further Rom. 5⁹ ᶠ· 2 Cor. 1²⁰ 5¹⁸ ᶠ· Col. 1¹⁶· ¹⁹ ᶠ·. On ἐν ὀνόματι (II 3⁶ Col 3¹⁷) and διά τοῦ ὀνόματος (1 Cor. 1¹⁰), see below on II 3⁶.

(2) *True Consecration* (4³⁻⁸).

The divine exhortation (ἐν κυρίῳ, v. ¹) and the divine command (διὰ κυρίου, v. ²) now becomes the divine will (θέλημα τοῦ θεοῦ, v. ³). The meaning of τὸ πῶς (v. ¹) and τίνας (v. ²) which are resumed by τοῦτο (v. ³) is first stated generally as "your consecration," that is, "that you be consecrated." This general statement is then rendered specific by two pairs of infinitives in apposition to ὁ ἁγιασμὸς ὑμῶν, namely, ἀπέχεσθαι and εἰδέναι, κτᾶσθαι and ὑπερβαίνειν. The principle is that true consecration being moral as well as religious demands sexual purity. Along with the principle, a practical remedy is suggested: The prevention of fornication by having respect for one's wife; and the prevention of adultery by marrying not in lust but in the spirit of holiness and honour. As a sanction for obedience, Paul adds (vv.·⁶ᵇ⁻⁸) that Christ punishes impurity; that God calls Christians not for impurity but for holiness; and that the Spirit, the gift of God unto consecration, is a permanent divine power resident in the individual Christian (5²³) so that disobedience is directed not against the human but against the divine.

The appeal to the Spirit as the highest sanction in every problem of the moral life is characteristic of Paul; *cf.* 1 Cor. 6¹⁹ and McGiffert, *Apostolic Age,* 263 *ff.* The reason for presenting the Christian view of consecration involving a Christian view of marriage is to be found not simply in the fact that the converts had as pagans looked upon sexual immorality as a matter of indifference, but also in the fact that such im-

10

morality had been sanctioned by their own religious rites (see on ἀκα-θαρσία, 2³). The temptation was thus particularly severe and some of the converts may have been on the point of yielding. The group as a whole, however, was pure, as 1³ 3⁶ and καθὼς καὶ περιπατεῖτε (v. ²) make plain.

³*God's will is this, that you be consecrated, that is, that you ab-stain from fornication,* ⁴*that each of you respect his own wife; that each of you get his own wife in the spirit of consecration and honour* ⁵*not in the passion of lust, as is the case with the Gentiles who know not God,* ⁶*to prevent any one of you from disregarding or taking ad-vantage of his brother in the matter. For the Lord is an avenger for all these matters, as indeed we have predicted and solemnly affirmed;* ⁷*for God has not called us Christians for impurity but to be conse-crated;* ⁸*consequently the rejecter rejects not man but God who puts his Spirit, the consecrating Spirit, into you.*

3. τοῦτο γάρ κτλ. "Well, to be explicit, God's will is this." With the explanatory γάρ, τὸ πῶς and τίνας (v. ²) are resumed by τοῦτο, a predicate probably, placed for emphasis before the sub-ject θέλημα τοῦ θεοῦ; and are further explained in ὁ ἁγιασμὸς ὑμῶν. By saying "God's will," Paul lays stress once more on the divine sanction already evident in the introduction (vv. ¹⁻²), "in" and "through" the Lord Jesus.

Though ἁγιασμὸς ὑμῶν and ἀπέχεσθαι are in apposition with τοῦτο, it is yet uncertain whether τοῦτο is subject (Lft. and most comm.) or predicate (De W. Dob.). Since τοῦτο resumes the objects τὸ πῶς and τίνας, and since the prompting subject is Christ (διὰ τοῦ κυρίου) who expresses the will of God, it is perhaps better to take θέλημα τοῦ θεοῦ as subject and τοῦτο as predicate. On τοῦτο γάρ, cf. especially 5¹⁸; also 4¹⁵ 2 Cor. 8¹⁰ Col. 3²⁰, etc. In Paul regularly (except 1 Cor. 7³⁷ Eph. 2³) and in Lxx. frequently, θέλημα refers to the divine will. In Paul we have either τὸ θέλημα τοῦ θεοῦ (Rom. 12² Eph. 6⁶; with κατά, Gal. 1⁴ (cf. 1 Esd. 8¹⁶); or ἐν, Rom. 1¹⁰); or θέλημα θεοῦ (5¹⁸; with διά, Rom. 15³² 1 Cor. 1¹, etc.) like εὐαγγέλιον θεοῦ (Rom. 1¹). We expect here either τὸ θέλημα τοῦ θεοῦ (A) or θέλημα θεοῦ (D; so BD in 5¹⁸ where ℵ has θέλημα τοῦ θεοῦ). The omission of only one article here may be due to the influence of the Hebrew construct state (Bl. 46⁹). But neither here nor in 5¹⁸ is the total will of God in mind; *multae sunt voluntates* (Bengel). Paul does not use θέλησις; cf. ἡ θέλησις τοῦ θεοῦ (Tob. 12¹⁸ 2 Mac. 12¹⁶).

ὁ ἁγιασμὸς ὑμῶν = τὸ ὑμᾶς ἁγιάζεσθαι. God's will is "your consecration"; that is, either that you may be consecrated or better that you consecrate yourselves. The word ἁγιασμός denotes both the process of consecration (as here) and the state of the consecrated (as vv. ⁴· ⁷; see SH. on Rom. 6¹⁹). The consecrating power is God (5²³), Christ (1 Cor. 1²· ³⁰), or the Spirit (v. ⁸ II 2¹³; cf. Rom. 15¹⁶). Though in itself, as Vorstius (apud Poole) observes, ἁγιασμός is a general term, yet the immediate context, ἀπέχεσθαι . . . πορνείας, and the contrasts between ἁγιασμός and πάθος ἐπιθυμίας (vv. ⁴⁻⁵) and between ἁγιασμός and ἀκαθαρσία (v. ⁷) suggest the restriction to impurity.

In the N. T. ἁγιασμός is chiefly in Paul; but only here do we have the article or the personal pronoun (cf. Ezek. 45⁴). On ἐν ἁγιασμῷ, cf. vv. ⁴· ⁷ Test. xii, Benj. 10¹¹ Ps. Sol. 17³³ 1 Clem. 35²; on ἐν ἁγιασμῷ πνεύματος II 2¹³ 1 Pet. 1²; on εἰς ἁγιασμόν, Rom. 6¹⁹· ²² Amos 2¹¹. For ἁγιασμός = ἁγιωσύνη, cf. Test. xii, Levi 18⁷ (πνεῦμα ἁγιασμοῦ) with 18¹¹ and Rom. 1⁴ (πνεῦμα ἁγιωσύνης).

ἀπέχεσθαι . . . πορνείας. "That you hold aloof from fornication"; for true consecration to God is moral as well as religious. Every kind of impurity is a sin not simply against man but against God (cf. v. ⁸ and Ps. 50⁶: σοὶ μόνῳ ἥμαρτον).

What was unclear in τὸ πῶς (v. ¹), τίνας (v. ²), and τοῦτο (v. ³) and what was still general in ὁ ἁγιασμὸς ὑμῶν, now (vv. ³ᵇ⁻⁶ᵃ) becomes clear and specific in the two pairs of infinitives, ἀπέχεσθαι and εἰδέναι, κτᾶσθαι and ὑπερβαίνειν, placed in asyndetical apposition with ὁ ἁγιασμὸς ὑμῶν. Dibelius thinks it unnecessary to take the infin. as appositive, "since the infinitive often appears in such hortatory enumerations (see Pseudophokylides)"; on such infinitives, but without subject, cf. Rom. 12¹⁵ Phil. 3¹⁶ and Bl. 69¹. In the Lxx. ἀπέχεσθαι takes either the genitive alone or the gen. with ἀπό (both constructions in Sap. 2¹⁶); classic Gk. prefers the former, Paul the latter (5²²). Paul uses the plural πορνεῖαι (1 Cor. 7²) but not πᾶσα πορνεία (so F here); the word itself suggests all forms of sexual immorality. On the generic τῆς, cf. 1 Cor. 6¹³· ¹⁸.

4. εἰδέναι . . . σκεῦος. "That each of you respect his own wife." Usually εἰδέναι is understood in the sense of "learn how to," "savoir" (Phil. 4¹²) and so is construed with κτᾶσθαι as its com-

plement: "that each one of you learn how to get (or 'possess') his own vessel ('wife' or 'body') in holiness and honour"; in the light, however, of 5^{12} where εἰδέναι = "respect," it is tempting to take it also here = "regard," "appreciate the worth of." In this case a comma is to be put after σκεῦος to indicate the separation of κτᾶσθαι from εἰδέναι. With this punctuation, the parallelism of ἀπέχεσθαι and εἰδέναι, κτᾶσθαι and τὸ μὴ ὑπερβαίνειν becomes at once obvious.

εἰδέναι here and 5^{12}, like ἐπιγινώσκειν in 1 Cor. 16^{18} Mt. 17^{12}, is employed in a sense akin to that in the common Lxx. phrase εἰδέναι (v. ^{5} II 1^8 Gal. 4^8) or γινώσκειν (Gal. 4^9) θεόν, the knowledge involving intelligent reverence and obedience; cf. Ign. Smyr. 9^1: θεὸν καὶ ἐπίσ-κοπον εἰδέναι. For ἕκαστον, B^2 or B^3, the Latins, et al. read ἕνα ἕκαστον as 2^{11} II 1^3.—(1) In the usual view which takes εἰδέναι with κτᾶσθαι and which rightly sees in vv. $^{3b-8}$ a reference solely to ἀκαθαρσία, the point is that "first πορνεία is prohibited; then a holy use of its natural remedy affirmatively inculcated; and lastly the heinous sin of μοιχεία, especially as regarded in its social aspects, formally denounced" (Ell.). (2) In favour of the alternative view which takes εἰδέναι = "respect" and so separates it from κτᾶσθαι is the position of κτᾶσθαι not before τὸ ἑαυτοῦ σκεῦος as we should expect from Phil. 4^{12}, and as DG, et al., here actually have it, but after; the apparent parallelism of the four infinitives; the fact that εἰδέναι . . . σκεῦος is complete in itself, balancing ἀπέχεσθαι . . . πορνείας; and the fact that εἰδέναι in 5^{12} = "to respect," "appreciate." In this alternative view we have two pairs of parallel infinitives, ἀπέχεσθαι and εἰδέναι, κτᾶσθαι and τὸ μὴ ὑπερβαί-νειν. In the first pair, ἀπέχεσθαι, though first in order, is really subordinate to εἰδέναι, the point being: "abstain from fornication by appreciating the worth of your wife." In the second pair, ὑπερβαίνειν, as τὸ μή (v. infra) intimates, is explicitly subordinate to κτᾶσθαι, the thought being: "marry in the spirit of holiness and thus prevent adultery with a brother's wife." The arrangement of the four infinitives is chiastic; in each pair a practical remedy for temptation is provided.

Spitta (Zur Geschichte und Litteratur, I, 1893, 131^2) was evidently the first to suggest the separation of κτᾶσθαι from εἰδέναι; but his own view that εἰδέναι = ידע (Gen. 4^{17}, etc.) is apparently untenable, for ידע = "know carnally" is rendered in Lxx. not by εἰδέναι but by γινώ-σκειν (Judg. 21^{11} is not an exception). Born. and Vincent rightly take εἰδέναι here as in 5^{12} to mean "respect," but assume for κτᾶσθαι the improbable sense (v. infra): "to do business." Wohl., after taking the position that both impurity and dishonesty in business are discussed in vv. ³ᵇ⁻⁸, suggests for consideration in a foot-note (90²) an interpretation similar to the alternative view here proposed, but does not elaborate it.

τὸ ἑαυτοῦ σκεῦος. "His own vessel," that is, "his own wife." Paul has in mind married men and the temptation to unholy and dishonourable relations with women. The ἑαυτοῦ intimates a contrast between a σκεῦος πορνείας and a σκεῦος γάμου τιμίου. As εἰδέναι κτλ., parallel to and explanatory of ἀπέχεσθαι κτλ. shows, the way of escape from πορνεία is the appreciation of the worth of the wife. This estimate of marriage is essential to true consecration and is God's will.

σκεῦος is rare in Paul; it is used literally of a utensil in the household (Rom. 9²¹), and metaphorically, with some qualifying description, of an implement for some purpose (e. g. Rom. 9²² ᶠ· σκεύη ὀργῆς, ἐλέους; 2 Cor. 4⁷ ὀστράκινα σκεύη—"a metaphor from money stored in earthen jars," as Bigg (ICC. on 1 Pet. 3⁷) notes). The absolute τὸ σκεῦος in a metaphorical sense appears to be unique in the Gk. Bib.   (1) On the analogy of the other Pauline passages, the reference here is to a vessel adapted to a purpose; and the emphasis on ἑαυτοῦ and the contrast with πορνεία suggest the woman as the vessel, not, however, for fornication but for honourable marriage. This meaning for σκεῦος has a parallel not in 1 Pet. 3⁷ (where both the man and the woman are vessels), but in rabbinical literature (cf. Schöttgen, Horae Hebraicae, I, 827), where כלי = σκεῦος = woman. This interpretation of σκεῦος is taken by the Greek Th. Mops. as well as by Augustine and most modern commentators.   (2) On the other hand, many commentators (e. g. Tertullian, Chrys. Theodoret, Calv. Grot. Mill. Dibelius) understand σκεῦος as = "body." In support of this opinion, passages are frequently adduced (see Lün. and cf. Barn. 7³ 11¹⁹) in which the context rather than the word itself (σκεῦος, ἀγγεῖον, vas) indicates that the vessel of the spirit or soul is the body. But even if σκεῦος of itself is a metaphor for body (cf. Barn. 21⁸), it is difficult so to understand it here, if κτᾶσθαι and ἑαυτοῦ have their usual meaning.   (1) κτᾶσθαι in the Gk. Bib. as in classic Gk. means "to get" a wife (Sir. 36²⁹), children (Gen. 4¹), friends (Sir. 6⁷), enemies (Sir. 20²³ 29⁶), gold (Mt. 10¹⁹), etc.; also "to buy" (Acts 1¹⁸ 8²⁰ 22²⁸). The sense "dem Erwerb nachgehen" (Born.), "pursue gain-getting" (Vincent) is doubtful, although we have the absolute ὁ κτώμενος "the buyer" (Deut. 28⁶⁸ Ezek. 7¹² ᶠ· 8³); κέκτησθαι (not in N. T.) in Lxx. as in classic Gk. means "to have gotten" (a wife, Ruth 4¹⁰), "possess" (Pr. 16²²), "own" (ὁ κεκτημένος, "the owner," Ep. Jer. 58). "Cum κτᾶσθαι significat acquirere non potest σκεῦος significare corpus suum sed uxorem" (Wetstein). This conclusion, however, is bereft of its force if in Hellenistic Gk. κτᾶσθαι = κέκτησθαι (so Mill. who quotes P. Tebt. 5²⁴¹ ᶠᶠ· and P. Oxy. 259⁶; and, following him, Dibelius). (2) But the difficulty with ἑαυτοῦ remains: "to possess his *own* body." This may be obviated by assuming that here, as often in later Gk., ἑαυτοῦ like ἴδιος (*cf.* I Cor. 7²) has "lost much of its emphatic force" (Mill. on ἑαυτῆς, 2⁷; and Moult. I, 87 *ff.*). If, however, κτᾶσθαι and ἑαυτοῦ retain here their normal meaning, then σκεῦος probably = "woman," "wife."

κτᾶσθαι. "That each of you get in marriage his own wife" (*sc.* τὸ ἑαυτοῦ σκεῦος). Wetstein notes Sir. 36²⁹: ὁ κτώμενος γυναῖκα ἐνάρχεται κτήσεως (*cf.* also Ruth 4¹⁰). Paul has now in mind unmarried men and the temptation especially to adultery. The ἑαυτοῦ is contrasted with the brother's wife implied in v. ⁶. True consecration, which is God's will, is not simply that a man should marry in order to avoid adultery (*cf.* I Cor. 7²: διὰ τὰς πορνείας ἕκαστος τὴν ἑαυτοῦ γυναῖκα ἐχέτω), but, as the ἐν ἁγιασμῷ καὶ τιμῇ prescribes, should marry in purity and respect for his wife, and not in the passion of lust. As the clause with εἰδέναι explained that the married man is to appreciate his wife and so be kept from fornication, so the clause with τὸ μὴ ὑπερβαίνειν indicates that the unmarried man is to marry in holiness and honour and so be kept from invading the sanctity of his brother's home.

The subject ἕκαστον and the object τὸ ἑαυτοῦ σκεῦος hold over; *cf.* Sir. 51²⁵ (κτήσασθε αὐτοῖς ἄνευ ἀργυρίου), where αὐτήν is to be supplied.

ἐν ἁγιασμῷ καὶ τιμῇ. "In holiness and honour." The ἐν designates the atmosphere in which the union of the man and woman takes place (Ell.). ἁγιασμός is here equivalent to ἁγιωσύνη, the state of those who are consecrated to God. Religious feeling is to pervade marriage; but whether this feeling is to be expressed in prayer is not stated. Wohl. notes Ignatius to Polycarp 5²: "It is fitting for men who marry and women who are married to unite themselves (τὴν ἕνωσιν ποιεῖσθαι) with the consent of the bishop ἵνα ὁ γάμος ᾖ κατὰ κύριον καὶ μὴ κατ' ἐπιθυμίαν." The marriage is likewise to be "in honour"; that is, the woman is not a σκεῦος πορνείας but a σκεῦος γάμου τιμίου, and honour is due her as a person of worth (εἰδέναι).

Paul's statement touches only the principles; Tobit 8¹ ᶠᶠ· is more specific. "Even were κτᾶσθαι taken as = 'possess,' a usage not quite impossible for later Greek, it would only extend the idea to the duties of a Christian husband" (Moff.).

5. μὴ ἐν πάθει ἐπιθυμίας κτλ. Without connecting particle, the positive statement is further elucidated by a negative and the contrast between Pauline and pagan ideals of marriage sharply set forth: "not in the passion of lust as is the case with the Gentiles who do not recognise and obey the moral requirements of God." That pagan marriage was marked by the absence of holiness and respect for the wife and by the presence of passionate lust is the testimony of one familiar with the facts, one who is "as good a source for the life of the people as any satirist" (Dob.).

πάθος signifies any feeling; to 4 Mac. it consists of ἡδονή and πόνος; in Paul it is always used in a bad sense (Rom. 1²⁶ Col. 3⁵). ἐπιθυμία in Paul has usually a bad sense, but sometimes a good sense (2¹⁷ Phil. 1²³; cf. κακὴ ἐπιθυμία, Col. 3⁵). On καθάπερ καί, see 3⁶. Ellicott, with his wonted exactness, notes the καί as having here "its comparative force and instituting a comparison between the Gentiles and the class implied in ἕκαστον ὑμῶν." On τὰ μὴ εἰδότα τὸν θεόν, a Lxx. phrase (Jer. 10²⁵ Ps. 78⁶), cf. II 1⁸ Gal. 4⁸ 1 Cor. 1²¹, and contrast Rom. 1²¹. If the Thessalonians in their pagan state had held πορνεία to be sanctioned by religion, and had also considered πάθος ἐπιθυμίας to be compatible with honourable marriage, the clause with καθάπερ would be particularly telling. See Jowett, II, 70 ff. "On the Connexion of Immorality and Idolatry."

6. τὸ μὴ ὑπερβαίνειν καὶ πλεονεκτεῖν. "To prevent (τὸ μή) any one of you (sc. τινὰ ὑμῶν from ἕκαστον ὑμῶν, v. ⁴) from disregarding and taking advantage of his brother in the matter." Just as appreciation of the wife (εἰδέναι) is tacitly regarded as a preventive of fornication (ἀπέχεσθαι), so pure and honourable marriage (κτᾶσθαι) is expressly (τὸ μή) regarded as preventing the invasion (ὑπερβαίνειν) of the sanctity of the brother's home.

The meaning of τὸ μή is uncertain. Many take it as final in the sense of τοῦ μή (Schmiedel) or ὥστε (Lft.); others regard it as not merely parallel to the anarthrous εἰδέναι but as reverting "to the preceding ἁγιασμός, of which it presents a specific exemplification more immediately suggested by the second part of v. ⁴" (Ell.); Dob., who inclines to the view of Ell., concludes that the article indicates the beginning of a new and second main point, the matter of dishonesty in business; Dibelius suggests that the article is merely a cæsura in delivery, designed to show that the μή is not parallel to the μή in v. ⁵, but the beginning of a new clause. On the other hand, τὸ μή (cf. 3²) may be due to the idea of hindering implied in the clause with κτᾶσθαι, a clause thus to be closely connected with τὸ μὴ ὑπερβαίνειν κτλ., as indeed the asyndetical construction itself suggests. In classical Greek, τὸ μή is used with many verbs and expressions which denote or even imply hindrance or prevention (GMT. 811, where inter alia the following are noted: Æschylus, Agam. 15: φόβος παραστατεῖ τὸ μὴ βλέφαρα συμβαλεῖν ὕπνῳ ("stands by to prevent my closing my eyes in sleep"); and Soph. Antig. 544: μήτοι, μ' ἀτιμάσῃς τὸ μὴ οὐ θανεῖν). In this case there is no reason for assuming a change of subject in v. ⁶.—ὑπερβαίνειν, only here in N. T., is used in the Lxx. literally, "cross over" (2 Reg. 22³⁰ Pr. 9¹⁸ A), "pass by" (2 Reg. 18²³ Job 9¹¹); and metaphorically "surpass" (3 Mac. 6²⁴), "leave unnoticed," "disregard" (Mic. 7¹⁸: ἐξαίρων ἀνομίας καὶ ὑπερβαίνων ἀσεβείας). Since the meaning "disregard" suits perfectly here (cf. Ell. who notes Isæus 38⁶ 43³⁴ and other passages), it is unnecessary to take ὑπερβαίνειν absolutely, or to supply, instead of the natural object τὸν ἀδελφὸν αὐτοῦ, either ὅριον or νόμον (see Wetstein, who also quotes Jerome: concessos fines praetergrediens nuptiarum). πλεονεκτεῖν occurs elsewhere in Gk. Bib. apart from Paul (2 Cor. 2¹¹ 7² 12¹⁷ ᶠ·) only Judg. 4¹¹ Ezek. 22²⁷ Hab. 2⁹; it means "get the advantage of," "defraud," the context not the word itself indicating the nature of the advantage taken, whether in money, as usually in Paul, or not (2 Cor. 2¹¹). Here the object of greediness (cf. πλεονεξία, 2⁵) is the brother's wife as the context as a whole and ἐν τῷ πράγματι particularly suggest.

ἐν τῷ πράγματι. "In the matter," "the meaning of which is sufficiently defined by the context" (Lft.), as in 2 Cor. 7¹¹. It is probable that the phrase is not a specific reference either to πορνεία, as if the article were anaphoristic, or to μοιχεία, as if the article referred to the matter immediately in hand, but is "a euphemistic generalisation for all sorts of uncleanness" (Lillie), as περὶ πάντων τούτων in this clause and ἀκαθαρσία in v. ⁷ suggest.

τῷ, not the enclitic τῳ, which is without parallel in the N. T., is to be read.—πρᾶγμα like res and דבר is a euphemism for anything abominable. Wetstein cites in point not only 2 Cor. 7¹¹ but also Æschines, Timarch.

132 *ff.* and Isæus, *de haered. Cironis*, 44; *cf.* also Pirque Aboth 5²³ and Taylor's note.—In this connection it may be noted that many commentators (*e. g.* Calv. Grot. De W. Lün. Born. Vincent, Wohl. Dob.) deny the view of Chrys. Th. Mops. Bengel, and most English interpreters (see the names in Lillie) that Paul in vv. ³ᵇ⁻⁸ is referring solely to impurity, and assert, either on the ground that Vulg. translates ἐν τῷ πράγματι by *in negotio* or that Paul frequently associates uncleanness with avarice (*cf.* Test. xii, Benj. 5¹ ἄσωτοι and οἱ πλεονεκτοῦντες), that with τὸ μή a new point begins, dishonesty in business (*cf.* especially Dob. *Die urchristlichen Gemeinden*, 1902, 283). In this view, πρᾶγμα = "business"; and the article is either anaphoristic, if with Born. and Vincent κτᾶσθαι = "to do business," or generic, business in general. Against this opinion is the consideration that "no other adequate example of πρᾶγμα in this sense in the singular has been produced" (Mill.). To obviate this consideration, Dibelius looks beyond 1 Cor. 6¹ (πρᾶγμα ἔχειν) to the papyri for πρᾶγμα in the sense of "case" at court, without explaining τῷ, and refers v. ⁶ to disputes: "*nicht Uebergriffe machen und beim Zwist den Bruder übervorteilen.*"—To interpret v. ⁶ of sexual immorality is considered forced exegesis by Calv. and Dob. On the other hand, Ell. pertinently remarks: "To regard the verse as referring to fraud and covetousness in the general affairs of life is to infringe on the plain meaning of τῷ πράγματι; to obscure the reference to the key-word of the paragraph ἀκαθαρσία (v. ⁷); to mar the contextual symmetry of the verses; and to introduce an exegesis so frigid and unnatural as to make us wonder that such good names should be associated with an interpretation seemingly so improbable."

τὸν ἀδελφὸν αὐτοῦ. Not neighbour in general, not both neighbour and Christian brother, but simply the Christian brother is meant. Obviously the point is not that it is permissible thus to wrong an outsider, but that it is unspeakable thus to wrong a brother in Christ. Zanchius (*apud* Poole) compares aptly 1 Cor. 6⁸: ἀδικεῖτε καὶ τοῦτο ἀδελφούς.

6ᵇ–8. With διότι, γάρ (v. ⁷) and τοιγαροῦν (v. ⁸), Paul passes to motives for obeying these commands, not his but God's commands. First he appeals, as he had done before when he was with them, to the sanction of the judgment when Christ will punish all these sins of the flesh (v. ⁶ᵇ). Next he reminds them that God's call had a moral end in view, holiness (v. ⁷). Finally he points out that the indwelling, consecrating Spirit, the gift of God, is the resident divine power in the individual, so that disobedience strikes not at the human but at the divine (v. ⁸).

διότι ἔκδικος κτλ. διότι = "because" as in 2⁸. As a sanction for present obedience to the will of God as specified in vv. ³ᵇ⁻⁶ᵃ, Paul points to the future judgment (2 Cor. 5¹⁰, Rom. 14¹⁰). κύριος is not θεός (GF) but Christ (3¹²), as the emphatic ὁ θεός (vv. ⁷⁻⁸) intimates. He is the one who inflicts punishment directly or indirectly (cf. II 1⁸), the avenger (ἔκδικος) "for all these things," that is, for fornication, adultery, and all such uncleanness.

ἔκδικος means here, as always in Gk. Bib. (Rom. 13⁴ Sir. 30⁶ Sap. 12¹² 4 Mac. 15²⁹; cf. ἐκδικητής Ps. 8³), "avenger." This characterisation of God is so common in the Lxx. (ἐκδικῶν or ποιῶν ἐκδίκησιν, Ps. 98⁸ Nah. 1² Mic. 5¹⁵, etc.), that the phrase ἔκδικος κύριος here need not be a literary allusion to Ps. 93¹: ὁ θεὸς ἐκδικήσεων κύριος, ὁ θεὸς ἐκδικήσεων.

καθὼς καὶ προείπαμεν κτλ. Paul tactfully reminds them, as in vv. ¹⁻², that this eschatological sanction is not new to them. When he was with them he had "predicted" and "solemnly affirmed" that Christ would avenge all manner of unchastity. Apparently neither the temptation nor the exhortation was new. But whether Timothy had brought news of the yielding to temptation in some case or cases, since Paul's departure, as ὁ ἀθετῶν (v. ⁸) rather strongly intimates, or whether the exhortation is simply prophylactic, is uncertain.

On the comparative καί (A omits) after καθώς, see 3⁴; the καί after ὑμῖν is the simple copula; on the position of ὑμῖν, cf. v. ¹ ἐρωτῶμεν ὑμᾶς. προείπαμεν (cf. Gal. 5²¹ where it is contrasted with προλέγω) is predictive as in 3⁴; on the mixed aorist (AKL read προείπομεν), see Bl. 21¹. διαμαρτύρεσθαι, only here in Paul but common elsewhere in Gk. Bib., is possibly stronger than μαρτύρεσθαι (2¹²; but cf. Kennedy, Sources, 37); it means either "call to witness" (Jer. 39¹⁰· ⁴⁴ Deut. 4²⁶ 31²⁸) or "solemnly affirm or protest"; etiam apud Att. notio testes invocandi evanescit (Blass on Acts 2⁴⁰).

7. οὐ γὰρ ἐκάλεσεν κτλ. The γάρ, parallel to διότι (v. ⁶), introduces a second motive for obedience, the moral goal of God's call. "For God called us Christians not that we should be impure (ἐπί denoting the purpose or object) but that we should be holy" (ἐν indicating the state of holiness resulting from the call-

ing). Such being the moral purpose of the call, it would be sin to disregard these commands which express God's will.

On χαλεῖν, which is mediated by the preaching of the gospel (II 2¹⁴), see 2¹²; on ἀκαθαρσία, which sums up περὶ πάντων τούτων, see 2³. ἁγιασμός is here, as in v. ⁴, holiness, the state of those whom God consecrates to himself through the Spirit. ἐπί indicates either the condition or basis on which, or the "object or purpose for which, they were (not) called" (Ell.); cf. Gal. 5¹³ Eph. 2¹⁰ and Bl. 43³; also Sap. 2²³ ὁ θεὸς ἔκτισεν τὸν ἄνθρωπον ἐπ' ἀφθαρσίᾳ (Mill.). ἐν is not for εἰς (Piscator) but is a "natural abbreviation for ὥστε εἶναι ἐν ἁγιασμῷ as the sense requires" (Lft. who notes Eph. 4⁴). For ἐν introducing the result of χαλεῖν, Col. 3¹⁵ is pertinent. Other expositors (e. g. Bengel, Hofmann, Riggenbach, Wohl. Dob.) understand ἁγιασμός as an act of God and ἐν as indicating the essential character of the call.

8. τοιγαροῦν. With τοιγαροῦν, "therefore," "consequently," Paul draws a sharp inference from vv. ³⁻⁷. Since the specific commands, making for a consecration that is moral, are the express will of God who not only judges but calls unto holiness, he that sets aside these injunctions sets aside not man but God, the God who through his Spirit is the energising, consecrating power in the hearts of the believers.

As in Is. 21² (ὁ ἀθετῶν ἀθετεῖ, ὁ ἀνομῶν ἀνομεῖ), so here the present participle is timeless and equivalent to a substantive, "the rejecter," "the despiser." The omission of the object (Vulg. qui haec spernit) serves to "call attention not so much to what is set at naught as to the person who sets at naught" (Ell.). The omission of the article before ἄνθρωπον suggests a reference not to man generically nor to some particular man (e. g. τὸν ἀδελφόν who has been wronged), but to any individual, with perhaps a "latent reference to the Apostle" (Ell.; cf. Dob. who compares 2 Cor. 12²) who was God's spokesman. The contrast between man and God is unqualified (cf. 2¹³ Gal. 1¹⁰ Exod. 16⁸ 1 Reg. 8⁷); it is not a man's will but God's will that is here in question. τοιγαροῦν, elsewhere in N. T. only Heb. 12¹ and a dozen times in Lxx., is similar to but stronger than διὰ τοῦτο (2¹³), διό (3¹) or ὥστε (4¹⁸), and like these introduces a logical conclusion from a preceding discussion. Usually it begins the sentence (Heb. 12¹ Job 22¹⁰; cf. Epictetus); sometimes it is the second word (4 Mac. 13¹⁶ 17⁴ Job 24²², etc.). ἀθετεῖν (cf. Soph. Lex. sub voc.) is a late Gk. word common in Lxx.; it signifies "put away," "set aside"; hence "reject," "spurn," "despise" (cf. Jude 8 with 2 Pet. 2¹⁰).

τὸν διδόντα κτλ. "Who puts his Spirit, the holy, consecrating Spirit into you," that is, εἰς τὰς καρδίας ὑμῶν (Gal. 4⁶). This addition, phrased in language reminiscent of the Lxx. (cf. Ezek. 37¹⁴: καὶ δώσω τὸ πνεῦμά μου εἰς ὑμᾶς καὶ ζήσεσθε), is a tacit reminder that they as well as Paul are ἐν κυρίῳ (v. ¹) and as such responsible for their conduct not to Paul but to God who dwells in them by Christ or the Spirit. Three points are evident in this appended characterisation of God, each of them intimating a motive for obedience. (1) Not only is God the one who calls and judges, he is also the one who graciously puts into their hearts his Spirit whose presence insures their blamelessness in holiness when the Lord comes (3¹³). In gratitude for this divine gift, they should be loyally obedient. (2) This indwelling Spirit is a power unto holiness, a consecrating Spirit. Devotion to God must consequently be ethical. (3) The Spirit is put not εἰς ἡμᾶς (A) "into us Christians" collectively, but εἰς ὑμᾶς "into you" Thessalonians, specifically. Hence each of them is individually responsible to God who by the Spirit is resident in them. In despising, the individual despises not a man but God.

διδόντα (ℵBDEGFI) is a general present participle and timeless; it describes God as the giver of the Spirit (cf. ὁ καλῶν ὑμᾶς, 2¹²). δόντα (AKL, Vulg.) is due to ἐκάλεσεν (v. ⁷; cf. ℵA in 2¹², καλέσαντος); the aorist points to the time when God gave (Rom. 5⁵ 2 Cor. 1²² 5⁵) or sent (Gal. 4⁶) the Spirit into their hearts. The new point emphasised by τὸν διδόντα is made explicit by ℵDGFKL, Vulg. et al., which insert καί after τόν (cf. ℵGP in II 2¹⁴ which read καί before ἐκάλεσεν, and A in II 3² which inserts καί before στηρίξει). Here BAEI omit καί, as do BADKL in II 2¹⁴ and ℵBD and most in 3⁸. In our passage, most textual critics including Weiss (112) insert καί; but WH. do not allow it even as an alternative reading. The phrase διδόναι πνεῦμα εἴς τινα is apparently found elsewhere in Gk. Bib. only Ezek. 37⁶·¹⁴. For διδόναι πνεῦμά τινι, cf. Rom. 5⁵ 11⁸ 2 Cor. 5⁵ Eph. 1¹⁷; Is. 42⁵; for διδόναι πνεῦμα ἔν τινι, cf. 2 Cor. 1²² 3 Reg. 22²³ Ezek. 36²⁶ ff. 4 Reg. 19⁷ 2 Ch. 18²²; for διδόναι πνεῦμα ἐπί τινα, cf. Num. 11²⁹ Is. 42¹. The εἰς is for dative or for ἐν; "give to be in," "put in."—The whole phrase τὸ πνεῦμα αὐτοῦ τὸ ἅγιον is unusual in Paul; he uses, indeed, τὸ πνεῦμα αὐτοῦ (Rom. 8¹¹), τὸ ἅγιον πνεῦμα (2 Cor. 13¹³), and τὸ πνεῦμα τὸ ἅγιον τοῦ θεοῦ (Eph. 4³⁰; cf. 1¹³ and Is. 63¹¹); but more often he has simply πνεῦμα ἅγιον (1⁵ f·, etc.; Ps. Sol. 17⁴²). On the phrase here, cf. Ps. 142¹⁰: τὸ πνεῦμά σου τὸ ἅγιον, and Is. 63¹⁰: αὐτοὶ δὲ ἠπείθησαν καὶ παρώξυναν τὸ πνεῦμα τὸ ἅγιον αὐτοῦ. Paul's emphasis on τὸ ἅγιον is especially appropriate to the theme ἁγιασμός, consecration which is ethical as well as religious. Some codices (AI) put αὐτοῦ before πνεῦμα.

(3) Love to the Brothers (4⁹⁻¹⁰ᵃ).

As the exhortation to ethical consecration (vv. ³⁻⁸) recalls ἀμέμπτους ἐν ἁγιωσύνῃ (3¹³), so the new point "concerning love to the brothers" recalls περισσεύσαι τῇ ἀγάπῃ εἰς ἀλλήλους (3¹²). The form in which the new section (δέ) is introduced, περὶ δὲ τῆς φιλαδελφίας, suggests (cf. 1 Cor. 7²⁵ 8¹ 12¹ 16¹ (2 Cor. 9¹) 16¹²) that the Thessalonians had written Paul expressly for advice in this matter. They would scarcely have done so, if there had been no disturbing elements in the brotherhood, namely, as vv. ¹⁰ᵇ⁻¹² intimate, idleness on the part of some leading to poverty and meddlesomeness in the affairs of the brotherhood. In his reply, Paul at first says (vv. ⁹⁻¹⁰ᵃ) that it is unnecessary for him to write anything about the matter because they have been taught of God to love one another and are, moreover, practising this love among the brethren not only at home but throughout all Macedonia. This excellent practice, however, does not prohibit his exhorting them not simply in general to abound the more in brotherly love (περισσεύειν μᾶλλον) but also in particular to be tranquil in mind, to attend to their own affairs, and work with their hands (vv. ¹¹⁻¹²), any more than the fact that they were walking so as to please God (v. ¹) prevented his urging them not simply in general to abound the more in such walking (ἵνα περισσεύητε μᾶλλον) but also in particular to abstain from fornication, etc. (vv. ³⁻⁸). To affirm,, as some do, that although vv. ¹⁰ᵇ⁻¹² are closely joined syntactically with vv. ⁹⁻¹⁰ᵃ yet exegesis is not justified in joining them materially appears to miss not only the obvious connection of the two sections but also the parallelism of approach already observed between vv. ⁹⁻¹¹ and vv. ¹⁻³. It is for convenience only that we subdivide into Love to Brothers (4⁹⁻¹⁰ᵃ) and Idleness (4¹⁰ᵇ⁻¹²).

⁹*Now concerning love to the brothers, you have no need of our writing to you, for you yourselves are taught of God to love another;*

[10]*in fact you are also doing it toward all the brothers who are in the whole of Macedonia.*

9. φιλαδελφίας. The brother who is the object of love is not the brother by birth, nationality, or alliance, but the brother ἐν Χριστῷ. Affection for the brotherhood (1 Pet. 2[17]) does not exclude ἀγάπη εἰς πάντας (3[12]).

In the Lxx. (4 Mac. 13[23. 26] 14[1]) as in classical Gk. φιλαδελφία (*cf.* also φιλάδελφος 2 Mac. 15[14]) designates love of the brother by birth (*cf.* ἀδελφότης of the brotherhood by alliance in 1 Mac. 12[10. 17]); in the N. T. it denotes always love of the Christian brother (Rom. 12[10] Heb. 13[1] 1 Pet. 1[22] 2 Pet. 1[7]; *cf.* 1 Clem. 47[5] 48[1]). See Kennedy, *Sources*, 95 *f.*

οὐ χρείαν ἔχετε κτλ. "You have no need that we (*sc.* ἡμᾶς) write to you." The explanation of this "simple statement of fact" (Mill.) is then introduced by γάρ. But instead of saying, "for you yourselves know how to love one another" (*cf.* 5[1]) or "for we know that you are loving one another" (*cf.* 2 Cor. 9[1]), he says "for you yourselves (αὐτοὶ ὑμεῖς contrasting with ἡμᾶς understood before γράφειν) are taught of God to love one another," thus resuming the point made in v. [8] that it is not the apostles who teach but God speaking by the indwelling Spirit or Christ. In virtue of this divine inspiration, they are θεοδίδακτοι (Barn. 21[6]), that is, διδακτοὶ θεοῦ (Is. 54[13]) or ὑπὸ τοῦ θεοῦ (Ps. Sol. 17[35]).

ἡμᾶς (Riggenbach) not τινά or ἐμέ is to be supplied before γράφειν. The difficulty created by γράφειν instead of γράφεσθαι (5[1]) may account for the reading ἔχετε γράφεσθαι (H, *et al.*; *cf.* 5[1]) and ἔχομεν γράφειν (DGF, *et al.*; *cf.* 1[8]). B (*cf.* am. *habuimus*) has εἴχομεν, which may suggest (Dob.) that Paul had already written a letter, and that he now justifies his failure to mention therein φιλαδελφία. If εἴχομεν, however interpreted, is original (so Weiss), then ἔχομεν is a correction and ἔχετε a conformation to 5[1] as H shows. I seems to read ειχε [τε γρα] φιν. Most editors read ἔχετε with אAHKL, *et al.*, and γράφειν with most uncials. Θεοδίδακτος occurs only here in Gk. Bib.; Lft. notes it in the later Barn. 21[6], Athenag. *Leg.* 11 and Theoph. *ad Autol.* 2[9]. On compounds with θεο-, *cf.* Rom. 1[30] 2 Tim. 3[16] 2 Mac. 6[23] and Ignatius. For the idea, see Is. 54[13] Jn. 6[45] Jer. 31[33 ff.]. εἰς τό limits θεοδίδακτοι (*cf.* Phil. 1[23] and *BMT.* 413). On the characteristic Johannine ἀγαπᾷν ἀλλήλους, *cf.* Rom. 13[8] 1 Pet. 1[22].

10. καὶ γὰρ ποιεῖτε κτλ. "For you are also doing it," that is, τὸ ἀγαπᾶν ἀλλήλους. With καὶ γάρ (3⁴), Paul "confirms the statement that they had already been divinely instructed in regard to it" (Lillie) and strengthens the reason for οὐ χρείαν ἔχετε (v. ⁹). Two points are in mind (cf. 1⁸): (1) not only are they taught it, they also practise it; (2) they practise it not only at home but also throughout all Macedonia. These two points are so combined that the proof of love at home is found in the love exhibited toward all the Macedonian Christians, an argument from the greater to the less (Calvin).

On ποιεῖν εἰς, cf. 1 Cor. 10³¹. B alone puts a καί before εἰς, marking the advance from ἀλλήλους to πάντας. BKLH (?) repeat τούς after ἀδελφούς (cf. 1⁸ 2¹); אADGF, et al., omit; it is hard to tell whether it has been inserted as an improvement of style (Zim. Dob.) or whether it is original, the omission being due to partial haplography; cf. Phile. 6 ἀγαθοῦ τοῦ (AC omit τοῦ). ὅλη may be enthusiastic (cf. 1⁷⁻⁸), but Thessalonica as well as Philippi and Beroea may have been a centre of influence for Macedonia as a whole; cf. 2 Cor. 1¹ τοῖς οὖσιν ἐν ὅλῃ τῇ Ἀχαΐᾳ. The disposition to love all the Macedonian Christians may have expressed itself both in hospitality to visiting brothers, Philippians, Beroeans, and others (Dob.), and "in ministering to the necessity of other churches" (McGiffert, EB. 5041). Mill. (XLVII) quotes a remark of Jerome, in his commentary on Galatians (Migne, PL. 26, 356), that reveals the charitable disposition of the Macedonians of his day: *Macedones in charitate laudantur et hospitalite ac susceptione fratrum.*

(4) *Idleness* (4¹⁰ᵇ⁻¹²).

Though the readers are practising brotherly love, yet (δέ) Paul urges them both generally "to abound the more" (cf. v. ¹) in that virtue, and specifically "to strive to be calm, and to mind their own business, and to work with their hands." This last injunction at least (ἐργάζεσθαι) is not new (cf. II 3¹⁰), as he forthwith proceeds to add (καθὼς ὑμῖν παρηγγείλαμεν; cf. v. ²); it is repeated here (v. ¹²) to the end (1) that the readers may behave themselves becomingly, having in mind the opinion of non-Christians, and (2) that they may be dependent on no one for support.

Precisely what the situation is to which Paul speaks, beyond the fact that it has to do with brotherly love, is not clear. It may be assumed that the belief in the coming of the Lord had created in the minds of some of the converts a feeling of restlessness and excitement which manifested itself outwardly in idleness and meddlesomeness in the affairs of the brotherhood. The idlers, we may imagine, being in want, had asked support from the church, and being refused on the ground that they were able to support themselves, had attempted to interfere in the affairs of the group. The peace of the brotherhood was disturbed and Christianity was falling into disrepute with unbelievers. Being in doubt as to how brotherly love was to be exhibited in such a case, the leaders wrote Paul for advice.

The clue to the interpretation of vv. $^{10b-12}$ is given in II 3^{6-15} without which our verses would remain obscure. But neither I nor II tells us precisely wherein the meddlesomeness, alluded to in πράσσειν τὰ ἴδια and expressed in περιεργάζεσθαι (II 3^{11}), consists. For idleness, while it naturally leads to poverty and to demands upon the brotherhood for support (Theodoret, Estius, Lft.), does not of itself involve interference with the affairs of the church. But as the position of πράσσειν τὰ ἴδια before ἐργάζεσθαι intimates, meddlesomeness, the result of idleness, is the disturbing factor. Some light may be thrown on the situation by hints given in $5^{12 \, ff.}$. In 5^{12-13}, for example, the readers are urged to appreciate the worth of (εἰδέναι as v. ^{4}) "those who labour among you," those, namely, who act as leaders and function as νουθετοῦντες; and to regard them highly in love on account of their work. Furthermore, the readers are commanded to be at peace not with them, but among themselves; and also to warn the idlers (5^{14}). In 5^{19-22} they are exhorted not to quench the operations of the Spirit, not to despise the gift of prophecy; and again are bidden to test all sorts of charismata, holding fast to such as make for edification and holding aloof from every evil kind of charismata. In 5^{23} the God of peace is invoked; and in 5^{27} this letter is ordered read to *all* the brethren. From these statements we may surmise that the idlers (οἱ ἄτακτοι, 5^{14}) are the disturbing element in the brotherhood, their idleness being due to a religious cause, namely, the excitement occasioned by the expectancy of the coming of the Lord. They became poor and asked "the workers among them" for assistance, only to be refused on the ground that the applicants were able but unwilling to support themselves, and were thus acting in direct violation of what Paul had taught (II 3^{10}: εἴ τις οὐ θέλει ἐργάζεσθαι μηδὲ ἐσθιέτω, a passage which suggests that καθὼς ὑμῖν παρηγγείλαμεν (I 4^{11}) is to be restricted to ἐργάζεσθαι). The leaders were

probably not tactful, as εἰρηνεύετε ἐν ἑαυτοῖς (5¹³) implies and II 3¹². ¹⁵
confirms. Possibly the demand of the idlers was made "in the Spirit,"
on the analogy of Did. 11¹²: ὃς δ' ἂν εἴπῃ ἐν πνεύματι· Δός μοι ἀργύρια
ἢ ἕτερά τινα, οὐκ ἀκούσεσθε αὐτοῦ. Such a misuse of spiritual gifts may
well have led "the workers among you" to distrust the validity of the
χαρίσματα; in which case the exhortation in 5¹⁹⁻²² is *ad hoc*. The invocation of the God of peace in 5²³ is pertinent; the solemn adjuration
that the letter be read to *all* the brethren intimates that some of the
idlers had asserted that they would give no heed to the epistolary injunctions of Paul, a suggestion confirmed by II 3¹⁴· ¹⁷.

¹⁰ᵇ*We urge you, however, brothers to abound the more, *¹¹*and to
strive to be calm and to mind your own business, and to work with
your hands as we charged you, *¹²*in order that you may behave yourselves becomingly in reference to the unbelievers and may have need
of no one to support you.*

11. φιλοτιμεῖσθαι ἡσυχάζειν. "Strive to be calm." Paul
recognises that the source of meddlesomeness and idleness is
inward, the excitement created in the minds of some by the expectation that the day of the Lord was at hand. With Lam. 3²⁶
he might have said: "It is good that a man should hope and
quietly wait for the salvation of the Lord" (Lxx.: καὶ ὑπομενεῖ
καὶ ἡσυχάσει εἰς τὸ σωτήριον κυρίου). Inward tranquillity
once restored, outward idleness and meddlesomeness would cease.

ἡσυχάζειν, only here in Paul, is used elsewhere in Gk. Bib. to denote
silence after speech (Acts 11¹⁸), rest after labour (Lk. 23⁵⁶), peace after
war (Judg. 3¹¹, etc.), and the like; also tranquillity or peace of mind, the
antithesis being expressed (Job 3²⁶ Pr. 1³² Is. 7⁴) or implied (Ex. 24¹⁴
Lam. 3²⁶ and here); *cf.* II 3¹²: μετὰ ἡσυχίας ἐργαζόμενοι. Many commentators, influenced doubtless by Plato's *Rep.* VI, 496 D, where the
philosopher retires from public life and pursues his studies in retirement
ἡσυχίαν ἔχων καὶ τὰ αὐτοῦ πράττων (*cf.* Dio Cass. 60²⁷: τὴν ἡσυχίαν
ἄγων καὶ τὰ ἑαυτοῦ πράττων), find the opposite of ἡσυχάζειν implied
in the opposite of πράσσειν τὰ ἴδια and interpret ἡσυχάζειν objectively
as leading the quiet life after busying themselves with affairs not their
own, as, for example, entering into public life, discussing the *Parousia*
in the market-place and elsewhere, and thus bringing the Christian
circle into discredit with the Gentiles (Zwingli, Koppe, Schott, Dob.
and others). But the Thessalonians are not philosophers but working
people, and the context (περὶ τῆς φιλαδελφίας) points to church rather
than to public affairs.

11

φιλοτιμεῖσθαι occurs elsewhere in Gk. Bib. only Rom. 15²⁰ 2 Cor. 5⁹ and 4 Mac. 1³⁵ (A). In later Gk. it is used absolutely in the sense "love honour," "be ambitious," or "act with public spirit" (Mill.); and with a complementary infinitive in the sense of "strive," "be eager," "try" (so in papyri (Mill.); cf. Polyb. I, 83², where φιλοτιμεῖσθαι is balanced by ποιεῖσθαι μεγάλην σπουδήν). The meaning here = σπουδάζειν in 2¹⁷; see Wetstein, ad loc. and SH. on Rom. 15²⁰. On the Pauline phrase παρακαλοῦμεν ... ἀδελφοί, cf. 5¹⁴ Rom. 15³⁰ 16¹⁷ 1 Cor. 1¹⁰ 16¹⁵; also I 5¹² II 2¹ (where ἐρωτῶμεν (v. ¹) takes the place of παρακαλοῦμεν). With παρακαλεῖν, Paul uses the ἵνα clause (v.¹ II 3¹²); or the infinitive, either alone or with εἰς τό (2¹¹) or τὸ μή (3²); or the imperative (5¹⁴ 1 Cor. 4¹⁶).

πράσσειν τὰ ἴδια καὶ ἐργάζεσθαι κτλ. The outward expression of inward restlessness was meddlesomeness and idleness. Paul refers first not to idleness but to meddlesomeness (περιερ·γάζεσθαι II 3¹¹) because in this case the disturbing element in the peace of the brotherhood was not simply that some were idle and in their want had asked support from the church, but also that, being refused, they had attempted to interfere in the management of its affairs. Furthermore, in putting second ἐργάζεσθαι, the cause of meddlesomeness, he seems to intimate that καθὼς ὑμῖν παρηγγείλαμεν is to be taken not with all three preceding infinitives (ἡσυχάζειν, πράσσειν, and ἐργά·ζεσθαι) but solely with the last, as indeed the clause of purpose v. ¹² (especially μηδενὸς χρείαν ἔχητε) and the parallel II 3¹⁰ (εἴ τις οὐ θέλει ἐργάζεσθαι μηδὲ ἐσθιέτω) suggest. To meet this situation, he urges first that they attend to their own affairs and not interfere with the affairs of the church; and second, repeating an injunction already given, that they work with their hands, that is, support themselves instead of begging assistance from the church (μηδενὸς χρείαν ἔχητε, v. ¹²).

πράσσειν τὰ ἴδια is unique in the Gk. Bib. but common in the classics (see Wetstein); cf. μὴ πολυπραγμονεῖν (Plato, Rep. IV, 433 A) and ἰδιοπραγεῖν (Soph. Lex.). GF. read πράττειν. ἐργάζεσθαι ταῖς χερσίν (1 Cor. 4¹² Eph. 4²⁸; cf. Sap. 15¹⁷) denotes manual labour; but whether skilled or unskilled is not certain. Influenced by ἴδια (Weiss, 91), אAKL, et al., prefix ἰδίαις to χερσίν, an unnecessary insertion in view of ὑμῶν. In 1 Cor. 4¹² Eph. 4²⁸, where ὑμῶν fails, ἰδίαις is to be read, though B omits it in Eph. 4²⁸.

12. ἵνα περιπατῆτε κτλ. The purpose of παρακαλοῦμεν is twofold, (1) that the converts may behave themselves becomingly with a view to the opinion of non-Christians (τοὺς ἔξω), the point being that the idleness of some of the Christians tended to bring Christianity into discredit with the unbelievers; and (2) that they may have need of no one to support them, the point being that they should support themselves instead of trespassing on the hospitality of the church.

Ell. thinks that ἵνα περιπατῆτε εὐσχημόνως refers mainly to ἡσυχάζειν and πράσσειν, and μηδενὸς χρείαν ἔχητε refers to ἐργάζεσθαι. This reference is due to the fact that ἡσυχάζειν is interpreted as leading a quiet life after a bustling interest in public affairs. Ewald and Dob. take the clause with ἵνα as the object of παρηγγείλαμεν; but the change from the infinitives to ἵνα after παρακαλοῦμεν strongly intimates that Paul is passing from the object to the purpose of the exhortation (*cf.* 1 Cor. 10³² ᶠ·: γίνεσθε . . . καθὼς . . . ἵνα). εὐσχημόνως, which is used elsewhere in the Gk. Bib. only Rom. 13¹³ (περιπατεῖν) and 1 Cor. 14⁴⁰ (parallel to κατὰ τάξιν), denotes "becomingly," "honestly" in the sense of *honeste*, so that no exception can be taken; *cf.* Epictetus, *Diss.* II, 5²¹ εὐσχημόνως ἀνεστράφης. οἱ ἔξω in Paul (1 Cor. 5¹² ᶠ· Col. 4⁶) indicates non-Christians, irrespective of race (contrast οἱ ἔσω, 1 Cor. 5¹²). The Jews had a similar designation for non-Jews; *cf.* οἱ ἔξωθεν (Josephus, *Ant.* 15³¹⁶; also 1 Tim. 3⁷) and οἱ ἐκτός (Sir. *prol.*); and see Schöttgen on 1 Cor. 5¹² and Levy, *Neuhebr. u. Chald. Wörterbuch* on רוצח. πρός = "with an eye to," as in Col. 4⁵; not *coram*, "in the eyes of." On the gender of μηδενός, Vorstius (*apud* Poole) remarks: "*perinde est sive* μηδενός *in neut. gen. sive in masc. accipias.*" Nor does it matter logically, for in either case the reference is to dependence upon the brotherhood for support. Grammatically, the usage of χρείαν ἔχειν is inconclusive; contextually, the masculine is probable (τοὺς ἔξω); Vulg. has *nullius aliquid.*

(5) *The Dead in Christ* (4¹³⁻¹⁸).

This section is separated from the previous paragraphs "concerning brotherly love" (vv. ⁹⁻¹²) but is closely related to the following question "concerning times and seasons" (5¹⁻¹¹), as the repetition of ἅμα σύν (v. ¹⁷) in 5¹⁰ intimates. The faint-hearted (οἱ ὀλιγόψυχοι 5¹⁴) are anxious both about their dead (4¹³⁻¹⁸) and about their own salvation (5¹⁻¹¹).

Since Paul's departure, one or more of the Thessalonian Christians had died. The brethren were in grief not because they did not believe in the resurrection of the saints, but because they feared that their dead would not have the same advantages as the survivors when the Lord came. Their perplexity was due not simply to the Gentile difficulty of apprehending the meaning of resurrection, but also to the fact that Paul had not when he was with them discussed explicitly the problem of the relation of survivors to dead at the *Parousia*. Since they had received no instruction on this point (contrast vv. 1-2. 6. 9. 11 5²), they write to Paul for advice "concerning the dead."

That the question is not: Will the Christians who die before the *Parousia* be raised from the dead? but: Will the Christians who die before the *Parousia* be at the *Parousia* on a level of advantage with the survivors? is made plain by the consideration that in v. 14 Paul says not ἐγερεῖ but ἄξει σὺν αὐτῷ (which presupposes resurrection); and that he singles out for emphasis not only in v. 14 but also in the summarised agraphon (v. 15), in the explanation of v. 15 given in vv. 16-17 (as far as ἀέρα), and in the consequence drawn in v. 17 (καὶ οὕτως πάντοτε σὺν κυρίῳ ἐσόμεθα), not ἀναστήσονται but σὺν αὐτῷ (v. 14), ἅμα σύν (v. 17; *cf.* 5¹⁰), and σὺν κυρίῳ (v. 17). It may well be that during the previous seventeen or more years of Paul's Christian career relatively few Christians had died (*cf.* Acts 12²; also the death of Stephen when Paul was yet a Pharisee); but it is improbable that, because this passage is perhaps the first extant reference in Paul to the resurrection of believers, it is also the first time Paul had expressed himself, let alone reflected, on the subject; but see Lake, *Exp.* 1907, 494–507. In fact, if v. 15 is to be accepted, Jesus himself had given his disciples to understand that the survivors would not anticipate the dead at his coming, thus intimating that some might die before he came (*cf.* Mk. 9¹).

Similar but not identical questions bothered the writers of the Apocalypse of Baruch and Fourth Ezra; but their answers differ from that of Paul. Baruch says (11⁶ f.): "Announce in Sheol and say to the dead: Blessed are ye more than we who are living." Ezra writes (13¹⁶ ff.) that the seer first pronounces woe unto the survivors and more woe unto the dead, but concludes that it is better or happier for the survivors, a conclusion confirmed from on high with the words (13²⁴): "*magis beatifici sunt qui derelicti super eos qui mortui sunt.*" Paul's encouraging word is that living and dead are at the *Parousia* on a level of advantage, ἅμα σύν (v. 17 5¹⁰), *simul cum.*

In replying to the request for information, Paul states that his purpose in relieving their ignorance is that they, unlike the non-

Christians who sorrow because they have no hope of being with Christ, should not sorrow at all. The reason for this striking utterance, already tacit in ἔχοντες ἐλπίδα (v. 13), is first expressed in v. 14 where from a subjective conviction, drawn from Christian experience and hypothetically put: "if we believe, as of course we do, that Jesus died and rose again," he draws directly an objective inference: "so also God will lead on with Jesus those who died through him." This internal argument from the believers' mystic experience in Christ, the main purpose of which is to prove that the saints will be σὺν αὐτῷ, is further strengthened by an appeal to the external authority of an unwritten word of the Lord, summarised in Paul's language, to the effect that the surviving saints will not anticipate the dead at the *Parousia* (v. 15). Then in apocalyptic language, drawn from tradition but coloured with his own phraseology, Paul explains the word of the Lord by singling out such details in the procedure at the *Parousia* as bring to the forefront the point to be proved, ἅμα σὺν αὐτοῖς (vv. 16-17 as far as ἀέρα); and draws the conclusion, anticipated in v. 14, "and so we shall always be with the Lord." Finally (v. 18), uniting conclusion with exhortation, he bids them not to be encouraged but to encourage one another with the very words he himself has used.

13*Now as to those who sleep, brothers, we do not wish you to be in ignorance, that you may not grieve, as do the rest who have not hope.* 14*For if we believe that Jesus died and rose, so also God will lead on those who fell asleep through Jesus along with him.* 15*For this that follows, we, the writers, tell you, not on our own authority but in a word of the Lord, namely, that we, the writers and our Christian contemporaries, who live, that is, who survive until the coming of the Lord, shall by no means anticipate the dead;* 16*because the Lord himself at a command, namely, at an archangel's voice and a divine trumpet, will come down from heaven, and the dead who are in Christ will arise first of all;* 17*then we the living, the survivors, will with them at the same time be caught and carried by means of clouds to meet the Lord in the air. And so, we shall be always with the Lord.* 18*So then encourage one another with these words.*

13. οὐ θέλομεν δέ κτλ. With δέ and the affectionate ἀδελφοί,

Paul passes to a new section, "concerning the dead" in Christ, about which they had written (*cf.* v. ⁹) for instruction. The Pauline phrase that introduces the theme, οὐ θέλομεν δὲ ὑμᾶς ἀγνοεῖν, is negative in form but positive in meaning, as the clause with ἵνα μή (*cf.* Rom. 11²⁵) demonstrates.

This phrase, with some variation, is in the N. T. employed only by Paul and serves to emphasise a personal statement within a paragraph (Rom. 1¹³ 2 Cor. 1⁸), or to introduce a new point in a new paragraph (Rom. 11²⁵ 1 Cor. 10¹) or section (1 Cor. 12¹ and here). The positive form θέλω δὲ (γὰρ) ὑμᾶς εἰδέναι (1 Cor. 11³ Col. 2¹; *cf.* Phil. 1¹²) is "very common in the papyri" (Mill.). The fact that the clause with οὐ θέλομεν in 1 Cor. 12¹ precedes and here follows (*cf.* 2 Cor. 1⁸) the clause with περί does not exclude the probability (see v. ⁹) that the new point "concerning the dead," unconnected as it is with the preceding "concerning brotherly love," is a reply to a written request from the converts to Paul.

τῶν κοιμωμένων. The present participle is probably timeless, "the sleepers," that is, the dead, a euphemism not confined to Biblical writers. The word κοιμᾶσθαι itself does not throw light on the state of the Christian dead before the *Parousia*, but it is especially appropriate in Paul who considers the believers as being ἐν Χριστῷ not only before death and at death (1 Cor. 15¹⁸), but also from death to the *Parousia* (v. ¹⁶ οἱ νεκροὶ ἐν Χριστῷ). At the *Parousia*, they will be (v. ¹⁷) or will live (5¹⁰) σὺν κυρίῳ, the ultimate goal of the Christian hope.

"The designation of death as a sleep did not arise from the resurrection hope; for it is found in books that were unacquainted with this hope" (Charles, *Eschat.* 127, note 1; *cf.* Volz, *Eschat.* 134). As Paul is not here discussing the intermediate state, it is not certain from what he writes that he shared with Eth. Enoch 51¹ and 4 Ezra 7³² the view that at death the body went to the grave and the soul to Sheol; or that he regarded the existence in Sheol as "*ein trübes Schattenleben*" (Schmiedel). Clear only is it that in some sense, not defined, the dead as well as the living are under the power of the indwelling Christ (ἐν Χριστῷ).— κοιμᾶσθαι in the N. T. as in the classics (see Liddell and Scott, *sub voc.*) and Lxx. (*cf.* κοιμᾶσθαι μετὰ τῶν πατέρων Gen. 47³⁰ Deut. 31¹⁶ 2 Reg. 7¹² 1 Ch. 17¹¹, etc.; αἰώνιος κοίμησις Sir. 46¹⁹) is frequently a euphemism for ἀποθνήσκειν; so also καθεύδειν (5¹⁰; Ps. 87⁶ Dan. 12²); see especially Kennedy, *Last Things*, 267 *ff.* KL (DG) read the perfect **part.**

with 1 Cor. 15²⁰; 1912 reads the aorist with v. ¹⁴ and 1 Cor. 15¹⁸. The present is either timeless indicating a class, "the sleepers," or it designates the act of sleep as in progress (*cf.* 1 Cor. 11³⁰); the aorist views the act of sleep as entered upon in the past without reference to its progress or completion; the perfect regards the act as completed in the past with the added notion of the existing state (see *BMT. passim* and *cf.* 2 Mac. 12⁴⁴ ᶠ·); in all cases οἱ νεκροί are meant.

ἵνα μὴ λυπῆσθε κτλ. The purpose of οὐ θέλομεν ἀγνοεῖν = θέλομεν εἰδέναι is stated without qualification, "that you do not grieve." With καθὼς καί, a comparison is instituted which is also an antithesis: "as the non-Christians grieve (*sc.* λυποῦνται) who do not have, as you do, the hope of being with Christ." Just as καθάπερ καί (v. ⁵) does not mean, "in the same manner or degree of πάθος as the Gentiles," so καθὼς καί here does not mean that the Christians are indeed to grieve but not in the same manner or degree as the unbelievers (*cf.* Theodoret, *apud* Swete: οὐ παντελῶς κωλύει τὴν λύπην, ἀλλὰ τήν ἀμετρίαν ἐκβάλλει). Paul speaks absolutely, for death has a religious value to him, in that after a short interval the dead are brought to the goal of the Christian hope, σὺν αὐτῷ (*cf.* Phil. 1²¹ ᶠᶠ·). In view of this glorious consummation, present grief, however natural, is excluded (*cf.* Jn. 14²⁸).

In the light of the context which lays stress not on resurrection as such but on being with Christ, it is probable that the hope which the unbelievers do not have is not resurrection or immortality as such but the hope of being with Christ. It is striking that Paul seems to overlook the belief in immortality exemplified in the mysteries "especially of the orphic circles, but also in the cult of Attis, Isis, and Mithra, perhaps in that of the Cabiri as well" (Dob. 188). This oversight may be due either to the fact that neither the Jewish nor the pagan hope is a hope of εἶναι σὺν Χριστῷ, or to the fact that he has chiefly in mind the despair of the common people among the pagans whose life and aspirations he knew so well. In the latter case, a second-century papyri confirms Paul's estimate: "Irene to Taonnōphris and Philo, good comfort. I was as sorry (ἐλυπήθην) and wept over the departed one as I wept for Didymas. And all things whatsoever were fitting, I did, and all mine, Epaphroditus and Thermuthion and Philion and Apollonius and Plantas. But, nevertheless, against such things one can do nothing. Therefore comfort ye one another (παρηγορεῖτε οὖν ἑαυτούς)"; see Deiss. *Light*, 164; and *cf.* Mill. *Papyri*, 96, and Coffin, *Creed of Jesus*,

1907, 114–138. With this average pagan view may be contrasted the following from a contemporary Christian apologist, Aristides (noted by Dob.): "And if any righteous man among them passes from the world, they rejoice and offer thanks to God; and they escort the body as if he were setting out from one place to another near" (translation of D. M. Kay in *Ante-Nicene Fathers*, IX, 277). οἱ λοιποί, used absolutely here and 5⁶ Rom. 11⁷ 1 Cor. 7¹² 15³⁷ 2 Cor. 13² Phil. 1¹³, gets its meaning from the context; here it probably = οἱ ἔξω (v. ¹²) and denotes non-Christians in general. On μὴ ἔχοντες ἐλπίδα, cf. Eph. 2¹²; on καί in comparisons, rare after negations, cf. v. ⁶; with λυπεῖσθαι (Rom. 14¹⁵ Eph. 4³⁰ 2 Cor. 2² ᶠᶠ· 6¹⁰ 7⁸ ᶠᶠ·) indicating inward grief, contrast κλαίειν, θρηνεῖν, κόπτεσθαι and πενθεῖν (Lk. 6²⁵ 8⁵² 23²⁷).

14. εἰ γὰρ πιστεύομεν κτλ. The γάρ introduces the reason for ἵνα μὴ λυπῆσθε, already hinted at in ἔχοντες ἐλπίδα (v. ¹³): "for if we believe that Jesus died and rose, so also God will lead on those who fell asleep through Jesus along with him." The Greek sentence runs smoothly (cf. 1⁸), but there is an obvious compression of thought. Since οὕτως καί in the apodosis suggests a comparison, Paul might have said: "As we are convinced that Jesus died and that God raised him from the dead, so also must we believe, since the indwelling Christ is the guarantee of the resurrection of the believer, that God will raise from the dead those who died through Jesus and will lead them on along with him." There are, however, compensations in the compactness, for from a subjective conviction based on experience and stated conditionally, "if we believe, as we do, that Jesus died and rose," Paul is able to draw directly an objective inference, "so also God will," etc.

The fact of fulfilment lies not in the form of the condition but in the context (*BMT.* 242). The context here indicates that the Thessalonians are perplexed by doubts not as to the fact of the resurrection of the dead but as to whether the dead will have equal advantage with the survivors at the *Parousia*. By the insertion of ὁ θεός in the protasis, Paul makes clear that it is God who raised Jesus from the dead (1¹⁰ 1 Cor. 6¹⁴ 2 Cor. 4¹⁴ Rom. 8¹¹ 10⁹, etc.). On πιστεύειν in the sense of conviction, cf. πιστεύειν ὅτι in Rom. 6⁸ 10⁹.

ἀπέθανεν καὶ ἀνέστη. The death and resurrection of Jesus are inseparable in Paul's thought about salvation. As Christ died and rose actually, so does the believer die and rise with him mysti-

cally (Gal. 2¹⁹ Rom. 6³ ᶠᶠ· Col. 2²⁰ 3¹ ᶠᶠ·). The presence of Christ
or the Spirit in the Christian guarantees that when he actually
dies ἐν Χριστῷ (1 Cor. 15¹⁸) or διὰ Χριστοῦ (here), he will continue ἐν Χριστῷ (v. ¹⁶) during the interval between death and
resurrection, and will at the *Parousia* be raised from the dead by
God through the power of the same indwelling Christ or Spirit
(Rom. 8¹¹), and will attain the ultimate goal of Christian hope,
εἶναι σὺν Χριστῷ. This characteristically Pauline idea is the
probable link that unites the protasis and apodosis of our verse.

> Paul regularly uses ἐγείρειν (ἐξεγείρειν 1 Cor. 6¹⁴) for the resurrec
> tion; he uses ἀνιστάναι elsewhere only in Eph. 5¹⁴, a quotation, and
> below v. ¹⁶ in an utterance distinctly traditional in flavour. On the
> other hand, he uses ἀνάστασις (ἐξανάστασις Phil. 3¹¹), but not ἔγερσις
> (Mt. 27⁵³). On the name Ἰησοῦς, see 1¹⁰ and *cf.* Rom. 8¹¹ 2 Cor. 4¹⁴.
> For οὕτως καί without an expressed correlative, *cf.* Gal. 4³ Rom. 6¹¹
> 1 Cor. 2¹¹ 9¹⁴ 14⁹· ¹² 15⁴²· ⁴⁵. The reading of B, *et al.*, οὕτως ὁ θεὸς καί
> brings out the point that as God raised Jesus, so also he will raise the
> believers; *cf.* 1 Cor. 15¹⁸: ἄρα καὶ οἱ κοιμηθέντες ἐν Χριστῷ, where
> not only the dead but also (καί) the living (ὑμεῖς) ἀπώλοντο. Though
> οὕτως without an expressed correlative is frequent in Paul (*cf.* v. ¹⁷ II 3¹⁷
> Gal. 1⁶), yet the καί is placed here (*cf.* v. ¹⁰) by B to mark the connection
> with τοὺς κοιμηθέντας (Weiss, 136).

τοὺς κοιμηθέντας διὰ τοῦ Ἰησοῦ. "Those who fell asleep
through Jesus," that is, through the indwelling power of that
Jesus who died and rose again, the causal energy which operates
in the believers from baptism to actual resurrection from the
dead (*v. supra* on ἀπέθανεν). Though the union of διά with
κοιμηθέντας is striking, yet it is consonant with Paul's thinking,
is demanded by the parallelism of the sentence (Ell. Dob.),
and is the logical though not the grammatical equivalent of οἱ
κοιμηθέντες ἐν Χριστῷ in 1 Cor. 15¹⁸ (*cf.* v. ¹ ἐν κυρίῳ with v. ³
διὰ κυρίου).

> Those who join διὰ τοῦ Ἰησοῦ with the participle (*e. g.* Ephr. Chrys.
> Calv. Grot. Ell. Lft. Mill. Dob. Dibelius) do so on various grounds.
> Calvin (*apud* Lillie) says: "*dormire per Christum* is to retain in death
> the union (*coniunctionem*) which we have with Christ; for they who
> by faith are engrafted into Christ have their death in common with
> him, that they may be partners in his life." Lake (*The Earlier Epistles
> of St. Paul*, 1911, 88) thinks it probable "that it means martyrdom rather

than a natural death"; so before him Musculus (*apud* Lillie): "The
faithful die through Christ, when on his account they are slain by the
impious tyrants of the world." Lake further conjectures that the reference to the death "of the Lord Jesus and of the prophets" (2¹⁵) certainly suggests that persecution in Thessalonica "had already led to the
martyrdom of some Christians" (*loc. cit.*). Dob. contents himself with
a general statement: "*Sie sind gestorben, indem ein Verhältniss zu Jesus
dabei war.*" For Dibelius, the Pauline conception revealed in v. ¹⁴
"*wurzelt in den Mysterien.*"—On the other hand, many expositors
(*e. g.* Th. Mops. De W. Lün. Lillie, Schmiedel, Born. Wohl. Schettler,
Moff.) join διὰ τοῦ Ἰησοῦ with ἄξει. The reasons adduced are (1)
that it is unnecessary to designate the dead as Christian and (2) that
διά is made equivalent to ἐν. In reply it is urged that we have οἱ νεκροὶ
ἐν Χριστῷ (v. ¹⁶) and that the equivalence between διά and ἐν is not
grammatical but conceptual. In this alternative view, Jesus is God's
agent in both resurrection and ἄγειν (Th. Mops. and finally Schettler
(*op. cit.* 57): "*Gott wird sich Jesus bedienen, um die Toten zu erwecken
und die Erweckten zu sammeln*)."—The view that joins διὰ τοῦ Ἰησοῦ
with κοιμηθέντας is preferable not simply because it gives a distinctively
Pauline turn to the passage but also because it is grammatically better.
On the latter point, Ell. remarks vigorously: "The two contrasted
subjects Ἰησοῦς and κοιμηθέντας διὰ τοῦ Ἰησοῦ thus stand in clear
and illustrative antithesis, and the fundamental declaration of the sentence ἄξει σὺν αὐτῷ remains distinct and prominent, undiluted by any
addititious clause."

ἄξει σὺν αὐτῷ. In these words, the "fundamental declaration"
of Paul's reply (vv. ¹¹⁻¹⁸), just supported by an appeal to the internal evidence of the believer's experience of the indwelling
Christ, is succinctly stated. The believers are not to sorrow;
for the departed saints, as well as the survivors, will at the *Parousia* be in the company of Christ and follow his lead. What is
added in v. ¹⁵ confirms the same declaration on the external evidence of a summarised word of the Lord. How it is that the survivors will not anticipate the dead (v. ¹⁵) is then further explained
in vv. ¹⁶⁻¹⁷ where Paul selects from a traditional description of
the *Parousia* such points as bring into prominence his central
contention, εἶναι σὺν αὐτῷ.

Since σὺν αὐτῷ (v. ¹⁷ 5¹⁰ 2 Cor. 13⁴ Phil. 1²³) is the goal of ἐν Χριστῷ
(Deiss. *Neutestamentliche Formel "in Christo Jesu,"* 126), ἄγειν refers
to the final act when Jesus the victor over enemies (II 2⁸ 1 Cor. 15²⁴ ᶠᶠ·),
accompanied by his saints, leads the way heavenward to hand over the

kingdom to God the Father. The resurrection and ἐπισυναγωγή (II 2¹), the redemption, change, or transformation of the body (Rom. 8²³ 1 Cor. 15⁵¹ Phil. 3²¹), and the judgment are all presupposed. Paul is not here concerned with the details; even in the description vv. ¹⁶⁻¹⁷ only such pertinent features are sketched as prepare the readers for the conclusion which he draws: καὶ οὕτως πάντοτε σὺν κυρίῳ ἐσόμεθα. It is thus unnecessary to take σὺν αὐτῷ = εἰς τὸ εἶναι αὐτοὺς σὺν αὐτῷ, as Th. Mops. does: "*quoniam et illos suscitabit per Jesum ita ut et sint cum eo*"; for σὺν αὐτῷ begins both for living and for dead immediately at the *Parousia* and continues forever (πάντοτε v. ¹⁷).

15. *τοῦτο γάρ κτλ.* To confirm and explain, by an appeal to external authority, what was stated in v. ¹⁴ on the basis of religious experience, Paul proceeds: "This that follows, we, the writers of the letter, tell you, not on our own authority but in (the sphere of, by means of; *cf.* 1 Cor. 2⁷ 14⁶) a word of the Lord, namely, that we (ἡμεῖς, including both the writers and their Christian contemporaries) who live, that is, who survive until the coming of the Lord, shall by no means anticipate the dead."

Since γάρ gives not a second reason for v. ¹³ but explains and confirms the point of v. ¹⁴ on a new ground, τοῦτο is to be taken not with the preceding but with the following, and ὅτι is not causal (Zahn, *Introd.* I, 223) but resumptive as in 1 Cor. 1¹².

ἐν λόγῳ κυρίου. In this verse it is probable that the point only of the word of the historical Jesus is given, not the word itself; *cf.* Rom. 14¹⁴ 1 Cor. 9¹⁴. In the light of Mk. 9¹, it is not unlikely that Jesus may have expressed the opinion that those who survived until the coming of the Son of Man would not anticipate the dead. Since, however, no such "word of the Lord" exists in extant gospels (*cf.* Zahn, *Introd.* I, 224), the utterance here summarised in Paul's own words is an agraphon.

The presence of ἐν λόγῳ κυρίου of itself intimates that Paul has in mind not a general suggestion of the Risen Lord (Gal. 1¹² 2² 2 Cor. 13³ Eph. 3³) given by revelation (so Chrys. De W. Lün. Ell. Lft. Mill. Dob. Moff. and others) but a definite word of the historical Jesus (so Calv. Drummond, Wohl. Dibelius, and others). Even if he had written simply ἐν κυρίῳ (Eph. 4¹⁷), the content of the inward revelation would have an historical basis, as Rom. 14¹⁴, with its allusion to Mk. 7¹⁵, suggests: οἶδα καὶ πέπεισμαι ἐν κυρίῳ Ἰησοῦ ὅτι οὐδὲν κοινὸν δι' ἑαυτοῦ. Furthermore the analogy both of Rom. 14¹⁴ and of 1 Cor. 9¹⁴ (where Paul

alludes to but does not literally cite Mt. 10¹⁰ Lk. 10¹⁷ = 1 Tim. 5¹⁸), and
the fact that Paul does not affirm that the Lord says "we who live,"
etc. (contrast Acts 20³⁵: τῶν λόγων τοῦ κυρίου Ἰησοῦ (cf. 1 Tim. 6³)
ὅτι αὐτὸς εἶπεν) but affirms that "we tell you on the strength of a word
of the Lord that we we who live," etc., conspire to make probable that
here as in Rom. 14¹⁴ 1 Cor. 9¹⁴ we have not a citation of but an allusion
to a word of the Lord. The exact form of the agraphon is not recover-
able unless it is embedded in vv. ¹⁶⁻¹⁷ (Ropes, Dibelius).

Schmiedel, in an excellent note, after remarking that the word of the
Lord does not come from Mt. 24²⁹⁻³¹ or from 4 Ezra 5⁴¹ ff. (as Steck once
held), observes that it is not to be found in v. ¹⁶ᵃ (as von Soden held, SK.
1885, 280 f.), or in v. ¹⁶ without πρῶτον (so Stähelin, J. d. Th. 1874, 193 f.),
or hardly in v. ¹⁵ alone, since vv. ¹⁶⁻¹⁷ are too detailed, or in vv. ¹⁶⁻¹⁷,
since its beginning after the previous formulation in v. ¹⁵ would not be
sufficiently accentuated, but in vv. ¹⁵⁻¹⁷. If, however, it is admitted that
v. ¹⁵ gives the point of the agraphon, the only question at issue is
whether it is actually cited in vv. ¹⁶⁻¹⁷. At first sight, the "concrete
and independent character" of these verses (Ropes) does suggest a citation, even if it is granted that the citation is free (the Pauline phraseology being evident in αὐτὸς ὁ κύριος and ἐν Χριστῷ). On the other
hand, it is noteworthy that the salient point of vv. ¹⁶⁻¹⁷, the ἅμα σύν, does
not explicitly appear in the summary of the word v. ¹⁵. The impression, difficult to escape, is that Paul, remembering a traditional description of the *Parousia*, selects such points as explain the basal declaration
of the summarised word of the Lord in v. ¹⁵. On the question, see
Ropes, *Die Sprüche Jesu*, 1896, 152 ff. and *HDB.* V, 345; Titius, *Neutestamentliche Lehre von der Seligkeit* 1895, I, 24; Resch, *Paulinismus*,
338–341; Mathews, *Messianic Hope in N. T.* 1905, 73; and Askwith,
Exp. 1911, 66.

ἡμεῖς οἱ ζῶντες κτλ. The insertion of ἡμεῖς and the presence
of εἰς denoting the temporal limit make clear that the exact
contrast here is not between the living and dead at the *Parousia;*
not between "we Christians who are alive" *at* the *Parousia* and
the dead; but between "we Christians who live," that is, "who
continue to survive *until* the *Parousia*," and the dead. Paul
thus betrays the expectation that he and his contemporary
Christians will remain alive until Christ comes.

Paul's personal belief that the advent is at hand is constant (1 Cor. 10¹¹
16²² Rom. 13¹¹ Phil. 4⁵), a conviction shared also by other Christians of
the first century (1 Pet. 4⁷ Heb. 10²⁵ Jas. 5⁸ 1 Jn. 2¹⁸) and apparently by
the Master himself (Mk. 9¹). In our passage, Paul speaks, as often,
without qualifications. If questioned, he would probably have admitted

that he himself as well as other Christians might taste of death before the
Lord came. Such cases, however, would have been to him exceptional.
His hope is fixed not on a far-off divine event; not on the fact that "each
several generation, at whatever period existing, occupies during that
period the position of those who shall be alive at the Lord's coming"
(Bengel), but on the nearness of the *Parousia*, even if the exact day and
hour be unknown. Calvin tacitly admits the obvious force of ἡμεῖς
in observing that Paul by using it makes himself as it were one of the
number of those who will live until the last day. But Paul does this,
Calvin ingeniously explains, "to rouse the expectation of the Thessalonians, and so to hold all the pious in suspense, that they shall not
count on any delay whatever. For even supposing him to have known
himself by special revelation that Christ would come somewhat later,
still this was to be delivered as the common doctrine of the church that
the faithful might be ready at all hours" (quoted by Lillie, *ad loc.*).
Apart from Grotius and, less clearly, Piscator, most of the older expositors found difficulty in admitting that Paul at this point shared the
views of his time. Origen (*Cels.* V, 17), for example, in the only extant
quotation from his commentary on our letters, namely, on I 4¹⁵⁻¹⁷ (*cf.*
Turner, *HDB.* V, 496), allegorises; Chrys. Th. Mops. and others so interpret οἱ περιλειπόμενοι as to exclude Paul; still others think that
the ἡμεῖς is not suited to Paul, although Olshausen protests against
this *enallage personae* or ἀνακοίνωσις. On the older views, see Lün.
ad loc. Denney, however (177), queries: "Is it not better to recognise
the obvious fact that Paul was mistaken as to the nearness of the second
advent than to torture his words to secure infallibility?" See also
Kennedy, *Last Things,* 160 *ff.*

οἱ περιλειπόμενοι κτλ. The living are further defined as
those who continue to survive until the *Parousia*. With reference to these survivors including Paul, it is asserted on the
strength of the Lord's utterance that they will by no means take
temporal precedence over the dead.

The participle περιλειπόμενοι is present, the action being viewed as
going on to the limit of time designated by εἰς; contrast ἐν τῇ παρουσίᾳ
2¹⁹ 3¹³ 5²³ I Cor. 15²³. The word περιλείπεσθαι occurs elsewhere in
N. T. only v. ¹⁷; *cf.* 4 Mac. 13¹⁸ 12⁶. φθάνειν here, but not in 2¹⁶, is
used classically in the sense of προφθάνειν (Mt. 17²⁵), "*praevenire,*"
"precede," "anticipate." On οὐ μή with aorist subj. as the equivalent
of an emphatic future indic. (so K here), *cf.* 5³ and *BMT.* 172. For
κυρίου after παρουσίαν, B reads Ἰησοῦ, conforming to v. ¹⁴ (Weiss, 81).

16. ὅτι αὐτὸς ὁ κύριος. With ὅτι "because," parallel to γάρ
(v. ¹⁵; *cf.* 2¹⁴), the word of the Lord summarised in v. ¹⁵ is ex-

plained and elaborated.   The point of the Pauline phrase αὐτὸς
ὁ κύριος (cf. 3¹¹) is apparently that the very Jesus under whose
control the believers stand in life, at death (τοὺς κοιμηθέντας
διά, v. ¹⁴), and from death to resurrection (οἱ νεκροὶ ἐν Χριστῷ),
and whose indwelling spiritually guarantees their resurrection,
is the Lord who at the resurrection functions as the apocalyptic
Messiah.

ἐν κελεύσματι κτλ.   The descent of the Lord from heaven is
characterised by three clauses with ἐν.   Unlike the three dis-
connected clauses with ἐν in 1 Cor. 15⁵², the second and third are
here joined by καί, a fact suggesting that these two clauses
are in some sense an epexegesis of the first.   "At a command,
namely, at an archangel's voice and at a trumpet of God."   Precisely what Paul has in mind is uncertain.   It is conceivable
that God who raises the dead (v. ¹⁴), or Christ the agent in resurrection, commands the archangel Michael to arouse the dead;
and that this command is executed at once by the voice of the
archangel who speaks to the dead (cf. 1 Cor. 15⁵²) through a
divine trumpet.   But whatever the procedure in detail may be,
the point is clear that at the descent of the Lord from heaven,
the dead are raised first of all, and then the survivors and the
risen dead are together and simultaneously (ἅμα σύν) snatched
up and carried by means of clouds to meet the Lord in the air.

    Kabisch (Die Eschatologie des Paulus, 1893, 231) thinks that God gives
a command to Christ and that the archangel is only the messenger, the
voice which God makes use of (cf. Kennedy, Last Things, 190).   Teichmann (Die paulinischen Vorstellungen von Auferstehung und Gericht,
1896, 23) imagines that Christ on his way to earth commands the dead
(who through the cry of the archangel and the blowing of the trumpet
of God are awakened from their slumber) really to arise.   Paul's statement, however, is general; how far he would subscribe to the precise
procedure read into his account from extant Jewish or Christian sources,
no one knows.

    Most commentators agree with Stähelin (J. d. Th. 1874, 189) in tak-
ing the ἐν of attendant circumstance as in 1 Cor. 4²¹; but it may mean
"at the time of" as in 1 Cor. 15⁵² ἐν τῇ ἐσχάτῃ σάλπιγγι.   κέλευσμα,
found in Gk. Bib. here and Pr. 24⁶², is used classically (cf. Wetstein, ad
loc.) in various applications, the command of a κελευστής to his rowers,
of an officer to his men, of a hunter to his dogs, etc.   Ell. quotes Philo

(*de praem et poen.* 19) as using it of God's assembling the saints. The σάλπιγξ, like other touches in the description, appears in the account of the theophany on Mt. Horeb (Ex. 19¹⁶⁻¹⁹; *cf.* Briggs, *Messiah of the Apostles*, 88); here the trumpet, as in 1 Cor. 15⁵², is used not to marshal the hosts of heaven, or to assemble the saints (Mt. 24³¹, which adds to Mark μετὰ σάλπιγγος μεγάλης; Bengel says: *tuba Dei adeoque magna*), but to raise the dead.—The ἀρχάγγελος (in Gk. Bib. only here and Jude 9) may be Michael as in Jude; *cf.* Eth. En. 9¹ 20⁶. On Michael, see Lueken, *Der Erzengel Michael;* Bousset, *Relig.*² 374 *ff.*; Everling (*op. cit.* 79 *ff.*) and Dibelius, *Die Geisterwelt,* etc. 32 *ff.*

καὶ οἱ νεκροὶ ἐν Χριστῷ κτλ. With καί of simple narration, the results of the descent of the Lord are stated; first (πρῶτον) the resurrection of the dead saints, which removes their disadvantage by putting them on a level with the living; and then (ἔπειτα, v. ¹⁷), the rapture of both the risen dead and the survivors, presumably in changed, transformed, redeemed bodies (1 Cor. 15⁵¹ Phil. 3²¹ Rom. 8²³), to meet the Lord in the air. Striking here is it that Paul says not simply ἀναστήσονται οἱ νεκροί (Is. 26¹⁹) but οἱ νεκροὶ ἐν Χριστῷ. This phrase designates not "those who died in Christ" (1 Cor. 15¹⁸) but "the dead who are in Christ"; and intimates, without defining precisely the condition of the believers in the intermediate state, that as in life and at death so from death to the *Parousia,* the believer is under the control of the indwelling Christ or Spirit. This indwelling spiritual Christ, whose presence in the believer guarantees his resurrection, is also the very enthroned (Rom. 8³⁴) Lord himself (ὅτι αὐτὸς ὁ κύριος) who comes down from heaven to raise the dead.

17. ἔπειτα . . . ἁρπαγησόμεθα κτλ. "Then, presumably at no great interval after the resurrection, ἡμεῖς οἱ ζῶντες οἱ περιλειπόμενοι (as in v. ¹³; it is unnecessary here to add εἰς τὴν παρουσίαν τοῦ κυρίου) shall be caught up simultaneously (ἅμα) with the risen saints (σὺν αὐτοῖς) and carried by clouds to meet the Lord in the air." The rapture is a supernatural act as in Acts 8³⁹ Rev. 12⁵; *cf.* 2 Cor. 12² ᶠᶠ. The means (ἐν), not the agent (ὑπό; *cf.* Baruch 4²⁶), by which the rapture is executed is the clouds which, as in Elijah's case (4 Reg. 2¹¹), are conceived as a triumphal chariot. Slavonic Enoch 3¹ ᶠᶠ. (ed. Morfill and

Charles; noted also by Mill.) is in point: "These men (that is, angels) summoned me and took me on their wings and placed me on the clouds. And lo, the clouds moved. And again, going still higher, I saw the ether and they placed me in the first heaven."

ἅμα σύν occurs in Gk. Bib. only here and 5¹⁰; Vulg. has here *simul rapiemur cum;* in 5¹⁰, am. fuld. omit *simul.* In Gk. Bib. ἅμα is regularly an adverb (Pr. 22¹⁸, etc.); in Mt. 13²⁹ 20¹, it is a preposition. Ell. remarks: "We shall be caught up with them at the same time that they shall be caught up, ἅμα marking as usual connection in point of time." The phrase gives the most precise statement of the equality of advantage that we have; it does not appear in the summary of the agraphon in v. ¹⁵. GF m Ambst. omit οἱ περιλειπόμενοι; B has οι περιλειμενοι. In the syn. gospels, the cloud appears, apart from the transfiguration and Lk. 12⁵⁴, only in connection with the *Parousia* of the Son of Man. The influence of Dan. 7¹³ is felt where Lxx. has ἐπὶ τῶν νεφελῶν (Mt. 24³⁰ 26⁶⁴) and Th. μετά (Mk. 14⁶²; *cf.* Rev. 1⁷). The ἐν, however, is given by Mk. 13²⁶ = Lk. 21²⁷; see further Rev. 11¹² (ἐν), 4 Ezra 13³ (*cum*), and Ex. 34⁵ (κατέβη κύριος ἐν νεφέλῃ); and *cf.* Acts 1¹¹ with 1⁹.

εἰς ἀπάντησιν κτλ. With εἰς, the purpose of ἁρπαγησόμεθα is expressed, "to meet the Lord." The εἰς ἀέρα designates the place of meeting, probably the space between the earth and the firmament of the first heaven, as in Slav. En. 3¹ ᶠᶠ· quoted above. As it is probably to the air, not to the earth that the Lord descends from heaven, so it is into the aïr that all the saints are caught up into the company of the Lord and from the air that God will lead them on with Jesus (ἄξει σὺν αὐτῷ v. ¹⁴) to heaven where the fellowship with Christ begun in the air will continue forever; for, in summing up the point intended in the description of vv. ¹⁶⁻¹⁷, he says not καὶ ἐκεῖ ("and there," as if the air were the permanent dwelling-place; so apparently Kabisch (*op. cit.* 233) alluding to Ass. Mos. 10⁹) but καὶ οὕτως, drawing the conclusion from vv. ¹⁶⁻¹⁷, implicit in v. ¹⁴ (σὺν αὐτῷ), with the added emphasis upon the permanence of the fellowship, πάντοτε σὺν κυρίῳ ἐσόμεθα.

In the Lxx. συνάντησις, ἀπάντησις, ἀπαντή, ὑπάντησις and συναντή occur chiefly in phrases with εἰς and gen. or dat. The readings vary, but εἰς with ὑπάντησιν or συνάντησιν is rare. In the N. T. the readings also vary; *cf.* Mt. 25⁶ 27³² Acts 28¹⁵; also Mt. 8³⁴ 25¹ Jn. 12¹³. Here DGF read εἰς ὑπάντησιν τῷ Χριστῷ. Moulton (I 14²), who notes BGU, 362 (πρὸς ἀπάντησιν τοῦ ἡγέμονος; for πρός, *cf.* 3 Mac. 5²), thinks the special idea of the word is the "official welcome of a newly arrived dignitary. The case after it is entirely consistent with Greek idiom, the gen. as in our "to *his* inauguration," the dat. as the case governed by the verb"; see also Ex. 19¹⁷ εἰς συνάντησιν τοῦ θεοῦ.— The εἰς before ἀέρα is naturally taken with ἀπάντησιν, the usage being either classical, or εἰς for ἐν of place (Bl. 39³). Above the firmament is the αἰθήρ, a word not found in Gk. Bib. רקיע is rendered a few times in Sym. by αἰθήρ; in Lxx. (2 Reg. 22¹² = Ps. 17¹²) by ἀήρ. On the meaning of ἀήρ, *cf.* Slav. En. 3¹·², Ascen. Isa. 7⁹· ¹³ 10²; and see Moses Stuart in *Bibliotheca Sacra*, 1843, 139 *ff.* and Ezra Abbot in Smith's *DB*, I, 56 *f.*

καὶ οὕτως κτλ. "And so (*cf.* 1 Cor. 7¹⁷ Rom. 11²⁵ ᶠ·), as the result of the resurrection, the rapture, and the meeting of the Lord in the air, we shall be with the Lord, not for the moment only but forever" (πάντοτε), the point of v. ¹⁴ and the fruition of the Christian hope.

For σὺν κυρίῳ, B reads ἐν κυρίῳ which is "ganz gedankenlos" (Weiss, 56); *cf.* Phil. 1²³. The belief in the nearness of the coming of Christ is constant in Paul, but there is less emphasis on the traditional scenery in the letters subsequent to our epistles. Even in 1 Cor. 15²⁴·²⁶ where there is an allusion to the last conflict (*cf.* II 2⁸), the concrete imagery is less conspicuous (*cf.* Rom. 8¹⁸ ᶠᶠ· 2 Cor. 5¹·¹⁰). In the epistles of the imprisonment, the eschatology is summed up in hope (Col. 1⁵· ²³; *cf.* Eph. 1¹⁸ 4⁴), the hope of being with Christ (Col. 3³ ᶠ· Phil. 1²³; *cf.* 2 Cor. 13⁴). On καὶ οὕτως . . . ἐσόμεθα, Moff. remarks: "This is all that remains to us, in our truer view of the universe, from the naïve λόγος κυρίου of the Apostle, but it is everything."

18. ὥστε παρακαλεῖτε κτλ. "So then," as the result of the conviction drawn from the religious experience in Christ (v. ¹⁴), from the summarised word of the Lord (v. ¹⁵), and from the confirmatory description of the *Parousia* (vv. ¹⁶·¹⁷), do not grieve (v. ¹³), but "encourage one another (5¹¹) with these (τούτοις not τοιούτοις) words," the very words that have been used.

On ὥστε = διό (5¹¹) = τοιγαροῦν (4⁸) = διὰ τοῦτο (3⁷) with imperative, *cf.* 1 Cor. 10¹² 11³³ 14³⁹ 15⁵⁸ Phil. 2¹² 4¹. Paul does not simply offer encouragement; he bids them actively to encourage one another (*cf.* 2 Cor. 1³ ᶠᶠ·).—It is obvious that vv. ¹⁶·¹⁷ do not pretend to give a description in detail of the *Parousia*. Of the points not mentioned, we may assume that Paul would admit the following: the assembling of the saints; the redemption, change, or transformation of the body (Rom. 8²³ 1 Cor. 15⁵¹ Phil. 3²¹); and the judgment on all men (Rom. 14¹⁰ 2 Cor. 5¹⁰) without the resurrection of the wicked. On the other hand, since Paul does not elsewhere indicate a belief in the intermediate kingdom (*cf.* Charles, *Eschat.* 389 *ff.*), it is not to be looked for between πρῶτον and ἔπειτα here (*cf.* Vos, *Pauline Eschatology and Chiliasm*, in the *Princeton Theol. Rev.* for Jan. 1911). It is, however, probable that after the meeting of the Lord in the air, the Lord with his saints go not to earth but to heaven, as ἄξει σὺν αὐτῷ (v. ¹⁴) suggests, the permanent abode of Christ and the believers. Even in this description of the *Parousia* it is worth noting that the interest centres in the ultimate form of the hope, εἶναι σὺν κυρίῳ; and that only such elements are singled out for mention as serve to bring this religious hope to the forefront. Like the Master, Paul, out of the treasures of apocalyptic at his disposal, knows how to bring forth things new and old.

(6) *Times and Seasons* (5¹⁻¹¹).

The written request for information "concerning times and seasons" (*cf.* 4⁹· ¹³) appears to have been made at the suggestion of the faint-hearted who were concerned not only about their friends who had died (4¹³⁻¹⁸; *cf.* 5¹⁰) but also about their own salvation. In doubt about Paul's teaching in reference to the nearness of the advent and in fear that the day might catch them morally unprepared, they ask him, in their discouragement, for further instruction about the times and seasons. Paul, however, is convinced that they require not further instruction but encouragement (5¹¹). Accordingly, while reminding them that the day is to come suddenly and is to be a day of judgment on unbelievers (vv. ¹⁻³), he is careful to assure them that the day will not take them by surprise, for they, one and all of them, are sons of light and sons of day, that is, believers (vv. ⁴⁻⁵ᵃ). Furthermore, recognising that they need to be exhorted to moral alertness, an exhortation which not only they but all Christians require (hence the tactful change from "you" to "we" in v. ⁵), he urges that since they are sons of light and sons of day, they must be morally alert and sober, arming themselves with that faith and love, and especially that hope for future salvation,

without which they cannot realise their destiny (vv. 5b-8). There
is, however, no cause for anxiety, he assures the faint-hearted, for
God has appointed them unto salvation, the indwelling Christ
enables them to acquire it, and Christ died for their sins in order
that all believers, whether surviving until the *Parousia*, or dying
before it, might at the same time have life with Christ (vv. 9-10).
Hence they are to encourage and build up one another, as in
fact they are doing (v. 11).

*1Now as to the times and seasons, brothers, you have no need that
anything be written you; 2for you yourselves know accurately that the
day of the Lord so comes as a thief at night. 3When people are saying: "All is well and safe," then sudden destruction comes on them
as travail on her that is with child, and they shall in no wise escape.*

*4But you, brothers, are not in darkness that the day should sur-
prise you as thieves are surprised; 5for you are all sons of light and
sons of day.*

*We Christians do not belong to night or to darkness. 6So then
let us not sleep as do the unbelievers, but let us watch and be sober.
7For it is at night that sleepers sleep and at night that drunkards
are drunk. 8But we, since we belong to day—let us be sober, putting
on the breastplate of faith and love, and as a helmet the hope of salvation. 9For God has not appointed us to wrath but to the winning of
salvation through our Lord Jesus Christ, 10who died for us, that
whether we are watching or whether we are sleeping, we might together have life with him.*

*11So then encourage one another and build up one the other, as
in fact you are doing.*

1. περὶ δὲ τῶν χρόνων κτλ. With δέ, the second (*cf.* 4¹³) eschatological question about which the Thessalonians had written
(*cf.* 4⁹· ¹³) for information is stated: "Concerning the times and
seasons." Perceiving, however, that they really need not instruction but encouragement, he tells them, following the precedent of 4⁹ (contrast 4¹³-¹⁸) but varying the language: "you have
no need that anything (*sc.* τι) be written you."

The plural (*cf.* καιροὺς καὶ χρόνους Dan. 2²¹ 4³⁴ (Lxx.); contrast the
singular ἕως χρόνου καὶ καιροῦ Dan. 7¹²) does not here refer to a future
cycle of times and seasons, or to a past cycle now ending (*cf.* 1 Cor. 10¹¹),

but indicates in traditional language the time of the *Parousia*. The question put to Paul was an old one (*cf.* Jer. 25[11] 36[10] Dan. 9[25 ff.]) and was prevalent not only in Christian but in Jewish circles of the time (see Charles, *Eschat.* 168–175; Volz, *Eschat.* 162 *ff.*). Notwithstanding the warning of the Lord: οὐχ ὑμῶν γνῶναι χρόνους ἢ καιρούς (Acts 1[7]; *cf.* Mk. 13[32] Mt. 24[36]), it was impossible to quell curiosity as to the exact day and hour. Doubtless the converts particularly in mind in 5[1-11] were wondering what Paul's teaching meant, especially since they feared lest the day might find them morally unprepared. Though as Ammonius (*apud* Ell.) says: ὁ μὲν καιρὸς δηλοῖ ποιότητα χρόνος δὲ ποσότητα, yet in Jewish usage the terms are interchangeable (*cf.* Dan. 7[12] Sap. 7[18]). ℵ inserts τοῦ before γράφεσθαι; GF smooth χρείαν ἔχετε to χρεία ἐστίν.

2. αὐτοὶ γὰρ ἀκριβῶς κτλ. The reason why (γάρ as in 4[9]) it is unnecessary to write is not that he is unable to teach them anything new (Th. Mops.), but that, in view of the purpose of encouragement, it is inexpedient and superfluous (*cf.* Chrys.) to do any more than call attention to the facts which they already know accurately, namely (1), that the day of the Lord comes "as a thief at night comes" (*sc.* ἔρχεται), that is, suddenly and unexpectedly; and (2) that, as the explanation (vv. 3-5) indicates, although the day comes suddenly for both believers and unbelievers alike, it is only the latter (v. 3) and not the former (vv. 4-5a) who are taken by surprise.

On αὐτοὶ γὰρ οἴδατε, see 2[1]. ἀκριβῶς (Acts 24[22]) occurs elsewhere in Paul only Eph. 5[15] and elsewhere in Gk. Bib. about a dozen times. Findlay thinks that ἀκριβῶς is quoted from the letter sent to Paul. The O.T. (ἡ) ἡμέρα (τοῦ) κυρίου, which appears first in Amos 5[18] (see Robertson Smith, *Prophets*, 396, and Davidson, *HDB*. I, 736) is retained by Paul, though κύριος is Christ, as the context here and elsewhere (*e. g.* Phil. 1[10] 2[16] 1 Cor. 1[8] 2 Cor. 1[14]) attests. The omission of the articles (here and Phil. 1[6. 10] 2[16]; *cf.* Is. 2[12] 13[6. 9], etc.) indicates a fixed formula (*cf.* θεὸς πατήρ, 1[1]). A reads with Amos 5[18 a] ἡ ἡμέρα κυρίου. The mention of νύξ, literal here and v. 7, prepares the way for the metaphors in the contrasts between darkness and daylight (v. 4), darkness and light (v. 5), and night time and daytime (v. 5; *cf.* v. 8). On ὡς . . . οὕτως, *cf.* 1 Cor. 7[17] (οὕτως καί, Rom. 5[15. 18], etc.). As the emphasis is on ὡς κλέπτης not on ἔρχεται, the present tense is general or gnomic (*BMT.* 12), not present for future, or prophetic. For the early belief that the Lord would come at night, expecially Easter eve, see Lün. *ad loc.* who quotes Lactantius, *Inst.* 7[19], and Jerome on Mt. 25:

Paul does not tell us (contrast 4¹⁵) whence he derived the information assumed to be possessed by the readers. The comparison to a thief is in itself natural enough (cf. Jer. 29¹⁰ ὡς κλέπται ἐν νυκτὶ ἐπιθήσουσιν χεῖρα αὐτῶν; also Job 24¹⁴ Joel 2⁹); but the first extant comparison of the coming of the Lord to a thief appears to be the word of Jesus in Lk. 12³⁹ = Mt. 24⁴³: εἰ ᾔδει ὁ οἰκοδεσπότης ποίᾳ ὥρᾳ ὁ κλέπτης ἔρχεται. To be sure ἐν νυκτί does not appear in the logion, and it is the Lord himself (by context) not the day of the Lord that is compared to a thief. But despite these differences, it is better to see in our passage an allusion to that word of the Lord than to postulate an agraphon or a citation from an unknown Jewish apocalypse (as Brückner does in his *Entstehung der paulinischen Christologie*, 179 ff.). Ephr. (who wrongly takes ὅτι as = *quia*) remarks on οἴδατε: "*sicut didicistis etiam haec a nobis; quoniam et nos ex ipso evangelio Domini nostri didicimus.* 2 Pet. 3¹⁰ (where CKL add ἐν νυκτί) is evidently based on our passage.

3. ὅταν λέγωσιν κτλ. "When people are saying: There is (*sc.* ἐστίν) security and safety," etc. Starting from ἡμέρα κυρίου as a day of judgment, and from the idea of moral indifference suggested by ἐν νυκτί (*cf.* v. ⁴ οὐκ ἐστὲ ἐν σκότει), Paul proceeds, without connecting particle (*cf.* v. ⁵ οὐκ ἐσμέν; 1 Cor. 14²⁶ Col. 3⁴) to explain the bearing first on unbelievers of the sudden coming of the Lord (v. ²). Though λέγωσιν is impersonal (*cf.* 1 Cor. 10²⁰ and Bl. 30⁴) and αὐτοῖς is undefined, yet clearly unbelievers alone are in mind, as the sharply contrasted ὑμεῖς δὲ ἀδελφοί (v. ⁴) makes plain. By the phrase εἰρήνη καὶ ἀσφάλεια, we are reminded with Grot. of Ezek. 13¹⁰, λέγοντες εἰρήνη καὶ οὐκ ἦν εἰρήνη (*cf.* Jer. 6¹⁴ = 8¹¹); and of the false repose and safety of the people described in the word of the Lord (Lk. 17²⁶ ⁱ· =Mt. 24³⁷ ⁱ·) to which Ephr. alludes: "*istud est quod dixit Dominus noster: sicut fuit in diebus Noë et Loth*, etc.

The asyndeton (אAGF, *et al.*) is corrected by BD, *et al.*, which insert δέ, and by KLP, Vulg. (*enim*), *et al.*, which insert γάρ. For ὅταν δέ, *cf.* 1 Cor. 13¹⁰ 15²⁷, etc; ὅταν γάρ, 1 Cor. 3⁴ 2 Cor. 12¹⁰, etc. GF, *et al.*, read λέγουσιν (*cf.* στήκετε 3⁸). On ὅταν ... τότε, *cf.* 1 Cor. 15²⁸·⁵⁴ Col. 3⁴. For the present general condition, see *BMT.* 260, 312. εἰρήνη and ἀσφάλεια, united only here in Gk. Bib., are virtually synonymous (*cf.* Lev. 26⁵ ⁱ·); but Ell. would distinguish them: "εἰρήνη betokens an inward repose and security; ἀσφάλεια a sureness and safety that is not interfered with or compromised by outward obstacles."

αἰφνίδιος ὄλεθρος. That is, either "all of a sudden" (adjective for adverb; Bl. 44²) or "sudden" (adjective) "destruction comes on them." It is probable that ὄλεθρος, like θάνατος (2 Cor. 2¹⁵ 7¹⁰) and ἀπώλεια (II 2¹⁰ 1 Cor. 1¹⁸ 2 Cor. 2¹⁵ Phil. 1²⁸) is the opposite of σωτηρία; and that the point is not annihilation of existence but separation from the presence of Christ; hence ὄλεθρος may be αἰώνιος (II 1⁹) as well as αἰφνίδιος.

On the idea, see Kennedy, *Last Things*, 314. In 1 Cor. 5⁵, ὄλεθρος τῆς σαρκός is contrasted with the salvation (σώζεσθαι) of τὸ πνεῦμα; in 1 Tim. 6⁹, we have εἰς ὄλεθρον καὶ ἀπώλειαν. αἰφνίδιος is rare in Gk. Bib. (Lk. 21³⁴ Sap. 17¹⁵ 2 Mac. 14¹⁷ 3.Mac. 3²⁴); WH. edit here αἰφνίδιος (Bℵ), but in Lk. 21³⁴ ἐφνίδιος (so here, ADFLP, *et al.*). ἐφιστάναι, frequent in Lxx. appears in N. T. only here and 2 Tim. 4². ⁶, apart from Lk. Acts. It is construed with dat. (here and Sap. 6⁵. ⁸ Lk. 2⁹ 24⁴, etc.), or with ἐπί and accus. (Sir. 41²² Jer. 21², etc.; Lk. 21³⁴ Acts 10¹⁷ 11¹¹). On ἐπίσταται (BℵL, etc.) for ἐφίσταται (DEKP, *et al.*), see Bl. 6⁷. GF, read φανήσεται; B puts αὐτοῖς after ἐπίσταται.

ὥσπερ ἡ ὠδίν κτλ. "As travail comes upon (*sc.* ἐπίσταται) her that is with child." The point of the comparison is not ὁ πόνος τῶν ὠδίνων (*cf.* Is. 66⁷), as the common Lxx. phrase ὠδίνες ὡς τικτούσης might suggest (so Th. Mops.); not the certainty (an interpretation which Chrys. combats); but the suddenness as αἰφνίδιος indicates. The idea of inevitableness, brought out by οὐ μὴ ἐκφύγωσιν, arises probably not from the comparison but from ὄλεθρος.

For ὠδίνες ὡς τικτούσης, *cf.* Ps. 47⁶ Hos. 13³ Mic. 4⁹ Jer. 6²⁴ 8²¹ 22³³ 27⁴³; also Jer. 13²¹ Is. 13⁸; and Is. 26¹⁷ Eth. En. 62⁴. The singular (ℵB read ἡ ὠδείν) is rare in Gk. Bib.; but even if the plural were read with GF, there would be here no reference to the *dolores Messiae* (Mk. 13⁸ = Mt. 24⁸; *cf.* Volz, *Eschat.* 173 and Bousset, *Relig.*² 286). On ἐκφεύγειν (Rom. 2³ 2 Cor. 11³³), *cf.* Lk. 21³⁶; on οὐ μή with aor. subj. instead of fut. indic. (which DGF here read; *cf.* Gal. 4³⁰), see 4¹⁵ and *cf.* Rom. 4⁸ 1 Cor. 8¹³ Gal. 5¹⁶. It is unnecessary to supply an object with ἐκφύγωσιν; contrast 2 Mac. 6²⁶: τὰς τοῦ παντοκράτορος χεῖρας οὔτε ζῶν οὔτε ἀποθανὼν ἐκφεύξομαι. Here only does Paul use γαστήρ; elsewhere in N. T. apart from Tit. 1¹² Lk. 1³¹, it is used in the common Lxx. phrase, as here, ἔχειν ἐν γαστρί = εἶναι ἔγκυος.

Lft. remarks on v. ³: "The dissimilarity which this verse presents to the ordinary style of St. Paul is striking." To be sure, ὅταν . . . τότε,

ὥσπερ, ἐκφεύγειν, ὄλεθρος, or οὐ μή with aor. subj. need excite no wonder;
but the use of εἰρήνη = "security," of ἀσφάλεια, αἰφνίδιος, ἐφιστάναι and
ὠδίν, and of the impersonal λέγωσιν might suggest that Paul (a) is citing from a Jewish apocalypse, or (b) from an agraphon, or is writing
under the influence either (c) of a Jewish apocalypse or (d) a word of
the Lord (as in v. ²). In the light of v. ², (a) is improbable. In favour
of (d) rather than (c) is to be urged not Mk. 13⁸ = Mt. 24⁸, or Mk. 13¹⁷
and par., but Lk. 21³⁴⁻³⁶: "Take heed to yourselves that your hearts
be not dulled by debauches and μέθη and the distractions of life; and
take heed lest ἐπιστῇ ἐφ' ὑμᾶς ἐφνίδιος ἡ ἡμέρα as a trap (ὡς παγίς;
cf. Jer. 5²⁷). For it will surely come upon all those who sit on the face
of all the earth. ἀγρυπνεῖτε at every season, praying that ye may be
able ἐκφυγεῖν all these things which are going to happen, and to stand
before the Son of Man." This passage may have affected vv.⁴⁻⁸ below;
cf. Rom. 13¹¹ ᶠᶠ·. In favour of (b) is not the concrete and definite character
of the utterance (cf. 4¹⁶), but the indefinite αὐτοῖς. "If, as seems not
unlikely, the sentence is a direct quotation from our Lord's words, the
reference implied in the word αὐτοῖς is to be sought for in the context
of the saying from which St. Paul quotes" (Lft.).

4. ὑμεῖς δέ κτλ. The δέ is adversative by context and contrasts the brethren with the αὐτοῖς (v. ³) who are now seen to be
unbelievers. The latter are in the realm of night, as ἐν νυκτί
(v. ²) suggests, that is, of wickedness; and the day of the Lord
with its inevitable destruction comes on them suddenly and finds
them unprepared. The brethren on the other hand (δέ) are not
in darkness (ἐν σκότει), that is, in the realm of wickedness, and
the day of the Lord, now designated as the daylight in contrast
with the dark, while it comes suddenly for them also, does not
(and this is the point of the new comparison) surprise them as
thieves are surprised by the coming of the dawn.

"Christians are on the alert, open-eyed; they do not know when it
is to come, but they are alive to any signs of its coming. Thus there is
no incompatibility between the emphasis on the instantaneous character
of the advent and the emphasis in II 2³ ᶠ· on the preliminary conditions"
(Moff.). On σκότος, cf. Rom. 13¹² 1 Cor. 4⁵ 2 Cor. 6¹⁴, etc.; cf. ἡ ἐξουσία
τοῦ σκότους Col. 1¹³ Lk. 22⁵³. The clause with ἵνα is not of purpose but
of conceived result (cf. 2 Cor. 1¹⁷ and BMT. 218 f.). The daylight is a
metaphor for "the day," that is, ἡ ἡμέρα ἐκείνη (GF; cf. II 1¹⁰); on
ἡ ἡμέρα, cf. 1 Cor. 3¹³ Rom. 13¹²; also Rom. 2¹⁶ Ezek. 36³³. καταλαμβάνειν is here not "attain" (Rom. 9³⁰ 1 Cor. 9²⁴ Phil. 3¹² ᶠ·), or "understand" (Eph. 3¹⁸), but "overtake" (Gen. 19¹⁹ Sir. 7¹ Jn. 12³⁵), with a

touch of surprise and detection. GF read καταλάβοι. ADGF place ὑμᾶς before ἡ ἡμέρα. Rom. 13¹¹⁻¹⁴, where the time before the *Parousia* is designated as ὕπνος, σκότος, and νύξ, affords a striking parallel to vv. ⁴⁻⁷. The advent is ἡ ἡμέρα and Christians are to put on τὰ ὅπλα τοῦ φωτός and to conduct themselves ὡς ἐν ἡμέρᾳ, that is, are to avoid κώμοις, μέθαις κτλ., for ἡ νὺξ προέκοψεν ἡ δὲ ἡμέρα ἤγγικεν.

ὡς κλέπτας. "That the day should surprise you as thieves are surprised." As Grotius has observed, the comparison here is not the same as in v. ², though it follows naturally from it. In v. ², "the day of the Lord comes as a thief at night," suddenly and unexpectedly; here the day of the Lord (compared to the daylight) does not surprise the believers as it does the unbelievers (ὡς κλέπτας), that is, does not catch the Christians unawares and unprepared.

κλέπτας, read by BA Boh., is accepted by Lachmann, WH. De W. Ewald, Koch, Lft. Moff. and Field (*Otium Norv.* III, 123). Most commentators, however, prefer the numerically better attested κλέπτης (see Souter, *ad loc.*). In this case, the same comparison is used as in v. ², but here the point is not "suddenness" but "surprise." The usual objection to κλέπτας, that it spoils the metaphor (see on νήπιος 2⁷), is too incisive, in view of the inversion of metaphors in Paul, especially in this section (*cf.* καθεύδειν and γρηγορεῖν in vv. ⁶·¹⁰); see Lft. on 2⁷ and *ad loc.* Weiss (17) thinks that κλέπτας is a mechanical conformation to ὑμᾶς (*cf.* τύπους 1⁷). Zim. (*cf.* Mill. and Dibelius) suggests that κλέπτας involves a change of sense that overlooks the reference to Lk. 12³⁹ = Mt. 24⁴³.

5. πάντες γὰρ ὑμεῖς κτλ. The γάρ explains why "the day" should not surprise them; and the πάντες (*cf.* πᾶσιν II 1¹⁰) singles out the faint-hearted for special encouragement. The readers, one and all, are not "in darkness" but are "sons of light," that is, belong to Christ; and, with a slight advance of meaning, are "sons of day," that is, belong to the realm of future light and salvation, the unexpressed reason being that the indwelling Christ or Spirit guarantees their ability so to live a blameless life that they may even now, if they are vigilant and sober, be assured of the rescue from the wrath that comes (1¹⁰), and of an entrance into God's own kingdom and glory (2¹²; *v. infra*, vv. ⁹⁻¹⁰).

υἱὸς φωτός suggests the possible influence of the word of the Lord in Lk. 16⁸; cf. Jn. 12³⁶ Eph. 5⁸ (τέκνα); the phrase does not occur in Lxx. υἱὸς ἡμέρας is not found elsewhere in Gk. Bib. The use of υἱός with a gen. to denote the intimate relation of a person with a thing or person appears to be Semitic in origin (see on II 2³ and cf. Deiss. *BS*. 161–166); the idiom is common in the Gk. Bib.

οὐκ ἐσμέν κτλ. The change from ὑμεῖς (vv. ⁴⁻⁵ᵃ) to ἡμεῖς (vv. ⁵ᵇ⁻¹⁰) should not be overlooked. In saying that *all* the brethren are sons of light and sons of day, Paul seems already to be preparing the way tactfully for an exhortation that they conduct themselves as such, especially since blamelessness of life (3¹³) alone assures them of escape from judgment (cf. 2 Cor. 5¹⁰ Rom. 14¹⁰). Not wishing to discourage the faint-hearted but at the same time recognising that they need the warning, he includes in the exhortation not only them but himself and all other Christians, and proceeds (v. ⁵ᵇ) asyndetically: "We Christians, all of us, do not belong to night or to darkness." He thus prepares for the exhortation to sobriety and vigilance (vv. ⁶⁻⁷), and for the encouraging assurance of future salvation (vv. ⁹⁻¹⁰). This done, the ὑμεῖς of v. ⁵ᵃ (cf. v. ⁴) is resumed in v.¹¹. It is obvious that οὐκ ἐσμὲν νυκτὸς οὐδὲ σκότους forms the transition to the exhortation.

εἶναι νυκτός, σκότους, ἡμέρας (v. ⁸) is logically equivalent to υἱοὶ νυκτός, etc. In view of 1 Cor. 3²³ 2 Cor. 10⁷ Rom. 14⁸, etc., it is unnecessary to supply υἱοί. The arrangement of φωτός, ἡμέρας, νυκτός, σκότους is chiastic. Day and night are the periods; light and darkness the characteristics of the periods. GF put καί before οὐκ ἐσμέν to relieve the asyndeton. On οὐκ . . . οὐδέ, see 2³ and II 3⁸.

6. ἄρα οὖν μὴ καθεύδωμεν κτλ. "So then let us not sleep as do the rest (οἱ λοιποί as 4¹³) but let us watch and be sober." The figurative use of καθεύδειν and νήφειν is suggested, as v. ⁷ intimates, by the fact that sleepers sleep at night and drunkards get drunk at night. καθεύδειν covers all sorts of moral laxity; γρηγορεῖν, its opposite, denotes watchfulness, moral alertness, vigilance against the assaults of unrighteousness. The point of νήφειν is less certain; for since drunkenness may suggest either stupid unconsciousness or abnormal exaltation (B. Weiss, Dob.), νήφωμεν may be an exhortation either to perfect control of the senses without which vigilance is impossible or to quietness of mind (4¹¹) without which the peaceable fruits of righteousness essential to future salvation are unattainable.

Since καθεύδωμεν and γρηγορῶμεν are metaphorical, it is unlikely that νήφωμεν here (and v. ⁸) is literal, as if some of the converts were intemperate; or that it is both literal and metaphorical (Find.). At the same time, as v. ⁷ intimates, the sons of day and the sons of light in Thessalonica as elsewhere may have been tempted to indulge in habits characteristic of those who belong not to day but to night. ἄρα οὖν, found in Gk. Bib. only in Paul, is followed by the hortatory subj. (here and Gal. 6¹⁰ Rom. 14¹⁹); or by the imperative (II 2¹⁵). KLP read καθεύδομεν and GF νήφομεν; cf. Rom. 14¹⁹ (ℵBAG).—καθεύδειν is used by Paul only in this section and in the fragment of a hymn cited in Eph. 5¹⁴. In v. ⁷ it is literal; in v. ¹⁰ it is = κοιμᾶσθαι = ἀποθνήσκειν. ὡς καί, which DGF read here for the simple ὡς, is rare in Paul (Rom. 9²⁵ 1 Cor. 7⁷ ᶠ· 9⁵ Eph. 2³ 5²³), and is perhaps a reminiscence of Eph. 2³ ὡς καὶ οἱ λοιποί. γρηγορεῖν is infrequent in Paul (1 Cor. 16¹³ Col. 4²) and the Lxx. (cf. 1 Mac. 12²⁷: γρηγορεῖν καὶ εἶναι ἐπὶ τοῖς ὅπλοις, ἐτοιμάζεσθαι εἰς πόλεμον δι' ὅλης τῆς νυκτός). It is employed in the eschatological passages Mk. 13³³ ᶠᶠ· Lk. 12³⁷ ᶠᶠ· and Mt. 24⁴³ ᶠᶠ·; but in Lk. 21³⁶ and Mk. 13³³ we have ἀγρυπνεῖν.—νήφειν, rare in Gk. Bib., is used metaphorically in the N. T. (v. ⁸ 2 Tim. 4⁵ 1 Pet. 1¹³ 4⁷; 5⁸ (νήψατε, γρηγορήσατε); cf. ἐκνήφειν (1 Cor. 15³⁴ Joel 1⁵, etc.) and ἀνανήφειν (2 Tim. 2²⁶).

7. οἱ γὰρ καθεύδοντες κτλ. The exhortation to vigilance and sobriety is illustrated by a fact of observation familiar to the readers (cf. Rom. 13¹¹ ᶠᶠ·). "Those who sleep (usually) sleep at night (νυκτός; cf. 2⁹) and those who get drunk (usually) are drunk at night." These habits, characteristic of those who are not sons of day and sons of light, are mentioned, not without reference to the temptations to which all Christians, including the readers, are exposed.

The distinction between μεθύσκεσθαι "get drunk" (Eph. 5¹⁸ Lk. 12⁴⁵ Pr. 23³¹) and μεθύειν (B reads μεθύοντες) "be drunk" (1 Cor. 11²¹; cf. ὁ μεθύων Job 12²⁵ Is. 19¹⁴ 24²⁰, etc.) is doubted by Ell. Lft. and others. Since Paul does not say οἱ καθεύδοντες νυκτός εἰσιν κτλ., "the sleepers belong to night," etc., it is improbable that v. ⁷ is figurative (see Lün.). Schmiedel would exscind v. ⁷ as a marginal note, and v. ⁸ᵃ as a connecting link inserted by a later reader.

8. ἡμεῖς δὲ ἡμέρας κτλ. The emphasis on νυκτός (v. ⁷),
already implied in vv. ². ⁴⁻⁶, prepares for the contrast here, δέ
being adversative by context, and for the exhortation. Sleep
and drunkenness are the affairs of those who belong to the night;
"but let us, since we belong not to night (the realm of evil), but
to day (the future glory; *cf.* v. ⁵), be sober."

ἐνδυσάμενοι κτλ. "It is not sufficient to watch and be sober,
we must also be armed" (Chrys.). "Perhaps the mention of
vigilance suggested the idea of a sentry armed and on duty"
(Lft. who compares Rom. 13¹¹ ᶠᶠ·). As in 1³, Paul describes the
Christian life on the religious side as faith and on the ethical
side as love, and singles out for special remark the moral
quality of hope; hence to the breastplate he adds the helmet,
the hope for future salvation, thus giving to conduct an eschatological sanction.

> One is reminded here and even more strongly in Eph. 6¹⁴ of Is. 59¹⁷:
> καὶ ἐνεδύσατο δικαιοσύνην (*cf.* Job 29¹⁴) ὡς θώρακα (*cf.* Sap. 5¹⁸) καὶ
> περιέθετο περικεφάλαιαν σωτηρίου ἐπὶ τῆς κεφαλῆς. The figure, how
> ever, is natural to Paul (*cf.* Rom. 13¹² ἐνδυσώμεθα τὰ ὅπλα τοῦ φωτός
> and Eph. 6¹¹ ἐνδύσασθε τὴν πανοπλίαν τοῦ θεοῦ). The purpose of the ar
> mour, tacit here but expressed in Eph. 6¹¹, is probably: πρὸς τὸ δύνασθαι
> ὑμᾶς στῆναι πρὸς τὰς μεθοδίας τοῦ διαβόλου, the Satan who, as an
> angel of darkness, transforms himself into an ἄγγελος φωτός (2 Cor. 11¹⁴).
> ἐνδύεσθαι, a common word in Lxx., is used metaphorically by Paul with
> various objects (*cf.* Gal. 3²⁷ 1 Cor. 15⁵³ ᶠᶠ· Rom. 13¹⁴ Col. 3¹² Eph. 4²⁴).
> The aorist part. is of identical action (*BMT.* 139). θώραξ, here and Eph.
> 6¹⁴ in Paul, is quite frequent in Gk. Bib. (*cf.* ἐνδύεσθαι θώρακα 1 Reg. 17⁵
> Jer. 26⁴ Ezek. 38⁴ 1 Mac. 3³). περικεφάλαια, in N. T. only here and Eph.
> 6¹⁷, is literal in Lxx. except Is. 59¹⁷. On the complete armour of the
> *hastati*, see Polyb. VI, 23. The gen. πίστεως and ἀγάπης are appositional.

ἐλπίδα σωτηρίας. Salvation is both negatively freedom from
wrath (*cf.* 1¹⁰) and positively fellowship with Christ, as vv. ⁹⁻¹⁰
declare. Since σωτηρία is an eschatological conception (*cf.* Rom.
13¹¹), something to be acquired (v. ⁹), Paul says not σωτηρίαν
but ἐλπίδα σωτηρίας (objective gen. as 1³ Rom. 5² Col. 1²⁷).
The significance of this exhortation to hope lies in the conviction that without blamelessness of life (3¹³) even believers cannot escape the judgment (*cf.* Rom. 14¹⁰ 2 Cor. 5¹⁰). To be sure,

as Paul forthwith encourages the faint-hearted to remember
(vv. ⁹⁻¹⁰), this hope is virtually certain of realisation.

> Here and v. ⁹, he speaks generally of σωτηρία. In Rom. 8²³, he singles
> out the redemption of the body as the object of hope; "for by that hope
> we have been (proleptically) saved"; and in Phil 3²⁰ ᶠ·, Jesus Christ as
> σωτήρ is to transform the body of our humiliation that it may be con-
> formable to the body of his glory (note ἀπεκδεχόμεθα in both pas-
> sages and cf. Gal. 5⁵). Though Paul here may have this specific hope
> also in mind, he contents himself with a general statement, ἐλπὶς
> σωτηρίας (cf. Job 2⁹ for the objective gen.: προσδεχόμενοι τὴν ἐλπίδα τῆς
> σωτηρίας μου).

9-10. ὅτι οὐκ ἔθετο κτλ. With ὅτι "because," he confirms
the propriety of the exhortation to the ἐλπίδα σωτηρίας by encouraging the faint-hearted to be assured that that hope is bound
to be fulfilled. The ground of assurance is stated, first, negatively, "God did not appoint us Christians for wrath," that is,
for condemnation at the day of judgment (cf. 1¹⁰ 2¹⁶); and then
positively, "but to gain salvation." Since, however, it is impossible to work out one's own salvation (Phil. 2¹³) unless the divine
power operates in the believer, Paul next recalls the means by
which salvation is to be acquired, namely, "through" the causal
activity of the indwelling "Jesus Christ our Lord." Furthermore, since death and resurrection are inseparable factors in
the redemptive work of Christ (cf. 4¹⁴), he adds: "who died for
us," that is, for our sins, "in order that we might live, have life
with him," the future life in fellowship with Christ, which is
the consummation of Christian hope.

> The construction τιθέναι τινά εἰς τι, only here in Paul, but fre-
> quent in Lxx., is not the equivalent of Acts 13⁴⁷ = Is. 49⁶ (τέθεικά σε
> εἰς φῶς; contrast Rom. 4¹⁷ = Gen. 17⁵), but nevertheless "appears to
> have a partially Hebraistic tinge" (Ell.; cf. Ps. 65⁹ Hos. 4⁷ Mic. 1⁷
> Jer. 25¹², etc.). ἔθετο (= ἔθηκεν, Bl. 55¹) indicates the purpose of God,
> but like εἵλατο (II 2¹³) is less specific than ἐκλογή (1⁴); περιποίησις,
> rare in Gk. Bib., is used absolutely in the passive sense of "possession,"
> "remnant," in 2 Ch. 14¹³ Mal. 3¹⁷ Hag. 2⁹ Eph. 1¹⁴ 1 Pet. 2⁹; here, how-
> ever, and II 2¹⁴ Heb. 10³⁹, where a genitive follows, it is active, *acquisitio*
> (Vulg. Ell Mill. and most), "gaining," "winning," as indeed γρηγορῶ-
> μεν and νήφωμεν (Find.) and the clause with διά (Dob.) intimate.
> B and some minuscules invert the order to read ὁ θεὸς ἡμᾶς (cf. 2¹⁶).

διὰ τοῦ κυρίου ἡμῶν 'Ι. X. This clause is to be construed not
with ἔθετο but with the adjacent εἰς περιποίησιν σωτηρίας.
The διά indicates the causal activity of the risen Lord conceived
of as a spiritual power resident in the hearts of believers, ena-
bling them to bring forth the fruits of righteousness essential to
salvation and guaranteeing their resurrection from the dead
and eternal fellowship with himself.

> The phrase is the logical but not grammatical equivalent of ἐν τῷ
> κυρίῳ: see on 4². ¹⁴. On the divine name, see 1³; B Eth. omit Χριστοῦ
> (cf. 2¹⁹).

10. τοῦ ἀποθανόντος κτλ. The risen Lord through whose indwelling power the believer gains salvation is also he who died
for us, that is, for our sins (Gal. 1³ 1 Cor. 15³; cf. Rom. 5⁸ 4²⁵).

> Bℵ read περί (cf. Gal. 1³ where B has ὑπέρ), but most have ὑπέρ (cf.
> Rom. 5⁸); the distinction between these prepositions is becoming en-
> feebled (Moult. I, 105). By the phrases ἀποθνήσκειν ὑπέρ (Rom. 5⁶ ff.
> 14¹⁵ 1 Cor. 15³ 2 Cor. 5¹⁵), διδόναι περί (Gal. 1³), and παραδιδόναι ὑπέρ
> (Gal. 2²⁰ Rom. 8³²), Paul indicates his belief in the sufferings and es-
> pecially the death of Christ, the righteous for the unrighteous, as an
> atonement for sins (cf. Moore, EB. 4229 ff.). In speaking of the death of
> Christ for us, Paul uses regularly the category not of forgiveness (Rom.
> 4⁷ Col. 1¹⁴ Eph. 1⁷; cf. Col. 2¹³ 3¹³ Eph. 4³²) but of reconciliation (Rom.
> 5¹⁰ ff. 2 Cor. 5¹⁸ ff. Col. 1²⁰ ff.) and especially justification. "Forgive-
> ness he calls justification. It is the same thing as atonement, or recon-
> ciliation, terms in which somewhat different aspects of the same process
> are emphasised" (Ropes, Apostolic Age, 156). The absence of these
> terms in I, II, and the fact that this is the only passage in I, II in which
> the death of Christ for us is mentioned, suggests not that the significance
> of that death was not preached prominently in Thessalonica, but that
> the purpose of these letters did not call for a discussion of justification,
> law, works, etc. Nothing is here said explicitly of Christ's death "to
> sin" (Rom. 6¹⁰) or of the believers' dying and rising with Christ (Gal.
> 2¹⁹ f. Rom. 6³ ff. Col. 2¹². ²⁰ 3¹), but this conception may underlie both
> the passage (4¹⁴), "if we believe that Jesus died and rose," etc., and
> διὰ τοῦ κυρίου and ἐν κυρίῳ.

ἵνα . . . ζήσωμεν. The purpose of the death, stated in the
light of the cognate discussion (4¹³⁻¹⁸), is: "that whether we are
watching (living) or whether we are sleeping (dead), we might
together live with him." γρηγορῶμεν and καθεύδωμεν are to

be taken figuratively for ζῶμεν and ἀποθνήσκωμεν (Rom. 14⁸), as, indeed, Th. Mops. Chrys. Ephr. (*sive vivi simus sive mortui*), and most affirm. For survivors and dead, salvation comes simultaneously at the *Parousia*, as ἄξει σὺν αὐτῷ (4¹⁴) and πάντοτε σὺν κυρίῳ ἐσόμεθα (4¹⁷) prepare us to expect.

It is noteworthy that even in a casual statement about the significance of salvation, three distinctive points in Paul's conception are touched upon, forgiveness of sins through the death of Christ, moral renewal through the indwelling power of the spiritual Christ, and the final consummation of future fellowship with him. Ell. is again right in insisting that as in 4¹⁷ so here ἄμα and σύν be separated; "the ζῆν σὺν Χριστῷ forms the principal idea, while the ἄμα subjoins the further notion of aggregation"; Vulg., however, joins *simul cum* (contrast 4¹⁷). On καθεύδειν = "to die"; see 4¹³; but "to this particular use of γρηγορέω no Biblical parallel can be adduced" (Mill.). There seems to be no sharp difference in meaning between εἰ with the subjunctive (common in later Gk.; *cf.* Mill. and 1 Cor. 14⁵) and the expected ἐάν (Rom. 14⁸). Burton (*BMT.* 253), contrary to the opinion of many (*e. g.* Bl. 65⁴) thinks that the subjunctive "can hardly be explained as attraction since the nature of the thought (in our passage) calls for a subjunctive." A few minuscules read γρηγορούμεν and also with KLP καθεύδομεν. εἴτε, a favourite particle in Paul (*cf.* II 2¹⁵), is rare elsewhere in Gk. Bib. (1 Pet. 2¹³ *f.* Josh. 24¹⁵ Is. 30²¹ Sir. 41⁴, etc.).—A reads ζήσομεν; DE ζῶμεν; the aorist ζήσωμεν (אB, *et al.*) indicates the future living as a fact without reference to progress or completion, "that we might have life."

11. διὸ παρακαλεῖτε κτλ. "Wherefore" (3¹; *cf.* ὥστε 4¹⁷), since the day of the Lord, though it comes suddenly on all, believers and unbelievers, will not surprise you believers; and since the power of Christ makes possible that blamelessness of life which is necessary to salvation and so guarantees the realisation of your hope; do not be faint-hearted but "encourage one another" (παρακαλεῖτε ἀλλήλους, as was just said in 4¹⁸) "and build up one another." Then remembering the actual practice of the converts, and justifying, as it were, his writing when there was no need to write (v. ¹; *cf.* 4⁹), he adds tactfully as in 4¹⁰ (*cf.* 4¹): "as in fact (καθὼς καί; see 3⁴ 4¹) you are doing."

οἰκοδομεῖν, οἰκοδομή and ἐποικοδομεῖν are frequent words in Paul, especially in his letters to Corinth. From the figure of the church or the individual (1 Cor. 6¹⁹) as a temple of the Spirit, the further metaphor of "building up," "constructing" a character would naturally develop (see Lft. on 1 Cor. ʒ·²). The parallelism with ἀλλήλους demands for εἰς τον ενα a sense similar to ἀλλήλους and the accentuation εἰς τὸν ἕνα, "each one of you build up the other one." Lillie observes: "no edition has εἰς τὸν ἕνα, the construction adopted by Faber Stapulensis (*ad unum usque, to a man*), Whitby (*into one body*), Rückert (who understands by τὸν ἕνα Christ)." Blass (45²) remarks on the phrase: "quite unclassic but Semitic for ἀλλήλους." Of the many parallels cited by Kypke (II, 339), the closest is Theoc. 22⁶⁵: εἰς ἐνὶ χεῖρας ἄειρον. The exact phrase, however, recurs later in the *Greek Legend of Isaiah*, 2⁸ (in Charles's *Ascen. Isaiah*, 143); *Testament Job*, 27 (in James's *Apocrypha Anecdota*); and in Pseudo-Cyrill. Alex. X, 1055 A, εἰς τῷ ἐνί = ἀλλήλοις (noted by Soph. *Lex.* 427).

(7) *Spiritual Labourers* (5¹²⁻¹³).

There are still some ὑστερήματα (3¹²) which need to be adjusted. Hence the exhortations (4¹–5¹¹) are now continued, as δέ introducing a new point and ἐρωτῶμεν (*cf.* 4¹) intimate. The brethren as a whole are first urged to appreciate those who labour among them, two special functions of these labourers being selected for emphasis, that of leading and that of admonishing. But not only are they to appreciate the labourers, they are to do so very highly, and that too not from fear and distrust but from love, because of their work. Then changing from infinitive to imperative, he commands them to be at peace not "with them" but "among yourselves."

¹²*Furthermore, we ask you, brothers, to appreciate those who labour among you both acting as your leaders in the Lord and warning you;* ¹³*and to rate them very highly in love for the sake of their work. Be at peace among yourselves.*

There must be a reason for specifying two of the functions of "the workers" and for observing that in acting as leaders they do so in the Lord. Precisely what the reason is escapes our knowledge. It may be conjectured, however (see on 4¹¹), that the idlers in their want had appealed for assistance to those who laboured among them, managing the external affairs of the group including money matters and acting as spiritual advisers, and had been refused rather tactlessly with an admonition on the ground that the idle brothers though able were unwilling to support themselves, thus violating Paul's express command (4¹¹ II 3¹⁰). The result was friction between the idlers and "the workers" and the disturbance of the peace of the church. Paul recognises that there was blame on both sides; and so, addressing the brethren as a whole, for the matter concerned the entire brotherhood, he urges first, with the idlers in mind, that the workers be appreciated, that it be remembered that they manage the affairs of the church not on their own authority but on that of the indwelling Christ, and that they be highly esteemed because of the excellence of their services. He urges next, still addressing the church as a whole, but having in mind the attitude of the workers in admonishing, that they be at peace among themselves.

The arrangement of the exhortations in 5¹²⁻²² is not perfectly obvious. To be sure, παρακαλοῦμεν δέ (v. ¹⁴) is a fresh start, and vv. ¹⁶⁻¹⁸ and vv. ¹⁹⁻²² are distinct in themselves; but the division of the material in vv. ¹⁴⁻¹⁵ is uncertain. In the light, however, of the triplet in vv. ¹⁶⁻¹⁸, it is tempting to divide the six exhortations in vv. ¹⁴⁻¹⁵ into two groups of three each, putting a period after ἀσθενῶν and beginning afresh with μακροθυμεῖτε πρὸς πάντας. In this case, we may subdivide as follows: The Spiritual Labourers (vv. ¹²⁻¹³); The Idlers, The Faint-hearted, and The Weak (v. ¹⁴ᵃ⁻ᶜ); Love (vv. ¹⁴ᵈ⁻¹⁵); Joy, Prayer, and Thanksgiving (vv. ¹⁶⁻¹⁸); and Spiritual Gifts (vv. ¹⁹⁻²²).

12. ἐρωτῶμεν δέ κτλ. As already noted, the exhortations begun in 4¹ are here renewed. The phrase ἐρωτῶμεν . . . ἀδελφοί recurs in II 2¹. Here as in 4⁴ εἰδέναι means "respect," "appreciate the worth of." In τοὺς κοπιῶντας ἐν ὑμῖν καὶ προϊσταμένους καὶ νουθετοῦντας, we have not three nouns designating the official titles of the class of persons to be appreciated, but three participles describing these persons as exercising certain functions. Furthermore, the omission of the article before the last two participles indicates that only one set of persons is intended, "those who labour among you." Finally, the correlative καὶ . . . καί suggests that of the various activities involved in τοὺς κοπιῶντας ἐν ὑμῖν, two are purposely emphasised, leadership in practical affairs and the function of spiritual admonition.

Whether the two functions of "those who labour among you" "were executed by the same or different persons cannot be determined; at this early period of the existence of the church of Thess. the first supposition seems much the most probable" (Ell.). Though it is likely that the older or more gifted men would be conspicuous as workers, it does not follow that the class described not by title but by function is that of the official πρεσβύτεροι, a word found not in Paul, but in the Pastorals. Nor must we infer from the fact that later we have traces in another Macedonian church of ἐπίσκοποι and διάκονοι (Phil. 1¹) that such officials are in existence in Thess. at the time of writing I and II. Rather we are in the period of informal and voluntary leadership, the success of which depended upon the love of the brethren as well as upon the recognition that the leadership is ἐν κυρίῳ. Hence Paul exhorts the converts not only to esteem the workers but to esteem them very highly in love because of their work. See McGiffert, *Apostolic Age*, 666.

τοὺς κοπιῶντας ἐν ὑμῖν. In the light of ὁ κόπος τῆς ἀγάπης (1³), of Paul's habit of incessant work (2⁹ᶠ·), and of the exhortation to work (4¹¹), this quite untechnical designation of the persons in question as "those who work among you" is conspicuously appropriate. While such a designation is natural to Paul, the artisan missionary (*cf.* Deiss. *Light*, 316 *f.*), the choice of it here may have been prompted by the existing situation. It was "the idlers" (οἱ ἄτακτοι v. ¹⁴) who were fretting "the workers," as both 4¹¹ and the exhortation "be at peace among yourselves" make probable.

κοπιᾶν, "grow weary," "labour," with body or mind, is common in Gk. Bib. and frequent in Paul. With this word, he describes the activities of the women in Rom. 16⁶· ¹²; the missionary toil of himself (Gal. 4¹¹ 1 Cor. 15¹⁰ Phil. 2¹⁶ Col. 1²⁹) and others (1 Cor. 16¹⁶); and the manual labour incident thereto (1 Cor. 4¹² Eph. 4²⁸). The ἐν with ὑμῖν designates the sphere of the labour, *inter vos* (Vulg.); *cf.* 2 Reg. 23⁷.

καὶ προϊσταμένους καὶ νουθετοῦντας. "Both leading you in the Lord and warning you" (*cf.* 2¹¹ καὶ παραμυθούμενοι καὶ μαρτυρόμενοι). Though these participles may introduce functions different from but co-ordinate with τοὺς κοπιῶντας ἐν ὑμῖν (Dob.), yet it is more probable (so most) that they explain and specify τοὺς κοπιῶντας ἐν ὑμῖν, but without exhausting the departments of labour (*cf.* Lillie). Since such a phrase as ὁ κόπος τῆς ἀγάπης (1³) should seem to preclude any restriction whatever of the labour prompted by love, it is evident that the specifications here made are advanced not because they "were likeliest to awaken jealousy and resistance" (Lillie) but because they had actually awakened them.

13

προϊσταμένους ὑμῶν ἐν κυρίῳ. "Act as your leaders in the Lord." Attention is first called to the fact that the workers are leaders, that is, not simply rulers or chairmen but men who look after the general welfare of the group, especially the external matters, including the administration of the funds. That ἐν κυρίῳ is placed only after προϊσταμένους indicates not that the working (cf. Rom. 16¹²) and the warning are not in the Lord, but that it is necessary to remind the brethren, the idlers in particular, that the workers in taking the lead in temporal things are acting at the promptings not of personal interest but of the indwelling Christ.

προΐστασθαι, here and Rom. 12⁸ in Paul, is used in 1 Tim. 3⁴· ¹² (cf. 3⁵, 2 aor. act.) of managing the household; in Tit. 3⁸· ¹⁴ of attending to good works; and in 1 Tim. 5¹⁷ (perf. act.) of the ruling πρεσβύτεροι (cf. Hermas Vis. II, 4³). The word occurs also in Lxx. (e. g. 2 Reg. 13¹⁷ Amos 6¹⁰ Bel. (Lxx.) 8) and papyri (Mill.). Besides the basal meaning "be over," "rule," "act as leader," there are derived meanings such as "protect," "guard," " care for" (cf. Test. xii, Jos. 2⁶). In the light of 1 Tim. 3⁵ (where προστῆναι is parallel to ἐπιμελήσεται) and of προστατεῖν τινός = praesidio sum curam gero (Witk. 16), Dob. inclines to insist both here and in Rom. 12⁸ on the derived meaning, "fürsorgen."—ℵA read προϊστανομένους.

νουθετοῦντας ὑμᾶς. Apparently some of the brethren, presumably the idlers (see on 4¹¹), had refused to give heed to the spiritual counsels of the workers, with the result that relations between them were strained and the peace of the brotherhood disturbed. Hence the appropriateness of calling attention to the fact that the workers were not only leaders in things temporal but also spiritual advisers. νουθετεῖν denotes brotherly warning or admonition, as II 3¹⁵ makes plain.

νουθετεῖν appears in N. T., apart from Acts 20³¹, only in Paul; it is connected with διδάσκειν in Col. 1²⁸ 3¹⁶; cf. also νουθεσία 1 Cor. 10¹¹ Eph. 6⁴ (with παιδεία) and Tit. 3¹⁰. These words along with νουθέτημα are in the Lxx. found chiefly in the wisdom literature (cf. Sap. 12² ὑπομιμνήσκων νουθετεῖς).

13. καὶ ἡγεῖσθαι κτλ. It is not enough that the brethren appreciate the workers; they are to esteem them (ἡγεῖσθαι = εἰδέ-

ναι) very highly (ὑπερεκπερισσῶς), and that too not from fear or
distrust but from love (ἐν ἀγάπῃ); for the workers, because of
their work of faith (1³), deserve not only esteem but high and
loving esteem. "Those who labour among you," like Paul and
Timothy in 1 Cor. 16¹⁰, τὸ ἔργον κυρίου ἐργάζονται.

As the parallel with εἰδέναι demands, ἡγεῖσθαι is here not "consider" (II 3¹⁵ 2 Cor. 9⁵) but "esteem," a meaning, however, not elsewhere attested (Mill. Dob.). For this reason, some comm. find the
expected notion of esteem in the adverb and support their finding by
such phrases as περὶ πολλοῦ (Herod. II, 115) or περὶ πλείστου (Thucy.
II, 89) ἡγεῖσθαι. But these adverbial expressions are not identical
with ὑπερεκπερισσῶς. Other comm. (from Chrys. to Wohl.), on the
analogy of ποιεῖσθαι ἐν ὀλιγωρίᾳ (Thucy. IV, 5¹, VII, 3²) = ὀλιγωρεῖν, take
ἡγεῖσθαι ἐν ἀγάπῃ = ἀγαπᾶν, a meaning not sufficiently attested and
unlikely here because of the distance between ἐν ἀγάπῃ and ἡγεῖσθαι.
Schmiedel compares ἐν ὀργῇ εἶχον (Thucy. II, 18³ 21³ 65²); and Schott
notes even Job 35² τί τοῦτο ἡγήσω ἐν κρίσει. The unusual meaning
"esteem" is contextually preferable; cf. εἰς τὸν ἕνα (v. ¹¹) and εἰδέναι
(v. ¹² 4⁴). On ὑπερεκπερισσῶς (BDGF; ὑπερεκπερισσοῦ ℵAP), see 3¹⁰.
GF read ὥστε (Vulg. ut) before ἡγεῖσθαι. B has ἡγεῖσθε (cf. εἰρηνεύετε). P omits αὐτῶν as if ἡγεῖσθαι = "to rule." F has διό for διά.

εἰρηνεύετε ἐν ἑαυτοῖς. "Be at peace among yourselves,"
one with the other, ἑαυτοῖς for ἀλλήλοις (cf. Mk. 9⁵⁰). This
striking command, separated grammatically (note the change
from infinitive to imperative) but not logically from the preceding, suggests that the workers, in functioning both as managers
of the funds and as spiritual advisers, had been opposed by some
of the converts, presumably the idlers (4¹¹; cf. v. ¹⁴ νουθετεῖτε
τοὺς ἀτάκτους and II 3¹⁵), with the result that friction between
them arose and the peace of the group was ruffled. The fact that
Paul says not μετ᾽ αὐτῶν but ἐν ἑαυτοῖς further suggests that
the workers are in part to blame for the situation, in that their
admonitions to the idlers who had asked for aid had not been
altogether tactful (cf. II 3¹³· ¹⁵).

ἑαυτοῖς is read by BAKL, et al.; the tactfulness of Paul who includes both the workers and the idlers in the exhortation to peace is
lost sight of in the reading ἐν αὐτοῖς (ℵDP; cf. GF and Vulg. cum eis),
followed by Chrys. Th. Mops. (in eos), and most of the Greek comm.,
and by Erasmus, Calvin, and most recently Dibelius. Furthermore,

on the analogy of Rom. 12⁸ (*cf.* 3 Reg. 22⁴⁵), we should have expected not ἐν αὐτοῖς but μετ᾽ αὐτῶν (*cf.* Zim.). Swete (*op. cit. ad loc.*) remarks: "Ambst. who reads *inter vos* thinks only of mutual forbearance amongst the faithful: *pacificos eos esse hortatur*." Hermas has both εἰρηνεύετε ἐν αὐτοῖς (Vis. III, 9¹⁰) and ἐν ἑαυτοῖς (12³; 9² parallel with ἀλλήλοις; *cf.* 5¹).

(8). *The Idlers, The Faint-hearted, and The Weak* (5¹⁴ ᵃ⁻ᶜ).

From the beginning of his exhortations (4¹), Paul seems to have had in mind the needs of three classes, the meddlesome idlers (4¹¹⁻¹²; 5¹²⁻¹³), those who were anxious both about their friends who had died (4¹³⁻¹⁸) and about their own salvation (5¹⁻¹¹), and those who were tempted to unchastity (4³⁻⁸). To the same three classes he now refers once more (*cf.* Th. Mops.), specifying them respectively as "the idlers" (οἱ ἄτακτοι), who as most troublesome need to be warned; "the faint-hearted" (οἱ ὀλιγόψυχοι), who were losing the assurance of salvation and need to be encouraged; and "the weak" (οἱ ἀσθενεῖς), who being tempted to impurity are to be clung to and tenderly but firmly supported.

¹⁴*Further we urge you, brothers, warn the idlers, encourage the faint-hearted, cling to the weak.*

14. παρακαλοῦμεν ... ἀδελφοί. With δέ a new point in the exhortation is introduced. The similarity of the phrase (4¹⁰) to ἐρωτῶμεν ... ἀδελφοί (v. ¹²) and the repetition of ἀδελφοί make probable that the persons addressed are the same as in vv. ¹²⁻¹³, that is, not the workers only (Chrys.; Th. Mops. who says: "*vertit suum sermonem ad doctores*"; and Born. Find.) but the brethren as a whole. The only individuals obviously excluded are the recipients of the warning, encouragement, and support. "Those who labour among you," though they take the lead in practical affairs and admonish, have no monopoly of the functions of νουθετεῖν, παραμυθεῖσθαι and ἀντέχεσθαι.

On νουθετεῖν, see v. ¹². D omits ὑμᾶς. Instead of the expected infinitives after παρακαλοῦμεν (4¹⁰), we have imperatives (1 Cor. 4¹⁶; *cf.* above εἰρηνεύετε). GF, indeed, read νουθετεῖν, παραμυθεῖσθαι, and ἀντέχεσθαι (so D), perhaps intimating (and if so, correctly; *cf.* Wohl.) that with the imperative μακροθυμεῖτε, Paul turns from brotherly love (*cf.* 4¹⁰⁻¹²) to love (πρὸς πάντας; *cf.* εἰς πάντας, v. ¹⁵; εἰς ἀλλήλους v. ¹⁵ is of course included).

τοὺς ἀτάκτους. "The idlers." Since in 4¹¹⁻¹², to which these words evidently refer, people of unquiet mind, meddlesome, and idle are mentioned, most commentators content themselves here with a general translation, the "disorderly," "unquiet," "unruly," even when they admit that idleness is the main count in the disorder (Ephr.: "*inquietos, qui otiosi ambulant et nihil faciunt nisi inania*"). The certainty that the specific sense "the idlers" is here intended is given in II 3⁶ ᶠᶠ· where the context demands that ἀτακτεῖν and περιπατεῖν ἀτάκτως be rendered as Rutherford translates and as the usage in papyri allows, "to be a loafer," "to behave as a loafer" (*cf*. Theodoret: "τοὺς ἀτάκτους τοὺς ἀργίᾳ συζῶντας οὕτως ἐκάλεσεν).

In the N. T., ἄτακτος occurs only here, ἀτακτεῖν only in II 3⁷, and ἀτάκτως only in II 3⁶· ¹¹. Chrys. notes that they are originally military words, the τάξις being that of troops in battle array, or of soldiers at their post of duty. By a natural extension of usage, they come to describe various types of irregularity such as "intermittent" fevers, "disorderly" crowds, and "unrestrained" pleasures; and, by a still further extension, "disorderly" life in general (*cf*. 3 Mac. 1¹⁹; Deut. 32¹⁰ Ezek. 12²⁰ 4 Reg. 9²⁰ (Sym.); Test. xii, Naph. 2⁹; 1 Clem. 40² Diogn. 9¹). In an exhaustive note, Milligan (152–154) has called attention to several papyri concerned with contracts of apprenticeship (*e. g*. P. Oxy. 275, 724–5) where ἀτακτεῖν and ἀργεῖν are used interchangeably. In a letter to the present editor under date of February 12, 1910, Dr. Milligan refers "to a still more striking instance of ἀτακτέω = 'to be idle' than the Oxyrhyncus passages. In BGU, 1125⁸ (13 B.C.)—a contract— the words occur ἃς δὲ ἐὰν ἀρτακτήσηι ἢι ἀρρωστήσηι. Evidently ἀτακτήσηι is to be read, with a confusion in the writer's mind with ἀργήσηι (Schubart)." In a paper in the volume entitled *Essays in Modern Theology* (in honour of Dr. Briggs), 1911, 191–206, reasons are advanced in some detail for concluding that ἀτακτεῖν and its cognates, as employed by Paul, are to be translated not "to be idle," etc. (*cf. AJT*. 1904, 614 *ff*.) but "to loaf," etc. In II 3¹⁰, the idleness is a refusal to work, a direct violation of instructions orally given (παράδοσις 3⁶), of Paul's own example (3⁷ ᶠ·), and of the gospel utterance (τῷ λόγῳ ἡμῶν 3¹⁴). To express this notion of culpable neglect, Paul chooses not σχολάζειν (*cf*. Exod. 5⁸· ¹⁷), a word he prefers to use in the sense "to have leisure for" (1 Cor. 7⁵; *cf*. Ps. 45¹¹); not ἀργεῖν (*cf*. Sir. 30³⁶; also ἀργός Sir. 37¹¹ Mt. 12³⁶ 20³· ⁶ 1 Tim. 5¹³ Tit. 1¹²), a word which Paul does not use; but ἀτακτεῖν (ἀτάκτως, ἄτακτος), a word which distinctly implies the wilful neglect of the "golden rule of labour" (Dob.). In English, this notion of neglect is conveyed best not by "to be idle," etc., but by "to be a loafer," etc. as Rutherford saw in II 3⁶· ⁷ but not in I 5¹⁴.

· τοὺς ὀλιγοψύχους. "The faint-hearted." These "men of little heart" (Wiclif) were worried not only about their dead (4¹³⁻¹⁸) but also about their own salvation (5¹⁻¹¹). They are not troublesome like the idlers; hence they require not warning but encouragement (παραμυθεῖσθε; cf. 2¹¹; see also παρακαλεῖτε 4¹⁸ 5¹¹ and the discussion in II 1³⁻2¹⁷).

Theodoret (cf. Chrys.) explains τοὺς ὀλιγοψύχους both as τοὺς ἐπὶ τοῖς τεθνεῶσιν ἀμετρίως ἀθυμοῦντας (cf. Col. 3²¹) and as τοὺς μὴ ἀνδρείως φέροντας τῶν ἐναντίων τὰς προσβολάς. The first reference is probable; but in place of the second reference, namely, to persecution, an allusion to the lack of assurance of salvation (5¹⁻¹¹) is more probable. In the prayer of 1 Clem. 59⁴ there is an interesting parallel: ἐξανάστησον τοὺς ἀσθενοῦντας, παρακάλεσον (cf. παρακαλεῖτε 4¹⁸ 5¹¹) τοὺς ὀλιγοψυχοῦντας. In the Lxx., ὀλιγόψυχος (only here in N. T.; cf. Pr. 14²⁹ 18¹⁴ Is. 25⁵ 35⁴ 54⁶ 57¹⁵), ὀλιγοψυχεῖν (not in N. T.), and ὀλιγοψυχία (not in N. T.) are regularly used, with the exception of Jonah 4⁸ (where physical faintness is meant; cf. Isoc. 19³⁹), of the depressed and the despondent in whom little spirit is left; so Is. 57¹⁵: ὀλιγοψύχοις διδοὺς μακροθυμίαν καὶ διδοὺς ζωὴν τοῖς τὴν καρδίαν συντετριμμένοις.

ἀντέχεσθε τῶν ἀσθενῶν. "Cling to the weak." In this connection, the reference is to the weak not physically (1 Cor. 11³⁰) but morally. Furthermore, since "the idlers" and "the faint-hearted" refer to classes already exhorted (4¹¹⁻¹²; 4¹³⁻5¹¹), it is probable that "the weak" are not generally the weak in faith (Chrys. Ephr. and others) but specifically those who are tempted to impurity (4³⁻⁸; so Th. Mops.: *de illis qui fornicatione deturpabantur*). Being persons of worth, they are not to be despised (cf. Mt. 6²⁴ = Lk. 16¹³) but are to be held to and tenderly but firmly supported.

ἀντέχεσθαι, always middle in Gk. Bib. except 4 Mac. 7⁴, is construed with the gen. either of persons (Mt. 6²⁴ = Lk. 16¹³ Pr. 4⁶ Zeph. 1⁶ Is. 57¹³) or of things (Tit. 1⁹ Is. 56⁴, etc.). For a different connotation of οἱ ἀσθενεῖς, cf. 1 Cor. 8⁹ 9²².

(9) Love (5¹⁴ ᵈ⁻¹⁵).

With μακροθυμεῖτε πρὸς πάντας, Paul seems to turn from the specific needs of the three classes just named to a need of the group as a whole in reference to one another and especially to

all men, namely, not simply brotherly love but also love. The
exhortation, directed to all the converts, that they be slow to
anger, and that they see to it that no one of their number retaliate a wrong done but that they rather seek earnestly the good
toward one another and toward all, suggests, though the exhortation is general and characteristic of Paul, a specific situation,
namely, that the friction between workers and idlers within, and
chiefly the persecutions from without at the hands of Gentiles
directly and Jews indirectly, had stirred up a spirit of impatience
destined to express itself, if it had not done so already, in revenge. To prevent this violation of the moral ideal, τὸ ἀγαθόν,
that is, love in which Paul had previously prayed (3¹²) that the
Lord would make them abound εἰς ἀλλήλους καὶ εἰς πάντας
the present injunction is apparently intended.

πρὸς πάντας includes all men (Gal. 6¹⁰), the Thessalonians (vv. ²⁶⁻²⁷)
and their fellow-Christians (4¹⁰) and the Gentiles and Jews (εἰς ἀλλήλους
καὶ εἰς πάντας v. ¹⁵ 3¹²). It is probable, therefore, that μακροθυμεῖτε
goes not with the preceding which has to do solely with brotherly love
(so most) but with the following (so Wohl.). It is perhaps not accidental
that, as in vv. ¹⁶⁻¹⁸ (χαίρετε, προσεύχεσθε, εὐχαριστεῖτε), and in vv. ¹²⁻¹³
(εἰδέναι, ἡγεῖσθαι, εἰρηνεύετε), so now in v. ¹⁴ᵃ⁻ᶜ (νουθετεῖτε, παραμυθεῖσθε,
ἀντέχεσθε) and vv. ¹⁴ᵈ⁻¹⁵ (μακροθυμεῖτε, ὁρᾶτε, διώκετε) we have the arrangement in triplets.

¹⁴ᵈ*Be patient with all men;* ¹⁵*see to it that no one pays back to
any one evil for evil, but do you always follow the good toward one
another and toward all.*

14ᵈ. *μακροθυμεῖτε.* "Be patient with all men," literally, "long-
tempered," slow to anger and retaliation, as opposed to the disposition of the ὀξύθυμος who, unable to endure much, acts ill-
advisedly (Pr. 14¹⁷) and stirs up strife (*cf.* Pr. 26²⁰ (A): ὅπου δὲ
οὐκ ἔστιν ὀξύθυμος, ἡσυχάζει μάχη). Patience is a fruit of the
Spirit (Gal. 5²²) and a characteristic of love (1 Cor. 13⁴ ἡ ἀγάπη
μακροθυμεῖ).

In Paul μακροθυμία is several times closely joined with χρηστότης
(Gal. 5²² 2 Cor. 6⁶; *cf.* 1 Cor. 13⁴); it is used not only of men but of
God (Rom. 2⁴ 9²²; *cf.* μακρόθυμος καὶ πολυέλεος Exod. 34⁶ Ps. 85¹⁵
102⁸, etc.). In Gk. Bib. μακροθυμεῖν is regularly construed with ἐπί
(Sir. 18¹¹ Jas. 5⁷, etc.), once with εἰς (2 Pet. 3⁹); *cf.* μετά Ign. Polyc. 6².

15. ὁρᾶτε κτλ. The group as a whole are held responsible for any single member (τις) whose patience is exhausted and who is ready to retaliate an injury done him by brother or outsider (τινί includes both as the parallel εἰς ἀλλήλους καὶ εἰς πάντας indicates). The ancient principle of retaliation (cf. Exod. 21²³ ᶠ· Deut. 19²¹ Lev. 24¹⁹ ᶠ·) had undergone modifications in keeping with the advancing moral insight of Israel (cf. Pr. 20¹² 24⁴⁴ 25²¹ ᶠ· Sir. 28¹⁻⁷), but it was left to the Master to put the case against it in the unqualified injunction beginning ἀγαπᾶτε τοὺς ἐχθροὺς ὑμῶν (Mt. 5⁴⁴ = Lk. 6²⁷). It was perhaps the difficulty of living up to such an imperative in the present circumstances that prompted Paul to write not simply "render not evil for evil" (Rom. 12¹⁷) but, evoking the responsibility of the Christian society for the individual, "see you to it that no one pay back to any one evil for evil."

ὁρᾶτε μή occurs only here in Paul (cf. Mt. 18¹⁰ Josh. 9¹³) who prefers βλέπετε μή (Gal. 5¹⁵ 1 Cor. 8⁹ 10¹² Col. 2⁸). On ἀποδιδόναι, cf. Rom. 12¹⁷ 1 Pet. 3⁹ Pr. 17¹³. ℵGF read ἀποδοῖ (a subj. from ἀποδόω); D reads ἀποδοίη. The opposite of κακός in Paul is both ἀγαθός (Rom. 7¹⁹ 12²¹, etc.) and καλός (Rom. 7²¹ 12¹⁷, etc.). ἀντί is rare in Paul (Rom. 12¹⁷ 1 Cor. 11¹⁵ Eph. 5³¹; II 2¹⁰ ἀνθ' ὧν).

ἀλλὰ . . . διώκετε κτλ. "But," on the contrary, "always," no matter how trying the circumstances, "follow," that is, strive earnestly after "the good." It is difficult to avoid the conviction that τὸ ἀγαθόν, the moral ideal (here opposed to κακόν, "an injury") is for Paul love, seeing that ἡ ἀγάπη τῷ πλησίον κακὸν οὐκ ἐργάζεται (Rom. 13¹⁰), the neighbour including both the believer and the unbeliever (εἰς ἀλλήλους καὶ εἰς πάντας, as in 3¹²). He might have said διώκετε τὴν ἀγάπην (1 Cor. 14¹).

It is questionable whether in Paul's usage τὸ ἀγαθόν and τὸ καλόν (v. ²¹) can be sharply differentiated (see Ell. on Gal. 6¹⁰). Both terms represent the ethical ideal of Paul, which, as a comparison of Rom. 12⁶ ᶠᶠ· and Gal. 5²² with 1 Cor. 13 makes plain, can be described as ἡ ἀγάπη. On τὸ ἀγαθόν, cf. Rom. 7¹³ 12⁹ 13⁴ Gal. 6¹⁰, etc.; τὸ καλόν Rom. 7¹⁸·²¹ Gal. 6⁹ 2 Cor. 13⁷, etc. For διώκειν in a similar metaphorical sense, cf. Rom. 9³⁰ Sir. 27⁸; Rom. 12¹³ 14¹⁹ Ps. 33¹⁵ ζήτησον εἰρήνην καὶ δίωξον αὐτήν. See also Epict. IV, 5³⁰ διώκειν τὸ ἀγαθὸν φεύγειν τὸ κακόν. The καί which BKLP (cf. Weiss, 114) insert before εἰς ἀλλή-λους is to be omitted with ℵADEGF, et al.; cf. 3¹² 4¹⁰.

(10) *Joy, Prayer, Thanksgiving* (5¹⁶⁻¹⁸).

The injunction to constant joy and prayer and to thanksgiving in every circumstance is characteristic of Paul (*cf.* 3⁹ ᶠ·). The fact, however, that he notes, as in 4³, that this exhortation is God's will makes probable that the special circumstances of persecution from without and friction within are here in mind as in vv. ¹⁴⁻¹⁵. In adding that this will of God operates in Christ Jesus, he designates that will as distinctively Christian, the will of the indwelling Christ who is the personal and immediately accessible authority behind the injunction (*cf.* 4⁷ ᶠ·). In adding still further εἰς ὑμᾶς, he intimates that the will of God in Christ is for their advantage, and implies that the Christ in them, the source of joy (1⁶ Phil. 4⁴), prayer (Eph. 6¹⁸ Rom. 8²⁶), and thanksgiving (*cf.* διὰ Χριστοῦ Rom. 1⁸ 7²⁵ Col. 3¹⁷) is the power that enables them to carry out the difficult imperative.

¹⁶*Always rejoice;* ¹⁷*continually pray;* ¹⁸*in everything give thanks; for this is God's will operating in Christ Jesus for you.*

16. πάντοτε χαίρετε. Paul has already revealed his own joy because of the converts (2¹⁹ ᶠ· 3⁹ ᶠ·), and has used the fact of their joy in the midst of persecution as a proof of their election (1⁶). It is natural for him now, with the persecutions from without and the disturbances in the brotherhood in mind, to urge them not only to rejoice (Rom. 12¹⁵ 2 Cor. 13¹¹ Phil. 3¹ 4⁴, etc.), but to rejoice "always" (πάντοτε as Phil. 4⁴; *cf.* ἀεί 2 Cor. 6¹⁰). This feeling of joy, expressed or unexpressed, is a joy before God (*cf.* 3⁹ ᶠ·), as the following references to prayer and thanksgiving make probable. The source and inspiration of this religious joy is the indwelling Christ, as ἐν Χριστῷ presently explains (*cf.* Phil. 4⁴ χαίρετε ἐν κυρίῳ πάντοτε; GF insert ἐν κυρίῳ here; *cf.* Phil. 3¹).

17. ἀδιαλείπτως προσεύχεσθε. The way to constant joy in the midst of persecution is constant prayer (*cf.* Chrys.) unuttered or expressed. The exhortation to be steadfast in prayer (Rom. 12¹² Col. 4²), to pray ἐν παντὶ καιρῷ (Eph. 6¹⁸) is characteristic of Paul's teaching and practice (3¹⁰ II 1¹¹). In this context, prayer would include especially supplication ὑπὲρ τῶν διωκόντων

(Mt. 5¹⁴ Lk. 6²⁸ Rom. 12¹⁴). That they can thus pray as they ought is possible because of the indwelling Christ (ἐν Χριστῷ Ἰησοῦ; cf. Rom. 8²⁶ Eph. 6¹⁸).

προσεύχεσθαι (v. ²⁵ II 1¹¹ 3¹) is common in Gk. Bib.; it is a general word (τὸ ὁμιλεῖν τῷ θεῷ, Theophylact), including δεῖσθαι (3¹⁰), ἐντυγχάνειν (Rom. 8²⁶· ³⁴), etc. On ἀδιαλείπτως, see 1³.

18. ἐν παντὶ εὐχαριστεῖτε. "Whatever happens, give thanks to God." Since in 2 Cor. 9⁸ ἐν παντί is distinguished from πάντοτε we must supply here not χρόνῳ or καιρῷ but χρήματι, "in every circumstance of life," even in the midst of persecutions and friction within the brotherhood. Even when τῷ θεῷ is not expressed, it is to be understood after εὐχαριστεῖν (cf. Rom. 1²¹ 1 Cor. 10³⁰ 11²⁴ 14¹⁷ Eph. 1¹⁶). Constant joy with constant prayer leads to the expression of thankfulness to God at every turn of life. The stimulating cause of thanksgiving is the Christ within (ἐν Χριστῷ Ἰησοῦ; cf. the διά in Rom. 1⁸ 7²⁵ and especially Col. 3¹⁷).

The parallelism here between πάντοτε and ἀδιαλείπτως, and the usage of πάντοτε or ἀδιαλείπτως with εὐχαριστεῖν (1² 2¹³. II 1³ 2¹³ 1 Cor. 1⁴ Phil. 1³ Eph. 5²⁰ Phile. 4), χαίρειν (Phil. 4⁴; ἀεί 2 Cor. 6¹⁰), μνημονεύειν (1²), μνείαν ἔχειν (3⁶) or ποιεῖσθαι (Rom. 1⁹), προσεύχεσθαι (II 1¹¹; ἐν παντὶ καιρῷ Eph. 6¹⁸) make it tempting to take ἐν παντί = πάντοτε (so Chrys. τὸ ἀεὶ εὐχαριστεῖν τοῦτο φιλοσόφου ψυχῆς, Flatt and Dob.). But the usage of ἐν παντί, in the N. T. only in Paul, quite apart from 2 Cor. 9⁸, is against that interpretation (cf. 1 Cor. 1⁵ 2 Cor. 4⁸ 6⁴ 7⁵· ¹¹· ¹⁶ 8⁷ 9¹¹ 11⁶· ⁹ Eph. 5²⁴ Phil. 4⁶· ¹²). In the Lxx., ἐν παντί is rare and never temporal (Pr. 28⁵ Sir. 18²⁷ 37²⁸ Dan. (Lxx.) 11³⁷ 4 Mac. 8²); in Neh. 13⁶ ἐν παντὶ τούτῳ, it is τούτῳ not παντί which demands a χρόνῳ or καιρῷ. Had Paul wished to indicate a temporal reference, he would have added χρόνῳ or καιρῷ (Eph. 6¹⁸; cf. Lk. 21³⁶ Acts 1²¹ Tobit 4¹⁹ Ps. 33¹ 1 Mac. 12¹¹ Hermas, Mand. V, 2³), or written διὰ παντός (II 3¹⁶ Rom. 11¹⁰) instead of ἐν παντί. On εὐχαριστεῖν, εὐχαριστία (cf. εὐχάριστος Col. 3¹⁵), which are frequent words in Paul, see on 1² 3⁹; cf. Epict. I, 4³² 10³ χαίρων καὶ τῷ θεῷ εὐχαριστῶν. For the collocation of thanksgiving and prayer, apart from the epistolary outline, see 3⁹ Phil. 4⁶ Col. 4².

τοῦτο γὰρ θέλημα θεοῦ κτλ. "For this," namely, that you rejoice and pray always and give thanks to God whatever happens, "is God's will." As in 4³, Paul insists that what he exhorts

is not of his own but of divine authority. But instead of stopping
here, leaving the readers to infer that God was inaccessible and
his will impersonal, Paul adds characteristically, using his pregnant phrase ἐν Χριστῷ Ἰησοῦ (2¹⁴; see on 1¹), that God's will,
the authority that has the right to give the difficult injunction,
operates in Christ Jesus, thus indicating that the will is distinctively Christian and that Christ in whom God operates is an
accessible personal power whose right to command is recognised
both by Paul and by his readers (cf. 4⁷ ᶠ·). With the further addition of εἰς ὑμᾶς, which would be superfluous if ἐν X. 'I. meant
simply that the will of God was declared by Christ, Paul implies not only that the distinctively Christian will of God is
directed to the believers but also that it is to their advantage
(cf. 2 Cor. 13⁴ εἰς ὑμᾶς ℵAD); and he succeeds in hinting that it
is the Christ in the believers who guarantees their ability to execute even this most difficult exhortation.

Since joy, thanksgiving, and prayer are related ideas (cf. 3⁹ ᶠ·), and
since the change from πάντοτε and ἀδιαλείπτως to ἐν παντί does not
compel the singling out of εὐχαριστία as the only element in the will
of God requiring immediate emphasis, it is probable that τοῦτο refers
not simply to εὐχαριστεῖτε (so Th. Mops. Chrys. Ephr. Ell. Wohl.),
or to εὐχαριστεῖτε and προσεύχεσθε (Grot.), but to all three imperatives. While it is possible to understand ὁ before ἐν Χριστῷ (cf. 2 Cor.
5¹⁹ Eph. 4³²), it is probable in the light of Rom. 8³⁹ (τῆς ἀγάπης τοῦ θεοῦ
τῆς ἐν X. 'I.) that τό is to be understood (cf. 2¹³ Phil. 3¹⁴). Though the
stress here is on the will of God as operating in Christ, yet such operation presupposes the presence of God in Christ. The omission of articles
in θέλημα θεοῦ indicates either a fixed formula or that one part of the
divine will is meant (Ell.). Influenced by 4³, DEFG add ἐστίν after
γάρ; and ℵA insert τοῦ before θεοῦ. L omits Ἰησοῦ. By putting εἰς
ὑμᾶς before ἐν X. 'I., A yields the less pregnant sense "will of God directed to you who are in Christ Jesus" (so Dob.).

(11) *Spiritual Gifts* (5¹⁹⁻²²).

From the distinctively Pauline conception of Christ or the
Spirit as the permanent ethical power in the life of the believer
(ἐν Χριστῷ Ἰησοῦ), the Apostle turns to the ancient but equally
Pauline conception of the Spirit (cf. Rom. 15¹⁸ Eph. 4¹¹ of Christ)

as the source of the extraordinary phenomena in the Christian life, the spiritual gifts (τὸ πνεῦμα). Though the gifts of the Spirit (χαρίσματα) are as valid to Paul as the fruits of the Spirit, he is ever at pains to insist that the validity of the former depends on their serving an ethical end, namely, love (1 Cor. 12-14).

The presence of the exhortation at this point makes probable the conjecture (see 4¹¹) that the idlers had demanded ἐν πνεύματι that the workers, in whose hands as leaders was the control of the funds, give them money. This demand was refused on the ground that Paul had enjoined orally that if a man refused to work he should not receive support (II 3¹⁰; I 4¹¹). The effect on the workers of this misuse of the Spirit was an inclination to doubt the validity not of the Spirit in the ethical life but of the Spirit as manifested in χαρίσματα. Hence the first two exhortations, though addressed to all, refer especially to the attitude of the workers. In general, Paul says, the operations of the Spirit are not to be extinguished; and in particular, the manifestations of the Spirit in prophecy are not to be despised. Then, still addressing all, but having in mind especially the idlers who had misinterpreted the Spirit, he urges them to test all things, that is, πάντα εἴδη πνευμάτων (cf. 1 Jn. 4¹), including prophecy; and then, as a result of the test, to hold fast to the good, that is, those manifestations of the Spirit that make for edification or love, and to hold aloof from every evil sort of πνεῦμα or χάρισμα; for while the good is one, the evil is manifold.

> Th. Mops. refers the five injunctions to spiritual gifts (cf. Ephr.); so Chrys. who, however, first interprets τὸ πνεῦμα of the fruits of the Spirit. The triple arrangement of vv. ¹²⁻¹⁸ is here succeeded by a fivefold, 2 + 3. If, as is almost certain, πάντα δὲ δοκιμάζετε is to be restricted to spiritual gifts in general and prophecy in particular, it follows that both κατέχετε and ἀπέχεσθε, which designate the positive and negative results of the testing, are likewise so to be restricted (cf. Th. Mops.). Indeed K, et al., indicate this interpretation by reading δοκιμάζοντες for δοκιμάζετε.

¹⁹*Quench not the gifts of the Spirit;* ²⁰*do not make light of cases of prophesying;* ²¹*on the other hand, test all gifts of the Spirit, holding fast to the good* ²²*and holding aloof from every evil kind.*

19. τὸ πνεῦμα μὴ σβέννυτε. "Quench not the Spirit," that is, the divine Spirit operating in believers. The reference, however, is not to the ethical fruits of the Spirit (*cf.* 1⁵⁻⁶ 4⁸ II 2¹³) but, as προφητείας makes certain, to the extraordinary gifts of the Spirit, the charismata. Furthermore, τὸ πνεῦμα is not to be restricted to a specific charisma (Ephr. *qui loquuntur in linguis spiritus*) but is to be understood of the totality of the extraordinary operations (Calvin). To quench, to put out the fire of, the Spirit is to prohibit or repress those who ἐν πνεύματι are ready with psalm, teaching, revelation, tongue, interpretation, etc. (1 Cor. 14²⁶). To repress the believer is or may be to repress the Spirit. This exhortation is of course not incompatible with the injunction that all things be done εὐσχημόνως, κατὰ τάξιν, and πρὸς οἰκοδομήν (1 Cor. 14⁴⁰· ²⁶).

That 1 Cor. 12–14 (*cf.* 2 Cor. 12²⁻⁴ Rom. 12⁶⁻⁹) happens to be the *locus classicus* on spiritual gifts is due to the fact that Paul is there replying to a written request for information περὶ τῶν πνευματικῶν. The Thessalonians had made no such specific request; but, if our conjectural reconstruction is correct, Paul refers to the matter here in order to warn both the workers and the idlers. This brief allusion, however, yields information that tallies exactly with what may be learned *in extenso* from the passages noted above. In Thessalonica, as in Corinth, the Christian life was accompanied by the same spiritual phenomena.

Three main groups of χαρίσματα may be detected: (1) Healing, both of ordinary (ἰάματα) and of extraordinary (δυνάμεις) disease. (2) Revelation, including (*a*) γλώσσαις λαλεῖν, an unintelligible utterance requiring, in order that it might be πρὸς οἰκοδομήν, ἑρμηνία, another charisma; (*b*) προφητεία (see below, v 20); (*c*) διακρίσεις πνευμάτων (see below, v. 21); and (*d*) διδασκαλία. (3) Service, embracing "apostles, governments, helps" (*cf.* Rom. 12⁸ 15²⁵ 1 Cor. 16¹). While Paul rejoices in all these extraordinary gifts and especially in prophecy (1 Cor. 14), he makes plain that they all must be used for the upbuilding of the church, and that without love even prophecy is of no avail (1 Cor. 13). On the Spirit in general, see Gunkel, *Die Wirkungen des Geistes*, 1888; Weinel, *Die Wirkungen des Geistes und der Geister*, 1899; Briggs, *JBL.* 1900, 132 *ff.*; Gloël, *Der Heilige Geist in der Heilsverkündigung des Paulus*, 1888; Wood, *The Spirit of God in Biblical Literature*, 1904; Arnal, *La Notion de L'Esprit*, I, 1908 (*La Doctrine Paulienne*); and Volz, *Der Geist Gottes*, 1910. On the charismata in particular, see Schmiedel, *EB.* 4755 *ff.*; McGiffert, *Apostolic Age*, 517 *ff.*; and J. Weiss (in Meyer) and Robertson and Plummer (in *ICC.*) on 1 Cor.

12–14; also Harnack, *Das hohe Lied von der Liebe* (in *SBBA*. 1911, 132 *ff.*). For the particular situation in Thessalonica, see Lütgert, *Die Volkommenen in Phil. und die Enthusiasten in Thess.* 1909, 55 *ff.*

Since σβεννύναι is used of putting out fire or light (see Wetstein), the Spirit is here conceived metaphorically as fire (*cf.* Rom. 12¹² Acts 2³ Mt. 3¹¹ = Lk. 3¹⁶ 2 Tim. 1⁶). In Lxx. σβεννύναι is used with θυμός (4 Reg. 22¹⁷ = 2 Ch. 34²⁵ Jer. 4⁴ 7²⁰), ὀργή (Jer. 21¹²), ψυχή (Sir. 23¹⁶) and ἀγάπη (Cant. 8⁷ where ἐξουδενοῦν also occurs). On the hellenistic ζβέννυτε (BDGF), see Bl. 3⁹.

20. προφητείας μὴ ἐξουθενεῖτε. From the general τὸ πνεῦμα, he passes to the particular, the charisma of prophecy (Calvin). This gift is singled out for mention, perhaps, because the idlers had exercised it wrongly and because the workers made light of it especially. The plural (*cf.* 1 Cor. 13⁸) is chosen either because prophecy has many forms of expression or because individual cases are in mind. προφητεία to Paul is not the science of interpreting Scripture (Calvin), not the gift of foretelling the future and explaining the past, but the proclamation of the utterance of God, so that the prophet (1 Cor. 12²⁸ ᶠ· 14²⁹ ᶠᶠ·) is the revealer of the will of God operating in the indwelling Christ or Spirit.

προφητεία to Paul is apparently the greatest χάρισμα (1 Cor. 14), though it is worthless unless it makes for love (a comprehensive term for the ethical, non-charismatic fruits of the Spirit). Though it may arise in an ἀποκάλυψις or ὀπτασία (2 Cor. 12²⁻⁴ Gal. 2²), it is, unlike speaking with tongues, an intelligible utterance, making directly, without ἑρμηνία, for edification, comfort, and encouragement (1 Cor. 14³). There is a control by the Spirit but the νοῦς is active, as it is not in γλώσσαις λαλεῖν. What is prompted by the Spirit can be remembered and imparted, though the control of the Spirit is greater than in διδασκαλία. It may be that such passages as Rom. 8¹⁸ ᶠᶠ· 1 Cor. 13, 15⁵⁰ ᶠᶠ· owe their origin to prophecy. ἐξουθενεῖν is quite frequent in Paul (Gal. 4¹⁴ Rom. 14³· ¹⁰, etc.), and in the Lxx. (*cf.* ἐξουθενοῦν and ἐξουδενοῦν); in meaning it is akin to καταφρονεῖν and ἀποδοκιμάζειν (*cf.* Mk. 8³¹ with 9¹²).

21. πάντα δὲ δοκιμάζετε. "Test all things," that is, πάντα εἴδη πνευμάτων (1 Cor. 12¹⁰), including προφητεία. Though Paul insists, over against the doubts of the workers, that no operation of the Spirit is to be repressed, and that no case of prophecy is to be despised, yet he recognises and insists equally as well, over against the misuse of the Spirit by the idlers, that all χαρίσματα must be subject to test. Hence δέ, contrasting the two attitudes, is adversative. That this is Paul's meaning is confirmed by 1 Cor. 12¹⁰ where the charisma of διακρίσεις πνευμάτων is mentioned; *cf.* also 14²⁹: "Let two or three prophesy" καὶ οἱ ἄλλοι διακρινέτωσαν, that is, "and let the others exercise the gift of discerning" whether a given utterance ἐν πνεύματι makes for good or is evil.

It is noteworthy that the utterances of the Spirit are to be tested. Calvin rightly infers that the spirit of judgment is conferred upon believers that they may discriminate so as not to be imposed upon. This power, he thinks, must be sought from the same Spirit who speaks by his prophets. In fact, as 1 Cor. 12¹⁰ 14²⁹ prove, the power to discern is itself a charisma, διακρίσεις πνευμάτων (*cf.* Grot.). It is further noteworthy that the nature of the test is not stated. In view, however, of the place given to οἰκοδομή and especially to ἀγάπη (see Harnack, *op. cit.*) in 1 Cor. 12-14, it is probable that the test of the spiritual is the ethical, the value of the Spirit for the life of love. In his note on τὸ καλόν, Ephr. says: *id est quod adaequatur evangelio*, a pertinent statement in the light of 2¹³ ᶠ·. In 1 Jn. 4¹ where δοκιμάζειν τὰ πνεύματα occurs, the test is objective, the belief that Jesus is the Christ come in the flesh; in 2 Jn. 10 the same test recurs with the added point of φιλαδελφία; these two being the elements in the διδαχὴ Χριστοῦ emphasised in view of the docetic and separatist (1 Jn. 2¹⁹) movement. In the *Didache*, δοκιμάζειν is likewise referred to (*e. g.* 11¹⁻¹² 12¹); especially pertinent to the probable situation in Thess. is 11¹²: "Whoever says in the Spirit: Give me silver or anything else, ye shall not hearken unto him; but if he tell you to give on behalf of others that are in want, let no man judge him." δέ, omitted by ℵA, *et al.*, is probably to be read after πάντα with ℵᶜBDGFP, Vulg. (*autem*), *et al.*

τὸ καλὸν κατέχετε κτλ. The brethren are not to rest content with the testing and the discovery whether a given utterance of the Spirit in a man tends to the good or is an evil kind, but are (*a*) to hold fast to the good and (*b*) to hold aloof from every evil kind. The positive injunction of itself includes the negative; but the mention of the negative strengthens the appeal and adds a new point—the good is one, but the evil many. τὸ καλόν designates the utterance of the Spirit as making for οἰκοδομή (1 Cor. 14³⁻⁵· ¹²· ²⁶) or specifically love (1 Cor. 13; *v. supra* v. ¹⁵ τὸ ἀγαθόν).

κατέχειν is common in Gk. Bib. and has a variety of meanings. Luke uses the word differently in each of his four instances; "hold fast to" (λόγον Lk. 8¹⁵), "get hold of," "occupy" (τόπον Lk. 14⁹), "restrain from" (Lk. 4⁴² τοῦ μὴ πορεύεσθαι; Paul never has κατέχειν τοῦ (τὸ) μή), and "put in" (of a ship, Acts 27⁴⁰). Mill. (155–157), in illustrating the use of the word in papyri, groups the meanings under two heads (1) "hold fast" and (2) "hold back." Examples of (1) are "hold fast to" (= κρατεῖν) with λόγον (1 Cor. 15²), and παραδόσεις (1 Cor. 11²; cf. 2 Thess. 2¹⁵ κρατεῖτε); "possess," "get possession of" (1 Cor. 7³⁰ (absolute) 2 Cor. 6¹⁰ Exod. 32¹³ Josh. 1¹¹, etc.; cf. Sir. 46⁹ Lk. 14⁹); "grip," "control," "cripple" (cf. Deiss. Light, 308) "overpower" (2 Reg. 1⁹ Job 15²⁴ Jer. 6²⁴ 13²¹ Ps. 118⁵³ 138¹⁰, etc.; cf. P. Oxy. 217¹ κατέχει τὰ πράγματα ἡ σὴ βασιλεία; also 3 Mac. 5¹² ἡδίστῳ καὶ βαθεῖ (ὕπνῳ) κατεσχέθη τῇ ἐνεργείᾳ τοῦ δεσπότου; and Jn. 5⁴ (v. l.) νοσήματι κατείχετο, of demon possession as in Lk. 13¹⁶). Examples of (2) are "detain" (Phile. 13 Gen. 24⁵⁶ Judg. 13¹⁵· ¹⁶ (A has βιάζειν) 19⁴); as in prison (Gen. 39²⁰ 42¹⁹); "restrain" (cf. Deiss. Light, 308), "restrain from" "hinder" (Lk. 4⁴²). The exact shade of meaning is not always easy to discover (e. g. II 2⁶ Rom. 1¹⁸ 7⁶ Is. 40²²). Reitzenstein (Die hellenistischen Mysterienreligionen, 1910, 71 ff.) admits that κατέχεσθαι, κάτοχος, and κατοχή may be used of possession; but in the references to the Serapeum he holds with Mill. that κάτοχος = δέσμιος, κατοχή = the prison (temple), and κατέχεσθαι = "to be detained." See further on II 2⁶.

22. εἴδους πονηροῦ. "Evil kind" of χάρισμα or πνεῦμα (cf. 1 Cor. 12¹⁰ 1 Jn. 4¹). As a result of testing it appears that there is but one kind of operation of the Spirit that can really be called such, namely, that which makes for the good; while the kinds which are attributed to the Spirit, but which prove themselves evil, are many. Hence, instead of ἀπὸ τοῦ πονηροῦ to balance τὸ καλόν, we have ἀπὸ παντὸς εἴδους πονηροῦ, "from every evil sort hold yourselves aloof" (ἀπέχεσθε as 4³).

If τὸ καλὸν κατέχετε is general (Lft. Born. Wohl. et al.), then ἀπέχεσθε is likewise general; if, however, the former is specific (Lün. Ell. et al.), then the latter is likewise specific. The objection (Lün.) that the specific sense would require ἀπὸ τοῦ πονηροῦ is not cogent, for in v. ¹⁵ κακόν is balanced by τὸ ἀγαθόν; and furthermore Paul purposes to contrast the one good with the many evil forms. Whether πονηροῦ is a noun (De W. Lün. Ell. Schmiedel, Born. Vincent, Find. Wohl. Mill. and most) or adjective (Erasmus, Bengel, Pelt. Lft. Dob. et al.) is uncertain; in either case the meaning is the same (Calv.). The absence of the article "does not contribute to the decision" (Ell.); nor the possible allusion to Job 1¹ = 1⁸ (ἀπεχόμενος ἀπὸ παντὸς πονηροῦ

πράγματος) or 2³ (ἀπεχόμενος ἀπὸ παντὸς κακοῦ).   Apart from ὁ πονηρός
(II 3² 1 Cor. 5¹³ Eph. 6¹⁶) and τὸ πονηρόν (Rom. 12⁹), πονηρός in Paul
is an adjective and anarthrous (II 3² Col. 1²¹ Eph. 5¹⁶ 6¹³), unless Gal.
1⁴ (ἐκ τοῦ αἰῶνος τοῦ ἐνεστῶτος πονηροῦ) is an exception.—εἶδος is rare
in N. T. but common in Lxx.   It may mean (1) that which is seen
whether "physical form" (Jn. 5³⁷ Lk. 3²²; frequently in Lxx. of the
human form καλός or αἰσχρὸς τῷ εἴδει) or "look," "mien" (Lk. 9²⁹
Job 41¹⁰ Pr. 7¹⁰, etc.), or physical "appearance," "manifestation," *quod
aspicitur* (*e. g.* 2 Cor. 5⁷ Exod. 24¹⁷ Num. 9¹⁵); or (2) "sort," "kind,"
"class" (Jer. 15³ Sir. 23¹⁶ 25²; *cf.* P. Tebt. 58²⁰ ᶠ. ἀπὸ παντὸς εἴδους
(πυροῦ); *cf.* Witk. 78).   This meaning fits our passage admirably.
Calvin, however, misled by *species* (Vulg.), understands εἶδος as "appearance" over against reality, "abstain not simply from evil but from
all appearance of evil."   This interpretation puts the stress not on
πονηροῦ (which τὸ καλόν demands) but on εἴδους and introduces a
meaning of εἶδος which is doubtful lexically.—From Hänsel (*SK.* 1836,
170–184) to Resch (*Agrapha*,² 112–128), it has been held frequently
that in vv. ²¹⁻²² there is an allusion to an agraphon, γίνεσθε δόκιμοι
τραπεζῖται (on this agraphon, see Ropes, *Sprüche Jesu*, 141–143, or
HDB. V, 349).   Rutherford seems to have this in mind when he translates: "Rather, assay all things thereby.   Stick to the true metal; have
nothing to do with the base."   There is, however, no mention of τραπεζῖται or νόμισμα in this context; and, as we have seen, δοκιμάζειν is,
in the light of vv. ¹⁹⁻²⁰, naturally to be understood of the testing of
πνεύματα.

V. PRAYER (5²³⁻²⁴).

Recognising that the exhortations (4¹–5²²) especially to ethical
consecration (4³⁻⁸) and peace (5¹²⁻¹³; *cf.* 4¹⁰⁻¹²) would be of no
avail without the divine assistance; and recognising further the
necessity of the consecration not only of soul but of body (4³⁻⁸),
—a consecration which would be impossible unless the Spirit of
God as immanent in the individual were inseparably bound to
the human personality, body and soul; he prays first in general that God may consecrate them through and through, and
then specifically that he may keep their spirit, the divine element, and the soul and body, the human element, intact as an
undivided whole so that they may be blameless when the Lord
comes.   That the prayer will be answered is certain, for God
the faithful not only calls but also consecrates and keeps them
blameless to the end.

14

²³*Now may the God of peace himself consecrate you through and through, and may your spirit and soul and body be kept intact so as to be blameless at the coming of our Lord Jesus Christ.* ²⁴*Faithful is he who calls you; who also will do this very thing.*

23. αὐτὸς δέ κτλ. Following the exhortation (4¹-5²²), a new epistolary section is introduced, the prayer. In this connection, δέ is slightly adversative as if Paul had said: "I have exhorted you to ethical consecration and to the things that make for peace, but God himself is the only power that can make the exhortation effective."

ὁ θεὸς τῆς εἰρήνης. An apt designation in the light of vv. ¹²⁻¹³. This "peace," however, is not to be restricted to harmony within the brotherhood; but is to be understood of the spiritual prosperity (1¹) of which God is the author (Estius) and without which concord in the community is impossible. A similar appeal to the underlying religious sanction is seen in 1 Cor. 14³³ where, after a reference to disorder among the prophets, God is called a God not of confusion (ἀκαταστασίας) but of peace (εἰρήνης, instead of the expected εὐσχημόνης or τάξεως).

ἁγιάσαι ὑμᾶς ὁλοτελεῖς. "Consecrate you throughout," "through and through" (Luther). The note of consecration already struck in 3¹³ and 4³⁻⁸ is heard again. As in those passages so here consecration includes not only religion, devotion to God, but conduct, ethical soundness. Furthermore, since Paul has in mind the consecration not only of the soul but of the body (4³⁻⁸), it is probable that ὁλοτελεῖς is to be taken not qualitatively "so that you may be perfect" (Ambst. Lft. Dob. *et al.*) but quantitatively "wholly," *per omnia* (Vulg.), that is, σώματι καὶ ψυχῇ (Theophylact; *cf.* Grot. De W. Lün. Ell. Schmiedel, Born. Wohl. Mill. *et al.*).

On αὐτὸς δέ, see 3¹¹. The phrase ὁ θεὸς τῆς εἰρήνης (not in Lxx.) is mainly Pauline (Rom. 15³³ 16²⁰ 1 Cor. 14³³ 2 Cor. 13¹¹ Phil. 4⁹ Heb. 13²⁰; *cf.* ὁ κύριος II 3¹⁶).—ἁγιάζειν is rare in Paul (active here and Eph. 5²⁶, passive in Rom. 15¹⁶ 1 Cor. 1² 6¹¹ 7¹⁴), but common in Lxx. (Exod. 31¹³ ἐγὼ κύριος ὁ ἁγιάζων ὑμᾶς, Lev. 11⁴⁴ 21⁸ Ezek. 37²⁸). Though the consecrating power of Christ or the Spirit possesses the believers at baptism so that they become a καινὴ κτίσις, yet the consecration is not fully perfected (*cf.* 3¹³). For the optative ἁγιάσαι,

GF have the future indic. ὁλοτελής occurs only here in Gk. Bib.;
Field notes it in Lev. 6²³ Ps. 50²¹ (Aq.); *cf.* Aristotle, *de plantis*, 817 *f.*
ὁ κόσμος ὁλοτελής ἐστιν καὶ διηνεκής; also Hermas, Mand. IX, 6, Vis.
III, 6⁴ 10⁹ 13⁴.

καὶ ὁλόκληρον κτλ. "And—to specify more exactly (Ell.),
may your spirit and soul and body . . . be kept in their en-
tirety," as an undivided whole.   So important for the readers
is the prayer for the consecration not only of soul but of body
that Paul repeats it, explaining the ἁγιάσαι ·with ἀμέμπτως
τηρηθείη; the ὑμᾶς with ὑμῶν τὸ πνεῦμα, ἡ ψυχή, τὸ σῶμα;
and the ὁλοτελεῖς with ὁλόκληρον.   In doing so, he makes
clear that God not only consecrates the believers but keeps
them ("from the baptism to the coming of Christ," Ephr.) so
that they are blameless when the Lord comes.

> ὁλόκληρον like ὁλοτελεῖς which it resumes is in the predicate posi-
> tion and is to be interpreted not qualitatively "so as to be ethically
> perfect" but qualitatively "in their entirety," "intact," *integer* (Vulg.),
> the point being that no part of the Christian personality should be lack-
> ing in consecration. Though closely connected with πνεῦμα, ὁλόκληρον
> like the unemphatic ὑμῶν is to be construed with all three substantives.
> —ὁλόκληρος differs etymologically from ὁλοτελής but is in meaning
> virtually synonymous with it. The former word occurs elsewhere in
> the Gk. Bib. Jas. 1⁴; Zech. 11¹⁶ (of physical soundness; *cf.* ὁλοκληρία
> Acts 3¹⁶ Is. 1⁶ *v. l.*); Ezek. 15⁵ (of wood not yet cut for fuel); Deut.
> 27⁶ Josh. 9² 1 Mac. 4⁴⁷ (of the unhewn stones for the altar); Deut. 16⁹
> (A) Lev. 23¹⁵ (of the seven Sabbaths); Sap. 15³ (of δικαιοσύνη); 4 Mac.
> 15⁷ (of εὐσέβεια); *cf.* Hermas, Mand. V, 2³ τῶν τὴν πίστιν ἐχόντων
> ὁλόκληρον; also A in 1 Ch. 24⁷ = 25⁹ where B has ὁ κλῆρος.

ὑμῶν τὸ πνεῦμα κτλ.   Judging from the Pauline conception of
the Christian as the man into whom there has entered a supernatural divine power, Christ or the Spirit (Gal. 4⁶ Rom. 8¹¹
1 Cor. 6¹⁹ 2 Cor. 1²²), and from the fact that Paul is addressing
Christians, it is probable but not certain that "your spirit" (*cf.*
1 Cor. 14¹⁴) designates that portion of the divine Spirit which as
dwelling permanently in the individual as τὸ πνεῦμα τὸ ἐκ τοῦ
θεοῦ constitutes τὸ πνεῦμα τοῦ ἀνθρώπου τὸ ἐν αὐτῷ (1 Cor. 2¹¹).
The believer and the unbeliever are so far alike that their individuality consists of an inner (ψυχή, νοῦς, καρδία, ὁ ἔσω ἄνθρωπος) and an outer part (σῶμα); but the believer differs from

the unbeliever in that he has received from God the divine Spirit which controls and redeems his former individuality, so that at the *Parousia* he is raised from the dead and enters upon a life with Christ in a spiritual body. Without the indwelling πνεῦμα, man at his best (ψυχικός) is mere man, unregenerate, σαρκικός (1 Cor 3³ 15⁴⁴ ᶠᶠ·), incapable of resurrection and life with Christ. Hence the emphasis on ὁλόκληρον at this point; the divine in man and the human individuality must be kept intact, an undivided whole, if the believer is to be blameless at the *Parousia*.

This view, shared substantially by Dob., appears in an anonymous catena quoted by Swete (Th. Mops. II, 39): οὐδέποτε ἐπὶ ἀπίστου τὰ τρία τέθεικεν, πνεῦμα, ψυχήν, καὶ σῶμα, ἀλλ᾽ ἐπὶ μόνων τῶν πιστευόντων· ὧν ψυχὴ μὲν καὶ σῶμα τῆς φύσεως, τὸ δὲ πνεῦμα τῆς εὐεργεσίας, τουτέστιν, τὸ χάρισμα τῶν πιστευόντων. Th. Mops. (who seems to take ὁλόκληρον with πνεῦμα and ἀμέμπτως with ψυχή and σῶμα) Chrys. and Theodoret interpret ὑμῶν τὸ πνεῦμα as the direct equivalent of τὸ πνεῦμα in v. ¹⁹. —The contrast between "my," "our" spirit with the divine Spirit (1 Cor. 5¹⁴ Rom. 8¹⁶) does not of necessity compel the conclusion that the human spirit in a psychological sense (= ψυχή, νοῦς, etc.) is here meant, for in 1 Cor. 14¹⁴ where "my spirit" is contrasted with "my νοῦς," it is evident that "my spirit" is that portion of the divine Spirit which is resident in the individual. Occasionally Paul uses τὸ πνεῦμα ὑμῶν as a designation of the Christian personality (Gal. 6¹⁸ Phil. 4²³ Phile. 25) instead of ὑμεῖς (v. ²⁸ II 3¹⁸) or the popular ψυχή (Rom. 2⁹ 11¹³ 13¹ 16⁴ 2 Cor. 1²³ Phil. 2³⁰; also 1 Thess. 2⁸ 2 Cor. 12¹⁵); and this is probably the case in 1 Cor. 16¹⁸ 2 Cor. 2¹³ 7¹³ (*cf.* Mt. 11²⁹ and ἡ σάρξ ὑμῶν 2 Cor. 7⁵); ἐκ ψυχῆς (Col. 3²³ Eph. 6⁶) is equivalent to ἐκ καρδίας as Rom. 6¹⁷ makes probable. ψυχή is rare in Paul compared with πνεῦμα, σῶμα or even καρδία; it is less frequent than νοῦς. Ten of the thirteen instances have been mentioned already; in 1 Cor. 15⁴⁵ = Gen. 2⁷, Paul contrasts sharply πνεῦμα and ψυχή under the influence of his conception of the ψυχικός as σαρκικός; in Phil. 1²⁷ (στήκετε ἐν ἑνὶ πνεύματι, μιᾷ ψυχῇ συναθλοῦντες), where, as here, ψυχή appears alongside of πνεῦμα, πνεῦμα is the divine Spirit as such or as individualised in the believer.—Didymus (*de spiritu sancto*, 55, quoted by Swete (*op. cit.*), 39) thinks that it would be incredible and blasphemous for the Apostle to pray that the Holy Spirit *integer servetur, qui nec imminutionem potest recipere nec profectum;* and hence refers "your spirit" to the human spirit. Whether his objection is cogent depends on the interpretation of 1 Cor. 5⁵ and 2 Cor. 7¹ (if σάρξ here as in Col. 2⁵ = σῶμα; *cf.* 2 Cor. 7⁵). Pelagius (noted by Dob.) remarks: *gratia spiritus, quae quamvis in se semper integra sit, non tamen in nobis integra nisi ab integris habetur* (Souter). If with Didymus Paul here speaks *de humano spiritu*, then πνεῦμα is a distinctively psychological term appropriate to believers and unbelievers alike, and the collocation with ψυχή which is unusual (Phil. 1²⁷ 1 Cor. 15⁴⁵) is to be understood either (1) as rhetorical (De W. Jowett, and many), or at least as "a popular statement, not an expression of the Apostle's own psychology" (Charles, *Eschat.* 410); or (2) as the "distinct enunciation of the three component parts of the nature of man" (Ell.; so most after Origen, Jerome, Apollinaris of Laodicea). Lft. *ad loc.* says: "The spirit which is the ruling faculty in man and through which he holds communication with the unseen world —the soul, which is the seat of all his impulses and affections, the centre of his personality—the body, which links him to the material world and is the instrument of all his outward deeds—these all the Apostle would have presented perfect and intact in the day of the Lord's coming."

In the O. T. man is regularly divided into an inner (spirit or soul) and an outer (body) part,—a view which prevails in the simple psychology of late Judaism (Bousset, *Relig.*² 459) and in the N. T. Concurrent with this view is another (to Charles the more primitive), namely, that *ruach* is the breath of life which quickens man, body and soul, and returns at death to God (Charles, *Eschat.* 44),—a view which occasionally appears in apocalyptic literature (*ibid.* 194-232). Charles (*ibid.* 409 *ff.*) understands πνεῦμα in Paul of the higher nature of man which is created anew by God in order to make possible communion with him; it of course survives death; ψυχή is a mere function of the body and perishes with it. Dob. doubts this and refers to 2 Cor. 1²³ 12¹⁵.

Neither Plato nor Aristotle has a trichotomy (Dob. 230 *ff.*); they divide man into σῶμα and ψυχή and subdivide ψυχή into three parts or powers. When νοῦς comes alongside of ψυχή, it is a function of the latter, "the instrument by which the soul thinks and forms conceptions" and it has "no reality at all prior to the exercise of thought" (Arist. *de anima*, III, 4 (429), in Hammond, *Aristotle's Psychology*, 1902, 113). In Philo, "the πνεῦμα is not a part of human nature but a force that acts upon it and within it. The dichotomy of human nature remains" (Hatch, *Essays*, 128). In Christianity, trichotomy does not seem certain until the second century; outside of Christianity, it is not clear before the Neoplatonists with their σῶμα, ψυχή, νοῦς (Dob.).—On the question at issue, see Wendt, *Die Begriffe Fleisch und Geist*, 1879; Dickson, *St. Paul's Use of the Terms Flesh and Spirit*, 1883; Hatch, *Essays*, 94-130 (for psychological terms in Lxx. and Philo); Davidson, *Old Testament Theology*, 1904, 182 *ff.*; Charles, *Eschat.*; Bousset, *Relig.*² 459 *ff.*; and Lft. Ell. and Dob. on our passage.

ἀμέμπτως . . . τηρηθείη. "May your spirit and soul and body as an undivided whole be kept blamelessly (that is, so as to be

blameless) at the coming of our Lord Jesus Christ" (3^{13}). Since
ἀμέμπτως τηρηθείη resumes ἁγιάσαι, the logical subject of the
passive optative is God. The verb τηρεῖν of itself intimates that
the process of keeping intact the divine and human element in
man has been going on since the baptism (Ephr.) when first
the Spirit entered into the believer. The adverb ἀμέμπτως lays
stress not so much on the manner of God's activity as on the
result; hence the adverb may be interpreted as an adjective (so
Lillie, Pelt: ὥστε ὑμᾶς ἀμέμπτους ἐν τῇ παρουσίᾳ; cf. Bl. 76^1
and see above on 2^{10} and on 3^{13} where BL read ἀμέμπτως).

Grot. Piscator, Lft. Dob. *et al.* take ἐν as brachyology for εἰς; *cf.*
Bl. 41^1 and 1 Cor. 11^{18}. τηρεῖν (1 Cor. 7^{37} 2 Cor. 11^9 Eph. 4^3) is common in Gk. Bib.; *cf.* Sap. 10^5 of σοφία: εὗρεν τὸν δίκαιον καὶ ἐτήρησεν
αὐτὸν ἄμεμπτον θεῷ.

24. πιστὸς ὁ καλῶν κτλ. The prayer of v. ^{23} will certainly be
answered, for God is faithful. "This happens not from my prayers, he says, but from the purpose with which he called you"
(Chrys.). This faithfulness of God has already been manifested
when in keeping with his eternal choice (1^4) he called them (2^{12})
through the preaching of the gospel (II 2^{14}). But if the caller is
faithful, he may also (καί) be relied upon to perform the very
thing involved in the call, namely, that for which Paul prayed,
τὸ ἁγιάσαι καὶ τὸ τηρηθῆναι.

In stating this assurance of faith (*cf.* 4^{9-10}) in the fewest words, Paul
succeeds in putting in the forefront the main point, the faithfulness of
God as caller and doer. It is to be observed that he does not even
say that ὁ καλῶν ὑμᾶς (the participle is timeless as in 2^{12}) is God,
though that is self-evident without recourse to v. ^{23}, or to the Pauline
turn πιστὸς ὁ θεός (1 Cor. 1^9 10^{13} 2 Cor. 1^{18}; *cf.* κύριος 2 Thess. 3^3);
nor does he say for what (2^{12} 4^7) or through what (II 2^{14}) they are called;
nor does he state the precise object of ποιήσει (*cf.* 2 Cor. 8^{10} f. Ps. 36^5
51^{11}, etc.). It is better, however, to supply the object from v. ^{23} (Ell.
Lft. and most) than to interpret generally: "will perform as surely as
he calls, and everything promised or implied in the call" (Lillie, who
notes Pelagius *quod promisit* and Œcumenius ἐφ' ᾧ ἐκάλεσεν). Indeed
some minuscules actually add from 2 Cor. 1^7 τὴν ἐλπίδα (ὑμῶν) βεβαίαν
(see Poole *ad loc.*). On the faithfulness of God, Grot. notes Is. 49^{17}
πιστός ἐστιν ὁ ἅγιος (τοῦ) Ἰσραήλ, καὶ ἐλεξάμην σε (*cf.* Deut. 7^9 32^4, etc.).

VI. FINAL REQUESTS (5^{25-27}).

With an affectionate address ($\dot{a}\delta\epsilon\lambda\phi o\acute{\iota}$), Paul makes three more requests (note the triple exhortations in vv. $^{12-22}$ except vv $^{19-20}$) before closing the letter with the customary invocation of the grace of Christ. First, he bids the brethren in their prayers (v. ^{17}) for themselves and others to remember also himself and his associates (v. ^{25}). Next he bids them to greet for him all the brethren, with a tactful inclusion of the idlers (v. ^{26}). Finally, with an abrupt change to the first person, he adjures them to see to it that the letter be read to all the brethren, presumably a covert admonition of the idlers who had apparently threatened to pay no heed to the epistolary injunctions of Paul.

^{25}*Brothers, pray for us as well (as for yourselves and others).* ^{26}*Greet for us the brothers, all of them, with a holy kiss.* ^{27}*I adjure you by the Lord that the present letter be read to the brothers, all of them.*

25. $\pi\rho o\sigma\epsilon\acute{\nu}\chi\epsilon\sigma\theta\epsilon$ $\kappa a\grave{\iota}$ $\pi\epsilon\rho\grave{\iota}$ $\dot{\eta}\mu\hat{\omega}\nu$. When the brethren pray without ceasing (v. ^{17}), they are to bear in mind not only themselves and others but Paul and his fellow-missionaries as well ($\kappa a\acute{\iota}$),—a human touch showing how heavily Paul leaned upon the sympathy of his converts (*cf.* II 3^1 Col. $4^{2\ f.}$).

> On requests for prayer (but without $\kappa a\acute{\iota}$), *cf.* Rom. 15^{30} Eph. 6^{19} Phil. 1^{19} and Heb. 13^{18}. For $\pi\epsilon\rho\acute{\iota}$ (II 3^1 Col. 4^3; Gen. 20^7 Ps. 71^{15} 2 Mac. 1^6), GFP read $\dot{\nu}\pi\acute{\epsilon}\rho$ (Col. 1^9 1 Reg. 1^{27}); on these prepositions, see Moult. I, 105. $\kappa a\acute{\iota}$ is read by BD*, a few minuscules, Syr. (hl. pal.), Arm. Gothic, Orig. Chrys. Th. Mops.; but is omitted by אAD^{c}EGFI KLP, Vulg. Pesh. Boh. Eth. Ambst. (Souter). Both Zim. and Dob. think that the $\kappa a\acute{\iota}$ comes from Col. 4^3. Assuming $\kappa a\acute{\iota}$ to be original, we must translate not "you also pray for us as we have just prayed for you" but "you pray for us as well as for yourselves and others," the reference being not to v. ^{23} but to v. ^{17} (Weiss, 111). Failure to see this reference accounts for the omission of $\kappa a\acute{\iota}$ (B. Weiss, *ad loc.*). I reads $\pi\rho o\sigma\epsilon\acute{\nu}\chi\epsilon\sigma\theta a\iota$.

26. $\dot{a}\sigma\pi\acute{a}\sigma a\sigma\theta\epsilon$ $\kappa\tau\lambda$. The second request takes the form of a salutation characteristic of contemporary epistolary literature. "Because being absent he could not greet them with the kiss, he greets them through others, as when we say: Kiss him for me" (Chrys.). The fact that instead of the expected ἀλλήλους (Rom. 16¹⁶ 1 Cor. 16²⁰ 2 Cor. 13¹²; 1 Pet. 5¹⁴) Paul writes τοὺς ἀδελφοὺς πάντας indicates not that he is turning from the brethren addressed in v. ²⁵ to the workers who take the lead and admonish, but that he is tactfully including in the number of those to be greeted for him not only the workers, the faint-hearted, and the weak, but also the idlers (cf. Phil. 4²¹ ἀσπά-σασθε πάντα ἅγιον without exception). The kiss is holy be-cause it is the expression not of romantic but of Christian love (ἐν φιλήματι ἀγάπης 1 Pet. 5¹⁴).

On the salutation in epistolary literature, see the references given in the note on 1¹. Greetings (ἀσπάζεσθαι or ἀσπασμός or both) are found in all Paul's letters except Gal. and Eph. In Rom. 16¹⁶ 2 Cor. 13¹², ἀλλήλους is parallel to οἱ ἅγιοι πάντες, in 1 Cor. 16²⁰ to οἱ ἀδελφοὶ πάν-τες. Over against De W. Lün. Ell. Find. Born. and others who find the leaders addressed, Hofmann, Wohl. Mill. Dob. Moff. rightly see the brethren as a whole.

φίλημα, apart from the passages noted above, occurs in the Gk. Bib. only Lk. 7⁴⁵ 22⁴⁸; Pr. 27⁶ Cant. 1² (φιλήματα). "In the ancient world one kissed the hand, breast, knee, or foot of a superior, and the cheek of a friend. Herodotus (I, 134) mentions kissing the lips as a custom of the Persians. Possibly from them it came to the Jews" (Toy, ICC. on Pr. 24²⁶—the only distinct reference to kissing the lips, since Gen. 41⁴⁰ (see Skinner, ICC. ad loc.) is doubtful). That the "holy kiss" is kissing the lips, or that the kiss was given promiscuously cannot be inferred from our verse (Cheyne in EB. 4254, who notes Neil, Kissing: Its Curious Bible Mentions, 1885, 27 ff., 78 ff.). The Jewish and Christian attitude is probably expressed in that of Bunyan (Grace Abounding, 316): "Some indeed have urged the holy kiss, but then I have asked why they made baulks? Why did they salute the most handsome and let the ill-favoured go? Thus how laudable soever such things have been in the eyes of others, they have been unseemly in my sight." Cheyne states that Conybeare (Exp. 1894, 461) "points out two passages in Philo's quaestiones in Ex. preserved in Armenian, which seem to imply that the "kiss of peace" or "of concord" was a formal institution of the synagogue,"—an opinion which Schultze (article Friedenskuss in PRE.³ VI, 274 f.) thinks possible.—This kiss is mentioned in Justin (Apol. I, 65), ἀλλήλους φιλήματι ἀσπαζόμεθα παυσάμενοι τῶν εὐχῶν. It came before the eucharistic prayer and after the other prayers (Tert. de orat. 18; the references in ad uxorem, II, 4 (iam vero alicui fratrum ad *osculum convenire*) and in *de virg. vel.* 14 (*inter amplexus et oscula assidua*) are uncertain, but seem to point to the extension of the custom). It is probable (so Cheyne and Schultze) that the φίλημα was not originally promiscuous, and that the ordinances of the *Apostolical Constitutions* (II, 57[12], VIII, 11[41]) arose in view of the abuse. For the history of the custom in Christian worship, see, in addition to Cheyne and Schultze, the article *Kiss* in the *Dictionary of Christian Antiquities* and the note of Robertson and Plummer in *ICC.* on 1 Cor. 16[20].

27. ἐνορκίζω κτλ. Had Paul written ποιήσατε ἵνα ἡ ἐπιστολὴ πᾶσιν τοῖς ἀδελφοῖς ἀναγνωσθῇ (*cf.* Col. 4[16]), it would have been natural to suppose that he intended simply to emphasise the importance of the present letter (τήν; Vulg. *haec; cf.* II 3[14] Rom. 16[22] Col. 4[16]) not only to the weak who by it might be supported, and to the faint-hearted who by it might be encouraged, but also to the idlers who might by it be induced to heed the admonition (*cf.* Ephr.). The sudden change, however, from the second to the first person (but without ἐγώ; *cf.* 2[18] 3[5]), and the introduction of the solemn adjuration directed to the group as a whole (ὑμᾶς) suggest the existence of a serious situation, namely, either that the leaders had intimated to Paul that they would not read his reply to all the brethren (*cf.* Th. Mops. Calv. B. Weiss) or, and more probably in the light of II 3[14], that they had informed Paul that the more recalcitrant of the idlers had asserted that they would pay no heed to the epistolary injunctions of Paul. Hence the solemn adjuration by the Lord Jesus that the brethren as a group see to it (*cf.* v. [15]) that all the brethren, including the idlers, hear this letter read.

On the theory of Harnack, shared also by Lake (*The Earlier Epistles of St. Paul*, 1911, 89) that πᾶσιν here, like πάντας in v. [26], implies the existence of a Jewish Christian church in Thessalonica between which and the Gentile Christian church addressed in I there was a line of cleavage, *v. supra*, p. 53 *f.* From this verse, called forth by a particular need, it can neither be affirmed nor denied that Paul had written letters to communities visited (*cf.* Gal. 1[21]) or that the reading of his letters, if written, in the church had become a fixed custom.—Though ἀναγινώσκειν both in classics and in papyri (Mill.) may mean not only "read aloud" but also "read," it is yet probable that the former sense, usual in classics, is always intended by Paul (2 Cor. 1[13] 3[2. 15] Col. 4[16] Eph. 3[4]; *cf.* 1 Mac. 14[19] ἐνώπιον ἐκκλησίας). Whether all the artisans in Thess. could read, we do not know. The aor. infin. ἀναγνωσθῆναι (object of ἐνορκίζω; cf. BMT. 391) indicates "the being read" as an act without reference to its progress, repetition, or result.—ἐνορκίζω (BADE, et al.) is found elsewhere in Gk. Bib. only Neh. 13²⁵ (A); the simple ὁρκίζω (Neh. 13²⁵ (B) Mk. 5⁷ Acts 19¹³) is read by אGFP, et al. (cf. ὁρκόω 4 Reg. 11⁴; also ἐξορκίζω Mt. 26⁶³ Gen. 24³ Judg. 17² (A) 3 Reg. 22¹⁶). These verbs are construed either with two accus. as here (Mk. 5⁷ Acts 19¹³ Gen. 24³) or with accus. and κατά with gen. (Mt. 26⁶³ 2 Ch. 36¹³; Hermas Sim. IX, 10⁵; see Deiss. BS. 28 ff.). On the infin. instead of ἵνα (Gen. 24³ Mt. 26⁶³ and the Hermas passage), cf. Joseph. Ant. VIII, 104: λέγειν αὐτῷ τ' ἀληθὲς οὗτος ἐνωρκίσατο.—P. omits τὴν ἐπιστολήν; ἁγίοις (א°AKLP, et al.) is an insertion influenced by φιλήματι ἁγίῳ (Dob.), and though retained by Weiss (91) is probably to be omitted with א*BDEGF, et al. πάντες οἱ ἅγιοι is common in Paul (Rom. 16¹⁵ 2 Cor. 1¹ 13¹², etc.), but οἱ ἅγιοι ἀδελφοί is unexpected and redundant. Moff. notes Apoc. Bar. 86¹: "When therefore ye receive this my epistle, read it in your congregations with care."

VII. BENEDICTION (5²⁸).

28. ἡ χάρις κτλ. "The grace of our Lord Jesus Christ be (sc. ἔστω or εἴη; see 1¹) with you." The place of the epistolary "farewell" (ἔρρωσο; ἔρρωσθε; cf. Acts 15²⁹) is in Paul's letters taken by the invocation of "grace" (Col. 4¹⁸) or "the grace of (our) Lord Jesus (Christ)."

ἡ χάρις μεθ' ὑμῶν (Col. 4¹⁸) is the shortest concluding benediction in Paul; with our verse cf. II 3¹⁸ which inserts πάντων and Rom. 16²⁰. The ἀμήν (cf. 3¹³), retained by אAEKLP, et al., is probably to be omitted with BDGF, et al.—Like the inscription (see on 1¹), the subscription ΠΡΟΣ ΘΕΣΣΑΛΟΝΙΚΕΙΣ Α (אB), to which GF prefix ἐτελέσθη and to which AKL add ἐγράφη ἀπὸ Ἀθηνῶν, is late and forms no part of the original letter; see Sod. Schriften des N. T. I, 296 ff.

COMMENTARY ON THE SECOND EPISTLE TO THE THESSALONIANS.

I. SUPERSCRIPTION (1¹⁻²).

¹*Paul and Silvanus and Timothy to the assembly of Thessalonians in God our Father and the Lord Jesus Christ. *²*Grace to you and peace from God the Father and the Lord Jesus Christ.*

1-2. The superscription differs from that of I 1¹ (*q. v.*) in adding after πατρί the ἡμῶν, thus expressing the sense of common fellowship in the Father (*cf.* I 1³); and in adding after εἰρήνη the clause with ἀπό which makes explicit the source of the divine favour and spiritual prosperity, God the Father and the Lord Jesus Christ.

> The clause with ἀπό appears in all Pauline superscriptions except I; Col. 1¹, however, omits καὶ κυρίου ᾽Ι. Χ. Usually ἡμῶν (ℵA, *et al.*, omit) is found after πατρός (BD, *et al.*, here; ℵA, *et al.*, in Gal. 1³), except in Gal. 1³ (BD, *et al.*) where it is put after κυρίου. On the inscription πρὸς Θεσσ. Β′ (ℵBA, *et al.*), see on I 1¹.

II. THANKSGIVING AND PRAYER (1³⁻¹²).

Word has come to Paul, probably by letter, informing him of the increased discouragement of the faint-hearted (1³–2¹⁷) and the continued troublesomeness of the idlers (3⁶⁻¹⁵). Cast down by the persistent persecution, worried by the assertion of some that the day of the Lord is present, and anxious lest they might not be deemed worthy of entrance into the kingdom, the faint-hearted had given utterance to their despair by saying that they were not entitled to the praise of their faith and love, and especially of their endurance which Paul had generously given in his first epistle. To these utterances, reflected in the letter from Thessalonica, Paul replies at once in the Thanksgiving (vv. ³⁻¹⁰) and Prayer (vv. ¹¹⁻¹²) by insisting that he ought to thank God for them, as is most proper under the circumstances because their

219

growth in faith and brotherly love is steady (v. ³). In fact, contrary to their expectations, he is boasting everywhere of their endurance and faith in the midst of persecution (v. ⁴). They need not worry about their future salvation, for their constant endurance springing from faith is positive proof that God the righteous Judge will, in keeping with his purpose, deem them worthy of entrance into the kingdom on behalf of which they as well as Paul are suffering (v. ⁵). It will not always be well with their persecutors, for God, since he is righteous in judgment, will recompense them with affliction as he will recompense the converts with relief from the same, a relief which Paul also will share (vv. ⁶⁻⁷ ᵃ). God will do so at the Great Assize (vv. ⁷ᵇ⁻¹⁰) when the wicked, those, namely, who do not reverence God and do not obey the gospel of the Lord Jesus, will receive as their punishment separation forever from Christ, on the very day when the righteous in general, and, with an eye to the faint-hearted, all who became believers will be the ground of honour and admiration accorded to Christ by the retinue of angels. In order to reach this glorious consummation, however, the converts must be blameless in goodness and love; hence Paul prays as the converts were praying not only that God may deem them worthy of his call, that is, acquit them at the last day, but also, to insure this acquittal, that he may perfect them morally; in order that finally the name of the Lord Jesus may be glorified in virtue of what they are, and that they may be glorified in virtue of what the name of our Lord Jesus has accomplished. This glorification is in accordance with the divine favour of our God and the Lord Jesus Christ.

That the purpose of 1³⁻2¹⁷ is the encouragement of the faint-hearted is evident from the emphasis put on the certainty of the readers' salvation (1⁵⁻¹² 2¹³⁻¹⁷), and from the express statement, purposely added after the destruction of the *Anomos*, that the advent of the *Anomos* is intended not for believers, but for unbelievers who have doomed themselves (2⁸⁻¹²). That Paul is replying to a letter from Thessalonica is a hypothesis (not excluded by ἀκούομεν 3¹¹) which admirably accounts for the emphasis on ὀφείλομεν (v. ³ 2¹³), καθὼς ἄξιον (v. ³), αὐτοὺς ἡμᾶς (v. ⁴) and καί in εἰς ὃ καί (v. ¹¹), and for the exegetical difficulties in 3¹⁻⁵. See Bacon, *Introd.* 72.

*³We ought, brothers, to thank God always for you, as it is proper,
because your faith is growing exceedingly and the love for one
another of each one of you all is increasing, ⁴so that we ourselves
are boasting of you in the assemblies of God, of your endurance and
faith in all your persecutions and afflictions which you bear—
⁵p. vof positive of the righteous judgment of God that you should be
deemed worthy of the kingdom of God for which you too as well as
we are suffering;—righteous judgment of God, we say, ⁶if indeed
(as it certainly is) righteous in God's sight to recompense affliction
to those who afflict you; ⁷and to you who are afflicted, relief with us,
at the revelation of the Lord Jesus from heaven, with his angels of
power, ⁸in fire of flame, rendering vengeance to those who know not
God and to those who obey not the gospel of our Lord Jesus: ⁹who
shall be punished with eternal destruction from the face of the Lord
and from the glory of his strength, ¹⁰when he shall come to be glorified
in his saints and admired in all those who became believers (for our
testimony to you was believed) in that day. ¹¹To which end we too,
as well as you, pray always for you that our God may deem you
worthy of the calling and may fulfil every resolve after goodness and
work of faith in power; ¹²in order that the name of our Lord Jesus
may be glorified in you and you in it, according to the grace of our
God, and the Lord Jesus Christ.*

3. εὐχαριστεῖν ὀφείλομεν κτλ. "We ought, as is manifestly
fitting, proper, worth while, in spite of your remonstrances, to
thank God always for your growing faith and brotherly love."
To account for the emphasis on ὀφείλομεν, a word only here and
2¹³ in Paul's thanksgivings, and on καθὼς ἄξιον which resumes it,
it may be assumed that Paul is replying to the utterances of the
faint-hearted, communicated to him in a letter from Thessalonica, to the effect that they did not consider themselves
worthy of the kingdom or entitled to the praise accorded them
in the first epistle.

Since καθώς in Paul is slightly causal (Bl. 78¹), it cannot indicate the
degree (Th. Mops.) or the manner (Wohl. who refers to 1 Cor. 8²) of
εὐχαριστεῖν, but must resume and explain ὀφείλομεν (Born. Dob.). If
ὀφείλομεν stood alone, it might be interpreted as a general expression
of personal obligation (Rom. 15¹) in view of the progress of the read-

ers, or as a liturgical formula (1 Clem. 38⁴; Barn. 5³ ὀφείλομεν (ὑπερ)
εὐχαριστεῖν). Similarly if we had had εὐχαριστοῦμεν and καθὼς ἄξιόν
ἐστιν, the latter clause might have expressed what was proper in view
of the growth of the converts or have been purely liturgical (cf. 1 Mac.
12¹¹ ὡς δέον ἐστὶν καὶ πρέπον). The resumption, however, of ὀφείλομεν
in καθὼς κτλ. reveals not liturgical tautology (Jowett) but an emphasis,
due to special circumstances.—That Paul is no slave of epistolary
form is evident from the present thanksgiving. Here as in 1 Cor. 1⁴
Col. 1³, the πάντων of the common πάντοτε περὶ πάντων ὑμῶν (I 1²) is
omitted; the prayer which is usually associated with the thanksgiving
(I 1²) is omitted here as in 1 Cor. 1⁴; here as in Rom. 1⁸ he passes
directly from εὐχαρ. to ὅτι, while the prayer comes in Rom. 1¹⁰ and here
in v. ¹¹. In Phil. 1³ Col. 1³, the thanksgiving and prayer are closely
united as in I 1², but a further προσεύχεσθαι is added in Phil. 1⁹ Col. 1⁹
as in v. ¹¹ below. The address ἀδελφοί usually comes later (I 1⁴ Gal. 1¹¹,
etc.: it does not appear at all in Col. Eph.); its place here at the start
betrays at once Paul's affection for his converts.—ἄξιος is rare in Paul,
but common elsewhere in Gk. Bib.; on ἄξιον cf. 1 Cor. 16⁴ 4 Mac. 17⁸.
Th. Mops. takes it as = δίκαιον (Phil. 1⁷); its presence here prepares the
way for καταξιωθῆναι (v. ⁵) and ἀξιώσῃ (v. ¹¹).

ὅτι ὑπεραυξάνει κτλ. With causal ὅτι dependent on εὐχαριστεῖν (I 1¹ 2¹³), he gives the reason for the thanksgiving, namely,
the very abundant growth (ὑπεραυξάνει) of the tree of religious
life (πίστις), and the abundance (πλεονάζει) of the fruit of the
same (cf. Phil. 4¹⁷ Col. 1⁶·¹⁰) in their ethical life as manifested in
the brotherhood (ἡ ἀγάπη (sc. ἡ and cf. I 3¹²) εἰς ἀλλήλους, or
φιλαδελφία).

This thanksgiving differs from that in I where "work of faith,"
"labour of love," and "endurance of hope" are mentioned, and
also from I 3⁶ where faith and love (not φιλαδελφία) are referred
to. In thus singling out brotherly love, Paul expresses his appreciation of the fact that love to brothers (I 4⁹) is abounding
as he exhorted (I 4¹⁰) and prayed (I 3¹²) in his first letter. But
in order to make plain that he includes in his praise each and
every one of them, even the idlers who are troublesome (3⁶⁻¹⁵),
he adds to ἡ ἀγάπη εἰς ἀλλήλους not only the individualising
ἑνὸς ἑκάστου ὑμῶν (I 2¹¹) 'but also πάντων, which precludes
any exception.

ὑπεραυξάνειν, only here in Gk. Bib., is classic. Paul is fond of compounds with ὑπέρ (see I 3¹⁰); if he does not find them he coins them.

On the simple αὐξάνειν (with πίστις), see 2 Cor. 10¹⁵; on πλεονάζειν, here as usual intransitive, see I 3¹²; on ἡ πίστις ὑμῶν, see I 1⁸ 3² ᶠᶠ. αὐξάνειν and πλεονάζειν, only here in Gk. Bib., are in synonymous parallelism; cf. πλεονάζειν and περισσεύειν in I 3¹² (cf. 2 Cor. 4¹⁵). Olshausen (apud Lün.) takes ὑπεραυξάνει as indicating that the converts were guilty of extravagance in their religious zeal, thus introducing a thought like that of Ps. Sol. 5¹⁹ (cf. 5⁶) ἐὰν ὑπερπλεονάσῃ ἐξαμαρτάνει. Schrader and Pelt suggest that I 3¹² is in mind, and that the omission of καὶ εἰς πάντας shows that the converts do not love the Gentiles. Schmiedel and Holtzmann, on the assumption that II is a forgery, find here a literary reminiscence of I 2¹¹ (ἑνὸς ἑκάστου) and 3¹². Wrede (85) is less certain, but thinks that πάντων might easily come from I 1² (so Schmiedel).—The emphasis on the progress of faith (ὑπεραυξάνει, not αὐξάνει, as Chrys. notes) is evidence that II is written after, not before (Grot. Ewald), I.

4. ὥστε αὐτοὺς ἡμᾶς κτλ. The consequence (ὥστε) of their progress in faith and brotherly love is that Paul and his associates (ἡμᾶς) can and do boast of them everywhere. We have, however, not ἡμᾶς alone but αὐτοὺς ἡμᾶς; a contrast is intended. In I 4⁹, αὐτοὶ ὑμεῖς finds its antithesis in ἡμᾶς supplied from the subject of γράφειν; here no antithesis to αὐτοὺς ἡμᾶς is distinctly stated, though ἐν ὑμῖν, the emphatically placed object of καυχᾶσθαι, suggests the Thessalonians. Precisely what prompts the expression is uncertain; probably Paul has in mind the utterances of the faint-hearted to the effect that their faith and love, and especially their endurance (which, as ὑπέρ κτλ. shows, is the main theme of Paul's exultation) were not worthy of the praise bestowed by the Apostle in I. To these remonstrances he replies: "So that we ourselves, contrary to your expectations, are boasting."

Had Paul written not αὐτοὺς ἡμᾶς but καὶ ἡμᾶς, the point would have been that the converts as well as Paul found the Thess. an object of boasting; or that Paul as well as others in general or in particular the αὐτοί of I 1⁹ found the Thess. an object of boasting. But αὐτοὺς ἡμᾶς indicates not a reciprocal relation but a contrast. Bacon (Introd. 74) interprets differently: "The Thess. had written that they boasted of the apostles against the slanderers; cf. 2 Cor. 1¹⁴." In this "significant and inimitable ὥστε αὐτοὺς ἡμᾶς" κτλ. (Bacon), Wrede (cf. Schmiedel) finds an assertion of apostolic dignity ("if we boast of any one, that means more than if others do it"), and also a literary reminiscence of I 1⁸⁻⁹ ὥστε . . . ἡμᾶς . . . αὐτοί.—In αὐτοὺς ἡμᾶς (Bℵ, *et al.*; *cf.* αὐτὸς ἐγώ Rom. 7²⁵ 9³.15¹⁴ 2 Cor. 10¹ 12¹³), αὐτούς gets the emphasis; in ἡμᾶς αὐτούς (ADGFKL, *et al.*; *cf.* 1 Cor. 5¹³ 7³⁵ 11¹³ Rom. 16²) ἡμᾶς.

ἐν ὑμῖν ἐνκαυχᾶσθαι κτλ. The two clauses with ἐν specify respectively the object and the place of boasting. By putting the contrasted persons ἡμᾶς and ἐν ὑμῖν side by side, and by choosing ἐνκαυχᾶσθαι instead of καυχᾶσθαι, he intensifies the point (*cf.* ὑπεραυξάνει). The place is described, as in 1 Cor. 11¹⁶, without geographical limitations, as "the churches of God" (I 2¹⁴). To insist that every church founded up to this time has heard Paul boast, orally or in writing, of the Thessalonians, or to restrict the reference to the churches of God in Corinth and its vicinity (or more exactly to the church of God in Corinth and the brethren round about), is to forget the enthusiasm of Paul and the compliment which he is paying to his readers (*cf.* ἐν παντὶ τόπῳ I 1⁸).

On this interpretation, see Dob. For ἐνκαυχᾶσθαι (BℵA; ἐγκαυχᾶσθαι P), DEKL, *et al.*, have καυχᾶσθαι, and GF καυχήσασθαι. The compound is rare in Gk. Bib. (Ps. 51³ 73⁴ 96⁷ 105⁴⁷; *cf.* 1 Clem. 21⁵); it is always construed with ἐν of the object. Of the mainly Pauline words καυχᾶσθαι, κατακαυχᾶσθαι, καύχημα and καύχησις (I 2¹⁹), καυχᾶσθαι is in Gk. Bib. usually construed with ἐν, rarely with ἐπί (Ps. 5¹² 48⁷ Sir. 30² Pr. 25¹⁴); *cf.* Rom. 5² with 5³. Here, as in Gal. 6¹³, the clause with ἐν precedes the verb. Polycarp 11³ has our verse in mind when he writes *de vobis etenim gloriatur in omnibus ecclesiis; cf.* 11⁴ *et non sicut inimicos tales existimetis* with 3¹⁵ of our letter.

ὑπὲρ τῆς ὑπομονῆς κτλ. The clause with ὑπέρ resumes ἐν ὑμῖν, and specifies the qualities about which he boasted, namely, their endurance and faith manifested in persecutions. Though faith and persecution are inseparable, as the omission of the article before πίστεως reveals, the ethical (ὑπομονή) takes precedence of the religious (πίστις) from which it springs and of which it is the fruit and evidence (Calvin). The selection not of faith and brotherly love (v. ³) but of faith and endurance, and the position of ὑπομονή before πίστις (*cf.* Phile. 5) are probably due to the utterances of the faint-hearted who had remonstrated against Paul's praise of their endurance and faith (I 1³) in his first epistle.

Here ὑπέρ (contrast 2 Cor. 7¹⁴ 9² 12¹⁵) is equivalent to περί (2 Cor. 10⁸; see below 2¹ and *cf.* I 5¹⁰). In view of the context and of the usage elsewhere in I, II, πίστις is "faith" not "faithfulness" (Bengel, Lün. Born.; *cf.* Gal. 5²²). Unnecessary is the assumption of a hendiadys whether *fidei vestrae firmitatem* (Th. Mops.) or ὑπομονὴ ἐν πίστει (Grot.).

ἐν πᾶσιν τοῖς διωγμοῖς κτλ. The fourth prepositional phrase in this verse (*cf.* I 3⁷⁻⁸ for a similar heaping up of prepositions), namely, ἐν πᾶσιν ... ἀνέχεσθε, states the circumstances in which (I 3³) their endurance and faith were manifested: "in all your persecutions and afflictions that you are bearing." The ὑμῶν binds together the virtually synonymous διωγμοῖς and θλίψεσιν (*cf.* I 2⁹ τὸν κόπον ἡμῶν καὶ τὸν μόχθον); and the αἷς (attraction for ὧν), which refers to both nouns, agrees in gender with the nearer. The πᾶσιν intimates that the persecutions have been repeated ("not in one but in all," Ephr.); and the ἀνέχεσθε (*cf.* Gal. 2⁴ τὴν ἐλευθερίαν ἡμῶν ἣν ἔχομεν), that they are still going on; while the emphasis on both πᾶσιν and ἀνέχεσθε serves to convey rare praise for the unexceptional constancy of their endurance and faith.

The construction assumed above is on the whole the simplest. Some commentators (*e. g.* Lün.), forgetting that the presence of ταῖς (which DGFP omit) does not prevent ὑμῶν from uniting the synonymous words (*cf.* I 2⁹ where there is an article before μόχθον), attach πᾶσιν to διωγμοῖς alone (*cf.* 2 Cor. 8⁷), making αἷς ἀνέχεσθε parallel to ὑμῶν (*cf.* Phile. 5, and Col. 1⁴ τὴν πίστιν ὑμῶν καὶ τὴν ἀγάπην ἣν ἔχετε, where faith and love are not synonymous): "in all the persecutions you have and the afflictions which you are bearing." On the other hand, Dob., who takes ἔνδειγμα as a predicate noun after αἷς ἀνέχεσθε, breaks the rhythm by putting a comma after θλίψεσιν, and is also led to understand ἀνέχεσθε of the necessity of enduring: "which you have to endure as a proof," etc. In the Gk. Bib., διωγμός means usually not "pursuit" (2 Mac. 12²²) but "persecution" (Lam. 3¹⁹ Mk. 4¹⁷ Mt. 13²¹ Rom. 8³⁵ 2 Cor. 12¹⁰). On the meaning of θλῖψις, see I 1⁶. The persecutions which marked the beginnings of Christianity in Thessalonica (I 1⁶ 2¹⁴) and which were going on when Paul wrote I (3³; *cf.* 2¹⁴ ᶠᶠ.) still continue, as the presents ἀνέχεσθε and πάσχετε show.—Since ἀνέχεσθαι in Gk. Bib., when not used absolutely, is construed not with dat. but either with gen. (Gen. 45¹ Is. 46⁴ 63¹⁵ 2 Mac. 9¹² and N. T.) or with accus. (Job 6²⁶ (where A has gen.) Is. 1¹³ 3 Mac. 1²² 4 Mac. 13²⁷), αἷς is probably not directly governed by ἀνέχεσθε (Fritzsche, who notes Eurip.

15

Androm. 981, Lft. Mill.) but is an attraction for ὧν, or less likely for
ἅς. Cod. B gets rid of the difficulty of the unusual attraction by reading ἐνέχεσθε, a rare word in Gk. Bib. (with dat. Gal. 5¹ 3 Mac. 6¹⁰;
with ἐν and dat. Ezek. 14⁴· ⁷). But not even Weiss (35) accepts the
reading of B. On the change of ἀν— and ἐν—, see Gal. 5¹ where D and
a few minuscules read ἀνέχεσθε. With our passage, compare 1 Cor.
4¹² διωκόμενοι ἀνεχόμεθα. The ἐν which K reads before αἷς comes from
the preceding—σιν (Zim.).

5. ἔνδειγμα κτλ. The faint-hearted need not worry about
their future salvation, for the fact of their unexceptional endurance and faith in all their persecutions is itself a "token," "guarantee," "positive evidence" of the righteous judgment of God
(Rom. 2⁵), already in purpose and soon to be declared, that they
be deemed worthy of the kingdom of God, for which they, and
Paul too, are continually suffering. The εἰς τὸ καταξιωθῆναι
expresses the purpose of δικαίας κρίσεως.

Since the object of boasting specified in v. ⁴ is not suffering, but the
constancy of their endurance and faith in the midst of persecution, ἔνδειγμα is to be taken not with the idea of suffering alone, whether with
ἀνέχεσθε or with ἐν πᾶσιν . . . ἀνέχεσθε (Calv. *et al.*), but with the idea
of endurance and faith in spite of persecutions, that is, with ὑπὲρ . . .
ἀνέχεσθε (De W. Lün. Lillie, Ell. Lft. Mill. and others). ἔνδειγμα is
probably an accus. in direct apposition with the preceding (*cf.* Rom.
8³ 12¹); but it may be a nominative, in which case ὅ ἐστιν is to be supplied on the analogy of Phil. 1²⁸. Ephr. and some minuscules read
ἐνδείγματι; Theophylact and Codex 442 have εἰς ἔνδειγμα (*cf.* Rom.
3²⁵); so similarly g, Vulg. Ambst. Syr. Arm. have *in exemplum*. The
distinction between the passive ἔνδειγμα (only here in Gk. Bib., but
classic; *cf.* Plato, *Critias*, 110 C) and the active ἔνδειξις (in Gk. Bib.
confined to Paul; Rom. 3²⁶ ᶠ· 2 Cor. 8²⁴ Phil. 1²⁸) is negligible; the meaning is *demonstrationem* (Th. Mops.), *ostentamen* (Tert. *apud* Swete).
That εἰς τό κτλ. is to be connected not with ἀνέχεσθε (Bengel) leaving
ἔνδειγμα . . . θεοῦ as a parenthesis, or with ἔνδειγμα . . . θεοῦ (Schott),
or with ἔνδειγμα (Wohl.), but with δικαίας κρίσεως is usually admitted
(De W. Lün. Lft. Vincent, Dob. *et al.*). But εἰς τό, since the telic
sense is not always evident in Paul (see I 2¹²), might denote either the
content of the judgment (Theophylact ὅπερ ἐστὶν καταξιωθῆναι), or
the "object to which it tended" (Ell.; Lillie), or the result conceived
or actual (Lün.). In Paul, εἰς τό is most frequently of purpose (*BMT.*
409); and this is the probable meaning here (so among others De W.
Alford, Ewald, Dob.). καταξιόω, only here in Paul (but frequent in

Ignatius), means either "beseech" (2 Mac. 13¹²) or, as elsewhere in Gk. Bib., "deem worthy" (Lk. 20³⁵ Acts 5⁴¹ 4 Mac. 18²). It intensifies the simple ἀξιόω (a word used by Paul only in v. ¹¹, but found elsewhere in the N. T. and frequently in Lxx.). In the N. T. καταξιόω and ἀξιόω (except Acts 15³⁸ 28²² where the meaning is "beseech," "command," as regularly in the Lxx.) are to be rendered not "make worthy," but "deem worthy" (cf. SH. 30 ff.). Dalman (Worte Jesu, I, 97) observes that "to be worthy of the future æon" is a common rabbinical expression. On βασιλεία, see I 2¹².

ὑπὲρ ἧς καὶ πάσχετε. "For which you too (as well as we, that is, the writers) are suffering." The present tense (πάσχετε; cf. v. ⁴ ἀνέχεσθε) designates the sufferings as going on; ὑπὲρ ἧς makes plain that the motive or goal of suffering is none other than the future kingdom of God; καί implies a fellowship in present sufferings of readers (at home) and writers (in Corinth), and prepares the way for the significant ἄνεσιν μεθ' ὑμῶν (v. ⁷).

It is probable that καί here and μεθ' ἡμῶν (v. ⁷) are due to Paul's experiences in Corinth (cf. 3²); on καί, cf. I 2¹³ 3⁵ 5²⁵ 2 Cor. 1⁶. Most commentators, however, interpret καί (which F omits) as implying a correspondence not between Paul and his readers in reference to suffering, but between present suffering and future glory; so, for example, Lft., who compares 2 Tim. 2¹², and Ell. who notes Rom. 8¹⁷ Acts 14²² and says: "καί with a species of consecutive force supplies a renewed hint of the connection between suffering and the καταξιωθῆναι κτλ." (cf. also Wohl. Dob. and others). In the phrase πάσχειν ὑπέρ (Phil. 1²⁹ 1 Pet. 2²¹ Acts 9¹⁶), ὑπέρ may indicate advantage (Lft.), "object for which" (Ell.), the motive or goal ("to gain which"; Lün. Schmiedel, Dob.); but it is probably equivalent to περί (cf. v. ⁴ 2¹; also πάσχειν περί 1 Pet. 3¹⁸ B and 2²¹ A). On the thought of v. ⁵, cf. especially Phil. 1²⁸⁻³⁰.

6–7ᵃ. εἴπερ δίκαιον κτλ. The "righteous judgment of God" (v. ⁵) is not only positive, the salvation of the readers (v. ⁵), but also (δίκαιον παρὰ θεῷ resuming τῆς δικαίας κρίσεως τοῦ θεοῦ) positive and negative, in keeping with the principle of recompense sharply stated as the ius talionis, namely, θλίψις for your persecutors and ἄνεσις for you who are persecuted (cf. Lk. 16²⁵). The principle is put conditionally (εἴπερ), "not indeed as if there were the least doubt respecting the righteousness of any part of the divine procedure in judging the world. On the con-

trary, it is the very certainty of that truth, as something altogether beyond cavil, that emboldens the writer, by a sort of
logical meiosis, to argue from it conditionally" (Lillie; *cf.* Pelagius: *hic "si tamen" confirmantis sermo est, non dubitantis*).
ἄνεσιν μεθ᾽ ὑμῶν. As there is a present fellowship of readers
and writers in suffering (καὶ πάσχετε v. ⁵), so also will there be a
future fellowship in "rest" or "relief" from suffering,—a genuinely Pauline touch (*cf.* 1 Cor. 4⁸ 2 Cor. 1⁶ ᶠᶠ· Phil. 1³⁰).

On the positive side, ἄνεσις is entrance into the kingdom (v. ⁵) and
eternal fellowship with the Lord (v. ¹⁰ as contrasted with v. ⁹; *cf.* I 4¹⁷
πάντοτε σὺν κυρίῳ). θλίψις is, according to v. ⁹, eternal separation from
Christ, the precise opposite of I 4¹⁷. The moral ground of ἄνεσις, not
expressed at this point, is faith leading to endurance as v. ⁴ shows, the ὑμῖν
who are persecuted being those who have exhibited an unusual endurance
inspired by faith. The same stress on faith is seen in v. ¹⁰, "all who
became believers," and in the explanatory clause with ὅτι. The moral
ground of θλίψις, not stated in our verse, is, in the light of v. ⁸, which describes "those who do not reverence God and do not obey the gospel of
our Lord Jesus," the lack of faith and its moral expression. Though the
ius talionis is here exhibited in its clearest form (Ell.), the persecutors of
the readers are not the only ones who are to receive θλίψις, as is evident
from Rom. 2⁸ ᶠᶠ· where the disobedient receive ὀργὴ καὶ θυμός, θλίψις καὶ
στενοχωρία (*cf.* also I 4⁶ Rom. 12¹⁹ 2 Cor. 5¹⁰ Col. 3²⁴ᶠᶠ·, etc.). In Rom.
8¹⁸ ᶠᶠ·, the believers are to get δόξα for their παθήματα; in 2 Cor. 4¹⁷,
δόξα for θλίψις. On the Mosaic *lex talionis*, see the notes of Charles
on Jub. 4³¹ 48¹⁴ and Montefiore on Mt. 5³⁸ ᶠᶠ·.—εἴπερ is found in Gk.
Bib., apart from Paul, only Judith 6⁹ Sus. (Th.) 54, 4 Mac. 11⁷. The
condition is of itself colourless, the truth or error of the assumption being
found, if at all, in the context; here and elsewhere (unless 1 Cor. 8⁵
is excepted), the context implies the truth of the condition with εἴπερ
(Rom. 3³⁰ 8⁹· ¹⁷ 1 Cor. 15¹⁵ 2 Cor. 5³). Chrys. makes εἴπερ = ἐπείπερ.—
παρὰ θεῷ (1 Cor. 7²⁴) or παρὰ τῷ θεῷ (so A here; *cf.* Rom. 2¹¹· ¹³ Gal. 3¹¹ 1
Cor. 3¹⁹) = "in the eyes of," *iudice Deo;* the day of judgment may here
be in mind.—On δίκαιον, *cf.* Phil. 1⁷; on θλίβειν, I 3⁴; on ἀνταποδιδόναι (I
3⁹) as the expression of judicial recompense, *cf.* Rom. 12¹⁹ = Deut. 32³⁵;
also Is. 35⁴ 59¹⁸ 63⁷ 66⁴· ⁶ Jer. 28⁶· ²⁴· ⁵⁶ ᶠ· Sir. 32¹¹, etc.—ἄνεσις (2 Cor.
2¹² 7⁵ 8¹³; Acts 24²³; Lxx.) denotes a let up from restraint; hence "liberty," "license," or, as here and 2 Cor. 7⁵ 8¹³, "relief" as opposed to
θλίψις; *cf.* ἀνάψυξις Acts 3¹⁹. ἡμῶν refers here not to all Christians
(De W.), not to the saints in Israel (Bengel, Ewald), but, in view of the
specific ὑμᾶς and ὑμῖν and of καὶ πάσχετε, which balances μεθ᾽ ἡμῶν, to
Paul and his two associates (Lün. Ell. Lft. Born. Mill. Dob.). In

μεθ' ἡμῶν as in αὐτοὺς ἡμᾶς (v. ⁴), Schmiedel inclines to see the hand of a forger putting Paul in a position of apostolic eminence. On the other hand, Dob. remarks on μεθ' ἡμῶν: "these two little words belong to the genuine Pauline touches for the sake of which no one, with any feeling for the way in which the mind of Paul works, can give up the authenticity of this brief epistle."

7ᵇ-10. The description of the advent unto judgment begins with a temporal phrase, ἐν τῇ ἀποκαλύψει κτλ., which is to be attached to ἀνταποδιδόναι κτλ. (v. ⁶). First, with three prepositional adjuncts (*cf.* I 4¹⁶), the external features of the revelation are described; then the function of the person revealed is indicated, the punishment (διδόντος ἐκδίκησιν) of those who deserve it; then (v. ⁹), with οἵτινες resuming τοῖς μὴ εἰδόσιν κτλ. and with δίκην τίσουσιν resuming διδόντος ἐκδίκησιν, the character of the punishment is exhibited, eternal separation from Christ; and finally, with ὅταν ἔλθῃ (v. ¹⁰), which is grammatically connected with τίσουσιν, the beginning of the eternal fellowship of the saints and all believers with their Lord is suggested, in that, because of what they are, honour and admiration are ascribed to Christ. In writing πᾶσιν τοῖς πιστεύσασιν to balance τοῖς ἁγίοις αὐτοῦ, instead of τοῖς πιστεύουσιν, Paul passes purposely from the general to the specific, having in mind the faint-hearted, as the parenthetical clause with ὅτι which refers distinctly to the welcome accorded to the gospel demonstrates. The ἐν τῇ ἡμέρᾳ which belongs with the infinitives is suspended temporarily by the parenthesis, only to take its place at the end with a solemn effectiveness. As in I 4¹⁶-¹⁷ so here it is Paul himself who is responsible for the rhythmical description in which only such features are mentioned as serve both to bring out the value of the judgment and to inspire hope and assurance in the hearts of the faint-hearted. Though the description abounds in reminiscences from the Lxx., there is but one approximately exact citation, ἀπὸ προσώπου ... ἰσχύος αὐτοῦ (Is. 2¹⁰; *cf.* ὅταν ἔλθῃ 2¹⁰ and ἐν τῇ ἡμέρᾳ ἐκείνῃ 2¹¹).

The passage abounds in allusions to or reminiscences of the Lxx., but the only exact quotation is in v. ⁹, taken from the refrain of Is. 2¹⁰ which is repeated in 2¹⁹· ²¹: ἀπὸ προσώπου τοῦ φόβου κυρίου καὶ ἀπὸ τῆς δόξης τῆς ἰσχύος αὐτοῦ, ὅταν ἀναστῇ θραῦσαι τὴν γῆν; *cf.* ἐν τῇ ἡμέρᾳ

ἐκείνη 2¹¹· ¹⁷. Though the citation is evident, τοῦ φόβου is omitted.
Furthermore in v. ⁸ there is an apparent allusion to Is. 66¹⁵: ἰδοὺ γὰρ
κύριος ὡς πῦρ ἥξει καὶ ὡς καταιγὶς τὰ ἅρματα αὐτοῦ ἀποδοῦναι ἐν θυμῷ
ἐκδίκησιν αὐτοῦ καὶ ἀποσκορακισμὸν αὐτοῦ ἐν φλογὶ πυρός. Paul, however, is composing not copying, as the unique parallelism τοῖς μὴ εἰδόσιν θεὸν καὶ τοῖς μὴ ὑπακούουσιν κτλ. suggests. At the same time,
such passages as Jer. 10²⁵ (cf. Ps. 78⁶): ἔκχεον τὸν θυμόν σου ἐπὶ ἔθνη τὰ
μὴ εἰδότα σε καὶ ἐπὶ γενεὰς αἳ τὸ ὄνομά σου ἐπεκαλέσαντο and Is. 66⁴:
ὅτι ἐκάλεσα αὐτοὺς καὶ οὐχ ὑπήκουσάν μου, ἐλάλησα καὶ οὐκ ἤκουσαν
(cf. Is. 65¹²) may have been running in his mind. In v. ¹⁰, where ἐνδοξασθῆναι and θαυμασθῆναι are in parallelism (cf. the description of God
in Exod. 15¹¹), there seems to be a reminiscence of Ps. 88⁸: ὁ θεὸς ἐνδοξαζόμενος ἐν βουλῇ ἁγίων, μέγας καὶ φοβερὸς ἐπὶ πάντας τοὺς περικύκλῳ
αὐτοῦ, and of Ps. 67³⁵ (א): θαυμαστὸς ὁ θεὸς ἐν τοῖς ἁγίοις αὐτοῦ; cf.
also Is. 49³ and 66⁵: εἴπατε, ἀδελφοὶ ἡμῶν, τοῖς μισοῦσιν ὑμᾶς καὶ βδελυσ-
σομένοις, ἵνα τὸ ὄνομα κυρίου δοξασθῇ (cf. v. ¹² of our chapter) καὶ ὀφθῇ
ἐν τῇ εὐφροσύνῃ αὐτῶν, καὶ ἐκεῖνοι αἰσχυνθήσονται. Other words and
phrases suggest the influence of non-canonical Jewish literature; e. g.
ἀποκάλυψις (cf. Apoc. Bar. 29³ with the note of Charles), ἀγγέλων
δυνάμεως αὐτοῦ (cf. Test. xii, Jud. 3¹⁰ and Eth. En. 61¹⁰ "the angels of
power"), ὄλεθρος αἰώνιος (4 Mac. 10¹⁵ (A); cf. Eth. En. 84⁵ Ps. Sol. 2³⁵
(cf. 3¹²) ἀπώλεια αἰώνιος or (Gebhardt) αἰῶνος). On the other hand,
τίνειν δίκην, a classic expression, is not found elsewhere in Gk. Bib.
(Lxx. uses with δίκην either ἀποδιδόναι or ἀνταποδιδόναι or ἐκδικεῖν; so
also the construction διδόναι ἐκδίκησίν τινι (Lxx. has, however, ἀποδιδόναι
or ἀνταποδιδόναι; cf. Num. 31³ Sir. 12⁶ 32²³). The aorist πιστεύσασιν
(v. ¹⁰) instead of the present is due to the situation. It happens that
"the gospel of our Lord Jesus" like "the gospel of his Son" in Rom. 1⁹
is unique in Paul.

While McGiffert (EB. 5054) throws out the hint that vv. ⁶⁻¹⁰ are a possible interpolation, Born. (cf. Find. lvii and Moff. Introd. 80) suggests
that in vv. ⁶⁻¹⁰ᵃ or vv. ⁷ᵇ⁻¹⁰ᶜ Paul is citing or alluding to a Christian hymn.
It has also been conjectured (cf. Encyc. Brit.¹¹ XXVI, 841) that in
vv. ⁷ᵇ⁻¹⁰ Paul is adapting to his own purposes a fragment of a Jewish
apocalypse or a psalm like one of the Psalms of Solomon. The adapta-
tion would consist in the insertion of Ἰησοῦ (vv. ⁷· ⁸) and of the parenthesis ὅτι . . . ἐφ' ὑμᾶς (v. ¹⁰); and in the substitution of εὐαγγελίῳ (v. ⁸)
for, say, λόγῳ (cf. 2 Ch. 11⁴ A), and of πᾶσιν and πιστεύσασιν (v. ¹⁰) for,
say, πιστεύουσιν (Is. 28¹⁶ B). The insertion of Ἰησοῦ would occur to
any Christian; but the change from λόγῳ to εὐαγγελίῳ betrays the
hand of Paul, for ὑπακούειν τῷ εὐαγγελίῳ is found elsewhere in N. T.
only Rom. 10¹⁶ (First Peter would have used not ὑπακούειν but ἀπει-
θεῖν); and the change from πιστεύουσιν to πᾶσιν πιστεύσασιν is, as the
inserted clause with ὅτι demonstrates, due to one of the two main purposes of the epistle, the encouragement of the faint-hearted. Attrac-

tive as the hypothesis is and accounting as it does excellently for the position of ἐν τῇ ἡμέρᾳ ἐκείνῃ, it is unnecessary (cf. Clemen, *Paulus*, I, 119). For Paul himself, it must be remembered, is quite competent in the Spirit to produce a rhythmical psalm, apocalypse, or prophecy. The description is fragmentary; expected details such as the burning fire, the angels of punishment, the torture of the wicked in the fire of hell in the presence of the righteous are conspicuously absent. The external features of the revelation are few in number and are selected with a view to enhancing the dignity of the Judge. The reason why he executes judgment is clearly stated; the sentence is pronounced simply as eternal separation from Christ, with no details as to the manner of executing the sentence or the nature of the separation. The reward of the righteous, the character of the future felicity is not dwelt upon; in fact, the reward is only intimated—in virtue of what the believers are, Christ receives glory and admiration. The concentration upon the essential and the sole interest in values which signalise the description point rather to the free composition of Paul, influenced by O. T. and later Jewish literature, as is also the case in I 4^{16-17}.

7^b. ἐν τῇ ἀποκαλύψει κτλ. With this clause, the time of the ἀνταποδοῦναι (v. ⁶) is indicated, "at the revelation of the Lord Jesus" = "when the Lord Jesus is revealed" (cf. v. ¹⁰ ὅταν ἔλθῃ). "The advent is here conceived of not as a *Parousia* (cf. I 2¹⁹ 3¹³ 5²³ ἐν τῇ παρουσίᾳ) but as a revelation (so 1 Cor. 1⁷; cf. Lk. 17³⁰) of the Messiah, just as in the first epistle of Peter" (Briggs, *Messiah of the Apostles*, 90 ff.; cf. 1 Pet. 1⁷· ¹³).

Of the twenty-two instances of ἀποκάλυψις in the Gk. Bib., thirteen are in Paul. In the Lxx. the word is used literally of uncovering (1 Reg. 20³⁰) and metaphorically of disclosing works or secrets (Sir. 11²⁷ 22²² 42¹). In Paul, it denotes regularly a prophetic revelation in the Spirit; here, however, and in 1 Cor. 1⁷, it is equivalent to παρουσία. Underlying this use of ἀποκάλυψις may be the idea that the Son of Man is hidden before God and that the elect, though they know him in the Spirit, do not behold him visibly until he comes to function as Messiah (cf. Eth. En. 48⁶ 62⁷; also *revelabitur* of the Messiah in 4 Ezra 13³² Apoc. Bar. 39⁷, etc.; see J. Weiss in Meyer on 1 Cor. 1⁷). Mill., however, who discusses carefully (141–151) ἀποκάλυψις in connection with ἐπιφάνεια (2⁸) and παρουσία concludes that ἐπιφάνεια or manifestation is also a "revelation of the divine plan and purpose which has run through all the ages, to find its consummation at length in the 'one far-off divine event' to which the whole creation is slowly moving." On ὁ κύριος Ἰησοῦς, see I 2¹⁵; L reads τοῦ κυρίου ἡμῶν Ἰ. Χ.

ἀπ' οὐρανοῦ κτλ. With three prepositional phrases (cf. I 4¹⁶), the revelation is described in reference to the place "from heaven," to the attendant retinue "with his angels of power," and to the manner "in a fire of flame." (1) The ἀπ' οὐρανοῦ seems to imply that the Messiah is hidden in heaven, concealed from the sight of men, though he operates in the souls of believers; hence he must be revealed "from heaven" (cf. Rom. 1¹⁸), namely, by coming down from heaven (I 4¹⁶) either toward the earth and within the range of human vision, or to the earth. (2) The ἄγγελοι δυνάμεως αὐτοῦ suggests the ἄγγελος δυνάμεως (Test. xii, Jud. 3¹⁰) and "all the angels of power and all the angels of principalities" (Eth. En. 61¹⁰); and invites the translation "his angels of power" (cf. αὐτοῦ in Rev. 13³ Heb. 1³ Col. 1¹³). (3) The manner in which the revelation is pictured, ἐν πυρὶ φλογός, is in keeping with the descriptions of theophanies in the O. T., for example, Exod. 3² where the ἄγγελος κυρίου appears ἐν πυρὶ φλογὸς ἐκ τοῦ βάτου and Is. 66¹⁵ κύριος ὡς πῦρ ἥξει (cf. Ps. 49³, etc.).

Usually αὐτοῦ is taken solely with δυνάμεως and the gen. is explained as possessive: "which serves to mark that to which the ἄγγελοι appertained and of which they were the ministers; exponents and instruments of his power" (Ell.). Dob. regards "his power" as a periphrasis for "his." Calv. observes: *angelos potentiae vocat in quibus suam potestatem exseret* (cf. Bengel and Schmiedel). Some Gk. fathers (e. g. Theophylact and Œcumenius) and some moderns (e. g. Piscator, Flatt, Jowett) interpret with A. V. "his mighty angels." Still others (see Lillie, *ad loc.*), taking δύναμις = "host" (cf. Ps. 32⁶ 4 Reg. 21⁵, etc.), translate "the host of his angels" (cf. Pesh.). Hofmann avoids the difficulty but spoils the rhythm by joining αὐτοῦ with διδόντος. Since the position of αὐτοῦ allows it, it is simpler to take "angels of power" as a class and αὐτοῦ as a gen. poss. governing both ἄγγελοι and δυνάμεως. On ἄγγελοι, see on I 4¹⁶ and Charles's notes on Eth. En. 61¹⁰ and Slav. En. 20¹.—The phrase ἐν πυρὶ φλογός (ℵAKLP, etc.) is found also in Sir. 8¹⁰ 45¹⁹ (+ αὐτοῦ) Exod. 3² (B) Ps. Sol. 12⁵ Acts 7³⁰ (ACE); the easier reading ἐν φλογὶ πυρός (BDEGF, *et al.*) occurs also in Is. 66¹⁵ Exod. 3² (AF) Acts 7³⁰ (ℵDB, *et al.*); compare the rather frequent φλὸξ πυρός (Is. 29⁶ Dan. 7⁹ Sir. 21⁹, etc.). The reference is to the glorious brilliancy of the revelation. Some commentators however (see Lillie), because of the present connection with judgment, assume that the fire is a burning, purifying fire (cf. the ποταμὸς πυρός in Dan. 7¹⁰) as in 1 Cor. 3¹³; and join the ἐν closely with διδόντος, thus specifying the manner or instrument of punishment. Still others (e. g. Lft. Dob.) are inclined to make the fire do double service. On the idea involved, see Bousset, *Relig.*² 320.

8. διδόντος ἐκδίκησιν κτλ. The revelation of the Lord Jesus is further described by the loosely attached διδόντος (agreeing not with φλογός, which is feminine, but with τοῦ κυρίου Ἰησοῦ) as a revelation unto judgment, resuming the thought of v. ⁶ but putting it generally. The objects of the divine justice are defined in a unique parallelism as "those who do not know (that is, respect and worship) God and those who do not obey the gospel of our Lord Jesus." Since ἔθνεσιν does not appear in the first member (contrast I 4⁵ Jer. 10²⁵ Ps. 78⁶), and since the repetition of the article is not incompatible with synonymous parallelism (cf. Ps. 35¹¹), it is not certain, though the usage of Paul makes it probable, that the Gentiles are in mind in the first member (cf. I 4³ Gal. 4⁸ Rom. 1²⁸ Eph. 2¹²) and the Jews in the second member (cf. especially Rom. 10¹⁶). Though the statement is general, Paul may have had in mind distinctly τοῖς θλίβουσιν ὑμᾶς (v. ⁶) who were both Gentiles, the official persecutors and Jews, the instigators of persecution.

The distinction, assumed above as probable, is made among others by Ephr. Grot. Lün. Lillie, Ell. Dob. On the other hand, since ἔθνεσιν is omitted and the article repeated in the second member is unobjectionable, the parallelism may be synonymous (cf. v. ¹⁰ ἁγίοις and πιστεύσασιν), and non-Christians, irrespective of race, may be meant (e. g. Calv. Vincent, Mill.); in fact, Paul refers to the disobedience of the Gentiles (Rom. 11³⁰); but does not, as the O. T. (e. g. Jer. 9⁶) does, speak of the Jews as not knowing God. Still other interpreters, while distinguishing two classes, take the first member as referring to the Gentiles with a distinct allusion to Jer. 10²⁵, and the second as referring to both Jews and Gentiles (e. g. Lft. Schmiedel, Born. Wohl.).—Though the first member of the parallelism may have been influenced unconsciously by Jer. 10²⁵ and the second by Is. 66⁴, yet the parallelism as a whole is unique and the second member distinctly Pauline; for ὑπακούειν τῷ εὐαγγελίῳ is not found in Lxx. Ps. Sol. Test. xii, or Apost. Fathers, and is found elsewhere in N. T. only Rom. 10¹⁶.—The exact phrase "the gospel of our Lord Jesus" is, like "the gospel of his Son" in Rom. 1⁹, unique in the N. T. The substitution of "our Lord Jesus" for "Christ" is natural in view of the divine name ὁ κύριος ἡμῶν Ἰησοῦς (see on I 2¹⁹); and in Rom. 1⁹ "the gospel of his Son" is natural in view

of Rom. 1³ τοῦ υἱοῦ αὐτοῦ. In our passage, אAGF add Χριστοῦ to Ἰησοῦ.
—On διδόναι ἐκδίκησίν τινι, cf. Num. 31³ Sir. 12⁶ (ἀποδιδόναι) and Deut.
32⁴³ Sir. 32²³ (ἀνταποδιδόναι); more frequent in Lxx. is ποιεῖν ἐκδίκησιν
ἔν τινι (Exod. 12¹² Num. 33⁴ Ezek. 25¹⁷, etc.). On ἐκδίκησις (Rom. 12¹⁹
2 Cor. 7¹¹), see ἔκδικος I 4⁶.—GF insert καί before ἐν πυρί; DGF read
διδούς for διδόντος; Stephanus begins v. ⁸ with *in flamma ignis*; PL
insert τόν before θεόν conforming to I 4⁵.—ὑπακούειν (Rom. 6¹² ff.) is
common in Lxx. and construed usually with gen., sometimes with dat.
(2 Ch. 11⁴ (A) Jer. 3²⁵).

9. οἵτινες δίκην κτλ. "Men who shall pay the penalty of
eternal destruction from the presence of the Lord Jesus and from
the glory of his strength." With οἵτινες, designating a class,
τοῖς μὴ εἰδόσιν . . . Ἰησοῦ (v. ⁸) is resumed; similarly with
δίκην τίσουσιν, the διδόντος ἐκδίκησιν (v. ⁸) is resumed. An
advance over v. ⁸ is, however, made in that the penalty is an-
nounced as an eternal banishment from Christ.

ὄλεθρον αἰώνιον. This phrase, in apposition with δίκην, occurs
elsewhere in the Gk. Bib. only 4 Mac. 10¹⁵ (A); it is equivalent
(see I 5³) to ἀπώλεια αἰώνιος or αἰῶνος in Ps. Sol. 2³⁵ (cf. Eth.
En. 84⁵). The destruction resulting from the supernatural conflict or as here from a forensic judgment involves for Paul not
the annihilation of the wicked (for they exist after death even
if they are not raised from the dead) but their separation from
Christ, as the defining clause with ἀπό intimates. In the light
of αἰώνιος, ὄλεθρος might mean the definitive supernatural act
belonging to the age to come; but in view of ἀπό κτλ., it must
rather refer to the destruction whose consequences are age-long,
that is, to Paul and to the N. T. in general, "eternal" (Mk. 3²⁹
Mt. 25⁴⁶; cf. Dan. 12²). Beyond the statement of the fact of an
eternal banishment and separation, Paul does not go; he says
nothing of πῦρ αἰώνιον (Jude 7 Mt. 18⁸ 25⁴¹).

ἀπὸ προσώπου κυρίου κτλ. The banishment from Christ is
expressed in language drawn from the refrain of Is. 2¹⁰· ¹⁹· ²¹:
ἀπὸ προσώπου τοῦ φόβου τοῦ κυρίου καὶ ἀπὸ τῆς δόξης τῆς
ἰσχύος αὐτοῦ. In citing this passage, however, Paul omits τοῦ
φόβου, leaving προσώπου (see I 2¹⁷) to be explained as "face,"
"presence," and ἀπό as a preposition after an implied verb of
separation. Then in the second member of the virtually synony-

mous parallelism, "face" becomes "glory," the halo of majesty
which lightens the face of the Lord; and "the Lord" becomes
"his strength," the *fons et origo* of the glory (ἰσχύος being a
genitive of origin). Thus, with a concentration upon the essential, the θλίψις of v. ⁶ is defined as an eternal separation
from the glorious presence of Christ, this penalty being the
direct opposite of the reward of the believer (v. ¹⁰), namely, as
I 4¹⁷ states that reward, πάντοτε σὺν κυρίῳ.

The classic distinction between ὅς and ὅστις (found in every letter
of Paul except I and Phile.) is apparently observed by Paul (Bl. 50¹);
hence *quippe qui*, "men who" (Ell. Lft. Mill.; also SH. on Rom. 1²⁵).
—δίκη, a classic word, rare in N. T. (Jude 7 Acts 28⁴) but common in
Lxx., means either "justice" (Sap. 1⁸), "suit at law" (Job 29¹⁶) or "punishment" (Sap. 18¹¹ 2 Mac. 8¹¹· ¹³ 4 Mac. 6²⁸ 9³²). τίνειν is found elsewhere in Gk. Bib. only Pr. 20²² 24²²· ⁴⁴ 27¹² (τίειν); the phrase τίνειν
δίκην is classic, but is not found elsewhere in Gk. Bib.; it is equivalent
to τίνειν ζημίαν (Pr. 27¹²), or ζημιοῦν (1 Cor. 3¹⁵); *cf.* ἐκδικεῖν δίκην
(Lev. 26²⁵ Ezek. 25¹²); ἀποδιδόναι or ἀνταποδιδόναι δίκην (Deut. 32⁴¹· ⁴³).
—With the phrase ὄλεθρος αἰώνιος (see Vincent, *ad loc.*) is to be compared ζωὴ αἰώνιος (Rom. 2⁷ 5²¹ 6²² ᶠ· Gal. 6⁸), destruction being the opposite of life. The adjective or its equivalent αἰῶνος is common in the
Lxx. (*e. g.* Sir. 15⁶ 17¹² 45¹⁵; Ps. Sol. 2³⁵); its meaning is to be determined not from Greek etymology but from the usage of עולם, that is, long
duration whether looking forward or backward, to futurity or antiquity
(BDB.). The exact duration intended depends upon the writer; in Eth.
En. 10¹¹ the ζωὴ αἰώνιος is five hundred years; in Daniel as in the N. T.
the age to come is of unlimited duration; hence αἰώνιος "belonging to
the age" means to Paul "eternal" and "everlasting." A reads ὀλέθριον
(*cf.* 3 Reg. 21⁴² Sap. 18¹⁵). On the duration of punishment in Jewish
literature, see Bousset, *Relig.*² 320, Volz. *Eschat.* 286 *ff.*, and Kennedy,
Last Things, 316; on αἰών, see Dalman, *Worte Jesu*, I, 120 *ff.*—That ἀπό
is local, as in Gal. 5⁴ Rom. 9³ 2 Cor. 11³, is generally admitted (Piscator,
Riggenbach, Lün. Ell. Lft. Born. Vincent, Mill. Dob. *et al.*). Grammatically possible, however, is (1) the causal sense of ἀπό, frequent in Lxx.,
but infrequent in N. T. (Bl. 40³), "at the presence of," the thought being
that the very face of the Lord causes destruction. In this interpretation, no hint is given that destruction consists in eternal separation.
"It is sufficient that God comes and is seen and all are involved in punishment and penalty" (Chrys. *apud* Ell.). (2) The ἀπό may indicate
source,—"the eternal destruction which proceeds from the face," etc.
(*cf.* Acts 3¹⁹; so apparently Grot. Schmiedel, Find. Wohl.). (3) Possible also grammatically but "pointless in sense" (Find.) is the expla-

nation of ἀπό as temporal, "from the time of the revelation of the Lord" (see Lillie for names). Much simpler is it to take ἀπό of separation. That Paul says not ἀπό but ἀπὸ προσώπου (only here in Paul; *cf.* Acts 5⁴¹ 7⁴⁵ Rev. 6¹⁶ 12¹⁴ 20¹¹) κυρίου is due to the influence of Isa. 2¹⁰.—On δόξα, see I 2⁶; on ἰσχύς (Eph. 1¹⁹ 6¹⁰), rare in N. T. but common in Lxx., see especially 1 Ch. 16²⁸ Ps. 146⁵.—DGF omit τοῦ before κυρίου.—In his references to the destruction of the wicked (vv. ⁶ᵃ· ⁸⁻⁹), Paul refrains from details, contenting himself with the fact of eternal separation. Furthermore, since ἐν πυρὶ φλογός describes not the means of punishment but the manner of the Christophany, it is probable that "his angels of power" are not the angels of punishment (Eth. En. 62¹¹ ᶠ·) but the attendant retinue of angels who accord to Christ glory and admiration by reason of his saving work manifested in the saints and believers who stand before the βῆμα Χριστοῦ (v. ¹⁰).

10. ὅταν ἔλθῃ κτλ. With this relative conditional sentence designating the time of δίκην τίσουσιν, Paul resumes the point of vv. ⁵· ⁷ᵃ and indicates the beginning of the future salvation of the readers which is eternal fellowship with the Lord. This indication is put in a unique parallelism the language of which betrays the influence of the Lxx.: "when he comes (ὅταν ἔλθῃ balancing ἐν τῇ ἀποκαλύψει τοῦ κυρίου v. ⁷) to be glorified in his saints (that is, in virtue of what they are; *cf.* Gal. 2²⁴ ἐδόξαζον ἐν ἐμοὶ τὸν θεόν) and to be admired in all who became believers . . . in that day." Though the parallelism is synonymous, the presence in the second member of πᾶσιν and of the aorist τοῖς πιστεύσασιν (instead of the expected present τοῖς πιστεύουσιν; *cf.* I 2¹⁰· ¹³) indicates an advance from the general to the specific. Included in the number of the saints are particularly the faint-hearted Thessalonians who became believers when they welcomed the word (I 1⁶ ᶠᶠ· 2¹³ ᶠᶠ·); "for," as the parenthetical clause with ὅτι (separating "in that day" from the infinitives to which it belongs) explains, "our witness (= our gospel) which was directed to you was believed" (ἐπιστεύθη being suggested by πιστεύσασιν).

Both ὅταν and ἐν τῇ ἡμέρᾳ (a phrase only here in Paul; *cf.* Lk. 10¹² 17³¹ 2 Tim. 1¹⁸ 4⁸) seem to have been influenced by Is. 2¹⁰ ᶠᶠ·; on the other hand, the total phrase ἐνδοξασθῆναι . . . τοῖς πιστεύσασιν, though it shows traces of resemblance to Ps. 88⁸ 67³⁶ (א) Is. 49³ 66⁵, is unique. The verb ἐνδοξάζεσθαι, here and v. ¹² (*cf.* Is. 66⁵), like ἐνκαυχᾶσθαι (v. ⁴),

is unclassic; it is found about thirteen times in the Lxx., usually with
ἐν (cf. Exod. 15¹¹ δεδοξασμένος ἐν ὑμῖν, θαυμαστὸς ἐν δόξαις). This ἐν
(which is also frequent with the more common δοξάζεσθαι) is in the Lxx.
to be explained either as (1) of place where (Ps. 88⁸ ἐνδοξαζόμενος ἐν
βουλῇ ἁγίων; Ps. 67³⁶ (א) θαυμαστὸς ἐν τοῖς ἁγίοις αὐτοῦ; cf. 1 Mac.
3¹⁴ א); (2) of instrument (Is. 49³ (B); cf. δοξάζεσθαι ἐν Is. 5¹⁶, etc.);
or (3) of ground (Is. 45²⁵ Sir 38⁶; cf. δοξάζεσθαι ἐν Sir. 48⁴; θαυμάζεσθαι
ἐν Is. 61⁶ (B). The ἐν is not διά (Sir. 10³⁰) or ὑπό (Sir. 3²⁰)). Were Paul
distinctly quoting Ps. 88⁸ 67³⁶, it would be natural to take ἐν of place
where, "among" (Michaelis, Van Ess., and others noted by Lillie; so
also Dob.), in spite of the fact that the local sense does not fit v. ¹²
(ἐν αὐτῷ). This theory, however, does not compel us to assume that the
persons who accord the glory and admiration are not "his angels of
power" but Christians. On the other hand, since Paul is not quoting,
and since his interest is not in the external features of the judgment but
is in the character of the people (cf. v. ⁸) present, it is more probable that
ἐν is to be understood not of place, or even of instrument (Chrys. Bengel;
ἐν = διά with gen.), but of ground (Grot. Lün. Ell. Lillie, Lft. Schmiedel, Born. Find. Wohl. Mill. et al.); cf. Pelagius: "he himself is to
be glorified in his members which shall shine with the brightness of the
sun" (on this ἐν, see Gal. 1²⁴ 1 Cor. 6²⁰). In virtue of what the saints
and all believers are (by reason of the death and the indwelling of Christ),
the attendant angels ascribe glory and admiration to Christ. This view
of ἐν is also applicable to the ἐν of v. ¹². There is no hint that the glory
which proceeds from the Lord has already entered into the Christians.
—On θαυμάζεσθαι ἐν, cf. Sap. 8¹¹ (ἐν of place), Sir. 33⁴ (א; ἐν of instrument), and Is. 61⁶ (B; ἐν of ground).—οἱ ἅγιοι αὐτοῦ is in synonymous
parallelism with πάντες οἱ πιστεύσαντες; both refer to Christians irrespective of race.—That ὅτι . . . ὑμᾶς is parenthetical was noted by Th.
Mops. Zim. and Wohl. less naturally connect ὅτι with the preceding
infinitives, "to be glorified and admired in the fact that our witness,"
etc.—τὸ μαρτύριον (see I 1⁵) = τὸ εὐαγγέλιον (v. ⁸); τὸ μαρτύριον ἡμῶν
(which is equivalent to τὸ εὐαγγέλιον ἡμῶν 2¹⁴ I 1⁵ and τὸ κήρυγμα ἡμῶν
1 Cor. 15¹⁴) is the witness, inspired by God (1 Cor. 2¹) or Christ (1 Cor.
1⁶), which we preach. It is the witness which (sc. τό) is (not "against"
you; Lk. 9⁵ Num. 35³⁰ A; but) "over" you (1 Mac. 2³⁷ μαρτυρεῖ ἐφ᾽
ὑμᾶς ὁ οὐρανὸς καὶ ἡ γῆ).—ἐπιστεύθη = "was believed," as πιστεύσασιν
suggests, the reference being to the welcome given to the gospel at the
beginning. It is interesting that πιστεύεσθαι in this sense is used with
an impersonal subject elsewhere in the N. T. only Rom. 10¹⁰ (contrast
1 Tim. 3¹⁶). Lft. joins ἐπιστεύθη with ἐπί and paraphrases thus:
"belief in our testimony directed itself to reach you." Hort and Moff.
accept Markland's conjecture ἐπιστώθη (which Cod. 104 reads). Hort
explains in connection with vv. ⁴⁻⁵ that "the Christian testimony had
been confirmed and sealed upon the Thessalonians." He compares

238 2 THESSALONIANS

1 Cor. 1⁶ Ps. 92⁴·⁵ and πιστοῦσθαι ἐπί τινα 1 Ch. 17²³ (which is doubtful) and 2 Ch. 1⁹. The conjecture, however, is unnecessary.

11–12. Though the faint-hearted may thus be assured of their
being deemed worthy of the kingdom, yet (cf. I 5⁸ ᶠᶠ·) they must
be blameless (cf. I 3¹³) in order to enter into the same. Since
blamelessness is possible only through the power of God, Paul
adds a prayer: "to which end (namely, the future salvation implied in v. ¹⁰; cf. ἄνεσιν v. ⁸ and εἰς τὸ καταξιωθῆναι v. ⁵), we
too as well as you pray always that our God may deem you
worthy (that is, acquit you at the judgment) of the calling (of
God mediated by the preaching of our witness; cf. 2¹⁴) and (that
the acquittal may follow) bring to completion every resolve after
goodness and every work inspired by faith in power" (that is,
of the Spirit). This prayer for moral perfection is to the eventual
end "that (ὅπως) the name of our Lord Jesus may be glorified in
you (that is, as in v. ¹⁰, in virtue of what you are) and you may
be glorified in it" (that is, in virtue of what his name accom-
plishes). And this blessed consummation is "in accordance with
the divine favour of our God and the Lord Jesus Christ."

11. εἰς ὃ καὶ προσευχόμεθα κτλ. Though εἰς ὅ is loosely attached to the preceding and refers to the idea of salvation implied in v. ¹⁰, it is yet tempting (with Lft.) to connect it directly
with εἰς τὸ καταξιωθῆναι (v. ⁵), the controlling idea of vv. ⁵⁻¹²
being that the faint-hearted may be assured of their being deemed
worthy of the kingdom. In this case, εἰς ὅ denotes purpose "to
which end," and is resumed by ἵνα (likewise telic) ἀξιώσῃ (cf.
ἄξιον v. ³). The καί before προσευχόμεθα is interesting. In the
letter from Thessalonica to Paul it appeared that the faint-
hearted, though anxious about their salvation, were nevertheless praying constantly that God would equip them with the
Spirit whose presence guaranteed a blameless life and the acquittal at the last day. This prayer Paul reciprocates, "we too
as well as you pray" (καί as in I 2¹³; cf. Col. 1⁹).

That εἰς ὅ indicates purpose is recognised by De W. Riggenbach,
Lillie, Lft. Born. Vincent, Find. Mill. and others. The objection that
it is logically impossible (e. g. Lün. Dob.) overlooks Paul's recognition of the facts of religious experience and his interest in righteousness

as essential unto future salvation (cf. I 3¹³ 5⁸⁻⁹). To be sure salvation is assured to those who are in Christ, but the test of being in Christ is ethical. Those who deny the telic force of εἰς ὅ take it of reference (Lün. Ell. Schmiedel, Dob. *et al.*). On εἰς τοῦτο ἵνα, *cf.* Rom 14⁹ 2 Cor. 2⁹; on ἵνα . . . εἰς ὅ καί, *cf.* Col. 1²⁸ ᶠ·; on εἰς ὅ, see further 2¹⁴ Phil. 3¹⁶.—Bacon sees the force of καί but interprets differently: "it is clear that they had assured him of their prayers in his behalf, as requested I 5²⁵" (*Introd.* 72). Others see in καί the intimation of a correspondence between prayer on the one hand and on the other hope (Ell.), witness (Find.), or thanksgiving (Riggenbach, Wohl. Dob. Moff.). —Influenced by I 5²⁵ D inserts a second καί before περὶ ὑμῶν. On πάντοτε, see I 1²; on προσεύχεσθαι περί, see I 5²⁵. For the prayer at this point, *cf.* Phil. 1⁹ Col. 1⁹.

ἵνα ὑμᾶς ἀξιώσῃ κτλ. Since ἵνα resumes εἰς ὅ, it is to be taken not epexegetically as introducing the content of the prayer, but finally, "to which end, namely, that." The ὑμᾶς, emphatically placed, resumes the specific ὑμᾶς of vv. ¹⁰· ⁵. "The calling" (1 Cor. 7²⁰ Eph. 4¹) is, in view of "our God," to be interpreted not as "your calling" (1 Cor. 1²⁶ Eph. 4⁴) but as "God's calling" (Rom. 11²⁹ Phil. 3¹⁴; *cf.* Vulg. *vocatione sua*), the reference being to God's act of calling in the past (I 2¹² 4⁷ 5²⁴) mediated through the preaching of the gospel (2¹⁴), *i. e.* "our witness to you" (v. ¹⁰). ὁ θεὸς ἡμῶν, a characteristic phrase in our letters (see I 2²), intimates that just as there is a common suffering of Paul and his readers (καὶ πάσχετε v. ⁵), and a common relief (μεθ᾽ ὑμῶν v.⁷), so also there is a common fellowship in God, the ultimate source of salvation.

Many interpreters find difficulty in referring κλῆσις to the past, on the ground, apparently, that the historical call of God of itself involves future salvation. Paul, however, while practically certain that all believers will be acquitted at the βῆμα Χριστοῦ because of the presence in them of Christ or the Spirit as the power unto righteousness, reckons with the possibility that believers may fall out of the realm of grace and disregard the promptings of the Spirit (*cf.* I 3¹³ 5⁸ ᶠᶠ· Gal. 5⁴ 2 Cor. 6¹, and the implications of Phil. 2¹²). To avoid the supposed difficulty, κλῆσις, contrary to Paul's usage, is understood of the future glory and blessedness (Th. Mops. *ut dignos vos bonorum illorum exhibeat deus, in quorum et vocati estis fruitionem; cf.* Calv. Riggenbach, Ell. Lft. Mill. *et al.*) either on the analogy of Phil. 3¹⁴, of ἐλπίς in Col. 1⁵, or of the Synoptic "invitation" to the Messianic Supper (Mt. 22³· ⁸; *cf.* Chrys. Schmiedel,

Wohl. *et al.*). Others, contrary to usage, take ἀξιόω to mean "to make
worthy" (Grot. Flatt, Dob. *et al.*). Better Pelagius: "that ye may be
found worthy of that to which you have been called" (*cf.* Ephr. Born.
Find. *et al.*). G reads τῆς κλήσεως ὑμῶν; KL ὁ θεὸς ὑμῶν. Outside of
Paul, κλῆσις occurs infrequently in the Gk. Bib. (2 Tim. 1⁹ Heb. 3¹
2 Pet. 1¹⁰ Judith 12¹⁰ (A) Jer. 38⁶ 3 Mac. 5¹⁴).

καὶ πληρώσῃ κτλ. Since ἀξιώσῃ means not "make worthy"
but "deem worthy," πληρώσῃ is not synonymous with ἀξιώσῃ
but rather, as Lillie remarks, "regards the process by which
alone the object of the Apostle's heart could be secured. Whom
he counts worthy, he first makes worthy." In order that God
may acquit the believers at the judgment, he must by the power
of the Spirit perfect in them every resolve after goodness and
every work that faith inspires.

πᾶσαν εὐδοκίαν ἀγαθωσύνης. The first of the parallel objects
of πληρώσῃ touches the inner purpose, "every resolve (not 'desire,' as if with Cod. 17 ἐπιθυμίαν were read) that they have
after goodness" (the genitive is objective). The phrase εὐδοκία
ἀγαθωσύνης does not appear elsewhere in the Gk. Bib. In εὐδοκία as in εὐδοκεῖν (I 2⁸), the prominent thought is that of
"will," "resolve," "consent." "Goodness" (ἀγαθωσύνη, elsewhere in N. T. only Gal. 5²² Rom. 15¹⁴ Eph. 5⁹) is a fruit of the
Spirit (Gal. 5²²) akin to χρηστότης; over against κακία it denotes singleness of heart (Sap. 1¹; *cf.* Col. 3²² Eph. 6⁵).

καὶ ἔργον πίστεως. "And every (*sc.* πᾶν) work of faith."
This second of the parallel objects of πληρώσῃ refers to the activity inspired by faith, that is, not specifically endurance in persecution (Chrys.), but generally, as the omission of the articles
(in keeping with εὐδοκίαν ἀγαθωσύνης) suggests, love (*cf.* I 1³).
Paul prays that God may perfect not only the resolve but the
accomplishment of the same.

ἐν δυνάμει. "In power," that is, in the power of God (Ephr.).
The phrase, which is to be construed with πληρώσῃ, puts the
stress on the energy exercised by the divine (Rom. 1⁴ Col. 1²⁹).
The δύναμις θεοῦ is Christ (1 Cor. 1²⁴) or the Spirit (I 1⁵) without whose aid the resolve after goodness and the attainment of
love would be impossible.

ἀγαθωσύνη is quite frequent in Koheleth; *cf.* also Neh. 9²⁵· ³⁵; εὐδοκία, apart from Lk. 2¹⁴ 10²¹ Mt. 11²⁶, is employed in N. T. only by Paul (of God Phil. 2¹³ Eph. 1⁵· ⁹; *cf.* Sir. 32⁵ 41⁴; of men Rom. 10¹ Phil. 1¹⁵); on its meaning, see SH. or Zahn on Rom. 10¹, also Kennedy, *Sources*, 131.—Since εὐδοκία need not refer to God's good will, "goodness which is his good pleasure" (Grot.), "his good pleasure proceeding from his goodness" (Calv.), or "his good pleasure in the goodness of men" (Dob.), it is unnecessary, especially in a context in which moral excellence is in mind, to take ἔργον πίστεως = "work which is faith" (gen. of apposition), that is, God's work of faith (Calv. Dob.). In fact most commentators rightly refer both εὐδοκία and ἔργον to the Thessalonians (De W. Lün. Ell. Lillie, Lft. Mill. and especially Schmiedel and Wohl. who note the progress from will (εὐδοκία) to deed (ἔργον)).

12. ὅπως ἐνδοξασθῇ κτλ. The clause with ὅπως (dependent on ἵνα v. ¹¹) states the ultimate purpose of the prayer in language reminiscent of Is. 66⁵, and similar to but more specific than (not ἐν τοῖς ἁγίοις αὐτοῦ but ἐν ὑμῖν) that of v. ¹⁰: "that the name of our Lord Jesus may be glorified in you," that is, in virtue of (ἐν of ground as in v. ¹⁰) what you are at the last day, blameless in holiness. Following the usage of the O. T., ὄνομα signifies what is involved in the Christian estimate of Jesus, namely, his Lordship and Messiahship (κύριος and Χριστός, Acts 2³⁶ Phil. 2⁹ ᶠᶠ·). Here, however (contrast Phil. 2¹¹ 1 Cor. 1²· ¹⁰ 6¹¹ Eph. 5²⁰), only the Lordship is mentioned (AGP, *et al.*, add Χριστοῦ); the name is not simply Jesus, but "our Lord Jesus" (1 Cor. 5⁴; *cf.* Col. 3¹⁷). The idea underlying the clause with ὅπως seems to be that at the last judgment, at the beginning of the eternal fellowship with Christ, the name "our Lord Jesus" is named with loud acclaims (perhaps by the attendant angelic hosts), in virtue of the goodness and love of the Thessalonians perfected by God through the Spirit. What was in God's purpose, "that they be deemed worthy of the kingdom of God" (v. ⁵), will then be realised.

καὶ ὑμεῖς ἐν αὐτῷ. Advancing beyond v. ¹⁰, Paul here states explicitly that the relation in glory between the Lord Jesus and his servants is reciprocal; they too are accorded honour and glory in virtue of what the name of our Lord Jesus has done for them: "and that you may be glorified in (ἐν of ground) it," that is, the name.

16

κατὰ τὴν χάριν κτλ. The glorification for which prayer is made is in accordance with the divine favour (I 1¹) of "our God" (v. ¹¹) and the Lord Jesus Christ, just as it is with the purpose of God (v. ⁵). The statement is put positively; a contrast with human effort is not here indicated (contrast with Lft. Rom. 4¹⁶ 11⁵ ᶠ· Eph. 2⁵· ⁸).

In view of v. ¹⁰ and of ὅπως after ἵνα, it is all but certain that the reference here is not to the present (Dob.) but to the future glorification (so most). In Paul, ὅπως is much less frequent than ἵνα; for the sequence here, cf. 1 Cor. 1²⁷ ᶠᶠ· 2 Cor. 8¹³ ᶠ·.—On ὄνομα, cf. Ps. 85⁹· ¹² Is. 24¹⁵ 42¹⁰ Mal. 1¹¹ Dan. 3²⁶, and see Deiss. BS. 35 ff. 143 ff., NBS. 24 ff., and TLZ. 1904, 199 ff. The parallelism makes probable that αὐτῷ refers to ὄνομα (Hofmann, Lün. Schmiedel, Wohl. Dob.); the meaning would be the same were the reference to "our Lord Jesus." Neither here nor in v. ¹⁰ is there a clear hint of δόξα entering into the believer.—GF omit καὶ ὑμεῖς . . . Χριστοῦ.—In the salutations ἀπὸ θεοῦ πατρὸς (ἡμῶν) καὶ κυρίου Ἰησοῦ Χριστοῦ, the article is omitted as the formulæ are fixed. The presence of τοῦ here before θεοῦ has led some scholars to think that one person alone is meant, "Jesus Christ, our God and Lord." Hofmann, Riggenbach, and Wohl. find the justification for Christ as God in Rom. 9⁵ (cf. Tit. 2¹³ Jn. 20²⁸ 2 Pet. 1¹· ¹¹); Dob. would delete καὶ κυρίου Ἰ. Χ. as a gloss; Hilgenfeld sees in the phrase an evidence of the spuriousness of II. Inasmuch, however, as ὁ θεὸς ἡμῶν (not θεὸς ἡμῶν) is characteristic of our letters (see I 2²), and κύριος Ἰησοῦς Χριστός, without the article, is a fixed formula, it is probable that we should, with most interpreters, distinguish between "our God" and "the Lord Jesus Christ." K omits τοῦ; the Latins naturally do not help.

III. EXHORTATION (2¹⁻¹²).

The discouragement of those converts who feared that they were not morally prepared for the day of judgment (1³⁻¹²) was intensified by the assertion of some, perhaps the idle brethren, supported, it was alleged, by the authority of Paul, that the day of the Lord was actually present. Paul, who receives news of the situation orally or by letter, together with a request for information about the *Parousia* and *Assembling*, is at a loss to understand how anything he had said in the Spirit, orally, or in his previous epistle, could be misconstrued to imply that he was responsible for the misleading assertion, "the day of the Lord is

present." Believing, however, that the statement has been innocently attributed to him, and feeling sure that a passing allusion
to his original oral instruction concerning times and seasons will
make plain the absurdity of the assertion, and at the same time
quiet the agitation of the faint-hearted, he answers the request
in words not of warning but of encouragement (*cf.* also vv. [13 f.]).
"Do not be discouraged," he says in effect, "for the day of the
Lord, though not far distant, will not be actually present until
first of all the *Anomos* comes; and again be not discouraged, for
the advent of the *Anomos* is intended not for you believers, but
solely for the unbelievers, and destruction sudden and definitive
is in store both for him and for them."

> The exhortation falls roughly into four parts (1) the object of the ex-
> hortation (vv. [1-2]); (2) the reason why the day of the Lord is not present
> (vv. [3-8 a]); (3) the triumph of the good over the evil in the destruction of
> the *Anomos* (v. [8 b. c]); and (4) the spiritual significance of the *Parousia*
> of the *Anomos* (vv. [9-12]). There is no formal counterpart in I either of the
> exhortation or of the preceding prayer (1[11-12]); furthermore the material
> of 2[1-12] like that of 1[5-12] is, compared with I, almost wholly new.

[1]*Now brothers, in reference to the coming of our Lord Jesus
Christ and our gathering together to meet him, we ask you* [2]*not to be
readily unsettled in your mind or to be nervously wrought up by the
statement made by Spirit, orally, or by letter, as if we had made it,
that the day of the Lord is present.*
   [3]*Let no one deceive you in any way whatever: for (the day of the
Lord will not be present) unless first of all there comes the apostasy
and there be revealed the man of lawlessness, the son of perdition;*
[4]*the one who opposes and exalts himself against every one called God
or an object of worship so that he sits (or, attempts to sit) in the
temple of God and proclaims (or, attempts to proclaim) that he himself is really God.* [5]*You remember, do you not, that when I was yet
with you, I used to tell you these things?* [6]*And as to the present
time, you know the spirit or power that detains him (or, is holding
sway), in order that he (the lawless one) may be revealed in his appointed time.* [7]*For, the secret of lawlessness has already been set in
operation; only (the apostasy will not come and the Anomos will
not be revealed) until the person who now detains him (or, is now*

holding sway) is put out of the way. ⁸*And then will be revealed
the Anomos whom the Lord Jesus will slay with the breath of his
mouth and will destroy with the manifestation of his coming.*

⁹*Whose coming, according to the energy of Satan, attended by all
power and signs and wonders inspired by falsehood* ¹⁰*and by all
deceit inspired by unrighteousness, is for those destined to destruction; doomed because they had not welcomed the love for the truth
unto their salvation.* ¹¹*And so for this reason, it is God that sends
them an energy of delusion that they may believe the falsehood;*
¹²*that (finally) all may be judged who have not believed the truth
but have consented to that unrighteousness.*

1–2. First stating the theme as given him in their letter, "concerning the advent and the assembling to meet him" (v. ¹), Paul
exhorts the readers not to let their minds become easily unsettled,
and not to be nervously wrought up by the assertion, however
conveyed and by whatever means attributed to him, that the
day of the Lord is actually present (v. ²).

1. ἐρωτῶμεν δὲ ὑμᾶς ἀδελφοί. In this phrase (which = I 5¹²),
δέ marks a transition from the thanksgiving and prayer (1³⁻¹²)
to a new epistolary section, the exhortation (vv. ¹⁻¹²). But the
same people are chiefly in mind here as in 1³⁻¹², the faint-hearted,
though the converts as a whole are addressed, and that too affectionately, "brothers" (1³).

ὑπὲρ τῆς παρουσίας κτλ. The prepositional phrase, introduced
by ὑπέρ = περί (see 1⁴ and I 3² 5¹⁰), announces the two closely
related subjects (note the single τῆς) about which the readers of
I had solicited information, "the coming of our (B and Syr. omit
ἡμῶν) Lord Jesus" and "our assembling unto him." The addition of ἐπ' αὐτόν intimates that not only the well-known
muster (ἐπισυναγωγή) of the saints (cf. Mk. 13²⁷ = Mt. 24³¹)
that precedes the rapture (I 4¹⁷) is meant, but also the sequel of
the rapture (σὺν κυρίῳ εἶναι, I 4¹⁷).

Since ἐρωτάω is rare in Paul (see on I 4¹), it is not strange that ἐρωτάω
ὑπέρ is unique in Paul; he uses, however, παρακαλεῖν ὑπέρ (see on I 3²)
as well as παρακαλοῦμεν δὲ ὑμᾶς ἀδελφοί (I 4¹⁰ 5¹⁴; cf. Rom. 15³⁰ 16¹⁷
1 Cor. 1¹⁰ 16¹⁵); cf. further οὐ θέλομεν ἀγνοεῖν περί (I 4¹³ 1 Cor. 12¹, and
2 Cor. 1⁸ (אAC, et al.) where BKL have ὑπέρ). On the exact phrase

ἡ παρουσία κτλ., cf. I 5²³.—ἐπισυναγωγή (elsewhere in Gk. Bib. only 2 Mac.
2⁷ Heb. 10²⁵; cf. Deiss. *Light*, 101 *ff*.) refers to the constant hope of the
Jews that their scattered brethren would be gathered together in Palestine (Is. 27¹³ Sir. 36¹³ 2 Mac. 2¹⁸; cf. the ἐπισυνάγειν under the leadership
of the Messiah in Ps. Sol. 17²⁸· ⁵⁰), a hope which passed over, with some
changes, into Christian apocalyptic; see for details Schürer, II, 626 *ff*.;
Bousset, *Relig.*² 271 *ff*.; and Volz. *Eschat.* 309 *ff*. Swete (on Mk. 13²⁷)
observes that ἐπισυναγωγή in Heb. 10²⁵ "is suggestively used for the
ordinary gatherings of the church, which are anticipations of the great
assembling at the Lord's return." On ἐπί for πρός, here due to the substantive, cf. Gal. 4⁹ and especially Hab. 2⁵ (B; AQ have πρός).

2. εἰς τὸ μὴ ταχέως κτλ. The object (εἰς τὸ μή) of ἐρωτῶμεν
is specified by two infinitives, one aorist σαλευθῆναι which looks
at the action without reference to its progress or completion;
the other present, θροεῖσθαι which defines the action as going
on; hence, "we urge you not to be easily unsettled and not to be
in a constant state of nervous excitement." The phrase σαλευθῆναι ἀπὸ τοῦ νοός, which is not found elsewhere in the Gk. Bib.,
suggests that the readers were driven from their sober sense like
a ship from its moorings. The word νοῦς, frequent in Paul (cf.
Rom. 14⁵), means here not "opinion" (Grot.) but, as elsewhere
in the N. T., "mind," the particular reference being not so much
to the organ of thought as to the state of reasonableness, "their
ordinary, sober, and normal state of mind" (Ell.). Thus driven
from their mind, they fell into a state of alarm, agitation, nervous excitement which, as the present tense (θροεῖσθαι) shows,
was continuous.

On the analogy of παρακαλεῖν εἰς τό (I 2¹²) or τὸ μή (I 3³) and δεῖσθαι
εἰς τό (I 3¹⁰) or τὸ μή (2 Cor. 10²), ἐρωτῶμεν εἰς τὸ μή is natural, and
that too as an object clause (*BMT*. 412). Parallel to this negative
exhortation is the independent negative prohibition μή τις κτλ. (v. ²).
Wohl., however, takes εἰς τὸ μή as final and finds the content of the
exhortation in μή τις κτλ. a construction which is smoother and less
Pauline.—σαλεύειν, only here in Paul but common elsewhere in Gk. Bib.,
is used literally "of the motion produced by winds, storms, waves," etc.
(Thayer; cf. Ps. 17⁸ and σάλος Lk. 21²⁵), and figuratively of disturbance
in general (Ps. 9²⁷ 12⁵; cf. especially Acts 17¹³ of the Jews in Bercœa). It
is sometimes parallel to (Job 9⁶ Nah. 1⁵ Hab. 2¹⁶) or a variant of (Is. 33²⁰
1 Mac. 9¹³) σείειν; and it is construed with ἀπό in the sense of "at"
(Ps. 32⁸), "by" (1 Mac. 9¹³ (A) Ps. Sol. 15⁶), or as here "from" (cf. 1⁹);

Vulg. has *a vestro sensu* (*cf.* 4 Reg. 21⁸ = 2 Ch. 33⁸ Dan. (Th.) 4¹¹). DE add ὑμῶν after νοῦς; *cf.* 1 Cor. 14¹⁴.—θροεῖσθαι, indicating a state of alarm (*cf.* θροῦς Sap. 1¹⁰ 1 Mac. 9³⁹), occurs elsewhere in Gk. Bib. only Cant. 5⁴, and Mk. 13³⁷ = Mt. 24⁶, an apocalyptic word of the Lord which, so some surmise (Wohl. Mill. Dob.), Paul has here in mind. On θροεῖσθαι, see Kennedy, *Sources*, 126, and Wrede, 48 f.—On μή . . . μηδέ, *cf.* Rom. 14²¹; EKLP, *et al.*, have μήτε due probably to the following sequence where D has μηδέ, μηδέ, μήτε, and F μηδέ, μήτε (corrected to μηδέ), μηδέ. Though μήτε is common in Gk. Bib. (3 Reg. 3²⁶ Hos. 4⁴, etc.), it occurs only here in Paul; see Bl. 77¹⁰.

διὰ πνεύματος κτλ. The instrument or means (διά not ὑπό) by which the σαλευθῆναι and θροεῖσθαι are effected is specified in three parallel clauses standing together in negative correlation (the triple μήτε being due to μηδέ), διὰ πνεύματος, διὰ λόγου and δι' ἐπιστολῆς. In the light of I 5¹⁹, πνεῦμα (anarthrous as often in Paul) refers clearly to the operation of the Spirit in the charisma of prophecy; λόγος, in the light of ἐπιστολῆς, means probably an oral as contrasted with an epistolary utterance (v. ¹⁵ Acts 15²⁷); and ἐπιστολή is probably an allusion not to a forged or an anonymous letter, but to I.

Chrys. apparently understands πνεῦμα either of the spirit of prophecy or of false prophets who deceive by persuasive words (διὰ λόγου; *cf.* Ephr.). λόγος is sometimes understood of the "reckoning" of times and seasons, or of a real or falsified λόγος κυρίου (see Lün.); but it is usually explained as an oral utterance inspired (= διδαχή 1 Cor. 14⁶· ²⁶; *cf.* λόγος σοφίας and γνώσεως 1 Cor. 12⁸) or uninspired.

ὡς δι' ἡμῶν. "As if said by us." Since this clause is separated from the construction with the triple μήτε, it is not to be construed with the infinitives σαλευθῆναι and θροεῖσθαι; and since the three preceding phrases with διά are closely united in negative correlation, ὡς δι' ἡμῶν is to be connected not with ἐπιστολῆς alone, not with both ἐπιστολῆς and λόγου, but with all three prepositional phrases. The reference is thus not to the unsettlement and agitation as such, and not to the instruments of the same, but to the unsettling and agitating cause conveyed by these instruments, the statement, namely, "that the day of the Lord is present." While it is possible that some of the converts, perhaps the idle brethren, had themselves said in the Spirit, or in an address, that the day had actually dawned, and had supported their assertion by a reference to an anonymous letter attributed innocently to Paul, it is probable, in view of the unity of the negative correlation with the triple μήτε, that an actual utterance of Paul in the Spirit, or in an address, or in his first epistle (*cf.* Jerome, Hammond, Kern and Dob.) had been misconstrued to imply that Paul himself had said that "the day of the Lord is present," thus creating the unsettlement and nervous excitement.

That the three instruments specified do not exhaust the number of actual instruments about which Paul was informed, or of possible instruments which he thinks may have been employed, is a natural inference from v. ³: "let no one deceive you in any way," the ways mentioned or other possible ways. In writing ὡς δι' ἡμῶν, Paul does not deny that he has used such instruments, or that he has expressed himself in reference to times and seasons; he disclaims simply all responsibility for the statement: "the day of the Lord is present." The context alone determines whether or not ὡς (1 Cor. 4¹⁸ 7²⁵ 9²⁶ 2 Cor. 5²⁰, etc.) indicates an erroneous opinion.

That ὡς δι' ἡμῶν is to be joined with all three substantives is regarded as probable by Erasmus, Barnes, Lft. Mill. Dob. Harnack, Dibelius, *et al.* (1) Many scholars, however (from Tertullian to Moff.), restrict the phrase to ἐπιστολῆς, and interpret it as meaning ὡς δι' ἡμῶν γεγραμμένης (Thayer, 681), or ὡς ἡμῶν γεγραφότων αὐτήν (Bl. 74⁶; P reads παρ' ἡμῶν). According to this construction, some of the converts either (*a*) ἐν πνεύματι (or *ex falsis visionibus quas ostendunt vobis*, Ephr.), or (*b*) in an oral address (Chrys.; *cf.* Ephr. *ex commentitiis sophismati verbis quae dicunt vobis*) or in the charisma of διδαχή, or (*c*) in a forged letter (Chrys. Theodoret, Ell. and many others; *cf.* Ephr. *per falsas epistolas minime a nobis scriptas tamquam per nos missas*) asserted that the day is present. But while some of the converts might innocently make such an assertion in the Spirit or in an address, inspired or not, they could not innocently forge a letter. And if they had done so, Paul would scarcely have written as he now writes. Hence, many commentators content themselves with the supposition that an anonymous letter had been attributed, innocently or wilfully, to Paul; or that Paul suspected that a letter had been forged. (2) Still other scholars (Theodoret, Grot. De W. Lün. Lillie, Ell. Schmiedel, Vincent, *et al.*), influenced doubtless by v. ¹⁵, join ὡς δι' ἡμῶν with both λόγου and ἐπιστολῆς. According to this view, πνεῦμα is understood of an utterance of some of the converts in the Spirit, λόγος of a pretended oral word of Paul, and ἐπιστολή of an anonymous or a forged letter. (3) A more recent theory

(Dods, Askwith in his *Introd. to Thess. Epistles*, 1902, 92 *ff.*, and Wohl.)
connects ὡς δι' ἡμῶν closely with the infinitives, and explains that Paul
is here disclaiming not the Spirit, or word, or letter, but simply the "responsibility for the disturbance which has arisen"; and that ὡς δι' ἡμῶν
means "as if such disturbance came through us." This attractive suggestion seems to overlook the evident detachment of ὡς δι' ἡμῶν from
the negative correlation with the triple μήτε (*cf.* Dibelius).

ὡς ὅτι ἐνέστηκεν κτλ. The actual statement of some of the
converts, based on a misconstruction of Paul's utterance by
Spirit, by word, or by his first epistle, is now given: "that the
day of the Lord is present." That this statement is not a word
of Paul has already been indicated by ὡς δι' ἡμῶν. The second
ὡς may be separated from ὅτι, in which case the judgment of
the first ὡς is reiterated, "as if we said that"; or ὡς ὅτι may be
equivalent to a simple ὅτι "that," in which case the utterance
is quoted without further qualification: "to wit that the day of
the Lord is present" (*cf.* 2 Cor. 5¹⁹). ἐνέστηκεν means not "is
coming" (ἔρχεται I 5²), not "is at hand" (ἤγγικεν Rom. 13¹²),
not "is near" (ἐγγύς ἐστιν Phil. 4⁵), but "has come," "is on
hand," "is present." The period indicated by ἡμέρα has dawned
and the Lord is expected from heaven at any moment. Paul of
course had not expressed any such opinion; and it is with a trace
of impatience that, after noting what first must come, he asks:
"Do you not remember," etc. (v. ⁵). It is this misleading assertion that accounts both for the increased discouragement of the
faint-hearted to encourage whom Paul writes 1³–2¹⁷, and for
the increased meddlesomeness of the idle brethren to warn
whom Paul writes 3¹⁻¹⁸.

ὡς ὅτι occurs elsewhere in Gk. Bib. 2 Cor. 5¹⁹ 11²¹ 2 Reg. 18¹⁸ (A; B
omits ὡς) Esther 4¹⁴ (B; A omits ὡς); for other examples, mostly late
(since recent editors no longer read ὡς ὅτι in Xen. *Hellen.* III, 2¹⁴; Dion
Hal. *Antiq.* 9¹⁴; Josephus, *Apion*, I, 58), see Wetstein on 2 Cor. 5¹⁹ 11²¹.
In late Gk. ὡς ὅτι = ὅτι = "that" (Sophocles, *Lex. sub voc.*). Moulton
(I, 212), however, urges that this usage appears "in the vernacular at a
rather late stage" and so takes ὡς ὅτι = *quasi* with most interpreters.
But while the sense "as if," "on the ground that" would fit most of the
instances in Gk. Bib., it does not fit 2 Cor. 5¹⁹. Since ὡς ὅτι cannot
mean "because," and since the reading ὅτι (Baljon, Schmiedel) for
ὡς ὅτι in 2 Cor. 5¹⁹ is pure conjecture, there remains only the sense "to

wit that" (so Dob. here, and Bernard, *EGT.* on 2 Cor. 5¹⁹ 11²¹).—ἐνί-
στημι is used in N. T., apart from 2 Tim. 3¹ Heb. 9⁹, only by Paul; in
Rom. 8³⁸ 1 Cor. 3²², ἐνεστώς is contrasted with μέλλων. "The verb
is very common in the papyri and inscriptions with reference to the
current year" (Mill.; *cf.* Esther 3¹³ τοῦ ἐνεστῶτος ἔτους). Lillie cites
Josephus, *Ant.* XVI, 6² οὐ μόνον ἐν τῷ ἐνεστῶτι καιρῷ ἀλλὰ καὶ ἐν τῷ
προγεγενημένῳ "where the former reference equally with the latter excludes all idea of future time." That ἐνέστηκεν = "is present" is recognised by many commentators (*e. g.* Œcumenius, Kern (*jetz eben vor-
handen*), Riggenbach, Alford, Ell. Lillie, Find. Wohl. Mill.). Many
other interpreters, however, perhaps "from the supposed necessity of the
case rather than from any grammatical compulsion" (Lillie), are inclined to explain "is present" to mean "is at hand." Grot. notes that
it is "common to announce as present what is obviously just at hand"
and interprets, *nempe hoc anno;* Bengel defines by *propinquitas;* Schmiedel and Dob., on the assumption that the Thess. could not have meant
"is present," understand ἐνέστηκεν of the future which is almost present. Against all such restrictions, see Lillie's exhaustive note in defence of the translation "is present."—On ἡ ἡμέρα τοῦ κυρίου (1 Cor.
5⁵), see I 5²; D omits ἡ and GFP omit τοῦ; K, *et al.*, read Χριστοῦ for
κυρίου.

3–8ᵃ. Allow no one, Paul continues, to delude you into such a
belief whatever means may be employed (v. ³ᵃ). Then, choosing
to treat the question given him (v. ¹) solely with reference to the
assertion (v. ²), and having in mind the discouragement of the
faint-hearted, he selects from the whole of his previous oral teaching concerning times and seasons only such elements as serve to
prove that the assertion (v. ²) is mistaken, and proceeds to remind
them that the day of the Lord will not be present until first of all
the apostasy comes and a definite and well-known figure, variously described as the man of lawlessness, the son of destruction,
etc., is revealed,—allusions merely with which the readers are
quite familiar, so familiar, indeed, that the Apostle can cut short
the characterisation (v. ⁴), and appeal, with perhaps a trace of
impatience at their forgetfulness, to the memory of the readers
to complete the picture (v. ⁵). Then, turning from the future to
the present, he explains why the apostasy and the revelation of
the *Anomos* are delayed, and so why the day of the Lord is not
yet present. To be sure, he intimates, the day of the Lord is not
far distant, for there has already been set in operation the secret

of lawlessness which is preparing the way for the apostasy and
the concomitant revelation of the *Anomos;* but that day will
not actually be present until the supernatural spirit which detains the *Anomos* (or, which is holding sway) for the very purpose that the *Anomos* may be revealed only at the time set him
by God, or the supernatural person who is now detaining the
Anomos (or, who is now holding sway), is put out of the way
(vv. [6-7]). And then there will be revealed the lawless one (v. [8a]).

3. ὅτι ἐὰν μὴ ἔλθῃ. The ὅτι introduces the reason why the
readers should not be alarmed or excited (v. [2]), or, more directly,
why they should not allow themselves to be deceived about the
time of the day of the Lord in any way whatever, the ways mentioned in v. [2] or in any other way; and at the same time it starts
the discussion of the theme (v. [1]) "concerning the advent and the
assembling unto him." However, in the treatment of the theme,
only such points are brought to the memory of the readers as
make clear (1) that the *Parousia* will not be present until first
of all there comes the apostasy and there be revealed the *Anomos*
(vv. [3-4]); (2) why the day of the Lord is not yet present (vv. [5-8]);
and (3) what the significance is of the advent of the *Anomos*,—
points selected with a view to the encouragement of the faint-
hearted. The clause with ὅτι remains unfinished; from v. [2] we
may supply after ὅτι "the day of the Lord will not be present"
(ἡ ἡμέρα τοῦ κυρίου οὐκ ἐνστήσεται).

> On the rare prohibitory subj. in the third person (1 Cor. 16[11]), see
> *BMT.* 166; in view of 1 Cor. 16[11] 2 Cor. 11[16], it is unnecessary to con-
> strue μή τις with ἐρωτῶμεν, and to take εἰς τὸ μή (v. [2]) as indicating
> purpose. The clause with μή τις is quite independent; it is not prob-
> ably parenthetical, although ὅτι κτλ. may be connected directly with
> vv. [1-2].—As θροεῖσθαι (v. [2]) suggests the μὴ θροεῖσθε of Mk. 13[7] = Mt.
> 24[6], so ἐξαπατήσῃ recalls the βλέπετε μή τις ὑμᾶς πλανήσῃ of Mk. 13[5] =
> Mt. 24[4]. ἐξαπατάω, frequent in Lxx., is in the N. T. used chiefly by
> Paul.—On κατὰ μηδένα τρόπον, "evidently a current phrase" (Mill.),
> which strengthens μή τις, *cf.* 3 Mac. 4[13] 4 Mac. 4[24] 10[7]; also κατὰ πάντα
> τρόπον Rom. 3[2]. Though κατά (v. [9] 1[12] 3[6]) is common in Paul, it does
> not appear in I.

ἡ ἀποστασία. The article suggests that "the apostasy" or
"the religious revolt" is something well known to the readers; in

fact, instruction upon this and cognate points had already been given orally by Paul (vv. ⁵ ᶠᶠ· I 5¹). The term itself is at least as old as the time of Antiochus Epiphanes who was "enforcing the apostasy" (1 Mac. 2¹⁵), that is, of Judaism to Hellenism; thereafter, as one of the fearful signs of the end (cf. Eth. En. 91⁷), it became a fixed element in apocalyptic tradition (cf. Jub. 23¹⁴ ᶠᶠ· 4 Ezra 5¹ ᶠᶠ· Mt. 24¹⁰ ᶠᶠ·). Paul, however, is probably thinking not of the apostasy of Jews from Moses, or of the Gentiles from the law in their hearts, or even of an apostasy of Christians from their Lord (for Paul expects not only the Thessalonians (I 5⁹ II 2¹³ ᶠᶠ·) but all believers (1 Cor. 3¹⁵) to be saved), but of the apostasy of the non-Christians as a whole, of the sons of disobedience in whom the prince of the power of the air, the evil spirit, is now operating (cf. Eph. 2²). This apostasy or religious revolt is not to be identified with "the mystery of lawlessness" (v. ⁷), for that mystery, already set in operation by Satan, precedes the apostasy and prepares the way for it; it is therefore something future, sudden, and final, like the revelation of the *Anomos* with which apparently it is associated essentially and chronologically. Whether this definitive religious revolt on earth synchronises with the revolt of Satan (Rev. 12⁷ ᶠᶠ·) in heaven, Paul does not say.

On the term, see Bousset, *Antichrist*, 76 ff., and Volz. *Eschat.* 179. That the revolt is not political, whether of all peoples (Iren. V, 25²) or of Jews (Clericus, *et al.*) from Rome, and not both political and religious (see Poole, *ad loc.*, and Wohl.), but solely religious, is probable from the fact that elsewhere in the Gk. Bib. ἀποστασία is used of religious apostasy (Josh. 22²² (B) 3 Reg. 20¹³ (A) 2 Ch. 29¹⁹ 33¹⁹ (A) Jer. 2¹⁹ 1 Mac. 2¹⁵ Acts 21²¹), and from the fact that in vv. ³⁻¹², as elsewhere in the apocalyptic utterances of Paul, there is no evident reference to political situations. (It is not evident that τὸ κατέχον and ὁ κατέχων ἄρτι in vv. ⁶⁻⁷ refer to Rome). Furthermore, it is unlikely (1) that heresy is in mind, since "the doomed" here (v. ¹⁰) and elsewhere in Paul are outside the Christian group, "the saved" (Hammond and others (see Poole) find the prophecy fulfilled (cf. 1 Tim. 4¹ ᶠᶠ·), while Cyril of Jerusalem (*Cat.* 15⁹) sees the fulfilment in the heresies of his own day); or (2) that ἡ ἀποστασία = ὁ ἀποστάτης (cf. Iren. V, 25 *apostata*, and Augustine, *de civ. dei*, 20²¹, *refuga*), the abstract for the concrete (so Chrys. and others); or (3) that Belial is meant, on the ground that this word is rendered once in

Lxx. by ἀποστασία (3 Reg. 20¹³ A) and several times in the later Aquila (e. g. Deut. 15⁹ Judg. 19²² 1 Reg. 2¹² 10²⁷ 25¹⁷ Ps. 16²⁷ Nah. 1¹¹).—Whether πρῶτον (without a following ἔπειτα I 4¹⁷ or δεύτερον 1 Cor. 12²⁸) belongs to both ἔλθῃ and ἀποκαλυφθῇ, indicating that the coming and revelation are contemporaneous,—"the day will not be present until, first of all, these two things happen together" (Schmiedel, Dob.); or whether καί is consecutive (Ell. Find. Mill.), pointing out the result of the coming, is uncertain (cf. Lft.). In any case, the two things are not identical, although they are apparently associated both essentially and chronologically.

ἀποκαλυφθῇ. The *Anomos*, described in the following words, is indeed in existence, concealed, perhaps imprisoned, somewhere, as ἀποκαλυφθῇ intimates; but the place of concealment, whether in heaven (cf. Eph. 6¹²), in the firmament, on earth, or in the abyss, is not stated. That he is influencing "the doomed" from his place of concealment is nowhere suggested; it is hinted only (vv. ⁶⁻⁷) that at present (that is, in the time of Paul) there is a supernatural spirit or person that directly by detaining him (or keeping him in detention) or indirectly (by holding sway until the appointed time of the coming of the *Anomos*) prevents his immediate revelation. This function of τὸ κατέχον or ὁ κατέχων ἄρτι is not, however, permanent; indeed, it is exercised for the purpose (God's purpose) that the *Anomos* may be revealed in his proper time, the time, namely, that has been appointed by God. Not until then will the *Anomos* be revealed, then when the supernatural spirit or person is removed.

Since Paul does not describe the place or conditions of concealment, it is impossible to ascertain precisely what he means. His interest is not in the portrayal of the movements of the *Anomos* but is in his character (vv. ³⁻⁴) and his significance for the unbelievers (vv. ⁹⁻¹²). Paul uses φανερόω (Col. 3³) and ἀποκάλυψις (1⁷ 1 Cor. 1⁷) of the advent of Christ, but not ἀποκαλύπτειν (contrast Lk. 17³⁰ 4 Ezra 7²⁸ 13³²). The revelation or *Parousia* of the *Anomos* (v. ⁹) is perhaps intended as a counterpart of that of the Messiah (1⁷); but whether Paul is responsible for the idea or is reproducing earlier Christian or Jewish tradition is uncertain. In the later Asc. Isa. 4¹⁸, the Beloved rebukes in wrath "all things wherein Beliar manifested himself and acted openly in this world."

ὁ ἄνθρωπος τῆς ἀνομίας = ὁ ἄνομος (v. ⁸), for ἄνθρωπος ἀνομίας like υἱὸς ἀνομίας (Ps. 88²³) is a Hebraism, designating a person as belonging to a lawless class or condition. This phrase, like ὁ υἱὸς τῆς ἀπωλείας, ὁ ἀντικείμενος καὶ ὑπεραιρόμενος κτλ., and ὁ ἄνομος, is not a proper name but a characterisation of a person, and that too a definite person, as the article in each of the four phrases makes plain. It is evident that the figure in question is not Satan but a man, a unique man, however, in whom Satan dwells and operates. Chrys. observes: "Who is this person? Satan? Not at all; but ἄνθρωπός τις πᾶσαν αὐτοῦ δεχόμενος τὴν ἐνέργειαν." So complete is the control of Satan over his peculiar instrument that it is natural to hold with Th. Mops. that the parallel between the incarnation of Christ and the indwelling of Satan in the *Anomos* is all but complete.

While (ὁ) ἄνθρωπος (τοῦ) θεοῦ is quite frequent in the Lxx. (*cf.* also 1 Tim. 6¹¹ 2 Tim. 3¹⁷), ἄνθρωπος with an abstract gen. (Sir. 20²⁶ 31²⁵ Lk. 2¹⁴) is less frequent than ἀνήρ. For the equivalence of ἄνθρωπος, ἀνήρ, and υἱός in this construction, *cf.* ἄνθρωπος αἱμάτων (Sir. 31²⁵) with ἀνὴρ αἱμάτων (2 Reg. 16⁷ ᶠ· and often in Psalms; see Briggs, *ICC.* on Ps. 5⁷); and *cf.* υἱὸς θανάτου (1 Reg. 20³¹ 2 Reg. 12⁵) with ἀνὴρ θανάτου (3 Reg. 2²⁶).—Instead of ἀνομίας (Bℵ, Tert. *et al.*), the majority of uncials (ADEGFKLP, *et al.*) read ἁμαρτίας. In the Lxx., A frequently reads ἁμαρτία where B reads ἀνομία (*e. g.* Exod. 34⁷ Is. 53¹² Ezek. 16⁵¹ 29¹⁶); occasionally A has ἀνομία where B (Ezek. 36¹⁹) or ℵ (Ps. 108¹⁴) has ἁμαρτία. As these variants and the parallelism in Job 7²¹ Ps. 31⁵ Is. 53⁵ show, the two words are similar in meaning, ἁμαρτία being the more general (*cf.* 1 Jn. 3⁴). Though common in Lxx., both ἀνομία (Rom. 4⁷ 6¹⁹ 2 Cor. 6¹⁴) and ἄνομος (1 Cor. 9²¹) are rare in Paul. Unless Bℵ revised in the light of vv. ⁷⁻⁸ (Weiss), or substituted ἀνομίας for ἁμαρτίας in the light of an exegesis which understood "the man of sin" to be Belial, the more specific ἀνομίας is the preferable reading.—It is tempting to identify the figure described in the four phrases with Belial (Beliar), though we cannot be sure (*cf.* Dob. Dibelius) that Paul would assent to this identification. This identification seems probable to Bousset (*Antichrist*, 1895, 99) and "all but certain" to Charles (*Ascension of Isaiah*, 1900, lxii; *cf.* also Mill. and Moff.). The origin and meaning of the word Belial are alike uncertain; Moore (*ICC.* on Judg. 19²²) observes: "The oldest etymology of the word is found in *Sanhedrin, 111 f.* . . . 'men who have thrown off the yoke of Heaven from their necks' (בלי + עול). So also Jerome in a gloss in his translation of Judg. 19²²: *filii Belial, id est absque iugo*"; but the word is "without analogy in the language" (*ibid.*); see further, Cheyne in *EB.* 525 ff. In the Hebrew O. T. Belial is not certainly a proper name, though in Ps. 18⁵ = 2 Sam. 22⁵ "torrents of Belial" (Briggs) is parallel to "cords of Sheol" and "snares of Death." In the Lxx. בליעל is rendered by υἱοὶ βελιάμ (Judg. 20¹³ A), ἀποστασία (3 Reg. 20¹³ A; so frequently in the later Aquila), παράνομος (frequently; cf. Judg. 20¹³ B, where A has βελιάμ; Judg. 19²², where Th. has βελιάλ), ἀνόμημα (Deut. 15⁹), ἀνομία (2 Reg. 22⁵ Ps. 17⁵, parallel with θάνατος and ᾅδης), etc.; see Moore, loc. cit. In the Test. xii (see Charles on Reub. 2¹), Jub. (see Charles on 15³³ "sons of Beliar"), and Asc. Isa. (see Charles on 1⁸), Belial or Beliar is definitely a Satan or the Satan (cf. 2 Cor. 6¹⁵).

Charles (Asc. Isa. lxi ff.) not only identifies "the man of lawlessness" with Belial but elaborates an hypothesis to account for the Antichrist as he appears in Paul and in later N. T. literature. The Anomos of Paul, a god-opposing man, a human sovereign armed with miraculous power, is the resultant of a fusion of two separate and originally independent traditions, that of the Antichrist and that of Beliar. The Antichrist is not, as Bousset supposes, originally the incarnate devil but a god-opposing being of human origin. The first historical person to be identified with Antichrist is Antiochus Epiphanes; and the language applied to him "recalls, though it may be unconsciously, the old Babylonian saga of the Dragon's assault on the gods of heaven." Beliar, on the other hand, is a purely Satanic being. "It is through the Beliar constituent of the developed Antichrist myth that the old Dragon saga from Babylon gained an entrance into the eschatologies of Judaism and Christianity." This fusion of Antichrist with Beliar "appears to have been effected on Christian soil before 50 A.D.," and is attested by 2 Thess. 2¹⁻¹². The subsequent history of Antichrist was influenced by the incoming of the Neronic myths; for example, Rev. xiii betrays the fusion of the myth of Antichrist with that of Nero Redivivus; Sib. Orac. III, 63–74, reflects the incarnation of Beliar as Antichrist in Nero still conceived as living; and Asc. Isa. 4²⁻⁴ (88–100 A.D.; Harnack and Bousset put the passage much later) suggests the incarnation of Beliar as Antichrist in the form of the dead Nero: "Beliar . . . will descend from his firmament in the likeness of a man, a lawless king," etc.

ὁ υἱὸς τῆς ἀπωλείας = ὁ ἀπολλύμενος, a Hebraism indicating the one who belongs to the class destined to destruction (v. ¹⁰ οἱ ἀπολλύμενοι) as opposed to the class destined to salvation (1 Cor. 1¹⁸ οἱ σωζόμενοι). The same description is applied to Judas Iscariot in Jn. 17¹².

Abaddon is in Lxx. rendered by ἀπώλεια, and appears in parallelism with ᾅδης (Job 26⁶ Pr. 15¹¹), θάνατος (Job 28²²) and τάφος; cf. ἀνομία (Belial) with θάνατος and ᾅδης in Ps. 17⁵. Bousset (Antichrist, 99) calls attention to the angel of the abyss in Rev. 9¹¹ whose name is 'Αβαδδών in Hebrew and ᾿Απολλύων in Greek. The abyss is apparently "the abode of the ministers of torment from which they go forth to do hurt" (Taylor in *ERE*. I, 54). It is not, however, probable that ὁ υἱὸς τῆς ἀπωλείας refers to the demonic angel of the abyss, for (1) Paul's usage of ἀπώλεια is against it (Rom. 9²² Phil. 1²⁸ 3¹⁹; *cf.* Is. 57⁴ τέκνα ἀπωλείας, σπέρμα ἄνομον; Pr. 24²²ᵃ υἱὸς ἀπωλείας; Jub. 10³ Apoc. Pet. 1²); and (2) in Rev. 17⁸, the beast that ascends from the abyss is to go off ultimately εἰς ἀπώλειαν.

4. ὁ ἀντικείμενος κτλ. In the further characterisation of Satan's peculiar instrument, three points are prominent (1) his impious character, "the one who opposes and uplifts himself against every one called God or an object of worship"; (2) the tendency of his spirit of opposition and self-exaltation, "so that he sits in the sanctuary of God"; and (3) the blasphemous claim, intended by the session, "proclaiming that he himself is really God." The words of the first clause are evidently reminiscent of a description already applied to Antiochus Epiphanes by Daniel (Th. 11³⁶ ᶠᶠ·): καὶ ὑψωθήσεται ὁ βασιλεὺς καὶ μεγαλυνθήσεται ἐπὶ πάντα θεόν, καὶ λαλήσει ὑπέρογκα (*i. e.* ἐπὶ τὸν θεὸν τῶν θεῶν, Lxx.) . . . καὶ ἐπὶ πᾶν θεὸν οὐ συνήσει, ὅτι ἐπὶ πάντας μεγαλυνθήσεται. In alluding to this passage and in quoting ἐπὶ πάντα θεόν, Paul inserts λεγόμενον to prevent the possibility of putting the would-be gods on a level with the true God; but whether λεγόμενον refers solely to the would-be gods designated as such, "so-called" (*cf.* Iren. V, 25¹ *super omne idolum*, Wohl. Dob.), or whether it embraces both the would-be gods and the true God, "which is called God," rightly or wrongly (so most interpreters), is uncertain.

Since both ἀντικείμενος and ὑπεραιρόμενος are united by one article, it is probable but not certain (De W. Lün. Ell.) that the former is not a substantive referring to Satan (1 Tim. 5¹⁴ 1 Clem. 51¹) or ὁ διάβολος who stands at the right hand of Joshua in Zech. 3¹ τοῦ ἀντικεῖσθαι αὐτῷ. —Apart from Paul (2 Cor. 12⁷) ὑπεραίρεσθαι is found in Gk. Bib. Ps. 37⁴ 71¹⁶ Pr. 31²⁹ 2 Ch. 32²³ Sir. 48¹³ 2 Mac. 5²³; the construction with ἐπί (only here in Gk. Bib.; *cf.* ὑπέρ in Ps. 71¹⁶ and the dat. in 2 Mac. 5²³) is due, perhaps, to the allusion in ἐπὶ πάντα θεόν.—Since ἀντικεῖσθαι (common in Gk. Bib.; *cf.* the substantive participle in Is. 66⁶ 1 Cor. 16⁹ Phil. 1²⁸) is regularly construed with the dative, a zeugma is here to be assumed, unless the possibility of ἀντικεῖσθαι ἐπί = "against" be admitted (Schmiedel, Dob.).—The rare σέβασμα (Acts 17²³ Sap. 14²⁰ 15¹⁷ Dan. (Th.) Bel 27; *cf.* Sap. 14²⁰ with 14¹² εἴδωλα, 14¹⁵ εἰκών, and 14¹ᵉ τὰ γλυπτά) indicates not a divinity (*numen*) but any sacred object of worship.—On λεγόμενος, *cf.* 1 Cor. 8⁵ Col. 4¹¹ Eph. 2¹¹.—The omission by א* of καὶ ὑπεραιρόμενος is not significant.

ὥστε αὐτὸν καθίσαι κτλ. The session in the sanctuary of God is tantamount to the assumption of divine honours, "proclaiming that he himself is really (ἔστιν) God." The attempt to sit in the sanctuary of God is made quite in the spirit of the king of Babylon (Is. 14¹³ ᶠᶠ·) and the prince of Tyre (Ezek. 28²); but whether the attempt is successful or not (*cf.* Lk. 4²⁹ ὥστε κατακρημνίσαι αὐτόν) is not indicated certainly by ὥστε with the infinitive.

τὸν ναὸν τοῦ θεοῦ. This is apparently the earliest extant reference to the session of the Antichrist in the temple of God (Bousset, *Antichrist*, 104 *ff.*). It is, however, quite uncertain whether the temple is to be sought in the church (on the analogy of 1 Cor. 3¹⁶ ᶠᶠ· 6¹⁹ 2 Cor. 6¹⁶), in Jerusalem (Ps. 5⁸ 78¹ 137²), "in the high mountains toward the north" (Is. 14¹³), "in the heart of the sea" (Ezek. 28²), or in the holy heavenly temple where God sits enthroned; *cf.* Ps. 10⁴ κύριος ἐν ναῷ ἁγίῳ αὐτοῦ, κύριος ἐν οὐρανῷ ὁ θρόνος αὐτοῦ (see Briggs, *ad loc.*, and *cf.* Is. 66¹ Mic. 1² Hab. 2²⁰ Ps. 17⁷). If the reference is to the heavenly temple, then there is a reminiscence, quite unconscious, of traits appearing in the ancient saga of the Dragon that stormed the heavens, and (beginnings being transferred in apocalyptic to endings) is to storm the heavens at the end (*cf.* Bousset, *loc. cit.*). In this case ὥστε with the infinitive will indicate either (1) that the tendency of the spirit of defiance and self-exaltation is toward self-deification, the reference to the temple not being pressed; or (2) that after his revelation or advent, the *Anomos*, like the Dragon, attempts an assault on the throne of God in his holy temple in heaven, but is destroyed in the act by the breath of the mouth of the Lord Jesus.

Dibelius thinks that the original saga has been humanised by the insertion of the temple in Jerusalem, and compares Rev. 13⁶ βλασφημῆσαι τὴν σκηνήν. Other commentators who find here a reference to the temple in Jerusalem hold either that the prophecy has been (Grot.) or will be fulfilled (*e. g.* Iren. V, 25⁴ 30⁴; Hippolytus (*Dan.* 4⁴⁹ *Antichrist*, 6) has the temple rebuilt; and Cyril of Jerusalem (*Cat.* 15⁵) has it rebuilt on the ruins of the old temple). When the significance of ὥστε with the infinitive is faced, it is held either (1) that the *Anomos*, when he comes, actually takes his seat in the temple, and exercises therefrom his demonic powers until his destruction, the exact manner in which ὥστε is realised being left indeterminate; or (2) that ὥστε indicates tendency or purpose not realised, the description being intended to set forth the trend of defiance and self-exaltation, and the reference to the temple not being forced. Still other commentators interpret the temple as equivalent to the church (Th. Mops. Chrys. Theodoret, Jerome, *et al.*), an interpretation which makes easy the application to heresy (Calv.), or when necessary, by Protestants, to the Pope sitting in the *cathedra Petri*.

The difficulty with the reference to the temple in Jerusalem is that the evidence adduced for this interpretation is not convincing. Neither Antiochus who erected a heathen altar on the altar of burnt-offering, and presumably placed thereon a statue of Zeus Olympios (*cf.* 1 Mac. 1⁵⁴ Dan. 9²⁷ 11³¹ 12¹¹ ; Mk. 13¹⁴ Mt. 24¹⁵), nor Caligula who ordered Petronius to set up his statue in the temple (Josephus, *Ant.* 18⁸) is conceived as sitting or attempting to sit in the sanctuary of God. Contrast our verse with Asc. Isa. 4¹¹: "He (Beliar) . . . will set up his image before him in every city." The temple then is probably to be sought in heaven; and there is in the allusion an unconscious survival of traits in the ancient tradition of the Dragon. On this saga, *cf.* Bousset, *Antichrist*, 104 *ff.*; Gunkel, *Schöpfung und Chaos*, 221 *ff.*; Cheyne in *EB.* 1131 *ff.*; Mill. 163 *f.*; and Dob. or Dibelius, *ad loc.*—καθίζειν is intransitive; on εἰς (Exod. 16²⁹ 1 Reg. 5¹¹ 2 Reg. 15²⁵ (A) Lam. 2¹⁰), see Bl. 39³. The ναὸς τοῦ θεοῦ (1 Es. 5⁵² Judith 5¹⁸ Dan. (Th.) 5³ Mt. 26⁶¹, etc.; or κυρίου Lk. 1⁹ and often in Lxx.) is elsewhere in Paul used metaphorically; the Christians are the temple of God, or the body is the temple of the Spirit. —ἀποδείκνυμι (1 Cor. 4⁹) may mean "exhibit," "prove" (Acts 25⁷), "appoint" (Acts 2²²), or "designate" (a successor, 2 Mac. 14²⁶ (A); *cf.* Polyb. V, 43⁴, Josephus, *Ant.* 6³⁵ 7²³⁸). The latter meaning in the sense of "nominate" or "proclaim" is here preferred by Lft. and Mill. The participle ἀποδεικνύντα (AGF, *et al.*, read ἀποδεικνύοντα) denotes either purpose (Acts 3²⁶) or attendant circumstance (*BMT.* 449). Before καθίσαι, KL, *et al.*, put ὡς θεόν.

5. οὐ μνημονεύετε κτλ. With an unfinished sentence behind him (vv. ³⁻⁴), Paul abruptly reminds his readers that they have already been instructed in the matter of the times and seasons, particularly the signs which must precede the *Parousia* of Christ

17

(ταῦτα referring strictly to vv. ³⁻⁴). With a trace of impatience it may be (contrast μνημονεύετε in I 2⁹) he asks: "Do you not remember that when I was yet with you, I was repeatedly telling you these things?"

Paul is wont to appeal not only to the knowledge of his readers (cf. I 2¹, etc.), but also, and specifically, as Chrys. has seen, to his previous oral communications (3¹⁰ I 3⁴).—On πρὸς ὑμᾶς εἶναι, cf. 3¹⁰ I 3⁴.—Even without πολλάκις (Phil. 3¹⁸), ἔλεγον may denote customary or repeated action.—On the first person sing. without ἐγώ, cf. 3¹⁷; with ἐγώ, I 2¹⁸ 3⁵.— For ἔτι ὤν, DE have ἔτι ἐμοῦ ὄντος; so also Ambst. (Souter). On the view that ἔτι (a word found in the Major Epistles and Phil. 1⁹; cf. Lk. 24⁶· ⁴⁴) excludes a reference to Paul's visit and indicates a reference to Timothy's visit, and that therefore Timothy is here proclaiming himself that he is really the author of II (Spitta), see Mill. xc.

6–8ᵃ. In these verses, Paul is evidently explaining the delay of "the apostasy" and of the revelation or *Parousia* of the *Anomos*, and consequently the reason why the day of the Lord is not yet present. As the readers are not receiving new information, it is sufficient for Paul merely to allude to what they know already. Unfortunately, the allusions are so fragmentary and cryptic that it is at present impossible to determine precisely what Paul means. The conspicuous difficulty lies in the interpretation of τὸ κατέχον and ὁ κατέχων ἄρτι (*v. infra*). Since the reference is unknown, it is impossible to determine whether κατέχειν is to be translated "withhold" or "detain," an object αὐτόν (= ἄνομον) being supplied; or, "hold sway" "rule" (κρατεῖν), κατέχειν being intransitive. It is worth noting, however, that in vv. ⁶⁻¹² there is nothing obviously political. The thought runs in the sphere of the supramundane; the categories are concrete and realistic; and the interest, as in apocalyptic at its best, is religious and moral, the assertion of faith that the universe is moral, the justification of the ways of God to men. Though the Devil controls his own, his movements are directed by the purpose of God. Indeed, as vv. ⁹⁻¹² make clear, God first of all endeavours through his Spirit to stir up within men the love for his truth unto their salvation. When they refuse to welcome the heavenly visitor, then God as judge prepares them for

the consequences cf their refusal.   It is thus God himself who
sends an "operation unto delusion" into the souls of those who
have destroyed themselves by refusing to welcome the love for
the truth unto their salvation.   Since then there is no obvious
reference in vv. [6-12] to a political power, it is antecedently probable that τὸ κατέχον and ὁ κατέχων ἄρτι refer not to the Roman
Empire and emperor as a restraining principle or person, but to
a supernatural spirit or person conceived either as an unknown
being who keeps the *Anomos* in detention as the Dragon of the
saga is kept (*cf.* Dibelius), or as a well-known spirit or person,
possibly the Devil himself who is in control of the forces of evil,
the prince of the power of the air that operates in the sons of
disobedience (*cf.* Schaefer).

The Meaning of τὸ κατέχον and ὁ κατέχων ἄρτι.

The sphere of conjectural interpretations of τὸ κατέχον and ὁ κατέχων ἄρτι seems to be limited by the following probabilities: (1) The presence of ἄρτι with ὁ κατέχων indicates that ὁ κατέχων (and similarly τὸ
κατέχον, notwithstanding the fact that we do not have τὸ νῦν κατέχον
or τὸ κατέχον νῦν) is not a proper name but a description of a definite
and well-known figure whose activity in κατέχειν is in progress at the
time of Paul; (2) the ἄρτι is "now" to Paul; the τότε is of his expectation, and is not a far-distant "then"; (3) κατέχειν has the same
meaning in both participial phrases (so Boh. "that which layeth hold"
(Horner) and Syr.), though the Vulg. (Th. Mops. Ambst.) renders the
former *quid detineat* and the latter *qui tenet nunc.* Within the limits
of these probabilities, two types of opinion may be briefly sketched,
the one based on the "contemporary-historical," the other on the
"traditional-historical" method of interpretation.

I. The usual conjecture finds a reference in both τὸ κατέχον and ὁ κατέχων ἄρτι to the Roman Empire.   The older expositors (*e. g.* Tert. *de
resur.* 24, and Chrys.) stretch the limits of τότε and include in ἄρτι both
their own and Paul's present.   Modern writers, following the example of
Wetstein (who thinks of Nero), Whitby (who thinks of Claudius), and
Hitzig (who unlocks the pun *qui claudit*), are inclined to adhere firmly
to the contemporary reference.   Bacon (*Introd.* 77; *cf.* Spitta, *Zur Geschichte und Litteratur*, 1893, I, 146 *ff.* and Dob. *ad loc.*) states the prevailing conjecture cogently: "We need not assume with Hitzig a play upon
the name Claudius, ncr deny that 'the restrainer' may well be a primeval element of the Antichrist legend; but in the present application
of the word, first neuter, then masculine, the reference is certainly to

Paul's unfailing refuge against Jewish malice and persecution, the usually incorruptible Roman magistracy (Rom. 13¹⁻⁶) which at this very period was signally befriending him (Acts 18¹²⁻¹⁷)." The difficulty with this generally accepted interpretation is (1) that while the fall of Rome is one of the signs of the Messianic period (4 Ezra 5³ Apoc. Bar. 39⁷; *cf.* for the rabbinical literature Klausner, *Die Messianischen Vorstellungen*, etc. 1904, 39 *ff.* and Rabinsohn, *Le Messianisme*, etc. 1907, 63 *ff.*), the notion of Rome as a restrainer does not appear in Jewish apocalyptic literature (*cf.* Gunkel, *Schöpfung*, etc. 223). To obviate this objection, it is assumed that the trait is due to Paul or to contemporary Christianity (*cf.* Dob.). (2) A second difficulty is the fact that Paul the Roman citizen, although he does not identify the Roman Empire or emperor with the Antichrist (contrast Rev.), is compelled with grim apocalyptic determinism to put the Roman emperor, if not also the empire, ἐκ μέσου when once he, if not also it, has performed his service as restrainer. Augustine, in his interesting review of conjectural explanations (*de civ. dei*, xx, 19), notes the opinion of some that Paul "was unwilling to use language more explicit lest he should incur the calumnious charge of wishing ill to the empire which it was hoped would be eternal," and concedes that "it is not absurd to believe" that Paul does thus refer to the empire as if it were said: "Only he who now reigneth, let him reign until he is taken out of the way." But while the conjecture is not absurd, it creates the only political reference not simply in this passage but in Paul's apocalyptic utterances as a whole. A theory which is not open to this objection would be distinctly preferable.

II. Passing by other opinions, as, for example, that the Holy Spirit is meant (noted by Chrys.), or a friendly supernatural being (Hofmann thinks of the angel prince of Daniel), or Elijah (Ewald, who notes Mt. 17¹¹ Rev. 11³), we turn to the distinctively "traditional-historical" interpretations. (1) Gunkel (*Schöpfung*, 223 *ff.*) remarks that the heavenly or hellish powers who are to appear at the end are already in existence, and that the natural query why they have not yet manifested themselves is answered by the reflection that there must be something somewhere that holds them back for the time. The idea of κατέχων is originally mythical. Gunkel thinks that to Paul the κατέχων is probably a heavenly being, Elijah. (2) Dibelius in his *Geisterwelt im Glauben des Paulus*, 1909, 58 *ff.* and in his commentary (1911) on our passage attaches himself to Gunkel's method, and makes the acute suggestion, supported by such passages as Job 7¹² Rev. 13¹ Apoc. Bar. 29⁴ 4 Ezra 6⁵² and by instances from mythology and folk-lore, that τὸ κατέχον or ὁ κατέχων is the something somewhere (Paul does not know who or what it is exactly, and therefore shifts easily from neuter to masculine) which keeps the *Anomos* in detention until the time appointed by God for his advent. The trait is thus mythical, as Gunkel suspected. It is of interest to observe that while Gunkel takes κατέχειν in the sense of κωλύειν (so most from Chrys. on), Dibelius understands it in the equally admissible sense (see on I 5²¹) of κρατεῖν, confirming the meaning by an apt quotation from the *Acta Pilati*, 22², where Christ, in delivering Satan to Hades, says: λαβὼν αὐτὸν κάτεχε ("*in Banden halte*") ἀσφαλῶς ἄχρι τῆς δευτέρας μου παρουσίας. (3) Schaefer in his commentary (1890) agrees with Döllinger in taking κατέχειν intransitively and in translating it "*herrschen*," "rule," "hold sway." In his exegesis of the passage he comes to the conclusion not only that τὸ κατέχον is the mystery of lawlessness and that αὐτόν (v. ⁶) is Christ, but also that ὁ κατέχων is Satan. This indentification of ὁ κατέχων with Satan, original apparently with the Roman Catholic scholar, has the advantage of fitting admirably into Paul's thinking both here and elsewhere. Assuming Schaefer's identification as a working hypothesis and applying it in our own way, we suggest first of all that just as Christ is to Paul both the exalted Lord and the Spirit operating in believers, so Satan is both (1) "the god of this age" (2 Cor. 4⁴), "the prince of the power of the air" (Eph. 2²), the (temporary) ruler (ὁ κατέχων ἄρτι) of the spiritual hosts of wickedness, and (2) the evil spirit (τὸ κατέχον) that energises in the sons of disobedience (Eph. 2²). The effect of the operation of Satan, the spirit or person who is now holding sway, is characterised as "the mystery of lawlessness," that is, the lawlessness which is secretly growing in unbelievers under the spell of Satan. This control of Satan is in accordance with the divine purpose, for it prepares the way for the revelation of the *Anomos* in the time set him by God and not before, the reason being that the mystery of lawlessness, which Satan sets in operation, is to culminate in a definitive apostasy on earth which is the signal for the advent of Satan's instrument, the *Anomos*. But this apostasy will not come, and the *Anomos* will not be revealed until Satan, who is now holding sway, is put out of the way. The notion that a limit has been set to the authority of Satan has recently received fresh confirmation in a manuscript of the Freer collection (*cf.* Gregory, *Das Freer Logion*, 1908), where between Mk. 16¹⁴ and 16¹⁵ we read: "This age of lawlessness (ἀνομίας) is under Satan who (which) does not permit τὰ ὑπὸ τῶν πνευμάτων ἀκάθαρτα to understand the true power of God"; and further, in words attributed to Christ: πεπλήρωται ὁ ὅρος τῶν ἐτῶν τῆς ἐξουσίας τοῦ Σατανᾶ ἀλλὰ ἐγγίζει ἄλλα δεινά. But the unsolved difficulty in our passage is the reference intended by ἐκ μέσου γένηται. It is just possible that Paul is alluding to the war in heaven (Rev. 12⁷ ᶠᶠ·), the religious revolt led by Satan, which is the signal for the sudden apostasy on earth. In this case, ἐκ μέσου refers to Satan's expulsion from heaven to earth. Though he is thus removed, he makes use of his peculiar instrument, the *Anomos*, who now issues forth from his place of concealment, and gives him all his power, just as the Dragon (Rev. 13²) gives the beast his power, his throne, and great authority. Equipped with this power, the *Anomos*, whose advent is for the doomed alone, gathers his forces for war against Christ (*cf.* 1 Cor. 15²⁴ ᶠᶠ·), attempts the assault on the throne of God in his holy temple in heaven, but is slain in the attempt by the Lord Jesus with the breath of his mouth and is destroyed with the manifestation of his advent. To this conjecture, based on Schaefer's identification of ὁ κατέχων with Satan, it may be objected not that Satan is described in reference to his function of κατέχειν, for Paul calls Satan ὁ πειράζων (I 3⁵), but that (1) Paul might not subscribe either to the identification or to the deductions therefrom indicated above, and (2) that ἐκ μέσου, which to be sure designates only the fact not the manner (forced or voluntary) of the removal, does not at first blush suggest an ἐκβάλλεσθαι εἰς τὴν γῆν (Rev. 12⁹).

This brief review of conjectures only serves to emphasise the fact that we do not know what Paul had in mind, whether the Roman Empire, or a supernatural being that keeps the *Anomos* in detention, or Satan who is temporarily in control of the forces of evil, or something else quite different. Grimm (1861), for example, thinks of the *Anomos* himself and Beyer (1824) of Paul; see other conjectures in Lün. (ed. Gloag, 222–238). It is better, perhaps, to go with Augustine who says on v. ⁶: "Since he said that they (the Thessalonians) know, he was unwilling to say this openly. And thus we, who do not know what they knew, desire and yet are unable even *cum labore* to get at what the Apostle meant, especially as the things which he adds (namely, vv. ⁷⁻⁸ᵃ) make his meaning still more obscure"; and to confess with him: *ego prorsus quid dixerit me fateor ignorare* (*de civ. dei*, xx, 19).

6. καὶ νῦν τὸ κατέχον οἴδατε. "And as to the present, you know that which restrains him" (if the reference is to the Roman Empire), or "detains him" (if the reference is to a supernatural being that keeps the *Anomos* in detention), or "is holding sway" (if the reference is to Satan). From things to come (vv. ³ᵇ⁻⁴), Paul turns with καὶ νῦν to things present (vv. ⁶⁻⁷); and then, having indicated the reason for the delay of the advent of the *Anomos* and so of Christ, he reverts in v. ⁸ with τότε to the future. The νῦν (*cf.* I 3⁸) is not logical but temporal, calling attention to what is going on in the present in contrast not with the past (v. ⁵) but with the future (vv. ³⁻⁴; *cf.* the next clause ἐν τῷ αὐτοῦ καιρῷ and καὶ τότε v. ⁸). τὸ κατέχον is not a title, but the description of a supernatural being (or the Roman Empire) that is functioning as κατέχον in Paul's present.

Some commentators (especially Lün.) explains νῦν in the temporal sense: "and now to pass to a further point." This explanation puts so great a stress on the new point as such as to demand νῦν δέ (*cf.* 1 Cor.

12²⁰, one of the few instances of logical νῦν in Paul). Since, however, the
readers have already been instructed (Lün.) and need only to be reminded again of the point, and that too allusively, it is more likely that
the emphasis is laid not on the new point as such but on the present
situation involved in κατέχον as contrasted with the future situation
when ὁ κατέχων ἄρτι will be removed, and the prophecy of v. ³ will be
realised; and that therefore νῦν is temporal (so most). But to seek the
contrast in ἔτι (v. ⁵) is to be forced to assume that the readers had never
heard of τὸ κατέχον until now, and that from the cryptic utterances of
vv. ⁶⁻⁸ᵃ they could divine, without previous knowledge, Paul's meaning.
Dob. asks too much of the readers when he remarks: "*Paulus muss
seiner Sache in dieser Hinsicht sehr sicher gewesen, dass er sich mit dieser
Andeutung begnügt.*—The καὶ νῦν is detached and emphatic (*cf.* Jn. 4¹⁸),
"*und für jetzt*" (Dibelius).—If κατέχειν = "restrain" or "detain,"
αὐτόν = ἄνομον is to be supplied here and in v. ⁷; if it means "hold
sway" "rule," it is intransitive.

εἰς τὸ ἀποκαλυφθῆναι κτλ. The divine purpose (εἰς τό; *cf.*
1⁵) of the present action designated by τὸ κατέχον is "that he
(namely, the *Anomos; cf.* ἀποκαλύπτεσθαι vv. ³· ⁸) may be revealed in his time," that is, the time set him by God, and not
before. It is already evident (as v. ⁷ explains) that the terminus
of the function indicated by τὸ κατέχον is the apostasy and the
concomitant revelation of the *Anomos.*

The emphatically placed αὐτοῦ (ℵAKP, *et al.*) is misunderstood by
BDEGFL, *et al.*, and changed to ἑαυτοῦ (Zim.; *cf.* Rom. 3²⁵). The καιρός
(*cf.* I 2¹⁷ 5¹) is a day γνωστὴ τῷ κυρίῳ (Zech. 14⁷; *cf.* Ps. Sol. 17²³).—It
is to be observed that we have εἰς τὸ ἀποκαλυφθῆναι κτλ., not τὸ μή
or τοῦ μὴ ἀποκαλυφθῆναι πρὸ τοῦ καιροῦ αὐτοῦ (*cf.* Lk. 4⁴²) or ἕως αὐτὸς
ἀποκαλυφθῇ ἐν τῷ αὐτοῦ καιρῷ.

7. τὸ γὰρ μυστήριον κτλ. "For" (γάρ), to explain the connection between the present action intimated in τὸ κατέχον and
the future revelation of the *Anomos,* "the secret, namely, of lawlessness has already been set in operation" (by Satan), and is
preparing the way for the definitive apostasy on earth and its
concomitant, the revelation of the *Anomos* (v. ³). "Only," that
apostasy will not come and the *Anomos* will not be revealed,
"until he who is now holding sway (or, detains or restrains him)
is put out of the way; and then will be revealed the *Anomos.*"
The phrase τὸ μυστήριον τῆς ἀνομίας, the secret whose content
is lawlessness, or "the mystery of which the characterising feat-

ure, or, so to say, the active principle is ἀνομία " (Ell.), is unique
in the Gk. Bib. The exact meaning cannot at present be made
out; but with some probability it may be referred not to the
ἀποστασία (v.³) itself, but to the secretly developing lawlessness
which is to culminate in the definitive apostasy on earth (cf.
Dob.). As ἐνεργεῖται suggests, an evil power sets in operation
"the secret of lawlessness"; and since it is improbable that
ἀνομίας = ἀνόμου, this evil power is not the Anomos (the instrument of Satan) operating from his place of concealment, but
Satan himself (cf. Schaefer), or more precisely, if we may identify
τὸ κατέχον with Satan, τὸ κατέχον, the spirit that holds sway,
energising in the sons of disobedience. In this case, τὸ κατέχον
(present participle) and τὸ μυστήριον (note the ἤδη) are connected both essentially and temporally.

In the light of I 2¹³ ἐνεργεῖται may be middle "is already operating,"
or passive "has already been set in operation." In the latter case, the
present tense with the adverb is to be rendered by the English perfect;
cf. I 3⁶ ἔχετε πάντοτε and BMT. 17.—It is to be observed in passing
that in vv. ⁶⁻⁷ Paul not only exposes the absurdity of the allegation that
the day is present (v. ²) but also intimates (ἤδη ἐνεργεῖται) that that
day is not far distant.—On μυστήριον, which may have been suggested
by ἀποκαλυφθῆναι, cf. 1 Cor. 2¹, etc. (with τοῦ θεοῦ), Col. 4³, etc. (with
τοῦ Χριστοῦ), Eph. 1⁹ (with θελήματος; cf. Judith 2² with βουλῆς), and
Eph. 6¹⁹ (with εὐαγγελίου); also ἀποκαλύπτειν μυστήρια Sap. 6²² Sir. 3¹⁸
27¹⁶ ff. Dan. (Lxx.) 2²⁸ f. (Th.) 2¹⁹. ³⁰. ⁴⁷. See further, Hatch, Essays, 57 ff.;
SH. on Rom. 11²⁵; Lft. on Col. 1²⁶; Swete on Mk. 4¹¹; and Robinson,
Ephesians, 235 ff.

μόνον ὁ κατέχων ἄρτι κτλ. There is an ellipsis here; and since
the clause with μόνον is evidently the link between the present
action implied in τὸ κατέχον and the terminus of that action at
the revelation of the Anomos, it is natural to supply not only
"that apostasy, which is the culmination of the secret of lawlessness, will not come," but also, in the light of vv. ⁶ᵇ and ⁸ᵃ, "the
Anomos will not be revealed." Both the ellipsis and the position
of ἕως have a striking parallel in Gal. 2¹⁰: μόνον τῶν πτωχῶν ἵνα
μνημονεύωμεν.

On the probable meaning of these obscure words, v. supra, pp. 259 ff.—
Since Gal. 2¹⁰ explains satisfactorily both the ellipsis and the inverted
order of the words, it is unnecessary to resort to other expedients, as,

for example, that of the Vulgate: *tantum ut qui tenet nunc, teneat, donec de medio fiat*. Many commentators think it needless "to supply definitely any verb to complete the ellipsis. The μόνον belongs to ἕως, and simply states the limitation involved in the present working of the μυστήριον τῆς ἀνομίας; it is working already, but only with unconcentrated action until the obstacle be removed and Antichrist be revealed." (Ell.). —The conjunction ἕως occurs in Paul only here and 1 Cor. 4⁵ (ἕως ἄν; so GF in our passage; *cf. BMT.* 323).—ἐκ μέσου is rather frequent in Gk. Bib. with αἴρειν (Col. 2¹⁴ Is. 57², ἐκ μέσου being absolute in both instances), ἐξολεθρεύειν (Exod. 31¹⁴ with λαοῦ), and ἁρπάζειν (Acts 23¹⁰ with αὐτῶν); but ἐκ μέσου with γίνεσθαι occurs only here in the Gk. Bib. Wetstein notes Plut. *Timol.* 238 B: ἔγνω ζῆν καθ' ἑαυτὸν ἐκ μέσου γενόμενος. The fact not the manner of the removal (*cf.* Fulford) is indicated: "to be put out of the way." See further, Soph. *Lex. sub* μέσος and Steph. *Thesaurus,* 6087.

8. καὶ τότε . . . ὁ ἄνομος. With καὶ τότε (*cf.* 1 Cor. 4⁵ Mk. 13²¹·²⁶ᶠ·) balancing καὶ νῦν (v. ⁶), Paul turns from the present (vv. ⁶⁻⁷) to the future, to the fulfilment of the condition stated in vv. ³⁻⁴. The words "and then will be revealed the *Anomos*" (note ὁ ἄνομος = the Hebraistic ὁ ἄνθρωπος τῆς ἀνομίας v. ³) close the argument of vv. ⁶⁻⁷ and open the way for two important points, the description of the destruction of the *Anomos* introduced by ὅν (v. ⁸ᵇ·ᶜ) and the estimate of the significance of the advent of the *Anomos* introduced by the parallel οὗ (vv. ⁹⁻¹²). In passing directly from the revelation to the destruction of the *Anomos* without pausing to describe the *Parousia* of the Lord Jesus, Paul creates the impression that he is interested not in external details (*e. g.* the description of the advent of Christ, of the conflict apparently involved in the destruction of the *Anomos*, and of the action of the *Anomos* intimated in ὥστε κτλ. v. ⁴) but in spiritual values, the triumph of apocalyptic faith in the victory of the good over evil.

ὃν κύριος ἀνελεῖ κτλ. The description of the destruction moves in synonymous parallelism. The first member may be an allusion to Is. 11⁴: καὶ πατάξει γῆν τῷ λόγῳ τοῦ στόματος αὐτοῦ καὶ ἐν πνεύματι διὰ χειλέων ἀνελεῖ ἀσεβῆ. Paul's phrase, however, τῷ πνεύματι τοῦ στόματος αὐτοῦ, unique in the N. T., is probably an unconscious reminiscence of Ps. 32⁶ where the same phrase balances the creative word of God (τῷ λόγῳ τοῦ κυρίου). The second member is synonymous but not quite identical with the first, for instead of "breath of his mouth" we have "manifestation of his *Parousia*." The words ἐπιφάνεια and παρουσία are ultimately synonymous, the former being the Hellenistic technical term for the appearance of a god, and the latter (see I 2¹⁹), the Christian technical term for the expected coming of Christ. If any distinction between the terms is intended, the former will emphasise the presence, the latter, the arrival. The point is that the manifest presence itself is sufficient to destroy the *Anomos*; *cf.* Chrys. ἀρκεῖ παρεῖναι αὐτόν.

In the phrase "with the breath of his mouth" (*cf.* Is. 27⁸ Sap. 11¹⁹ ⁻. Job 4⁹), the means of destruction is not the word (*cf.* Eth. En. 62² Ps. Sol. 17²⁷; also Eth. En. 14² 84¹) but the breath itself. Dibelius sees in the phrase traces of the primitive conception of the magical power of the breath and refers to a passage in Lucian (*The Liar*, 12) where the Babylonian magician gathered together all the snakes from an estate and blew upon them (ἐνεφύσησε), "and straightway every one of them was burnt up by the breathing" (κατεκαύθη ὑπὸ τῷ φυσήματι).—Against the majority of witnesses (אAD*G, *et al.*, the versions and most of the fathers), BDᶜK, *et al.*, omit Ἰησοῦς after κύριος (so Weiss (84) who thinks Ἰησοῦς is added to explain κύριος; *cf.* B in 1 Cor. 5⁵ 11²³).—The reading ἀνελεῖ (BAP) is, according to Dob., supported by ἀνέλοι (DGF), an impossible word from which arose ἀναλοῖ (א* and Orig. in three-fourths of the quotations). Thereupon this present (derived from ἀναλόω = ἀναλίσκω), in view of the future καταργήσει, became ἀναλώσει (DᶜEKL, *et al.*). Weiss (40) thinks that א knew the emendation ἀναλώσει, and formed ἀναλοῖ to approximate to the original ἀνελεῖ. Zim. observes that ἀνέλοι points not to ἀνελεῖ, for the interchange of οι and ει is without parallel, but either to ἀναλοῖ or to a fusion of ἀναλοῖ and ἀνελεῖ; and he concludes that the present ἀναλοῖ, the harder reading, is original (so Lft. Find.). On ἀναιρεῖν (Lxx. and Lk. Acts) = "remove," "slay," a word only here in Paul (if ἀνελεῖ is read), see Plummer, *ICC.* on Lk. 22². On ἀναλόω = ἀναλίσκω, "consume," which is rarer in Gk. Bib. than ἀναιρεῖν, *cf.* Gal. 5¹⁵ Lk. 9⁵⁴.—καταργεῖν, a favourite word of Paul, occurs rarely elsewhere in Gk. Bib. (2 Tim. 1¹⁰ Lk. 13⁷ Heb. 2¹⁴; *cf.* Barn. 2⁶ 5⁶ 9⁴ 15⁵ (καταργήσει τὸν καιρὸν τοῦ ἀνόμου) 16²; Ign. Eph. 13² where it is parallel with καθαιρεῖν and λύειν); it denotes in Paul "annul," "abolish" (*e. g.* νόμον), "destroy," etc., (1 Cor. 15²⁴· ²⁶ of the evil powers including death; *cf.* 2 Tim. 1¹⁰ Barn. 5⁶).—In the N. T. ἐπιφάνεια appears elsewhere only in the Pastorals, where the Christian παρουσία is supplanted by the Hellenistic ἐπιφάνεια; in the Lxx. (mainly 2, 3 Mac.), it is used of the manifestation of God from the sky; *e. g.* ἡ τοῦ θεοῦ ἐπιφάνεια (2 Mac. 15²⁷ Ven.); *cf.* ὁ ἐπιφανὴς κύριος (2 Mac. 15³⁴), and ὁ ἐπιφανὴς θεός (3 Mac. 5³⁵; *cf.* also Driver's *Daniel*, 191 *f.* for coins inscribed "of King Antiochus, god manifest"). Mill. (151) remarks: "ἐπιφάνεια draws attention to the 'presence' as the result of a sublime manifestation of the power and love of God, coming to his people's help." Deissmann (*Light*, 374, 378) notes a third-century (B.C) inscription which records a cure at the temple of Asclepius at Epidaurus: τάν τε παρουσίαν τὰν αὐτοῦ παρενεφάνιξε ὁ Ἀσκλάπιος, "and Asclepius manifested his *Parousia.*" In view of the equivalence of ἐπιφάνεια and παρουσία, the former does not mean "brightness," *illustratio* (Vulg.); *cf.* Bengel: "Sometimes the *apparitio* is spoken of, sometimes, and in the same sense, *adventus* (v. ¹); but here the *apparitio adventus* is prior to the coming itself, or at least is the first gleam of the advent, as ἐπιφάνεια τῆς ἡμέρας" (quoted by Lillie who renders our phrase, "with the appearing of his coming or presence").

9–12. Careless of chronological order but careful of spiritual values (*cf.* v. ⁸), Paul reverts in vv. ⁹⁻¹² to the *Parousia* of the *Anomos*. The section, introduced by οὗ parallel to ὅν (v. ⁸), is intended both as a justification of the universe as moral and as an encouragement (*cf.* vv. ². ¹³ ᶠᶠ·) of the disheartened among the readers. Concerned primarily in the description with the character of the advent of the *Anomos*, he assures the faint-hearted that his *Parousia*, inspired by Satan and attended by outward signs and inward deceit prompted by falsehood and unrighteousness, is intended not for believers but for unbelievers, "the destined to destruction" like "the son of destruction himself (vv. ⁹⁻¹⁰ᵃ). Then justifying the ways of God to men, he observes that the advent of the *Anomos* is for "the doomed" because they have already put themselves into this class by refusing to welcome the heavenly visitor, the influence of the Spirit designed to awaken within them the love for the truth of God which is essential to their salvation (v. 10ᵇ). As a consequence of their refusal, God as righteous judge is himself bound (for he, not Satan or the *Anomos*, is in control of the universe) to send them "an inward working to delude them" into believing the falsehood of the *Anomos* (v. ¹¹), in order that, at the day of judgment, they might be condemned, all of them, on the moral ground that they believed not the truth of God but consented to the unrighteousness of the *Anomos* (v. ¹²).

9. οὖ ἐστιν ἡ παρουσία κτλ.   Instead of ἡ ἀποκάλυψις (1⁷),
which in view of ἀποκαλύπτεσθαι (vv. ³·⁶·⁸) might have been expected, we have Paul's regular word παρουσία, its use here being
due doubtless to association of ideas (τῆς παρουσίας αὐτοῦ v. ⁸).
The collocation of οὖ, which resumes ὅν (v. ⁸ = τὸν ἄνομον), with
αὐτοῦ is more difficult to the eye than to the ear.   The ἐστίν does
not describe something in the process of happening (γίνεται),
but, like πέμπει (v. ¹¹), looks upon the "is to be" as "is" (cf.
ἔρχεται I 5² and ἀποκαλύπτεται 1 Cor. 3¹³).   This advent is first
described as being "in accordance with, in virtue of (κατά), the
energy, that is, the inward operation of the indwelling spirit of
Satan," *daemone in eo omnia operante* (Th. Mops.), the parallel
between the Spirit of holiness in Christ (Rom. 1⁴)· and the indwelling of Satan in the *Anomos* being thus strikingly close (cf.
Th. Mops.)

The grammatical arrangement of the clauses following παρουσία is
uncertain.   Many commentators (*e. g.* Lün. Riggenbach, Born. Dob.)
"connect ἐστίν closely with ἐν πάσῃ δυνάμει κτλ. for the predicate and
treat κατ' ἐνέργειαν τοῦ Σατανᾶ as a mere explanatory appendage; but
with no advantage either to the grammar or the sense" (Lillie).   In the
light of the succession of dative clauses in such passages as Rom. 15¹⁸ ff.
Col. 1¹¹, etc., it is natural to construe ἐστίν with each of the dative
clauses, the καί before the second ἐν (v. ¹⁰) serving to unite the parallel
clauses with ἐν (ἐν πάσῃ δυνάμει κτλ. v. ⁹ and ἐν πάσῃ ἀπάτῃ κτλ. v. ¹⁰);
or we may take ἐστίν with τοῖς ἀπολλυμένοις for the predicate, leaving
the three prepositional phrases under the government of an unexpressed
article after the subject παρουσία: "the *Parousia*, which is κατά, ἐν, and
ἐν, is for the doomed."   But the arrangement is uncertain (see Wohl.).
Logically, however, the advent of the *Anomos* is for the doomed, and the
ἐνέργεια manifests itself both in outward wonders and in inward deceit.
—In the N. T. ἐνέργεια appears only in Paul; it denotes the inward operation (see on ἐνεργεῖν I 2¹³) of God (Eph. 1¹⁹ 3⁷ with κατά) and of Christ
(Col. 1²⁹ Phil. 3²¹ with κατά).   This single instance of ἐνέργεια in reference to Satanic activity is in keeping with the usage of ἐνεργεῖν in
v. ⁷ and Eph. 2².   In the Lxx. ἐνέργεια is found only in Sap. and 2, 3 Mac.;
it indicates among other things the operation of God (Sap. 7²⁶ 2 Mac. 3²⁹
3 Mac. 4²¹ 5¹²· ²⁸).   ἐνέργεια differs from δύναμις with which it is sometimes associated (as here and Sap. 13⁴ Eph. 3⁷), as "operative power"
from "potential power" (Mill.); cf. Reitzenstein, *Poimandres*, 352, l. 24:
δαίμονος γάρ οὐσία ἐνέργεια.   On Satan, see I 2¹⁸.

ἐν πάσῃ δυνάμει κτλ. The advent of the *Anomos* is further described in a second prepositional clause as being "in (that is, 'clothed with,' 'attended by') all power and signs and portents that originate in falsehood." Paul co-ordinates δύναμις, the abstract potential power, with σημεῖα καὶ τέρατα, the concrete signs and portents, intending no doubt by δύναμις the specific power to perform miracles. Since he seems to feel no difficulty with this co-ordination, we need not hesitate to construe πάσῃ both with δυνάμει and (by zeugma) with σημείοις καὶ τέρασιν (a common phrase in the Gk. Bib.). It follows that ψεύδους is likewise to be taken with all three substantives (*cf.* v. ² ὡς δι' ἡμῶν). The reality of the capacity and of its expression in outward forms is not denied; but the origin is stigmatised as falsehood.

While many expositors connect πάσῃ and ψεύδους with all three nouns (*e. g.* Lün. Ell. Lillie, Lft. Schmiedel, Wohl. Mill.), some (*e. g.* Calv. Find. Dob.), feeling troubled it may be by the abstract δύναμις, restrict πάσῃ to the first and ψεύδους to the last two nouns, "in all power—both signs and wonders of falsehood" (*cf.* Vulg.).—The ἐν is variously understood, "in the sphere or domain of" (Ell. Mill. *et al.*), "consisting in" (Born. Dob.), or *"verbunden mit"* (Wohl.). The gen. ψεύδους is interpreted as of "origin" (Dob.), "quality" (Chrys. Find. Mill.), "object" (Ambst. Grot. De W. Lün. Ell.), or "reference" in the widest sense (*e. g.* Riggenbach, Alford, Wohl.).—As all Christians are empowered ἐν πάσῃ δυνάμει (Col. 1¹¹), and as the indwelling Christ works in Paul ἐν δυνάμει σημείων καὶ τεράτων (Rom. 15¹⁹), so Satan operates in the *Anomos* with the result that his advent is attended by all power to work wonders. Since elsewhere in Paul we have not the singular "a power" (Mk. 6⁵ 9³⁹) but the plural δυνάμεις (2 Cor. 12¹²; *cf.* Acts 2²² Heb. 2⁴) in reference to miracles, the rendering "with every form of external power" is evidently excluded. The phrase σημεῖα καὶ τέρατα is common in the Gk. Bib. (Exod. 7³ 11⁹, etc.; Rom. 15¹⁹ 2 Cor. 12¹² Heb. 2⁴, etc.), σημεῖα suggesting more clearly than τέρατα (which in N. T. appears only with σημεῖα) that the marvellous manifestations of power are indications of the presence of a supramundane being, good or evil. ψεῦδος, a rare word in Paul, is opposed to ἀλήθεια (vv. ¹¹⁻¹² Rom. 1²⁵ Eph. 4²⁵) and parallel with ἀδικία (vv. ¹⁰· ¹²).—Paul is quite content with a general description of the circumstances attending the advent of the *Anomos;* but later descriptions of the Antichrist delight in the details, *e. g.* Rev. 13¹³ Asc. Isa. 5⁴ Sib. Orac. 3⁶³ ᶠ· 2¹⁶⁷‿ᶠᶠ·; see Bousset, *Antichrist,* 115 *ff.* and Charles on Asc. Isa. 5⁴.

10. καὶ ἐν πάσῃ ἀπάτῃ ἀδικίας. "And with all deceit that
originates in unrighteousness." While the preceding clause with
ἐν (v. ¹⁰) directed attention to the accompaniment of the advent
of the *Anomos* mainly on the objective side, this closely related
clause, united to the former by καί, directs attention to the subjective side. Hand in hand with the external signs and wonders
prompted by falsehood goes deceit, the purpose to deceive,
inspired by unrighteousness; *cf.* Rev. 13¹³ ᶠ· καὶ ποιεῖ σημεῖα
μεγάλα . . . καὶ πλανᾷ.

τοῖς ἀπολλυμένοις. Finally the class is designated for whom
alone the *Parousia*, with its attendant outward signs and inward
deceit, is intended "the perishing," those whose end (Phil. 3¹⁹)
like that of "the son of destruction" is ἀπώλεια. The tacit opposite of οἱ ἀπολλύμενοι (a Pauline expression; *cf.* 1 Cor. 1¹⁸ 2 Cor.
2¹⁵ 4³) is οἱ σωζόμενοι (1 Cor. 1¹⁸ 2 Cor. 2¹⁵; *cf.* Lk. 13²³ Acts 2⁴⁷),
a phrase that characterises the remnant in Is. 37³² (*cf.* 45²⁰ Tobit
14⁷). As "the saved" are the believers so "the doomed" are
the unbelievers irrespective of nationality.

The phrase ἀπάτη ἀδικίας (DKLP prefix τῆς) is unique in the Gk.
Bib. For ἀπάτη, in the active sense of "deceit," *cf.* Col. 2⁸ Eph. 4²²
Eccl. 9⁶ 4 Mac. 18⁸; for the genitive, *cf.* Mk. 4¹⁹ Heb. 3¹³ and contrast
Test. xii, Reub. 5⁵. ἀδικία is a common word in Gk. Bib.; in Paul
it is sometimes opposed to ἀλήθεια (v. ¹² Rom. 1¹⁸ 2⁸ 1 Cor. 13⁶).—The
present participle ἀπολλυμένοις is general, indicating a class; a timeless aorist might have been used (*cf.* οἱ σωθέντες Is. 10²⁰ Neh. 1²).
Bousset (*Antichrist*, 13) restricts "the doomed" to the Jews, a restriction which is "permitted neither by the expression nor by the context"
(Dob.). The ἐν (before τοῖς) inserted by KLP, *et al.*, may have been influenced by 2 Cor. 2¹⁵ 4³. In the light of Mt. 24²⁴ 2 Cor. 4³, Lillie is disposed to take τοῖς ἀπολλυμένοις not with ἐστίν but with ἀπάτῃ ἀδικίας;
so also Dob. on the ground that the deceit is only for unbelievers while
the miracles could be seen by both believers (but without injury to
them) and unbelievers.

ἀνθ᾽ ὧν τὴν ἀγάπην κτλ. That the advent of the *Anomos* is
for "the doomed" (vv. ⁹⁻¹⁰ᵃ) is their own fault "because (ἀνθ᾽
ὧν) they had not welcomed the love for the truth intended for
their salvation." The phrase τὴν ἀγάπην τῆς ἀληθείας, only
here in the Gk. Bib., suggests that God had sent them the divine

power (Christ or the Spirit) to create in them a love for the truth
of God (Rom. 1²⁵), or Christ (2 Cor. 11¹⁰; hence DE add here
Χριστοῦ), or the gospel (Gal. 2⁵·¹⁴ Col. 1⁵); and that they had
refused to welcome the heavenly visitor. Having thus refused
the help designed (εἰς τό) for their salvation, they must take
upon themselves the consequences of their refusal as stated in
vv. ¹¹⁻¹².

ἀνθ' ὧν, very common in Lxx. (cf. Amos 5¹¹), is used elsewhere in the
N. T. only by Luke; it means regularly "because," but occasionally
"wherefore" (Lk. 12³); cf. Bl. 40¹.—In Paul, ἡ ἀλήθεια, which is often
used absolutely (vv. ¹²⁻¹³ Rom. 1¹⁸ 2⁸·²⁰ 1 Cor. 13⁶, etc.), means not
"truthfulness," or "the truth" in general, but specifically the truth of
God, of Christ, or of the gospel preached by Paul as contrasted with
the falsehood of the *Anomos* (v. ¹¹; cf. Rom. 1²⁵ 3⁷). In the light of
πιστεύειν τῇ ἀληθείᾳ (v. ¹²), ἀληθείας is genitive of the object. Elsewhere in Paul ἡ ἀγάπη is used with the gen. (subjective) of the person,
θεοῦ (so Lk. 11⁴²), Χριστοῦ, πνεύματος (Rom. 15³⁰), to denote the divine
love for men. Chrys. explains "the love of truth" as equivalent to
Christ; Primasius takes ἀληθείας as = Christ (cf. Jn. 5⁴³ 14⁶). The phrase,
however, is natural in view of the use of ἀγαπᾶν with various impersonal
objects (Eph. 5²⁵; cf. 2 Tim. 4⁸·¹⁰ Heb. 1⁹ = Ps. 44⁸ Jn. 3¹⁹; also ἀγαπᾶν
ἀλήθειαν Ps. 50⁸ 83¹² Zech. 8¹⁹). The divine offer, made through Christ
or the Spirit, is not simply the gospel which might be intellectually ap-
prehended, but the more difficult love for it, interest in it; contrast
this refusal with the welcome which the readers gave to the gospel
(δέχεσθαι I 1⁶ 2¹³).—εἰς τό (I 2¹²) may indicate purpose (ἵνα σωθῶσιν
I 2¹⁶) or intended result (εἰς τὴν σωτηρίαν αὐτῶν; cf. ὥστε v. ⁴). On
the variant ἐξεδέξαντο, cf. Sir. 6²³.

11. καὶ διὰ τοῦτο πέμπει. "And for this reason (because they
did not welcome the love for the truth), God sends (is to send)
them an inward working of delusion." The καί may be consecutive, "and so," or it may designate the correspondence of guilt
and punishment. The πέμπει refers not to the time previous
to the revelation of the *Anomos* (ἐνεργεῖται v. ⁷) but, as ἐστίν
(v. ⁹) intimates, to the time when the apostasy comes and the
Anomos is revealed.

ὁ θεὸς ἐνέργειαν πλάνης κτλ. The position of ὁ θεός is emphatic. In appearance, Satan is responsible for the future success of the *Anomos* with "the doomed"; in reality it is God

who is in supreme control, working out his moral purposes
through the agencies of evil. Since the divine influence designed
to stir up a love for the gospel is unwelcome, God sends another
visitor, the ἐνέργεια πλάνης, whose function it is, as a servant
of the divine purpose, to prepare the way for final judgment
(v. ¹²) by first deluding the minds of "the doomed" into believing the falsehood of the *Anomos*.

τῷ ψεύδει balances τῆς ἀληθείας (v. ¹⁰) and εἰς τό introduces the
primary purpose of πέμπει. In the striking phrase ἐνέργεια πλάνης,
only here in Gk. Bib., πλάνης is a genitive of the object, and denotes the
goal of the active inward energy, namely, "delusion," the state of being
deceived (see on I 2³): "an energy unto delusion." On διὰ τοῦτο, see
I 2¹³; for πέμπειν τινί, cf. 1 Cor. 4¹⁷ Phil. 2¹⁹. D omits καί; GF, et al.,
omit αὐτούς; F omits τῷ; KLP, et al., forgetting ἐστίν (v. ⁹) read πέμψει.
On διὰ τοῦτο πέμπει, cf. Rom. 1²⁴· ²⁶ διὸ παρέδωκεν.

12. ἵνα κριθῶσιν κτλ. The ultimate purpose of πέμπει is
contingent upon the fulfilment of the initial purpose in εἰς τὸ
πιστεῦσαι; hence ἵνα depends on εἰς τό. Wishing to insist that
the basis of judgment (cf. 1⁵⁻¹⁰) is "believing the falsehood,"
Paul repeats the thought in a parallelism which designates "the
doomed" negatively as "all who have not believed the truth"
of Christ, and positively, "who have consented to the unrighteousness" of the *Anomos* (cf. ἀδικίας v. ¹⁰). The antithesis of
"truth" and "unrighteousness" (cf. Rom. 2⁸ 1 Cor. 13⁶) intimates that "truth" is regarded more on the moral than on the
purely intellectual side, the truth of God, Christ, or the gospel as preached by Paul; and the parallelism of πιστεύειν and
εὐδοκεῖν hints that in believing the will is an important factor.

The phrases πιστεύειν τῷ ψεύδει (v. ¹¹) and τῇ ἀληθείᾳ do not occur
elsewhere in the Gk. Bib. πιστεύειν with dative is employed elsewhere
by Paul only in citations (Rom. 4³ τῷ θεῷ; Rom. 10¹⁶ τῇ ἀκοῇ; cf. the
accus. 1 Cor. 13⁷ πάντα πιστεύει). For the impersonal object, cf. πίστις
with εὐαγγελίου (Phil. 1²⁷) and ἐνεργείας (Col. 2¹²). The construction
εὐδοκεῖν τινι (1 Esd. 4³⁹ Sir. 18³¹ (A) 1 Mac. 1⁴³) does not appear elsewhere in N. T.; Paul construes εὐδοκεῖν elsewhere with the infinitive
(see I 2⁸) and with ἐν and dative (1 Cor. 10⁵ 2 Cor. 12¹⁰; so here AEKLP,
et al.).—κρίνεσθαι (opposed to σώζεσθαι v. ¹⁰) gets here by context the
meaning κατακρίνεσθαι (cf. Heb. 13⁴); κρίνειν is common in Gk. Bib.

(Rom. 2¹² 3⁷ Is. 66¹⁶, etc.).—Exegetically it is unimportant whether
πάντες (BDEKLP, *et al.*) or ἅπαντες (אAGF, *et al.*) is read (*cf.* Gal. 3²⁸);
WH. read ἅπας but once in Paul (Eph. 6¹³). The expression ἅπας ὁ or
ὁ ἅπας is chiefly Lukan (also Mt. 28¹¹ Mk. 16¹⁵ 1 Tim. 1¹⁶; *cf.* Gen. 19⁴,
etc.); on πάντες οἱ πιστεύοντες (which K reads here), see I 1⁷; on
πάντες οἱ πιστεύσαντες, *cf.* 1¹⁰.—On the contrast between ἀλήθεια and
ἀδικία, *cf.* Rom. 2⁸ 1 Cor. 13⁶; on the thought of vv. ¹¹⁻¹², *cf.* Born. *ad*
loc. and Rom. 1¹⁸⁻³².

The Origin and Significance of the Anomos.

On the basis of what has been said above on vv. ³⁻⁷, a general
word may be added as to the origin of the *Anomos* and the significance of the same to Paul. The name "Antichrist," com-
monly employed to designate the being variously described by
Paul as "the man of lawlessness"="the lawless one," "the son
of destruction," "the one who opposes and exalts himself against
every one called God," etc., does not appear in extant literature
before First John (2¹⁸· ²² 4³; *cf.* 2 Jn. 7). In that epistle, the
Antichrist, who is assumed to be a familiar figure, is both the
definite being who is to come and the spirit already in the world
(κόσμος), possessing men so that they are themselves called
"Antichrists" (2¹⁸), and leading them both to deny that Jesus
is the Christ, Son of God, come in the flesh (4²) and to separate themselves from their fellow-Christians (2¹⁹). Whether the
name was coined by the Ephesian school is unknown.

But while the designation "Antichrist" is later than Paul, the
idea for which it stands is evidently pre-Christian. On the one
hand, the opponent of Israel and so of God is identified with a
heathen ruler, for example, with Antiochus Epiphanes by Daniel
(the earliest instance; *cf.* Pompey in Ps. Sol., and "the last
leader of that time" in Apoc. Bar. 40¹); on the other hand, the
opponent of God is conceived as a Satanic being, Beliar (*e. g.*
Jub. and Test. xii). But the *Anomos* of Paul is neither a heathen
tyrant, nor a political ruler, nor a Zealotic false-Messiah (Mk.
13²² = Mt. 24²⁴ and possibly Jn. 5⁴³), but is an extraordinary man
controlled completely by Satan,—a non-political conception that
suggests the original influence of the Babylonian myth of Tiâ-
mat, the sea-monster that opposes Marduk and is vanquished,

18

but who at the end is to revolt only to be destroyed. In fact, due to the researches of such scholars as Gunkel, Bousset, Charles, and Gressmann, it is not infrequently held that traces of that primeval myth, however applied, are discoverable in the O. T. (*cf.* Daniel's description of Antiochus), in subsequent Jewish apocalyptic, and in the apocalyptic utterances in the N. T.; and it is confidently expected by some that from the same source light may shine upon the hitherto inexplicable technical terms of apocalyptic. The precise question, however, whether the *Anomos* of Paul is the indirect result of the conception of the Antichrist as originally a humanised devil (Bousset) or is the direct result of the fusion of the Antichrist conceived as purely human and of Belial conceived as purely Satanic (Charles, whose sketch of the development of the idea of Antichrist, especially in the period subsequent to Paul when the figure of Antichrist is further affected by the Neronic myths, is particularly attractive) may perhaps be regarded as still open.

In estimating the significance of apocalyptic in general, it is to be remembered that actual experiences of suffering compelled the Jews, a people singularly sensitive to spiritual values, to attempt to reconcile these experiences with the ineradicable conviction that the Lord is righteous and that they are his elect, and that the apocalyptic category, whatever may have been the origin of its component elements, is the means by which the assertion of their religious faith is expressed. The Book of Daniel, for example, is considered as a classic instance not only of apocalyptic form but also of the venture of faith in the triumph of righteousness,—a judgment sustained by the immediate effect of that "tract for the times," and by its subsequent influence not only on apocalyptic writers in general but also on the Master himself. The literary successors of Daniel are not to be reckoned as purely imitators; they adhere indeed closely, sometimes slavishly, to the classic tradition; but they also proclaim, each in his way, their originality by what they retain, omit, or insert, and by what they emphasise or fail to emphasise; and still further, they keep alive the old religious faith, even if they differ widely from one another in spiritual insight.

Into the apocalyptic and eschatological tradition and faith of
late Judaism, Paul entered as did the Master before him. But
Paul, to refer only to him, brought to his inheritance not only
his own personal equation but also his religious experience in
Jesus the Christ. Through that experience, his world became
enlarged and his sympathies broadened. To him, Christianity
was a universal religion in which Jesus the Messiah was not a national political factor but the world-redeeming power and wisdom
of God. While holding to the traditional conceptualism of apocalyptic and to the essence of its faith, he demonstrates the originality of his religious insight in his attitude to the traditional forms.
This scribe who had been made a disciple to the kingdom knows
how to bring forth out of his treasures things new and old. The
political traits of the Antichrist being uncongenial, he reverts,
quite unconsciously, in the attempted session of the *Anomos* in
the heavenly temple of God, to elements of the non-political
primeval myth; and equips the *Anomos* with Satanic power
not for political purposes, but to deceive the doomed (*cf.* the
false prophet in Rev. 16[13] 19[20] 20[10]). On the other hand, his
mystical experience in Christ leads him to make the parallel between the Spirit of holiness in Christ and the operation of the
spirit of Satan in the *Anomos* almost complete. This fusion of the
old and new in the mind of the Christian Paul gives an original
turn to the conception of the Antichrist. With a supreme disregard for externals and with a keen sense for the relevant, he
succeeds in making pre-eminent his faith that God is Abba, that
the world is moral, that righteousness triumphs; and his confidence is immovable that a day will come when the sway of the
sovereign Father of the Lord Jesus Christ will be recognised, for
obstacles will be removed and the believer will be delivered from
the evil one. And Paul is at pains to observe that even Satan
and his peculiar instrument, the *Anomos*, are under the control
of the divine purpose; that "the destined to destruction" destroy themselves by refusing to welcome the heavenly influence
which makes for their salvation; and that therefore it is really
God himself who on the ground of their refusal sends to the
doomed an ἐνέργεια πλάνης. "It must have been a great,

deeply religious spirit who created this conception, one proof
more for the genuinely Pauline origin of our epistle" (Dob. 296).

The literature of the subject is enormous. Of especial importance are
Schürer; Bousset, *Relig.*[2]; Charles, *Eschat.* (together with his editions
of apocalyptic literature and his articles in *EB.* and *Ency. Brit.*[11]);
Söderblom, *La Vie Future d'après le Mazdéisme*, 1901; Volz. *Eschat.*;
Gunkel, *Zum religionsgeschichtlichen Verständniss des N. T.* 1903;
Klausner, *Die Messianischen Vorstellungen des jüdischen Volkes im
Zeitalter der Tannaiten*, 1904; Gressmann, *Der Ursprung der Israel
itschen-jüdischen Eschatologie*, 1905; Mathews, *The Messianic Hope in
the N. T.* 1905; Bousset's commentary on Revelation in Meyer, 1906;
J. H. Gardiner, *The Bible as English Literature*, 1906, 250 *ff.*; Rabinsohn,
Le Messianisme dans le Talmud et les Midraschim, 1907; Oesterley,
Evolution of the Messianic Idea, 1908; Clemen, *Religionsgeschichtliche
Erklärung des N. T.* 1909; Dibelius, *Die Geisterwelt im Glauben des
Paulus*, 1909; and Moffatt's commentary on Revelation in *EGT.* 1910.
Likewise of special importance are such specific works as Gunkel's
Schöpfung und Chaos, 1895; Bousset's *Antichrist*, 1895 (in English,
1896; *cf.* his articles on *Antichrist* in *EB. ERE.* and *Ency. Brit.*[11]);
Wadstein's *Eschatologische Ideengruppe: Antichrist*, etc., 1896; Charles's
Ascension of Isaiah, 1900, li *ff.*; Friedländer's *Der Antichrist in den
vorchristlichen jüdischen Quellen*, 1901; the articles on *Antichrist* by
Louis Ginsberg in the *Jewish Ency.*, and by Sieffert in *PRE.*; and the
discussions by Briggs in his *Messiah of the Apostles*, and by Born. Find.
Schmiedel, Wohl. Mill. Dob. and Dibelius in their respective commentaries. For the later history of the Antichrist, see, in addition to Bousset's
monograph, Preuss, *Die Vorstellung vom Antichrist im späteren Mittelalter,
bei Luther*, etc. 1906 (and Köhler's review in *TLZ.* 1907, 356 *ff.*). For
the history of the interpretation of 2[1-12], see the commentaries of Lün.
Born. and Wohl.; Mill. (166–173) gives an excellent sketch.

IV. THANKSGIVING, COMMAND, AND
PRAYER (2[13-17]).

Like the thanksgiving and prayer (1[3-12]) and the exhortation
(vv. [1-12]), this new section (vv. [13-17]), though addressed to the
converts as a whole, is intended especially for the encouragement of the faint-hearted whose assurance of salvation was wavering, and who had become agitated by the assertion (v. [2]) that
the day of the Lord was actually present. With a purposed repetition of 1[3], Paul emphasises his obligation to thank God for

them notwithstanding their discouraged utterances, because, as was said in the first epistle (I 1⁴ ᶠᶠ·), they are beloved and elect, chosen of God from everlasting, and destined to obtain the glory of Christ (vv. ¹³⁻¹⁴). Thus beloved and elect, they should have no fear about the future and no disquietude by reason of the assertion that the day is present; on the contrary, remembering the instructions received both orally and in the first epistle, they should stand firm and hold to those deliverances (v. ¹⁵). Aware, however, that only the divine power can make effectual his appeal, and aware that righteousness, guaranteed by the Spirit, is indispensable to salvation, Paul prays that Christ and God who in virtue of their grace had already commended their love to Christians in the death of Christ and had granted them through the Spirit inward assurance of salvation and hope for the ultimate acquisition of the glory of Christ, may vouchsafe also to the faint-hearted readers that same assurance of salvation, and strengthen them in works and words of righteousness.

This section differs from 1³⁻¹², and from I 2¹³–3¹³ which it resembles closely in arrangement (*cf.* αὐτὸς δέ vv. ¹⁶⁻¹⁷ with I 3¹¹, and the repeated thanksgiving v. ¹³ with I 2¹³), in having the command (v. ¹⁵).

¹³*Now we ought to thank God always for you, brothers beloved by the Lord, because God chose you from the beginning of time to be saved by consecration of the Spirit and by faith in the truth;* ¹⁴*and to this end he called you by the gospel which we preach, namely, to the obtaining of the glory of our Lord Jesus Christ.* ¹⁵*So then, brothers, stand firm and hold fast to the instructions that you have been taught whether we delivered them orally or by letter.* ¹⁶*Now may our Lord, Jesus Christ himself and God, our Father, who loved us (Christians) and gave us, in virtue of grace, eternal encouragement and good hope,* ¹⁷*encourage your hearts, and make you steady in every good work you do and word you utter.*

13. ἡμεῖς δὲ ὀφείλομεν κτλ. The similarity in thought and language between the first clause of this verse and that of 1³ suggests of itself a purposed return to the obligation there expressed "to give thanks to God always for you, brothers"; and the differences observable in our verse, the order of ὀφείλομεν εὐχαριστεῖν and the insertion of ἡμεῖς, tend to confirm the suggestion. By putting ὀφείλομεν first, Paul lays stress on the obligation and at the same time, by the very emphasis, intimates that the repetition of 1³ is intentional.   By inserting ἡμεῖς (*i. e.* Paul, Silvanus, and Timothy as in I 2¹³· ¹⁷) he reiterates emphatically what was implied in 1³ that he and his fellow-writers are morally bound to thank God, notwithstanding the fact that the readers, voicing the discouragement of the faint-hearted, had declared to Paul by letter that they were not worthy of salvation and that therefore Paul ought not to thank God for them as he had done in his former epistle.   If this is the case, δέ is not adversative, contrasting in some manner with vv. ⁹⁻¹², but introduces, as in v. ¹, a new point.

That δέ introduces a resumption of 1³ is frequently admitted (B. Weiss, Dob. Dibelius, *et al.*).   Usually, however, a contrast is discovered between ἡμεῖς and the doomed in v. ¹⁰ (*e. g.* Lün. Ell. Lft.), a contrast which is pertinent only if ἡμεῖς referred to the Thessalonians or all Christians.   To obviate this difficulty, ἡμεῖς is put over against God who sends the energy of delusion;   or over against the *Anomos;* or over against the mystery of lawlessness (Hofmann, Riggenbach, Denney, *et al.*);   but these interpretations are, as Wrede insists (21), somewhat forced.   On the other hand, the contention of Wrede (and Schmiedel) that ἡμεῖς is taken over mechanically from I 2¹³ arises from the neces-sity of explaining the workings of the *falsarius.*   A similar resumption of the thanksgiving occurs in I 2¹³ (from 1²; *cf.* 3⁹);   but in I 2¹³ we have καί not δέ, and the main point of I 2¹⁻¹² is resumed as well as the thanks-giving of 1².   Contrast with our verse I 2¹⁷ (ἡμεῖς δέ) where δέ is adver-sative: "we apostles" over against the Jews who insinuated that we did not wish to return.

ἠγαπημένοι ὑπὸ κυρίου. The readers are addressed not simply as brothers (1³ 2¹) but as brothers "beloved by the Lord," that is, "whom Christ loved and loves."   The phrase ἠγαπημένοι ὑπὸ κυρίου does not appear in 1³ ᶠᶠ·, though the idea of election is there implied in the statement that the endurance and faith of the readers is evidence of God's purpose to deem them worthy of the kingdom.   In I 1⁴, however, where Paul openly draws the conclusion that the readers are elect from the fact that the Spirit is at work not simply in him (1⁵) but especially in the Thessa-

Ionians who welcomed the gospel (1^{6-10}), the same estimate is given: ἀδελφοὶ ἠγαπημένοι ὑπὸ τοῦ θεοῦ. The repetition here of these words of appreciation which recall the love of Christ (v. ^{16}) who died for them (I 5^{10}) and who as Spirit quickens within them the sense of the divine love (3^5), and which suggest (cf. Rom. 1^7 Col. 3^{12}) that as beloved they are elect (I 1^4), is evidently designed for the purpose of encouraging the faint-hearted with the assurance of salvation, and of awakening within them, as elect and beloved, the obligation to fulfil their Christian duty (v. ^{15} ἄρα οὖν).

On the phrase, cf. Test. xii, Iss. 1^1 (v. l.) ἠγαπημένοι ὑπὸ κυρίου and Deut. 33^{12}; and see note on I 1^4. On the perfect participle "implying a past action and affirming an existing result," cf. BMT. 154 and ἐκκέχυται Rom. 5^5.—(ὁ) κύριος is used frequently in Paul of the Lord Jesus; but it is especially characteristic of the Macedonian letters, fourteen times in I, eight times in II, and ten times in Phil. In our letters it appears in reminiscences from the Lxx. (I 4^6 II 1^9 2^{13}); in such phrases as ὁ λόγος τοῦ κυρίου (I 1^8 4^{15} II 3^1), ἐν κυρίῳ (I 3^8 5^{12}; cf. Gal. 5^{10} Rom. $16^{2\,\text{ff.}}$ and eight times in Phil.), and ἡμέρα κυρίου (I 5^2 II 2^2; cf. 1 Cor. 5^5); in prayers (I 3^{12} II $3^{5.\,16}$); and in other connections (I 1^6 4^{15-17} 5^{27} II 3^3). In the light of this usage, κύριος here (contrast I 1^4) and 3^{16} (contrast I 5^{23}) is natural; cf. παρὰ θεῷ II 1^6 with ἔκδικος κύριος I 4^6 in the light of βῆμα θεοῦ (Rom. 14^{10}) or Χριστοῦ (2 Cor. 5^{10}). On the use of ὁ κύριος, see especially Mill. 136 ff. and Zahn, Introd. I, 254.—D corrects to θεοῦ; ℵA, et al., read τοῦ κυρίου.

ὅτι εἵλατο ὑμᾶς κτλ. In advancing the reason why (ὅτι = "because" as in I 2^{13} II 1^3) he ought to thank God always for them, Paul lets his religious imagination range from everlasting to everlasting,—from the choice of God unto salvation before the foundation of the world, to the divine invitation in time extended to the readers through the preaching of the gospel, and to the consummation in the age to come, the acquiring of the glory which Christ possesses and which he will share with those who are consecrated to God by the Spirit and have faith in the truth of the gospel. The purpose of this pregnant summary of Paul's religious convictions (cf. Rom. 8^{28-30}) is the encouragement of the faint-hearted. Not only are they chosen, they are chosen from all eternity (ἀπ' ἀρχῆς); not only are they chosen,

they are also called; and not only are they called, they are also
destined to acquire the fulness of salvation in eternity.

The order of words, εἵλατο ὑμᾶς ὁ θεός (cf. I 5⁹) not ὑμᾶς εἵλατο,
tells against the suggestion that the readers are contrasted with "the
doomed" (v. ¹⁰). K reads εἵλετο (cf. προείπομεν (AKL) in I 4⁶, and
see, for mixed aorists, Bl. 21¹). For ὑμᾶς (BAGFP, et al.), ℵD, et al., read
ἡμᾶς; so also for ὑμᾶς after ἐκάλεσεν in v. ¹⁴, BAD read ἡμᾶς, a reading
which takes the nerve out of Paul's intention and which in v. ¹⁴ leads to
the impossible.—αἱρεῖσθαι (Phil. 1²² Heb. 11²⁵), like ἐκλέγεσθαι (1 Cor.
1²⁷ ff. Eph. 1⁴), προγινώσκειν (Rom. 8²⁹ 11²) and προορίζειν (Rom.
8²⁹ f.; 1 Cor. 2⁷ πρὸ τῶν αἰώνων; Eph. 1⁵· ¹¹), is used of God's election
as in Deut. 26¹⁸ (cf. προαιρεῖσθαι Deut. 7⁶ f· 10¹⁵); cf. τιθέναι I 5⁹,
καταξιοῦν II 1⁵, and ἀξιοῦν 1¹¹. The idea of election is constant, but
the words expressing it vary,—a consideration that accounts for the
fact that elsewhere in the N. T. αἱρεῖσθαι is not used of the divine election.—The reading ἀπ' ἀρχῆς (ℵDEKL, Pesh. Arm. Eth. Chrys. Th.
Mops. Ambst. et al.) suits Paul's purpose of encouraging the faint-
hearted better than ἀπαρχήν (BGP, Vulg. Boh. Didymus, Ambrose,
et al.). The former reading is harder in that elsewhere Paul uses not
ἀπ' ἀρχῆς but πρὸ τῶν αἰώνων (1 Cor. 2⁷), ἀπὸ τῶν αἰώνων (Col. 1²⁶) or
πρὸ καταβολῆς κόσμου (Eph. 1⁴) to express the idea "from eternity,"
while ἀπαρχή, apart from Jas. 1¹⁸ Rev. 14⁴, is found in the N. T. only
in Paul (seven times; it is common in Lxx., especially in Ezek.). Most
commentators prefer ἀπ' ἀρχῆς and interpret it as = ἀπ' αἰῶνος (cf. Ps.
89²); a few, however (so recently Wohl.), seek to refer ἀπ' ἀρχῆς to the beginnings of Christianity either as such or in Thessalonica, a view possible
in itself (cf. 1 Jn. 2⁷· ²⁴), though more appropriate to a later period in
Paul's career, but not probable in Paul who, when he refers to ἐν ἀρχῇ
(Phil. 4¹⁵) adds not only τοῦ εὐαγγελίου (cf. 1 Clem. 47²) but also ὅτε
ἐξῆλθον ἀπὸ τῆς Μακεδονίας. As already indicated, ἀπ' ἀρχῆς does not
occur elsewhere in Paul; it is, however, common in the Gk. Bib. as a
designation of beginnings whether in eternity or in time (cf. Is. 63¹⁶ Sir.
24⁹ 1 Jn. 2¹³ Mt. 19⁴, etc.; also 2 Reg. 7¹⁰ Ps. 73² Lk. 1², etc.). Apart
from our passage and Phil. 4¹⁵, ἀρχή denotes in Paul "power" or, in
plural, "powers."—The reading ἀπαρχήν which, under the influence of
the Vulg. primitias (Wiclif: "the first fruytis"), was current in Latin
exegesis (Dob.), implies that "believers have been, as it were, set aside
for a sacred offering, by a metaphor taken from the ancient custom of
the law" (Calvin, who, however, prefers ἀπ' ἀρχῆς "which almost all the
Gk. Mss. have"). The reference in ἀπαρχή is (1) to the Thessalonians
as first-fruits consecrated to God in opposition to the mass of "the
doomed" (Hofmann, who notes Rev. 14⁴; but see Swete on that passage); (2) to the Thessalonians or Macedonians as first-fruits "con-

trasted with others yet to follow" (Moff., ἀπαρχή here as in 1 Cor. 15²⁰
implying others to come); or (3), combining an estimate of worth with
the idea of historical priority, to the fact that the Thessalonians are
consecrated for a possession (Jas. 1¹⁸ Rev. 14⁴), and are, along with
the Philippians and others, especially a first-fruit from paganism (B
Weiss).—It is noteworthy, however, that, apart from Rom. 11¹⁶ where
the reference to the cult (Num. 15¹⁹ f.) is obvious, Paul elsewhere qualifies ἀπαρχή with a genitive as in Rom. 16⁵ 1 Cor. 16¹⁵ (cf. Rom. 8²³
1 Cor. 15²⁰· ²³; and 1 Clem. 24¹). The absence of the qualifying genitive
in this passage suggests either that the Thessalonians are first in value,
a choice fruit, which is improbable; or that they are the first in time,
which is impossible, for they are not even the first-fruits of Macedonia.
Grot. obviates the difficulty by supposing that our letter was written as
early as 38 A.D., that is, before Paul came to Thessalonica, and was addressed to Jason and other Jewish Christians who had come thither
from Palestine. Harnack likewise (v. supra p. 53 f.) thinks that our letter
was addressed to Jewish Christians in Thessalonica, a group of believers
that formed a kind of annex to the larger Gentile Christian church,
and interprets ἀπαρχήν as referring specifically to the Jews who were
the first-fruits of Thessalonica (Acts 17⁴). But apart from the fact
that, in a section written for the encouragement of those who were losing the assurance of salvation, ἀπ' ἀρχῆς (cf. Sir. 24⁹) is more appropriate than ἀπαρχήν, it is difficult to understand, on Harnack's theory,
the omission of the expected τῆς Θεσσαλονίκης or the τῶν Θεσσαλονικέων,
for in the letter to Corinth, a city in which two distinct groups of Christians, Jewish and Gentile, are unknown, the familia of Stephanas is
called not simply ἀπαρχή but ἀπαρχὴ τῆς 'Αχαίας (1 Cor. 16¹⁵).—In
passing it is to be noted not only that D in Rom. 16⁵ and ℵ in Rev.
14⁴ change the forceful ἀπαρχή to the meaningless ἀπ' ἀρχῆς, but also
that in Sir. 24⁹ (Bℵ), πρὸ τοῦ αἰῶνος ἀπ' ἀρχῆς ἔκτισέν με, A changes
ἀπ' ἀρχῆς to ἀπαρχήν.

εἰς σωτηρίαν κτλ. The eternal choice of God includes not
only the salvation (I 5⁹) of the readers (εἰς σωτηρίαν = εἰς
τὸ σωθῆναι ὑμᾶς; cf. v. ¹⁰ I 2¹⁶), but also the means by which
(ἐν = διά, Chrys.) or the state in which (cf. I 4⁸) salvation is
realised (Denney). The ἀγιασμὸς πνεύματος designates the total
consecration of the individual, soul and body, to God, a consecration which is inspired by the indwelling Holy Spirit, and which,
as the readers would recall (I 4³⁻⁸ 5²³), is not only religious but
ethical. The phrase πίστις ἀληθείας, "faith in the truth" of
the gospel, is prompted by πιστεύειν τῇ ἀληθείᾳ (v. ¹²). Faith
is man's part; but behind the will to believe is the consecrating

Spirit of God (τὸ πνεῦμα αὐτοῦ τὸ ἅγιον I 4⁸). To be sure, man may refuse to welcome the heavenly influence designed for his salvation; but, if he does, he takes upon himself the consequences of his choice (vv. ¹¹⁻¹²). A similar interaction of the divine and human in salvation is referred to in another Macedonian letter (Phil. 2¹² ᶠ·). The fact that the means or state of salvation is included in the eternal choice, and that it is mentioned before the calling (when the means or state is historically manifested) suggests that Paul is choosing his words with a view to the encouragement of the faint-hearted. To know that they are elect from everlasting, and hence destined to the future salvation to which they were called, they have only to ask themselves whether the consecrating Spirit is in them and whether they have faith in the truth of the gospel. By the same token, Paul, in I 1 ⁴ ᶠᶠ·, expresses the conviction that the readers are elected, namely, by the presence of the Spirit in the readers who heard him and welcomed his gospel. "We find in ourselves a satisfactory proof (of election) if he has sanctified us by his Spirit, if he has enlightened us in the faith of his gospel" (Calvin).

Grammatically ἐν ἁγιασμῷ κτλ. is to be construed not with εἵλατο alone (Wohl.), or with σωτηρίαν alone (Riggenbach, Schmiedel, Born.), but with εἵλατο εἰς σωτηρίαν (Lün. Ell. Lft. Dob. *et al.*). In the light of I 5²³, πνεύματος is not the human (Schott. Find. Moff. *et al.*) but the divine Spirit (Calv. Grot. and most); and the gen. is not of the object but of the author. The phrase ἐν ἁγιασμῷ πνεύματος in 1 Pet. 1² "probably comes from 2 Thess. 2¹³" (Hort). On ἁγιασμός, see I 4³ ᶠᶠ·; on πίστις ἀληθείας, see vv. ¹⁰⁻¹² and *cf.* Phil. 1²⁷ Col. 2¹².

14. εἰς ὃ ἐκάλεσεν κτλ. "To which end," "whereunto" (1¹¹), that is, "to be saved in consecration by the Spirit and faith in the truth." The eternal purpose is historically manifested in God's call (καλεῖν I 2¹² 4⁷ 5²⁴; κλῆσις II 1¹¹), an invitation extended through the gospel which Paul (*cf.* Rom. 10¹⁴ ᶠᶠ·) and his associates preach (ἡμῶν; *cf.* I 1⁵). That is, οὓς δὲ προώρισεν τούτους καὶ ἐκάλεσεν (Rom. 8³⁰).

εἰς περιποίησιν δόξης κτλ. With this clause, standing in apposition to εἰς ὅ, Paul proceeds to the final consummation of the purpose of God in election and calling, explaining εἰς σωτηρίαν as the acquisition of divine glory, "to the obtaining of the glory of our Lord Jesus Christ." The "glory of Christ" (1⁹), like the glory of God (to which he calls in I 2¹²), is the glory which Christ possesses, and which he shares (cf. Rom. 8¹⁷) with "the beloved of the Lord." In other words, οὓς ἐκάλεσεν . . . τούτους καὶ ἐδόξασεν (Rom. 8³⁰). The repetition, in this appositional explanation, of a part of the language of I 5⁹ (εἰς περιποίησιν σωτηρίας διὰ τοῦ κυρίου ἡμῶν Ἰησοῦ Χριστοῦ) where the faint-hearted are likewise encouraged is undoubtedly purposed.

Lillie properly remarks: "There is no reason for restricting εἰς ὅ to any one (σωτηρίαν, as Piscator, Bengel, et al.; or πίστει, as Aretius, Cocceius, et al.), or any two (ἁγιασμῷ . . . καὶ πίστει, as Grotius, Flatt, Schott, de Wette, Hofmann, et al.), of the three; though, inasmuch as salvation is the leading idea and ultimate end, this is repeated and defined in the latter clause of the verse, εἰς περιποίησιν κτλ." Most commentators agree with the above in referring εἰς ὅ to σωτηρίαν ἐν ἁγιασμῷ . . . πίστει (Theophylact, Lün. Ell. Lft. Find. et al.); but B. Weiss refers it to εἵλατο "with reference to which election" (cf. εἰς ὅ in 1¹¹ which resumes εἰς τὸ καταξιωθῆναι 1⁵).—A few codices read εἰς ὃ καί (אPGF, Vulg.), the καί coming probably from 1¹¹ (but see Weiss, 112); cf. I 4⁸ τὸν καὶ διδόντα (אDGF, Vulg. et al.), and contrast the simple εἰς ὅ in Phil. 3¹⁶.—On διὰ τοῦ εὐαγγελίου, cf. Eph. 3⁸ 1 Cor. 4¹⁵.—In vv. ¹³⁻¹⁴ (on which see especially Denney in *Expositor's Bible*, 1892), which are "a system of theology in miniature" (Denney), nothing is expressly said of the death and resurrection of Christ, or of the specific hope of believers for a redeemed and spiritual body conformed τῷ σώματι τῆς δόξης αὐτοῦ (Phil. 3²¹; 1 Cor. 15⁴² ᶠᶠ.; Rom. 8²³ ᶠ.). But these essential convictions of Paul, who is already a Christian of over seventeen years' standing, are given in the very words "our gospel."

15. ἄρα οὖν κτλ. With his characteristic ἄρα οὖν (I 5⁶), to which an affectionate ἀδελφοί is added (as in Rom. 8¹²), Paul commands the brethren to fulfil their Christian duty, their good work and word. This imperative is based on the fact that they are beloved of Christ and elected and called of God to obtain the glory of Christ, and is expressed (1) in στήκετε (a word of Paul; see I 3⁸), "stand firm" and (2) in κρατεῖτε τὰς παραδόσεις, "hold to the deliverances or instructions which you have been taught by us whether by our word or by our letter," ἡμῶν being construed with both substantives. Since ἐδιδάχθητε has in mind instructions hitherto conveyed by Paul, Silvanus, and Timothy (ἡμῶν; *cf.* v. ¹⁴) to the Thessalonians, λόγος refers to the oral teaching during the first visit; and "our letter" (not δι᾽ ἐπιστολῶν "our letters") refers specifically to the first epistle. While these instructions comprehend the various elements, religious and moral, communicated by Paul and his associates to the Thessalonians orally or by letter up to the time of the writing of II (ἐδιδάχθητε), the presence of στήκετε, recalling the σαλευθῆναι of v. ², goes to show that Paul has in mind not only generally "our gospel" as outlined in vv. ¹³⁻¹⁴ but also specifically the instructions concerning the *Parousia* which he had given orally (I 5² II 2⁵) and had touched upon in the first epistle (5¹⁻¹¹ which has the faint-hearted in mind). Knowing, as they should remember (v. ²), that the day is not actually present, and aware that, as elect and beloved (I 1⁴ ᶠᶠ·), they are put not for wrath but for the acquiring of salvation (I 5⁹), they should not be agitated and nervously wrought up (v. ²), but should stand firm and stick to the deliverances that they had been taught, "whether we conveyed them by word of mouth when we were yet with you or by our letter," that is, the first epistle (*sive per verbum praesentes sive et absentes per litteras* Th. Mops.; *cf.* also Theodoret: λόγους οὓς καὶ πάροντες ὑμῖν ἐκηρύξαμεν καὶ ἄποντες ἐγράψαμεν).

As Dob. (*ad loc.*) and J. Weiss (in Meyer on 1 Cor. 11²) have pointed out, the use of παράδοσις betrays the Jewish training of Paul who as a Pharisee outstripped many of his comrades in his zeal for τῶν πατρικῶν μου παραδόσεων (Gal. 1¹⁴). Here, as in 1 Cor. 11² (ὅτι καθὼς παρέδωκα ὑμῖν τὰς παραδόσεις κατέχετε), the deliverances are not defined; contrast the single tradition below 3⁶ which is stated in 3¹⁰; and note also the comprehensive ἡ παράδοσις τῶν ἀνθρώπων (Col. 2⁶⁻⁸; *cf.* Mk. 7⁸) which is antithetical to Christ. In our passage, Paul might have said τὴν διδαχὴν ἣν ὑμεῖς ἐμάθετε (Rom. 16¹⁷; *cf.* Phil. 4⁹ Col. 1⁷ 2⁶ ᶠᶠ. Eph. 4²⁰; also 1 Cor. 4¹⁷); or, on the analogy of I 4¹⁻² 1 Cor. 7¹⁰, τὰς παραγγελίας ἃς ἐδώκαμεν ὑμῖν. The thought is constant, but the language varies. Paul is ὁ διδούς, ὁ παραδιδούς, ὁ διδάσκων, ὁ παραγγέλλων, and ὁ γνωρίζων (1 Cor. 15¹); and the readers or hearers receive (παραλαμβάνειν Gal. 1⁹ 1 Cor. 15¹ Phil. 4⁹ Col. 2⁶ I 4¹ II 3⁶), learn (μανθάνειν Phil. 4⁹ Rom. 16¹⁷ Col. 1⁷ Eph. 4²⁰), and are taught (διδάσκεσθαι Col. 2⁷ Eph. 4²¹; *cf.* Gal. 1¹²); and they likewise "hold fast to the instructions" (here and 1 Cor. 11²; *cf.* 15²). While the source of these words, deliverances, teaching, commands, etc., is for Paul the indwelling Christ, and may thus be opposed to human authority (Gal. 1¹²) or his own opinion (1 Cor. 7¹⁰ ᶠᶠ·), still they are historically mediated by the O. T., sayings of Jesus, and the traditions of primitive Christianity (1 Cor. 15³). —κρατεῖν is used elsewhere by Paul only Col. 2¹⁹ (κεφαλήν); *cf.* Mk. 7³· ⁸ κρατεῖν τὴν παράδοσιν; but παράδοσις, apart from Paul, appears in Gk. Bib. only Mk. 7³ ᶠᶠ· = Mt. 15² ᶠᶠ·, and in 2 Es. 7²⁶ Jer. 39⁴ 41² of "delivering up" a city.—The construction διδάσκεσθαί τι is found elsewhere in Gk. Bib. 1 Ch. 5¹⁸ Cant. 3⁸ Sap. 6¹⁰ (but *cf.* Gal. 1¹²); on δι-δάσκειν, *cf.* 1 Cor. 4¹⁷ Col. 2⁷ Eph. 4²¹.—The implication of this specification of alternative modes of conveying instruction, διὰ λόγου and δι' ἐπιστολῆς (εἴτε being disjunctive as in I 5¹⁰), is that each is equally authoritative; *et par in utroque auctoritas* (Grot.). Paul had previously referred to both these modes (vv. ²· ⁵ I 5²· ²⁷); but the reminder here may imply an intentional contrast both with the erroneous inferences drawn by some from Paul's oral utterances (inspired or not) and from his first epistle (v. ²), and (probably) with the statement implied in I 5²⁷ that some of the brothers (presumably "the idlers") would give no heed to the letters of Paul (*cf.* below 3¹⁴).—ἐπιστολή with an article· may refer to "this" present letter (I 5²⁷ II 3¹⁴ Rom. 16²² Col. 4¹⁶; *cf.* P. Oxy. 293⁸ ᶠ· (A.D. 27) τῷ δὲ φέροντί σοι τὴν ἐπιστολήν), or to a previous letter, "that" letter (1 Cor. 5⁹ 2 Cor. 7⁸), the context determining in each instance the reference. The plural ἐπιστολαί indicates with the article previous past letters in 2 Cor. 10⁹⁻¹⁰; and without the article, either letters to be written (1 Cor. 16³) or the epistolary method (2 Cor. 10¹¹).

16–17. αὐτὸς δέ κτλ. The δέ, which introduces a new point (*cf.* I 3¹¹ 5²³ II 3¹⁶), is here, as in I 5²³, slightly adversative. "We have commanded you to stand firm and hold to the instructions which you have received, and we have based our imperative on the fact that you are beloved and elect; but after all (δέ), the only power that can make the appeal effective, that can encourage your purposes and strengthen them in the sphere of righteousness, is Christ and God, to whom consequently we address our prayer for you." As in I 3¹¹, so here the divine names are united and governed by a verb in the singular; there, however, God, as usual, takes the precedence; here (as in Gal. 1¹ 2 Cor. 13¹³) Christ is named first, perhaps because the good hope is pictured as the sharing of the glory of Christ (v. ¹⁴). Due to the position of the name of Christ, the arrangement of the divine names is chiastic, "Our Lord, Jesus Christ," and "God, our Father" (the phrase ὁ θεὸς ὁ πατὴρ ἡμῶν being unique; see on I 1³).

ὁ ἀγαπήσας ἡμᾶς καὶ δούς. "Who loved us (Christians; contrast ὑμῶν v. ¹⁷) and so gave us (sc. ἡμῖν) eternal encouragement and good hope in virtue of grace" (both the love and the gift arising from the divine favour (I 1¹) of God and Christ unto salvation; cf. κατὰ τὴν χάριν 1¹² and ἐν δυνάμει 1¹¹). On the analogy of I 3¹¹, it is evident that ὁ ἀγαπήσας καὶ δούς is to be referred to both Christ and God (contrast Gal. 1¹, "through Jesus Christ and God the Father who raised him from the dead," where ἐγείραντος logically excludes the double reference). Since the aorists look upon the past event simply as an event without reference to its progress or existing result (*BMT.* 38), it is probable (1) that ὁ ἀγαπήσας alludes chiefly to the love of God (Rom. 5⁸) or Christ (Gal. 2²⁰) manifested in his sufferings and death, though the aorist does not exclude the idea of the continued love of God and Christ ("who has loved us"; cf. I 1⁴ II 2¹³ ἠγαπημένοι, and Rom. 8³⁵ ᶠᶠ·); and (2) that the δούς, which is closely attached to ἀγαπήσας under the governance of one article, refers to the initial gift of the Spirit (I 4⁸ Gal. 4⁶ Rom. 5⁵), though the aorist does not exclude the idea of the permanent possession of the gift ("and has given us").

παράκλησιν αἰωνίαν καὶ ἐλπίδα ἀγαθήν. In choosing these phrases (which are evidently unique in the Gk. Bib.), Paul, though speaking of Christians in general, has especially in mind the needs of the faint-hearted who had been losing confidence and hope. παράκλησις is the courageous confidence, inspired by the Spirit, that nothing, whether persecutions (1⁴ I 3³) or disquieting utterances touching the time of the *Parousia* (vv. ²⁻³) can prevent the beloved and elect from sharing the future glory of Christ. This "encouragement" is αἰωνίαν, not because it belongs to this present æon (ὁ αἰὼν οὗτος), but because it holds good for and reaches into the æon which is to come (ὁ αἰὼν ὁ μέλλων), a present and lasting encouragement. The "good hope" springs from the "eternal encouragement" (cf. Rom. 5¹ ᶠᶠ·), and is likewise a present possession (cf. Rom. 8²³) due to

the Spirit. It is "good" not only negatively in contrast with
the empty hope of non-Christians (I 4¹³) but also positively in
that it is genuine and victorious (Rom. 5⁵), certain to be realised in the future kingdom of God.

17. παρακαλέσαι . . . καὶ στηρίξαι κτλ. Having named
the divine persons and recalled their gracious love and gift to
all Christians (v. ¹⁶), Paul petitions Christ and God (the two
persons being united here as in I 3¹¹ by the singular optatives)
first of all (1) to "encourage" the inward purposes or will of the
faint-hearted among the readers (ὑμῶν τὰς καρδίας as 3⁵ I 3¹⁵;
note the change from the general ἡμᾶς (v. ¹⁶) to the specific
ὑμῶν), that is, to put into their hearts the confident assurance
of salvation, the "eternal encouragement" of which he had just
spoken (παρακαλέσαι resuming παράκλησιν). Then (2), recognising still the needs of the faint-hearted and gently reminding
them that the future salvation, though it is assured by the indwelling Spirit, is contingent upon righteousness (cf. 1¹¹⁻¹² I 3¹³
5⁶ ᶠᶠ·; Rom. 14¹⁰ 2 Cor. 5¹⁰ 1 Cor. 3¹³ ᶠᶠ· Phil. 1⁶), he petitions
further (as in 1¹¹ I 3¹³) Christ and God to "establish (στηρίξαι;
cf. I 3². ¹³ and στήκετε above v. ¹⁵) their hearts (sc. ὑμῶν τὰς
καρδίας; KL, et al., insert ὑμᾶς) in every good work that they
do (contrast περιεργάζεσθαι 3¹¹) and in every good word that
they speak" (contrast v. ²).

On αὐτὸς δέ, see 3¹⁶ I 3¹¹ 5²³. Most codices have Ἰησοῦς Χριστός; but
A reads Ἰησοῦς ὁ Χριστός, and B Χριστὸς Ἰησοῦς (cf. Rom. 16²⁵ Eph. 5²⁰;
also D in 1¹ above). The unique ὁ θεὸς ὁ πατὴρ ἡμῶν is given by אGF;
BD omit ὁ before θεός, yielding an equally unusual phrase; θεός (K)
or ὁ θεός (APL) καὶ πατὴρ ἡμῶν (AKLP) is conformation to Paul's regular usage.—Paul speaks elsewhere of the love of God (3⁵ Rom. 5⁵ 8³⁹
2 Cor. 13¹³) and of the love of Christ (Rom. 8³⁵· ³⁷ 2 Cor. 5¹⁴); of God as
the author of παράκλησις (Rom. 15⁵ 2 Cor. 1³) and of Christ as the inspiration of the same (Phil. 2¹); of God as the author of hope (Rom. 15⁵)
and of Christ in us the hope of glory (Col. 1²⁷); and of the grace both of
God and of Christ (see I 1¹). There is no intrinsic difficulty therefore
in referring ὁ ἀγαπήσας καὶ δούς to both Christ and God.—In the present
context, παράκλησις, which anticipates παρακαλέσαι in v. ¹⁷, means not
"consolation" but "encouragement" (Find.; cf. I 3²).—On the feminine ending αἰωνία instead of the common αἰώνιος (which GF have here;
cf. 1⁹), cf. Heb. 9¹² Num. 25¹³ Jer. 20¹⁷, etc.—For ἐλπὶς ἀγαθή (which,

like παράκλησις αἰωνία, is unique in the Gk. Bib.), see Goodwin's note on Demosthenes, *de cor.* 258. On διδόναι ἐλπίδα, *cf.* Job 6⁸ Sir. 13⁶; on ἀγαθός, see I 3⁶ and on ἐλπίς I 1³. Is. 57¹⁸ may be cited: παρεκάλεσα αὐτὸν καὶ ἔδωκα αὐτῷ παράκλησιν ἀληθινήν.—The adverbial expression ἐν χάριτι (*cf.* 1¹¹ ἐν δυνάμει) is to be construed not with παρακαλέσαι (B. Weiss), and not with δούς alone, but with the two closely united participles ὁ ἀγαπήσας καὶ δούς (De W. Lün. Lft. *et al.*). The ἐν indicates the sphere or more precisely the ground of the divine love and gift (*cf.* 1¹⁰· ¹² Rom. 5¹⁵ Gal. 1⁶ 2 Cor. 1¹²).—Why Paul writes not "word and work" (so GFK, *et al.*; *cf.* Col. 3¹⁷ Rom. 15¹⁸ 2 Cor. 10¹¹) but "work and word" (not elsewhere in Paul; but *cf.* Lk. 24¹⁹), and adds ἀγαθῷ (which, like παντί, is to be connected with both ἔργῳ and λόγῳ) is quite unknown.—On the analogy of I 2⁴ (τὰς καρδίας ἡμῶν), אA put ἡμῶν after καρδίας. For the phrase παρακαλεῖν τὰς καρδίας, *cf.* Col. 4⁸ Eph. 6²² Sir. 30²³.—Ell. notes Chrys. on στηρίξαι: βεβαιῶσαι, ὥστε μὴ σαλεύεσθαι μηδὲ παρακλίνεσθαι.

V. FINALLY (3¹⁻⁵).

This section, as τὸ λοιπόν and ἀδελφοί make clear, is new, and serves not as a conclusion of the foregoing (2¹³⁻¹⁷) but as an introduction to the following discussion (3⁶⁻¹⁶), as παραγγέλλομεν (v. ⁴ and vv. ¹⁰· ¹¹) and ποιήσετε intimate; in other words, vv. ¹⁻⁵ form a transition (analogous to I 4¹⁻²) from the first to the second main point of the epistle, from the faint-hearted (1³⁻2¹⁷) to the idle brethren (3⁶⁻¹⁵). The structure is abrupt (*cf.* δέ in vv. ³· ⁴· ⁵) more so than in I 5¹⁴⁻²²; and the transitions, based on association of ideas (πίστις to πιστός and, less obviously, to πεποίθαμεν), do not quite succeed either in relieving the abruptness or in making definite the underlying connection of thought. The situation may best be explained on the assumption not that a forger is at work (Wrede), or that in 2¹⁶⁻3⁵ considerable material has been deleted (Harnack), but that Paul is replying informally to remarks made by his converts in their letter to him.

Wishing to get their willing obedience to the command of vv. ⁶⁻¹⁵, he seeks their sympathy in requesting their prayers for him and his cause, and delicately commends their faith (vv. ¹⁻²). Finding, it may be, in the letter from the converts that the idle brethren are disposed to excuse their idleness on the ground that the Tempter is too strong for them, Paul bids them to remember

that Christ is really to be depended on to give them strength
sufficient to resist temptation (v. ³). Still wishing to get their
willing obedience, Paul in the same Christ avows tactfully his
faith in them that they will be glad to do what he commands,
as indeed they are even now doing (v. ⁴). But as a stimulus to
obedience, they need especially a vivid sense of God's love for
them, and the reminder that Christ can give them an endurance
adequate to the situation. Accordingly, Paul addresses a prayer
for them to Christ the source of power (v. ⁵).

¹*Finally, pray, brothers, for us, asking that the word of the Lord
may run its race and be crowned with glory, as it does with you;
²and that we may be delivered from those unrighteous and evil men,
—for not for all is the Christian faith. ³Faithful, however, the Lord
really is, and he will make you firm and guard you from the evil
one. ⁴Moreover, prompted by the Lord, we have faith in you that
the things which we command, you both are doing and will continue
to do. ⁵However, may the Lord incline your hearts to a sense of
God's love and to the endurance that Christ alone inspires.*

1. τὸ λοιπόν. Though τὸ λοιπόν, like λοιπόν (I 4¹ and GF
here), is often found at the end of a letter intimating that it is
drawing to a close (2 Cor. 13¹¹; contrast 1 Cor. 1¹⁶ 4² 7²⁹), yet
it does not of necessity imply that "what remains to be said" is
of secondary importance, as the instances in the other Macedonian letters demonstrate (I 4¹ Phil. 3¹ 4⁸). In fact, just as
I 4¹⁻² paves the way for the important exhortations in I 4³–5²²
(which are placed, like vv. ¹⁻¹⁵ here, between two prayers, αὐτὸς
δέ I 3¹¹⁻¹³ 5²³ and II 2¹⁶⁻¹⁷ 3¹⁶) so vv. ¹⁻⁵, introduced as I 4¹⁻² by
(τὸ) λοιπόν and the affectionate ἀδελφοί, serve as a tactful
introduction to the important injunction in vv. ⁶⁻¹⁵.

προσεύχεσθε κτλ. This appeal for the prayers of the readers
is characteristic of Paul (1¹¹ I 5²⁵ Rom. 15³⁰ ᶠ· Col. 4². ¹⁸ Phile. 22;
also 2 Cor. 1¹¹ Phil. 1¹⁹); it is inspired here by the circumstances
in which he is writing, namely, as καὶ πάσχετε (1⁴) has already
intimated, by persecutions, and that too at the instigation of
Jews, as οὐ γὰρ πάντων ἡ πίστις in the light of I 2¹⁵⁻¹⁶ suggests,
and as the typical instances narrated in Acts (18⁵ ᶠᶠ·) corroborate.
This appeal for sympathy is intended not to remind the readers

19

that they are not the only victims of Jewish opposition, but, as the tacit praise of their faith (καθὼς καὶ πρὸς ὑμᾶς) suggests, to stir up within them such love for him that they will obey with alacrity the command which he is about to give (vv. 6-15).

ἵνα ὁ λόγος τοῦ κυρίου κτλ. The prayer requested is not so much for Paul and his companions personally (περὶ ἡμῶν) as for them as preachers of the gospel (2¹⁴) and as sufferers in the common cause of the kingdom of God (1⁴). Hence the object of the prayer (ἵνα being here not, as in 1¹¹, of the purpose, but of the object as in Phil. 1⁹ Col. 1⁹; cf. v. ¹² below and I 4¹ 2 Cor. 8⁶) is both (1) that the word of the Lord (I 1⁸) may run its race unhindered by the weight of opposition, and be crowned with glory; and (2) that the missionaries of the gospel of Christ may be delivered from those well-known unrighteous and evil men. In each of the clauses with ἵνα there is an additional remark (a) in reference to the faith of the readers, καθὼς καὶ πρὸς ὑμᾶς; and (b) in reference to the adversaries common to Paul and the readers, the Jews whose hearts are hardened, οὐ γὰρ πάντων ἡ πίστις.

On Paul's prayers and requests for prayer, see especially E. von der Goltz, *Das Gebet in der ältesten Christenheit*, 1901, 112 ff. The language here (προσεύχεσθε ἀδελφοὶ περὶ ἡμῶν) is natural enough in itself (Heb. 13¹⁸) and is quite Pauline (Col. 4²); but the phrase as a whole reminds one of I 5²⁵ (ἀδελφοὶ προσεύχεσθε καὶ περὶ ἡμῶν). The agreement between our phrase and that of I 5²⁵ is not, however, exact. The καί of I is not present here, a fact that makes the usual reference to 2¹⁶-¹⁷ less distinct (Chrys. Œcumenius: "above he prayed for them, now he asks prayer from them"). Furthermore the position of ἀδελφοί is different; from I 5²⁵ (cf. I 4¹ 2 Cor. 13¹¹ Phil. 3¹ 4⁸), we should expect it to precede (as GF, *et al.*) not to follow (אBA, *et al.*) προσεύχεσθε (cf. DE, *et al.*, which put ἀδελφοί after ἡμῶν). Finally, unlike I 5²⁵, the object of the prayer is here stated. The significance, if there is any, of the emphatic position of προσεύχεσθε is unknown. Since "those unrighteous and wicked men" (v. ²) are evidently well known to the readers, it is not improbable that in their letter to him they had prayed for him in Corinth. If this surmise be correct, the present imperative (which, however, is regularly used in the Macedonian letters, the only aorists being ἀσπάσασθε I 5²⁶ Phil. 4²¹ and πληρώσατε Phil. 2²) with which Paul replies may perhaps be rendered: "Keep on praying as you are, brethren, for us."

τρέχῃ καὶ δοξάζηται. "That the word of the Lord may run and be glorified." This, the first object of the prayer, expressed

in a collocation (τρέχειν καὶ δοξάζεσθαι) which is not found elsewhere in the Gk. Bib., is to the general effect that the gospel of
Christ "may have a triumphant career" (Lft.). The word τρέχειν (used absolutely here as elsewhere in Paul) is, in the light
of 1 Cor. 9²⁴ ff. (cf. Rom. 9¹⁶ Gal. 2² 5⁷ Phil. 2¹⁶), probably a metaphor derived from the races in the stadium. The word of the
Lord is ὁ τρέχων (Rom. 9¹⁶), competing for the βραβεῖον (1 Cor.
9²⁴) or στέφανος (I 2¹⁹ 1 Cor. 9²⁵), that is, for the acceptance of
the gospel as the power of God unto salvation. But to indicate
the victory of the runner, Paul adds, not, as we should expect,
στεφανῶται (cf. 2 Tim. 2⁵), or λαμβάνῃ στέφανον (1 Cor. 9²⁵),
but, with a turn to the religious, δοξάζηται "be glorified," that
is, "crowned with glory" (compare the kingly crown in Ps. 8⁶
Heb. 2⁷· ⁹). But while the general point of the metaphor is clear,
the exact force of it is uncertain. In the light of v. ², however, it
is probable that τρέχῃ means not "to fulfil its course swiftly
(Ps. 147⁴ ἕως τάχους) and without hindrance" (so Riggenbach
and many others); not "to run, that is, unhindered, and make
its way quickly through the world" (Dob., who notes the
hope expressed in Mk. 13¹⁰ Mt. 24¹⁴); but to run its race un-
encumbered by obstacles (not self-imposed (cf. Heb. 12¹) but)
superimposed by adversaries, in this context, the Jews (cf.
Theodoret ἀκωλύτως).

In view of the unique collocation, τρέχειν καὶ δοξάζεσθαι, and of
Paul's fondness for metaphors from the race-course, it is unnecessary
to see here a literary allusion either to "the faithful and expeditious
messenger" (Briggs) of Ps. 147⁴, or to Ps. 18⁵ ὡς γίγας δραμεῖν ὁδὸν αὐτοῦ
where "the path of the sun in the heavens is conceived as a race-course"
(Briggs), or to Is. 55¹¹. In this phrase, evidently coined by Paul, the
present tenses (contrast in v. ² ῥυσθῶμεν) regard the race and victory as
in constant progress. Each person or group of persons is constantly
recognising the gospel at its true worth and welcoming it as the word not
of man but of God. The transition to the complimentary καθώς κτλ.
is thus easily made.—On ὁ λόγος τοῦ κυρίου, see I 1⁸ where א has τοῦ
θεοῦ (cf. I 2¹³) as do GFP, et al., here. On δοξάζεσθαι, see 1¹⁰· ¹².

καθὼς καὶ πρὸς ὑμᾶς. "As it is running and is being glorified
with you"; or succinctly, "as it does in your case." The praise
implied in the prayer that the gospel may succeed with all as it

succeeds with the readers is designed probably as an incentive not to their prayers for him but to their obedience to the command in mind (v. ⁶). Sympathy for Paul is to create a willing compliance; if they love him, they will keep his commands. πρός (I 3⁴) is to be construed with both τρέχῃ and δοξάζηται.

2. καὶ ἵνα ῥυσθῶμεν. The ἵνα (parallel to ἵνα in v. ¹) introduces the second object of προσεύχεσθε: "that we may be delivered." The aorist (contrast the present tenses in v. ¹) regards the action of deliverance simply as an event in the past without reference to progress. As in 2 Cor. 1¹¹ where the prayer requested is for deliverance (ῥύεσθαι) from the danger of death, and as in Rom. 15³⁰ ff. where it is for deliverance from those that are disobedient in Judæa (ἵνα ῥυσθῶ ἀπὸ τῶν ἀπειθούντων), so here person and cause are inseparable.

τῶν ἀτόπων καὶ πονηρῶν ἀνθρώπων. "From those unrighteous and evil men." The τῶν points to a definite class of adversaries (cf. Rom. 15³¹) and well known to the readers. That persecutions in Corinth are here referred to is likewise suggested by καὶ πάσχετε in 1⁴; and that the Jews are the instigators of persecution is the natural inference both from οὐ γὰρ πάντων ἡ πίστις when compared with I 2¹⁵⁻¹⁶, and from the typical instances recorded in Acts 18⁵ ff.

οὐ γὰρ πάντων ἡ πίστις. "For not for all is the faith"; "it is not everybody who is attracted by the faith" (Rutherford). "The faith" (Gal. 1²³) is not "the word of the Lord" (v. ¹), "the truth" (2¹⁰· ¹²), or "the gospel" (cf. 2¹⁴), but the faith which the gospel demands, the faith without which the gospel is not effective as the power of God unto salvation. The γάρ explains not the prayer for deliverance, as if "only deliverance from them is to be requested since their conversion is hopeless" (Schmiedel), but the reason why those unrighteous and evil men exist. The explanation is set forth not in terms of historical fact, "for not all have believed" (cf. Rom. 10¹⁶ οὐ πάντες ὑπήκουσαν τῷ εὐαγγελίῳ), but in terms of a general principle based on observation (ἐστίν, which GF, et al., read, is to be supplied here as often elsewhere in Paul), "for not for all is the faith" (πάντων being either an objective or a possessive genitive; cf. Acts 1⁷ 2 Cor. 2³

Heb. 5¹⁴). In view of the fact that under similar circumstances Paul had expressed himself similarly as regards the conversion of the Jews (I 2¹⁵⁻¹⁶) it is quite likely that here too, in spite of πάντων, he has in mind the obstinacy of the Jews. It was their rejection of Jesus as the Messiah that raised a serious problem not only for Paul (Rom. 9–11) but for others (Mk. 4¹⁰⁻¹² Acts 28²⁶ ᶠᶠ· Jn. 12³⁷ ᶠᶠ·). Here, however, the mystery alone, not its solution, is stated.

> ἄτοπος is used of persons only here in the Gk. Bib.; elsewhere, chiefly in Lk. Acts, Job, it is neuter; e. g. πράσσειν ἄτοπα (Job 27⁶ 36²¹) or ἄτοπον (Pr. 24⁵⁵ 2 Mac. 14²³; cf. Lk. 23⁴¹) and ποιεῖν ἄτοπα (Job 34¹²; cf. Polyc. Phil. 5³). "From its original meaning 'out of place,' 'unbecoming,' ἄτοπος came in late Greek to be used ethically = 'improper,' 'unrighteous'; and it is in this sense that, with the exception of Acts 28⁶, it is always used in the Lxx. and N. T." (Milligan, Greek Papyri, 72). For other instances of the word, see Wetstein and Loesner, ad loc., and on Lk. 23⁴¹, and the former on Acts 28⁶. The prevailing ethical meaning makes unlikely the rendering "unbelieving" which the context might suggest (cf. I 2¹⁶ θεῷ μὴ ἀρεσκόντων). For a conspectus of proposed translations such as "unreasonable," "perverse," "unrighteous" (Thayer), etc., see Lillie's note; compare also Hatch-Redpath, Concordance, where under ἄτοπος in Job 36²¹ both ἄδικα and ἄνομα are noted as variants of ἄτοπα.—On πονηρός, see I 5²²; D in Lk. 23⁴¹ reads πονηρόν for ἄτοπον. On ῥύεσθαι ἀπό, see I 1¹⁰.—Born. (533), whom Wrede follows, finds an almost verbal dependence on Is. 25⁴: ἀπὸ ἀνθρώπων ῥύσῃ αὐτούς. But Ps. 139¹ would serve as well: ἐξελοῦ με κύριε ἐξ ἀνθρώπου πονηροῦ, ἀπὸ ἀνδρὸς ἀδίκου ῥῦσαί με. Dob. (cf. Harnack, op. cit.) sees a reference to 1 Mac. 14¹⁴ where Simon ἐξῆρεν πάντα ἄνομον καὶ πονηρόν; cf. Is. 9¹⁷ πάντες ἄνομοι καὶ πονηροί. However this may be, it is evident both that Paul read the Lxx. and that the collocation ἄτοπος καὶ πονηρός is not found elsewhere in the Gk. Bib.

3. πιστὸς δέ ἐστιν ὁ κύριος κτλ. "The Lord (Christ) is really (2⁴) faithful (cf. Rom. 3³), and as faithful will surely strengthen you and protect you from the evil one." Prompted it may be by a passage in their letter to him saying that some of the converts, probably the idlers, were disposed to excuse their conduct on the ground that the Tempter was too strong for them, and being "more anxious about others than about himself" (Calvin), Paul turns somewhat abruptly (δέ) from the situation in Corinth and his own trials to the similar situation, so

far as persecution is concerned (1^4), in Thessalonica, and the
moral dangers to which the devil exposed the readers (ὑμᾶς,
not ἡμᾶς which Bentley and Baljon conjecture). With πιστός,
here naturally suggested by πίστις (v. ²), and with an emphatic
ἐστίν (which is unexpected in the phrase πιστὸς ὁ θεός or κύριος),
Paul reminds them that Christ is really to be depended on
to give them strength sufficient to resist the enticement of the
devil. Paul assures them not that they will be delivered from
persecution (cf. I 3^4) but rather that they will be strengthened
both in faith (I 3^2) and conduct (I 3^{13} II 2^{17}), and thus be shielded
from the power of Satan (I 2^{18} II 2^9), that is, from the ethical
aberrations, perhaps specifically the idleness and meddlesomeness to which the Tempter (I 3^2), by means of persecution, en-
tices some of them. The similarity of 1 Cor. 10^{13} has not escaped
Calvin's notice: There hath no temptation taken you but such
as man can bear; πιστὸς δὲ ὁ θεός, ὃς οὐκ ἐάσει κτλ.

The usual phrase in Paul is not πιστὸς δέ ἐστιν ὁ κύριος but simply
πιστὸς ὁ θεός (1 Cor. 1^9 10^{13} 2 Cor. 1^{18}; cf. I 5^{24}). The change from θεός
to κύριος = Christ (v. ⁵) is in keeping with the tendency of II already
mentioned (v. 2^{12}). In fact, the frequency of ὁ κύριος in vv. ¹⁻⁵ (four
times) has an interesting parallel in another Macedonian letter, Phil.
4^{1-5} (where ὁ κύριος occurs four times). The unexpected ἐστίν (G, et al.,
omit, conforming to Paul's usage), which emphasises the reality of the
faithfulness of Christ, may be due simply to the contrast with the faith-
lessness of the Jews; or it may intimate, as said, that in a letter to
Paul the converts, perhaps specifically not the faint-hearted (2^{17}) but
the idle brothers, had expressed the feeling that the evil one was too
strong for them, thus accounting for their yielding to temptation. Paul's
reply, emphasising the faithfulness of Christ who is stronger than the
devil, serves both as a reminder that persecutions are not an excuse for
idleness and as an incentive to do what Paul is about to command
(vv. ³⁻⁴· ⁶⁻¹⁵).—ὁ κύριος stands in victorious antithesis to ὁ πονηρός; for,
although grammatically τοῦ πονηροῦ may be either masculine (Eph. 6^{16})
or neuter (Rom. 12^9), yet the masculine, in view not only of I 2^{18} 3^5
II 2^9 but also of Paul's conception in general of the evil world (cf. 2 Cor.
6^{15}), is the more probable gender (so Calv. and most modern expositors).
For supposed allusions in this passage to the Lord's Prayer, see on the
one side Lft. and Chase (The Lord's Prayer in the Early Church, 1891),
and on the other Dibelius, ad loc.—On στηρίζειν, see I 3^2. Elsewhere in
the N. T. the future is στηρίξει (as ℵADP, et al., here); in the Lxx. it is
regularly στηριῶ. The reading of B (στηρίσει) has a parallel in Jer.

17¹; that of GF (τηρήσει) is due either to a previous στηρήσει (*cf.* B in Sir. 38³⁴) or to an approximation to φυλάξει (Dob.); *cf.* Sir. 4²⁰ συντήρησον καιρὸν καὶ φύλαξαι ἀπὸ πονηροῦ.—φυλάσσειν is found apart from the Pastorals but twice elsewhere in Paul, Gal. 6¹³ Rom. 2²⁶ (used in reference to the law). On the construction here, *cf.* Ps. 120⁷. The collocation στηρίζειν and φυλάσσειν is without a parallel in Gk. Bib.

4. πεποίθαμεν δέ κτλ. With δέ again, introducing a new point, and with the Pauline phrase πεποίθαμεν ἐν κυρίῳ (Gal. 5¹⁰ Phil. 2²⁴ Rom. 14¹⁴, but not in I), Paul, who is still intent on gaining the willing obedience of the converts, avows with tact his faith that what he commands they will do as they are doing. This confidence is defined as inspired by the indwelling Christ (ἐν κυρίῳ), and as directed to the readers (ἐφ᾽ ὑμᾶς; *cf.* 2 Cor. 2³; also εἰς ὑμᾶς Gal. 5¹⁰). The insertion of ποιεῖτε (*cf.* I 5¹¹) tactfully prepares for ποιήσετε, as καθὼς καὶ περιπατεῖτε (I 4¹) prepares for περισσεύητε μᾶλλον (I 4¹). Though the words are general, "what (that is, *quae* not *quaecumque*) we command, both you are doing and will continue to do" (the future being progressive; *BMT.* 60), yet it is natural in view both of παραγγέλλομεν (*cf.* vv. ⁶·¹²) and ποιήσετε to find a specific reference, namely, not to the faint-hearted (as if vv. ⁴⁻⁵ were a doublet of 2¹⁵⁻¹⁷), and not to the request for prayer (vv. ¹⁻² Lft.), but to the command in vv. ⁶⁻¹⁵ (Calvin).

The underlying connection between v. ⁴ and v. ³ is not evident. Indeed, πεποίθαμεν is less obviously dictated by πιστός than πιστός is by πίστις. The connecting idea may be that since Christ is really faithful and will surely protect the readers from the wiles of the devil, Paul may dare to express his faith in them, prompted by Christ, that they (probably the idlers) will no longer seek to excuse their idleness but will be willing, as they are able (v. ²), to do what he commands. Or it may be that v. ⁴ is suggested by something else said in the letter to Paul. In any case, v. ⁴ prepares for vv. ⁶⁻¹⁵, as most admit (Lün. Riggenbach, Ell. Wohl. Mill. *et al.*; so Find. who, however, refers ποιεῖτε to vv. ¹⁻²). —πείθειν is characteristic of Paul, though the word is not confined to his writings; the perfect tense here denotes the existing state, "I am confident." The specifically Pauline ἐν κυρίῳ (see I 3⁸) does not always appear in this phrase (πέποιθα ἐπί or εἰς). While v. ³ hints that the readers are "in the Lord," the position of ἐφ᾽ ὑμᾶς intimates only that Paul is in the Lord, the one who inspires his confidence in the converts; contrast Gal. 5¹⁰, πέποιθα εἰς ὑμᾶς ἐν κυρίῳ. πείθειν is construed with ἐφ' ὑμᾶς (2 Cor. 2³ Mt. 27⁴³ and often in Lxx.), with εἰς (Gal. 5¹⁰ Sap. 16²⁴) with ἐν (Phil. 3³), and with ἐπί and dative (2 Cor. 1⁹, etc.).—The expected ὑμῖν after παραγγέλλομεν (I 4¹¹; cf. below, vv. ⁶. ¹⁰) is inserted by AGFKLP, et al.; but אBD, et al., omit. On ὅτι, cf. Gal. 5¹⁰ Phil. 2²⁴ 2 Cor. 2³, etc.; on παραγγέλλειν, see I 4².—καὶ ποιεῖτε καὶ ποιήσετε is read by P and Vulg. and (without the first καί) by אAD; GF have καὶ ἐποιήσατε καὶ ποιεῖτε; B alone is comprehensive with καὶ ἐποιήσατε καὶ ποιεῖτε καὶ ποιήσετε. Either B is original with its unexpected aorist after the present παραγγέλλομεν, or the seat of the trouble is the itacism ποιήσατε which D preserves.

5. ὁ δὲ κύριος κτλ. The new point, introduced by δέ, is slightly adversative. Although Paul has confidence in the Lord that they will do what he commands (v. ⁵ looks not to ποιεῖτε but to ποιήσετε), yet he is certain that the help of the Lord is indispensable to incline their hearts to keep his command. What they need especially is a sense of God's love to them and a reminder that Christ can give them an endurance adequate to face the persecutions. Hence the prayer: "May the Lord (=Christ) direct (I 3¹¹) your hearts (I 3¹³ II 2¹⁷) unto the love of God and the endurance of Christ."

In Paul, ἡ ἀγάπη τοῦ θεοῦ (Rom. 5⁵ 8³⁹ 2 Cor. 13¹³) means not our love to God but God's love to us, the thought here being that their inner life may be directed to a sense of the divine love (see SH. on Rom. 5⁵). With an appreciation of the meaning of God's love, there would be no temptation to infringe upon φιλαδελφία by the continuance of idle habits (cf. I 4⁹⁻¹²).—Since elsewhere in Paul ὑπομονή = "endurance," the rendering patientem exspectationem (Beza), "patient waiting" (AV), which demands the objective genitive, is here improbable (see Vincent); see, however, Lft. Schmiedel, and Dob. and compare Ign. Rom. 10³, ἐν ὑπομονῇ Ἰησοῦ Χριστοῦ, an expression which is "probably derived from St. Paul" (Lft.). Taking ὑπομονή = "endurance," Χριστοῦ may mean either the endurance which Christ possesses and shares (cf. δόξα τοῦ κυρίου in 2¹⁴), or which is characteristic of him, and hence an object of imitation as in Polyc. Phil. 8²; or it may mean the endurance which Christ inspires, as ὁ θεὸς τῆς ὑπομονῆς (Rom. 15⁵) suggests (cf. Moff.).— ὁ Χριστός is not found elsewhere in II; cf., however, I 2⁶ 3² 4¹⁶, and see Mill. 136. The total phrase ἡ ὑπομονὴ τοῦ Χριστοῦ appears to be found only here in the Gk. Bib.—The phrase κατευθύνειν (or εὐθύνειν) τὰς καρδίας (or τὴν καρδίαν) occurs frequently in the Lxx. (1 Ch. 29¹⁸ 2 Ch. 12¹⁴ 19³ 20³³ Pr. 21², etc.); on εἰς (cf. πρός in I 3¹¹), see Sir. 51²⁰ Judith 12⁸. DE, Vulg. have τὰς καρδίας ὑμῶν (I 2⁴); but ὑμῶν referring to ἐφ' ὑμᾶς in v. ⁴ is emphatic (B. Weiss).

VI. COMMAND AND EXHORTATION (3⁶⁻¹⁵).

This section contains the second main point of the letter, prepared for in vv. ¹⁻⁵, "the case of the idlers" (Find.). Word has come to Paul (v. ¹¹) orally and by letter to the effect that the idle minority, in spite of his oral (v. ¹⁰ I 4¹¹) and written (I 4¹¹⁻¹² 5¹⁴) instructions are still begging and meddlesome, some of them still refusing to obey his epistolary injunctions (I 5²⁷ and below, v. ¹⁴). The case having become acute, Paul orders the majority to take severer measures against the idle minority, to add to νουθετεῖν (v. ¹⁵ I 5¹⁴), στέλλεσθαι (v. ⁶) and μὴ συναναμίγνυσθαι (v. ¹⁴). Insisting, however, that the delinquents are brothers (vv. ⁶· ¹⁵), and surmising that the majority have not always dealt tactfully with the excited idlers (vv. ¹³· ¹⁵), Paul is careful to explain just why he gives the command (vv. ⁷⁻¹²) and to have it understood that the discipline, being intended for reformation, is to be administered in love (vv. ¹⁴⁻¹⁵). In fact, his attitude throughout is not that of an apostle exercising his apostolic authority but that of a brother appealing to brothers in the name of a common authority, the Lord Jesus Christ. He believes that his word will suffice; but he contemplates the probability that a few of the idlers will persist in being recalcitrant.

> The connection of thought is clear, the divisions being marked by δέ (vv. ⁶· ¹²· ¹³· ¹⁴) and γάρ (vv. ⁷· ¹⁰· ¹¹). Though the brethren as a whole are addressed throughout the section (even in v. ¹²), it is really the majority whom Paul has in mind and upon whom he places the responsibility for the peace of the brotherhood.

⁶*Now we command you, brothers, using the name of the Lord Jesus Christ, to keep away from every brother who walks in idleness and not in accordance with the instruction which you received from us.* ⁷*For you yourselves know how you ought to imitate us, for we were not idle among you, nor did we receive the means of support from any one without paying for it;* ⁸*but in toil and hardship, night and day we kept at our work in order that we might not put on any of you the burden of our maintenance,—*⁹*not because we have no right to free support, but that we might give in ourselves an example*

for you to imitate. ¹⁰*For also, when we were with you, this we used to command you: "If any one refuses to work, neither let him eat."* ¹¹*For we are informed that some among you are walking in idleness, not working themselves but being busybodies.* ¹²*Now such as these we command and exhort, prompted by the Lord Jesus Christ, that with tranquillity of mind they work and earn their own living.* ¹³*Now as for you, brothers, do not grow tired of doing the right thing.* ¹⁴*In case, however, any one is not for obeying our word expressed in this letter, designate that man; let there be no intimate association with him; in order that he may be put to shame;* ¹⁵*and so count him not as an enemy, but warn him as a brother.*

6. παραγγέλλομεν δὲ ὑμῖν κτλ. With a particle of transition (δέ), the point prepared for in vv. ¹⁻⁵ (especially παραγγέλλομεν and ποιήσετε v. ⁴) is introduced, the responsibility of the majority in reference to the case of the idlers. The command (I 4¹¹ and 4²) is addressed by a brother to brothers, and is based on the authority not of Paul but of Christ. The phrase "in the name of the Lord Jesus Christ" differs from "in the Lord Jesus Christ" (with which the idlers are indirectly commanded and exhorted in v. ¹²), and from "through the Lord Jesus" (I 4²), in that it is not subjective "prompted by the indwelling name or person of the Lord Jesus Christ," but objective, "with," that is, "using" that name. By the actual naming of the name, Paul draws attention not only to the authoritative source of his injunction, but also to the responsibility which the recognition of that supreme authority entails.

στέλλεσθαι ὑμᾶς κτλ. The substance of the command is "that you hold aloof from (cf. I 4³ ἀπέχεσθαι ὑμᾶς ἀπό) every brother who walks idly (or, with Rutherford, "not to be intimate with any of your number who is a loafer") and not according to the deliverance which you have received from us." The persons to be avoided are not enemies but brothers (v. ¹⁵). Their fault lies in the realm of conduct; they "walk" (cf. I 2¹² 4¹· ¹²), that is, "live" (Chrys.), "behave themselves" as idlers (ἀτάκτως). The reference in περιπατεῖν ἀτάκτως is to the refusal, on the part of a small fraction of the converts (v. ¹¹ τινάς) to work and earn their own living, and to the resultant idleness, want, and meddle-

some demand for support from the church, which are mentioned
in I 4¹¹⁻¹² and warned against in I 5¹⁴ (νουθετεῖτε τοὺς ἀτάκτους;
cf. below, v. ¹⁵). As the adverbial clause μὴ κατὰ τὴν παράδοσιν
κτλ., parallel to and explanatory of ἀτάκτως, intimates, this disobedient idleness was contrary to the express instruction given
when Paul was with them (v. ¹⁰ and I 4¹¹ καθὼς παρηγγείλαμεν)
and reiterated in the first epistle (4¹¹⁻¹²; cf. 5¹⁴).

On the phrase ἐν ὀνόματι, cf. 1 Cor. 5⁴ 6¹¹ Col. 3¹⁷ Eph. 5²⁰ Acts 16¹⁸
Ign. Polyc. 5¹; also 1 Cor. 1¹⁰ (διὰ τοῦ ὀνόματος); on the meaning
of the phrase, see Heitmüller, *Im Namen Jesu*, 1903, 73.—ἡμῶν after
χυρίου is to be omitted with BD, *et al.*, "as a likely interpolation" (Ell.).
—στέλλεσθαι is found several times in the Lxx. but only once elsewhere
in the N. T. (2 Cor. 8²⁰). From the root meaning "set," the further idea,
"set one's self for," "prepare" (Sap. 7¹⁴ 14¹ 2 Mac. 5¹), or "set one's
self from," "withdraw" (cf. 3 Mac. 1¹⁹ 4¹¹, and especially Mal. 2⁵ ἀπὸ
προσώπου ὀνόματός μου στέλλεσθαι αὐτόν in parallelism with φοβεῖσθαι),
is easily derived. The meaning, which is somewhat uncertain in 2
Cor. 8²⁰, is clear here, "withdraw one's self from," "hold aloof from"
= χωρίζεσθαι (Theodoret), or ἀπέχεσθαι (which is parallel to στέλλεσθαι
in Hippocrates, *Vet. Med.* 10, as quoted by Liddell and Scott); it differs
little from ὑποστέλλειν ἑαυτόν (Gal. 2¹²) and ὑποστέλλεσθαι (cf. GF
in 2 Cor. 8²⁰). On the word, see Loesner, *ad loc.*, and Wetstein on 2 Cor.
8²⁰; also Mill on our passage. For the subject accusative ὑμᾶς resuming
ὑμῖν, see Bl. 72⁵.—It has already been stated (see I 5¹⁴) that ἀτάκτως
may be either general "disorderly" or specific "idly." That the specific
sense is intended is evident from vv. ⁷⁻⁹ where ἡ παράδοσις is indirectly
explained by the reference to Paul's habitual industry (ἐργαζόμενοι);
from v. ¹⁰ where ἡ πάραδοσις as orally communicated by Paul is quoted:
"if any one refuses to work (ἐργάζεσθαι), he shall not eat"; and from
v. ¹² where ἀτάκτως is defined as μηδὲν ἐργαζομένους. The fault is not
idleness but deliberate, disobedient idleness. What was probable in
I 4¹¹⁻¹² 5¹⁴ now becomes certain; the second epistle explains the first.
D, *et al.*, by reading περιπατοῦντος ἀτάκτως (as in v. ¹¹) blunt the emphasis on the adverb. On μή, see *BMT*. 485.—Precisely how much is
involved in the command to the majority "to hold aloof from" the idle
brethren is uncertain, even in the light of the further specifications in
vv. ¹⁴⁻¹⁵. The idlers are deprived to some extent of freedom of association with the rest of the believers, though to μὴ συναναμίγνυσθαι (v. ¹⁴)
there is not added, as is the case with the incestuous person in 1 Cor. 5¹¹,
a μηδὲ συνεσθίειν. It is not Paul's intention to exclude the idlers from
the brotherhood, for he insists that the admonitions even to the recalcitrant among the idlers, being designed to make them ashamed of them-

selves and return to their work, be tempered with love (*cf.* Chrys.). Furthermore, the fact that στέλλεσθαι, as interpreted in vv. ¹⁴⁻¹⁵, is an advance over νουθετεῖν (v. ¹⁵ I 5¹⁴) and calls for a slightly severer attitude to the delinquents suggests that, in the interval between I and II, the idlers, influenced both by the belief that the day of the Lord was near and by the severity of the persecutions (vv. ¹⁻⁵), had become more meddlesome and contumacious than at the time of writing I (see note on πράσσειν τὰ ἴδια I 4¹¹). It is evident that some of them persist in refusing to obey Paul's orders as conveyed by letter (v. ¹⁴ I 5²⁷); and it is not improbable that some of the more excited idlers were responsible for the disquieting assertion that the day of the Lord is present (2²).— Most recent editors prefer the excellently attested reading παρελάβοσαν (אA), which is supported by ἐλάβοσαν (D), and, with corrected orthography, by παρέλαβον (EKLP). On the other hand, this reading puts an emphasis upon the idlers which would lead one to expect in the sequel not οἴδατε (v. ⁷) but οἴδασιν. Hence παρελάβετε (BG, *et al.*), which fits both ὑμᾶς and οἴδατε, is the preferable reading, leaving παρελάβοσαν (on the ending, see Bl. 21³) to be explained either (1) as an emendation (Weiss, 57) in accord with the adjacent παντὸς ἀδελφοῦ (Pesh. *et al.* have παρέλαβε), or (2) as a scribal error arising from "an ocular confusion with —οσιν (παράδοσιν) in the corresponding place of the line above" (WH. *App.*² 172). For παρ' ἡμῶν, B reads ἀφ' ἡμῶν (1 Cor. 11²³); *cf.* G in I 2¹³.

7–11. In these verses, Paul gives the reasons why he commands the readers to hold aloof from the idle brethren among them, the separate points being introduced respectively by γάρ (v. ⁷), καὶ γάρ (v. ¹⁰), and γάρ (v. ¹¹). (1) First with γάρ (v. ⁷), he reminds them of himself as an example of industry, how he worked to support himself when he was with them, so as to free them from any financial burden on his account, strengthening the reminder by referring to the fact that though he, as an apostle, was entitled to a stipend, yet he waived that right in order that his self-sacrificing labour might serve as an example to them of industry (vv. ⁷⁻⁹). (2) Next with καὶ γάρ (v. ¹⁰), he justifies the present command (v. ⁶) by stating that the instruction to the idlers referred to in v. ⁶ (ἡ παράδοσις) is but a repetition of what he had repeatedly commanded when he was with them, namely, "if any one refuses to work, neither let him eat" (v. ¹⁰). (3) Finally with γάρ (v. ¹¹), he wishes it to be understood distinctly that he issues the command because he is informed that some among them are idle and meddlesome.

In reminding the converts both of himself as a visible example of industry (vv. ⁷⁻⁹) and of his repeated oral teaching in reference to idleness (v. ¹⁰), it would appear that Paul intends not only to arouse the majority to a sense of their own responsibility in the matter, but also to furnish them with arguments that would have weight even with those who might persist in refusing to obey this command as conveyed by letter (v. ¹⁴ I 5²⁷). At all events, this latter consideration helps to explain why Paul refers them not to what he had written in I, but to what he had said and done when he was yet with them. To be sure v. ⁸ is an exact reminiscence of I 2⁹, and v. ¹² recalls what was written in I 4¹¹⁻¹²; but both the example of Paul (vv. ⁷⁻⁹) and the precept in v. ¹⁰ (cf. καθὼς παρηγγείλαμεν, I 4¹¹) hark back to the time of the first visit.

7. αὐτοὶ γὰρ οἴδατε κτλ. With an appeal to the knowledge of the readers quite in the manner of I (2¹ 3³ 5²; cf. 1⁵ 2². ⁵, etc.), Paul advances the first reason (γάρ) for commanding the readers to hold aloof from every brother who walks idly and not in accordance with the specific instruction received. The reason is that they themselves know, without his telling them, the manner in which they ought to imitate him, namely, by working and supporting themselves. Though addressed to all, the appeal is intended for the idlers. On the analogy of I 4¹, we expect πῶς δεῖ ὑμᾶς περιπατεῖν ὥστε μιμεῖσθαι ἡμᾶς (Lft.); but the abridged expression puts an "emphasis on μιμεῖσθαι and gives the whole appeal more point and force" (Ell.).

ὅτι οὐκ ἠτακτήσαμεν . . . οὐδέ κτλ. The ὅτι is not "that" (I 3³) resuming πῶς, but "for," explaining why they know how to imitate Paul. The explanation is stated (1) negatively, and in two co-ordinated clauses (οὐκ . . . οὐδέ), namely, (a) "because we were no loafers when we lived among you" (Rutherford), and (b) because "we did not receive our maintenance from any one for nothing"; and (2) positively (v. ⁸), "but we worked toiling and moiling night and day rather than become a burden to any of you" (Rutherford). That ἀτακτεῖν (only here in the Gk. Bib.) is not general "to be disorderly" but specific "to be idle," "to be a loafer" (Rutherford) has already been pointed out (see on τοὺς ἀτάκτους in I 5¹⁴). ἐσθίειν ἄρτον is apparently a Hebraism for ἐσθίειν (v. ¹⁰). In view of παρά τινος (not τινί as in Tobit 8²⁰ ℵ), it means not "take a meal," and not simply "get food," but more broadly "receive the means of support," "get a living." Paul received maintenance, lodging probably with Jason; but unlike the idle brothers who were begging support from the church, he did not receive it "gratis," that is, without paying for it (*cf.* 2 Cor. 11⁷ ᶠᶠ·; also Exod. 21¹¹ δωρεὰν ἄνευ ἀργυρίου).

On πῶς δεῖ, *cf.* I 4¹, and Col. 4⁶ εἰδέναι πῶς δεῖ ὑμᾶς; μιμεῖσθαι, here and v. ⁹ in Paul, is rare in Gk. Bib. (Heb. 13⁷ 3 Jn. 11 4 Mac. 9²³, etc.); on μιμητής, a word found chiefly in Paul, see I 1⁶.—The phrase ἐσθίειν ἄρτον, only here and v. ¹² in Paul (*cf.* Mk. 3²⁰ 7⁵, etc., and Lxx. *passim*), represents the Hebrew אכל לחם (see BDB. *sub voc.* and Briggs, *ICC.* on Ps. 14⁴), which, like the simple אכל, denotes "take a meal," "get food," and, by a further extension of meaning "to spend one's life" (or, "to earn a livelihood"; see Skinner, *ICC.* on Gen. 3¹⁹); so Amos 7¹² where Lxx. has καταβιοῦν. But the total phrase ἐσθίειν ἄρτον παρά τινος seems to be unique in Gk. Bib., Lev. 10¹² (A) Lk. 10⁷ Phil. 4¹⁸ not being exact parallels. A few minuscules, bothered with ἐφάγομεν παρά, read ἐλάβομεν παρά.—For the adverbial accusative δωρεάν, which is common in Lxx., *cf.* in N. T. Rom. 3²⁴ Gal. 2²¹. For οὐκ . . . οὐδέ . . . ἀλλά, see I 2³.—The fact that Paul states not only that he was not idle but also that he did not beg is doubtless due to the consideration that the idlers were begging support from the church (*cf.* the emphatic ἑαυτῶν in v. ¹²); the reference in I 5¹² to μηδενὸς χρείαν now becomes definite.

8. ἀλλ᾽ ἐν κόπῳ κτλ. "We were not idle (οὐκ), and we did not receive support from any one without paying for it (οὐδέ), but on the contrary (ἀλλά, this strong adversative being antithetical here as in I 2³ to both the negative clauses) we were working," etc. But instead of proceeding "working in order that we might give ourselves as an example for you to imitate us" (v. ⁹ᵇ), and thus coming directly to the point introduced by μιμεῖσθαι (v. ⁷), Paul interjects two considerations designed to increase enormously the value of his example. (1) First, he calls attention to the fact, with which the readers are already acquainted and to which he had alluded in another connection in his first epistle (2⁹), that his labour was (*a*) exacting, "in toil and hardship," (*b*) incessant, "by night and by day," and (*c*) solely in their interests, "so as not to put on any one of you a financial burden"; and secondly (2), he observes characteristically that he worked

to support himself, not because he had no right to demand, as
an apostle of Christ, support from the church, but worked, waiving his right to maintenance, in order that he might give in himself a visible and constant example of self-sacrificing industry
for them to imitate.

The participle ἐργαζόμενοι is loosely attached to both ἠτακτήσαμεν
and ἐφάγομεν, a construction not uncommon in Paul (see I 2¹² 2 Cor. 7⁵).
—Some expositors separate the adverbial clauses, putting ἐν κόπῳ καὶ
μόχθῳ in sharp opposition to δωρεάν, and taking νυκτὸς . . . ἐργαζόμενοι as an explanatory parallel of ἐν κόπῳ καὶ μόχθῳ, "more remotely
dependent on the foregoing ἐφάγομεν" (Ell.; so also De W. Wohl.
Schmiedel, et al.).   But as Lillie, who inclines to the separation, remarks: "Grammatically, however, the words ἐν κόπῳ . . . ἐργαζόμενοι
may just as well be taken together in one antithetical clause," antithetical we may repeat, in the light of I 2³, to both οὐκ ἠτακτήσαμεν and
οὐδὲ ἐφάγομεν.—The reference to the manner and purpose of his work
is evidently advised.   But whether the reminiscence of I 2⁹, which is
almost verbal (except that ἐν κόπῳ καὶ μόχθῳ is closer to 2 Cor. 11²⁷
than to I 2⁹), is likewise conscious is not certain.—ℵBG read here νυκτὸς
καὶ ἡμέρας as in I 2⁹; ADEKLP, et al., emphasise the duration of the
labour by reading the accusative. On the repeated phrase as a whole, see
on I 2⁹.

9. οὐχ ὅτι κτλ.   Using a common ellipsis (οὐχ ὅτι . . . ἀλλά),
Paul qualifies the preceding statement with a view not simply
to asserting his apostolic right to support from the church, but
also to strengthening the force of his example by reminding the
readers that he waived that right.   Both the assertion and the
waiving of rights are characteristic of Paul, especially as regards
the right to receive remuneration for his missionary labour.   In
1 Cor. 9¹⁴, he fortifies his contention by quoting the point of a
word of the Lord (Mt. 10¹⁰=Lk. 10⁷).   The language in which he
expresses here his right differs from that in I (2⁶; see notes on
2⁵⁻⁸· ⁹) where the same claim is made and waived, and agrees
with that in 1 Cor. 9⁴ ᶠᶠ· μὴ οὐκ ἔχομεν ἐξουσίαν φαγεῖν καὶ
πεῖν; μὴ οὐκ ἔχομεν ἐξουσίαν ἀδελφὴν γυναῖκα περιάγειν
(even the wives of missionaries being entitled to support), and
especially ἢ μόνος ἐγὼ καὶ Βαρνάβας οὐκ ἔχομεν ἐξουσίαν μὴ
ἐργάζεσθαι.   In the light of the latter citation, we may supply
here after the absolute ἐξουσίαν a μὴ ἐργάζεσθαι.

ἀλλ' ἵνα κτλ. "But (we worked, waiving our rights) in order
that we might give ourselves as an example to you with a view to
your imitating us." Since Paul says not σχῆτε (cf. Phil. 3¹⁷
ἔχετε τύπον ἡμᾶς) but δῶμεν ὑμῖν, it is likely that he intends to
empha; ise the self-sacrifice involved in this waiving of his rights,
an emphasis which is conspicuous in a similar connection in
the first epistle (2⁸ μεταδοῦναι . . . τὰς ἑαυτῶν ψυχάς). The
ἑαυτούς here is likewise more emphatic than the ἡμᾶς just cited
from Phil. 3¹⁷; Paul gives not simply the command to work
(v. ¹⁰), but also himself as an example of industry.

On the ellipsis οὐχ ὅτι (cf. 2 Cor. 1²⁴ 3⁵ 7⁹ Phil. 4¹⁷), whose origin is
forgotten in usage (cf. Phil. 4¹¹), see Bl. 81¹; and on the ellipsis after
ἀλλά, see Bl. 77¹³. In the first case we may supply "we worked," in
the second, "we worked, waiving the right," or simply "we did it."
For ἀλλ' ἵνα, cf. 2 Cor. 2⁴ 13⁷ Eph. 5²⁷.—ἐξουσίαν is here not potestatem
but ius, not "liberty of action" but moral "right" or authority; see
Mill. and cf. ἔχειν ἐξουσίαν in Rom. 9²¹ 1 Cor. 7³⁷ 9⁴⁻⁶ 11¹⁰.—On τύπον,
see I 1⁷; on the use of διδόναι here, cf. Eph. 4¹¹ ᶠ·

10. καὶ γὰρ ὅτε κτλ. "For also when we were with you (cf.
I 3⁴ II 2⁵) this (that follows, τοῦτο being resumed by the ὅτι
recitative as in I 4¹⁵) we were wont to command you (παρηγ-
γέλλομεν; contrast παρηγγείλαμεν in I 4¹¹), namely," etc. The
γάρ is parallel to γάρ in v. ⁷, and the καί co-ordinates the first
reason for the command of v. ⁶, that is, the example of industry
(vv. ⁷⁻⁹), with the second reason, namely, the oral precept repeatedly given when he was with them (v. ¹⁰). The παράδοσις
of v. ⁶, which is now stated (εἴ τις οὐ θέλει κτλ.), is not a truism:
"if any one does not work, he has nothing to eat," but an ethical
imperative: "if any one refuses to work, he shall not eat";
"nolle vitium est" (Bengel). In characterising as Christian this
"golden rule of labour" (Dob.), Paul is true to the traditions of
his Jewish teachers and to the example of the Master himself
(Mk. 6³). The very phrase itself may well be the coinage of Paul,
for the Thessalonians were mainly working people.

Many parallels to this word of Paul, both Jewish and Greek, have
been suggested (see Wetstein); but the closest is that found in *Bereshith
Rabba* on Gen. 1² (a midrash "redacted according to Zunz in Palestine

in the sixth century"; see Schürer, I, 140): "if they do not work, they have nothing to eat." But, as Dob. rightly urges, both in the passage cited and in other parallels that have been adduced, "the full valuation of labour as a moral duty" (Dob.), which is the point of Paul's words, is absent. Deissmann would have it (*Light*, 318) that Paul was "probably borrowing a bit of good old workshop morality, a maxim coined perhaps by some industrious workman as he forbade his lazy apprentice to sit down to dinner." Be that as it may, it is the industrious workman Paul who introduces this phrase, with its significant emphasis on θέλει, into the realm of Christian ethics. On the imperative in the apodosis, *cf.* 1 Cor. 3¹⁸ 7¹², etc. For οὐ which negates θέλει, instead of μή (which D reads) in conditional sentences, see *BMT.* 370 *f.* The presence of μηδέ instead of μή (1 Cor. 7¹²) is due to οὐ (*cf.* 1 Cor. 10⁷ ᶠᶠ. Eph. 5³, and Bl. 77¹⁰). B* and א* read ἐργάζεσθε; L reads θέλῃ.

11. ἀκούομεν γάρ κτλ. With γάρ (parallel to γάρ in vv. ⁷·¹⁰), Paul explains (just why we do not know) that he is giving the command of v. ⁶ on the basis of information received orally or by letter, or both. "For we are informed that some among you are living in idleness." In saying "some (τινάς) among them" (ἐν ὑμῖν, not ὑμῶν v. ⁸, or ἐξ ὑμῶν; *cf.* Rom. 11¹⁴), Paul speaks indefinitely (*cf.* Gal. 1⁷ 2¹² 2 Cor. 10²· ¹², etc.); but he has in mind definite persons whose names may have been known to him from his source of information. Idleness is an affair of the brotherhood (I 4⁹⁻¹² 5¹²⁻¹⁴), and the brethren as a whole are responsible for the few among them who "do nothing but fetch frisks and vagaries" (Leigh).

μηδὲν ἐργαζομένους ἀλλὰ περιεργαζομένους. In a *paronomasia elegans* (Wetstein), common to both Greek and Roman writers, Paul defines περιπατεῖν ἀτάκτως (*cf.* v. ⁶) both negatively "working not at all," and positively "being busybodies." The point is not simply that some of the brethren are living in idleness, but also that these idlers, instead of minding their own business (I 4¹¹), are meddling in the affairs of the brotherhood (ἐν ὑμῖν), seeking in their poverty and want to exact funds from the treasury of the group (see on πράσσειν τὰ ἴδια I 4¹¹), instead of working to support themselves as they are able and as they ought to do.

The present tense ἀκούομεν (*cf.* 1 Cor. 11¹⁸, and contrast the aorist in Col. 1⁴ Eph. 1¹⁵) indicates not "we have just heard," but either "we

20

keep hearing," a progressive present, or "we hear, are told, are informed," a present for the perfect (*BMT.* 16; Vulg. has *audivimus*). ἀκούειν may refer to hearsay (Find. Dob.; *cf.* 1 Cor. 5¹ 11¹⁸); but it may just as well indicate information received by letter, by word of mouth, or both (*cf.* Lk. 4²³ Acts 7¹² 3 Jn. 4); note in P. Oxy. 294 ἀντιφώνησις of a "reply" to a letter, and ἀκούειν φάσιν, "to get word" by letter.—If there is a distinction (*cf.* Bl. 73⁵) between ἀκούειν with an infinitive (1 Cor. 11¹⁸) and ἀκούειν with the participle, the former construction will refer simply to the fact that they walk, the latter, to the continuous state of walking.—In the light of ἠτακτήσαμεν ἐν ὑμῖν (v. ⁷), the περιπατοῦντας ἀτάκτως may be joined directly with ἐν ὑμῖν; since, however, Paul does not elsewhere use περιπατεῖν ἐν in the sense of "walk among," it may be better to connect ἐν ὑμῖν with τινας, the separation being emphatic; *cf.* 1 Cor. 10²⁷ (possibly also 3¹⁸ 15¹²), and Schmiedel, Moff. Dob. Rutherford. D, *et al.*, obscure the emphasis by reading τινὰς ἐν ὑμῖν περιπατοῦντας; Vulg. has *inter vos quosdam ambulare.*—To illustrate the "elegant paronomasia," commentators refer among others to Demosthenes (*Phil.* IV, 72) ἐργάζῃ καὶ περιεργάζῃ, and to Quintilian (VI, 3⁵⁴) *non agere dixit sed satagere.* Various translations have been attempted (see Lillie); *e. g.* "*keine Arbeit treibend sondern sich herumtreibend*" (Ewald); "*doing nothing, but overdoing;* not busy in work, but busybodies" (Edward Robinson, *Lex.* 1850); "working at no business, but being busybodies" (Ell.). For other instances in Paul of this play on words, Lft. refers to Phil. 3⁸ 1 Cor. 7³¹ 2 Cor. 1¹³ 3² 6¹⁰ 10¹²; see also Bl. 82⁴.—περιεργάζεσθαι is found elsewhere in Gk. Bib. only Sir. 3²³ (*cf.* Sap. 8⁵ א); *cf.* Test. xii, Reub. 3¹⁰ and Hermas, Sim. IX, 2⁷; it is sometimes equivalent to πολυπραγμονεῖν (2 Mac. 2³⁰). See further, Deissmann, *NBS.* 52, and *cf.* περίεργος in 1 Tim. 5¹³.

12. τοῖς δὲ τοιούτοις κτλ. Having explained in vv. ⁷⁻¹¹ why he commands the brothers to hold aloof from every brother who lives in idleness, Paul now turns (δέ) to command the idlers to work and earn their own living in tranquillity of mind, the τοῖς τοιούτοις being in contrast with ὑμῖν (v. ⁶). Paul, however, says not "we command you idlers," or even "those idlers," but indirectly and impersonally "such as these." Furthermore, though he uses παραγγέλλομεν as in v. ⁶, he adds to it a παρακαλοῦμεν, tempering the command with an exhortation. And still further, wishing it to be understood that he speaks on the authority not of himself but of the indwelling Christ, he adds "in the Lord Jesus Christ." The tone of the verse is obviously tactful. Paul speaks as one of them, not as an apostle but as a babe (I 2⁷);

and he is confident that this word from him will suffice for most
of the idlers, though in v. ¹⁴ he faces the contingency that a few
of them will continue to be disobedient (I 5²⁷).

ἵνα μετὰ ἡσυχίας κτλ. Not without reference to his own example, Paul commands and exhorts them (ἵνα introducing the
object) to work and earn their own living, and that too with
tranquillity of spirit. They are to depend for their maintenance
not upon others (I 4¹²) but upon their own exertions (Chrys. notes
the emphatic ἑαυτῶν). In the light of ἡσυχάζειν (I 4¹¹ q. v.),
μετὰ ἡσυχίας is to be understood as the opposite not of περιεργάζεσθαι, as if "without meddlesomeness" were meant, but of
the feverish excitement of mind stimulated by the belief that
the *Parousia* was at hand, or, in its new and erroneous form
(2²), was actually present, a belief which together with the persecutions (vv. ¹⁻⁵) accounts for the increase of idleness and
meddlesomeness since the writing of I.

On τοιοῦτοι, which defines the τινάς with reference to them individually or as a class, see Bl. 47⁹ and *cf.* Rom. 16¹³ 1 Cor. 16¹⁶ ᶠᶠ., etc.
—παραγγέλλειν (I 4¹¹) and παρακαλεῖν (I 2¹¹) are not combined elsewhere in Paul; on the ἵνα with παρακαλεῖν, *cf.* I 4¹¹; with παραγγέλλειν
Paul elsewhere employs the infinitive (v. ⁶ 1 Cor. 7¹⁰; contrast 1 Tim. 5⁷).
After παρακαλοῦμεν, supply αὐτούς or τοὺς τοιούτους.—On the divine
name with ἐν, see I 1¹; P omits Χριστῷ; KL, *et al.*, read the logically
synonymous διὰ τοῦ κυρίου ἡμῶν Ἰ. Χ. with Rom. 15³⁰ (see on I 4²).—
On ἡσυχία, *cf.* Acts 22² 1 Tim. 2¹¹ ᶠ· Sir. 28¹⁶; μετά marks the quality
of mind with which working and earning their own living are to be
associated.—On ἐσθίειν ἄρτον, see v. ⁸.

13. ὑμεῖς δέ, ἀδελφοί κτλ. "O brothers, do not tire of doing
the right" (Rutherford). With δέ and an affectionate ἀδελφοί,
Paul turns from the idlers (v. ¹²) to the brethren addressed in
v. ⁶. The new point, general in form (since καλοποιεῖν is
applicable to all) but specific in reference (as v. ¹⁴ intimates), is
a direct hint to the majority, perhaps definitely to "those that
labour among you" (I 5¹²), that they keep on trying to do the
right thing for the delinquents. The words may imply that in
warning the idlers (I 5¹⁴) the brethren had become impatient
and tactless.

Chrys., however, thinks that the majority are here reminded that they are not to permit the idlers to perish with hunger. Calv., taking the words generally, interprets Paul as fearing that their experience of the abuse of liberality will tend to make the leaders uncharitable, even to the deserving members of the church.—With the exception of Lk. 18¹, the verb ἐνκακεῖν is found elsewhere in Gk. Bib. only in Paul; cf. Gal. 6⁹, τὸ δὲ καλὸν ποιοῦντες μὴ ἐνκακῶμεν. On the spelling ἐνκακεῖν (BD), ἐγκακεῖν (ℵA; cf. Sym. Pr. 3¹¹ Is. 7¹⁶, etc.), or ἐκκακεῖν (GFKLP; cf. Sym. Jer. 18²), see WH. App.² 157 f. From the literal meaning "to behave badly in" (Thayer), ἐνκακεῖν comes to mean also "flag," "falter," "tire," "be weary." On the μή here, see BMT. 162.—καλοποιεῖν, a word found elsewhere in the Gk. Bib. only Lev. 5⁴ (F), is equivalent to καλῶς ποιεῖν (Lev. 5⁴ 1 Cor. 7³⁷ f. Phil. 4¹⁴, etc.); it means probably not "to confer benefits" (Chrys. Calv. Dob. et al.) but, as most take it, "to do the right." Elsewhere Paul uses not καλὸν ποιεῖν (GF; cf. Jas. 4¹⁷) but τὸ καλὸν ποιεῖν (Gal. 6⁹ Rom. 7²¹ 2 Cor. 13⁷).

14. εἰ δέ τις κτλ. Anticipating the probability (cf. I 5²⁷) that some of the idlers would refuse to obey his evangelic utterance (τῷ λόγῳ ἡμῶν referring especially to v. ¹²) expressed in this letter, he orders the brethren, if the case should arise, to proceed to discipline, not with a view to excluding the disobedient among the idlers from the brotherhood, but in the hope of inducing them to repent and amend their idle ways. (1) First of all, he commands: σημειοῦσθε, "designate that man." Just how they are to note him, whether in writing or by naming him publicly at a meeting, is not explained. (2) Then with an infinitive for an imperative (Rom. 12¹⁵ Phil. 3¹⁶), he continues, interpreting the στέλλεσθαι of v. ⁶: μὴ συναναμίγνυσθαι αὐτῷ, "let there be no intimate association with him." The advance from νουθετεῖν (I 5¹⁴) to "hold aloof from," "do not associate with," is necessary, and the severer measures are justified. It will be remembered that Paul had given orders to the idlers when he was present (v. ¹⁰ I 4¹¹), had repeated them in the first epistle (I 4¹¹⁻¹²; cf. 5¹⁴), and has just reiterated them in a conciliatory manner in vv. ⁶⁻¹² (cf. vv. ¹⁻⁵), hinting at the same time (v. ¹³) that the majority must be tactful in their treatment of their delinquent brothers. If, however (εἰ δέ), in spite of all this, some of the idle brothers persist in disobeying his orders as conveyed by letter (I 5²⁷), then they must be deprived of intimate association with the rest of their fellows (*cf.* 1 Cor. 5⁹· ¹¹). But even so, absolute separation from the companionship of the brethren is not in mind; for Paul does not add here, as he does in 1 Cor. 5¹¹, the μηδὲ συνεσθίειν; and above all he does add here the significant v. ¹⁵. (3) Finally, the purpose of the discipline is explicitly mentioned, ἵνα ἐντραπῇ "that he may be shamed." Reformation, not exclusion from the brotherhood, is intended.

ὁ λόγος ἡμῶν (2 Cor. 1¹⁸) could be the equivalent of τὸ εὐαγγέλιον ἡμῶν (2¹); here, however, it refers most probably to that element of the message of the gospel which is specified in v. ¹². The obedience required (*cf.* Phil. 2¹²) is not to Paul's word as such but to his word as inspired by Christ (ἐν κυρίῳ v. ¹²). B, *et al.*, read ὑμῶν for ἡμῶν; *cf.* Bℵ in 2 Cor. 6¹¹ (καρδία ὑμῶν).—διὰ τῆς ἐπιστολῆς refers naturally to the present letter (so most from Chrys. and Th. Mops. to Dob.); but the presence of the article (τῆς) is not conclusive for this interpretation, as 1 Cor. 5¹⁰ shows. However, were Paul alluding to a letter that the converts are to send him (Erasmus, Calv. Grot. *et al.*), there would be no point in specifying the procedure to be followed (Lün.); and furthermore in that case we should expect σημειοῦσθε τοῦτον δι' ἐπιστολῆς (GF omit τῆς). The phrase διὰ τῆς ἐπιστολῆς is to be joined closely with τῷ λόγῳ ἡμῶν, the article τῷ being supplied on the analogy of I 1¹ ἐκκλησίᾳ (τῇ) ἐν θεῷ.— On εἰ δέ τις, *cf.* v. ¹⁰; for the condition, see *BMT*. 242.—σημειοῦσθαι (BA have the imperative; ℵDGFP the infinitive) is found elsewhere in Gk. Bib. only Ps. 4⁷; it occurs in Polybius and Philo; and frequently in papyri, of the signature in writing (*e. g.* P. Oxy. 42, 5⁸ (A.D. 323) σεσημείωμαι ἐμῇ χειρί). See further, 1 Clem. 43¹, and Sophocles, *Lex. sub voc.*—συναναμίγνυσθαι is found elsewhere in the Gk. Bib. only 1 Cor. 5⁹· ¹¹ Hos. 7⁸ (A) Ezek. 20¹⁸ (A). The command is not direct "don't you associate," but indirect "let there be no intimate association with him." BℵA, *et al.*, read the infinitive (not of purpose, but equivalent to an imperative); EKLP, *et al.*, have the imperative. To relieve the asyndeton, GFKLP, *et al.*, insert καί before μή. In Hos. 7⁸ Ezek. 20¹⁸, B has the imperative, AQ the infinitive.—ἐντρέπειν occurs in Gk Bib. only 1 Cor. 4¹⁴; the more common ἐντρέπεσθαι is used either absolutely or with the accus. (Mk. 12⁶ Lk. 18² Sap. 2¹⁰ 7⁶, etc.); for the passive here, compare the refrain in Ps. 34⁴ 69² (39¹⁵) αἰσχυνθείησαν καὶ ἐντραπείησαν.

15. καὶ μὴ ὡς ἐχθρόν κτλ. Even the disobedient idler is a brother, and to do the right thing (v. ¹³) for him means that the warning is to be administered in the spirit not of hate but of love. "And so" (καί), that is, "that the moral result aimed at (ἵνα

ἐντραπῇ) may not be hindered, this *of course* must be the spirit
and style of your discipline" (Lillie), "regard him not as an
enemy, but on the contrary warn him as a brother" (*cf.* I 5¹⁴
νουθετεῖτε τοὺς ἀτάκτους). This significant sentence is so
formed that the stress is laid not on the νουθετεῖτε but on the
ἡγεῖσθε, as if the majority needed a warning as well as the minority. Evidently Paul wishes the majority to see as he sees
that the idlers, even the recalcitrant among them, are brothers,
not enemies; and to have a care that the discipline be administered in love and with the sole purpose of repentance and reform.
Furthermore, it now becomes clear that "to keep away from"
(v. ⁶), and "not to associate with" (v. ¹⁴) are far from suggesting
the removal of the disobedient idlers from the influence of their
brothers. It is noteworthy that the last word is not στέλλεσθαι
and συναναμίγνυσθαι, but νουθετεῖτε as in I 5¹⁴, the advance
here being in the words ἡγεῖσθε ὡς ἀδελφόν, a point which the
brethren appear to have been in danger of forgetting (v. ¹³; see
on εἰρηνεύετε I 5¹³).

Chrys., who sees the fatherly heart of Paul manifested in vv. ¹³⁻¹⁵, is
inclined to suppose that the admonition is to be given not publicly but
privately. On ἡγεῖσθαι, see I 5¹³; on ἐχθρός, *cf.* Rom. 12²⁰. The ὡς, if
not a Hebraism (Bl. 34⁵; *cf.* Job 19¹¹ ἡγήσατο δέ με ὥσπερ ἐχθρόν, 33¹⁰
41²²), is at least pleonastic, marking "the aspect in which he is not to
be regarded" (Ell.). D, *et al.*, omit the καί before μή.

VII. PRAYER (3¹⁶).

*Now may the Lord of peace himself give you peace continually,
in every circumstance. The Lord be with you all.*

16. αὐτὸς δέ κτλ. The prayer for peace addressed to Christ,
the Lord of peace, is prompted by the situation which the command (vv. ⁶⁻¹⁵) is designed to meet. The command alone, however, without the assistance of the indwelling Christ, will not
suffice to restore harmony within the brotherhood; hence, to
insure this concord, the Lord of peace himself must give them
a sense of inward religious peace, and that too continually, in
every circumstance of life. In the added prayer: "May the

Lord (= Christ) be (sc. ἔστω or εἴη) with you all," the πάντων may be intentional (cf. I 5²⁶ II 1³· ¹⁰ 3¹⁸; but note also Rom. 15³³); both the majority and the idlers need the personal presence as well as the peace of Christ as a surety for harmony and concord within the brotherhood.

A similar situation evokes a similar prayer to the God of peace in I 5²³⁻²⁴, following the exhortations of 4¹–5²². On εἰρήνη, see I 1¹ and 5²³; on κύριος = Christ, see 2¹³. GFL, *et al.*, read θεός conforming to Paul's regular usage (see on I 5²³). On δώη, *cf.* Rom. 15⁵ and the note of SH.; on διδόναι εἰρήνην, *cf.* Num. 6²⁶ Is. 26¹².—διὰ παντός occurs elsewhere in Paul only Rom. 11¹⁰ = Ps. 68²⁴; it is equivalent to ἀδιαλείπτως, ἀεί, πάντοτε, ἐν παντὶ καιρῷ (*cf.* the parallelism in Ps. 33²); see on I 5¹⁶ ᶠᶠ·. —ἐν παντὶ τρόπῳ (ℵBEKLP, *et al.*) is used elsewhere in Gk. Bib. only 3 Mac. 7⁸ (A); *cf.* παντὶ τρόπῳ (Phil. 1¹⁸ 1 Mac. 14³⁵) and κατὰ πάντα τρόπον (Rom. 3² Num. 18⁷). As Ven. in 3 Mac. 7⁸, so ADGF, the Latins, Chrys. and Ambst. here have the more common expression ἐν παντὶ τόπῳ (I 1⁸).

VIII. SALUTATION (3¹⁷).

The greeting by the hand of me Paul; this fact is a token of genuineness in every letter; this is the way I write.

17. ὁ ἀσπασμός κτλ. It would appear that Paul, like his contemporaries, occasionally wrote (Phil. 19) but regularly dictated (Rom. 16²²) his letters; and that, again like his contemporaries, he was in the habit of adding to every dictated letter a few concluding words in his own handwriting. Sometimes, and for varying reasons, he calls attention to the autographic conclusion, thus purposely authenticating his letter; so for example in 1 Cor. 16²¹ Col. 4¹⁸ where as here we have ὁ ἀσπασμὸς τῇ ἐμῇ χειρὶ Παύλου (the genitive being in apposition with ἐμοῦ implied in ἐμῇ); see also Gal. 6¹¹ = Phile. 19 ἔγραψα τῇ ἐμῇ χειρί. It is not at all necessary to assume in any of these instances that a particular suspicion of forgery prompted the summons to attention, though it is not inconceivable in our passage that mention is made of the autographic conclusion in view of the fact that some of the idle brethren (I 5²⁷ II 3¹⁴) may have excused their intention to disregard Paul's epistolary injunctions on the score that the letter to be read was not genuine.

ὅ ἐστιν σημεῖον κτλ. "Not 'which salutation,' nor 'which hand,' as if ὅ were attracted by σημεῖον; but 'which autographic way of giving the salutation'" (Lillie). The σημεῖον = "token" refers to what Paul has written in his own hand; it is a proof of authenticity. In view of the ancient habit of writing, or at least of signing a letter, just as we sign with our pen a letter written or typewritten by the stenographer, it is quite unnecessary to limit the scope of the phrase "in every letter." The οὕτως γράφω refers not to the fact but to the manner of the autographic conclusion; "mark the handwriting" (Rutherford). The Thessalonians had already received a letter from Paul, in which, according to epistolary custom, he had himself written a few closing words (I 5²⁸ or ²⁶⁻²⁸). His handwriting, which was characteristic (Gal. 6¹¹), is assumed to be known. In case of necessity, the majority could direct the attention of the recalcitrant among the idlers to the same hand in I and II.

Deissmann (*Light*, 153, 158 *f.*) calls attention to ancient procedure in the matter of writing autographic conclusions in evidence of authenticity, and properly urges that it is a begging of the question to assume that Paul "only finished off with his own hand those letters in which he expressly says that he did." In a very brief letter from Mystarion to a priest, dated September 13, 50 (BGU, 37), a reproduction of which is given by Deissmann (*ibid*, 157), the ἔρρωσο and the date are written in another hand, that is, "in Mystarion's own hand," a circumstance that "proves that somebody at that date (about the time of our letter) closed a letter in his own hand without expressly saying so." In the Passalacqua papyrus (Deissmann, *BS.* 212 *f.*, Witk. 35), a σύμβολον = σημεῖον is given, as a token of genuineness, to the messenger along with the letter: ἀπεδόθη τάδ᾽ αὐτῷ καὶ τὸ σύμβολον τῶν ἐγ. (Deissmann, ἐμῶν); on the other hand, there is no parallel for a σύμβολον = σημεῖον as contained in the letter itself. The extent of the autographic writing here and elsewhere is uncertain, naturally enough, for we do not possess the original. In our passage, Th. Mops. Chrys. Wohl. and others restrict it to v. ¹⁸; Ell. Lft. Mill. and others include vv. ¹⁷⁻¹⁸; Schmiedel, Dob. and others include vv. ¹⁶⁻¹⁸; and Dibelius includes both v. ¹⁸ and the date now lost.

IX. BENEDICTION (3¹⁸).

18. ἡ χάρις κτλ. "The grace of our Lord Jesus Christ be with you all." The benediction is the same as I 5²⁸ with the exception that πάντων is inserted, as in v. ¹⁶, to include "the censured as well as the steady members" (Moffatt).

Most codices add a liturgical ἀμήν after ὑμῶν; Bא and a few others omit.—The subscription πρὸς Θεσσαλονικεῖς β (אB), to which GF prefix ἐτελέσθη, and to which AKL, *et al.*, add ἐγράφη ἀπὸ Ἀθηνῶν, is late, and forms no part of the original letter; see on I 5²⁸.

INDEXES.

I. SUBJECTS AND AUTHORS.

ABBOTT, T. K., 98.
Achaia, 85.
Agrapha, 171, 183, 209.
Ambrosiaster, 58 *f.*, 65, 82, and *passim.*
Angels, 139, 174, 232.
Anomos, origin and significance of the, 273.
Antichrist; see *Anomos.*
Apostasy, the, 250.
Apostle, 68, 99.
Aquila and Priscilla (Prisca), 69.
Aristarchus, 5.
Askwith, E. H., 42, 172, 248.
Auberlen and Riggenbach, 42, 63 *ff.*
Augustine, 60, 260, 262.
Authenticity of the epistles, 37–54.

BACON, B. W., 9, 27, 42, and *passim.*
Baur, F. C., 37, 40, 115.
Belial, 253.
Bengel, 62 *f.*, 65, 92, and *passim.*
Bernard, J. H., 249.
Berœa, 8, 84, 110.
Beza, 61, 81, and *passim.*
Bigg, C., 149.
Blass, 72, 74, and *passim.*
Bornemann, W., 40, 42, 59 *f.*, 63, 65, 74, and *passim.*
Bousset, 41, 42, 70, and *passim.*
Briggs, C. A., 42, 44, 45, 60 *ff.*, 90, 140, 175, 197, 205, 231, 253 *f.*, 256, 276, 291, 302.
Brother, 78.

Burkitt, F. C., 58, 115, 116.
Burton, E. D., 2, 96, and *passim.*

CABIRI, 95 *f.*, 167.
Call of God, 105, 154, 214, 282.
Calvin, 60 *f.*, 65, 77, and *passim.*
Charles, R. H., 41 *f.*, 115, and *passim.*
Chrysostom, 59, 65, 69, and *passim.*
Church, 4 *ff.*, 109, 224.
Clemen, C., 7, 10, 42, 45, 115, and *passim.*
Commentaries on the epistles, 59–65.
Consecration, 138, 145 *ff.*, 281.
Contents of the epistles, 12–17, 20–24.
Conybeare, F. C., 58, 116, 119, 216.

DALMAN, G., 225, 235.
Date of the epistles, 9, 19–20.
Day of the Lord, 77, 180 *ff.*, 236, 248.
Death of Christ, 111, 168 *f.*, 189, 286.
Deissmann, A., 9, 43, 53, 67, 70, and *passim.*
Demas, 5.
Denney, James, 64 *f.*, 173, 278, 281, 283.
Destruction, 182, 234, 270.
De Wette, 40, 63, 65, 94, and *passim.*
Dibelius, M., 42, 54, 63, 75, and *passim.*
Dichotomy and trichotomy, 212 *f.*

Disposition of the epistles, 17, 27–28.
Dobschütz, E. von, 7, 38, 42, 45, 47, 55, 59, 63, 65, 68, 71, and *passim*.
Drummond, James, 39, 63, 99, 171.

ELECTION, 77 *f.*, 279.
Ellicott, 63, 65, 79, and *passim*.
Endurance, 76, 110, 224, 296.
Ephraem, Syrus, 59, 75, and *passim*.
Epictetus, 141, 155, 163, 200, 202.
Epistolary literature, 67.
Eschatology, 43 *f.*, 88 *f.*, 122 *f.*, 139, 163 *ff.*, 178 *ff.*, 243 *ff.*
Estius, 61 *f.*, 140, 160, 210.
Everling, 121 *f.*, 175.
Ewald, P., 121.

FAITH, 76, 86, 131, 168, 187, 222, 236, 240, 292.
Findlay, G. G., 42, 45, 55, 63 *ff.*, 75, and *passim*.
Flatt, 62, 99, and *passim*.

GALLIO, 9.
Gardner, Percy, 70.
Gilbert, G. H., 59.
Glory, 105, 236, 241, 282, 291.
Good, the, 200.
Goodwin, W. W., 89, 125, 152, 288.
Gospel of God, 79 *f.*
Grace, 71, 218 *f.*, 242, 286.
Gregory, C. R., 55 *ff.*, 69, 261.
Gressmann, H., 276.
Grotius, 43, 61 *f.*, 65, 99, and *passim*.
Gunkel, 41, 70, 105, 205, 250, 260, 276.

HAMMOND, H., 61 *f.*, 65, 81, and *passim*.
Harnack, 42 *f.*, 53 *f.*, 78, and *passim*.
Harris, Rendel, 67, 87, 107.
Hatch, E., 86, 213, 264.
Heart, 96, 118, 138, 287.

Heaven, 89, 174, 232.
Heitmüller, 299.
Hollmann, 41 *f.*, 45, 52.
Holtzmann, H. J., 37, 40 *ff.*, 45, 63, 64, 109, and *passim*.
Hope, 76, 167 *f.*, 187, 286.
Howson, J. S., 2.

IDLENESS, 159 *ff.*, 197, 297 *ff.*
Impurity, 11, 95, 145 *ff.*

JASON, 4 *ff.*
Jesus Christ, death of, 111, 168 *f.*, 189, 286; resurrection of, 168 *f.*; indwelling of, 69 *f.*, 144 *f.*, 169, 188.
Jews, the, 73, 90, 105 *ff.*, 117 *ff.*, 292.
Jowett, B., 63, 151, 213, 222, 232.
Joy, 83, 123, 133 *f.*, 201.
Judæa, 105 *ff.*
Judgment, the final, 89, 113 *ff.*, 188, 228, 233 *ff.*, 272.
Jülicher, 37, 42.

KABISCH, 121, 174, 176.
κατέχων ἄρτι, ὁ, the meaning of, 259.
Kennedy, H. A. A., 58, 102, and *passim*.
Kern, 40 *ff.*, 52, 247, 249.
Kingdom of God, 105, 226 *f.*
Kiss, the holy, 216.
Klausner, J., 260, 276.
Knowling, R. J., 4, 42.

LAKE, K., 7, 27, 42, and *passim*.
Language of the epistles, 28–34.
Lex talionis, 227 *ff.*
Lightfoot, J. B., 42, 47, 63, 65, 76, and *passim*.
Lillie, John, 42, 59, 64 *f.*, 76, and *passim*.
Literary resemblances between II and I, 45–51.
Lock, W., 42, 116.

Lord = Christ, 279.
Lord Jesus Christ, significance of the name, 71.
Love, 76, 131, 137, 157 *f.*, 187, 195, 198 *ff.*, 222, 270, 296, 309.
Lueken, 43, 63, 175.
Lünemann, 37 *f.*, 42, 63, 65, 85, and *passim.*

MACEDONIA, 86, 157.
McGiffert, 8, 27, 38, 42 *f.*, 43, 45, 52, 68, 100, 107, 121, 145, 159, 193, 205, 230.
Man of lawlessness; see *Anomos.*
Mathews, S., 5, 172, 276.
Mayor, J. B., 108, 122.
Michael, 174 *f.*
Milligan, George, 42 *f.*, 45, 63, 65, 67 *f.*, and *passim.*
Moffatt, James, 37 *ff.*, 42 *f.*, 45, 53, 64, 67 *f.*, and *passim.*
Moore, G. F., 88, 189, 253, 254.
Moulton, J. H., 75, and *passim.*
Mystery of lawlessness, 263.

NÄGELI, 32.
Name of Christ, in the, 298 *f.*
Nestle, 58, 72, 128.

ŒCUMENIUS, 60, 142, 214, 232, 249. 290.

Parousia, of Christ, 88, 122 *f.*, 139, 173, 212, 231, 244; of the *Anomos,* 265, 268 *ff.*
Peace, 71, 195, 210, 219, 310.
Pelagius, 59 *f.*, 142, 212, 214, 228, 237, 240.
Pelt, 59, 62, 99, and *passim.*
Persecutions, 82, 108 *ff.*, 127 *ff.*, 225, 294.
Personal equation of the epistles, 34-37.
Pfleiderer, 37, 40.

Place of writing of the epistles, 9, 19-20.
Plummer, A., 116.
Plural, epistolary, 68.
Politarchs, 2, 4, 121.
Poole, M., 61 *f.*, 65, 115, and *passim.*
Prayer, 75, 134 *ff.*, 201, 209 *ff.*, 215, 238 *ff.*, 285 *ff.*, 289 *ff.*, 296 *ff.*, 310.
Priority of II, 38-39.
Prophesying, gift of, 204 *ff.*

RABINSOHN, M., 260, 276.
Ramsay, W. M., 2 *f.*, 121.
Reinach, Th., 112.
Reitzenstein, R., 70, 208, 268.
Religious convictions of II, 24-27.
Resch, A., 172, 209.
Resurrection of Christ, 168 *f.*; of believers, 168 *f.*
Retaliation, 200, 227 *ff.*
Robinson, J. A., 67, 72, and *passim.*
Ropes, J. H., 172, 189, 209.
Rutherford, W. G., 93, and *passim.*

SALVATION, 112, 188, 270, 281.
Sanday and Headlam, 58, 71, and *passim.*
Sanders, H. A., 56.
Satan, 121 *f.*, 127 *ff.*, 268, 293 *f.*
Schaefer, A., 64, 261 *ff.*
Schettler, A., 145, 170.
Schmiedel, 37, 39 *ff.*, 45, 63, 65, 68, 85, and *passim.*
Schott, 62, 137, 161, 195, 226, 282 *f.*
Schürer, 245, 276, 305.
Schweitzer, A., 70.
Secundus, 5.
Silvanus, 68, 219.
Soden, H. von, 40, 55, 67, 69, and *passim.*
Söderblom, N., 276.
Sophocles, E. A., 94, 99, and *passim.*
Souter, A., 55 *f.*, and *passim.*

Spirit, the Holy, 81, 83, 155 *f.*, 203 *ff.*, 246.

Spitta, F., 43, 45, 126, 148, 258 *f.*

Swete, H. B., 59, 64, 80, and *passim.*

Synagogue, 109.

Tafel, 2.

Teichmann, E., 174.

Temple of God, 256.

Text of the epistles, 55–58.

Thackeray, H. St. John, 101, 114.

Thayer, J. H., 245, 247, 293, 308.

Theodore of Mopsuestia, 59, 65, 108, and *passim.*

Theodoret, 59, 99, and *passim.*

Theophylact, 60, 93, and *passim.*

Thessalonians, founding of the Church of the, 1–5; character of the Church of the, 5–7.

Thessalonica, the city of, 2.

Timothy, 68, 126, 131, 219.

Tischendorf, 55 *ff.*, 82, and *passim.*

Titius, A., 172.

Toy, C. H., 109, 216.

Tradition, 143, 284, 304.

Turner, C. H., 9, 59 *f.*, 173.

Versions, 58.

Vincent, M. R., 42, 140, 148 *f.*, 153, 208, 226, 233, 235, 238, 245, 296.

Viteau, 101.

Volz, P., 70, 166, and *passim.*

Vorstius, 62, 147, 163.

Vos, 178.

Weiss, B., 42, 55, 63, 78, and *passim.*

Weiss, J., 38, 81, 122, 205, 231, 284.

Weizsäcker, 40 *f.*, 52.

Wendland, P., 88.

Wernle, P., 42, 45.

Westcott and Hort, 28, 55, 82, and *passim.*

Wetstein, 62, 101, and *passim.*

Will of God, 146, 202.

Witkowski, S., 67, 72, and *passim.*

Wohlenberg, G., 42, 63, 65, 75, and *passim.*

Work, 102, 162, 191 *ff.*, 302 *ff.*

Wrath, 89 *f.*, 113 *ff.*, 188.

Wrede, W., 40, and *passim.*

Zahn, Th., 27, 42, 45, 53, 68, 71, and *passim.*

Zimmer, F., 55, 82, and *passim.*

II. GREEK WORDS AND PHRASES.

ἀγαθός, I 3⁶ II 2¹⁶· ¹⁷; τὸ ἀγαθόν, I 5¹⁵.
ἀγαθωσύνη, II 1¹¹.
ἀγαπᾶν, I 4⁹ II 2¹⁶; ἀδελφοὶ ἠγαπημένοι ὑπὸ τοῦ θεοῦ (I 1⁴), κυρίου
  (II 2¹³).
ἀγάπη, I 1³ 3⁶ 5⁸· ¹³; εἰς ἀλλήλους, I
  3¹² II 1³; τῆς ἀληθείας, II 2¹⁰; τοῦ
  θεοῦ, II 3⁵.
ἀγαπητοί, I 2⁸.
ἄγγελοι δυνάμεως, II 1⁷.
ἄγειν, I 4¹⁴.
ἀγιάζειν, I 5²³.
ἀγιασμός, I 4³· ⁴· ⁷; ἐν ἀγιασμῷ πνεύματος, II 2¹³.
ἅγιοι αὐτοῦ, I 3¹³ II 1¹⁰; ἅγιον with
  πνεῦμα, I 1⁵· ⁶ 4⁸; with φίλημα, I 5²⁶.
ἀγιωσύνη, I 3¹³.
ἀγνοεῖν, οὐ θέλομεν ὑμᾶς, I 4¹³.
ἀγών, I 2².
ἀδελφός, I 3² and passim; ἀδελφοί, I
  1⁴ and passim.
ἀδιαλείπτως, I 1³ 2¹³ 5¹⁷.
ἀδικία, II 2¹⁰· ¹².
ἀήρ, I 4¹⁷.
ἀθετεῖν, I 4⁸.
'Αθῆναι, I 3¹.
αἱρεῖσθαι, II 2¹³.
αἰφνίδιος, I 5³.
αἰώνιος, ὄλεθρος, II 1⁹; παράκλησις
  αἰωνία, II 2¹⁶.
ἀκαθαρσία, I 2³ 4⁷.
ἀκοῆς, λόγος, I 2¹³.
ἀκούειν, II 3¹¹.
ἀκριβῶς, I 5².
ἀλήθεια, ἡ, II 2¹²; ἡ ἀγάπη τῆς ἀληθείας, II 2¹⁰; πίστις ἀληθείας, II 2¹³.
ἀληθινός, θεός, I 1⁹.

ἀληθῶς, I 2¹³.
ἀλλά, I 1⁸ and passim; ἀλλὰ καί, I
  1⁵ 2⁸.
ἀλλήλους, I 4⁹· ¹⁸ 5¹¹; εἰς ἀλλήλους
  I 3¹² 5¹⁵ II 1³.
ἄλλοι, I 2⁶.
ἅμα σύν, I 4¹⁷ 5¹⁰.
ἁμαρτίας, τάς, I 2¹⁶.
ἄμεμπτος, I 3¹³.
ἀμέμπτως, I 2¹⁰ 5²³.
ἀναγινώσκειν, I 5²⁷.
ἀνάγκη, I 3⁷.
ἀναιρεῖν τῷ πνεύματι τοῦ στόματος,
  II 2⁸.
ἀναμένειν, I 1¹⁰.
ἀναπληροῦν, I 2¹⁶.
ἄνεσις, II 1⁷.
ἀνέχεσθαι, II 1⁴.
ἄνθρωπος, I 2⁴ and passim; ὁ ἄνθρωπος τῆς ἀνομίας, II 2³.
ἀνιστάναι, I 4¹⁴· ¹⁶.
ἀνομία, II 2³· ⁷.
ἄνομος, ὁ, II 2⁸.
ἀνταποδιδόναι, I 3⁹ II 1⁶.
ἀντέχεσθαι, I 5¹⁴.
ἀντί, I 5¹⁵; ἀνθ' ὦν, II 2¹⁰.
ἀντικείμενος, II 2⁴.
ἄξιόν ἐστιν, II 1³.
ἀξιοῦν, II 1¹¹.
ἀξίως τοῦ θεοῦ, περιπατεῖν, I 2¹².
ἀπαγγέλλειν, I 1⁹.
ἀπάντησιν, εἰς, I 4¹⁷.
ἅπαξ καὶ δίς, I 2¹⁸; cf. Phil. 4¹⁶.
ἀπάτη ἀδικίας, II 2¹⁰.
ἀπέχεσθαι ἀπό, I 4³ 5²².
ἀπό, I 1⁸ and passim; ἀπὸ προσώπου,
  II 1⁹.

319

ἀποδεικνύναι, II 2⁴.
ἀποδιδόναι, I 5¹⁵.
ἀποθνήσκειν, I 4¹⁴ 5¹⁰, of Christ.
ἀποκαλύπτεσθαι, II 2³·⁶·⁸, of the Anomos.
ἀποκάλυψις, ἡ, II 1⁷, of Christ.
ἀποκτείνειν, I 2¹⁵.
ἀπολλύμενοι, οἱ, II 2¹⁰.
ἀπορφανίζεσθαι ἀπό, I 2¹⁷.
ἀποστασία, ἡ, II 2³.
ἀπόστολοι Χριστοῦ, I 2⁶.
ἀπωλείας, ὁ υἱὸς τῆς, II 2³.
ἆρα οὖν, I 5⁶ II 2¹⁵.
ἀρέσκειν θεῷ, I 2⁴·¹⁵ 4¹; ἀνθρώποις, I 2⁴.
ἀρπάζεσθαι, I 4¹⁷.
ἄρτι, I 3⁶ II 2⁷.
ἄρτον, ἐσθίειν, II 3⁸·¹².
ἀρχάγγελος, I 4¹⁶.
ἀρχῆς, ἀπ', II 2¹³.
ἀσθενεῖς, οἱ, I 5¹⁴.
ἀσπάζεσθαι ἐν φιλήματι ἁγίῳ, I 5²⁶.
ἀσπασμὸς τῇ ἐμῇ χειρὶ Παύλου, II 3¹⁷.
ἀσφάλεια, I 5³.
ἀτακτεῖν, II 3⁷.
ἄτακτοι, οἱ, I 5¹⁴.
ἀτάκτως, περιπατεῖν, II 3⁶·¹¹.
ἄτοποι καὶ πονηροί, II 3².
αὐτός, passim; αὐτὸς δὲ ὁ θεός, I 3¹¹ 5²³; ὁ κύριος, II 2¹⁶ 3¹⁶; cf. I 4¹⁶.
τὰ αὐτὰ καθώς, I 2¹⁴.
Ἀχαία, I 1⁷·⁸.

βάρει εἶναι, ἐν, I 2⁶.
βασιλεία, ἡ ἑαυτοῦ, I 2¹²; ἡ βασιλεία τοῦ θεοῦ, II 1⁵.

γάρ, I 1⁸ and passim; αὐτοὶ γὰρ οἴδατε, I 2¹ 3³ 5² II 3⁷; καὶ γάρ, I 4¹⁰; καὶ γὰρ ὅτε, I 3⁴ II 3¹⁰.
γαστρί, ἔχειν ἐν, I 5³.
γίνεσθαι, passim; with dat. I 1⁵·⁷ 2⁸·¹⁰; with εἰς, I 1⁵ 3⁵; with ἐκ μέσου, II 2⁷.

γινώσκειν, I 3⁵.
γράφειν, I 4⁹ 5¹ II 3¹⁷.
γρηγορεῖν, I 5⁶·¹⁰.

δέ, I 2¹⁶ and passim.
δεῖ, πῶς, I 4¹ II 3⁷.
δεῖσθαι εἰς τό, I 3¹⁰.
δέχεσθαι (τὸν) λόγον, I 1⁶ 2¹³; τὴν ἀγάπην τῆς ἀληθείας, II 2¹⁰.
διά with gen., I 3⁷ and passim; τοῦ Ἰησοῦ, I 4¹⁴; τοῦ κυρίου Ἰησοῦ, I 4²; τοῦ κυρίου ἡμῶν Ἰ. Χ., I 5⁹; πνεύματος, II 2². With accus., I 1⁵ 3³ 5¹³; διὰ τοῦτο, I 2¹³ 3⁵·⁷ II 2¹¹.
διαμαρτύρεσθαι, I 4⁶.
διδάσκεσθαί τι, II 2¹⁵.
διδόναι, I 4² II 1⁸ 2¹⁶ 3⁹·¹⁶; εἴς τινα, I 4⁸.
δικαία κρίσις, II 1⁵; δίκαιον, II 1⁶.
δικαίως, I 2¹⁰.
δίκην, τίνειν, II 1⁹.
διό, I 3¹ 5¹¹.
διότι, I 2⁸·¹⁸ 4⁶.
διωγμοὶ καὶ θλίψεις, II 1⁴.
διώκειν τὸ ἀγαθόν, I 5¹⁵.
δοκιμάζειν, I 2⁴ 5²¹.
δόλῳ, ἐν, I 2³.
δόξα, I 2⁶·²⁰; I 2¹², of God; II 2¹⁴, of Christ; τῆς ἰσχύος αὐτοῦ, II 1⁹.
δοξάζεσθαι, II 3¹.
δουλεύειν θεῷ, I 1⁹.
δύναμις, II 1⁷ 2⁹; ἐν δυνάμει, I 1⁸ II 1¹¹.
δύνασθαι, I 2⁶ 3⁹.
δωρεάν, II 3⁸.

ἐάν, I 2⁸; with μή, II 2³; with indic., I 3⁸.
ἑαυτοῦ, I 2⁷ and passim.
ἐγείρειν ἐκ τῶν νεκρῶν, I 1¹⁰.
ἐγώ, I 2¹⁸.
ἔθνη, τά, I 2¹⁶ 4⁵.
εἰ, I 4¹⁴; εἴ τις οὐ, II 3¹⁰·¹⁴.

εἶδον, I 3⁶; τὸ πρόσωπον, I 2¹⁷ 3¹⁰.
εἶδος, I 5²².
εἴδωλα, τά, I 1⁹.
εἶναι, I 2¹³ and *passim*.
εἴπερ, II 1⁶.
εἰρηνεύειν, I 5¹³.
εἰρήνη, I 5³ II 3¹⁶; with χάρις, I 1¹ II 1²; ὁ θεὸς (ὁ κύριος) τῆς εἰρήνης, I 5²³ II 3¹⁶.
εἰς, I 1⁵ and *passim;* εἰς ὅ, II 1¹¹. ¹⁴; εἰς τό with infin., I 2¹². ¹⁶ 3². ⁵. ¹⁰. ¹³ 4⁹ II 1⁵ 2². ⁶. ¹⁰. ¹¹ 3⁹.
εἷς ἕκαστος, I 2¹¹ II 1³; εἷς τὸν ἕνα, I 5¹¹.
εἴσοδος, I 1⁹ 2¹.
εἴτε, I 5¹⁰ II 2¹⁵.
ἐκ, I 1¹⁰ 2³. ⁶; ἐκ μέσου γίνεσθαι, II 2⁷.
ἕκαστος, I 4⁴; with εἷς, I 2¹¹ II 1³.
ἐκδίκησίν τινι, διδόναι, II 1⁸.
ἔκδικος κύριος, I 4⁶.
ἐκδιώκειν, I 2¹⁵.
ἐκείνη, ἐν τῇ ἡμέρᾳ, II 1¹⁰.
ἐκκλησία Θεσσαλονικέων, ἡ, I 1¹ II 1¹; αἱ ἐκκλησίαι τοῦ θεοῦ, I 2¹⁴ II 1⁴.
ἐκλογὴ ὑμῶν, ἡ, I 1⁴.
ἐκφεύγειν, I 5³.
ἐλπίς, I 1³ 2¹⁹ 4¹³ 5⁸ II 2¹⁶.
ἐμός, II 3¹⁷.
ἔμπροσθεν, with God I 1³ 3⁹. ¹³; with Christ, I 2¹⁹.
ἐν, *passim;* ἐν θεῷ πατρὶ (ἡμῶν), I 1¹ II 1¹; ἐν τῷ θεῷ ἡμῶν, I 2²; ἐν κυρίῳ, I 3⁸ 5¹²; ἐν κυρίῳ Ἰησοῦ (Χριστῷ), I 4¹; I 1¹ II 1¹ 3¹²; ἐν Χριστῷ (Ἰησοῦ), I 4¹⁶; 2¹⁴ 5¹⁸; ἐν πνεύματι ἁγίῳ, I 1⁵; ἐν δυνάμει, I 1⁵ II 1¹¹.
ἐναντίος, I 2¹⁵.
ἔνδειγμα, II 1⁵.
ἐνδοξάζεσθαι, II 1¹⁰. ¹².
ἐνδύεσθαι, I 5⁸.
ἐνέργεια τοῦ Σατανᾶ, II 2⁹; πλάνης, II 2¹¹.
ἐνεργεῖσθαι, I 2¹³ II 2⁷.

ἐνέστηκεν ἡ ἡμέρα τοῦ κυρίου, II 2².
ἐνκακεῖν, II 3¹³.
ἐνκαυχᾶσθαι, II 1⁴.
ἐνκόπτειν, I 2¹⁸.
ἐνορκίζω ὑμᾶς τὸν κύριον, I 5²⁷.
ἐντρέπεσθαι, II 3¹⁴.
ἐξαπατᾶν, II 2³.
ἐξέρχεσθαι, I 1⁸.
ἐξηχεῖσθαι, I 1⁸.
ἐξουθενεῖν, I 5²⁰.
ἐξουσίαν, ἔχειν, II 3⁹.
ἔξω, οἱ, I 4¹².
ἔπειτα, I 4¹⁷.
ἐπί with gen., I 1²; with dat., I 3⁷. ⁹ 4⁷; with accus., I 2¹⁶ II 1¹⁰ 2¹. ⁴ 3⁴.
ἐπιβαρῆσαί τινα ὑμῶν, πρὸς τὸ μή, I 2⁹ II 3⁸.
ἐπιθυμία, I 2¹⁷ 4⁵.
ἐπιποθεῖν ἰδεῖν, I 3⁶.
ἐπιστολή, I 5²⁷ II 2². ¹⁵ 3¹⁴. ¹⁷.
ἐπιστρέφειν πρὸς τὸν θεόν, I 1⁹.
ἐπισυναγωγὴ πρὸς αὐτόν, ἡ ἡμῶν, II 2¹.
ἐπιφάνεια τῆς παρουσίας, ἡ, II 2⁸.
ἐργάζεσθαι, I 2⁹ 4¹¹, II 3⁸. ¹⁰. ¹¹. ¹².
ἔργον, I 5¹³; (τὸ) ἔργον (τῆς) πίστεως, I 1³ II 1¹¹; ἔργῳ καὶ λόγῳ, II 2¹⁷.
ἔρχεσθαι, I 1¹⁰ 2¹⁸ and *passim*.
ἐρωτῶμεν καὶ παρακαλοῦμεν, I 4¹; ἐρωτῶμεν δὲ ὑμᾶς ἀδελφοί, I 5¹² II 2¹.
ἐσθίειν, II 3¹⁰; with ἄρτον, II 3⁸. ¹².
ἔτι, II 2⁵.
εὐαγγελίζεσθαί τι, I 3⁶.
εὐαγγέλιον, τό, I 2⁴; with ἡμῶν, I 1⁵ II 2¹⁴; with τοῦ θεοῦ, I 2². ⁸. ⁹; with τοῦ κυρίου ἡμῶν Ἰησοῦ, II 1⁸; with τοῦ Χριστοῦ I 3².
εὐδοκεῖν, with infin., I 2⁸ 3¹; with dat., II 2¹².
εὐδοκία ἀγαθωσύνης, II 1¹¹.
εὐσχημόνως, I 4¹².
εὐχαριστεῖν, I 1² 2¹³ 5¹⁸; with ὀφείλομεν, II 1³ 2¹³.
εὐχαριστία, I 3⁹.

ἐφιστάναι, I 5³.

ἔχειν, I 1⁹ 3⁶ 4¹³ 5³ II 3⁹; with χρείαν, I 1⁸ 4⁹· ¹² 5¹.

ἐχθρός, II 3¹⁵.

ἕως (conj.), II 2⁷.

ζῆν, I 1⁹ 3⁸ 5¹⁰; ἡμεῖς οἱ ζῶντες, I 4¹⁵· ¹⁷.
ζητεῖν, I 2⁶.

ἤ, I 2¹⁹ II 2⁴.

ἡγεῖσθαι, I 5¹³; with ὡς, II 3¹⁵.

ἤδη, II 2⁷.

ἡμέρα, I 5⁸; ἡ ἡμέρα, I 5⁴; ἐκείνη, II 1¹⁰; τοῦ κυρίου, I 5² II 2²; υἱοὶ ἡμέρας, I 5⁵; νυκτὸς καὶ ἡμέρας, I 2⁹ 3¹⁰ II 3⁸.

ἡσυχάζειν, I 4¹¹.

ἡσυχία, II 3¹².

θάλπειν, I 2⁷.

θαυμάζεσθαι, II 1¹⁰.

θέλειν, I 2¹⁸ 4¹³ II 3¹⁰.

θέλημα (τοῦ) θεοῦ, I 4³ 5¹⁸.

θεοδίδακτος, I 4⁹.

θεός, passim; θεὸς ζῶν, I 1⁹; ὁ θεὸς ἡμῶν, I 2² 3⁹ II 1¹¹· ¹²; θεὸς πατήρ, I 1¹ II 1² (1¹); ὁ θεὸς καὶ πατὴρ ἡμῶν, I 1³ 3¹¹· ¹³ (II 2¹⁶); ἐν θεῷ πατρὶ (ἡμῶν), I 1¹ II 1¹; ἐν τῷ θεῷ ἡμῶν, I 2².

Θεσσαλονικεύς, I 1¹ II 1¹.

θλίβειν, I 3⁴ II 1⁶· ⁷.

θλίψις, I 1⁶ 3³· ⁷ II 1⁴· ⁶.

θώραξ, I 5⁸.

ἴδιος, I 2¹⁴ 4¹¹.

Ἰησοῦς, I 1¹⁰ 4¹⁴; (ὁ) κύριος (ἡμῶν) Ἰησοῦς, I 2¹⁵ 4¹· ² II 1⁷ 2⁸; I 2¹⁹ 3¹¹· ¹³ II 1⁸· ¹²; ὁ κύριος (ἡμῶν) Ἰησοῦς Χριστός, I 1¹ II 1¹· ²· ¹² 3⁶· ¹²; I 1³ 5⁹· ²³· ²⁸ II 2¹· ¹⁴· ¹⁶ 3¹³; ἐν Χριστῷ Ἰησοῦ, I 2¹⁴ 5¹⁸.

ἵνα, I 2¹⁶ and passim.

Ἰουδαία, I 2¹⁴.

Ἰουδαῖοι, I 2¹⁴.

ἰσχύς, II 1⁹.

καθάπερ, I 2¹¹; with καί, I 3⁶· ¹² 4⁵.

καθεύδειν, I 5⁶· ⁷· ¹⁰.

καθίζειν εἰς, II 2⁴.

καθώς, I 1⁵ and often in I; II 1³; καθὼς καί, I 2¹⁴ 3⁴ 4¹· ⁶· ¹³ 5¹¹ II 3¹.

καί, passim; καὶ γάρ, I 3⁴ 4⁹ II 3¹⁰.

καιρός, II 2⁶; καιροί, I 5¹; πρὸς καιρὸν ὥρας, I 2¹⁷.

κακὸν ἀντὶ κακοῦ, I 5¹⁵.

καλεῖν, of God, I 2¹² 4⁷ 5²⁴ II 2¹⁴.

καλοποιεῖν, II 3¹³.

καλόν, τό, I 5²¹.

καρδία, I 2⁴· ¹⁷; ὑμῶν τὰς καρδίας, I 3¹³ II 2¹⁷ 3⁵.

κατά with accus., II 1¹² 2³· ⁹ 3⁶.

καταβαίνειν ἀπ' οὐρανοῦ, I 4¹⁶.

καταλαμβάνειν, I 5⁴.

καταλείπεσθαι, I 3¹.

καταξιοῦσθαι, II 1⁵.

καταργεῖν, II 2⁸.

καταρτίζειν, I 3¹⁰.

κατευθύνειν τὴν ὁδὸν πρός, I 3¹¹; τὰς καρδίας εἰς, II 3⁵.

κατέχειν, I 5²¹; ὁ κατέχων ἄρτι, II 2⁷; τὸ κατέχον, II 2⁶.

καυχήσεως, στέφανος, I 2¹⁹.

κεῖσθαι εἰς, I 3³.

κέλευσμα, I 4¹⁶.

κενός, I 2¹; γίνεσθαι εἰς κενόν, I 3⁵.

κηρύσσειν εἰς ὑμᾶς τὸ εὐαγγέλιον τοῦ θεοῦ, I 2⁹.

κλέπτης, I 5²· ⁴.

κλῆσις, II 1¹¹.

κοιμηθέντες, οἱ, I 4¹⁵; διὰ τοῦ Ἰησοῦ, I 4¹⁴; οἱ κοιμώμενοι, I 4¹³.

κολακία, I 2⁵.

κοπιῶντες ἐν ὑμῖν, οἱ, I 5¹².

κόπος, I 3⁵; ὁ κόπος τῆς ἀγάπης, I 1³; κόπος καὶ μόχθος, I 2⁹ II 3⁸.

κρατεῖν τὰς παραδόσεις, II 2¹⁵.

κρίνειν, II 2¹².

κρίσις τοῦ θεοῦ, ἡ δικαία, II 1⁵.
κτᾶσθαι, I 4⁴.
κύριος, I 1⁶· ⁸ 3⁸· ¹² 4⁶· ¹⁵· ¹⁶· ¹⁷ 5²· ¹²· ²⁷
 II 1⁹ 2²· ¹³ 3¹· ³· ⁴· ⁵ 3¹⁶. See also
 above under ἐν and Ἰησοῦς.
κωλύειν, I 2¹⁶.

λαλεῖν, I 1⁸ 2⁴· ¹⁶; with εὐαγγέλιον,
 I 2².
λέγειν, I 4¹⁵ 5³ II 2⁵; λεγόμενος, II 2⁴.
λόγος, I 1⁵ 2⁵· ¹³ 4¹⁸ II 2²· ¹⁵· ¹⁷; ὁ
 λόγος, I 1⁶ II 3¹⁴ (ἡμῶν); λόγος
 ἀκοῆς, I 2¹²; ὁ λόγος τοῦ θεοῦ,
 I 2¹³; τοῦ κυρίου, I 1⁸ (4¹⁶) II 3¹.
λοιπὸν ἀδελφοί, (τό), I 4¹ II 3¹; οἱ
 λοιποί, I 4¹³ 5⁶.
λυπεῖσθαι, I 4¹³.

Μακεδονία, I 1⁷· ⁸ 4¹⁰.
μακροθυμεῖν πρός, I 5¹⁴.
μᾶλλον, περισσεύειν, I 4¹· ¹⁰.
μαρτύρεσθαι, I 2¹².
μαρτύριον ἡμῶν, τό, II 1¹⁰.
μάρτυς, θεός, I 2⁵· ¹⁰.
μεθύειν, I 5⁷.
μεθυσκόμενοι, οἱ, I 5⁷.
μέλλειν, I 3⁴.
μέν, I 2¹⁸.
μέσου, γίνεσθαι ἐκ, II 2⁷; ἐν μέσῳ
 ὑμῶν, I 2⁷.
μετά with gen., I 1⁶ 3¹³ 5²⁸ II 1⁷
 3¹²· ¹⁶· ¹⁸.
μεταδιδόναι, I 2⁸.
μή, I 1⁸ and passim; οὐ μή, I 4¹⁵ 5³;
 μή πως, I 3⁵.
μηδέ, II 2² 3¹⁰.
μηδείς, I 3³ 4¹² II 2³ 3¹¹.
μηκέτι, I 3¹· ⁵.
μήτε, II 2².
μιμεῖσθαι, II 3⁷· ⁹.
μιμητής, I 1⁶ 2¹⁴.
μνεία, I 1² 3⁶.
μνημονεύειν, I 1³ 2⁹ II 2⁵.
μόνον, I 1⁵· ⁸ 2⁸ II 2⁷.

μόνος, I 3¹.
μόχθος, κόπος καί, I 2⁹ II 3⁸.
μυστήριον τῆς ἀνομίας, τό, II 2⁷.

ναὸς τοῦ θεοῦ, ὁ, II 2⁴.
νεκρός, I 1¹⁰; οἱ νεκροὶ ἐν Χριστῷ,
 I 4¹⁶.
νεφέλη, I 4¹⁷.
νήπιοι, I 2⁷.
νήφειν, I 5⁶· ⁸.
νουθετεῖν, I 5¹²· ¹⁴ II 3¹⁵.
νοῦς, II 2².
νῦν, I 3⁸ II 2⁶.
νύξ, I 2⁹ 3¹⁰ 5²· ⁵· ⁷ II 3⁸.

ὁδός, I 3¹¹.
οἶδα, I 1⁴; εἰδέναι = "appreciate,"
 I 4⁴ 5¹²; εἰδέναι θεόν, I 4⁵ II 1⁸; οἴδατε, I 4² II 2⁶; αὐτοὶ γὰρ οἴδατε,
 I 2¹ 3³ 5² II 3⁷; καθάπερ οἴδατε,
 I 2¹¹; καθὼς οἴδατε, I 2²· ⁵ 3⁴; 1⁵.
οἰκοδομεῖν, I 5¹¹.
οἷος, I 1⁵.
ὄλεθρος, αἰφνίδιος, I 5³; αἰώνιος, II
 1⁹.
ὀλιγόψυχοι, οἱ, I 5¹⁴.
ὁλόκληρος, I 5²³.
ὅλος, I 4¹⁰.
ὁλοτελής, I 5²³.
ὁμείρεσθαι, I 2⁸.
ὄνομα, of Christ, II 1¹² 3⁶.
ὁποῖος, I 1⁹.
ὅπως, II 1¹².
ὁρᾶν, I 5¹⁵.
ὀργή, I 1¹⁰ 2¹⁶ 5⁹.
ὅς, I 1¹⁰ and passim.
ὁσίως, I 2¹⁰.
ὅστις, II 1⁹.
ὅταν, I 5³ II 1¹⁰.
ὅτε, I 3⁴ II 3¹⁰.
οὐδέ, I 2³ 5⁵ II 3⁸.
ὅτι, I 1⁵ and passim; ὡς ὅτι. II 2².
οὐ, I 1⁵ and passim.
οὖν, ἄρα, I 5⁶ II 2¹⁵.

οὐρανόι, οἱ, I 1¹⁰; ἀπ᾽ οὐρανοῦ, I 4¹⁶
　　II 1⁷.
οὔτε, I 2⁵· ⁶.
οὗτος, *passim*.
οὕτως, I 2⁴· ⁸ 4¹⁴· ¹⁷ 5² II 3¹⁷.
οὐχί, I 2¹⁹.
ὀφείλειν with εὐχαριστεῖν, II 1³ 2¹³.

πάθος, I 4⁵.
πάντοτε, I 1² 2¹⁶ 3⁶ 4¹⁷ 5¹⁵· ¹⁶ II 1³· ¹¹
　　2¹³.
παρά with gen., I 2¹³ 4¹ II 3⁶· ⁸; παρὰ
　　θεῷ, II 1⁶.
παραγγελία, I 4².
παραγγέλλειν, I 4¹¹ II 3⁴· ⁶· ¹⁰· ¹².
παράδοσις, II 2¹⁵ 3⁶.
παρακαλεῖν, I 2¹¹ 3²· ⁷ 4¹· ¹⁰· ¹⁸ 5¹¹· ¹⁴
　　II 2¹⁷ 3¹².
παράκλησις, I 2³ II 2¹⁶.
παραλαμβάνειν, I 2¹³ 4¹ II 3⁶.
παραμυθεῖσθαι, I 2¹¹ 5¹⁴.
παρουσία, ἡ, of Christ, I 2¹⁹ 3¹³ 4¹⁵ 5²³
　　II 2¹· ⁸; of the *Anomos*, II 2⁹.
παρρησιάζεσθαι, I 2².
πᾶς, I 1² and *passim;* ἐν παντί, I 5¹⁸;
　　ἐν παντὶ τόπῳ, I 1⁸; ἐν παντὶ τρόπῳ,
　　II 3¹⁶; διὰ παντός, II 3¹⁶.
πάσχειν, I 2¹⁴ II 1⁵.
πατήρ, of God, I 1¹· ³ 3¹¹· ¹³ II 1¹· ²
　　2¹⁶; figuratively of Paul, I 2¹¹.
Παῦλος, I 1¹ 2¹⁸ II 1¹ 3¹⁷.
πειράζειν, I 3⁵; ὁ πειράζων, I 3⁵; *cf.*
　　Mt. 4³.
πέμπειν, I 3²· ⁵ II 2¹¹.
πεποίθαμεν ἐν κυρίῳ, II 3⁴.
περί with gen., I 1³ and *passim.*
περιεργάζεσθαι, II 3¹¹.
περικεφαλαία, I 5⁸.
περιλειπόμενοι, οἱ, I 4¹⁷; εἰς, I 4¹⁵.
περιπατεῖν, I 4¹; ἀξίως τοῦ θεοῦ, I 2¹²;
　　ἀτάκτως, II 3⁶· ¹¹; εὐσχημόνως, I
　　4¹².
περιποίησις δόξης, II 2¹⁴; σωτηρίας,
　　I 5⁹.

περισσεύειν, I 3¹²; μᾶλλον, I 4¹· ¹⁰.
περισσοτέρως, I 2¹⁷.
πιστεύειν τῷ ψεύδει, II 2¹¹; τῇ ἀλη-
　　θείᾳ, II 2¹²; with ὅτι, I 4¹⁴; οἱ πισ-
　　τεύοντες, I 1⁷ 2¹⁰· ¹³; οἱ πιστεύσαντες,
　　II 1¹⁰; πιστεύεσθαι, I 2⁴ II 1¹⁰.
πίστις, ἡ, II 3²; ἡ πίστις ὑμῶν, I 1⁸
　　(ἡ πρὸς τὸν θεόν) 3²· ⁵· ⁶· ⁷· ¹⁰ II 1³· ⁴;
　　πίστις ἀληθείας, II 2¹³; (τὸ) ἔργον
　　(τῆς) πίστεως, I 1³ II 1¹¹; πίστις
　　καὶ ἀγάπη, I 3⁶ 5⁸; ὑπομονὴ καὶ
　　πίστις, II 1⁴.
πιστὸς ὁ καλῶν ὑμᾶς ὅς, I 5²⁴; πιστὸς
　　δέ ἐστιν ὁ κύριος ὅς, II 3³.
πλάνη, I 2³ II 2¹¹.
πλεονάζειν, I 3¹² II 1³.
πλεονεκτεῖν, I 4⁶.
πλεονεξία, I 2⁵.
πληροφορία, I 1⁵.
πληροῦν, II 1¹¹.
πνεῦμα ἅγιον, I 1⁵· ⁶; τὸ πνεῦμα αὐτοῦ
　　τὸ ἅγιον, I 4⁸; τὸ πνεῦμα, I 5¹⁹;
　　πνεῦμα, II 2²· ¹³; πνεῦμα, ψυχή,
　　σῶμα, I 5²³; τὸ πνεῦμα τοῦ στόμ-
　　ατος αὐτοῦ, II 2⁸.
ποιεῖν, I 1² 4¹⁰ 5¹¹· ²⁴ II 3⁴.
πολλῇ, ἐν, I 1⁵· ⁶ 2¹⁷; ἐν πολλῷ, I
　　2².
πονηρός, I 5²² II 3²; ὁ πονηρός, II 3³.
πορνεία, ἡ, I 4³.
ποτέ, I 2⁵.
πρᾶγμα, τό, I 4⁶.
πράσσειν τὰ ἴδια, I 4¹¹.
προεῖπον, I 4⁶.
προϊστάμενοι ὑμῶν, οἱ, I 5¹².
προλέγειν, I 3⁴.
προπάσχειν, I 2².
πρός with accus., I 1⁸ and *passim;*
　　πρὸς τὸ μή with infin., I 2⁹ II 3⁸.
προσευχαί, αἱ, I 1².
προσεύχεσθαι, I 5¹⁷ II 1¹¹; I 5²⁵ II 3¹.
πρόσωπον, I 2¹⁷; ἰδεῖν τὸ πρόσωπον
　　ὑμῶν, I 2¹⁷ 3¹⁰; ἀπὸ προσώπου κυ-
　　ρίου, II 1⁹.

πρόφασις, I 2[5].
προφητεῖαι, I 5[20].
προφῆται, I 2[15].
πρῶτον, I 4[16] II 2[3].
πυρὶ φλογός, ἐν, II 1[8].
πῶς, I 1[9]; (τὸ) πῶς δεῖ, I 4[1] II 3[7].

ῥύεσθαι ἐκ, I 1[10]; ἀπό, II 3[2].

σαίνεσθαι, I 3[3].
σαλεύεσθαι ἀπὸ τοῦ νοός, II 2[2].
σάλπιγξ θεοῦ, I 4[16].
Σατανᾶς, ὁ, I 2[18] II 2[9].
σβεννύναι, I 5[19].
σέβασμα, II 2[4].
σημεῖα καὶ τέρατα, II 2[9]; σημεῖον,
    II 3[17].
σημειοῦσθαι, II 3[14].
Σιλουανός, I 1[1] II 1[1].
σκεῦος, τό, I 4[4].
σκότος, I 5[4. 5].
σπουδάζειν, I 2[17].
στέγειν, I 3[1. 5].
στέλλεσθαι, II 3[6].
στέφανος καυχήσεως, I 2[19].
στήκειν, II 2[15]; ἐν κυρίῳ, I 3[8].
στηρίζειν καρδίας, I 3[13] (II 2[17]); στηρί-
    ζειν with παρακαλεῖν, I 3[2] II 2[17];
    with φυλάσσειν, II 3[3].
στόμα, II 2[8].
συμφυλέτης, I 2[14].
σὺν αὐτῷ, I 4[14]; σὺν κυρίῳ, I 4[17]; ἅμα
    σύν, I 4[17] 5[10].
συναναμίγνυσθαι, II 3[14].
συνεργὸς τοῦ θεοῦ, I 3[2].
σώζεσθαι, I 2[16] II 2[10].
σῶμα, I 5[23].
σωτηρία, I 5[8. 9] II 2[13].

ταχέως, I 2[2].
τέκνα, I 2[7. 11].
τέλος, εἰς, I 2[16].
τέρατα, σημεῖα καί, II 2[5].
τηρεῖν, I 5[23].

τιθέναι εἰς, I 5[9].
τιμή, I 4[4].
Τιμόθεος, I 1[1] 3[2. 6] II 1[1].
τίνειν δίκην, II 1[9].
τίς, I 4[2]; τίς γάρ, I 2[19] 3[9].
τις, I 1[8] 2[9] 5[15] II 2[3] 3[8. 10. 11. 14].
τοιγαροῦν, I 4[8].
τοιοῦτος, II 3[12].
τόπος, I 1[8].
τότε, I 5[3] II 2[8].
τρέχειν καὶ δοξάζεσθαι, II 3[1].
τρόπος, II 2[3] 3[16].
τροφός, I 2[7].
τύπος, I 1[7] II 3[9].

ὑβρίζεσθαι, I 2[2].
υἱὸς αὐτοῦ, ὁ, I 1[10]; ὁ υἱὸς τῆς ἀπ-
    ωλείας, II 2[3]; υἱοὶ ἡμέρας, φωτός,
    I 5[5].
ὑπακούειν τῷ εὐαγγελίῳ, II 1[8]; τῷ
    λόγῳ ἡμῶν, II 3[14].
ὑπέρ with gen., I 3[2] II 1[4. 5] 2[1].
ὑπεραίρεσθαι, II 2[4].
ὑπεραυξάνειν, II 1[3].
ὑπερβαίνειν, I 4[6].
ὑπερεκπερισσοῦ, I 3[10] 5[13].
ὑπό with gen., I 1[4] 2[4. 14] II 2[13].
ὑπομονὴ τῆς ἐλπίδος, ἡ, I 1[3]; ὑπο-
    μονὴ καὶ πίστις, II 1[4]; ἡ ὑπομονὴ
    τοῦ Χριστοῦ, II 3[5].
ὑστερήματα, τά, I 3[10].

φθάνειν, I 2[16] 4[15].
φιλαδελφία, I 4[9].
φιλήματι ἁγίῳ, ἐν, I 5[26].
φίλιπποι, I 2[2].
φιλοτιμεῖσθαι, I 4[11].
φλογός, ἐν πυρί, II 1[8].
φυλάσσειν ἀπό, II 3[3].
φωνὴ ἀρχαγγέλου, I 4[16].
φωτός, υἱοί, I 5[5].

χαίρειν, I 3[9] 5[16].
χαρά, I 1[6] 2[19. 20] 3[9].

χάρις, I 1¹ 5²³ II 1². ¹² 2¹⁶ 3¹⁸.

χείρ, I 4¹¹ II 3¹⁷.

χρείαν, ἔχειν, I 1⁸ 4⁹. ¹² 5¹.

Χριστός, I 1¹ and *passim;* see under
'Ιησοῦς; ἐν Χριστῷ, I 4¹⁶; ἐν Χριστῷ
'Ιησοῦ, I 2¹⁴ 5¹⁸; ἐν κυρίῳ 'Ιησοῦ
Χριστῷ, II 3¹².

χρόνοι καὶ καιροί, I 5¹.

ψεῦδος, II 2⁹. ¹¹

ψυχή, ἡ, I 5²³; ψυχαί, I 2⁸.

ὠδίν, I 5³.

ὥρας, πρὸς καιρόν, I 2¹⁷.

ὡς, I 2⁴. ⁶. ⁷. ¹¹ II 2² 3¹⁵.

ὡς, conj., I 2¹⁰. ¹¹; ὡς ὅτι, II 2².

ὥσπερ, I 5³.

ὥστε, I 4¹⁸; with infin., I 1⁷. ⁸ II 1⁴ 2⁶.